PIERS MORGAN

THE
INSIDER

To Mum and Dad,
'Greater love hath no parents than that they lay down
their *Daily Mail* for the *News of the World* and *Daily Mirror*.'

With my love, thanks, and apologies!

PIERS MORGAN

THE
INSIDER

EBURY
PRESS

A NOTE FOR THE READER

There are hundreds of people mentioned in these diaries,
often only by their first name. To help you keep track of
who I am talking about, you may find it useful to refer
to the Cast of Characters at the back of the book.

First published by Ebury Press in Great Britain in 2005

10 9 8 7 6 5 4 3 2 1

Text © Piers Morgan

Piers Morgan has asserted his right to be identified as the
author of this work under the Copyright, Designs and Patents Act 1988.

First published by Ebury Press

Random House, 20 Vauxhall Bridge Road, London SW1V 2SA

Random House Australia (Pty) Limited

20 Alfred Street, Milsons Point, Sydney, New South Wales 2061, Australia

Random House New Zealand Limited

18 Poland Road, Glenfield, Auckland 10, New Zealand

Random House South Africa (Pty) Limited

Endulini, 5A Jubilee Road, Parktown 2193, South Africa

The Random House Group Limited Reg. No. 954009

www.randomhouse.co.uk

A CIP catalogue record for this book is available from the British Library.

Cover Design by Two Associates

Interior Design by seagulls

Piers Morgan's Gulf War Diary commissioned by GQ July 2003, GQ © Piers Morgan

Diary column reproduced with permission of The Spectator magazine, © The Spectator

ISBN 0091905060

Papers used by Ebury Press are natural, recyclable products made from wood grown in sustainable forests.

Printed and bound in Great Britain by Clays Ltd, St Ives PLC

Cover photos: Tony Blair, Princess Diana, Gordon Brown, Cherie Blair, Jodie Kidd, Downing Street,
Richard Branson © Mirrorpix; Claudia Schiffer, Geri, Rachel Stevens © Richard Youn /Rex; Catherine Zeta
Jones © Dave Hogan; The Queen, Charles © PA Photos; Piers Morgan © Gemma Levine; Jordan © Dave
Bennett/Getty; Mo Mowlam © Alan Davidson; Clarkson, Finger © Times

Interior photos: David Mellor, Diana, Tony Blair, Peter Mandelson, Gordon Brown, Sarah Ferguson,
Ian Hislop, Ryan Parry © Mirrorpix; Rebekah Wade, Piers Morgan and Andy Coulson © Dave Bennett/
Getty; Kelvin McKenzie © Dave Hogan; Victoria Beckham © ITV

Every effort has been made to clear relevant copyright permissions.

Please contact the publishers with any queries or corrections.

ACKNOWLEDGEMENTS

The idea for this book came from Eugenie Furniss, my brilliant literary agent at the William Morris Agency in London, who came to me six months before I was sacked and convinced me that I should write my memoirs in diary form. She was so right, and I am so grateful both for that suggestion and for her tenacity, support and humour throughout the past year.

The driving force for the writing of the diaries was Jake Lingwood, my editor and publisher at Ebury Press, who almost single-handedly turned my erratic and sometimes rather hard-edged prose into something altogether more consistent and readable. Editors rarely like being 'edited' themselves. But I found it a remarkably pleasurable experience, thanks to Jake's skill, professionalism and inspiring devotion to the craft of good writing. I'd like to thank him, and his splendid staff at Ebury, for all their efforts on my behalf.

Editors, as Jake and I know only too well, are only as good as the teams around them.

I was lucky enough to have three wonderfully loyal and hard-working personal assistants – Vicky Bubb, Gilly Nolan and Kerrie Buckley. Kerrie deserves special praise for putting up with me for eight long years, right to the end of my *Mirror* career. We never argued, she never complained, and her remarkable discretion, loyalty and sense of humour kept me sane. Well, relatively, anyway. And then there were my various chauffeurs, another thankless job involving long, unpredictable hours and endless intrusion into their own lives. So cheers to Alan Mogg, Joe Sene, Damien Brady and Martin Parkinson for their patience, support and company over the years.

I'd also like to thank each and every one of those journalists and backroom staff who worked for me on the *News of the World* and *Mirror* – even those who didn't like me, ran off to rival papers, or landed me right in it from time to time. Nobody likes tabloid hacks very much, but I love them all.

I've had some amazing mentors. Kelvin MacKenzie, who knocked me – sometimes literally – into editor material at the *Sun*, and has given me such hilarious friendship and support ever since. And Rupert Murdoch, who gave me the greatest break any young journalist has surely ever had, and weekly masterclasses in tabloid journalism that even his billions couldn't buy. And I had some shrewd managers. David Montgomery, who took me to the *Mirror* and let me loose on a daily train set; and John Allwood, Philip Graf, Charlie Wilson, Roger Eastoe, Mark Haysom and Ellis Watson who successively manned the *Mirror* managerial engine rooms so skilfully as I careered away editorially – often out of control and with far too much steam.

I'd like to thank Trinity Mirror PLC Chief Executive Sly Bailey, of course, for so generously sacking me just when I needed the time to write this book. And, more seriously, the company's Chairman Sir Victor Blank, for backing me when many lesser chairmen would have turfed me into the ether, and for his amusing company.

Then there are the people at home who have to put up with so much crap from editors and their absurd jobs. My wife Marion, for giving me three amazingly entertaining and inspiring sons, and for supporting me during the good times and bad, and continuing to do so despite our separation four years ago. My parents, my grandmother, and the rest of my family for enduring all my highs and lows with good cheer and unflinching loyalty. It really mattered to me. And thanks, too, to my many friends, both in the media world and from my Sussex village of Newick. Two more different planets it would be hard to imagine, yet both have provided a constant source of fun, excitement and occasional solace.

And I'd finally like to thank Marina, my best friend, most amusing companion, and unpaid but razor-sharp proof reader.

INTRODUCTION

As a young cub reporter on the *Wimbledon News*, I kept a postcard from my mother on my desk showing a hippo flying with a flock of seagulls and the caption, 'Ambition knows no bounds'.

But even in my most wildly ambitious moments, I never imagined that I would end up editing two national newspapers for eleven years – and all before I was 40.

I'd always wanted to be a journalist. My family can remember me, aged six, reading the front page headline of the *Daily Mail* about some horrific sex attack and asking, 'Mum, what does being "rapped" mean?'

But my background didn't exactly scream 'editor'.

I was born in Guildford in 1965, brought up in an East Sussex village pub, educated at a smart prep school and then two local comprehensives, and always preferred three-card brag and cricket to maths revision. Yet from an early age I loved the smell and feel of newsprint, the excitement of breaking news, the funny headlines.

I dabbled with other jobs in my late teens, spending a tortuous year at Lloyds of London insurance market until I could weep no more tears of boredom and resigned – enrolling into a one-year journalism college in Harlow, Essex. From there, I did a two-year stint on local London papers before arriving at the *Sun* – where I began my brutal, blistering, and often hilarious, masterclass at the hands of its legendary editor, and fellow Harlow College old boy, Kelvin MacKenzie. It was there that I dropped the 'Pughe' from my surname, Pughe-Morgan, because of Kelvin's tabloid aversion to posh double-barrelled surnames.

It also was there that I somehow caught *Sun*-owner Rupert Murdoch's eye, while editing the paper's Bizarre showbiz column, and, to everyone's shock, not least my own, he appointed me editor of the *News of the World* at 28.

And that's where this book starts.

I have always wanted to write a book about newspapers. They are such exciting, funny and extraordinary places to work – yet most books about them read like the memoirs of a bank manager. So I have tried to create a book that would bring this crazy world to life in a way that would do it real justice.

At first, I thought the best way to do it would be to divide the book into themes. Politics, royals, showbiz, sport, and so on.

But that seemed too formulaic, and rather dull.

Then I read Alan Clark's wonderful political diaries again on holiday and realised, as my literary agent Eugenie had suggested, that the best way to do my story was as a similar journal. Because nothing beats the drama and sheer readability of a good diary.

The relentless daily grind of editing a national newspaper didn't allow for hours of patient diary-writing at the end of every, often long, evening. But I had kept regular contemporaneous notes of key moments, events, encounters and emotions – sometimes for my own amusement, often to make sure I had my back covered. And for eleven years, I would ask my PA at the end of each working day to chuck anything interesting into a box. Photos, letters, cuttings, scribbled memos of important meetings or phone calls, emails (once they started), taped interviews, faxes and memos, and every single front page of every edition of every paper I ever edited. A jackdaw would have been proud of me.

I never quite knew why I was doing it, but I guess I subliminally thought that it might come in handy one day.

The boxes would fill up, and we would start a new one. Each box brimming with all sorts of stuff that had sparked any kind of emotion, be it laughter, anger, tears or tantrums, or just mild curiosity. Literally thousands of items – as one friend put it, 'a veritable feast of deliciously intriguing memorabilia'.

I had also kept all my office day diaries and message books, recording every meeting and phone call I had throughout the whole time I edited papers. These alone were fascinating to revisit. Hour-by-hour, week-by-week, month-by-month, year-by-year – my working life charted like a hospital patient's bedside notes.

And so it wasn't a huge leap to convert this wealth of material into a fully formed diary. And being a diary, of course, it had to be completely honest.

Yes, there were great times, when we broke huge stories, won top awards, sold loads of papers, and when I brought genuine credit to the office of editing two of Britain's great journalistic institutions.

But there were also many times when my behaviour was rather less compatible with the editor's chair, occasions when I displayed a shocking lack of sensitivity or compassion, or got hideously drunk, had ugly violent brawls, abused my rivals and enemies in a deeply unpleasant way, and disgraced myself in front of major celebrities. Everything has stayed in, because I felt it was important not to hide those less graceful facets of my character. The truth is that you do get rather dehumanised editing a tabloid paper, and I should admit to it.

Part of that behavioural pattern was undoubtedly linked to the stress of managing a big daily newsroom, the sheer scale of which I only really appreciated when I was out of it.

And part of it was the intoxicating sense of power you feel as an editor, which, inevitably I think, creates an aura of invincibility and a massively over-inflated sense of one's own importance. I defy anyone not to be handed the biggest-selling newspaper in the world at 28 and not become a rather cocky little git.

There were times in my editing career when I was sanctimonious or hypocritical, and I've faithfully, if shamefacedly, detailed those moments too. Journalists are notoriously thin-skinned when it comes to our own failings. But much of what we do is notable for its conceit, moral double standards, and occasionally downright nastiness.

Conversely, I am very proud of many things I achieved as an editor.

My reporters on the *News of the World* and the *Daily Mirror* broke some fantastic scoops. Lady Buck and the Chief of Defence Staff, Alan Clark and his coven, James Hewitt's affair with Diana, Diana's cranky phone calls to Oliver Hoare and her romance with Dodi Fayed, BSE's link to humans, Paul Burrell's bombshell royal revelations, Sven's dalliance with Ulrika, and of course the undercover man at Buckingham Palace serving the Queen her Tupperware breakfast.

All firecracker stories that sold millions of extra papers, dominated the TV news for days, and eased the pain of almost constant circulation woes in a declining market.

And then there were the campaigns. From the fairly trivial, like trying to force Manchester United not to pull out of the FA Cup; to the populist, like winning a memorial for Princess Diana; to the deadly serious, like the *Mirror*'s campaign against the Iraq war. A great illustration of the genuinely important and responsible power a paper can wield when it wants to. If only we had been successful.

Clearing a front page for serious issues like war, or AIDS, or starving Africans, as I did fairly regularly, would never drive circulation as fast as Jordan's breasts. In fact it would often drive it down. But I never regretted it.

Away from all the revelations, gossip and stories, this book is also an often quite emotional and enlightening account of my personal editing journey – from carefree, aggressive, rather inhuman Thatcher-loving young shark on the *News of the World*, trashing people's lives, to a more mature (well, slightly!), less nasty, left-wing editor on the *Mirror*, trying to stop us blowing people up in places like Baghdad.

I changed a lot in the last decade, and without wishing to sound too pompous about it, that journey of discovery is in many ways the human substance that holds a lot of the content together.

The most overriding sense I had in reliving my career in these diaries, though, was the staggering degree of access I enjoyed for so long to the corridors of power and influence in this country.

At the time it seemed perfectly normal to be having breakfast with a tycoon like Philip Green, lunching with the Prime Minister, and dining with George Michael. Sometimes all on the same day.

Now it seems rather preposterous.

Bored one evening, I counted up all the times I had met Tony Blair. And the result was astonishing really, or slightly shocking – depending on your viewpoint.

I had 22 lunches, 6 dinners, 6 interviews, 24 further one-to-one chats over tea and biscuits, and numerous phone calls with him. That's a lot of face time with arguably Britain's most important person.

There were so many other surreal moments. Having lunch with Diana and a thirteen-year-old Prince William – served up by Paul Burrell. Riotous dinners with Fergie, Madonna and Bernard Manning (at the same time). Two hours spent strolling the surf on Miami's South Beach, barefoot and alone with Rupert Murdoch.

There were death threats, terrible clangers, and moments of such hilarity I thought I would choke to death with laughter.

This is not, I hope, a bitter book. I honestly, and perhaps surprisingly – even to myself – don't feel any bitterness about anything that happened to me. I always viewed editing a tabloid as an instinctive, high-octane, dangerous and ultimately short-lived pursuit. A bit like flying a fighter jet, constantly straddling the hard deck, trying to kill the opposition and avoid being killed yourself.

Eventually, the chances are that you're going to crash and burn.

But what a ride while it lasts!

Fleet Street can be a harsh, unforgiving place. But it can also be the most incredible fun. And on the really big news days, like 9/11, or Diana's death, or Dunblane, the adrenaline surges faster and stronger than on the highest, rockiest rollercoaster in the world. These were the times when the breathtaking professionalism of my colleagues shone through brightest. Tabloid hacks get a bad press, and a lot of it we deserve. But, my God, you should see the people I employed when they really had to sing for their supper. Their speed, quick thinking, creativity and phenomenal work-rate was breathtaking to watch.

The nature of a daily paper determines that it is not for the faint-hearted or the nine-to-five brigade. You have to be prepared to drop everything to get the story, be it Mother's Day lunches or Valentine's dinners. It's full of sacrifices, but never boring. Each day a new blank canvas to paint, a new story to tell. But all by 8pm. I hope this book exudes the excitement that kind of deadline pressure created.

This is essentially a story about people.

Hundreds of fascinating, hilarious, tedious, offensive, super-bright, or, in some cases, very dim people.

There's a lot of name-dropping in this book – of course there is. I met an awful lot of famous people. But I can count on one hand the number of 'celebrities' who I would consider to be personal friends. I have never been one to bring stars down to my local pub, or spend my precious weekends hobnobbing with the rich and fêted. Most of my real friends have nothing to do with the London media world, or the pages of *OK!* magazine.

A few legends, like Ian Botham, did become good mates. But that was more to do with a mutual love for cricket and hatred of all things Australian than anything else.

As for those who will inevitably squeal that I have breached confidences, I would respond that I have not. My experience of politicians, for instance, is that nothing is ever truly off the record. Politicians never fully trust journalists, whatever they say, and we never fully trust them. So our encounters are a reflection of that mutual prickliness. And both sides know that when the time suits, any information garnered from 'off-the-record' conversations will be used. I fully expect to be in Peter Mandelson's or Alastair Campbell's memoirs, and even possibly Tony Blair's – although I recognise I may have been slightly less important to his world than he was to mine!

So how did it all wash up?

Well, I hope you find this book informative, interesting and even vaguely historical. But most importantly, I hope it makes you laugh.

By way of research, I wined and dined endless friends and former colleagues, and we usually ended up howling away at all the ridiculous things that had happened.

I have been told many times that 'life's a serious business', normally by some bean counter telling me not to take the piss out of the Germans in the paper because it might not go down very well with our investors in Frankfurt. But life's as serious as you want it to be. This book is the story of a very lucky young man who rode his luck until his luck finally ran out. And even then, it turned out to be a lucky break.

I hope you laugh a lot as you read my story, and stay lucky.

DAILY Mirror

Saturday
May 1 2004

NEWSPAPER OF THE YEAR   45p

WORLD EXCLUSIVE

VILE

..but this time it's a **BRITISH**
soldier degrading an Iraqi

CAPTIVE'S TORMENT

A BRITISH soldier
urinates on an Iraqi
prisoner in a vile
display of abuse.
The captive was
beaten and hurled
from a moving
truck. Army chiefs
are investigating

MORE SHOCKING PHOTOGRAPHS

SEE PAGES
4 AND 5

PROLOGUE 2004

TUESDAY, 27 APRIL

We've been working on a potentially big story for weeks, involving photographs of British troops apparently abusing Iraqi civilians in Basra last summer. Two soldiers in the Queen's Lancashire Regiment came to us making pretty damning allegations about a culture of beatings, torture and – on at least one occasion – apparent murder. They've given us black-and-white photos to support their claims. They're very good quality, and, although the soldiers' heads have been cropped off, they show a hooded, battered Iraqi being urinated on by uniformed QLR squaddies, and having his head hit with a rifle butt. It is sickening stuff and should, of course, be exposed. But I'm not sure what to do with them. We caught a circulation cold during the war itself when the public watched our boys being shot at every morning on GMTV, and rejected us for not being gung-ho enough in our support of the war. I don't want to needlessly piss off a load more readers by 'betraying our boys' with this new story. We will have to think long and hard about it. Particularly as Jeremy has just flown out to Basra to join in the fun. Obviously, coming from a military family, I couldn't be more supportive of the armed forces. But I really hate them being used to fight such a senseless, illegal war, and I particularly loathe them apparently behaving in such a degrading manner to civilians of a country we have invaded and are now occupying against its people's will. Yet something is holding me back. And I told the newsdesk this afternoon that I wanted to think about it some more.

WEDNESDAY, 28 APRIL

Unbelievable coincidence. The American press have printed pictures of American soldiers abusing Iraqis in Abu Ghraib prison. These made our photos look like a tea party. One picture was of an inmate in a hooded outfit standing on a box with his head covered and wires attached to his hands. He'd been told that if he fell off the box, he would be electrocuted. Other images showed male and female guards laughing and joking above piles of naked, beaten prisoners who were being forced to simulate sex together, and holding snarling dogs inches from other terrified, naked men. It is all utterly horrible, and will do for this war what that picture of the Vietnamese girl running naked from the napalm attack did in the seventies. How can you sustain a moral position on removing Saddam for doing this kind of thing to his people, when you do it to them yourself?

THURSDAY, 29 APRIL

Blair's condemned the Abu Ghraib photos in unequivocal terms, clearly insinuating through his grim-faced rhetoric that this is not the kind of thing British armed forces would ever do. I looked again at the photos in my office of 'our boys' doing things that make that insinuation seem rather hypocritical, to say the least. The barriers to publication appear to have collapsed. Frankly, I now think we have a moral duty to publish them. Why should the British Government be able to distance themselves from American military misbehaviour, when it looks like we have been doing such unpleasant things ourselves? The public can make their own minds up whether this is the kind of thing our soldiers should be doing in our name. Be interesting to see what Jeremy thinks, particularly since his regiment has just replaced the one in our story.

FRIDAY, 30 APRIL

There was a lively debate in morning conference about whether we should publish the photos. Most executives thought we should, though one loud voice of dissent came from Steve Purcell, a normally reticent features man, who said it was 'unpatriotic and will be seen as such by our readers'. He very eloquently articulated the arguments about the effect of publication on morale in our troops, and also stressed the potential heightened danger we might be putting them in on the ground once the Iraqis saw the photos. Others were equally eloquent in demanding we publish, saying that to suppress them would look weak and hypocritical in light of the Abu Ghraib scandal. It was a lively, spirited debate, but in my mind I have decided to go for it. We've got several other independent claims about what the Queen's Lancashire Regiment were up to in Basra at the time these pictures were taken, and have been told that the army have been bracing themselves for it to be exposed for months. The *Sun* had something very similar-sounding involving the QLR all over its front page in February, to no denials. No photos, either. I got a front page mocked up on a computer showing the urination picture with a stark headline: 'VILE – but this time it's a BRITISH soldier degrading an Iraqi.' A new debate raged over whether you can put a urinating man on the front page at all – given that tomorrow is Saturday and most families will be looking at it together at breakfast. I overruled that one. This was the most powerful image. It depicted not just abuse, but total, abject humiliation. The victim was being degraded in a disgusting manner, whereas in the other pictures he was just being roughed up a bit. We sent the photos to the MoD mid-afternoon and they got back to us quite quickly saying there would be a statement later by the Chief of General Staff, General Michael Jackson. No denial.

This evening Jackson went live on TV and was visibly furious. His words pulled no punches: 'If proven, such appalling conduct is clearly unlawful, but also contravenes the British Army's high standards of conduct. Again, if proven, the perpetrators are not fit to wear the Queen's uniform and they have besmirched the Army's good name and conduct.' Downing Street made similar noises: 'We expect the highest standards of conduct from our forces in Iraq despite the difficulties they face.' And the Defence Minister, Adam Ingram, said the behaviour was 'clearly unacceptable'. Nobody is denying anything, nor are they trying to criticise us for damaging troop morale. The speed and ferocity of the response has been more than I expected. They obviously want to nip this in the bud right away. Fiona Bruce emailed me from BBC News: 'That is a great story. I knew it wouldn't only be the Yanks. We're going to lead on it.'

SATURDAY, 1 MAY

Terrible night's sleep. Big-story insomnia. The adrenaline just surging through the veins. Our scoop was leading every news bulletin and the general reaction was one of revulsion at the photos. Nobody was giving us any stick for publishing, there was a universal acceptance that this was appalling behaviour.

I went up to the Arsenal/Birmingham game at midday as a boardroom guest of City's boss Karren Brady, who also publishes the *Daily Sport*, so is, technically – very technically – a newspaper rival. I doubted they would be too aggrieved over there at missing this particular scoop. 'Fantastic story,' she cried, though, when I arrived. And that was the view of just about everyone else in the boardroom. There's nothing like the buzz of breaking a huge story and going somewhere quite public like this.

As the (very tedious) game progressed, I got a flurry of text messages from the *Mirror* picture and syndication departments telling me that the whole world's media was clamouring for the photos.

But listening to the radio as I drove back to Sussex afterwards, there were a few murmurs questioning the authenticity of the pictures. I know they're fine, of course. And we've done everything by the book. But I did feel uneasy enough to ring the newsdesk to check that there couldn't possibly be any question marks over the authenticity.

They assured me there weren't, but I took a call late this afternoon from the *Mail on Sunday*, who said the MoD were now casting 'serious doubt' on the photos. I laughed it off to them, saying, 'They would, wouldn't they?' but inside I was beginning to feel distinctly unsettled. If these pictures aren't real, it's a potential bloody disaster. I rang the newsdesk and relayed my concerns. They were confident there is no problem.

SUNDAY, 2 MAY

Slept very badly again. More fear than adrenaline today. Woke at 7am to see the BBC News leading on 'Fresh doubts over Iraq photos' and quoting Colonel 'Bonking' Bob Stewart saying everything from the troops' shoelaces to their floppy hats and type of rifle is wrong.

I wanted to be physically sick. I called the newsdesk and demanded: 'Get back to our two soldiers and find out what the fuck is going on here.' To my relief, the soldiers said they were standing completely by their story and – more importantly – the photographs, and were going to give us a load more pictures of them out in Iraq. I felt a bit more relaxed after all of this. I called Sly Bailey to explain what had been going on, and stressed that we have no reason to doubt the photos at this stage. She was supportive. But she's the chief executive, I'm the editor. This was my call, and it will be my head on the block if it goes pear-shaped.

I sent Steve White, our very experienced Northern news editor, to grill the soldiers, and he relayed very positive feedback afterwards. 'They are telling the truth,' he said. 'In fact, they are totally bemused as to why anyone would want to question what they have told us.'

But as the day wore on, the heat got more intense. Bank holiday weekends are great times to break a good story, because nothing ever happens, and everyone's desperate for anything to fill their airtime. Except for when things go a little awry like today, and we are the only story in town, with more and more 'experts' queuing up to berate us. The best form of defence in this kind of situation is attack. I issued a statement at 2.30pm, standing by the photos and saying: 'The Daily Mirror makes no apology for exposing this outrageous and unlawful behaviour, which has been common knowledge among disgusted British servicemen in Basra for many months. Nor do we believe there is any reason to think that these photographs have been faked in any way at all, given the powerful testimony we have received.'

The TV news guys gave us a fair crack with it, but it hasn't turned the tide. The knives have well and truly come out for us and the pressure is mounting. The first editions of tonight's papers confirmed my fears that the story is now the question of whether we've been hoaxed, not the question of whether British troops have been abusing Iraqis.

I don't like this at all.

MONDAY, 3 MAY

It was a lovely, sunny day today, and the boys were desperate to play football. But I was equally desperate to work out what was going on with these photos, and spent most of the time on the phone in the garden, to their mounting – and quite reasonable – fury. Eventually it came to a head.

'Dad,' said Spencer, 'you are so useless. Get off that phone before I throw it in the pool.'

I lost my rag. 'Listen, you ungrateful little wretch, I might get sacked over this, so for God's sake leave me alone to sort it.'

He looked shocked, upset, and worried – he's only eleven, after all. I instantly felt appallingly guilty. The job takes up enough of my time without it dominating precious bank holidays with them too. 'Sorry, mate – look, I'll be there in a minute. Just let me deal with this. I'm not going to get sacked, it's OK.'

But much as I wanted to switch off, my brain was racing with this unfolding crisis and I soon gave up trying to concentrate on being Thierry Henry and returned to the TV and phone.

We led tonight's paper on Soldiers A and B standing by their account under the headline WE TOLD THE TRUTH.

But Charles bloody Kennedy has gone on TV saying that, true or false, the damage is done and the pictures will put our troops in more danger than they are already.

That's not a line I want to run very far. The ultimate nightmare looming now is that British soldiers get killed in revenge for the photos.

I spoke to Jeremy in Basra. 'I think we both know what's going to happen now,' I joked. 'You're going to get kidnapped by Al Qaeda, and beheaded live on TV by some bloke clutching the Mirror front page.' He laughed, because he shares my black sense of humour, but we both realise this is not a laughing matter. He reckons the photos could be genuine, and the stories echo what he had heard had been going on before his regiment got out there. He said they all have floppy hats and wear bootlaces however they like, so a lot of the 'flaws' being claimed about the pictures are nonsense. But still the nagging doubt remains. Couldn't eat supper, and drank a bit too much wine.

TUESDAY, 4 MAY

I had a day off planned today and decided to take it anyway. Sometimes when things go wrong like this it's better to be out of the office and clear your head. But it did feel slightly surreal to be licking ice creams on the end of Brighton Pier under a sign saying 'End of the pier show' at the precise moment Adam Ingram was addressing the Commons about the scandal. Encouragingly he said: 'From the outset we have taken the allegations seriously and taken the photographs at face value and will continue to do so unless there is evidence to the contrary.'

I was asked by the MediaGuardian website what I thought of the *Express* calling us liars on their front page.

'Being called a liar by that lot is like being called a halfwit by the village idiot,' I said. 'A crushing blow, but you get on with the day as best you can.'

Des hasn't made any attempt to contact me since the storm broke. Not a single phone call. Quite incredible. What kind of a deputy is he? I finally sent him an angry email at 5pm, saying his behaviour was disgraceful. He feigned bemusement, but I suspect he's just sitting there, keeping his head down, and quietly hoping I get fired. 'Come and see me tomorrow morning,' I said.

WEDNESDAY, 5 MAY

Des shuffled sheepishly into my office.

'Sorry, I was at a family wedding in Ireland.'

'Don't they have newspapers or TV in Ireland, then?'

'I didn't hear about it, really sorry.'

'You're the deputy editor of the Daily Mirror and you didn't hear for three days that your own paper was leading every news bulletin in the fucking western world?'

'Nobody called to tell me. Bloody newsdesk, I've told them before about this …'

I cut him off.

'Nobody had to, for Christ's sake. You are paid enough to find out what is happening every day. This has been the biggest crisis I have probably ever faced and you have shown no interest in helping or even offering support. It's appalling.'

'Yes, sorry about that.'

He didn't give a damn. I could imagine him scurrying back into his office to call Carol Vorderman, his girlfriend, immediately after I'd finished with him and chortling: 'He's finished, I can tell. We're nearly there.'

He thinks they'll be the new Harry Evans and Tina Brown. Harry Redknapp and Tina Turner, more like.

Blair sent me a handwritten note today: 'Thank you for the *Mirror*'s renewed support, it's come at a good time.' Blimey. Is this what he calls support?

The families of Iraqi civilians killed by British troops appeared in the High Court today to challenge the MoD's refusal to consider legal responsibility for the deaths. The cases include the death of Baha Mousa, a hotel receptionist allegedly killed in Basra last September by soldiers from the Queen's Lancashire Regiment. This is obviously helpful. But Michael Howard turned the screw on me in Prime Minister's Questions by saying the photos had done 'enormous damage' and asking: 'Does the Prime Minister agree … that if the photos turn out to be false it will be a matter of the utmost seriousness for which the editor will have to take full responsibility?'

Blair dodged the question, but the matter of my resignation is now being openly discussed everywhere. Shit.

The Defence Select Committee have called me to appear before them, which is something I'd normally enjoy, but not this time. There are too many unanswered questions. I don't feel sure of my ground. Unlikely support came from Andrew Neil in his *Standard* column who said that whether the pictures are fake or not, I will survive because the story behind them is true. 'He is an editor with more lives than a cat,' he concluded. Prompting Rebekah over at the *Sun*, to bike round a talking toy cat … ho, ho, ho.

Stephen Glover, in the *Spectator*, said that I must quit. But that's the fourth time he has said that about me in ten years, so I see that as rather encouraging.

THURSDAY, 6 MAY

It never rains but it pours … I woke up to the joyous news that Naomi Campbell has won her appeal against us in the House of Lords. Three of the judges went with her, two with us.

I issued a suitably ill-tempered response, composed in the shower: 'This is a good day for lying, drug-abusing prima donnas who want to have their cake with the media and the right to then shamelessly guzzle it with their Cristal champagne.'

The timing could not have been worse, although it was tempered slightly by the fact that the official report into Ryan Parry's undercover Buckingham Palace investigation came out today as well, and was very good for us.

The Channel 4 lunchtime news was hilarious, with the first three stories all about the *Mirror*. They started with the photos and Krishnan Guru-Murthy concluded the report by saying: 'We invited the editor of the Daily Mirror to comment … but he declined.'

Next up was Naomi. Krishnan, by now semi-smirking, said at the end of that story: 'And we once again invited the editor of the Daily Mirror to comment … but he declined.'

The third item was Dame Elizabeth Butler-Sloss's Palace report. By now Mr Guru-Murthy was really struggling. 'And … ,' he giggled, 'as you may have guessed by now, we invited the editor of the Daily Mirror to comment … but he declined.'

It must have been the first time I had ever refused to comment on anything, and I'd done it three times in one day.

Victor Blank, our chairman, and Sly were grilled at the company's AGM about the photos, but stood by me and the paper.

Victor said: 'The core issue raised by the Mirror in the course of the last week or two is about very serious allegations of brutality and torture by rogue elements in the armed forces.'

And he's right, it is. But this isn't going away.

FRIDAY, 7 MAY

Time to come out fighting. I did an interview for this Sunday's *Observer*, pointing out that the Government and MoD have had a week to unequivocally knock down the story, but have failed to do so. I also confirmed my brother's presence in Basra, and added that the pictures have had no impact on the ground out there at all – making it obvious how I know this.

I was cheered by an email from Jeremy Bowen saying, 'Keep it going, Piers, you're doing some great journalism'.

And the ironic thing is that we are. More and more soldiers are coming forward to tell their own tales of abuse in Iraq, and to back up what we have been saying. But people are still obsessing about the veracity of these pictures. The atmosphere is increasingly febrile.

SUNDAY, 9 MAY

The *Observer* interview was positive and helpful. But they ran a separate news story about American investors in Trinity Mirror being unhappy about the row. We've been down this road with these guys before, over our coverage of the Iraq war itself. It amuses me that some jumped-up prat sitting in his New York investment bank believes he can influence editorial policy at the *Mirror* just because he owns a few shares in us. But I suspect it doesn't amuse Victor and Sly, who have to answer to these ghastly people.

I escaped to Wiltshire to attend my new nephew Finlay's christening at Charlotte's army house. His birth on New Year's Eve had been very traumatic, very premature and very nearly fatal for his poor mother, so it was an emotional but very happy day. Particularly for Mum, who has had quite a year so far with her various offspring.

General view of the military guests down there is that we were right to expose the abuse, and they all thought it had definitely happened.

MONDAY, 10 MAY

This morning the storm appeared to be abating somewhat. I relaxed for the first time in a week and thought we were probably over the worst.

If these photos were fake, then surely we'd have known for certain by now. At worst, I thought, it will remain a mystery. It's also a fact that no editor has ever had to resign or been fired over a hoax.

Then, just as I was sipping a self-congratulatory cup of tea, Geoff Hoon stood up in the Commons and said there were 'strong indications' that the truck in our photos was not in Iraq.

Cue instant nausea again. How can they be certain of that, for God's sake? All those trucks look the same, and are usually botched-up hybrids built from bits of numerous vans.

The TV news, which had been going away from the story, piled straight back in with Hoon's comments. And I got a new rash of calls asking if I was going to resign.

Bugger it.

We attacked Hoon in a statement for trying to deflect attention from the more important issue of whether the abuse was going on, abuse which has now been confirmed by the Red Cross and Amnesty International.

But this is now shaping up for a fight to the finish, and I can't be certain where it will end for me personally. I've been slightly unsettled by the increasing number of TV crews and newspaper reporters waiting outside my flat tonight, all shouting things like 'Are you going to quit, Mr Morgan?' Interesting experience to be on the receiving end. They were all polite but fierce. Like a shoal of friendly Hammerheads.

TUESDAY, 11 MAY

The *Sun*, which has restrained itself commendably for the last seven days, joined in the fun today with an interview with the father of a dead soldier saying I should be ashamed of myself, and a leader article demanding I apologise. It's a cheap shot but we'd do the same to them, I guess.

Hoon, who loathes me with a rare passion, ramped up the rhetoric further by telling Channel 4 News the photos were 'definitely a hoax'. I can tell he's loving this, as is Alastair Campbell, who told a parliamentary committee this afternoon that my position would be 'untenable' if the pictures were proved to be fake. And he added patronisingly: 'When you decide it's no longer enough to be a national newspaper editor, and you want to be a political player … when you decide to be a player, then sometimes you have to face up to the rules of the political game as well.'

Cheers, pal.

I lunched, by coincidence, with Greg Dyke and Alan Rusbridger, editor of the *Guardian*. Alan and I are trying to persuade Dyke to sell his memoirs to the *Mirror* and *Guardian* in a unique joint bid. We tried it with Robin Cook, but he preferred to take Murdoch's £400,000, even though all Murdoch's papers backed the war that Robin found so indefensible. Principles, eh?

Dyke was on good form, but seemed restless for real work again. Both men reckoned I'd survive this photo thing, though Greg warned, 'I wouldn't put anything past this Government, especially to do with the war. Be careful. They are fucking ruthless bastards and if they can get you out over this they will.'

He should know.

WEDNESDAY, 12 MAY

Fled to the Dover Street Wine Bar's 25th birthday party. George, the owner, sits next to me at Arsenal.

But any thoughts of unwinding were shattered when I got a phone call telling me that Adam Ingram is going to officially denounce the pictures as fake in the Commons tomorrow morning.

I got up, apologised, and went straight home, passing David Seaman on the way out – who just laughed and said, 'Good luck, mate.' I wish I could laugh too, but I am getting the sense this won't go away now until my head is skewered live on ITN. Spoke to Mum on the phone, and she's in turmoil. Her oldest son's facing the sack while her second son's facing bullets in Iraq. All this after her daughter's birth drama, her father dying in November and her mother having a stroke a month later.

I tried to reassure her. 'Mum, I've been through worse than this, don't worry.' But we both know it probably hasn't been worse than this.

THURSDAY, 13 MAY

Ingram did indeed say the photos were 'categorically not taken in Iraq', accused us of not co-operating, and directly challenged me to 'show the standards of honesty, openness and professionalism the Mirror expected of the army'.

I toyed with the idea of issuing a qualified apology if it was proven 'incontrovertibly' that the pictures were definitely a hoax, but decided against it.

We still don't know for sure, whatever the Government and the army say.

There are too many unanswered questions in my view to just throw our hands up and capitulate. The *Guardian* asked various editors and ex-editors if I should quit. Andrew Gowers, of the *Financial Times*, said yes, Rosie Boycott wasn't sure, and Peter Preston said only if I knew they were fakes – which is obviously not the case. Wish I did know!

I issued a new statement saying the Government still hasn't produced 'incontrovertible evidence'.

Andrew Marr rang to ask if I was thinking of resigning, always an ominous sign.

'There are two hopes of that,' I said; 'no hope and Bob Hope.' It was a line I'd trotted out many times at work.

'Can I use that?' he asked.

'Of course, been trying to get it on telly for eleven years.'

Seven minutes later I watched the *Six O'Clock News*, and saw a smirking Marr say, 'I spoke to Mr Morgan a few minutes ago and he told me there are two hopes of him quitting – no hope and Bob Hope.'

I laughed out loud. It was some welcome light relief in an otherwise very tense day.

But tonight's BBC News had their business reporter Jeff Randall saying several US investors were putting heat on Sly Bailey for me to go, and saying that her own position would be 'weakened' if she didn't take action. I am beginning to fear the worst now.

FRIDAY, 14 MAY

I woke to the unlikely sound of Roy Greenslade, historically one of my biggest detractors, defending me on the *Today* programme. I was determined not to say anything when I left the flat, but then saw all the TV crews waiting for me outside and thought I'd better give the panting dogs a bone.

Tried to sound suitably defiant, saying I definitely wasn't resigning and demanding answers from the Government: 'We revealed a can of worms, and if the Government ignores that, it's entirely up to them.'

It was hard not to laugh, even given the obvious severity of the situation. A dark part of me has been finding all this terribly funny.

There was a 'Should Morgan quit?' phone-in on Five Live and the split was about 60–40 in favour, which didn't seem too bad. As with all these scandals, if you can ride it out long enough, then the public and the media will eventually get bored and you can get on with your job. Alastair Campbell told me once you had to survive eleven days on a scandal, then it would always move on, and I'd always agreed with him.

Today is Day Thirteen.

I was supposed to be having lunch with Lorraine Heggessey, controller of BBC1, but cancelled it at 11am, saying, 'I think it might be a rather tricky day here, sorry.'

Instead, I had a Caesar salad from Waitrose on the grass outside the Canary Wharf tower in the sunshine and felt surprisingly calm.

A passer-by spotted me and shouted, 'Keep going, mate.'

At 2.30pm the Queen's Lancashire Regiment held a press conference at which a Colonel David Black said, 'It's not a Westminster game, there are real lives in danger. It is time that the ego of one editor is measured against the life of a soldier.'

Alastair Campbell couldn't have written it better himself. Perhaps he did, come to think of it.

For the next couple of hours the twentieth floor went horribly quiet. I tried emailing people down there, with increasing degrees of impatience, suggesting how we should respond to the QLR conference, but heard nothing.

The deadline for supplying a statement to the main evening news bulletins came and went, and I knew the game was probably up. I sent a last 'Back me or sack me' plea to Sly, but I think I knew in my heart it was too late for that now.

By an amazing coincidence, Kerrie was leaving tonight to have a baby, after eight and half years working as my personal assistant.

We'd never had a cross word.

I had flowers and champagne for her under my desk and was preparing to make a little speech in the newsroom.

As we stood alone together in my office for the last time, I said, only half-joking, 'Kerrie, how the hell will I ever survive here without you?' when the phone rang and I was asked to go and see Sly Bailey urgently.

Now this really did feel like Death Row. I felt the same horrible rush of fear and adrenaline I'd felt in 2000 when Suzy Jagger rang me from the *Telegraph* to ask if I had bought any Viglen Technology shares.

As I walked down the corridor on the twentieth floor to Sly's office, all the secretaries had their heads down.

They probably knew nothing, but it felt like they did.

I got to Sly's outer office and could tell from her PA's face that either my entire family had been wiped out in an air crash or I was about to be fired.

I smiled, and she led me into the execution chamber, where I found Sly and the company secretary Paul Vickers sitting on a sofa with faces longer than the Nile. I smiled again.

'Afternoon,' I said cheerily. Sly, ashen and stony-faced, invited me to sit down, then explained very matter-of-factly that there had been an emergency board meeting and as a result it had been decided it was 'no longer appropriate' for me to continue as editor of the *Daily Mirror*.

What a splendid way of putting it.

I just listened, half smiling and saying nothing, for the two or three minutes of corporate-speak for 'You're out, pal.' It's never an easy job, and I have no complaints with the way it was done.

Things got a little petty after that, though.

Sly asked for my security pass, and said she was very sorry but I'd have to leave the building immediately. To ensure this happened, the burly head of *Mirror* security arrived in the office to help Paul frogmarch me to the lift and out of the tower on to the concourse where I'd had my lunch. Both seemed rather embarrassed, and it was somewhat undignified after nearly ten years' loyal service, but I guess they didn't want any Greg Dyke-style rallies in the newsroom. Not that I would presume anything like that would have happened anyway.

Paul, who I'd worked with for nearly a decade, asked for my handheld Blackberry computer, which was quite upsetting because I'd only just got the hang of using the damn thing.

Then I borrowed his phone to call Kerrie and said: 'Hey, you know what I was saying ten minutes ago? Well we're never going to have to find out, I've been sacked.'

'*No!* You haven't?'

'Yes, 'fraid so. Can you bring my jacket and phone down for me?'

Kerrie arrived a few minutes later with tears in her eyes, and we exchanged an emotional farewell hug, the one we would have exchanged anyway in a few hours at her leaving party.

'God obviously realised I couldn't work without you,' I laughed, a bit lamely.

Kerrie laughed too: she was always great in a crisis. I got in my car and asked my driver to drive me home for the last time. I remember Derek Jameson always saying that the worst thing about getting sacked as an editor was losing the chauffeur, and he was right. It's like having a permanent free black cab at your disposal.

I phoned Conor Hanna and told him I'd been sacked, and asked him to pass on the news. He was shocked and upset. He'd fought like a Belfast terrier to save my neck for the last two weeks.

Next I phoned Martin Cruddace, who burst out laughing. 'Right, well don't say a word to anyone about anything. Or you won't get your money.'

I called Mum, who burst into tears. 'It's OK, Mum, I'm fine about it – honestly,' I said. Which was oddly true.

Then I called Marion so she could tell the boys their dad was now unemployed, which unfortunately meant they'd be seeing more of him now than they might like.

And then I just sat back and waited for my departure to break on the news. Just before it did, the mobile went and it was Ian Botham: 'Hey, buddy, I hear you've had a bit of bad news. If you want to escape from all the mayhem you can go to my new place in Spain, or come up to Yorkshire and do a bit of fishing or something. Whatever you want, mate.' I don't know how the hell he knew so quickly, but it was typical of him to be so instantly generous.

My in-car TV then crackled into frenzied excitement. I'd always wanted to be 'breaking news'.

'And we've just heard that Piers Morgan has stepped down as editor of the Mirror,' said ITN.

Stepped down? I hadn't bloody stepped down – I'd been sacked.

First call after it became public was from Mohammed Al Fayed: 'So the bastards got you too. Never mind, come and be a Harrods doorman for me.'

Then Marco Pierre White, another foul-weather friend: 'Come and have lunch with me and get drunk.'

It didn't surprise me that these three guys were first off the blocks. All are their own men, all have been through endless scrapes in their lives, and all inspire equal doses of admiration, fear and loathing.

My phone was now going into meltdown, with calls and text messages pouring in relentlessly from colleagues, other editors, family, friends. Even the odd foe, presumably just to make sure it was true.

It was all rather surreal, like I was living through my own death.

I got back to the flat before the media arrived and sat down in front of the TV with a glass of wine, feeling a bit shell-shocked, but otherwise alright.

It was over. I had ceased to be. I was, officially, an ex-editor.

Within an hour I'd been joined by Richard Wallace and Conor. Two finer pall-bearers a man couldn't wish for.

They brought plastic bags of expensive wine, and we ordered a lot of Chinese food. Ellis Watson arrived on his motorbike half an hour later. He'd been deliberately, and understandably, excluded from the decision today. I'm going to be his best man in three weeks, after all.

And finally Martin came. Wouldn't have been the same without him. He's always been there for my frequent 'local difficulties'.

We watched the TV, giggling at all the various hacks coming on to deliver their damning 'it's a personal tragedy, but he had to go' verdicts for £75 a pop.

A letter popped through the door from Fiona Bruce at BBC News. 'God, what a shock,' she'd written; 'I'm astonished, never thought this would happen. Would you consider doing an interview with me? I feel shameless in asking this, but it's the business we're in, so forgive me! PS And if you want to be cheered up, watch me tonight on the Ten. I've got an eye infection and look like an albino rabbit with dominatrix glasses. Viewers will be terrified.'

The coverage was absurdly over-the-top. Both the BBC and ITN dedicated more than ten minutes at the top of their news bulletins to my demise (we know because we timed them), prompting an incredulous Andy Coulson to send a text: 'This is bigger than bloody Blair going.' Rebekah sent similar thoughts: 'It's like the Queen Mother's died again, quite ridiculous.'

It was certainly a lot more than the departure of a tabloid editor warranted, however 'notorious'.

Fiona, in her jet-black Buddy Holly spectacles, did indeed look vaguely terrifying.

One enterprising TV crew infiltrated my block of flats and banged on my door. Ellis dealt with them: 'Mr Morgan is not speaking to the media, thank you very much.'

My phone was still in call and text meltdown. I left it on silent, taking some but leaving most.

By 9pm, I was already bored talking about it. What the hell is it going to be like in a month's time? More editors rang to offer support. Dominic Lawson, of course – a gentleman to the end. Roger Alton, sounding even more depressed than he must think I am about it. Simon Kelner, enjoying a drunken dinner with *GQ*'s Dylan Jones: 'Congratulations on a spectacular end.' And Alan Rusbridger, considerably more supportive on the phone than he'd been about me on TV earlier, I noted.

Perhaps the most difficult moment came when Marion called to say Bertie was a terrible state because he kept hearing on the news that I'd been fired and he thought that meant I'd been literally set on fire. I spoke to him and the poor little chap was crying uncontrollably. 'Daddy (sob) have they set you on fire (sob)? Are you on fire, Daddy? (sob)'

Throughout the whole day it was the only time I felt really upset, and the tears welled up a bit. 'No, no, Bertie, don't worry, I'm not on fire. I'm fine, don't worry.'

He wasn't remotely convinced, and went off still wailing. The other two boys were not quite as inconsolable.

Spencer was highly amused that I now appear to be some sort of 'disgrace', and Stanley just wanted to know how we're going to 'get revenge on that horrible Sly Bailey'. His suggestion? 'Dad, let's put dynamite in her pants and blow her up.' Spencer thought that was far too good for her. 'No, no, let's get a chainsaw and cut her into tiny pieces and strap them on to a rocket and send her to Pluto.'

The texts from the pubs of Canary Wharf grew more emotional as the booze levels increased. Some were transparently a bit self-serving, the sender not really giving a toss but thinking they ought to say something. Others were clearly heartfelt and very touching. A few of the more headstrong were threatening strikes and mutiny but I told them not to be so silly.

Fleet Street loves a drama, but we all know the rules. If the editor's chopped, then get pissed, tell him you love him and can't work without him, wake up, take some Resolve, and start sucking up to the new editor. It's a brutal world but I expect nothing else. I finally crashed out about 1am. There are only so many obituaries you can hear before you start to feel genuinely dead.

SATURDAY, 15 MAY

I woke at 7am, feeling restless, irritable, slightly unnerved – and unemployed for the first time in my life. I turned on Sky News and saw a guy reporting live from outside my flat, surrounded by a scrum of hacks.

'We believe Mr Morgan is still inside after having some sort of *party* last night,' he said, with a bemused look.

I made a cup of tea, surrounded by twenty empty wine bottles and half-eaten prawn balls, and read the papers.

Most of them had a large picture of my head, carefully selected to make me look miserable. But the general coverage was pleasingly over the top and surprisingly nice.

Particularly in the *Mail*, which did a small leader on page two saying I'm a 'brave and fearless' journalistic hero. Hilarious! It's almost certainly because I'm just a useful tool to have another whack at Blair, but I'll happily take the compliment because it means Middle England will now think that about me, such is the indisputable power of Paul Dacre's paper.

At 9am I got into to my car in the underground car park and drove out, expecting the scrum to be waiting. But not one of them had worked out where my car might be, so when I emerged from the only car-park exit they were all waiting fifty yards away. I waved theatrically, muttered 'halfwits', turned left, and drove off. When I got to Marion's house in Wandsworth ten minutes later to pick up the boys, there was the Sky guy saying: 'And we now think Mr Morgan has cleverly given us all the slip,' with an expression suggesting I had performed some typically cunning tabloid escape tactic. It wasn't that clever, mate, I thought, I just turned left. The boys were glued to the coverage, and started berating the TV reporters for their stupidity. One woman on BBC News 24 got particular stick for suggesting I might still be inside my flat. 'No, he's not, you idiot,' said Bertie (which was harsh, coming from a three-year-old), 'my dad's here.'

We headed up to Wandsworth Common to watch Stanley play cricket. His first proper match and a tremendously exciting moment for his cricket-mad father.

My phone was going mad again. Kelvin called, cackling at the coverage: 'Honestly, matey, I don't want to deflate your vast ego, but you're not JFK, you know.' He also gave me some great advice – 'Have a good break before you do anything, just clear your head. And remember that being fired by Sly Bailey can only be a good thing for your career! If you want a show on Talksport we'd love to have you.'

Typical Kelvin MacKenzie – piss-taking, funny, generous.

Then Fergie called to offer her sympathy. 'Believe me, Piers, I've been there,' she said, her voice quivering with emotion. 'If there is anything I can do, please let me know.' I wanted to laugh, but I've always liked Fergie and it was kind of her to call. 'Oh don't worry, I'm fine really. Just watching my son play cricket.' 'Oh, which one, Spencer or Stanley?' she replied. She has a quite staggering, and rather scary, memory for names.

We chatted for a few minutes and she said if I want lunch or something to cheer myself up then I only have to call. The thing is, she means it. And whenever I've had lunch or dinner with her, she has always made me laugh a lot.

After cricket, I loaded the two older boys into a taxi and the three of us went up to Highbury for the Leicester Premiership game – if we didn't lose, we'd have gone the whole season unbeaten. It seemed perfectly normal to me to be doing this, but everyone else seemed amazed. 'God, how brave,' said one ex-colleague when I said what I was doing. Brave? To watch Arsenal make history? Hardly.

There were no photographers waiting for me at Highbury, despite ITN reporting in their lunchtime bulletin that I 'may be on my way to Arsenal'. They were all presumably still standing outside my flat like lemmings.

The boys and I were guests of Frank Warren today in his box. Frank's been shot at, literally, so he knows what it's like to take a blow and survive. We had a jolly lunch, interrupted only by a call from Heather Mills-McCartney who said, 'Paul and I just want to say how sorry we are and to offer a bit of solidarity.'

Then David Seaman walked past the box, spotted me and came in to say hello. 'We've both had it,' I said; 'washed up has-beens before we're forty!'

Twenty minutes later, Andy Coulson texted me to say an amusing picture of me and Seaman laughing was running on the wires. The wonders of modern technology. 'Plays well, mate,' he said; ' "Morgan bounces back".'

We tabloid people have a habit of seeing our own lives in headlines.

Aware that the snappers were now sneaking their lenses on the box, I tried to ensure my face was in a perpetual grin. But I knew they'd bide their time and get a sad expression – not hard when Leicester scored just before half time. I suddenly got a new flurry of texts, all variations on the 'It never rains …' theme. Very droll.

It would have been truly ironic if we had lost our invincible record today of all days. But we turned it round in the second half and won 2–1, sparking a huge party on and off the pitch. Just what the doctor ordered. I came out of the stadium to be met by two snappers, who wanted me holding a Champions balloon. I obliged. Spencer, rather admirably, hated the attention and hid twenty yards behind. But Stanley loved it, and posed for all he was worth.

I picked up Bertie and drove the three boys to Sussex. Later in the evening,

Andy called to say the *Sunday Telegraph* had stuck a huge picture of me and Stanley in his Arsenal shirt all over the front page.

Stanley was delighted. 'I'm famous!' he cried, euphorically.

Spencer was pleased too when I had the page faxed over and he noticed that Stanley was scoffing a huge cake in the shot. 'You look like a nerd, you show-off,' he said.

I went down to the Royal Oak for a pint. There were ironic cheers as I arrived. 'Sorry, mate, but it's still your round.' We talked about today's league cricket match. They'd lost again without me.

Richard Branson has left a message on my phone. 'Piers, hi, it's Richard. Richard Branson. Erm, how are you?' Pause. 'Christ, what a stupid fucking thing to say. You've just been sacked, you're going to be bloody terrible!

WEDNESDAY, 19 MAY

Ian Botham was hosting a charity dinner for his leukaemia walks tonight and I bumped into Alastair Campbell there. He tried to snarl at me, but I just laughed in his face.

'Thanks for your help in getting me sacked, you twat,' I said. 'Pleasure,' he replied, and clearly meant it. It was a weird moment: after ten years of working together and against each other, here we were, both jobless, and ever so slightly less powerful and significant than we used to be.

'Missing it?' I said. 'Yes, to be honest,' he replied. 'It's taken a while to adjust. But I'm still in regular touch with Tony, which is good.' It doesn't interest me if he is or isn't, but Mandelson was the same when he went, constantly trying to reassure everyone he still had the PM's ear.

A photographer emerged and started snapping. I play-fought Campbell, slapping him and grabbing his neck – and it actually got quite nasty quite quickly before we both calmed down and realised it wouldn't be a very good idea to have a scrap, much as we'd probably both like to.

WEDNESDAY, 26 MAY

I've been taking up some of the endless kind offers of a 'long lunch to get over it'. Today was the big one – with Marco Pierre White at his smart new Drones club in Mayfair. We drank £500 bottles of Italian wine, ate sensationally good food, played spoof for ridiculous sums of money, and generally had a great drunken laugh. I staggered home at 5pm, put my head down for a nap and woke up at 3am totally disorientated. It was the best sleep I've had in years.

NEWS OF THE WORLD

BRITAIN'S MOST POPULAR NEWSPAPER

FEBRUARY 6, 1994   LAST WEEK'S SALE: 4,849,282   Price 50p   No.7826

PAGE 3 KATHY'S WACKY WEDDING

SEE PAGES 2 AND 3

WORLD PICTURE EXCLUSIVE

BARE HE IS!

We snap naked birdman swooping on Palace

MILLER: Trousers off

VIGNAUX: £1,500 romps

Defence chief in call-girl scandal

EXCLUSIVE
By ROGER INGALL

A DEFENCE chief with access to vital military secrets is dating a vice girl who has links with the IRA.

Ex-RAF intelligence officer Ian Vigneaux has spent more than £1,500 on seven sex romps with the hooker over the past fortnight.

He is under contract to the Ministry of Defence to design sophisticated security systems for key Air Force bases.

These include RAF Coltishall in Norfolk—home of the Jaguar fighter squadrons which saw action in the Gulf War and are now on standby for duty in Bosnia.

His fling with prostitute Susan Taylor leaves him wide open to blackmail.

Only last summer Susan, 24, was convicted of obtaining £10,000 from a wealthy client by deception. She is still serving a 12-month suspended jail

TURN TO PAGE 9

THIS is the heart-stopping moment a paraglider dropped out of the sky to run naked on the roof of Buckingham Palace.

With his private parts painted green, and a loud buzz coming from a propeller strapped to his back, James J. Miller sparked a massive security alert.

Seconds after his astonishing 7.30am landing, Miller—pictured here flying past trees in the palace grounds—stripped off his trousers and unhooked his engine. Then he

raced across the rooftop, giving a victory salute before being engulfed by a posse of armed police.

The 30-year-old American carried out similar stunts at last Monday's Bolton v. Arsenal match and at the Holyfield-Bowe world heavyweight boxing title fight in Las Vegas.

A police spokesman confirmed: "The man arrested was James Miller—and yes, he was covered in green paint. He's five pence short of a shilling."

By GARY JONES and CLIVE GOODMAN

FULL AMAZING STORY: PAGES 4 AND 5

GAZZA: TRUTH ABOUT TAYLOR, VENABLES AND ENGLAND PAGES 54 & 55

1994

FRIDAY, 10 DECEMBER, 1993

Tonight I had dinner with Rupert Murdoch in a private room at the Stafford Hotel in St James, opposite his London flat. Murdoch had asked Kelvin to get together some key *Sun* executives, old and young, to have a little verbal banter about the paper, the universe and life itself. Some wag sent me the invitation from Kelvin with a revised 'PS' stating: 'Dress down, Rupert's a casual kind of guy, be provocative and take him on if you don't agree with what he says, have a lot to drink because he will want to see you can take your liquor, and if you get the chance to pull a waitress then take it – he likes a man's man in his executives.' Fortunately I realised this was an invitation to commit suicide. We congregated in the restaurant, all bloody crapping ourselves. Deputy editor Stuart Higgins, leader writer Chris Roycroft-Davis, features supremo Neil Wallis, sports editor Paul Ridley, political editor Trevor Kavanagh – and me from the pop page.

Murdoch drifted in like a ghost, literally creeping up on us without any fanfare at all. I'd heard this was his deadliest weapon, his ability to just appear and scare the daylights out of you. It can be especially unnerving in the loo apparently. I mean, what the hell do you say standing next to the world's most powerful tycoon with your flies open? Dinner was fun. He was in a good mood, drinking his wine more enthusiastically than I thought he might, and the conversation was relaxed but challenging. I could sense him probing the table for the next creative genius, and coming up woefully short, I suspect. But we all gave it a good go. Some were too clever-dick, throwing all their great views on life at him like over-excited Jehovah's witnesses. Others were a bit too quiet and reverential, forgetting that he likes his executives to be confident leaders, not meek little mice. I just couldn't believe I was there, felt I'd got nothing to lose, and simply tried to engage in what I knew about and keep out of the stuff I didn't. Anything financial, for example – his area of undisputed global expertise – and my lips might as well have been stapled to the floor.

The key moment, though I didn't realise it at the time, came when the waiter asked if we would like a liqueur. Kelvin went first, saying no – because he's on the wagon. The others followed his lead, forgetting the crucial fact of his self-imposed month-long abstinence. When my turn came, I asked the waiter what he would recommend and he said, 'Peach brandy, sir.' I flashed a look at Murdoch, who seemed totally uninterested in whether I had one or not, and said, 'OK, one of those then, please.' Stuart Higgins next to me added chirpily, 'Make that two.' Then a loud Australian growl emanated from the head of the table: 'Make that three.' It emerged later that this was one of Murdoch's favourite after-dinner drinks. I finished the evening glugging my peach brandy contentedly.

FRIDAY, 21 JANUARY

I am on a plane to Miami in a bemused daze. Kelvin called me into his office this morning and looked even more conspiratorial than usual. 'The boss wants to see you.'

'Oh right, when, where – and more importantly why?'

Kelvin cackled, as he always does when he knows something juicy that nobody else knows. 'Miami, tomorrow – and never mind why, just go and see him. Might be nothing.' He handed me a plane ticket. I'd be leaving in two hours. No time to pack, just go to the airport and fly to Mr Murdoch. What the hell is going on here? Am I going to star in his next movie, run a TV station in Dallas, edit the *Melbourne Herald*? It could be anything. I reckon I'm a pretty good reporter, far too inexperienced for him to give me anything too big, admittedly, but I've got a chance here, a really amazing chance. One thing I mustn't be is under-prepared when I have my breakfast with him tomorrow morning. Which means I have got to rather quickly plug the yawning gaps in my knowledge of almost anything serious. So I've been flicking dementedly through *Newsweek*, *The Economist*, *Time* … anything they have on the plane that that looks remotely intelligent. I've read and re-read them until my insight into Clinton's foreign policy is probably greater than the President's himself.

9pm: I'm in my hotel now after a long flight. It's 3am in the UK and I've just called the features production desk to make sure everything is OK with the column. 'Oh yes, fine,' came the reply.

'Anything else going on?' I asked.

'Well, it's been a funny old day, hasn't it, what with Kelvin quitting?' said the sub. I tried to stay calm. Nobody apart from Kelvin knows where I am after all, and this is clearly now rather significant.

'Yes, yes, must have been. Sorry I missed it all. How did he explain where he was going …'

'Oh, he just said he was going to Sky and that was that; nothing too dramatic.' Sky? Bloody hell – Kelvin is quitting papers! This is like the Archbishop of Canterbury renouncing his faith to be a porn star. A genuine bombshell.

'What do you feel about his successor then?' I asked, wording the question as shrewdly as I could to hide my complete ignorance.

'They haven't announced it yet – no one knows what's happening.'

'No, no, sorry, of course, just thought you guys might have the inside track since I've been out of the loop a bit today.' I need a large scotch and a lie down. What the *fuck* is going on here?

SATURDAY, 22 JANUARY

This is all too ridiculous. I've been awake since 6am. I was shaking with nerves, and actually started pacing the room like some demented virgin in a brothel – talking to the mirror. 'Yes, Mr Murdoch, I agree that Clinton's been too aggressive in his macro-economic view of China.' And so on. I could barely think straight.

I called his room, at 8am as instructed. The growl came on: 'Allo.'

'Aha, hello, Mr Murdoch, it's Piers Morgan here. I believe you are expecting me to call.' Silence. Just long enough to make me think he hasn't got a bloody clue who or what I am.

'Ah yes, hi, Piers. Shall I meet you downstairs for breakfast in twenty minutes?'

I toyed with saying, 'No, no, half an hour's better for me, actually,' but managed to stop myself. It felt like twenty hours, not minutes. But then I saw him in the breakfast room, loping towards me. Casually dressed, and with a copy of *Newsweek* under his arm! Only question was … had he read it yet? We exchanged stilted banter about nothing in particular, then he asked how the news about Kelvin had gone down.

'Well, it's quite a shock I must say,' I told him. 'We sort of assumed that he'd go on forever, like Louis XIV or something.'

'Yes, well, he wanted a new challenge and he'll be great at Sky.'

'He's a genius,' I added, in a rather toadying way.

'Yes, he is. Completely mad, but a bloody great editor.' Breakfast arrived, but I was really struggling to consume a single morsel without accidentally spitting it straight on to his lap.

'What do you think of what Clinton's doing, then?' he asked. I almost gasped with joy: all that cramming on the plane had paid off. I embarked on a thorough, detailed analysis of all things Clinton. I was lucid, informed, mildly provocative (but only in a way I know he agrees with) and generally impressive. It was a world class display of bullshitting. Murdoch looked vaguely bemused, as if asking himself how a pop editor could possibly know this stuff. The rest of breakfast passed easily after that. I did OK.

Murdoch has an extraordinary mind, it races around all sorts of disparate subjects at high speed, pumping out completely unambiguous statements. He doesn't do middle ground. He is not a flashy dresser, and doesn't exude any Donald Trump-style flamboyance or showmanship. His power doesn't require him to impress anyone. He wasn't recognised by anyone in the room, there were none of the usual mutterings you see and hear if you go somewhere with someone like Richard Branson. But if, like me, you know who he is, then he holds your attention like Don Corleone in *The Godfather*. He is easy to talk to, and surprisingly funny. I really liked him.

At 10am, Murdoch left to prepare his speech for a big meeting of Fox Television affiliates and executives. He told me there was a party tonight to which I was invited, and he could see that I had perhaps come rather ill-prepared for such an event. 'Take my driver and get yourself some clothes,' he said. Minutes later I was plonked in the back of his Mercedes and being whisked around Miami searching for chinos and polo shirts – the News Corporation unofficial uniform. It all felt very, very surreal, mainly because I still had no idea what on earth was going to become of me.

At 3pm I met up again with The Boss, who suggested we go for a walk along the beach. *The beach*. I was going to walk along a *beach* with Rupert Murdoch. Christ alive. We boarded the Mercedes again, glided down to South Beach, and headed straight to the water's edge, where I was invited to take my shoes and socks off and the pair of us set off paddling through the breaking surf – with me trying not to giggle at the sheer absurdity of it all. Murdoch is bloody fit. Much fitter than my diseased, showbiz-damaged torso. He tore along at a pace that I found increasingly hard to match in the searing heat. And he chattered constantly, his extraordinarily quick mind whipping out thoughts and ideas for nothing in particular. We discussed the *Sun*, the *News of the World*, the two *Times* titles and some of our rivals. He tapped me for what I thought of the content, the editors, the staff.

I had nothing to lose, so I gave it to him straight, who and what I like and don't like. The *Sun*? 'Fantastic paper, driven by a fantastic editor.' I could never say anything disloyal about Kelvin. He can be monstrously cruel and impossible to work for at times, but his razor-sharp mind, journalistic genius and outrageous sense of humour have always inspired me and many others to greater heights. The *News of the World*? 'Great brand, but been off the boil a bit recently. Needs to break a few big stories.'

The Times? 'Well, I know someone must read it, but it's a bit too worthy for my liking.' He laughed. *Sunday Times*? 'I love Andrew Neil – editors should be like him, loud, opinionated, not afraid to get on TV and defend their papers and their stories. And he sets the agenda all the time.' Murdoch pondered this for a few seconds. 'Nah, editors should be anonymous and let their papers do the talking. Andrew is a good editor, he just doesn't need to tell everyone that all the time.' I didn't agree, but sensed I should let the moment pass. As we headed back to the car, I saw a young British tourist pointing at me. 'That's the bloke from the *Sun*, Pierce. You know 'im, does that Bizarre column. Bit of a prat.'

He didn't recognise Murdoch.

At 7.30pm Murdoch and I met up again in the hotel foyer to head off to the party. It was a relaxed affair, based around a huge swimming pool in a hotel nearby. The guest list was very corporate, with the odd Fox TV celebrity milling around from shows like *Beverley Hills 90210*. I was led around by Murdoch in a very solicitous manner, being introduced to everyone. Eventually we came across Dave Hill, the brash, brilliant, bearded Australian brain behind Sky Sports and now Fox Sports.

'Ah, Dave,' said Murdoch, 'this is a young friend of mine from London, Piers Morgan. He's going to be the new editor of the News of the World.'

Dave Hill pumped my hand. 'Congratulations, mate.'

I didn't know whether to laugh, cry, scream or just jump into the pool and ruin my new chinos.

I looked at Murdoch, who simply grinned back. 'Right, let's enjoy the party, shall we?'

And boy, did I enjoy the party. Murdoch left early, so I stuck about ten Budweisers down my neck and still my nerves were bursting.

At midnight I got back to the hotel. It was 5am in the UK. Too early to call anyone really, but I did think of one person who was probably awake and prowling. 'Kelvin, it's Piers. I think I've just been made editor of the News of the World.' Kelvin started to laugh, then completely lost it and began heaving with huge cackles. 'Has he done that, has he? Fucking hilarious, I can't believe it. Really? Christ ...'

SUNDAY, 23 JANUARY

I had a couple of hours' sleep, then got up feeling rather sore-headed to hear Murdoch address his Fox delegates. I sat in the wings watching the master at work. He was brief, devastatingly sharp, funny and supremely confident. Everything I hoped he would be, he is.

At midday he had finished and invited me up to his presidential suite at the Hyatt Regency to watch the NFL play-offs. It contained a grand piano, and in the middle of the giant sitting room lurked a chef with a barbecue, preparing burgers and hot dogs. There was also a large fridge full of ice-cold Buds. Murdoch's daughter Elisabeth was there, along with various chiefs of Fox movies and Fox TV, along with Dave Hill, and then there was a knock on the door and Barry Diller, boss of QVC Network, marched in, booming away about some TV deal so complex I couldn't work out what the hell he was on about. We watched the game, then Murdoch sidled over and announced, 'OK, Piers, I think it's time we went and talked newspapers. Meet me downstairs with your bag in ten minutes.' We boarded the Mercedes once more, and it headed to Miami International Airport where we drove straight on to the tarmac to a waiting Gulfstream jet. The crew were waiting on the steps, saluting. We ambled on, sat down and I was offered a chilled glass of Chablis, which I accepted. Murdoch sat back and promptly fell asleep as we took off. I was thus left sitting on my own in his new private plane peering out of the window, being asked to choose my main course for dinner (the coq au vin as it happens), and blinking in utter disbelief at the events of the past 24 hours.

Murdoch woke after an hour or so, and we talked papers. He was now entirely focused on the *News of the World*, ripping through an edition of the paper he'd brought with him, scrawling great red lines through page after page. 'This bloody headline busts, that story's a crock of shit, nobody cares about massage parlours any more, I have never heard of that so-called "star".' And so on. I agreed with almost everything he said, not audibly, just tacitly. His understanding of tabloid papers is phenomenal. He asked what I thought and I said, 'It is not rocket science. The News of the World just needs to break more big stories, project stuff more boldly, make it more saucy and less sleazy, and ramp up the sports coverage. It's been a very solid, very good paper. But it's looking a bit tired and needs an injection of fresh young talent. I think there's a fair amount of dead wood there that needs clearing out.' Murdoch didn't disagree with anything, which is hardly surprising, given that it was exactly the mantra any proprietor would want to hear.

We arrived at JFK in New York at 8pm, where yet another Mercedes was waiting on the tarmac to whisk us to the Hilton. I could get rather used to this style of travelling. No wonder he never seems jetlagged. Murdoch bounded out of the car, grabbed my bag from the boot and walked with me to the front desk. 'Right, Piers, that's it. Good luck, you'll be a great success and if you need me, just call.' 'Thanks, Mr Murdoch, I won't let you down.'

An hour later I was sitting in the bar of the hotel with a constant smirk on my face. The bartender asked why I was so happy. 'I've just been made editor of the News of the World in London,' I replied smugly.

'Never heard of it buddy, but hey if you're happy about it so am I. Let me get you another drink.' It was a suitably surreal end to a surreal weekend. Back in my room I called Mum to tell her the good news. There was a very long pause. 'The ... News of the World ... right ... I see ... well, how exciting darling, that's amazing.' I think if I'd told my mother I was going to be a mass murderer she might have been able to cope with it better.

But I know she will add it to her *Sunday Times* order, and quietly be delighted to cancel the *Sun* during the week.

TUESDAY, 25 JANUARY

Back in London, and rumours were flying around all day about my possible elevation. My computer messages amused.

'You can confide in me,' said Jamie Pyatt, a great guy but a serial office gossip and quite possibly the very last person on earth I think I'd confide in right at the moment.

John Kay, the chief reporter, *does* seem to know. 'On a totally serious note, may I be the first to congratulate you, an inspired appointment.' Kay's always the first to know everything.

Kelvin gives another considered and rational opinion of a major issue.

'All the boys from Arselickhan send their love, just in case it is true,' joked Peter Cox, the night editor.

The news was confirmed at 3pm. I was formally appointed 'acting editor' of the *News of the World*. The current editor, Patsy Chapman, has been on sick leave for months and is not coming back. But until the situation is sorted properly between her and the company, I will remain 'acting'. I also suspect it gives Murdoch a convenient space of time to see if I am up to it.

Stuart Higgins was made editor of the *Sun*. No 'acting'. A good day for peach brandy.

I made a short, anodyne statement for the press release: 'The *NoW* is a national institution and I look forward to the challenge of keeping it where it is, at No. 1.' No point in banging on too much before I've even got there.

Chris Roycroft-Davis, a man less than half as clever as he thinks he is and with a crude, Dick Emery-style humour, sent a computer message: 'I forgot to congratulate you in the toilet just now. Congratulations. It's one of the biggest I've seen. Nice colour too.'

WEDNESDAY, 26 JANUARY

The papers are all full of my appointment, and there has been general bemusement and shock that a kid of 28 has been put in charge of Murdoch's biggest-selling newspaper train-set. The *Guardian* summed it up with a headline saying GUNGE TANK VICTIM CHOSEN AS NEWS OF THE WORLD ACTING EDITOR. This was a reference to me being 'gunged' on *Noel Edmonds' House Party* last month. It does put the elevation into a certain perspective.

Pete Waterman visited my *huge* new office for a chat and showed an admirable lack of deference to my new status. 'Fuck me, Piers, how have you wangled this one, mate?' 'To be honest, Pete, I have no idea, but I'm just going to make the most of it.'

Grandpa sent a note congratulating me, but warning: 'The *NoW* newsdesk are noted as the hardest-nosed hacks in the business. Loyalty is a virtue unknown. The stick before the carrot is the message from GP.' Hmm. He would know, as a freelance investigative journalist he's dealt with them for years. And I've heard this from others, too.

THURSDAY, 27 JANUARY

My old prep school headmaster, Nick Milner-Gulland, sent a very funny note today: 'Another first for Cumnor House, I think … I have no doubt your first thought will be to raise the whole tone of the paper and that you will pull it up rather than let it pull you down! How will you manage to control all those dreadful reptiles?'

Pete Waterman sent a note: 'I have never seen anyone look so frightened as you did in your office today. I'm sure it was shell shock, but I know you'll cope

OK.' Wonder if he gives his acts the same confidence 'boost'. He's right though; underneath all the bluster I am bloody terrified.

My last Bizarre column appeared in the *Sun* today, suitably headlined END OF THE PIERS SHOW. Let's hope that's the last time I have to read that headline for a while.

FRIDAY, 28 JANUARY

It was Kelvin's leaving party at Planet Hollywood tonight and the great man received his obligatory framed front page, boasting the headline IF THAT'S A FAREWELL PAGE ONE MY PRICK'S A BLOATER. It also contained a spoof story written in Kelvinese: 'Worried *Sun* executives were last night searching for a gnat's arse. For that is everything they knew about journalism for the past 13 years.' Kelvin himself read out a message from his brilliant long-serving former news editor Tom Petrie: 'Thanks for not inviting me to your party. I wouldn't have fucking come anyway.' The mood was surprisingly sad, general consensus being that Kelvin may have been a monster but he was a bloody funny monster and a tremendously instinctive tabloid editor. I've never seen such a whirlwind of raw energy, and he kept it up from 7am to midnight, seven days a week. Days off and holidays were annoyances to him.

I remember one Christmas Day when his family lunch collapsed early amid furious rows and he stormed back to the office, screaming abuse at everyone and ripping the paper to pieces. And a Boxing Day when he rang my parents' home at 8am demanding to know where the hell I was (after agreeing I could have the day off) and then greeted my breathless arrival in the newsroom two hours later with the words, 'Oh, I was only joking, matey.' Seasons of goodwill are not huge priorities in Kelvin's life. Nor does he wish them to be anybody else's. All that mattered to him was the *Sun*, and crushing the opposition. Whatever happens now, the *Sun* will be a quieter, less volatile, probably more pleasant, but ultimately more boring place to work. I'm getting out at the perfect time.

MONDAY, 31 JANUARY

I got my first profile this morning, written in the *Guardian* by Roy Greenslade. He's tracked down my old associate editor at the *Sutton Herald* in South London, Joan Mulcaster, who says, 'Piers had this knack of getting old ladies to talk to him. He didn't get on with the editor though, because he was too good and he knew it.' Both allegations are pretty much right.

TUESDAY, 1 FEBRUARY

My first proper week started today at the *NoW*. And amid all the fawning and arse-licking a great letter arrived from Steve Sampson, a former *Sun* executive:

Piers, in many ways you've taken on the loneliest job in the world. Watch the room empty when the shit flies. Get two or three trusted people around you but don't be blind to what they say. Make one a production genius who can rip the paper apart for you on a Friday night. Don't listen to those who say you can't make the paper late off stone, if it's better it's worth it. Instincts are all. One of Kelvin's great assets was being visible. Everyone saw him and he saw everyone. I remember the night he spotted that sport were doing a single column on the back page about Don Revie having a terminal wasting disease, next minute it was the front page splash.

I read the letter several times. It's just what I needed to read.

Held my first morning conference today. Every Sunday paper has a morning conference on Tuesdays, usually around 11am, where the heads of the news, features, picture and sport departments present their schedules. It's the time when the editor gets to say what he/she likes or doesn't like, and for any opinions or gripes to be aired. They can be, from my experiences with Kelvin, very jolly or very brutal affairs. I tried to sound upbeat, vaguely intelligent, and on a mission. 'We need to break big stories, simple as that. You get them and I'll run them.'

WEDNESDAY, 2 FEBRUARY

The staff are still deeply uneasy about my appointment. I heard one of the older sub-editors whisper, 'Fuck me, he's younger than my grandson,' as I was given a proper tour of the newsroom. These are serious professionals, many with more than 25 years' experience on the biggest-selling newspaper in the world. They are not immediately impressed by this spotty little kid marching in from some pop column to tell them what to do. And I feel quite intimidated by the stares, the huddles, the murmurings. I'm a confident person by nature, but this is going to test that confidence more than anything in my life. I decided to stamp my mark by making the morning conference a daily event rather than the twice-weekly meetings of the past. 'We're going to have a daily paper ethic here,' I told the executive team, 'not the rather cosy gentlemen's club style you are clearly used to enjoying.' I also sent a memo to all staff declaring that the legendary three-hour drunken lunches – another *NoW* 'perk' – are over. More murmurings of discontent. It's written all over their faces – who does this little jumped-up prat think he is? But I reminded myself of the words of Douglas Jardine, the England cricket captain for the notorious bodyline tour to Australia of 1932/33, who, when told he wouldn't make many friends with his aggressive tactics, replied, 'I haven't come to make friends, I've come to win the Ashes.' And win them he did.

SATURDAY, 5 FEBRUARY

My first live day of editing. Stuart Higgins had warned me to get most of the paper done by close of play Friday night because 'nothing ever happens on a Saturday'. So I had it all done last night and it looked great. We were leading on a classic *News of the World* story about a defence chief, at the MoD and with access to intelligence secrets, having sex with a prostitute who has links to the IRA. And we'd got some great exclusive pictures of Page Three girl Kathy Lloyd getting married in an Elvis chapel in Las Vegas, plus a sensational interview with Gazza about England, Venables and Taylor. I spent hours crafting it all to make everything perfect and when Murdoch called about midday I was confident he'd like it. 'How's it going, Piers?' he asked cheerfully. 'Oh great, thanks, Mr Murdoch, we've got some brilliant stories at the front and back of the paper.' And I then talked him through the splash. 'Great story,' he said. 'That's the kind of thing the NoW should be doing.' I wanted to burst with joy. We chatted for about ten minutes and he couldn't have been more encouraging. 'You've got to get out there and kill 'em,' he said. 'Just shake it up, break big stories, and make the paper full of energy.' And so on. I felt like I'd just been transported to some celestial oasis where a harem of 100 beautiful women awaited me. I sat back in my chair and reflected on how easy this editing lark all seems. 'I'm a natural,' I told myself modestly.

Then, twenty minutes later, I was informed by a deadpan newsdesk exec that a man had parachuted on to the roof of Buckingham Palace half naked, with his genitalia painted green.

'Nothing ever happens on a Saturday' was all I could think of. My mind raced. I was going to have to change the paper, but how much? Time appeared to be moving rather quickly all of a sudden, and when I went outside my office there was a team of highly polished professionals waiting anxiously for this 28-year-old rookie to make his bloody mind up. This was real pressure, I knew. I felt it strongly. But I knew I had to deal with this test quickly and decisively. I marched over to the back bench and started giving some instructions. I kept telling myself to act the big player even if I felt like a minnow in a pool of piranhas. I wanted to keep the splash we had, but Harry Scott, the cheeky but talented No. 2 on the production desk, ended that thought process by saying, 'Boss, how many times does a bloke with green bollocks fly on to Buckingham Palace?' He was right: not very often. So we re-did the front page with a new banner headline, NAKED BIRD-MAN SWOOPS ONTO PALACE ROOF, and stuck the RAF scandal down the side, with Kathy and Elvis at the top. It looked a bit messy, but it seemed OK.

Kelvin rang to offer support, and I told him what we're doing. 'That's a crap headline for starters,' he sneered, quite rightly. 'Get them to come up with something better.' Trouble was that I'd already told them I liked it. But as I went over to change the headline I was shown a grainy photo of our birdman in mid-air over the Palace. It was terrible quality, but it was the only photo, and allowed me to change my mind about splashing it without losing too much face. 'Bare he is!' shouted Harry, who is slightly mad but great at headlines. I slapped the photo on the front with that headline and the page looked instantly better. The *NoW* first edition deadline is always 7.30pm and I worried and fretted over every tedious little detail until the moment came. Every minute you're late starting the presses – or 'off stone' as it's known in the trade – means sales lost. We were just about on time, and I took a few key execs into my office and got some wine out. They all told me it was a great paper, but then they would, wouldn't they? Our rivals' first editions came in during the next couple of hours and we dismissed their paltry efforts. Curiously, they all ran with the stories that my team had predicted earlier in the day. I left the office about 10.30pm feeling utterly drained, but totally exhilarated at the same time. It has been a very long day and I couldn't wait to get home to a large Jack Daniel's. It seems like a dream. But it's true – I am now doing one of the most exciting jobs in the entire world. And it's bloody great.

TUESDAY, 8 FEBRUARY
A Tory MP called Stephen Milligan has been found dead, hanging trussed up with electric flex, wearing women's stockings and suspenders, with a black bin liner over his head, and an orange suspiciously lying nearby. Nobody's quite sure what he was doing. But one thing's for sure, John Major's 'Back to Basics' speech probably didn't include this particular form of nocturnal pursuit.

SATURDAY, 12 FEBRUARY
We got wind late in the day that the *Sunday Mirror* were exposing a portly 47-year-old Tory MP called Hartley Booth for having an affair with a 22-year-old nude model called Emily Barr. Just to complete the amusement Booth is a lay preacher in his spare time. Emphasis on the word 'lay', clearly. What *is* it with these Tories? Ms Barr seems a game girl, admitting, 'Going to bed with a man no longer automatically means having full sex, though for me if it got to an orgasmic situation I'd feel a little guilty saying no …' Poor old Hartley never stood a chance. He denied having sex with her, which seems very unlikely given her earlier statement of intent, but he has resigned anyway, saying: 'I hate double standards and stood as an MP for the family.' Which is admirably honest.

We also ran a three-page wife-swapper exposé, including such delights as the hotdog seller who likes to 'do it with relish' at orgies in his village. I love these real life naughty stories, but Bob Warren – our most senior news executive and a veteran of 30 years at the *NoW* – threw a slight spanner of caution into my over-excited works.

'Piers, did you know that a teacher killed himself a few years ago over a similar wife-swapping exposé we ran?'

'No, I didn't.'

'I just think in light of that we need to think very carefully about the justification in each case.'

'Yes, of course. Thanks, Bob.'

I was a bit taken aback by this. It hadn't crossed my mind to 'justify' a wife-swapping story.

SATURDAY, 19 FEBRUARY

Another week, another shagging MP. But this time from the other side. We're exposing Labour's firebrand MP Dennis 'Beast of Bolsover' Skinner tomorrow as a 'loverat' under THE BEAST OF LEGOVER. He's been spending weekends with a wealthy American called Lois Blasenheim at her home in Carlisle Square – one of the poshest parts of London. Everyone will have a good laugh because dear old Dennis is always the first up on his feet in the Commons to hammer opponents who commit sins of the flesh. Who could forget his 'Crack the whip a bit harder' jibe at Norman Lamont after the Miss Whiplash scandal – or his 'Stop playing with yourself' entreaty to Cecil Parkinson after the Sara Keays affair blew up. Murdoch laughed out loud when I told him the story. 'That's great, he's had it coming for years. Of all the people … just goes to show they're all at it, aren't they?' I suspect they probably are. Later in the day I read Woodrow Wyatt's dreary political column and spotted that he was attacking the *Sunday Times*. I took out the offending line. It's senseless having a go at papers in our own stable. Wyatt seems a decrepit old dinosaur from the dark ages, and is already in my sights for early extinction.

THURSDAY, 3 MARCH

A fax arrived at 8am this morning from Woodrow Wyatt. 'I understand you censored my reference to the *Sunday Times* in my column at the weekend without even consulting me. Censorship is not acceptable to me. It has never happened to me before and I must make it clear it cannot happen now.' The pompous old fart. I am staggered by his arrogance. But slightly unnerved by it too. People only behave like this to their boss if they know something you don't. I made a few discreet enquiries and discovered he and Mr Murdoch go back a very, very long way, and he actually played a key role in helping The Boss buy the *News of the World* in the first place. But I'm not going to let that give him free rein to behave in this absurd manner. I fired back a fax saying that as long as I am editor, I will delete what the hell I like. He phoned immediately, chuckling, and said perhaps we ought to have lunch and 'talk about it'. Where's my gun?

FRIDAY, 4 MARCH

We've been offered the TV star Jonathan Ross's laptop computer for £20,000. When we asked the guy trying to flog it why on earth he thought it was worth so much, he leered and said, 'Because there's so much filth on it.' We had a look to see what he was on about and sure enough there was an extraordinary 2000 word missive from Jonathan to his wife Jane which could best be described as 'graphic', detailing precisely what depraved acts he'd like to get up to with his young bride. There were also all his contact numbers, scripts for new shows and business accounts. But Jonathan's a kind of mate, and I want to hire him as our new movie critic. So it was his lucky day that this guy came to us – claiming implausibly to have 'found the laptop in a taxi'. We persuaded the seller to part company with the computer for £3000, then handed it back to a rather relieved Jonathan on condition that he confirmed to our readers that he sends his wife disgusting 'love byte' letters – which he has done, hilariously confessing, 'It's embarrassing in this day and age to be exposed as an out-and-out heterosexual who still wants to have sex of the filthy variety with his wife, but there we go: I plead guilty.' Not sure I'll ever be able to look at him in quite the same way, though. I wonder if he knows a load of my staff have read the letter? Probably. He's quite media savvy.

TUESDAY, 8 MARCH

Max Clifford, an infamous PR man with a growing influence in Fleet Street, has offered us an amazing story about a woman called Lady Bienvenida Buck, a sexy Spaniard who claims to have had a lengthy affair with the married Chief of Defence Staff, Sir Peter Harding. She's got lots of letters, and her testimony is very detailed and credible. In light of all the recent fuss about soldiers from the lower ranks being punished for having affairs, this is topical and sensational, the perfect cocktail. There's also a handy 'security' aspect to it all, because she tells us how Harding used to give her all sorts of secret information about military plans and projects as they lay in bed. And how he 'didn't think much' of John Major. She also says she's a great 'friend' of Valerio Viccei, the notorious Knightsbridge bank robber, just to add even more intrigue to an already fantastic tale. Our negotiations with Max took a slight downturn this afternoon when my deputy editor Phil Hall agreed a very reasonable figure of around £40,000 with him, put the phone down, and said to me, 'Max is so thick sometimes. He could have got double that.' Unfortunately Phil then realised he hadn't hung the phone up properly. And yes, Max was still there, listening. 'Hello, Phil,' he said, not a trace of anger or bitterness in his voice; 'that's just cost you another forty thousand – not a bad minute's work for someone who's so thick.'

Phil and I looked at each other, and had to laugh. Most people would have seen that incident as a relationship-wrecking insult. Max just saw it as a financial opportunity.

Lady Buck's testimony is dynamite stuff, but we need to prove it beyond any doubt and that won't be easy given who Sir Peter Harding is and the tight security around him. Bienvenida has no such worries, though. 'Oh, I'll just ask him to take me to lunch at the Dorchester Hotel and you can photograph us coming out,' she says. It seems absurd that it will be this simple, but she is chillingly confident. Sure enough, he has instantly agreed to take her to lunch. Poor guy.

WEDNESDAY, 9 MARCH

Had my lunch today with Woodrow Wyatt at the House of Lords. He looked about 120. We had a glass of champagne and he told the full story of what a great mate he is of 'Rupert's' and why his column must never be touched, and so on. I wanted to exterminate the old buffer there and then but can see that might be politically tricky. He's definitely got some hold over Murdoch and I will just have to put up with him for the time being.

THURSDAY, 10 MARCH

Bienvenida Buck and Sir Peter Harding had their meeting at the Dorchester today as half my staff secretly invaded the place inside and out, in various disguises. If we'd been the IRA stalking him it couldn't have been easier, and he'd be a dead man. As it is, Bienvenida's nearly as lethal. She brought him right out to the steps of the entrance, gave the *NoW* van a quick knowing glance, kissed him passionately with their heads turned to where she knew our snappers were training their lenses, then let him lead her to a taxi where she snogged him again. It's all in the bag. What an operator she is.

SATURDAY, 12 MARCH

We laid out the story over the first five pages with the headline CHIEF OF DEFENCE IN SEX AND SECURITY SCANDAL. Then at 5pm we put the allegations to the army and an MoD spokesman called me back twenty minutes later to say 'It's all rubbish' and Sir Peter 'denies any impropriety'. I went into an ever-so-slight panic. What if she's a conwoman and it's all a set-up? What if she's just a social friend and that's why he let her kiss him? What if … the questions came thick and fast and I suddenly felt sick with worry. At that kind of moment you need stronger, wiser, more experienced heads. Step forward Tom Crone, our legal manager, who is now married to Pierce Brosnan's ex-girlfriend. Anyone who can nick James Bond's bird has got to be a cool customer, and Tom is everything you need in a newspaper lawyer. Superbright, fearless and cunning. He came into my office and shut the door. 'Look, Piers, this is a true story, I promise you. There is too much evidence. Ring the MoD back and read them one of the letters – then ask if they want to retract the denial before they look ridiculous.'

I made the call and read out an extract from one letter saying: 'Your face is serene, your eyes piercing, your neck elegant, your skin so fair, your nipples so delicately pink like a girl, your breasts so petite, your legs so gazelle-like, your smell so overpoweringly intoxicating.' I also pointed out that we have video of Sir Peter kissing Lady Buck outside the Dorchester on Thursday and will be releasing it to TV networks. I then gave the MoD guy ten minutes to come back to me before we publish his name and the denial on the front page, next to 'The Kiss'. He said he'd 'get back very quickly, sir'. Seven minutes later he was back on the phone. 'Erm, is it too late to withdraw our denial, Mr Morgan?' Bingo! I wanted to run outside and scream 'Hallelujah!' at passing strangers. The moment when you get the admission is such a buzz.

Later, I was told again what our rival tabloids were putting in their papers tomorrow. It seemed very early, and rather suspicious, to know all this so soon. There were sniggers when I asked how we come to be so well informed, and I decided not to ask too many questions in case I didn't like the answers I got back.

SUNDAY, 13 MARCH

Down to Sussex for a Mother's Day lunch with Mum, also attended by Jeremy, Charlotte, and her husband Patrick. As army officers Jeremy and Patrick were both somewhat alarmed by our big story. At 5.30pm we turned on the evening TV news and they were leading on Sir Peter Harding having just announced his resignation. There was a long silence. Then Jeremy exclaimed, 'God almighty, that's my boss. What the bloody hell have you done?' I wasn't quite sure, to be honest. Britain's most senior military man had quit over one of my stories. And I've only been editing a few weeks.

Patrick laughed. 'Well, on the positive side, he was RAF, and we'll probably get an army man in charge now.' I poured a large whisky. I was flushed with excitement and panic and adrenaline. It can't get bigger than this in our game. Harding's arguably the biggest establishment tabloid scalp since Profumo. Max Clifford rang to congratulate me. 'Well done, young man,' he said. 'I told you it would be big, didn't I? Now if you'd like to pay me a bit extra to reflect what's happened today, that would be very nice.'

Typical Max. And frankly, why shouldn't he get more out of it? He's been on every TV and radio show all day selling our story for us. Not so thick after all …

MONDAY, 14 MARCH

Sales went up 80,000 copies on the back of our story. A big result for an editorial property with no TV advertising to back it up. I have been bombarded all day with requests for interviews, notes of congratulations, flowers and champagne. I feel like I've won an Olympic gold medal for gutter journalism or something – utterly, deliciously intoxicating. I must admit this evening I have been thinking a bit about Sir Peter Harding, whose glittering career – and probably life – now lies in tatters. He's been a bloody fool, and deserves to be exposed for his hypocrisy and the stupid risks he's taken. But it's a high price to pay.

SATURDAY, 19 MARCH

Week Two of Lady Buck, and we've filmed a fantastic TV advert with her in very saucy underwear saying to the camera in a thick Spanish accent, 'I am Bienvenida Buck, the lady at the centre of the sex scandal rocking your country. Tomorrow I reveal how your Chief of Defence Staff was a tornado in my bed.' Well, I'd buy it. The interview was sensational – if only all kiss-and-tell women were this bright, funny and classy. 'Sir Peter liked a sex game called "Yellow Pages",' she said. 'He let his fingers do the walking all over my lips, legs, breasts and bottom.' She added that his 'lust exploded like an Exocet missile', and that Sir Peter 'kept the Prime Minister waiting as he fondled me under the table'. But our plans to wipe out page one for it again were changed at the last minute when we discovered that the *Sunday Mirror* were breaking a big story about Michael Aspel having an affair. The reason we knew this, I've now found out, is because we have one of the *Sunday Mirror's* journalists on our pay roll, bunging him £250 a week for a rundown on their stories, and more if he gives us a big one. It's a disgrace, of course, and totally unethical. But very handy. To make it even more amusing, he's their crime correspondent. We also, unbelievably, have a similar source on the *Sunday People*, a secretary who does the same for a bit less money. So for under £500 a week we always know exactly what our competitors are doing.

Our mole from the *Mirror* told us they'd finally nailed Aspel after a twelve-week investigation and were definitely running it tomorrow. But he's denying an affair so they are going to have a watered-down headline saying ASPEL'S SECRET TRYSTS WITH BLONDE. We promptly called Aspel's representatives and got a full confirmation of his relationship with the woman, Irene Clark, and the end of his marriage, enabling us to run with a much stronger headline, ASPEL'S SECRET AFFAIR. If I was their editor I'd want to top myself. The *Sunday Mirror* eventually changed their headline to our one for their last edition. The humiliation was complete.

THURSDAY, 24 MARCH

I took Bienvenida Buck to the Savoy Grill today for a celebratory lunch, with Phil Hall and Max Clifford. She tottered in wearing incredibly high stilettos and a revealing purple dress, leaving little of her splendid charms to the imagination. The effect on the whole room was extraordinary. Rich, powerful men dropped their knives and forks to gawp at her in wonderment. It's easy to see why Sir Peter found her so hard to resist. Almost every businessman and politician in this room would have taken her straight upstairs to one of the suites if they'd got the chance. We sat at a centre table, with Bienvenida holding everyone's attention like a brightly coloured piranha in an aquarium full of cod. She was hilarious company, intelligent, and very, very sexy for an older woman. 'Ooh, Piers,' she said at one stage, 'I do love a younger man with so much power in his fingertips.' Her delicate, bejewelled hand was resting on my left thigh under the tablecloth. 'Do you now … ,' I stammered, firmly placing her hand back on her own thigh. 'Yeeeesssss,' she purred, placing it back again. Then Max spotted an old mate, *Daily Express* editor Nick Lloyd, dining at another table with Bernard Ingham, Margaret Thatcher's former spokesman. Ingham, an insufferably pompous buffoon, has used his *Express* column this week to lambast our girl for her disgusting behaviour. We hatched a quick, mischievous plot that Bienvenida was only too pleased to play a starring role in.

Minutes later she stood up and walked slowly over to greet them, most of the room watching her every totter. 'Oohhh, Bernard,' she cooed, to his horror; 'how lovely to see you again. It's been such a long time.' Nick Lloyd burst out laughing, realising this was a glorious wind-up. But Bernard exploded with indignant, spluttering rage. '*What?* We have never met before, that is a monstrous lie.' He was bright red, foaming at the mouth, and generally self-imploding. Bienvenida reached over to give him a little peck on the check, pausing to make sure everyone in the room saw it, then returned to a round of applause from our table. Don't think Bernard will be bothering her again in his column.

SATURDAY, 16 APRIL

Murdoch's getting agitated about Major's Government and thinks we should call for a radical reshuffle in the summer, dumping 'dead wood like Douglas Hurd' at the foreign office and getting someone in as Chancellor who can raise a lot more money or, as he put it, 'bring the bacon home'. Murdoch isn't impressed by Major's demeanour: 'He's got to sort himself out. He looks miserable, doesn't he? I hear he's mostly on his own in Downing Street because Norma doesn't like coming up to town. That's not going to work.'

SUNDAY, 8 MAY

Tory MP Michael Brown was our front-page victim this week for having an illegal gay affair with a twenty-year-old toyboy he shares with an MoD official. All fairly grubby, and I'm not sure I can get too worked up about the 'illegal' aspect, frankly. But we drummed up the usual 'security risk' aspect, given that Brown's taken his boyfriend into the Commons. Major's brought all these exposés on himself, with that ludicrous 'Back to Basics' speech at the last Tory conference, but I am beginning to wonder where it will all lead. It strikes me that probably *every* Tory MP is up to some sexual shenanigans, but we can hardly get them all fired or there will literally be nobody left to run the country. Still, needs must. Brown's shenanigans will shift a few papers, get followed up everywhere and ensure the *NoW* leads the news agenda again. We're on a roll and it feels fantastic. The staff are much happier now: they haven't had such fun in ages and can see that although I may be a bit wet behind the ears at least I have the balls to run big stories, and with the *NoW* that's half the battle won.

Murdoch's been in town this week and he told me he had a secret dinner with Major and Woodrow. I said I knew because Woodrow couldn't wait to tell me he'd set it up. Murdoch laughed: 'Yes, I can imagine.' I asked what he thought of Major now he'd seen him. 'He's nice enough but he kept complaining about everything, the press in particular.' Woodrow told me Murdoch and Major had had a huge row over Europe, which appears to be an increasingly favourite subject for Murdoch's wrath. He hates Brussels, and thinks the single currency is a 'bloody bad joke'. Andrew Neil is quitting the *Sunday Times* and is going to do a TV show in America. He rang me today to say he's getting loads of money to do it, and had had enough of editing anyway. But I'm not convinced. Woodrow says he's been deliberately shuffled out because he backed Heseltine in the Tory leadership contest, and Murdoch's gone off Tarzan in a big way. I'm beginning to understand more about the true scope of Murdoch's influence, and the way he does business. And it's quite scary.

THURSDAY, 12 MAY

John Smith, the Labour leader and Prime Minister-in-waiting, has dropped dead from a heart attack. I am not a very political animal to be perfectly honest, but even I can see this could be a critical moment for Labour's chances of getting back into power. Smith was a straight, credible, highly electable man who has had Major on the ropes for months. Who replaces him may well decide who governs this country for the next decade. My political editor says Westminster's gone into an absolute frenzy of gossip and speculation. What a vile business politics is, almost as vile as journalism.

SATURDAY, 14 MAY

Murdoch rang today to see what the latest is on the Labour leadership battle. Luckily I'd been briefed. I told him that shadow Home Secretary Tony Blair is the favourite, and that senior Tories are telling us he's the one they fear because he's young, bright, and not too left wing. 'Yeah, I hear he's the one too. Brown seems to be drifting out of it,' he said.

Robin Cook and John Prescott are in the running too, but there's something about Blair that looks the part. He just doesn't seem as threatening as most of his socialist mates.

SATURDAY, 21 MAY

Murdoch rang again, and he's still only really interested in the Labour leader-ship race. I made him laugh by saying Cook is at the centre of a huge party row over whether he is too ugly to be leader. 'We're being briefed that Britain won't have a vandalised and terminally untelegenic garden gnome as Prime Minister,' I said. Murdoch laughed. 'You can't see many women rushing out to vote for him, can you?'

SUNDAY, 29 MAY

We exposed yet *another* Tory MP, Alan Clark, today for having an affair with a judge's wife *and* her two virgin daughters. Even by this legendary philanderer's standards, this seems pretty spectacular work. The judge, James Harkess, wailed, 'Call me an old fool, but I trusted the man.' An admission which does seem to suggest a certain failing in his ability to 'judge'. His wife Valerie, who admits she had 'forceful and selfish sex' with Clark, has called Clark a 'depraved animal'. And her daughters Alison (seduced when she was 'alone and upset in London') and Josephine ('coaxed into bed when I went to him for help') are equally distraught at his appalling behaviour. But this animal magnetism appears to be precisely why they all went to bed with him. There was a great letter from the man himself to the three Harkess women saying, 'My God you bitches, you temptresses, you looked fantastic, give me more.' We've been chasing this story since Clark published his infamous diaries, full of clues about them. Our chief feature writer, Stuart White, has done a brilliant job finding them in South Africa and persuading them to exact their revenge. When we confronted Clark last night, he said, 'I never comment on what ladies say about me.' His splendidly snobbish wife Jane added crushingly, 'If you bed people of below stairs class they will go to the papers.' Harkess meanwhile warns darkly, 'I'd like to have him horse-whipped.' All cracking stuff: this one will run for weeks.

WEDNESDAY, 1 JUNE

Patsy Chapman has officially stepped down as *NoW* editor for health reasons. Patsy was one of Fleet Street's first woman editors, a superb journalist and very popular with everyone who worked with her. But I can't pretend I am not delighted she's standing down.

I get confirmed as editor and a pay rise to £125k. It seems an absolute fortune, double what I was earning on the *Sun*.

SUNDAY, 5 JUNE

Another raft of great Alan Clark revelations from the 'coven', as the Harkess girls are now known. We've splashed on his claim to Valerie Harkess that he had a two-year-old lovechild called Billy by another mistress. It has been a very hard story to prove because the woman concerned doesn't want to talk and there's no father's name on the birth certificate. But we eventually gathered enough evidence for me to be reasonably satisfied. Our No. 2 lawyer, Daniel Taylor, came into my office late yesterday afternoon and I asked him what he thought. 'Well, Piers,' he smiled, 'do you feel lucky?'

I smiled back. 'Yes, I do, actually.'

And we let the dice roll, mainly in the belief that Clark has no reputation left to defend.

We've also revealed that he lusted after his mother-in-law and Maggie Thatcher, and used to flash his phallus at gay parties. He's already steaming, and this lot will lead to volcanic-force eruptions I suspect.

FRIDAY, 10 JUNE

We got an amusing story in today about Reggie Kray being visited by old foes

Charlie Richardson and 'Mad' Frankie Fraser in his prison cell for a cup of tea and biscuits. Harry Scott wrote the headline: I COULD MURDER ANOTHER MCVITIE. Magic.

SATURDAY, 2 JULY

Our Irish desk came over this morning raving about a story they've got concerning an expected visitation by the Virgin Mary to a young Yugoslavian girl in Dublin tomorrow at 5.40pm precisely. I burst out laughing. 'Let me get this straight. People actually believe the Virgin Mary is going to turn up?' 'Yes, boss, in a private home. This is serious, apparently this girl gets visitations all the time.' Now as a good Catholic boy, all I know about this is that a lot of other good Catholics in Dublin are going to get quite excited if anything actually happens. 'Splash on it,' I said. 'Just put "Virgin Mary to appear in Dublin at 5.40pm" and see what happens.'

SUNDAY, 3 JULY

Paul Gascoigne, England's soccer hero, sensationally confessed to us this week that he's been beating up his fiancée Sheryl Kyle for two years. It's a brilliant, shocking interview by Rebekah Wade, who is emerging as a real rising star.

Gazza admits, among other things: 'I hit her because she wasn't paying attention to me. The bruises used to frighten me. I've been a violent bastard and a coward and I want the world to know it.' He emerges as a pathetic character, and the Gazza halo may never recover its shine after this story.

MONDAY, 4 JULY

Unfortunately, the Virgin Mary didn't turn up. But 3000 Dubliners did, and most of them were clutching a *News of the World*. Sales rocketed, but it does feel a bit cheap. Still, next week I think we'll try PROPHET MOHAMMED TO APPEAR IN BRADFORD AT 9AM and see how we get on.

TUESDAY, 5 JULY

We've signed a reporter from the *Sunday People* called Phil Taylor, who has cultivated a brilliant relationship with Diana's 'friend' James Hewitt and reckons Hewitt is nearly ready to do the big confession interview about his love affair with the Princess. Hewitt agreed to Phil's request to meet me, Phil Hall, the deputy editor, and Rebekah Wade at the Carlton Towers Hotel in Knightsbridge. Rebekah booked a suite and sent over a little 'recce' team in the morning to kit it out with secret tape devices in various flowerpots and cupboards. If all else fails we can always expose him later for even thinking about ratting on Di. When he arrived, Hewitt was charming to the point of obsequiousness, but obviously nervous and suspicious. I cut to the chase. 'Look, James, everyone knows you had a relationship with Diana and it will all come out one day. You may as well get in first and make some money out of it. You know and trust Phil, and we are prepared to pay you five hundred thousand for a full interview.' His eyebrows flicked up. We knew from Phil that Hewitt likes his money, and had already flogged him various stories for bundles of cash in car parks. This would be the biggest cheque the *NoW* has ever paid anyone, but then he would be the biggest catch. 'What would I be expected to say?' he asked. 'Well, you'd be expected to confirm that you regularly slept with the future king's wife, James,' I replied. It was all rather dramatic.

'I … see … right … ,' he eventually said.

The rest of the meeting was spent talking about how and where such an interview might take place, and what else he might talk about. As he left, I joked, 'Of course, you could always do a book, James, and make a million out of it probably.'

He stared at me intently. Then said goodbye.

'Think he'll go for it?' I asked Phil Taylor.

'I don't know. He's definitely tempted though. You can see that.'

THURSDAY, 7 JULY

The newsdesk have unearthed an intriguing tale about a female switchboard operator who chatted up a caller and became obsessed with him, tracking down his address and then pestering him big time. It was a classic *NoW* story: Sex-mad phone girl stalks handsome stranger for illicit fun and games. Only the guy didn't find it funny and complained to the police. We were all set to run with it when the reporter I sent to confront her rang to say she'd broken down and pleaded for mercy, saying she had recently been released from a psychiatric hospital after trying to kill herself and the exposure would send her over the edge. And if we published she would try again. Her story checked out. And I pulled it. Lots of people break down when we confront them, and lots threaten to kill themselves. But there is a difference between paedophiles and lonely disturbed women like this. I could not have lived with myself if we had exposed her on page seventeen and then she had killed herself.

I am developing a curious moral code as I go. Sometimes the job does feel a bit like playing God with people's lives. I get, ultimately, to decide every week who lives and who dies by the *NoW* sword. And that sword can be a ruthless, highly destructive implement. I've not had any sleepless nights yet, but I can feel them coming. The obvious glee with which my newsdesk or features executives rehearse the weekly stories of misery and mayhem created by our revelations slightly unnerves, as well as excites, me. But editing a paper like this does not allow much room for sentiment.

FRIDAY, 8 JULY

Nigel Dempster, the *Daily Mail*'s famous gossip columnist, is rather unhappy about a piece we've run, accusing him of starting the false rumours that Lady

Sarah Chatto is pregnant. 'I object most strongly to having my name and the *Mail* diary dragged through sleaze by your so-called "Royal Editor",' he ranted in a letter to me. 'We wrote that a baby, perhaps next year, would seal the couple's happiness. Where does that suggest what you alleged? It is disgraceful you should implicate my good name to print this trash and I demand an apology.'

I replied: 'Dear Nigel, I never realised you were so sensitive. The Chatto tip probably came from one of your own diary staff anyway, didn't it?'

A lot of our stories come from people working on diaries like Dempster's, working long, hard days on relatively meagre shift rates while their celebrity boss is swilling away in some flash restaurant. They can make thousands of pounds secretly tipping us off about good stories behind their bosses' backs. It has crossed my mind that some of my own staff might be doing the same.

MONDAY, 18 JULY
When I was a young teen I used to correspond with the great Australian cricketer Sir Don Bradman after becoming obsessed with his amazing statistical career.

Last month I wrote again, suggesting he write an article or two on the forthcoming Ashes tour.

'You are kind in suggesting I might write for you, but please put the idea out of your head,' he replied, going on:

> I will be 86 next month and my writing days are over. I still get deluged with requests like this but have surrendered to the more youthful Benauds and others. I did my duty for 60 years and that was enough. I still struggle around the golf course, break my age occasionally, but get very frustrated at not being able to do the things which were once so simple. Your elevation to editor of the *News of the World* is certainly a big leap. What a responsibility, good luck. Don Bradman.

THURSDAY, 21 JULY
Tony Blair has become the new leader of the Labour Party, gaining 57 per cent of the vote. There's something about this guy that is very exciting. And obviously his party agrees.

TUESDAY, 2 AUGUST
Kelvin quit his job at Sky today after just seven months, citing a 'personality clash' with Sam Chisolm, the abrasive foul-mouthed Australian who runs the station. Nobody was particularly surprised. Put two jackals into a pit together and something's going to give. I phoned to offer support and found Kelvin in typically philosophical mood. 'Honestly man, life's just too short to wake up every morning and realise you have to work for a complete cunt.' I laughed and pointed out that that's exactly what *Sun* staff did for thirteen years. Kelvin

laughed too. He's always been able to laugh at himself just as much as he laughs at others. He doesn't know what he's going to do next, but I suspect it will be something where he's his own boss. Beneath the bravado, though, I can tell he's very hurt by Murdoch appearing to back Chisholm and not him in this battle of super-wills.

SATURDAY, 13 AUGUST

Murdoch's heading off for a holiday in Alaska, but has caused quite a stir by telling a German magazine he might back Blair in a general election. When he called today, I asked him if he meant it. 'No, no, I just said that I've backed Labour politicians before in Australia and wouldn't rule out backing one here like Blair. They just spun it up a bit. But Major's got to sort his Cabinet out, it's a mess. Hurd and Heseltine should go.' I can sense a massive mood change going on here. The Tories look like dying donkeys, and Blair is starting to resonate with the public as a fresh, dynamic, viable alternative. Murdoch doesn't back losers, and he is talking in a way that suggests he might ditch the Tories.

SATURDAY, 20 AUGUST

Gary Jones, my chief reporter, breezed into the office looking rather excited, flanked by news editor Alex Marunchak. 'Got rather a big one here, boss,' Gary said, with commendable understatement. 'Diana's a phone sex pest. The cops are investigating hundreds of calls she has made to a married art dealer called Oliver Hoare.' When I'd climbed down from the walls, I asked what evidence we had. 'Here's a read-out from the police report,' he said cheerfully. Now *that* is what I call evidence.

The details were fascinating. Hoare's been getting loads of silent calls for over a year, at all times of day and night, and eventually reported it to both BT and the police. BT set up a trace and discovered the calls were being made from Kensington Palace. When this was pointed out, Hoare admitted that he's been speaking regularly to Princess Diana about her separation from Prince Charles and has been 'consoling her and becoming quite close to her'. He adds that his wife is 'more on Prince Charles's side and doesn't like Diana'. And he thus believes it is Diana making the silent calls. The report says Hoare wanted to confront Diana about what's been going on but was advised not to by the police, but he could do so if she made another silent call.

Sensational stuff. Gary explained that the *Sunday Express* had the story, but it was pulled at the last minute because their owner Lord Stevens is a mate of Princess Diana's and didn't want to embarrass her. I have no such allegiance, thankfully. We put the story to Hoare, who asked for time to think, then called back and very politely said he didn't want to comment. No denial, though. Then a bizarre call came from Richard Kay, the *Daily Mail*'s superb royal reporter and a known confidant of Diana's, saying he 'might be able to help' get us something from the Princess if we told him what we have. Nice try, sunshine. Kay's allegiance would only ever be to the *Mail*.

We published the story over the first five pages under the headline DIANA'S CRANKY CALLS TO MARRIED ART DEALER. We used the word 'cranky' because we couldn't think of anything else that fitted, or that didn't accuse her of doing anything illegal. When I finally suggested 'cranky' everyone around me agreed it was brilliant. What they meant was 'Thank God for that, we've got something that fits, even if it does sound weird.' By midnight the world is erupting to the news that Di's a 'cranky' phone pest. Still sounds weird.

SUNDAY, 21 AUGUST

Every TV news bulletin led with the story all day and we were flying off the shelves. But at 10.30pm I got a worrying call from the newsdesk saying Diana had given a lengthy interview to the *Mail* denying making the calls and saying 'these wicked lies will ruin my life'. Richard Kay had done the chat in a car round the back of Paddington Station apparently, and it is pretty strong stuff. 'What have I done to deserve this?' she is said to have squealed tearfully. 'I feel I am being destroyed. There is absolutely no truth in it. Someone somewhere is going to make out that I am mad, that I am guilty by association, that the mud will stick.' And so on. Buried away in the text is a throwaway line that she did once hang up on Hoare because she thought his phone was being tapped. But otherwise she lets us have it with full barrels.

The news bulletins instantly started switching from our great scoop to Diana's furious denunciation. And there are, by midnight, already calls for me to resign if she is telling the truth. I feel decidedly uncomfortable about this.

MONDAY, 22 AUGUST

An extraordinary day. I slept very badly, waking every hour in a cold sweat. There is nothing like the joy of breaking a huge story, and nothing, as I am now finding, like the sheer horror of thinking you might have dropped an almighty clanger. I got up at 6am and read the *Mail*. It's hideous, a full denial in every way and so gut-wrenchingly emotive I can see no way of surviving this if we've got it wrong. She even cites specifics showing that she could not have been making the calls we printed at the time we said she did because she was a) in the cinema, b) having her hair done, c) at her lawyer's office, or d) (ironically) having lunch with Lady Stevens, wife of the *Express* boss.

Alex stood firm when I called him from home at 7am this morning. 'We've had the report read to us: she's lying,' he reassured me. But he knows we can't reveal this fact without potentially exposing our source, so where does that leave us? And what if the report is a forgery? I felt sick to the pit of my stomach. I couldn't eat or even drink a cup of tea. It was hellish.

The newsdesk told me the phones were going mad with media organisations wanting to know if I am going to quit! Christ.

I sought refuge in the shower, letting the water blast on my frazzled head for fifteen minutes. Then Marion tapped on the door with the immortal words, 'Mr Murdoch is on the phone.' I exited slowly, water dripping down my naked body. I'm half blind without my contact lenses and stumbled around for a few seconds trying to pick up the phone.

This was it, then, he'd heard what had happened and he was going to fire me right now like some Sicilian Don whacking an errant family member. I took the phone and said as brightly as I could, 'Good morning, Mr Murdoch.' There was a long, crackly silence. It was agony. 'Hi, Piers, I can't really talk for long but I just wanted you to know your story is one hundred per cent bang on. Can't tell you how I know, but I just know. So get on TV and tell the world she's a liar. Then say we're running another load of great stuff about it next week. OK?' I wanted to die with ecstasy on the spot. 'Yes, right, Mr Murdoch. Well, I never had any doubts, of course … as for the further revelations, though, we, erm, don't actually have any.' Pause. 'Oh, you will have by Sunday – don't worry. Gotta go. Good luck.' I put the phone down. Who the hell had he spoken to? Who cares? I am in the clear, and it feels fantastic. Right, she's going to get it now.

I called my PR team and ordered a series of interviews in which I suggested the Princess was being 'economical with the truth' and gloated for good measure that 'the Mail, I'm afraid, has fallen for a rather cynical royal stunt here by running her denial of a true story'. At 10.30pm I heard that the *Mail* was continuing to back Diana's version of events in their first edition. But there was more admission buried in the copy suggesting Diana 'was in the habit of ringing Mr Hoare and it is possible she may have replaced the receiver when he didn't answer' – but it was all perfectly innocent, etc. Which obviously confirms our story. What a mess the *Mail* is in. But you can hardly blame them, given that she has clearly fed them a pack of lies. I'd have run her interview too if she had called us: who wouldn't have?

TUESDAY, 23 AUGUST
The focus switched today to who leaked us the story. Everyone seemed to be blaming the police so I issued a statement saying it was categorically *not* a serving police officer, which is perfectly true.

SUNDAY, 28 AUGUST
A 105-year-old man is divorcing his 100-year-old bride in Iran. He said, 'She won't obey me any more.' She said, 'I'm tired of him after seventy-five years.'

I don't know why it's so funny, because it's quite sad, really, but it must be, because we all fell about laughing. Newsrooms are odd places.

SUNDAY, 11 SEPTEMBER
We splashed today on an interview I've done myself with Phil Collins, who's left his second wife Jill for a 22-year-old Swiss beauty called Orianne Cevey. It's

typical Phil, all heart on his sleeve and searing honesty. 'I know people will think I'm an old fool because I'm 43 and she's 22, but she's very bright, funny and so beautiful and makes me happy.' I've always got on well with him. He used to send me furious notes when I ran Bizarre, castigating me for mistakes.

We also carried a very funny story about Tony Blair's new press chief, a former *Mirror* hack called Alastair Campbell. I'd told our newsdesk to dig into his background a bit when his appointment was announced and it turns out he used to write lurid porn for *Forum* magazine, and wrote his prose around a sex-crazed, bagpipe-playing, bed-hopping hero called … Alastair Campbell.

Examples of his work appear to confirm he was some sort of gigolo on the French Riviera. One extract has him being seduced by a 40-year-old 'Mediterranean type' called Madame Ridaudo who set him up as a male prostitute in her bordello.

' "Are you good in bed?" asked Mme Ridaudo. "Yes," I said, "definitely." '

He then boasted of 'Pascaline, a 37-year-old wife of a fat German financier who paid me 2000 francs to spend three days on a yacht'. And of another encounter with a Dutch beauty, he drooled: 'Her nails bit into the flesh of my buttocks.' And then there was the 16-year-old German girl who stopped mid-bonk to ask his name:

' "Alastair Campbell," I replied, and returned to her crotch.'

When we confronted him about his literary past he admitted: 'It would be wrong to say there is *no* truth in any of it. It was youthful exuberance and a way to make some cash.'

I think we can safely conclude that Blair won't be leading any 'Back to Basics' campaign in light of this revelation.

Campbell rang tonight, laughingly confessing his shame, and inviting me to come in and meet him and Blair.

MONDAY, 12 SEPTEMBER

It was Rupert Murdoch's annual drinks party tonight at his London flat in Piccadilly. I met Tony Blair and his wife Cherie at the entrance to the lift and introduced myself.

Blair was very friendly and joked that he really ought to be getting the stairs. 'Yes,' I replied, 'it's a long way up and we don't really want another Labour leader to have a heart attack, do we …' Even as I said it, I realised it was in spectacularly bad taste. Tony politely semi-laughed. Cherie just looked appalled. Not a great start.

The party was great fun, though. Notably for my first meeting with my schoolboy heroine, Maggie Thatcher. She looked old and grimaced a lot – apparently this is because of appalling constant pain with her teeth, which numerous operations have failed to cure. She also drank extraordinary amounts of whisky from a vast tumbler. She must have literally swigged half a pint of the stuff in the half hour I stood talking to her. But her mind was still sharp, and when I suggested that recent interest rate rises were hurting ordinary people she exploded. 'What a load of nonsense. It's much better for them, because they'll have a lasting, smooth recovery without inflation coming back again, which it was tending to do.' I replied that, with all due respect, this was not going to help all those families with mortgages and there was a real fear we were heading for another meltdown on house prices as we did in the late 1980s.

She stared at me for a couple of seconds, aghast that someone my age was daring to confront her in this manner. Then she started physically jabbing me in the chest, raising her voice to semi-shout: 'You don't know what on earth you're talking about, young man, and I suggest you think very carefully before putting any of that rubbish in your newspaper.' Her jabs were hard and her bony little fingers induced not insignificant pain. The lady was not for turning, definitely. Nor did she seem remotely interested in listening to anything anyone apart from herself said. Which was perfectly understandable given her legendary status. Mr Murdoch came over at one stage, heard her berating me, and laughed: 'I wouldn't tangle with her if I were you, Piers: there will only be one winner.' Even The Boss was intimidated by her

Later she reclined on a sofa with another tumbler of whisky, chatting intimately to Woodrow Wyatt, who was also tucking into a large tumbler of the same medicine. I am starting to realise that Woodrow's tentacles spread far, wide and powerfully. I am going to have to tread rather carefully with him.

MONDAY, 19 SEPTEMBER

Alan Clark is not very happy about us saying in an editorial that 'we need protection from rotten apples like Alan Clark'. A furious letter arrived today, saying, 'The theme of this editorial was a personal attack on me for being a) "nasty", b) "little", c) owing my position in the Government to a "silver spoon", d) being "devious" over arms-to-Iraq, e) having made a "sneering" withdrawal from politics.'

He said he's 'mystified', explaining, 'You and I have never met, Mr Morgan, nor have I commented on either the quality of your paper or your own personal conduct and behaviour – which I have not the slightest interest in.' He then rebuffed the allegations:

a) It is not worth me contesting this but it is indicative of the prejudice you have against me. b) Since I am 6ft tall the term 'little' is pejorative rather than descriptive. c) Whether or not a silver spoon is a better or worse route to office can certainly be debated. But I take its use here to be a device to arouse jealousy and irritation in your readers. d) The charge of behaving 'deviously' over this matter is unusual given that it is my candour that has been the subject of universal and laudatory comment. e) Nothing I have said or written could ever be classified as 'sneering' and this is part of your general campaign to lower me in the esteem of the readership.

He goes on to claim the public were always on his side, citing a poll on *This Morning* as proof: 'They got 5,300 calls in 35 minutes in which I secured a 72 per cent approval rating compared to the Harkess family.'

Still raging, Clark accused me of ratcheting up the nasty coverage. 'Your charges got more and more vicious, wild and without substance. You claim I had a lovechild, and that I have a habit of exposing myself at gay parties. Both of which were deeply hurtful and insulting to my family and friends.' He concluded:

> Let me say that the gathering and dissemination of 'scandalous' news about public figures is (in my view at least) a perfectly legitimate pursuit which boosts circulation and is nearly always amusing to read. But in this case I am not alone in detecting a deliberate and contrived attempt to inflict personal damage by fabrication and embellishment, that amounts to a vendetta.

End.

It was a very Clark-like letter, articulate, funny, threatening.

TUESDAY, 20 SEPTEMBER

An agency put out some copy this afternoon on Kelvin secretly filming a pilot for a new Meridian TV chat show in Kent. It revealed that 'sources on the station said MacKenzie wrecked one run-through in front of a studio audience by shouting "Stop that fucking chattering" after hearing a director's instruction over his earpiece to move cameras'. I fear Kelvin's conversion to civilian life is a bit like that of a Vietnam veteran coming home to run a local corner shop. It's going to be a long, difficult journey of discovery.

WEDNESDAY, 21 SEPTEMBER

Had a cup of tea with Tony Blair and Alastair Campbell today in Blair's office at the Commons. He's very charming, and solicitous – even pouring the tea himself.

'I want a good relationship with you and your paper,' he admitted. 'It's important we have a constant dialogue and understand where each other is coming from. I don't want to get chewed up and spat out like Neil Kinnock was by the Sun.'

I liked him immediately. And Campbell. They're a couple of bright, young, focused and impressive men. The Tories are going to get a bit of a run for their money now, I reckon.

SUNDAY, 25 SEPTEMBER

My first Tory Party conference, and I couldn't have wished for a more entertaining start. I entered the Imperial Hotel to see a kerfuffle erupting in the foyer.

It was Alan Clark, haranguing Bob Warren and Rebekah Wade – who I've recently made features editor – about our exposé. I marched over and confronted him. 'Alan, Piers Morgan. Either punch me in the face or buy me a pint.' He stared at me for at least twenty long seconds, his expression a mixture of revulsion, bemusement and then mild amusement. Eventually he burst out laughing and said, 'Right, you little bastard, pint first – punch almost certainly later.' I laughed back. 'Of course, Alan, honestly I've been punched by much less impressive men than you, I assure you. It would be an honour to be floored by you.' We headed for the back of the bar and I bought a round of foaming pints. Not quite as foaming as Mr Clark, but foaming nonetheless.

Eight foaming pints later, and a lot of fun in the meantime, we got down to the negotiations.

'This is my suggestion for how we resolve things,' he said. 'For the distress you've caused my wife, ten thousand pounds. For the distress you've caused me, ten thousand. And for the distress you've caused my sons, twenty thousand. I can't look them in the face after you accused me of flashing my knob at gay parties.' I considered my position. 'Look, Alan, that's a bit on the pricey side to be honest. I've got a better idea. You give me fifty thousand and we won't disclose the other nine women who've come forward to say they had affairs with you.' He snorted loudly, then leant over towards me. 'Nine women … God – what were their names?'

TUESDAY, 27 SEPTEMBER

I love Michael Winner's restaurant review column in the *Sunday Times* and took him out to lunch today to try and persuade him to do a general news comment column for the *NoW* as part of my plan to move the paper a bit more into the mid-market. He was everything I assumed he would be – brash, name-dropping, amusing, very intelligent. And he insisted on paying the bill too. 'I always pay the bill, that gives me the right to say what I like about the food and service,' he said.

I called John Fraser, his 'fixer', later to offer Michael £120k a year, pointing out this would make him the paper's highest paid columnist, earning him even more than Woodrow Wyatt.

SATURDAY, 1 OCTOBER

James Hewitt's done a secret book about Diana and it's hitting the bookshops on Monday. The cheeky bastard. He's taken my joke seriously and blown us out of the water. I called in Phil Taylor and told him to empty his notes from our meeting with him. If Hewitt's going public about Diana then he must be admitting an affair, and we're going to expose him first.

I splashed the story huge on page one: MY 3-YEAR AFFAIR WITH DI. Even though everyone in Fleet Street's known the story for years, the public haven't, and it will cause a sensation.

WEDNESDAY, 5 OCTOBER

John Fraser faxed me with bad news. 'It seems highly unlikely we can proceed. The absolute minimum Michael would accept is £150k a year plus £20k expenses. We understand from impeccable sources that this is the sort of figure top columnists receive, even if your Mr Wyatt does not.' I have decided to play it long and didn't reply. He'll come down. He wants it too much.

THURSDAY, 6 OCTOBER

I attended the premiere of a new Disney movie tonight, *The Lion King*, and a rather dull affair was enlivened when Kris Thykier, a senior employee of Freud Communications, the PR firm running the event, decided to unceremoniously try and eject me and Stuart Higgins from the party afterwards in case we upset Elton John, another guest. Thykier is normally a pretty smart guy, but this was not his finest moment. 'Kris, with the greatest of respect, piss off,' I said, and Stuart was rather more abusive. We stayed where we were.

Ten minutes later, Elton John came over and started chatting quite happily to Stuart and me, saying how sorry he was for any misunderstanding and how it had nothing to do with him.

As we all laughed and joked together, I saw Mr Thykier in the corner of the room, surveying the scene with a face that said 'Beachy Head please, one way.'

I'll drive him there myself.

FRIDAY, 7 OCTOBER

I arrived, still steaming, in the office around 9am and ordered the executive team to remove every single thing from this week's paper or magazine, and anything forthcoming in the schedules, which involved any client represented by Freud Communications. They could whistle for it, frankly. I know it was a bit petty and I should have risen above it, but I want these people to get the message that we won't be dicked around by them. We scrapped several interviews, a big promotion and a news story. A panicky Matthew Freud called to ask what on earth was happening, and I told him that sadly the *NoW* was no longer going to work with his company on anything ever again and I explained why, adding that the only thing that might rescue the situation was the severed head of Kris Thykier. Within two hours, a grovelling fax arrived from Matthew, offering 'profound apologies and regret'. He says: 'Kris was instructed by a senior member of the film distribution staff to ask you to move to a different part of the room. This request was completely inappropriate and should have been ignored. I hope this very unfortunate incident does not affect our ongoing relationship, while understanding your irritation and anger.'

I decided to let him sweat for a bit, then lifted the ban. It won't happen again because the balance of power as to who needs who most has just been firmly established.

SATURDAY, 8 OCTOBER

Lord Longford's sent me a letter about Whitemoor Prison, subject of a recent break-out, defending Derek Lewis, head of the prison service, and attacking the Home Secretary Michael Howard – and he is not happy that I have refused to publish it.

In a second letter, he writes:

> I must conclude that, unlike your rival the *Sunday People*, you will never find room for a letter which criticises your line, however mildly. But I don't despair. I am hoping for early promotion to the editorship of the *Sunday Times*. Now there is a paper after my own heart. They published a letter from me recently AND ran a glowing review of my book. You continue to do more than well but remember 'humility and reliability'.

Longford is a lifelong friend of my grandfather and a great, kindly, eccentric guy. But we are not going to become a weekly platform for his interminable causes, I'm afraid.

SATURDAY, 15 OCTOBER

Jonathan Dimbleby's eagerly awaited book on Prince Charles is being serialised in the *Sunday Times* tomorrow and we spent all morning planning how to nick it from them. They, too, are part of the Murdoch empire and their offices are just a few corridors away. But they'd stepped up security and it wasn't going to be easy, particularly as John Witherow, the editor, told me to 'fuck off' when I asked for an early steer. But like all broadsheets they wouldn't have a clue how to repel my sophisticated operatives. I despatched Rebekah Wade to do her worst. Rebekah 'acquired' some News International cleaner's clothes and hid her distinctive flowing red hair under the uniform white hat. Then she headed down to the room where the *Sunday Times* inserts their sections into the main paper, and hid in the loo for two hours waiting for the presses to start. The plan worked a treat. As the *Sunday Times* started clicking off the press, Rebekah emerged from her hideaway, ran over, helped herself to a copy, then raced back to the *NoW*, with her hat falling off to reveal she may not be who they thought she was.

I had a copy of the *Sunday Times* before Witherow did, and it was sensational stuff. But he went completely berserk when he found out and sent security guards up to get the paper back. We hid it and played dumb. When they finally went away empty-handed, I got a call to go and see managing director John Dux urgently – Witherow had called him in after calling me first and shouting, 'Theft isn't journalism, Morgan – you bastard!' I left the team to crash all the text straight into the paper, literally lining up a dozen sub-editors with photocopies of each page to input it as fast as they could. 'Use every fucking word,' I said, laughing.

Witherow has wound me up all day, this is payback.

We missed the first edition, but the vast majority of our readers would get a paper headlined CHARLES: I'VE NEVER LOVED DIANA. This was based on the amazing third paragraph in the *Sunday Times* splash, which said: 'The Prince makes it clear he was never in love with Diana and felt he had to propose after he came under pressure from his father.' The detail from the book was just amazing. Charles says Diana slashed her wrists in front of him, his dad was mean to him, his mother never talked to him, and he was bullied at school. Quite what he hopes to achieve by coming out with all this is beyond me. But one thing's certain, Diana's going to flip her lid when she reads our front-page headline. We already had a paparazzi photo of her and Oliver Hoare speeding late last night out of Kensington Palace after some sort of secret tryst. What the hell is she plotting?

Meanwhile, back in John Dux's office, I arrived for my 9.30pm bollocking, and Witherow started ranting and raving like a lunatic, calling me a 'petty thief', and 'disgraceful crook'. Dux kept nodding, but I could see he was trying not to laugh. After all, he was going to win all ways up here. Both his papers were going to sell by the barrel-load. I quickly realised that the longer I could keep the row going, the longer our presses were going to run without anyone stopping them. I turned to Witherow and started shouting back, to his bewilderment, then fury. Then John started shouting and there we all are, bawling away in a back management office as thousands of *News of the World*s rolled out every minute with the hot story. When I finally got back to my office after 10pm, Murdoch called and I told him we were ripping into the 'brilliant Sunday Times stuff on Charles and Diana'. He would definitely have known from John Dux about what's been happening. But he just chuckled and said, 'Well, make sure you credit them.' He knows where his bread is buttered too.

SUNDAY, 16 OCTOBER

We have run an article by Labour's new leader Tony Blair today headlined: MAJOR'S FAILED AND HE KNOWS IT. This will enrage Major, and Woodrow Wyatt. So it has a double benefit. I do like Blair, he sounds so dynamic compared to Major and his ghastly old bores. He also sounds more centre ground and less threatening to the electorate than the Michael Foot and Neil Kinnock brigade. Murdoch agrees. 'He's an interesting guy this Blair, isn't he?' he said on the phone last night. 'Someone you could imagine people voting for.'

TUESDAY, 18 OCTOBER

Michael Winner faxed to give his latest views on his salary. 'I've been mulling over Winner's World and its possible glorious rebirth. I am driven to the view that I would feel uncomfortable working for less than other similar columnists receive. However I will go down a further £10,000 to £160,000 which would include £20,000 expenses so long as they are guaranteed.' God, he's a greedy sod. I've been round his house and it's worth squillions. But I guess this is how and why he's got squillions. I replied that we can go to £140k including expenses.

THURSDAY, 20 OCTOBER

Winner is still grasping for a few extra pennies: 'I say we split the difference and settle for £150k including expenses.'

I give up. 'We have, as you movie people like to say, a deal. Get your agent to call mine about the small print.'

SATURDAY, 22 OCTOBER

Our managing editor Stuart Kuttner has had a call from a Palace contact, ringing with the approval of Diana, saying the Princess was 'very distressed' by Charles's claim not to love her, and wondering if we remember pictures of her and her husband on their second honeymoon on an island in the Bahamas. The snaps, she believed, were not published at the time because they were deemed too intrusive, but she would have no argument if we wanted to run them now. Because 'they prove he loved me'. It's extraordinary that she would do this, but also an indication of how hurt she's been by this particular revelation. We checked the safe, and sure enough there was a set of amazing photos of Diana and Charles romping together in the surf, looking for all the world like the most loving couple imaginable. We ran them under the headline THE LIAR KING.

John Dux has sent clear guidelines to me and Witherow for this week's serialisation of the Dimbleby book. We are not to use anything until our third edition, we will restrict our coverage to the front page and three pages inside, credit the *Sunday Times* throughout and not claim it is our exclusive. The words 'horse' and 'bolted' spring immediately to mind. I have ordered the shortest ever print run of the first two editions so we can tuck into the *Sunday Times* nice and early. They'll never know.

SUNDAY, 6 NOVEMBER

We've exposed David Mellor for having a second affair, this time with a Lady Penelope Cobham. It had been a bit tricky standing the story up because the devious old dog has a flat in the same block as the Defence Secretary, Tom King, so security was tight. We cracked it by getting a female reporter to hang around by the door pretending she was pregnant until someone let her in. She went to the right floor and waited until she'd seen both Mellor and Lady Cobham go into the same room. When we put the allegations to Mellor he responded by announcing his immediate plans to divorce wife Judith. But refused to elaborate when we spoke to him directly, snarling at our reporter with no apparent sense of irony, 'You are a pompous prat.' The pair of them seem heartily relieved it's all out in the open. Certainly more pleased than Judith Mellor or Viscount Cobham appear to be.

MONDAY, 14 NOVEMBER

We ran a photo of Spike Milligan in yesterday's paper looking a bit unhappy under the headline CLOWN IN THE DUMPS. The intro read: 'Once the nation rocked with laughter at his funny voices, and crazy antics. Now he strolls the streets of London alone and unrecognised, a shadow of his former self. Spike got barely a second glance from passers-by. Get well Goon!'

Unfortunately I discovered today that the reason nobody recognised him was that … it wasn't him. As Dempster gleefully points out in his *Mail* diary this morning. Oh dear. Still, Spike will see the funny side, I'm sure. He's a comedian.

TUESDAY, 15 NOVEMBER

For a laugh I called Dempster's Diary pretending to be furious that they have slurred us over the Milligan photo without checking with us first – and demanding an apology. He wasn't there (when *is* he there?) so I left a message insisting he call asap.

WEDNESDAY, 16 NOVEMBER

Dempster took the bait. A letter arrived by fax still banging on about bloody Lady Sarah Chatto's baby plans. 'Until you issue an apology to me for what was one of the most dishonest ploys I have come across in thirty years of journalism, I will not address the matter you have raised.' He then managed to drop in that he's 'spoken to Lord Snowdon', who he claims backs him up. And he said he's also spoken to Spike Milligan, who is threatening to sue us. Dempster's such a ridiculous name-dropper. Still, he's a bit of a legend, I suppose, so I wrote back thanking him for his thoughts and offering lunch as an olive branch.

A loner weirdo called Colin Stagg's been cleared of killing a young mother, Rachel Nickell, on Wimbledon Common – despite most people thinking he probably did it.

One of my team has had the brilliant idea of putting Stagg through a proper lie detector test. We found a man who did police polygraphs for years and he agreed to do it, as did Stagg – a decision that in itself spoke volumes for his claim of innocence. He passed it easily, with the polygrapher declaring, 'There is no doubt he's innocent. He's a lonely, shy and dysfunctional man, but he didn't kill Rachel.' It's powerful stuff, and the pictures of him wired up are sensational.

THURSDAY, 17 NOVEMBER

Britain's most fearsome libel lawyer, Peter Carter-Ruck, has written on behalf of his client Spike Milligan, saying the photo was a 'deeply offensive, unpleasant and hurtful attack on our client which will have a most damaging effect on him professionally'. It went on to say that far from being a 'clown down in the dumps', Spike in fact has 'two books in the bestseller list for this year and has completely recovered from his operation, taking daily walks and swims of up to twenty lengths at his country home'.

It then demanded the usual compensation etc. I genuinely cannot believe how prickly Spike is being over this.

SUNDAY, 20 NOVEMBER

The National Lottery kicked off last night and was a massive instant success. We are, as I've always suspected, a nation of gamblers.

TUESDAY, 29 NOVEMBER

Sinead O'Connor has never been massively keen on me since I wrote a front page splash in the *Sun* headlined SINEAD THE SHE-DEVIL after she said support- ive words about Saddam Hussein in the 1991 Gulf War. But we had an extraor- dinary kiss-and-make-up moment late last year when she summoned me to an Irish pub in North London, gave me a great interview and posed for pictures kissing me. So when the picture desk showed me photos today of her kissing her husband in the street, suggesting they are back together, I dropped her a line by courier bike to try and squeeze a few quotes out of her.

She sent back a simple message: 'Tell him to fuck off.' I replied: 'Isn't life a bit short for all this? I liked you when we met but could rapidly go off you again if you keep telling me where to shove it. Come on … give me a call – it is the season of goodwill, after all.'

Dempster meanwhile says he'd be 'delighted' to have lunch. Whether my liver will remains to be seen.

WEDNESDAY, 30 NOVEMBER

Arsenal manager George Graham, who I've signed as an expensive commenta- tor for this season, has given a full interview to the *Evening Standard* about Paul Merson and drugs – a week after telling me he would never talk about it in the *NoW* or anywhere else. I was furious when I saw it and sent him a note saying: 'I am not prepared to carry on paying you £5000 a month for comparative bollocks while you save the best quotes for our rivals for free. I think we should have a chat asap.' I wonder how he'll react. He's so used to treating his players like some totalitarian general, I suspect rather badly.

Gary Farrow, agent and friend to many stars, rang me in a panic this morn- ing to say he is in deep shit with Elton John because someone's told Elton that Gary's been flogging me stories about him and other celebrity mates for years. Whoever it is has gone to the trouble of forging a letter from me confirming this. I sent an instant fax to Elton saying it's rubbish and pointing out the number of things he knows Gary must have seen and heard that never got printed. I say Gary's name doesn't appear on our contributions system at all, and 'nor does his granny's, his local publican's or his pet chihuahua's. He is no snitch, Elton, and never has been'.

This all sounds like a vicious smear. Gary had Elton, George Michael and Bob Geldof as godfathers round the font for his daughter's christening and turned down six-figure offers for the pictures. He may, by his own admission, be a shameless star-fucker, but he's not a grass.

THURSDAY, 1 DECEMBER

Elton John rang, and sounded unbelievably grateful for my letter, and incredibly relieved Gary was not guilty. 'It would have broken my heart,' he said. 'I couldn't believe it but the evidence looked damning. I am so glad it isn't true.' We then had a brief chat about 'sources' in general. 'Look, Elton,' I said, 'don't think we sit here thinking what great guys these people are when they ring us up shopping their celebrity friends or employers or relatives. We think they are scum, like you do. But we will pay them and we will publish what they say if it is true, because that's the game we're all in, and you know that as well as I do.'

He didn't sound overly impressed by my attitude. 'You always have the option *not* to pay them,' he said scornfully. 'Yes, Elton, and you have the option not to use my paper to help you flog the odd dodgy record, but you choose not to take that option either.' He had the good grace to laugh.

FRIDAY, 2 DECEMBER

George Graham's agent has replied to me because 'George is busy at the moment'. Never a good start when pacifying any editor. We tend to be quite 'busy' too, most of the time. George, of course, refutes every allegation of wrongdoing and demands an apology from me or he'll cancel his contract with us. I replied: 'If George discovered that Ian Wright was nipping off to White Hart Lane to score goals on Mondays after skipping Arsenal games claiming unfitness … I don't think he'd like it very much. But I'd like to move on amicably, and please assure him he's still the best manager in Britain.'

I've been a bit weak on this one, to be honest. I should have torn up his contract. But I've let my Arsenal heart rule my head.

SATURDAY, 10 DECEMBER

Sinead O'Connor has replied to my letter in a manner which I think confirms there's been a bit of a downturn in our relationship.

Peirs [sic], I couldn't care less if you like me or not frankly. You are nothing but a crawling sliming little gutter maggot. You have no right to bother me at my home, or pry into my life, or harass my friends on the phone. You have put myself and my family in severe danger on occasion with your lying stories like SINEAD THE SHE-DEVIL. You will get what you give out, you will get your come-uppance one of these days, so do your worst. I'm not afraid of the likes of you. You're just a big FAT fish in a tiny meaningless pond. So fuck off and die.

PS. The only thing your paper is any good for is wiping my arse.

PPS. Long live Ireland, free from the British and the Catholic Church. LIARS every one of you. But the truth always comes out …

I guess that's a no to the interview then. There was also a bizarre formal yellow

'Karma police report' attached, which said I had been found guilty of 'prying into the private lives of decent human beings'. My crimes, listed and ticked, include 'barefaced lying, cheating, disgusting thoughtlessness, hurting intentionally, being pompously prejudiced, rude and obnoxious, underhand, diabolical, blindly self-serving and self-obsessed, reprehensibly irresponsible, and' – hilariously – 'hopelessly spaced out and dangerously unaware'.

I am then ordered to make immediate amends and apologise to her or 'negative energy will reel around the planet right back into your life!' It was all signed 'Sinead O'Connor, Karma Police Officer.'

I think it may be time for a long lie down, love.

TUESDAY, 20 DECEMBER

I had my first invitation to No. 10 tonight for Christmas drinks with Major and his team. It was like the Tardis in *Dr Who* – much bigger than you think and full of robots. There were lots of journalists there, and Major hates most of us, so he came in for about three seconds, then left to deal with an 'urgent matter of state'. I was told by one of his staff that the reason he dislikes the press so much is that he insists on reading the first editions of the papers, then gets so enraged by all the abuse he can't sleep. Then he reads the later editions in the morning and gets even angrier. Maggie never read the papers, and that seems much more sensible to me.

WEDNESDAY, 21 DECEMBER

Lord Longford has written again, asking me to apologise for having a go at Myra Hindley. I replied that we'll never apologise to her for anything, and added: 'I know you to be a caring and compassionate man, as indeed I am on many issues. But I suggest we end all discussion on Myra Hindley because the mere mention of her name makes me shiver with fury and revulsion.'

THURSDAY, 22 DECEMBER

I've taken the plunge and, against my lawyers' advice, written direct to Spike Milligan. 'It looked like you, we were told it was you and we had no reason to think it wasn't you. However I now feel a complete plonker, particularly as I am one of your biggest fans. So how about a bit of festive forgiveness? Rather than printing some dreadfully serious apology why not pen us a comic note berating us, pose for a healthy smiling photo and we'll resolve things amicably. If you'd rather shove a red-hot poker up your arse I understand, but this has to be better than a court of law. I wish you peace, light and prosperity and will always be a fan regardless of this balls-up.' Surely this will do the trick?

FRIDAY, 23 DECEMBER

Spike was not amused by my letter. So we are going to have to do a deal and run this ridiculously serious apology: 'The photograph of Spike Milligan we published under the headline CLOWN IN THE DUMPS was not in fact him and he is not therefore a "shadow of his former self". We are happy to make it clear that Spike is fully fit and back at work, continues to write and has had two books in the bestseller list this year and is now touring the country to fulfil a programme of book-signing sessions. We apologise for any embarrassment and annoyance the article caused him.' We also have to pay him £1000 in damages.

And my opinion of Spike Milligan has changed forever, as I suspect will the opinion of a lot of our readers.

FRIDAY, 24 DECEMBER

A Christmas card arrived this morning from Alan Clark showing a photo of his castle, Saltwood, on a tempestuous day. The caption inside reads: 'Storm clouds over Saltwood, June 1994.' He underlines that and scribbles next to it: 'I'll get level, somehow, *personally*.'

NEWS OF THE WORLD

BRITAIN'S MOST POPULAR NEWSPAPER

JULY 2, 1995   LAST WEEK'S SALE: 4,633,156   Price 50p   No.7898

It's THAT tart in THAT dress

EXCLUSIVE

HUGH TOLD ME I WAS HIS SEX FANTASY

FILM idol Hugh Grant's hooker last night revealed exactly what happened when he picked her up for sex.

Speaking exclusively to the News of the World, Divine Brown said: "As I sat in his car he told me, 'I always wanted to sleep with a black woman. That's my fantasy.'"

Divine—pictured right in a Versace dress just like the one that made Grant's lover Liz Hurley famous—added:

By STUART WHITE and DAVID SHUMACHER

"At one point he got carried away and yanked my hair. I said, 'Honey, you can't be that rough'." Wealthy Grant (above) had paid Divine £40 for a sex act in his BMW.

The Los Angeles hooker added: "I told him that for 40 dollars more (about £26) we could've gone to a room—and never have been caught."

Photo: DAVID THORPE

Divine Brown tells her astonishing story inside

1995

SATURDAY, 31 DECEMBER 1994

It's been a bloody quiet week even by Christmas standards, and the story cupboard's remained unsettlingy bare. In desperation we settled for a ludicrous tale about a married *Emmerdale* star, Stan Richards – or Seth Armstrong as we know and love him – having an affair with a sex change redhead called Claire Hall, who used to be called Ian. I couldn't even begin to imagine how I could explain this to Murdoch and just prayed he was busy relaxing somewhere nice on holiday preparing for a New Year party or something. Anything to prevent him ringing. The front page headline was SETH'S 6-YEAR AFFAIR WITH GENDER-BENDER. And all I could think as I eyed this ghastly splash was Kelvin telling me once that Murdoch loathed stories about transsexuals, particularly kiss-and-tells, because 'they look so bloody awful, don't they?'

He's got a point. Our inside spread had a horrible photo of Ms Hall looking definitely more Ian than Claire, and the headline WE SHARED ANIMAL PASSION ON SHEEPSKIN RUG. By 6pm I reckoned I was in the clear and nipped down to the Old Rose pub outside the plant for a pint, leaving strict instructions that if The Boss called I would run back and take the call. Sure enough, I'd barely taken a sip when the call came to the pub that he was on the phone. I ran straight out and sprinted back to the office, a journey of about 800 yards – more than I've run in a few years. I didn't trust the lifts, so raced up the stairs, and arrived panting and sweating to take the call.

It had taken me about four minutes and I feared he might have gone when I gasped, 'Hello, Mr Murdoch.' But no, he was there.

'Hi Piers, where've you been, getting some great last-minute scoop?'

I tried to laugh but was almost unable to breathe. 'Erm … uh … um … yes, something like that.' I then had to stop talking and frantically suck air to stop myself passing out.

'Are you OK?' he asked. 'Yes, sorry, I've had this dreadful cold all week.' It was a barefaced lie and I suspected he knew it. But it wasn't going to stop him asking what the splash was.

'So, what are you splashing on?' he asked.

'Oh, we've got this fantastic story about a top soap star having an affair with a transsexual.'

Pause.

'Which top soap star?'

'Um, well, Seth Armstrong from Emmerdale.' 'What's Emmerdale?' came the distinctly uncomfortable response. 'Well, it's a huge new soap that everyone's watching and this guy's massive in it.'

Pause.

'How old is he?'

'Ahem, well, he's er … 64. But he's married with six kids and …' Murdoch cut me off. 'Let me get this straight. You're leading on some ancient old guy I've never heard of from a soap I've never heard of, having an affair with someone else I've never heard of and who's a woman who used to be a bloke?'

My turn to pause. 'Er, well, yes, Mr Murdoch, that's about the gist of it.' Long pause. 'And that's the most important story in Britain this week, is it?'

'I guess it is, yes. It's been a bit quiet, I'm afraid.'

I heard a snort of derision. 'A bit quiet, eh? Well, let's hope your highly paid reporters can make it a bit noisier next week, shall we? Happy New Year.' Click.

THURSDAY, 5 JANUARY

Dempster has cancelled lunch because Clive Goodman has written him a cheeky letter protesting at his claiming an *NoW* scoop as one of his own. 'It is a typically dishonest letter and in the circumstances I do not see much point in having lunch.'

I laughed out loud at the pomposity.

'Dear Nigel,' I replied, 'if you wish to cancel lunch because of your bizarre ongoing feud with Clive then so be it. It's a shame because I always thought you were above all that egocentric nonsense and my mother likes your column so she will be disappointed. But perhaps I'll take her out to lunch instead. Piers.'

FRIDAY, 6 JANUARY

Lord Longford was not impressed by my response to his plea for compassion towards Myra Hindley:

I'm afraid your letter would cause distress to anyone like myself who believes in you and has your future at heart. I am sure you are fundamentally a caring and compassionate man and that in years to come you will try to forget this unfortunate epistle. After years of crude abuse, I now get more letters favourable to Myra than unfavourable, although of course there is still the odd one beginning, 'What are you getting out of this, a bit of legover, I suppose?'

SATURDAY, 7 JANUARY

Dempster's responded. 'I hope your mother appreciates Château Lafite! Tell Goodman to run in the London marathon with my diary team. This will achieve two aims ... halting this sad fellow's unsociable smoking habit, and getting him fit so he can compete in the fantasy world of James Whitaker et al. Remember: *mens sana in corpore sano*. PS. A grand lunch on me when this is all over.'

I'm really not sure I have the strength for much more of this.

SUNDAY, 8 JANUARY

We've carried another big piece by Tony Blair headlined TRAITOR TORIES ARE INCOMPETENT, DESPISED AND RIDICULOUS. Think that might be a little hint as to where we're going ... and with a bit of luck it might give Woodrow a spontaneous heart attack too.

We've also launched Michael Winner's first column as part of a general relaunch of the paper designed to make us appeal to a wider, more affluent and middle class audience. It's boastful, funny, highly opinionated and very readable. But I daren't tell him or he'll be even more unbearable.

WEDNESDAY, 11 JANUARY

Rebekah and I took Sheryl Kyle to dinner at Quaglino's to try and persuade her to do a big interview with us. She was good fun, but definitely enjoys the fame of being Gazza's girlfriend. When we left, a scrum of paparazzi photographers started snapping away at me and Sheryl and she played up for the cameras a bit.

It was all good fun and none of the 'monkeys' seemed to be taking it terribly seriously, though since my recent separation from Marion the idea of the *NoW* editor having a secret fling with the lover of Britain's greatest footballer might grab a few headlines.

THURSDAY, 12 JANUARY

Chris Mullin, one of the harder left Labour MPs, has had a go at Murdoch and tabloids generally in one of his regular attacks on the 'gutter press'.

I've had enough of him and wrote to Blair: 'Dear Tony, idiots like Mullin shouting their mouths off about "loathsome tabloids" and my owner in such an offensive manner do nothing to help us forge the relationship between us and the Labour Party that you and I wish for. If he is like this *before* you get into power, what on earth can we expect afterwards?'

Be interesting to see how he responds.

TUESDAY, 24 JANUARY

Michael Winner took me, Rebekah and Phil Hall to Marco Pierre White's new place, The Restaurant, where he's just won his third Michelin star. Winner was determined to show us just how powerful and rich he is, barking orders to the terrified staff from the moment we arrived. He made a big show of ordering the wine, which was decanted before we drank it. It tasted pretty good and we wolfed it down.

Two bottles later, he said, 'Come on then, what do you think of the wine?'

'Very nice, Michael, very nice,' I replied.

'Nice? *Nice?* It's Château Latour 1961, one of the greatest wines ever made, and it's cost me £500 a bottle, so I expect a bit more than "nice".'

I performed an elaborate sniff of my glass again. 'Sorry, Michael, on second thoughts it smells a bit corked.' Later he calmed down enough to summon Marco from wherever he was celebrating his third star, and the great chef bounded in minutes later to join us.

It was a fun night, and Winner was a generous, and amusing, if breathtakingly boastful host.

WEDNESDAY, 25 JANUARY

Winner sent all three of us a signed copy of the bill, which came to £1828, and a scribbled note saying, 'Hope you enjoyed Dinner with Winner.'

I dropped him a line: 'Dear Michael, I will keep the bill on my loo wall as a constant reminder of what might have been had I gone into movies and not newspapers.'

Blair, meanwhile, has replied to my complaint about the idiot Mullin: 'Chris is one of Labour's strongest campaigners and has unwavering tenacity in pursuing causes about which he feels strongly. I am as keen as you to forge good relations between the shadow cabinet and your newspaper, but it is the nature of politics that there will be some Labour backbenchers with different views on this issue to mine, although they rarely match the vociferousness of the Tories' Roger Gale. But you should not doubt my commitment to ensure that Labour has a sensible adult approach to all sections of the media and I hope your newspaper will continue to have a similar approach to us. Incidentally I hope you will not see it as a transparently political move if I wish you luck in your move into the mid-market and congratulate you on the redesign of the leader page!'

It's typical Blair – firm but fair, and flush with charm and compliments. The guy's got manners, and style. I like him.

THURSDAY, 26 JANUARY

Winner has resigned. Because I asked him for extra copy for his column, and he demanded pro-rata extra money per word. I called his bluff:

Dear Michael, I am very sorry you are resigning, because you were my first suggestion to Mr Murdoch and your resignation will inevitably reflect badly on me. But I am not prepared to be held to ransom over the very occasional request for a few extra words to fill the page, especially after you informed me you would require space to apologise for libelling Tara Fitzgerald. It does seem extraordinary this should happen so soon after such a splendid night together, but you have obviously made your mind up and I will communicate the reasons to Mr Murdoch who I am sure will share my disappointment ...

He faxed back immediately: 'Dear Piers, you are a very naughty boy and you know it!!!! Anyway I wish you all the best and if you want to think it over and talk to me tomorrow please do. Love Michael.'

I ignored him, so another fax arrived: 'And I want another £50 for this fax!'

I ignored this too. Later he called in a panic demanding to speak to me. I let him wait a few minutes before taking the call.

'Michael, so sorry you're leaving,' I said nonchalantly.

'I don't want to leave, don't be so absurd,' he blustered.

'Sorry, it's too late,' I replied. 'I've told Mr Murdoch and he didn't seem too bothered and even suggested your Sunday Times column might have run its course –' Winner erupted: '*What! What!!!!* Where is Rupert, I must call him!'

I let a lengthy pause take its effect before telling him I was only joking.

I like him, but he's maddening.

SATURDAY, 28 JANUARY

Hilarious scenes next door at the *Sunday Times* this afternoon when a bunch of howling lesbians broke into their newsroom and chained themselves to the newsdesk in protest at some anti-gay article they'd published. The group, calling themselves Lesbian Avengers, spent an hour chanting 'Print the news, not your views' and 'Media lies, no surprise' as John Witherow pleaded with them to stop. We got a snapper up there who came back with fantastic photos of Witherow, the mob and some policemen which I ran on page thirteen under the immortal headline THE EDITOR, 60 COPPERS, 8 LESBIANS AND 4 PAIRS OF HANDCUFFS.

He took it well.

THURSDAY, 2 FEBRUARY

Felt as sick as a pig all day. Shivery and nauseous. Murdoch's in London and I have a big meeting with him tomorrow. I went home early, around 4pm, and retired to my bed to try and recover.

FRIDAY, 3 FEBRUARY

Alan, my driver, picked me up at 9am.

'God, you look bloody terrible,' he said.

'Well, so would you if you'd been sick all night, and I've got to see bloody Murdoch later. Can you go slowly?'

My head was pounding and sweating. Not the ideal physical conditions for a mental tussle with the world's most powerful media tycoon. By the time the meeting started at 3.15pm I was in a terrible state.

'You OK?' said Murdoch. 'Yes, yes, fine, thanks, Mr Murdoch. Just a bit of a cold.'

He must be starting to think I'm a sickly little child.

But it was more like full blown flu and I sneezed, wheezed and spluttered my way through the two hours like a zombie. As soon as it was over, I staggered back to my car and went home again to puke up bile.

Perhaps all *NoW* editors end up spewing bile, like the paper.

SATURDAY, 4 FEBRUARY

Felt a bit better and went back into the office. Marco Pierre White called to thank me for the interview we ran with him on Sunday to celebrate his third Michelin star. He sounded quite emotional, saying that his dad only realised his son was a success when he read it in the *News of the World*, a paper he'd taken for years.

'I will never forget what you have done for me,' he said.

THURSDAY, 9 FEBRUARY

I started giving Bill Anslow, our eccentric but brilliant production chief, a hard time this afternoon for not pushing pages through the system fast enough. Suddenly, he reached into a drawer, pulled out an iron bar, slapped it into his hand and yelled, 'Right, that's it, Morgan!'

Everyone was stunned into silence. Then, after a few tense seconds, he laughed. 'Got you, that time, didn't I?'

SATURDAY, 11 FEBRUARY

We were tipped off that Paula Yates is cheating on Bob Geldof with Michael Hutchence. A doorstep job outside the Halcyon Hotel in Holland Park confirmed this fact. I called their PR Matthew Freud with the good news.

He thought on his feet. 'Riiight. OK. Let me ask you something. If I could get you something good from Bob and Paula about their break-up would you splash on that and stick Hutchence inside somewhere?'

'Well, it will have to be pretty good, mate. Paula shagging another rock star is rather juicier than her and Bob having a break, to be honest.'

Two hours later Matthew was in my office clutching a piece of paper, looking slightly more pleased with himself than Neville Chamberlain returning from his tea with Hitler. It was a handwritten note from Bob saying the following:

After eighteen months of happiness together, Bob and Paula Geldof decided to have a break from each other for a while. Bob went off on tour to Europe and Paula didn't! They both love each other fantastically and adore their children and for them that's all that matters really. This is a break from 'being in each other's faces all the time.' Or to put it in what Bob calls the 'repulsive parlance of the day' they are 'giving each other some space'. They will see and speak and eat with each other daily, occasionally go out together and continue to love one another. They are each other's best friend. Having lived in the eye of the tabloid storm for eighteen glorious years both fully understand what a fantastic scoop this *News of the World* story is and as such, to avoid the inevitable ructions in its wake, the Geldof family have embarked en masse and together on a well-deserved winter holiday and wish everyone a very happy St Valentine's Day. Love Bob and Paula.

I looked at Matthew.

'How on earth did you persuade them to do that?'

'Been a bit of a nightmare, to be honest. Paula denied everything at first, but Bob forced it out of her and when she finally admitted it he started crying and punching the wall. It was awful. They eventually agreed a short statement when I explained their options, but it wasn't good enough. So I told them to make it better or you would just splash the affair. So they redid it and, well here we are.'

It had been ruthless but masterful PR work.

'OK, you've got a deal.'

The split went on page one, with just a little mention of the real reason behind it – the photos of her and Hutchence went inside. It's called damage limitation and Freud is very good at it, even if his clients don't realise at the time.

TUESDAY, 14 FEBRUARY

Andrew Neil wrote a load of ill-informed rubbish about us in the *Mail* last week and I wrote to Paul Dacre, the editor, to complain. He replied today:

I believe it is both tedious and counterproductive for papers to write about each other. I also believe however that columnists should be given considerable freedom to express their own views. I'm a huge admirer of the way you've reinvigorated your paper, you've had some remarkable exclusives. More power to your elbow. Paul.

I felt quite chuffed. He is an editor I respect hugely.

WEDNESDAY, 15 FEBRUARY

The England game against the Republic of Ireland had to be abandoned tonight after twenty minutes when appalling crowd trouble broke out. It looked well organised, and very, very nasty. You could hear chants of 'No surrender to the IRA', so it's a safe bet that far right groups like Combat 18 were involved. The scenes were horrible, little girls being taken away bleeding as huge skinhead yobs tore up seats and hurled the wooden debris on to stands below them.

THURSDAY, 16 FEBRUARY

I got a call first thing warning me that we might have a little 'local difficulty' with the England match because Vinnie Jones, who I had sent to cover the game as part of our team, got into some drunken brawl himself and bit the nose of a *Daily Mirror* journalist called Ted Oliver. This is all we need. What a berk. I called his agent and demanded some quick answers. He said he'd bring Vinnie in to explain himself.

Further details don't help his cause. It transpires that he never went to the game at all, didn't know it had been cancelled until hours later, went drinking all night with some mates and bit Oliver's nose 'for a laugh'. He is also alleged to have thrown bread rolls at Gary Lineker in the hotel restaurant during breakfast while shouting, 'Oi, Big Ears, get a load of this.'

The *Mirror* dropped late tonight with Mr Oliver's chewed nose all over the front page. Not a pretty sight.

FRIDAY, 17 FEBRUARY

Vinnie was a picture of contrition when he arrived in my office.

'I'm so sorry, Piers, I've let you down, the paper down, my country down.' I could hardly bear to look at him. Murdoch is going to hate this. 'Vinnie, you've been a complete disgrace and you're going to have to do a full apology in this Sunday's paper.' He asked if I was going to fire him, and I said we'd have to see how the story played out. Tears welled up in his eyes.

'Please, mate, give me a chance, I love my column. You know I can be an idiot sometimes.' I wasn't in the mood for charity. 'Vinnie, there's being an idiot and being an idiot. You were the biggest idiot ever on Wednesday night.'

He agreed, and trudged off to write his apologia for the paper. What makes this so much worse is that only last week we launched a 'Boot out the thugs' campaign designed to eradicate from football people that do precisely this kind of thing.

At lunchtime I went to the What The Papers Say awards at the Savoy. Appallingly, I saw on arrival that I'd been seated next to David Mellor. But far from being angry, he looked genuinely pleased to see me. And during a break in filming he leaned over to shake my hand and said, 'I just want to thank you for exposing me. If you hadn't done it when you did my wife wouldn't have given me a divorce. So you really did do me a huge favour.' All said with a vast grin. Quite amazing.

We won Scoops of the Year, and the citation said:

This is the first time we have made this award in the plural but during 1994 the *NoW* consistently produced front-page stories that set the agenda for the week and left other papers to catch up. The paper was essential reading for millions of people and has increased its circulation by 100,000 copies. There is no doubt that what the *NoW* does it does very well.

'Thanks so much for exposing me.' David Mellor shows his
gratitude at the What The Papers Say Awards.

The audience didn't know whether to laugh or cry as I marched up to get the award, but there was a mixture of grim-faced applause, tutting and even the odd boo. A perfect response for the *NoW* generally.

I got back to the office to find Vinnie's apology, which was stunningly grovelling. 'I was an idiot and I apologise to everyone. I've been stupid, dumb, even my best mates have slaughtered me and I will regret it to my dying day.' Etc. His agent kept asking if I was going to fire him. 'I don't know yet' was my truthful response. The trouble is we know he's a naughty boy and that's why we hired him. But this incident seems to have overstepped the boundaries of even the Vinnie Jones brand.

SATURDAY, 18 FEBRUARY

I fired Vinnie today. It's just not credible to spare him, given the severity of what he's done and the fact that the *Mirror*, quite rightly, are going to take him to court for assault. He took it very badly.

SATURDAY, 25 FEBRUARY

Frank Warren invited me and a few execs down to the London Arena to watch Nigel Benn fight an American boxer called Gerald McClellan tonight. It was the first time I'd ever seen a fight live, and we had ringside seats. The atmosphere was very, very intense. It seemed like half Millwall's home crowd had come down to join in the fun. I imagined it was the closest thing to those gladiatorial contests in Roman times. Looking at the angry, red-faced, ugly fat men screaming around me I sensed that what they really *really* wanted was Benn to kill his opponent.

But McClellan, who breeds pit bull terriers, is a fearsome fighter, and in the first round he just beat Benn up, laying hideous punch after hideous punch on him until Benn hurtled out of the ring altogether. I was shocked and slightly sickened by the ferocity of what I'd seen. Until you sit there a few feet from the action you have no idea of the power of the punching, or the amount of sweat and blood that flies off the boxers on to those around the ringside.

Benn looked finished, Warren looked very worried, and Frank Bruno, sitting next to me, looked slightly demented as he leapt to his feet and began pounding the ring with his fists shouting 'Focus, Nige, focus!' as the corner tried to revive him.

Incredibly, Benn fought back and the pair of them slugged it out in brutal fashion for ten rounds. At one stage I asked Warren if it was always like this when you're so close to the action. 'God, no,' he said, 'this is an unbelievable fight.'

In the tenth round, McClellan finally withered under another onslaught and was counted out. The crowd exploded into an orgy of chanting, and pocket fights broke out everywhere: it was complete mayhem. But there was something wrong. As Benn was carried on his trainer's shoulders shrieking, 'I fucking told you, I fucking told you,' McClellan collapsed in the corner. He looked very seriously hurt and only Warren seemed to notice. 'Get an ambulance, *now!*' he shouted.

It was a macabre, awful spectacle – Benn, oblivious to his opponent's condition, still celebrating; McClellan flat out, twitching. What made it even worse was the surreal presence at ringside of Michael Watson, who'd been left paralysed after a fight with Chris Eubank in 1991. As the minutes passed, and the efforts of the medical team appeared ever more frantic, it seemed that something tragic was happening in front of us. McClellan was eventually taken out and rushed to the Royal London Hospital with a blood clot on his brain. Benn then collapsed himself in his dressing room and was also taken to the same hospital. I left Warren, who just said, 'It's looking bad, very bad.'

I rushed back to the office and we drew up a new front page: BENN FIGHT HORROR. The photos of McClellan were just terrible, as were the condition reports from the hospital.

It's 1am now and I am going to sleep assuming McClennan will die overnight. It's all been a horrific experience.

FRIDAY, 3 MARCH
Lord Longford has written to congratulate me on our award, and says: 'In time to come I hope you will receive these at the *Sunday Times* and later still *The Times*. But for now, enough is enough.'

I love newspaper snobbery – it is such a British thing.

I'm going to Barbados tomorrow, which is Winner's favourite holiday place, and he's sent the manager of the famous Sandy Lane Hotel a note:

A friend of mine called Piers Morgan, who is editor of our most popular newspaper by far, is coming to Barbados and I have taken the liberty of telling him that if he'd like to sit on your beach you will extend that courtesy to him.

Hilarious.

He's also sent me a detailed map of the beach area, and the name of the guy I need to talk to: Archer.

MONDAY, 6 MARCH
Two days into the holiday and I decided to test Winner's generosity. I found a beach attendant at the Sandy Lane who pointed out Archer.

'Excuse me, Michael Winner sent me over to have a word with you –'

He sat bolt upright like I had just told him the island had been hit by a nuclear bomb.

'Winner … is *here* … *now*?' There was real and terrible panic and fear in those eyes.

'No, no, he's in England, don't worry.'

'Oh, thank the Lord!' he exclaimed.

Archer sorted us out some nice loungers and free beer – and seemed so relieved that Winner wasn't there he would probably have sorted us out a nice free suite too, if we'd asked.

FRIDAY, 17 MARCH

Ronnie Kray has died, and a nation's gangsters mourn. My dad told me tonight how he once barred Big Ron from coming into a London nightclub he worked in, called Churchill's, because he wasn't wearing a tie. Dad had no idea who he was until his manager saw what was happening, and raced ashen-faced to explain. The lights came on fast.

'Aha, Mr Kray,' said Dad, 'I'm so sorry, I thought you were somebody else – please come to your usual table. And of course a tie won't be necessary. Champagne on the house … ?'

FRIDAY, 31 MARCH

We've been offered an exclusive photo of Ronnie Kray lying in his open coffin. It's a fantastic news image, but there are some obvious little local difficulties to negotiate, not least of which is how we can run it without Reggie Kray ensuring I sleep with some Bethnal Green fishes. I'd crossed the 'family' a few years ago when I took the piss out of Charlie Kray's fake fur coat at the premiere of the Krays' movie – and got a call the next morning at work from a Cockney saying rather chillingly, 'The Krays read your article, Mr Morgan, and they were not amused.' Click.

You always know when that kind of thing is genuine because they are polite to you. Much more menacing than 'Oi, you wanker, we're gonna break your legs.'

I called Garry Bushell, the *Sun*'s TV critic and a 'friend of the Krays', and he said he'd try and help. Later in the day the phone rang and my PA said in a rather alarmed tone, 'Piers, there is someone claiming to be Reggie Kray on the phone from Maidstone Prison.'

I took the call. Obviously.

'Hi Reggie, how are you? Bearing up OK, I hope, after your terrible loss?' He didn't seem to hear me. Or perhaps he didn't want to hear me.

'Is that Pier? [sic] This is Reggie Kray.' The voice was surprisingly high-pitched and soft, a bit like Mike Tyson's when I met him once. Must be some weird vocal trait that ferocious killers develop. 'I understand you've got a photo of my brother.' The tone was deadly serious, and I was under no illusion that the way I handled this call might determine how much I have to look over my shoulder for the next twenty years in dimly lit car parks.

'Yes, Mr Kray.'

He sighed.

'Well, what does he look like?'

How the hell do you describe a picture of someone's dead twin brother to a man so obviously grief-stricken? Then a flash of inspiration came to me. 'Well, Mr Kray, he looks rather like Marlon Brando did in The Godfather.' Another long, terrifying pause.

'Does he? Does he? That's good, he'd have liked that. OK, well publish it then, with my blessing.' Click.

I was actually sweating. Only Mr Murdoch can do that to me normally.

SATURDAY, 1 APRIL

I laid out the front page in funereal black borders with a huge photo of Ronnie's corpse under the headline RONNIE KRAY – THE LAST PICTURE. It looked very dramatic and I had no doubts it would sell papers on the shock value alone. Then, at 5pm, the proprietor called for his weekly chat.

'Anything happening in the world then, Piers?' was his opening line, a favourite refrain. Murdoch loves gossip, stories, mischief. So long as I make him laugh with some salacious bit of tittle-tattle about a Cabinet minister, or reveal a shocking fact about one of his business mates, then I normally get off to a pretty good start in these conversations. I try to steer clear of my 'vulnerabilities', like the world economy, or the complexities of America's political arena, hoping he gets enough of that from his editors at The Times and the Sunday Times.

But today I was confident. 'We've got a great splash, Mr Murdoch. The only picture of Ronnie Kray lying in state.'

Pause.

'Who?' Not a great start.

'You know, the East End gangster, one of the notorious twins – he died last week.'

Another pause, slightly longer. 'Yeah, yeah. What? Dead? You're splashing on a dead body?'

'Erm, yes, Mr Murdoch.'

Pause.

'Look, it's not my job to edit the papers, but one thing I can tell you is that stiffs don't sell papers. They sell American magazines, the National Enquirer sold out twice with Elvis's corpse, but not papers. Ring your mate Kelvin and ask him about Grace Kelly, then call me back.'

I rang Kelvin and explained the conversation I'd just had.

He chuckled. 'Bloody Grace Kelly. Ha! Trouble is, he was right. I thought the photos of her lying in state would sell buckets of papers but the bloody sales fell off a cliff. And he'd warned me not to do it, so when he saw the figures he went mad. I'd ring him back and say you've had a rather dramatic re-think and decided not to splash on Ronnie Kray's rotting body if I were you.'

I did.

Mr Murdoch was pleased I had seen the light, and eager to help me fill the front page that was now gaping white space.

'Stick the picture inside if you like, you must have something else you can splash on, haven't you?' I scrabbled through the dummy lying in front of me until I stumbled across a page fifteen lead story about Earl Spencer's wife being in a clinic having treatment for alcohol and bulimia addiction.

'That sounds great, that's Di's sister-in-law, right? Good story, why don't you do that. OK, gotta go now. Thanks, Piers.'

I ran outside and ordered a rapid change on page one. Nobody understood why I'd gone off my sensational front page that I'd loved so much just minutes ago, but I didn't have time to explain.

'Have we got any photos with this story?' I screamed.

The picture editor said we did, but we weren't using them at the moment because there was a bit of a Press Complaints Commission issue, given that they are pictures of the Countess walking in the clinic grounds.

They're not overly intrusive, just rather evocative pictures of her looking sad and lonely. There was no time to really debate it anyway, so I just slammed the photo on the front and a bigger one inside, with the splash headline DI'S SISTER-IN-LAW IN BOOZE AND BULIMIA CLINIC. I've got to admit that it's probably, on balance, a better story in terms of broad appeal than a picture of a dead gangster. That's the really annoying thing about Mr Murdoch, he is hardly ever wrong. He'd make a great editor.

Ronnie's corpse went on pages six and seven with a full interview with Reggie to go with it. 'My brother looks so peaceful, like a statesman,' he said wistfully.

SUNDAY, 2 APRIL

Mayhem. Earl Spencer has been on TV railing about this 'disgraceful flagrant breach of the PCC code', and saying he will now be formally complaining to 'test the teeth of the PCC'. He looked mean and determined, and I felt a little queasy watching the bulletins. I should have spent more time thinking about that picture. We should have just run the story as we were going to originally. We should have stuck with bloody Ronnie Kray. Anything would have been better than the rather large pile of ordure that I suspect is now heading my way.

WEDNESDAY, 5 APRIL

Gary Jones won Reporter of the Year at last night's Press Gazette Awards for his string of big stories over the last year, including Oliver Hoare and Diana. I'm thrilled for him, he's a fantastic journalist. The *News of the World* hardly ever wins awards for anything, so we're breaking new ground here – and the troops love it. The newsroom has evolved into a younger, fitter, faster, better unit. I've paid off 18 of the 110 staff. Some went quietly, like one of our district correspondents who confessed – after a byline check revealed he'd written one story in a year – that he was an alcoholic who'd spent most of that year in the pub all day every day lying to the newsdesk.

Others were harder. Bill Bateson, legendary sports editor and a great character, was 58 and nearing retirement and I hated putting the pressure on him that I felt was necessary to implement the changes I wanted. Eventually I told him I wanted him to step down. He didn't like it, because he understandably wanted to go at his behest, not at that of some spotty 29-year-old.

I threw a big farewell dinner for him at the Savoy, with sporting icons like Richie Benaud and George Graham present, and read out a rare personal note of thanks from Murdoch. Then Bill's wife got up and made a very good, if pointed, little speech saying she always knew Bill might get fired one day – but was just rather surprised it was done by someone younger than their son. Touché.

He had four other leaving parties, including one where *Daily Mail* sportswriter Ian Wooldridge made a speech saying: 'Twenty years ago I got a few letters from a young lad asking for tips on how to be a journalist and I did what I could to help him. I watched his progress proudly and he went from strength to strength … his name was Piers Morgan, and he grew up to be the bastard who's just sacked my mate Bill.'

It was a tough call given Bill's stature and popularity, but I told him I wanted him to go off in style and he was gracious enough to write to me when the dust had settled to say, 'It must be rare for someone to enjoy their own execution, but I did. Thank you.'

SUNDAY, 9 APRIL

We've exposed a Tory MP called Richard Spring for having a three-in-a-bed sex romp with a Sunday school teacher and a business friend. The reason we're so sure of our facts is that she took a tape recorder into the bedroom for us. This recorded not only the dirty deed but also his hilarious observations on famous people.

On Norma Major: 'I quite fancy Norma, I think she and John only do it about 1.1 times a year.'

On Diana: 'Charles and she never hit it off in the sack.'

On Hugh Grant: 'Why does everyone fancy him so much – he's such a squirt?'

He resigned immediately when we put the story to him. My legal team were uneasy about running so much of the transcript on the basis that it's obvious she was wired up in the bedroom. But I ignored them, confident that Spring's so bang to rights it doesn't matter how we banged him.

TUESDAY, 11 APRIL

Woodrow Wyatt wrote a ridiculous article in *The Times* this morning, dumping all over the *News of the World* for exposing Spring. He's even demanded a privacy law to stop us doing this kind of thing again. All this from a wizened old sod who gets £150,000 a year to write a load of sycophantic drivel about John Major every week in the very paper he's castigating. I fired off a furious fax to him: 'Dear Woodrow, your article in this morning's *Times* was a disgrace. Piers.'

He replied: 'Dear Piers, I'm sure you know there's a Rupert Murdoch rule that writers and papers within the News International Group are free to criticise each other without censorship, whether the criticism affects the paper they are writing in or other titles. This rule has often been taken advantage of by the *Sunday Times* and the *Sun* in attacks on me. Cheer up, you become ever more famous, which can't be bad for business. And you're a brilliant editor.'

Yes, mate, I thought, and you are taking the piss. I sent an even angrier fax to Murdoch demanding Woodrow's head on a plate, preferably stuffed with his own fried genitals. 'Mr Murdoch, it is astonishing that one of our own columnists is publicly demanding a privacy law that can only damage us,' I ranted. 'I personally feel his views have become irrelevant anyway and we could do with an exciting new columnist in his slot.'

Murdoch, very unusually, sent a fax back. 'Thanks for your memo about Woodrow. I'll drop him a line. As you know, I think you're both wrong. He is wrong in principle and the *News of the World* was absolutely over the top about Richard Spring. There was no way in the world he deserved five pages of fairly hypocritical nonsense. You've been doing a wonderful job breaking news stories and giving the paper huge energy. I just wish you'd remember it is necessary to have a *balanced* product. Rupert.'

I was flattered by the rare praise, but not enough to desist from instantly planning to launch a full frontal attack on Wyatt in next Sunday's paper, changing his 'Voice of reason' byline boast to 'Voice of treason'. He can hardly complain, can he, given his view of this kind of incestuous criticism?

THURSDAY, 13 APRIL

A second memo from Mr Murdoch arrived. 'Following up on my memo of April 11, I should just say that I hope you don't have any editorial or other piece justifying last week's story. Equally, any reference to the Woodrow matter should be cut out.'

He's read my mind. He always reads my mind. I guess that's why he's the owner and I'm not.

WEDNESDAY, 19 APRIL

A terrible bomb has exploded in Oklahoma, killing 168 people, including many children. It was one of those days when I really missed being on a daily paper. It can be very frustrating editing a Sunday with six long days in between editions. I am starting to feel a bit bored during the week and that's worrying after just over a year at the helm.

MONDAY, 24 APRIL

Murdoch's come to town, and the building, as usual, has gone into paranoid meltdown. Editors and management executives swap information on his mood, his movements, his likely current interests. He, meanwhile, just prowls silently around – appearing in newsrooms out of nowhere, with no warning and no time to even hide the wine stash. It is hard to overstate the awesome power and influence he wields. He truly is Citizen Kane, though from my experiences so far nowhere near as malevolent. It makes me laugh when I read what a vile monster he is. Kelvin was far worse.

Lord Archer has protested about a story we ran on him being patron of a school where pupils have been going on a crime rampage. He insists he has had nothing to do with the school. I agreed to put a small correction in the paper.

SATURDAY, 29 APRIL

We've really been struggling to find anything to splash on and my temper has not improved at the prospect of Murdoch being in town reading a pile of old crap over his breakfast table. Bored and irritable, I read an interview Rebekah had done with Shane Richie, star of TV's *Lucky Numbers* show. It was a fairly interesting chat about his early days, when he was once so down on his luck he spent some time sleeping on a park bench. 'So he was a tramp, then,' I said, trying to muster some excitement about something.

'Er, well, not exactly, no,' replied Rebekah nervously. 'He did spend a few days sleeping rough, but I wouldn't say he was a tramp.'

'But if you sleep on a park bench then you're a tramp, aren't you?' Rebekah didn't like where I was going, but knew we were desperate for a splash and her name would be on it – always the main aim of every ambitious reporter on the paper each week.

'Yes, I suppose you are, yes.'

I laid out the front page: I WAS A TRAMP. Murdoch was not in a good mood when he called later and it was made worse by our useless scoop. 'Never heard of him, and so what if he lived rough?' He was right, of course. It was pretty ropey, but it would have to do. At 10.30pm we were all still in the office having a drink and reading the first editions when Rebekah's mobile went off and it was Shane Richie, going absolutely ballistic. He'd just finished a performance of *Grease* at the Dominion Theatre and gone outside to be confronted by a billboard with our headline on it.

'What the fuck have you done?' he yelled. 'I wasn't a fucking tramp. This is ridiculous, you're making me out to be some sort of wino.'

I could hear his yelling from my desk ten yards away. But I was fairly relaxed about it. He can't sue us because he admits sleeping rough. Rebekah calmed him down eventually: she's superb at making celebrities think a terrible story is actually very good for them.

But we've conned the readers, and that is never something the *News of the World* should resort to. The brilliance of the product is that you give the punters incontrovertible evidence of misbehaviour, not flim-flam stories spun up to be something they're not. Murdoch will know the truth when he reads it and he won't be happy.

MONDAY, 1 MAY

Lord Archer has written to thank me for my apology. Then added: 'My secretary has pointed out that many years ago I did send a cheque in support of a tour that the choir was doing at that school. So while I've got your attention I should like to plead guilty to 4012 other cases of supporting people over the years.'

Fascinating. He is basically admitting our story was true now, but at the same time, rather than apologising, he can't miss the chance to boast about what a great charity donor he is. Amazing front. I feel conned.

SATURDAY, 6 MAY

Clive Goodman pulled in a cracking story today. He'd been given a copy of a letter from Earl Spencer to a friend last week in which he said he's ditching his ailing wife and taking their kids with him to be a TV reporter in America. The letter read:

> Victoria is in a clinic called Farm Place in Surrey, she needs all her old friends around her now. Please don't tell her I encouraged you to get in touch – it's better if she thinks you just did it because you loved her. I'm off to work for an American TV station in New York for a couple of years. I'll be taking the children, too, but making sure that Victoria has frequent access. I think she might consider a move to the States herself, a couple of years away from Britain will be good for us all. Take care and I'll see you before I'm off hopefully. Charles.

Our source, the recipient of the letter, is a regular contact who tips us off about the Spencers from time to time. He's a good friend of the couple who doesn't like the Earl but does like Victoria, and his tips reflect that fact.

I laid out a front page saying 'DIANA'S BROTHER QUITS BRITAIN WITH HIS KIDS – New blow for sick countess' and let Spencer have it with both barrels in a thunderous leader article, calling him callous and heartless.

We put a call into his office for a comment at about 6pm but he didn't respond. Then at 9pm, an hour and a half after the presses had started rolling, he called my office.

'Mr Morgan, this is Earl Spencer, I've got you now, you bastard.' I was rather taken aback.

'What do you mean?'

'That letter was all made up. I suspected who your source was so I wrote it to him knowing he wouldn't be able to resist passing it on to you to publish. And it's all rubbish. Ha! What are you going to do now then, eh? Ha, ha!'

He sounded slightly bonkers.

'Why didn't you tell us before we started printing the paper? Wouldn't that have been more sensible?'

'Ha! Because if I had, you would have pretended I hadn't caught you out. You're going to have to admit you've printed lies now, aren't you, and apologise. Enjoy … ha!'

Then he rang off.

I sat back in my chair and started to palpitate. This was not good, not good at all. He'd done us up like kippers and a part of me had to admire the work. There's only one person to call when something like this happens.

'Kelvin, it's Piers, I have a slight problem which I would appreciate your advice on – rather quickly, please!'

Kelvin listened to the story, went quiet for a few seconds, then said slowly and deliberately, 'That sounds like a disgusting attempt by Earl Spencer to con News of the World readers, using his wife and kids to do so.'

I laughed out loud. 'Fantastic, thanks Kelvin.' The master had done it again.

I raced out of the office, explained what had been going on, and changed the paper to headline on 'WHAT A CHARLIE – Althorp invents pack of lies about wife and kids to trick *NoW* readers.'

We got it on to the second edition, which meant about 400,000 copies had already been sent out to foreign parts and far-flung places like Cornwall. It's about 1am now. I'm still nervous, but more confident than I would have been without Kelvin's help. Don't think this is going to play out quite how the Earl thought …

SUNDAY, 7 MAY

Spencer came out fighting early – slamming us for our 'disgraceful lies' and saying he has exposed a friend for selling him down the river. 'This man was able, with his boyfriend, to take hospitality repeatedly over the past few years and has repaid us in this shabby way. I am saddened one of my wife's closest friends has turned out to be a traitor.'

But the good Earl is getting hammered on TV for letting the fake story actually appear in the paper. It was a fatal strategic error. I laughed at the flak he's getting. That'll teach him to fuck with us.

MONDAY, 8 MAY

Everyone's attacking Spencer in the papers now, it's game over for him on this one – just when he thought he'd finally got me back for that row over those pictures of his wife in the clinic. He probably assumed other papers would support his con trick. But we tend to put traditional rivalries aside when someone pulls a stunt like this and back each other.

TUESDAY, 9 MAY

An exciting letter from Murdoch today. I've been invited to a News Corporation conference in Hayman Island later this summer, off the Great Barrier Reef in Australia. It all sounds incredibly glamorous, the resort is one of the best in the world and we've got the whole thing to ourselves apparently. Spent most of the day finding out who else has been invited – and more amusingly, who hasn't.

WEDNESDAY, 10 MAY

I took some of the sports desk to Paris for the Cup-Winners Cup Final between Arsenal and Real Zaragoza. As I drove to the airport, I called my home phone for messages and heard Andy Coulson, a diehard Spurs fan, saying, 'I've had a dream that Nayim [ex Spurs] is going to score the winner.'

At 9.45pm, Nayim scored a last-minute winning goal from the halfway line, lobbing it over a desperate David Seaman. It was without any doubt the worst moment of my football-watching life. And probably the best moment of Andy Coulson's.

THURSDAY, 11 MAY

I got back to the office tired and pissed off, to be further cheered by news that the PCC has upheld Earl Spencer's complaint over the photos of his wife in the clinic. And not only that, they've hammered me personally into the ground, for the first time taking their ultimate sanction of referring the matter to the offending newspaper's proprietor. I was called down to see Sir Edward Pickering, a wily old guy in his 80s who acts as Murdoch's fixer in the UK and smoothes over 'troublespots'. He was a great journalist and remains a very influential figure at News International behind the scenes.

'Pick' sat me down.

'Now look here, young man, I'm afraid we're in a spot of bother over this Spencer thing.' He peered at me sombrely over his spectacles. 'The PCC have got to show they have teeth, and I'm afraid their fangs have been set on you.' He passed me a copy of the adjudication, which was suitably damning.

Then he showed me Murdoch's response: 'While I will always support worthwhile investigative journalism as a community responsibility, it is clear in this case that the young man went over the top. Mr Morgan has assured me that his forthcoming apology to Countess Spencer on this matter is sincere and without reservation. I have no hesitation in making public this remonstration and I have reminded Mr Morgan forcefully of his responsibility to the Code to which he, as an editor, subscribes too in his terms of employment. The company will not tolerate its papers bringing into disrepute the best practices of popular journalism.'

Bloody cheek. None of this would have bloody happened if he hadn't stopped me doing Ronnie Kray's dead body.

Pick then handed me a copy of what I was required to say, which was a grovelling mea culpa and abject apology to the Spencers. I read it quickly and said, 'Look, Sir Edward, I've no problem saying sorry to Victoria, but I'm damned if I'm saying sorry to that lying toerag husband of hers.' He smiled, as if he had expected precisely that response.

I added, 'I can see what's happening here. I get a public thrashing, Mr Murdoch looks tough on his erring editors, and the PCC are seen to be effective. But please don't make me apologise to that prick.' Pick chuckled.

'OK, we'll delete the Earl from your statement.'

The rest of my lament read: 'I accept the ruling unreservedly. The decision to publish was mine and I apologise to the Countess for any distress our actions may have caused at a difficult time for her. Mr Murdoch has made his feelings on this subject very clear to me and I am determined that, as he says, the *NoW* strives to maintain the best practices of popular investigative journalism within the agreed parameters of the PCC Code of Conduct.'

I also wrote this evening to Countess Spencer saying how (genuinely) sorry I was for my mistake, wishing her a speedy recovery and pointing out that 'I am taking the rap over my knuckles from Mr Murdoch very seriously.'

The evening TV news went bonkers on my 'thrashing', affording me the same sort of public tributes as the Yorkshire Ripper.

FRIDAY, 12 MAY

My shame is everywhere in the papers. The *Independent* at least made me laugh with a cartoon showing a *NoW* front page and the headline EDITOR IN SPANKING ORDEAL. I told my PA to buy the original – but she discovered the PCC had got there first.

SATURDAY, 13 MAY

It never rains … The High Court has given Sir Nicholas Lyell, the Attorney General, leave to try and jail me for contempt of court over some obscure story we did exposing a drug dealer, where we revealed a bit too much personal detail. What we didn't know was he was already facing charges for other offences. I could be caged for years.

Turning into a good week, this.

SUNDAY, 14 MAY

We printed the Earl's apology in full, and I deliberately chose a picture of him looking suitably smug and jowly to go with it. It won't have much effect, but it made me feel better. I was supposed to be going to the Arsenal/Chelsea game at Stamford Bridge, but as I was leaving for the ground I got a frantic call from Mum. She'd been looking after Spencer – only 22 months old – and he'd gone into some sort of fit and was lying on her bed having spasms.

I drove illegally fast to Sussex, where he'd been taken to the local hospital in

Haywards Heath. They said it might be meningitis, because his temperature was raging above 105 degrees. Everything moved so fast, and the staff were clearly very worried. They decided to transfer him to a specialist children's unit in nearby Crawley where doctors said he had to have an immediate lumbar puncture, a procedure where they insert a needle into the base of his back to get spinal fluid out and see if it is meningitis or not. Marion and I were warned that some children suffer some form of paralysis as a result of this. I couldn't believe what I was hearing.

Spencer lay bright red on the bed, looking like a tiny boiling shrimp. I'd never felt such utter helpless despair. The lumbar puncture went OK though, and the good news came that it was not meningitis, but some other mystery, and very virulent, virus. But he was still burning up. The office called, but I wasn't interested. It's an old cliché, but my job seemed suddenly so absurdly irrelevant and unimportant. The nursing staff were amazing, they couldn't have been more caring or concerned if it had been their own child lying there.

MONDAY, 15 MAY

Spencer's been slowly recovering and is over the worst, but still looks so frail. There are lots of very sick kids in this place and it's obvious that some won't make it. I can hardly bear to look at them or their poor parents. We've been lucky this time, but for some of these people there is just a lifetime of misery and mourning ahead. Someone told me when Spencer was born that my attitude towards stories involving children would change dramatically now, and they were right. You put yourself into the shoes of the parents, whatever the story, and you feel more sympathetic and less inhuman. All editors should be parents, definitely.

WEDNESDAY, 17 MAY

Spencer came out of hospital today and seemed right as rain again. I can't believe how quickly he's got over it. 'Dad, you stink,' he said cheerfully, confirming a full recovery.

I thanked him for his thoughts and returned to the office in the afternoon to find a note from Lord Longford sending his condolences over the Murdoch rap. 'As you know, bad news for you is bad news for me.'

SATURDAY, 20 MAY

Typical. Murdoch arrives and we've got nothing in the story cupboard again. The best option was a tawdry exposé of a young girl called Davinia Murphy, the current lover of Manchester United star Ryan Giggs. Murdoch called for an update on the paper. 'Erm, well we've got this brilliant story about Ryan Giggs the footballer, his lover's doing the dirty on him and ...'

He interrupted me. 'How old is he?' 'Erm, twenty-one, Mr Murdoch.' 'And the girl?' 'Erm, she's seventeen.' 'Either of them married?' 'Not as such, no.' 'So let me get this straight. You're using the might of the NoW to turn over a kid who's saying stupid things about another kid.' I couldn't capitulate or he'd sense weakness. 'It's not like that, he's the hottest star in British football and she's tipped to marry him. It's a great story.'

'Well, you're the editor. I'll come and see you later.'

I stormed out of my office. 'Right, you lot. I need a new splash and I need it before the owner comes down here in about two hours' time.'

Controlled panic swept the newsroom. An hour later we got a massive stroke of luck. We'd heard from our usual inside source that the *Sunday Mirror* were breaking a story about Imran Khan fathering a lovechild by Sita White, daughter of the business tycoon Lord White. The picture desk sent a photographer straight to her home in Los Angeles, and when she opened the door he was able to take one quick shot inside. On closer examination of his picture he spotted a framed photo on the table in her hallway – with Sita and the lovechild, who bears a striking resemblance to his father. It blew up pretty well, and I cleared a new splash immediately: IMRAN'S SECRET LOVECHILD.

Murdoch will love this, I thought, Gordon White's a big player in his commercial world and he'll enjoy him squirming a bit. An hour later, The Boss came down to see me. 'Still splashing on that ridiculous football story?' he said, barely able to conceal his disgust. 'No, no, Mr Murdoch, that was never going to be the splash, I was only joking about that. We've got this brilliant story about Imran Khan fathering a child by Gordon White's daughter.'

Pause.

'You mean you bottled it, then?' He chuckled to himself and sauntered away to the *Sunday Times*. I was crushed.

MONDAY, 22 MAY

Murdoch asked to see me in his office this morning. He's never done that before. It is a very, very long walk up there from the *NoW* – at least ten minutes. So there was plenty of time to conjure up all sorts of terrible thoughts. The sack, 'resignation', or even worse, 'promotion' to some vacuous job in the far reaches of the News empire. The sort of ghastly fate that befell Andrew Neil when he was 'promoted' to present a TV show in America that never actually got to air. I waited outside his office, listening to him barking out orders on the phone. All the calls seemed abrupt; he deals with everything so quickly it is genuinely tiring just listening to him. God knows how he does it at his age, quite amazing. After a few minutes I was ushered in and he got up to shake my hand, which since there was no cheque in it seemed a positive start.

'Hi, Piers, how are you?' he said cheerily.

'Oh, fine thanks, boss, really enjoyed you humiliating me over Earl Spencer, thanks a bunch, *pal*,' was what I *wanted* to say.

But instead I said I was in great shape, the paper was in great shape and, well, everything's in great shape. The usual very bullish address to the Chief Bull. One thing I have learned is that he really doesn't want to hear you whining so there's no point going down that road. He just wants to hear precisely how you intend to smash the opposition into oblivion. 'I'm sorry about all that press complaining thingamajig,' he said, to my astonishment. He definitely used the word 'sorry'. And it was clear by his failure to even remember the name of the Press Complaints Commission that he doesn't really give a toss about it. 'We had to deal with it the way we did or they'd have all been banging on about a privacy law again and we don't need that right now. Anyway, it's done now. How are you going to sell me more papers?'

We didn't discuss it further.

TUESDAY, 23 MAY

Had my annual budget meeting with Murdoch this afternoon. We're nearly a million pounds overspent for the last year, so I'd planned my defence meticulously by compiling a bulky cuttings file with every follow-up to an *NoW* scoop in every other paper. I've also pointed out that sales are stronger than ever, and we've won loads of awards to boot.

Murdoch swung into the room like a prizefighter in a gipsy camp ready to pulverise all comers with his bare fists. 'Right, why have you spent so much of my money then, young man?' he growled.

'Erm, well, we've had to pay for all the great stories we've broken that everyone's followed up all year, Mr Murdoch,' I replied confidently, presenting my file with a flourish.

He studied it for a few minutes then laughed: 'OK, well how much do you want this year then?' We got pretty much all we asked for, The Boss is clearly happy with what we're doing. When I came out, all the other News International editors called to see what mood he was in. 'Oh, great,' I said smugly, 'though he did say that he was happier with our performance than some of the other papers.' That was an appalling lie of course, designed to unsettle and unnerve my fellow editors. They'd do the same to me.

SUNDAY, 28 MAY

Thatcher has publicly stated that Blair is 'the most formidable Labour leader since Hugh Gaitskell in the 1950s' and has 'genuinely moved' the party from far-left socialist to a more centre ground. Wonder if she's been dining with her old mate Murdoch, who seems to share that view precisely.

WEDNESDAY, 31 MAY

Winner's not happy. 'Up until last weekend the subbing of my column has been first-rate,' he moaned:

Whoever did it on Sunday needs a major telling off. It is full of changes to my copy, not for length, but because some idiot decided he knew how to write it better than I did. If he is right then perhaps he should do the whole column. May I give you just one example. At the end of the item about Nigel Mansell I wrote: 'Quite honestly, it cheers me up no end. Makes my mistakes look positively brilliant by comparison.' The sub changed it to 'Quite honestly, it cheers me up no end – by making my mistakes look positively brilliant by comparison.' There are many similar examples. Could you please tell these people that the way I write is the way I write and if they don't like it, just leave the page blank. Michael. PS. I'd be very happy to have the gentleman's name who did this and I will give him a sound bite on the telephone that he will remember for the rest of his life.

The sub is Lou Yaffa, a large and legendary Geordie production journalist who is superb at his job, very tough, and doesn't suffer fools. The idea of Winner berating him amused me, so I suggested he did indeed call Lou direct.

A fax arrived an hour later: 'Piers, Mr Yaffa tells me he doesn't like my writing style, that's why he changes it. Why don't you get him to write the column, he's cheaper. Michael.'

I replied:

Dear Michael, a) Mr Yaffa is very experienced and has done your column since you started. b) I understand you rewarded his efforts by telling him to 'piss off.' c) This is not conducive to a good working relationship between artiste and sub-editor. d) Mr Yaffa is cheaper, you're right. But although 'Yaffa's World' has an irresistible ring to it, I still feel your name is a slightly better property. At the moment. Piers. PS. Why don't you come in and sit next to Mr Yaffa as he does your page, I'm sure he'd love that. And you could also advise me on how to edit the paper while you're here.

Winner didn't give up: 'Excellently phrased letter, Piers, but wouldn't it be easier if we just agreed Clause 1 of our contract dated 27/10/94 which makes it clear that changes can be made for purposes of length not style. Michael. PS. "Piss off" is one of the milder remarks I utter when annoyed. On a scale of one to ten it is a weak three.'

I was up for this now. 'Dear Michael, The problem is occurring more when things are cut for length reasons than for style. I think the easiest thing is for you to read the final proof of every column on Saturday evening before publication.' I know he won't want to do this because he'll be guzzling some great meal somewhere expensive. I was right.

'No, darlink, I need only see the column in the morning so long as the sub-editor doesn't change things because he doesn't like my style as Mr Yaffa decided to do last week. Shortening for length has always been well done.'

FRIDAY, 2 JUNE

Got him.

> Dear Michael, Mr Yaffa has brought to my attention what appears to be a factual inaccuracy in this week's column. You state that 'euthanasia was officially sanctioned in Australia this week'. Mr Yaffa says that in fact it has only been sanctioned in the Northern territories, not the whole country. He is, understandably, reluctant to change this without your authorisation. What shall I do with this delicate problem?

He conceded:

> Mr Yaffa is of course right. But if you say heavy storms hit England yesterday you don't mean there were parts of England that didn't have them, do you? Or if you say Michael Winner died in London, you don't have to say Kensington, London. Anyway, up to you. Either say 1) Euthanasia was … in Australia's Northern Territories or 2) in Northern Australia or 3) in Australia. You choose it.
> Yaffa 1, Winner 0.

WEDNESDAY, 7 JUNE

I've gone to the Midlands on cricket tour with my village team and the office call today to say that the *Standard* diary has led with a story headlined GOTCHA! PIERS NABBED WITH GAZZA'S GIRL. It claims that the *Sun* were door-stepping Sheryl Kyle one night after a tip-off she had a new man – when they spotted me clambering down her drainpipes and killed the story.

Confirmation of our hot affair comes from Max Clifford, who says he introduced us. 'They're doing an album together called Tory Sleaze,' he is quoted as saying. 'They're certainly on good terms, and Piers will play the harmonica on the record.'

Then, to my horror, my mother is quoted saying, 'I expect mums are the last to know these things.'

What the hell is this all about? It is all complete and utter invention. I called Mum, who got immediately upset when she realised she'd tripped up after defying my strict lifetime ban on talking to the press. Mothers are always easy prey.

A second call to Max Clifford revealed he thought it was all some big wind-up so made up anything he could think of for personal amusement. By now rather angry, I called the *Standard* diary and gave a lady called Sarah Sands my views on their disgraceful piece of inaccurate intrusive journalism. Even as I said it, I realised it all sounded wrong coming from the editor of the *NoW*. I ploughed on anyway, giving it the full 'Do you have any fucking idea who you're dealing with?' line.

Ms Sands was very sorry and very understanding and promised to put the record straight tomorrow. That's showed 'em.

THURSDAY, 8 JUNE

Sands has stitched me spectacularly. 'The telephone rings,' ran her follow-up diary item. 'It's Piers Morgan, editor of the *NoW*. His fury is terrible. He says we caused his family distress and asks how we feel about his estranged wife having to read it. He says his holiday has been "ruined by all this shit". He wonders too how we'd feel if the *NoW* starts delving into our private lives. We wouldn't like it at all, and are eager to set the record straight.' I've emerged as a complete and utter hypocritical berk.

TUESDAY, 13 JUNE

Tony Blair went to the House of Lords today to address cross-bench peers about the unions, armed with a jokey Christmas present I sent him last year. When Woodrow Wyatt got up and started having a go at him about Labour's relationship with the unions, Blair stopped him dead in his tracks, fumbled under his seat and pulled out my framed picture of Woodrow in his old Labour campaigning poster with the caption 'Woodrow Wyatt says Labour is good for Britain and good for you'. Everyone, apart from Woodrow, fell about. He rang me later. 'You humiliated me,' he wailed. Yes, I thought, and this is just the start of it.

WEDNESDAY, 14 JUNE

Private Eye has carried the uncensored Sands conversation. 'You lot are fucking shit,' they quote me as ranting. 'How do you think my fucking family feel about this, you fucking dickheads.' Etc, etc, etc. All pretty accurate. And even more damning. The editor of the *NoW* bleating about his privacy, unbelievable. Never again.

Then it turned into an intriguing day. I got a call from David Montgomery, chief executive of the rival Mirror Group, and former Murdoch editor of the *News of the World* and *Today*. He wonders if I would like to meet for breakfast. It can only mean one thing – he wants to offer me the editorship of the struggling *Daily Mirror*. We arranged to meet at the Berkeley Hotel in Knightsbridge tomorrow morning for breakfast.

THURSDAY, 15 JUNE

Montgomery was, surprisingly, quite shy, but looked fit and focused. He didn't offer me the job outright, just asked if I would be interested if it became available. I didn't commit myself either, but said it had always been an ambition to edit a daily paper and I couldn't see me getting the *Sun* for a few years with Stuart Higgins doing so well.

'You must have been appalled by how Rupert humiliated you over the Earl Spencer business?' Montgomery goaded, pressing all the right buttons. 'Well, it wasn't massively supportive, I agree,' I said – pushing it far enough without being too disloyal. We both understood each other and agreed to talk again.

Later in the office, we received a tip that Who singer Roger Daltrey's teenage son has been suspended from his public school for drug abuse. Spencer's little health crisis has made me think a bit more about these sort of things. What if he was a teenager and had been caught doing this kind of stuff? I pinged Roger Daltrey a fax and was staggered when three hours later a fax whirled back saying, 'Dear Piers, There has been a disciplinary matter at Sevenoaks School involving ten pupils. One person has been expelled and nine suspended, for dabbling in cannabis. Unfortunately my son Jamie is one of those suspended for one week. We hope he has learned his lesson. Yours, Roger.'

No fuss, no nonsense, no raging PR or lawyer threatening us with courts and the PCC. Just a straightforward admission, and a very sensible quote from a concerned father. I've never met Daltrey, but I'm impressed. And we will, as a result, be kinder than usual with this story.

SUNDAY, 18 JUNE

Murdoch called and was totally dismissive about Major. 'He's a dead duck. The Tories are hopeless, they just have nobody to lead them.' 'What about Portillo?' I ask.

'He has some good ideas but he's a poofter, apparently,' Murdoch replied.

David Montgomery called again when I got home to say they'd like to take things a step further and wonders if I could see the Mirror chairman Sir Robert Clark for breakfast next week. They're warming up for a formal offer, I can see it coming.

WEDNESDAY, 21 JUNE

Had breakfast with Sir Robert Clark at his Mayfair office. He was a nice, avuncular guy and we had a very pleasant chat. Montgomery called later to say it went very well and he'd be in touch. I am excited by the possibility of being offered the *Mirror* because it's a paper on its knees and it would be fun turning it around. I've been getting more and more bored with the pace of a Sunday paper anyway, and I also think Murdoch's getting twitchy about all the mayhem I'm causing and thinks it's creating just a few too many problems for him in the corridors of power.

It might suit both of us for me to leave. I hope I don't get offered it before I have to go to the Hayman Island conference. It will be rather embarrassing going out there knowing I'm leaving.

THURSDAY, 22 JUNE

Winner's sent a vile fax to Rebekah whining about the removal of a photo of him from his column and replacing it with one of Carrie Fisher at the last minute: 'What a ghastly horrid mess the column looked this week! Carrie Fisher's photo would have been rejected by the Little Piddlington Gazette as too awful to print.

Staring eyes, dark, tacky in the extreme. Did you all just stick it in then go off to the pub early?'

Who does he think he is?

I replied: 'Dear Michael, I threw out your photo because it wasn't very good. I therefore resent your offensive remarks about that decision. As long as I am editor here I will make those decisions and I don't expect petty abuse from contributors as a result.'

SATURDAY, 24 JUNE

I was even more bored than usual today, and to alleviate the tedium decided to offer odds of 10–1 to anyone who fancied betting £20 on South Africa to beat New Zealand in today's rugby world cup final in Johannesburg. Ten people came forward to respond to my internal computer message, from messengers to executives and lawyers. I couldn't believe their stupidity. This All Blacks team has crushed everything in its wake.

After 90 minutes the score was 9–9 and I was an emotional wreck. Bookies only pay out on normal time, so I announced I had therefore won my bet. But I was shouted down by a chorus of hyped-up staff keen to relieve me of my wallet, so reluctantly agreed to extend the bet to the end of the match.

South Africa won, and I lost £2000.

TUESDAY, 27 JUNE

There is nothing quite as deathly as a Sunday tabloid newspaper newsroom on a Tuesday morning, with the possible exception of a leaving party for a particularly odious and ill-loved colleague. There's usually a smattering of low-key inquests into the previous edition, perhaps an angry exchange between features and news department reporters about alleged byline banditry and, on occasion, bitter recriminations relating to a wife-swapping exposé gone hideously wrong. But this was no ordinary Tuesday. This was going to be Divine Tuesday. Alex Marunchak burst into my office and declared, with all the portent his deadpan half-Ukrainian mustachioed visage can muster, 'Hugh Grant's been caught with a hooker in Hollywood.'

'What? How? When?' I over-excitedly spat out the usual garbled idiotic reply from an editor grappling with the sheer enormity of such extraordinary breaking news. Details are scant, but what we already know is quite enough. Mr Grant, the upper-crust, handsome, witty and urbane star of *Four Weddings and a Funeral*, has been caught quite literally with his pants down and is currently believed to be residing at the pleasure of the LAPD in Sunset Boulevard.

And he hadn't been caught with his fragrant, beautiful lover Elizabeth Hurley, but with a Miss Divine Brown, a tall, buxom prostitute. The curse of a Sunday paper dictates that all such bombshells erupt on a Monday or Tuesday. We thus had only one job to do, as the nation's leading moral arbiters and harbingers of grade-A gossip.

I ran out of my office punching the air delightedly and shrieking an order with somewhat embarrassing gusto: 'Get the hooker!'

By 4pm, flotillas of British journalists were boarding planes, boats, buses and taxis for Hollywood. Most of them employed by Mr R. Murdoch, owner of the *News of the World*. Divine Brown doesn't know it yet, but her little kiss and cuddle with this funny-speaking English guy is the biggest break of her entire professional life.

WEDNESDAY, 28 JUNE

It has been our lucky day. And Divine's. But not Hugh's. And definitely not Murdoch's bank manager's. Our brilliant American editorial team of Stuart White and David Schumaker have tracked down Miss Brown to her home in Oakland. Not the Oakland the rest of Fleet Street assumed from her police file – the one near Sunset. But the one an hour's flight away in California.

They called the number and a man claiming to be her uncle answered. My guys cut to the chase: 'Mr Brown, could you tell Divine that if she just waits at her house and refuses to talk to anyone who rings, we will be outside with a stretch limo filled with champagne and a thousand dollars in cash, in three hours' time?'

'I'll definitely tell her that,' chuckled the 'uncle'; 'that's something she will definitely be interested in hearing.' My boys duly turned up, and Divine duly got in the limo. 'We're going to have some fun,' they said. 'You bet your life we are,' she replied.

THURSDAY, 29 JUNE

The Fleet Street pack has been in hot pursuit ever since they realised they were all at the wrong Oakland. My team have had to move their precious quarry on every few hours, criss-crossing through America until finally arriving at a remote, palatial ranch in the Nevada desert. They booked the presidential suite, whose most recent inhabitants were, incredibly, Mr and Mrs R. Murdoch. Well, at least he'll know how expensive it is.

Divine's not in great shape. One of her cousins died yesterday in a shoot-out, and after much moral and ethical deliberation, Stuart decided he had to tell her, prompting an understandable deterioration in her emotional state. Stuart's an extraordinary operator – barely sleeping, constantly calling the office with updates, however trivial, and prowling the corridors of the hotel through the night with the demented attentiveness of an Israeli secret service agent.

Our friends at the *Sun* have no idea we've got Divine, and have taken to plastering 'Wanted' posters with her face on them all over Los Angeles, offering her $150,000 for her story. The biggest rivals the *News of the World* usually have lurk along the corridor in the *Sun* newsroom just fifteen feet away – owned by the same guy!

I had lunch today with Matthew Harding, an insurance tycoon I first met when I spent nine months working on an underwriting syndicate at Lloyds of London before I went to journalism college. He's now a top dog at Chelsea FC, and plotting hard to overthrow the chairman, Ken Bates.

We met at the Savoy, where he has a permanent table. He's an extraordinary character, a complete whirlwind of energy.

'Trouble with Ken is that he's such a miserable fucker,' he said, laughing so loud that other diners turned their heads.

Matthew showed me a playing card in his wallet with Glenn Hoddle's face on it. 'He's my hero: everyone should have heroes in life, shouldn't they, Piersy? I'm going to sign Glenn when I take over Chelsea. Might even pay the cash myself.'

He drinks like a fish, and after gulping down four gin and tonics he tucked into two bottles of wine. I tried to keep pace without getting too drunk for a possible Murdoch phone call later. Matthew's great fun, but physically and mentally exhausting. Eventually, at 3.30pm, I said I had to go and he exploded. 'Go? *Go?* Go where? You don't just have a lovely lunch with me and then go. You wait until I'm ready to go, then we'll leave, OK? Honestly, Piersy, have more fun in your life. You've got to live each day as if it's your last because one day you'll be right.' I finally staggered out at 4pm.

FRIDAY, 30 JUNE

Stuart Higgins's internal computer messages to me grew increasingly irate through the day as I pretended to know nothing about any deal with Divine Brown. This is how he responded to my dead bat answers:

12.07pm. I look forward to reading it Piers.

12.09pm. Stop lying.

12.11pm. Let me put this plainly, her story will be in the *NoW* this Sunday, yes, thank you and goodnight.

12.15pm. Don't fuck with me for one more second, tell me the fucking truth. I know you have her, don't deny it for another second.

12.28pm. Bloody disgusting.

12.32pm. Your attitude.

12.34pm. Yes, I'd have fucking told you and been fucking honest about it.

12.38pm. You've had her since Wednesday camel head.

12.42pm. If you haven't got her you can have my fucking house, my wife, my children, and my fucking garden shed and mountain bike. OK?

4.45pm. Don't start taunting me or I will get increasingly irate.

It's all very amusing.

We decided at 5pm to put Stuart and all our other rivals out of their misery and issued a statement to the world saying, 'To save our competitors any more fruitless searching, the *News of the World* can confirm that we have secured world rights to an exclusive interview with Divine Brown.' Within minutes it was flashing across TV screens all over the world. And Hugh Grant, after five days of hope, thinking he might just have got away with cavorting with the only hooker in the world who wouldn't sell her story, realised his worst possible nightmare was coming true. My joy was only slightly dimmed by a call from a disgruntled Stuart, who said Murdoch was furious with their 'Wanted' poster stunt, thinks Divine Brown's a two-bit sleazebag we shouldn't be paying a dime, and asked how all this is affecting the career prospects of his new best friend Hugh Grant – who has just signed a three picture deal with … Twentieth Century Fox … owned by one Rupert Murdoch. Shit.

I sense trouble. Big trouble.

SATURDAY, 1 JULY

A long, fitful night. Murdoch called mid afternoon. I knew he knew we had bought up Divine Brown's story. Yet he sounded cheerful and upbeat, and asked with apparent innocence: 'Hi, Piers, anything happening in England?'

'Erm, well, yes, Mr Murdoch, there is, actually.'

'Good, good, just so long as you haven't bought up that bloody tart.'

Silence.

'Um, which tart would that be, Mr Murdoch?' I stuttered, now aware of a hideous faultline developing in my gameplan.

'You know, that bloody Hugh Grant tart. Terrible woman.'

'Well, erm, ahem … well, you see …'

'You have, haven't you? Christ, have you gone *nuts*?' I was beginning to think that was exactly what had happened. It was time to step up to the plate.

'No, no, Mr Murdoch. This is a fantastic story and we've got her on our own. Everyone's been trying to get her.' Silence. At least ten seconds of silence. I could hear other voices in the background – I suspected the rather cocky tones of Los Angeles-based Fox Movie executives.

'I don't want to hear it. Christ, Piers, how could you pay a bloody hooker? Nobody wants to read a load of filth like that. It's just sleaze, sleaze, sleaze.' Well, yes, I thought. Not massively inconsistent with the traditional modus operandi of the *News of the World*. Then the killer punch: 'How much of *my* money have you paid her?' I had to lie. There was no way I could now admit to paying her at least £120,000 so far, including ever-spiralling expenses. 'Erm … forty.'

'Forty what?' he growled back.

'Forty thousand.'

'Dollars or pounds?'

'Erm … dollars.'

'So let me get this straight. You've given forty thousand of my bucks to some cheap tart to spill a load of sleaze on my new friend Hugh Grant?'

'Ahem, yes, Mr Murdoch, that's about the gist of it.' More silence, more mutterings that I couldn't quite hear properly. Then the pronouncement: 'I don't want you doing ... any more ... than two pages on it.'

I sensed a tiny opening, clutched from the jaws of abject, humiliating, hideous defeat. 'Right. Two pages.'

'Yes, and no more. What else is happening today?'

'Well, actually there is a good live situation on Hugh and Liz back together in their garden, having an animated chat about things.'

Silence.

'Right. Well, you can do another spread on that then. But that's *it*.'

The phone slammed. Murdoch had never done this before, but then we've never turned over a new movie superstar of his like this before either. His compromise instruction was breathtakingly brilliant. It pleased his Fox boys who clearly thought he'd all but killed the story, and he'd of course fully realised that we would still be OK, and the story would still be published in most of its gory details. I felt like Mike Tyson had splattered me all over Wapping with his bare mean fists, but let me rise at the count of nine to finish the fight.

No mention of the front page – which meant no ruling it off the front page, in my book. I informed my production boys that they now had to cram nine fantastic pages of undiluted sleaze about Mr Grant into two, with a live spread on the garden row. And in less than an hour. They exchanged knowing looks. They knew I'd had the arm put on me and there was no point asking too many questions. And thus it came to pass that tomorrow's *News of the World* will carry the most bizarre spread in its history – with more than 3,000 words packed into one page, and the other given over to pictures. And a page one that says simply HUGH TOLD ME I WAS HIS SEX FANTASY.

Well, I'd read it.

MONDAY, 3 JULY

Off to Wimbledon for a spot of tennis, caviar, scones and champagne. The perfect way to unwind from the pressures of ruining Hugh Grant's own break-fast, lunch, tea and dinner. I got back to the car to find six messages from the circulation manager of an increasingly over-enthusiastic nature.

Call one: 'Looks good, give me a bell.'

Call two: 'Blimey, it's coming in strong.'

Call three: 'This is fucking incredible, phone me.'

Call four: 'Shit, I mean fuck me sideways. It's flown out. Where are you?'

Call five: 'A thousand people have phoned asking for copies, it's a sell out everywhere. Mayhem. Where the hell have you gone?'

Call six (my favourite): 'It's bonkers, mate, bonkers.'

I finally got through to the poor man: 'Good sale, then?'

'You can say that again – two hundred and fifty-three thousand extra copies.'

God. That had to be the all-time *News of the World* record for an edition with no promotion or TV advertising. Just a great story, and the best promotional tool in journalism – rabid word of mouth. I wonder how Mr Murdoch will react.

TUESDAY, 4 JULY

Murdoch – we think for the first time ever – called the circulation department at 8am to ask for the *News of the World* sale. He was told the good news. Silence. An apparent murmer of 'wrong answer' and then he hung up.

John Major has won the Tory leadership contest. Woodrow rang boasting about how right he'd been all along. 'He'll lose the election,' I said. 'Rubbish,' retorted Woodrow. A word that springs to mind every time I read his turgid, toadying column.

THURSDAY, 6 JULY

There's two weeks to go to Hayman Island and still the *Mirror* haven't made a formal offer. It's getting ridiculous, so I called Montgomery this afternoon to ask what was happening and said I must know this week either way so I can plan what to do without compromising myself in Australia. He assured me I would know by the end of this week.

SUNDAY, 9 JULY

Still nothing from the *Mirror*, and something's not quite right about all this. Perhaps they have gone cold on the idea, or perhaps they think Murdoch will fight to keep me and might give me the *Sun* to stop me going. I don't think that's likely. But this is all pretty frustrating. It doesn't augur very well that they are dithering so much. I have resolved to go to Hayman Island and forget about the *Mirror* job. If they come back for me later, then fine, but I am going to put it to the back of my mind for now.

SUNDAY, 16 JULY

We got to Hayman Island via short stays in Hong Kong and Sydney. It's an amazing place. You arrive by speedboat right over the Great Barrier Reef. There are 500 staff for the 300 guests. In my room I found a huge parcel of News Corps freebies – baseball caps, T-shirts, shorts, everything you might need. I felt like getting it all on and running past the American Fox contingent chanting: 'One, two, three, four, Rupert Murdoch's News Corps.' There's quite a tough work agenda for the four days we're here, but there's a fair bit of leisure time too. All the key figures from News Corps worldwide are here – from the papers, the TV networks, the movie arm, everything. It's immediately obvious from early 'jovial' clashes that the Americans think we tabloid paper guys are scum. And since I think they're all suffering from American Superiority Complex too, that suits me fine, because it means I can hang out with the Brits and the Aussies and not worry about them.

MONDAY, 17 JULY

Dinner was a jolly affair last night, and I ended up playing snooker and drinking Jack Daniel's with the Murdoch sons, James and Lachlan, until 4am as most other 'delegates' had an early night to prepare to impress the Boss tomorrow. The Murdoch boys are a great laugh, totally unpretentious and up for partying. James has been running a record label, and told me with a laugh, 'I keep a gun under my desk because some of these rap guys come in to negotiate their contracts with Uzi machine guns stuffed into their jackets. Don't tell dad – he'd go mad!'

My alarm went off at 6.30am – I had forgotten I'd agreed to play tennis against a London executive called Chris Maybury. I felt like death but managed to get out there to play. He's a county standard player and thrashed me as I sweated neat bourbon. But at least it freshened me up a bit for the conference. The day went slowly and painfully. Lots of speeches and workshops, nothing too inspiring to be honest. I hate meetings.

At 4pm I got back to my room to have a little kip, and found 28 phone messages. What the hell was going on? I listened to the first one, from a reporter on the *Mail*.

'Mr Morgan, I wonder if you could call me urgently to comment on Sheryl Kyle's pregnancy.'

Oh, for Christ's sake, I thought, they can't be serious. The other 27 messages from other papers and news organisations confirmed they were. The tones were aggressive and persistent. I sat on my bed pondering what to do. I'd met this woman twice in my life, once in the newsroom, once at Quaglino's with Rebekah, and I'd never been near her in any intimate way. Yet the facts look damning.

I'm living on my own, Sheryl's had trouble with Gazza, we've been spotted coming out of a restaurant together … you do the maths, pal. To make things worse, they've all been ringing Gazza too, and he's gone potty, thinking there's no smoke without fire. I came to the decision that there was only one thing for it, and rang every editor to tell them personally it was all bullshit. They all sounded desperately sorry to hear it might not be true, and most of them clearly remained sceptical that I was telling the truth. I can only hope and pray they believe me when it comes to their presses running. Being hunted is not a nice experience. I'm getting a nasty taste of what my victims feel like. And it's horrible.

TUESDAY, 18 JULY

Nobody's run the story. Thank fuck for that.

Tony Blair made the keynote speech to the conference delegates here today, and went down an absolute storm. He spoke passionately of his 'new moral purpose' – particularly with regard to family life – and vowed to set free media companies from 'heavy regulation' and allow them to exploit their 'enterprise'. All just what Murdoch wanted to hear.

It was a pulsating speech, delivered with great energy and dynamism, and exuding confidence. As we walked out afterwards, Sam Chisolm grabbed me by the shoulders and virtually shrieked, 'That was an amazing speech – he's the new bloody JFK!'

Murdoch tried to make light of the mutual love-in that was going on by saying in his speech: 'If our flirtation is ever consummated, Tony, then I suspect we will end up making love like two porcupines. Very, very carefully.'

But there didn't seem to be anything prickly between them from where I was sitting.

Blair himself seemed elated when I had a quick word with him outside.

'You know, Piers, it was very important to me to come here and get the message over that New Labour is not going to strangle businesses like News Corporation. We believe in a vibrant free press and in commercial enterprise.'

Murdoch was, understandably, impressed. 'He's a very bright young man, and he made a great speech, didn't he?' he raved.

'Are we going to back him, then?' I asked.

'Too early to say that, but I could see people voting for him. He's a breath of fresh air.'

SUNDAY, 23 JULY

Sheryl has thankfully confirmed to Rebekah that I am *not* the father of her baby. But Gazza apparently still thinks I might be, and wants to kill me. Great. Just have to hope that when it arrives it has a big cheesy grin, blubs a lot and isn't overly blessed with cerebral mass. Then we'll know for sure it's Gazza's.

Or, as Rebekah said kindly, 'Actually, that would make it more likely to be yours.'

MONDAY, 24 JULY

This afternoon I played for the *News of the World* against a combined *Sunday Mirror/People* cricket team in Barnes, South London, and hit a century including 28 off one particularly awful over from their lawyer, Martin Cruddace. Hope if I go over there that his advice is better than his bowling.

MONDAY, 31 JULY

Lord Longford wrote to say he was disgusted by two 'revolting' letters we have published from readers about Myra. 'To rejoice in anyone's agony is beyond belief,' he said. 'I persuade myself that you didn't see them before publication. You tell me to accept defeat on this but you would think worse of me if I did.'

I did see them before publication, and agreed with them. I've written back to tell him this.

THURSDAY, 3 AUGUST

John Redwood came in for a drink at the *NoW*. He's a weird man, seemingly totally devoid of any humour. We did a front page with him morphed into Spock from *Star Trek*, which is his nickname because of his unemotional Vulcan-like demeanour. He looked at it, said 'How amusing' and sat down without a trace of a smile on his face. The rest of the meeting was just as deadly dull. He's obviously clever, but equally obviously a very, very boring man and hasn't got a hope in hell of being Prime Minister of this country. By contrast, when we had Michael Howard in after the Whitemoor prison break-out, we got some reporters to dress up in jailbird outfits and he loved it.

SUNDAY, 6 AUGUST

England rugby captain Will Carling's ex-PA Hilary Ryan has revealed to us, via Max Clifford (and £50,000), how Will and Princess Diana have been seeing each other secretly at Kensington Palace. She says it's a definite affair, but since he is married our lawyers are wary of going that far, and we've stuck to the hard incriminating fact that he has been slipping into the Palace up to three times a week for 'secret trysts'.

SATURDAY, 12 AUGUST

The Carling scandal has run all week everywhere and we've hoovered up another load of stuff on naughty Will from an ex-girlfriend for this weekend.

I rang his agent John Holmes for a comment. Holmes was in the press box at the test match, surrounded by cricket legends and writers. He seized his moment, shouting so they could all hear: 'Piers, you are the most odious, unpleasant, nasty, offensive and disgusting person in Fleet Street. I wish you an early fucking death. Now go away.' He sounded drunk.

A legal letter arrived later from the *Mail on Sunday* saying they had an exclusive interview with Will and Julia Carling and we must keep our grubby hands off. It's the usual futile effort papers make to stop everyone lifting great chunks of their scoop later in the night, and I laughed when I read it. As if we're just going to sit there, read this great interview, agree not to run a word of it and go to the pub.

To save time I just shouted to our lawyer across the newsroom: 'Hey Tom, how many fingers will this cost us if we nick it all?' He flicked five fingers at me: £50,000 maximum damages. Well worth a front page and two spreads inside.

We got the *Mail* at about 7pm and set about excavating every word with a journalistic JCB, crashing some of it into our first edition, thus making everyone think we have got the interview as well. It was great stuff, with Julia saying, 'This has happened to Diana before, but she's chosen the wrong couple this time.'

At 9pm we got another fax from the *Mail* legal team, issuing dire warnings about our 'flagrant breach of copyright' and saying they will be going for an injunction. We laughed again.

By the time they get a judge out of bed on a Saturday night after a long dinner we'll be printed and tucked up in our beds.

TUESDAY, 29 AUGUST

Had breakfast with David Montgomery at the Berkeley Hotel. He'd brought along my *Mirror* contract confirming my new salary of £175,000 with share options, bonus and other perks. It's much better than my *NoW* deal but the money doesn't really matter. I'm bored with Sunday papers. I returned to Wapping for what I assumed would be the last time to break the news.

I saw Les Hinton, the newly appointed chairman of News International, and told him I was leaving. He looked shocked, and immediately said I couldn't go. 'Look, Piers, it's very flattering to be offered the Mirror but your future is here at News. It would be madness to walk away now to work for those amateurs.'

Les was charming, flattering and determined to make me change my mind. Everything he said was true, but he was missing the main point. 'Les,' I said eventually, 'I want to edit a daily paper and you can't give me the Sun yet because Stuart's doing a great job there and the staff love him. So, since I don't want to work in TV or movies, or move abroad, my options are pretty limited here unless you see me editing The Times?' We both laughed.

Les said I was not to announce anything until he had spoken to Murdoch. 'He won't be happy about this,' he said. And I guess he won't be. But he might just understand it. I agreed to say nothing for 24 hours.

WEDNESDAY, 30 AUGUST

Les, having spoken to Murdoch, sent me a formal letter asking me to turn down the *Mirror* job, while conceding it was a 'feather in your cap'. He said everyone was 'very pleased with the way you have performed as editor at the *NoW* and wants you to stay in that very important role'. But then his tone grew a little more sinister and he reminded me I can't edit the *Mirror* for a year after the end of my six-month notice period – so not for another eighteen months. And if I do, then 'we will obviously have to take whatever steps are necessary to enforce your obligations'.

Newspaper buildings leak like sieves, and I started to get calls asking what's going on. There were wild rumours about me going to America, taking over the *Sun*, making a movie with Kevin Costner, having a terrible illness … The usual nonsense. At 4.30pm the late edition of the London *Evening Standard* dropped, and their diary led on my impending defection. Journalists started bombarding the company with calls asking if it was true. I called in a few select members of my staff and said I was leaving.

News International then surprised me by issuing a statement in the evening, saying I was still editor of the *NoW* and that they will be holding me to my contract. When the papers dropped later they all focused on me being at the centre of a tug-of-war, which obviously plays quite well if you're me.

THURSDAY, 31 AUGUST

I walked into the newsroom this morning and it was like a morgue. Journalists hate change, even if they hate their editor. New editors change things and sack people.

A few people came into my office to try and persuade me to stay. But I have already moved, in my mind, to the *Mirror*, and just want to get on with it now.

James Murdoch rang me. 'Piers, you can't leave now, you have a fantastic future with this company,' he said.

I gave him the speech I gave Les. 'James, I love working for your father and it's a great company, but daily papers don't come along very often and I have got to go and see if I can do it.'

He replied, 'Dad's really pissed at you: he can't believe you are doing this to him after he took such a gamble on you. He went mad when Les told him, he has great plans for you.'

The enormity of what I'm doing was beginning to hit home, but I had to stay firm.

'James, tell your dad I'm really sorry, but I am definitely leaving.'

He said he was really sorry again, but I could tell from the tone of his voice that he viewed my decision as treachery. The Murdochs are a very tight family; if you stiff one of them, you stiff them all. It's what makes them so strong, and so successful.

Les told me to stay at home tomorrow and await further instructions. He was still trying to be nice, but he knows I am going to be the enemy soon, and I suspect his mind is already moving to my replacement. I told him to appoint my deputy editor Phil Hall – that's what all editors should do, unless their No. 2 is a complete halfwit. They rarely get the job but they deserve your support.

FRIDAY, 1 SEPTEMBER

I was formally told this morning that I will have to serve my notice period at home, all twelve months of it. The *Mirror* lawyers say this is rubbish and it will be more like two or three at most. I'm not bothered, it will give me time to recharge the batteries and acquaint myself with the *Mirror* and its staff. News of my appointment has provoked mixed reaction, to put it mildly. Paul Foot, who quit the *Mirror* a few years ago, went on CNN to say it was 'very grim news. Piers Morgan has been editor of this utterly reactionary and despicable paper for a long time so I don't suppose he will change his ways very much at the Mirror.'

David English at the *Mail* sent a nice note, though: 'Editing a daily paper is so much more fun than running a Sunday. I have a particularly soft spot for the *Mirror* as it was the first paper I worked on in Fleet Street. It is a great paper and a great honour to edit it. I wish you the very best of luck and hope we can have lunch and a chat soon. Kelvin has told me so much about you.' I can imagine …

Lord Longford, of course, was thrilled: 'You will not be surprised to hear I never thought the *NoW* was good enough for you, you don't need me to spell out the meaning.'

And Michael Howard was amusing: 'Dear Piers, congratulations and best of luck. I am at the ready to visit the editor's office at the *Mirror* as I was at the *NoW*, but quite understand if the invitation is delayed.'

SATURDAY, 2 SEPTEMBER

News International issued a press release extolling the genius of new editor Phil Hall today. I got one line at the end: 'Piers Morgan will be leaving the company.'

Michael Winner sent me a card: 'Congratulations – my ma took the *Mirror* during the war. It was considered very daring then, and I am sure you will return it to its exuberance.'

I replied: 'Thanks, Michael. It's been a lot of fun and on a personal note, a lot of extremely amusing mutual aggravation!'

I'll miss the old devil.

WEDNESDAY, 6 SEPTEMBER

The UK *Press Gazette*, the newspaper industry trade mag, has come out with a ludicrous front-page splash headlined MORGAN WALKS OUT WITH MURDOCH PLANS. If he's got any, as I'm sure he has, he certainly wouldn't be sharing them with me. The whole piece smacks of News International spin designed to bill me as a cross between Philby and Judas.

THURSDAY, 7 SEPTEMBER

I was invited last night to a leaving drink with four or five executives at a bar in Docklands. When I got there I found almost the entire staff and felt really touched. One of them told me they tried to get a few hundred pounds from Stuart Kuttner, the *NoW* managing editor, to put behind the bar, but he refused, saying, 'That man is now persona non grata at this company.' Apparently rolling his tongue around the letter 'r' for extra effect.

I made a short speech and we all got pretty drunk. I will miss them: they're an eclectic and amusing group of very professional people, and we've had a lot of fun together.

FRIDAY, 8 SEPTEMBER

I've not heard a single word from Murdoch, so decided to write to him.

Dear Mr Murdoch, this letter may be wholly inappropriate under the circumstances, but I'd like to offer you an explanation for my decision to join the *Mirror*. I very much regret the manner in which my departure was conducted and in particular that I was not given the opportunity to discuss this with you personally. Perhaps it was naivety on my part, but

I assumed that when I informed Les of my job offer, then you would wish to see me. It was certainly never my desire to announce the move as a fait accompli before talking to you first. Unfortunately once the news became public, to my surprise and dismay, I was left in an utterly untenable situation. I can only say that when I had my initial conversation with Les I had not signed any contract with the *Mirror*. As for my decision to leave, I simply felt it was an opportunity I would be stupid to turn down. It has always been my ambition to edit a great national daily paper and these chances usually only come along once in a journalist's life. I have had a fantastic time at News International and your extraordinary gamble in appointing me to the *News of the World* gave me the opportunity most people only dream about. I am very acutely aware that you took a massive risk with me, and that because of that you will probably be viewing my decision as an unforgivable defection. But if there is one thing I learned more than anything else at News it was that life is about taking on challenges and opportunities. I cannot believe that anyone in my position would have been able to reject the chance to edit a paper that has so much to improve. By accepting the challenge I realise that I may have burned my bridges with you for ever, and that is not something I am either pleased about or proud of. You have been an extraordinary mentor to me and to work for you was an honour and a privilege I will never forget. I take nothing but great memories to the *Mirror*, where I know I will be competing with the best paper in the country, and one of the best editors in Stuart Higgins. Whatever else, it will be fun having a go. I hope one day in the future you might perhaps consider me for such a great job, but I guess at the moment you would rather have me hurled from the top of Canary Wharf into a pool of crocodiles. Thank you, Mr Murdoch, for giving me my break. I am personally very sorry at the way this has all ended, but resigned to perhaps the inevitability of a certain ill-feeling. Phil Hall is a brilliant journalist and I am sure the *NoW* will thrive under him … without the need for you to publicly bollock him, hopefully. Yours sincerely, Piers.

I sent it off, then re-read a copy of it tonight and realised I've come across as a bit of a fawning little creep. But I mean it.

Phil Hall biked me round a letter. 'Dear Piers, I'm afraid I've been told to get our fax machine back. Do you think you can return it? Regards, Phil.' I considered throwing it into the river and letting them pick it up when it floats past but decided against it.

SUNDAY, 24 SEPTEMBER
I am rather enjoying all this time off. One of my oldest village mates, Miles Caldwell, had his stag party at Butlins in Minehead yesterday, and I ended up

topless, covered in foam and chanting decidedly inappropriate songs to a hen party from Scunthorpe, in a truly terrible on-site nightclub called Bonkers.

WEDNESDAY, 27 SEPTEMBER

Ian Hislop invited me to the legendary Coach and Horses pub in Soho for a *Private Eye* lunch. All the *Eye* gang were there – from Richard Ingrams to Francis Wheen. I got horrendously pissed and started telling them endless gruesome Fleet Street stories that I'm sure will all start appearing in future issues. Must be their usual gameplan with lunch guests. They all absolutely revel in other people's misfortunes. It's like a drug for them. But my lasting memory will be Hislop's handshake, which has to be the weakest I've encountered since Larry Grayson caressed my hand like a wet dab.

MONDAY, 2 OCTOBER

I got down to Brighton for the Labour Party conference and played golf with my former *NoW* colleagues Bob Warren and Tom Crone. Halfway round the course, my phone rang and it was Stuart Kuttner, asking if I can give a job on the *Mirror* to his daughter Julia. I toyed with saying she's 'persona non grata', but decided not to sink to his level and just said I'd let him know when I got there. Breathtaking cheek.

Conference is an extraordinary business. Every politician and political journalist gathers together in a seaside town and gets pissed, from what I can see. And I mean really, really pissed. It's deemed 'not good form' to be in bed before 4am.

Great fun, but a complete waste of time and money as far as I can see.

TUESDAY, 3 OCTOBER

Saw Alastair Campbell in the evening and he was hopping mad because the BBC have led on O. J. Simpson being found not guilty of killing his wife, and not on Blair's conference speech. I suspect most of the public will be considerably more interested in Simpson, especially given the amazing live coverage inside the courtroom. But Campbell stormed off to remonstrate with the BBC, saying it's 'all a fucking plot. They hate us.' Bit paranoid.

WEDNESDAY, 4 OCTOBER

Bumped into John Prescott later, and introduced myself. He was suitably unimpressed. 'Ah, yes, you're the fucking Tory, aren't you?'

SATURDAY, 28 OCTOBER

Played golf today with Sir Nick Lloyd, editor of the *Express*, at his club, Woburn. I went round in 124 shots – terrible, even for a beginner like me. But to Nick's horror, and my utter amazement, I also got a hole in one. Something he had failed to do there for eighteen years.

Must be a lucky omen.

MONDAY, 30 OCTOBER

Two days before I start at the *Mirror* proper, and today I was invited to see Tony Blair at his Westminster office. 'Big move, leaving Murdoch,' he said.

'Yes, I loved working for him, but the chance of a daily paper was too good to turn down.'

Blair is clearly terrified of my ex-boss and what he might do to him. 'We can't afford to be put through the mincer like Neil Kinnock,' he said. 'Obviously the Mirror will always be our first port of call but we will have to have a good relationship with the other side too.'

We had a cup of tea and he asked what my plans for the *Mirror* were. 'To shake it up, take the Sun on a bit, and help you guys get elected,' I replied.

'Sounds good to me,' he said. 'If there's anything we can do to help, then just let me know.'

TUESDAY, 31 OCTOBER

The eve of my first day at the *Mirror* and I called the newsdesk to ask what they had in the locker for me. Bearing in mind they've had two months to prepare for this day, I was not overly impressed when they replied, 'We had five great stories but they've all fallen down.' I suggested they find something pretty sharpish or some of them might be 'falling down' too. My last words left my expectations very clear: 'I want to be on the lunchtime news on Thursday boasting about our great scoop.' I don't have any expectation of this expectation being realised. But I'm looking forward to a new start at work and at home – since I've moved back in with Marion this week too.

WEDNESDAY, 1 NOVEMBER

I arrived at 9am at Canary Wharf. The place was dead, just a few office workers, a couple of bars and restaurants, and that's your lot. Not very encouraging. I marched into the newsroom as confidently as I could, but I felt very nervous. It's an alien environment with alien people, most of whom will be at best distrustful of me until I can convince them otherwise.

My office is big, and right on a corner of the glass-fronted tower, 22 floors up. Which means I get quite amazing views over the whole of London. So much more civilised than the windowless Wapping offices of the *NoW*.

I summoned the newsdesk and asked what they had for me. They smirked and asked if I could wait until conference at 11am. I got the sense something was up and granted this request, but added: 'It had better be good.' More smirks.

When the time came, there were yet more smirks as Eugene Duffy, the news editor, announced: 'At six-forty this morning one of our reporters, Justin Dunn, got into Number Ten Downing Street and posed for photos outside John Major's private flat door. He used a security pass given to him by a former contract worker who'd been fired two weeks ago, and been jailed six times before that. It's a massive breach of security, they've all gone bonkers and we've got a cracking scoop.' Eugene paused for effect.

'You'll be on the lunchtime news tomorrow with this one, boss.' More smirks.

They'd pulled it out of the bag at the last minute, the jammy buggers. But I'm thrilled, it's a great story. Good for them.

I got back home to Wandsworth feeling knackered, but absolutely buzzing from the day.

THURSDAY, 2 NOVEMBER

The ITN lunchtime news led on our exposé – including an interview with the new editor of the *Daily Mirror* boasting about his paper's scoop. The circulation manager brought me more good news later that day: we sold an extra 40,000 papers too. A fantastic, dream start. The newsroom was buzzing all day.

A letter from Les Hinton arrived: 'Dear Piers, After the tense moments surrounding your departure from the *NoW*, I wanted to extend you my personal best wishes. Being on opposite sides means things are bound to become intense. Whatever takes place, please remember not to take it personally. Les,'

FRIDAY, 3 NOVEMBER

I had a little rant in morning conference about what I love and loathe in the paper, singling out the weekly offerings from Vanessa Feltz for special attention, saying, 'She is absolutely fucking hopeless – who cares what she has to say about anything. We're not running that column again.' Everyone nodded in agreement, not an uncommon experience when a new editor is making his first decrees.

When conference ended, I walked outside to find an enormous bunch of flowers from Vanessa Feltz, with a note saying: 'Dear Piers, congratulations from your adoring and adorable columnist Vanessa Feltz.'

I rang her agent to say thanks for the flowers, and to fire her client.

FRIDAY, 10 NOVEMBER

Peter Mandelson wrote to congratulate me on a 'great first week' and Gordon Brown also wrote to say how much he's 'looking forward to meeting me'. The Labour PR machine is off and running. It's obvious that they value the *Mirror* pretty highly. But the test will come when the election arrives and they have to appease our rivals.

FRIDAY, 17 NOVEMBER

Today newspaper shut down today, which is a great shame. I knew there were big problems keeping it going when I was at the *NoW*. In fact Murdoch was on the verge of selling it to Mohammed Al Fayed but canned the deal at the last minute, for some undisclosed reason, possibly after pressure from the Government.

John Major, by coincidence, came to lunch at the *Mirror* today. He was charming to start with, but soon got rattled when I asked if he accepted he was a ditherer because he never seemed to deal with badly behaved ministers like David Mellor until it was too late. 'Ditherer?' he said. *'I'm not a ditherer!'* He started banging his fist down on the table and looked like he wanted to beat me up, and in that moment I could tell all the Saint John stuff was crap. He's just as prickly and mean as most politicians when it comes to himself.

I took him on a tour of the newsroom and when I mentioned I was a cricket fan he instantly tried to catch me out by asking, 'Really? Who wrote a book called Whispering Death, then?'

'Michael Holding,' I instantly replied to his visible disappointment.

Later he visited Kelvin downstairs at Live TV, who took him to the twentieth-floor window and said, 'On a really good day, John, you can see a Tory voter if you're lucky.' He wasn't amused.

MONDAY, 20 NOVEMBER

Princess Diana went on *Panorama* tonight and opened her heart up in an astonishing way about absolutely everything. Why she adored James Hewitt, doesn't think Charles can be King, and so on. We sat on the back bench watching in breathless silence, interspersed with squeals of excitement. It was utterly sensational in every way, the most outrageous celebrity interview I have ever seen. She looked slightly potty, with too much eye make-up and a very intense delivery style. But the quotes were pure Class A infusion.

I cleared most of the paper and told the production team to try and cram every word in if they could. There isn't enough wood in the Amazon rain forest for the number of papers you could sell with this.

SATURDAY, 25 NOVEMBER

The *Sunday Mirror* journalist and *Sunday People* secretary who were flogging their papers' newslists to the *NoW* have both been fired. I'd given them a month to stop and incredibly they had just carried on, so I fried them.

SATURDAY, 30 DECEMBER

David English has given the *Guardian* his media predictions for the year ahead, including this one: 'Piers Morgan will be a bold and instinctive tabloid genius … But as in the case of his mentor Kelvin MacKenzie the risk of a spectacularly destructive own goal will remain high.'

DAILY Mirror

66 96

Monday, June 24, 1996   PEARCE IN OUR TIME   30p

ACHTUNG!

SURRENDER

For you Fritz, ze Euro 96 Championship is over

CUT OUT AND STICK IN YOUR WINDOW

Mirror declares football war on Germany

BY THE EDITOR

I AM writing to you from the Editor's office at Canary Wharf, London.

Last night the Daily Mirror's ambassador in Berlin handed the German Government a final note stating that, unless we heard from them by 11 o'clock that they were prepared at once to withdraw their football team from Wembley, a state of soccer war would exist between us.

I have to tell you now that no such undertaking has been received, and that consequently we are at soccer war with Germany.

Home

It is with a heavy heart we therefore print this public declaration of hostilities and urge every loyal subject to cut it out and place it in a prominent place in their home, office or car.

We desired a peaceful and honourable settlement but the German manager Herr Vogts would not have it.

Having over-run defenceless Russia the Czech Republic and Croatia, he has evidently made up his mind to attack England at the semi-finals on Wednesday.

His actions show that there is no chance that this man will ever give up his practice of using force, long balls and quick breaks to achieve his ends. He must be stopped.

Safe

The situation in which no team could feel their goalmouth safe has become intolerable.

The Mirror therefore, in fulfilment of our obligations, is going to the aid of our loyal forces, who are so bravely resisting this unprovoked assault in their determination to liberate the European Championship trophy.

You can imagine what a bitter blow it is to me that all my long struggle to win peace

● Turn to Page 6

1996

MONDAY, 8 JANUARY

Paula Yates is pregnant by Hutchence. She's taken to ringing me every now and again with secret updates on her various legal battles with Bob Geldof – despite the fact that she's a *Sun* columnist. I rang to congratulate her.

'Oh, I'm just so fucking thrilled,' she shrieked down the phone.

'You going to marry him, then?'

'Well, I'm not divorced yet. But the decree nisi is due soon, the baby's due at the end of July, and Michael is considering marrying me! I'd do it as soon as we can, but he is thinking about it. I can hang on a bit longer I guess. We can get married next year after the baby's born and when I am all slinky again.'

'How are things with Bob?'

'Oh, pretty awful. I am so worn out by it all. I just want a home. Bob doesn't want to give me anything, he thinks I have brought all this on myself. Michael is paying for the kids' taxis to school, it's ridiculous.'

Ridiculous is right – I don't believe Bob would behave this way towards his kids for a minute.

'How will it resolve, do you think?' I asked.

'I don't know how, I just don't know. Michael is such a nice good man and never throws it back in my face.'

THURSDAY, 18 JANUARY

There was a reception today to launch Childline's tenth birthday appeal at the Savoy Hotel and I went along for one reason – Diana was going to be there, and I'd never actually met her in the flesh. She didn't disappoint. All the guests were lined up in small groups after her speech, and we were told she would sweep round the room meeting as many of us as possible. I was in the tabloid corner so didn't fancy our chances very much. But she swept into the room and headed straight over to us, looking it must be said, absolutely stunning. I was introduced.

'Ah,' she said. 'The man who knows me *so* well.' The sarcasm dripped from her regal lips. 'Thank you, ma'am, I like to think so.' She wasn't sure if I was being serious, so made her position clearer. 'Honestly, you editors always think you know everything about me when we haven't even met.'

'Well, now's your chance to enlighten me, your royal highness,' I replied. She eyed me up. 'Hmm … I don't have the time, I'm afraid …' Then she giggled. 'Or the inclination, come to that!'

Then she moved on. It was fascinating watching her work the room. Everyone, and I include myself in this, just melted in her presence. She is radiant, sexy and very direct – so you get the feeling you're the only one she cares about for the few seconds she's talking to you. It's a class act. I must say I was impressed.

FRIDAY, 19 JANUARY

I'd agreed to do my first leaving party speech for a staff member at the London Press Club tonight. These things are always fraught with potential hidden dangers. But you have to do them if asked. I got a few funny stories from the leaver's colleagues, including one great one about how he secretly romanced a particular features writer without anyone on the paper knowing. The way it was told to me suggested that everyone knew now. Unfortunately as I cheerfully regaled it, I rapidly realised from the horrified expressions everywhere that they didn't and I had been monumentally stitched up.

WEDNESDAY, 24 JANUARY

Had dinner last night with Gordon Brown, Labour's Shadow Chancellor, in the Churchill room at the House of Commons. He's a fascinating and formidable man, who, as the wine flowed, opened up a bit and revealed a charming side to him the public don't see, but perhaps ought to more often. What struck me most was his determination to know what our readers really cared about. 'I want to know the issues they write to you about most,' he said. 'It's clear that the Tories have completely lost touch with the people of this country and I don't want us to make that mistake.'

Brown was scathing about the Conservatives. 'They're hopelessly divided, and Major just seems to be drifting along, letting the splits get wider and more dangerous. What we have now in the Labour Party is proper leadership and a proper purpose. It's time we were allowed to govern again and put right what the Tories have done to this country.'

He looked very intense at that point of the conversation, his eyes staring ahead in a vaguely demented way. I wouldn't want to challenge someone like this at the next election. Unlike the jovial chatty Blair, he exudes an air of quiet, brooding anger and determination that is quite scary.

Had lunch at the Howard Hotel today with David English, the *Mail* chief. He was sharp, mischievous, funny and splendidly indiscreet. By hilarious coincidence, the *Sunday Express* editor Sue Douglas was dining at another table with John Junor, now a *Mail on Sunday* columnist.

'Bugger it,' said David, with a cackle, 'that will cost me another ten thousand.'

He knew Junor wouldn't leave the paper, but he also knew the wily old devil would use the situation to screw a nice pay rise. Such is the way of Fleet Street.

THURSDAY, 25 JANUARY

Went to interview Tony Blair today, after his toughest week as leader. Harriet Harman, secretary of state for social security, had revealed she's sending her child to a selective grammar school – the ultimate Old Labour sin, and a decision which provoked a storm of flak from her own party members.

He looked a bit knackered, unsurprisingly.

I asked if he'd not been tempted to sack her as the furore mounted.

'No, I made my mind up when I became leader that I would take a view on these kind of things and stick to it however bad the flak got.'

I wonder if he'll be able to keep to that in years to come. The media is growing more powerful and more aggressive by the day.

'Isn't she just a terrible hypocrite, though?'

'No, she has made a human decision for her son and I respect that. The reason Harriet and other parents face this kind of tough choice is because of the damage the Tories did to the state education system in this country. We need to repair that damage.'

It was a cute answer, but I suspect a lot more of his ministers will follow the private path for their kids' education and it will cause him considerable grief.

MONDAY, 29 JANUARY

Ulrika Jonsson's agent, Melanie Cantor, sent me a terse note after we'd published photos of her client at her father's funeral last Friday. 'If you can't allow Ulrika a private life, at least allow her some private grief.' I'd normally be quite sympathetic to this kind of thing, but the tone of this letter and the fact it is Ulrika, the world's greatest self-publicist, makes me less inclined to feel bad about it.

'Dear Melanie, if Ulrika promises to stop selling interviews about her private life to anyone who will pay, then I will respect her private life.'

She hit straight back: 'Ulrika has only sold one interview about her private life … to the *Daily Mirror* in October 1993. Thirty–fifteen. Melanie.'

This is bullshit, she's sold it countless times to magazines like *OK!* and *Hello!,* and Melanie well knows it. But part of the agent's job is to constantly fib about their clients. They *all* do it.

'Dear Melanie, OK I give up. The *Mirror* is now an Ulrika-free zone. This, I know, will cause her more suffering than anything else. Piers.' Tonight, as I stuffed this correspondence in my files, I read my faxes again and realised I'd perhaps been a bit callous, given that Ulrika was mourning her father. But the problem is that I just know she will make money out of talking about it at some stage. She can't stop herself.

Is that a good enough excuse for us to pap her at her dad's funeral, though? Probably not.

MONDAY, 5 FEBRUARY

I gave an interview to Radio Four last week in which I responded to an allegation that I was just aping the *Sun* every day by saying, 'I would like to ape the Sun's circulation, that's for sure. They sell two million more than we do on some days.' It was a stupid thing to say. And sure enough, my friends at Wapping have made the most of my idiocy by taking out a whole-page colour advert in *Press Gazette* with the quote and a big mocked-up photo of me as an ape swinging on a tree.

FRIDAY, 9 FEBRUARY

Most Fridays on daily papers seem quieter than other weekdays, and I don't for the life of me know why. But certainly by 6pm, everyone in the newsroom is usually winding down and heading for a pub or restaurant for an end-of-the-week drink. Today was no exception and I was just tidying my desk for an early exit when our head of security appeared, looking nervous, saying there had been a coded IRA bomb warning about an attack at Canary Wharf.

'Is it serious?'

'Well, they've had a few that came to nothing, but seem to think this one might be, yes.'

I called the executive team into my office and we deliberated what to do, concluding that we'd just have to crack on and see what happened. Telling the staff to walk into a potential explosion didn't seem a sensible option, and the tower was not yet being evacuated so the risk seemed small.

At 7pm, an enormous bang suddenly went off behind me. I was literally blown an inch off my chair, and my office is 22 floors up. It had to be a bomb: nothing else could make that kind of noise. It felt quite sickening, a really deep thudding crash that ripped through you like some virtual grenade. I ran into the newsroom and there was general controlled panic. Most people had run to look out of the window and see what had happened.

The explosion had gone off at South Quay train station a few hundred yards from our tower. It was horribly close, and the consequences if it had been a bit closer were not lost on any of us. Most offices in the tower were emptying at high speed, but we are journalists and this was a huge story. I gathered everyone around and said that if anyone wanted to go home, particularly if they have families, then they must leave immediately. But I added that I was buggered if the IRA were going to stop us getting the paper out, and all those who wanted to stay and help would be very much appreciated.

Peter Cox, the night editor, immediately started ripping up pages, saying, 'This is fucking great, the IRA ceasefire's ended right on our doorstep.'

'Some of our staff might be down there in the middle of it,' cautioned another sub. 'People must have died.'

Peter, a brilliant production journalist who I used to work with on the *Sun*, quickly apologised, but I fully understood his emotions. It *was* a great story, just a bit too close to home this time. The mood was sombre but professional after that. We wiped out the front to catch the first edition with a big banner headline, IRA BOMB ROCKS THE WHARF. Details were, as ever, sketchy. But we could see the devastation below and we could see the ambulances everywhere, so there must have been casualties.

At 8.45pm we sent the page, just as two policemen burst on to the floor shouting at us all to get out.

They were evacuating the building after a second bomb warning. I grabbed one of them and asked if it was serious or a precaution.

'It's deadly serious. The BBC has had a coded warning that there is a second device inside the tower itself.' My heart flipped a few beats. We were caught right bang in the middle of an unfurling atrocity. I shouted at everyone to get out, but the lifts had automatically been stopped and we all had to march down 22 flights, which took over twenty minutes. I was bloody terrified. Eventually we got down and made our way to a nearby pub and considered what to do.

There was supposed to be a contingency plan for this kind of thing, but nobody seemed to have a clue what to do. What we did know was that we could produce pages for the *Mirror* at the Glasgow offices of our sister paper the *Daily Record*, because they have the same system. So we spent £4000 chartering a plane from City Airport and sent a team up within the hour. They got there before midnight and were able to access locked *Mirror* pages and release them for printing, as well as start preparing new ones. About the same time, Charlie Wilson, our managing director, rang me to say we could get back in. The police had officially said no, but unofficially they didn't want the IRA to stop us coming out either. So after a brief exchange of views (Cop: 'We don't much like you journalists at the best of times.' Me: 'No, well, we're not massively keen on you lot either.') I was allowed to troop back up the stairs to the newsroom with the only twenty or so members of staff still in the pub. We turned on the lights and went to work.

It was a disparate bunch, and didn't include some of our best production guys like Peter and Simon Cosyns, who had finally given up waiting and gone home thinking we'd never get back in. But we had enough skills between us to do ten pages – with the help of the team in Scotland. It wasn't the greatest paper I'd ever edited, but, by God, it was the most satisfying. At 3am, we ate takeaway pizzas on the newsdesk and reflected on the night's amazing events. I was knackered, but exhilarated. This was what we were all journalists for. This was what it was really all about.

SATURDAY, 10 FEBRUARY

I woke at 7.30am to the sound of the papers coming through the letterbox. I ran down and there was the ten-page *Mirror* special edition. I clenched it proudly and said a quiet 'fuck you' to the IRA.

MONDAY, 12 FEBRUARY

We ran a very sad story on the front page last week about a small-time TV star/model called Peter Donald who killed himself because he became obsessed with not looking good enough. His mother gave a heart-rending interview about him. But today she has written to me. Furious at our front-page headline, TOO UGLY TO LIVE TV STAR'S TORMENT. And rather than threaten me with the PCC or the law courts, she chose a much more direct and powerful approach. 'If you have a child or have one in the future, I hope you don't go through the double agony of losing that child and knowing he/she took his/her life. Believe me, your newspaper made this mother's agony even more excruciating with that headline.' I feel terrible. She's right, we've been insensitive. Dreadfully so. I wrote back along these lines, but the damage is done.

MONDAY, 26 FEBRUARY

Marje Proops has sent me an agony letter about her own salary. 'You expressed surprise when I mentioned it was only £70k the other day. Don't get me wrong, I love doing the job, but my salary does seem pretty meagre compared to what others receive. I am feeling underpaid and undervalued and would like you to do something about it.'

SATURDAY, 2 MARCH

James Hewitt's cashing in on Diana yet again with a TV interview, so we decided to have a little fun with him, putting his car number plate, home address and home phone number in the paper and urging our millions of readers to let him know what they think of him.

We also sent our West Country reporter Geoff Lakeman down to make a citizen's arrest on him for treason.

At 9am this morning, the newsdesk called me, laughing, and said a BT van had arrived to change his line. 'He's had a few thousand calls of support,' they said.

SUNDAY, 3 MARCH

Frances Shand-Kydd, Diana's mother, has written to me accusing one of my reporters of reading a fax on her machine through a window at her Scottish home. She says it was a 'despicable, untenable violation' and what made it worse was our man discussing the contents of the fax that night in the local pub. 'The fax machine was fairly obscure, at the side of my desk in a room at the back of my house, so your reporter must have spent some time and been fairly athletic to see the contents of the fax, which was facing him upside down.'

She is demanding a response within fourteen days or she will go to the PCC. I asked the journalist concerned whether it was true, and he explained that he had spotted a rival's fax on the machine and rang him mischievously to ask if he'd had a reply yet. That journalist had then, for a 'laugh', sent another fax to the machine saying: 'If you boys from the press can read this you're obviously still looking through the window.' No wonder Ms Shand-Kydd is a bit pissed off.

I called her back, offering to pay some money to her local church charity to resolve the issue. She was quite feisty on the phone, and I suspected a little 'tipsy', and suggested £5000 to charity might ease the pain. I suggested £2500 was a more appropriate fee 'in my humble opinion', and offered to put my man in stocks outside her house for an hour. She accepted my offer because:

1) It must be your lucky day.
2) You consider your opinion humble.
3) You think I am a lady and reasonable.
I reject however your offer of the stocks for one hour as it would be overwhelming temptation and I don't like a man with a soprano voice.

I sent a thank-you note later, and asked if she'd ever do an interview about Diana since we're now getting on so famously. She faxed straight back: 'I will decline the invitation to "chirrup" about my youngest daughter, which won't surprise you I'm sure: personal choice and conviction rule. It is a fact that photographs and descriptions of my solo lifestyle in the press brought me three stalkers for two years. I think you'd agree that anyone who has had that experience would elect to avoid publicity.'

SATURDAY, 9 MARCH
Our February ABC figures are great, up 50,000 on January. And the *Sun*'s have fallen by the same amount. We've retaliated for the ape advert by buying one ourselves with a spoof 'Dear Marje' letter headed HE CAN'T GET IT UP! and featuring a fake letter from Ellis Watson, the *Sun*'s marketing chief and a good friend of mine for years, saying: 'I have a serious problem, for the last month I've been shouting my mouth off about what a brilliant job I'm doing, but now our sales have plummeted and the *Mirror*'s have shot up. I feel a complete fool and don't know what to tell the boss. Do you have any advice? Ellis.' 'Marje' replies: 'I am sorry but your problem will only get worse and there's nothing I can do to help. Have you considered resigning?'

Very childish, I know, but very funny all the same.

MONDAY, 11 MARCH
Paula Yates rang in a state, saying she's £100,000 in debt and facing eviction

from her house. 'I'm months behind on my mortgage payments, and they've said they'll repossess it in three weeks,' she said, crying. 'I'm desperate, Piers, I'm pregnant, for God's sake, and I'm going to end up homeless.'

'Why doesn't Michael help you?' I asked, not unreasonably I thought, given his fortune.

'Why the fuck should he? It's not Michael's problem, and it's not his responsibility, I'm not going to sponge off him – wait, he wants a word with you.'

Hutchence came on the phone, sounding out of it as usual.

'Are you saying I'm not helping Paula?'

'No, I asked if you were, that's all. She's in a bad way, Michael, and you have got loads of money.'

'Yeah, well, I will be helping her, of course I will. But she's a proud woman, you know. But if Paula and the kids are likely to lose their home I'll stop that happening. I have enough to help, and that's what I'll do.'

'You sound angry about all this.'

'I am, fucking angry. Everyone goes on about Saint Bob Geldof, and make out Paula's some sort of Rose West figure and I'm the Evil Stepfather. It makes me sick.'

I tried to lighten the mood: 'You looking forward to being a dad, then?'

'Oh yeah, mate, definitely. We're expecting a girl, the scans showed it. I'm very excited, and really looking forward to becoming a father. I know some people don't think I will stick around very long because rock stars don't do that sort of thing. But Paula and I are truly very happy together. We love each other and I feel very protective towards her at the moment.'

Paula came back on the line, and we talked for another ten minutes about her plight.

'Piers, just do what you can in the paper to help, can you, please?'

'Well, how about we run all this stuff we've been talking about?'

'Yes, OK, fuck it – why not.'

We splashed on Paula's new heartache, attributing the quotes to 'friends of Paula'. I wonder what Bob would think if he knew it was his wife making the calls.

TUESDAY, 12 MARCH

Marje is thrilled at the extra £10k I've given her. 'I feel very valued again, and big-headed too after all the nice things you said,' she writes. 'I'd better get on with some work now and regain a sense of reality.'

WEDNESDAY, 13 MARCH

A quiet morning, with nothing much happening. Then, just after 10am, the newsdesk told me there were reports of a shooting at a school in Scotland. I was not immediately that interested. Scottish stories rarely get into the English edition unless they are pretty spectacular, because it's considered almost a foreign country, and we have a Scottish staff who produce a completely different Scottish edition of the *Mirror* anyway.

But as the minutes passed, it soon became clear that this was no local incident. 'The gunman's still shooting,' Eugene shouted over. 'There are loads of kids in there and parents are starting to arrive from all over the place, hysterical.'

I turned on the TV and there were appalling images of dozens of mainly mothers sprinting desperately to the school, in a small hamlet called Dunblane. The pictures were instantly haunting. Can there be anything worse in the world than hearing some nutcase is firing a gun around your child's school? As more details came in, it got increasingly serious. The attacker, a local man named Thomas Hamilton, had gone into the school gym and just blazed away at a group of five- and six-year-olds inside before shooting himself. I was sickened, like all my colleagues. There were none of the usual black jokes to lighten the mood.

I thought of Spencer, now nearly three and at his nursery right now in Putney, and my eyes started to sting. Every parent will feel the same. It's such a uniquely terrible outrage. To deliberately target children like this is just beyond understanding. There was a terrible gloom in the newsroom by early evening: I have never seen it like this. Everyone just staring at the TV screens, many in tears. But this was also a huge story and we had to get on with preparing a brilliant newspaper around it.

About 8pm, a photo of the class that was gunned down arrived. It was black and white, and unbelievably upsetting. All these sweet young kids with big grins looking forward excitedly to the rest of their lives. Now most of them were dead, those aspirations shattered by a lunatic. Most papers, I was sure, would use the picture in its current shape. But I always prefer to be unpredictable on big news days, and jumped at a suggestion by our art supremo Simon Cosyns to prepare a dramatic front page with each of the faces of the dead cut out into squares bordering the perimeter, and a photograph of Hamilton in the middle with the simple headline HE KILLED THEM ALL.

FRIDAY, 15 MARCH

The world's media have converged on Dunblane, more than a thousand of them, and even the most hard-nosed of them is struggling to come to terms with what has happened. The local police are not used to this kind of thing – who is? – and took the panicky step of asking all the media to leave the town so the funerals can take place in privacy.

I called one of the senior detectives and suggested he think rather carefully about the precedent he is setting. 'Look,' I said, 'I understand why you think we should all leave, but don't be so sure that the families don't want us to record the funerals. When I was a local reporter I remember being invited into many homes of people who had just died so they could pay tribute to their loved ones in the local paper. Isn't the answer to allow a small group of journalists and photographers to cover each funeral and let everyone have the words and pictures? That way the tributes will be properly recorded, but the families won't have to deal with the media scrum.'

The policeman, to his great credit given the huge pressure he was under, listened to me and said he'd go and ask the families what they wanted. They all consented to a small media presence, as I thought they would.

Later in the evening I heard that one of my reporters in Dunblane, a strong character who has covered all kinds of tragic stories in the past, had been found by two of his colleagues sobbing his heart out in his hotel room, and he wasn't sure he could stay on the job.

I understood completely, and said he could go home to his family if he wanted to, but he said he'd stay. Nobody criticised him for his reaction. This has been no ordinary story. It tears into the heart and soul. If my staff didn't feel this way there would be something wrong with them. I cleared the front page for a call to Britain for a minute's silence in memory of those who died and for their families. I hope it is not seen as some sort of theatrical stunt. My gut instinct just says the public need some sort of focal point for their feelings, and this might be an appropriate way of satisfying that need.

MONDAY, 25 MARCH

Paula Yates rang. 'I'm going to walk the kids home from school today in the rain because I can't afford a taxi. If you take some pictures, then Bob might feel shamed into helping me properly.'

I could hardly believe what I was hearing, but it would be a good picture so I agreed. Sure enough, they turned up on time, in the rain, shuffling home. Undignified is not the word. For any of us involved in this sorry ongoing farce.

THURSDAY, 28 MARCH

The *Press Gazette* awards at the Royal Lancaster Hotel tonight. I recklessly led the *Mirror* table in giving the presenter, Clive Anderson, a bit of stick. 'You finished yet?' was one of my 'wittier' quips.

'No, Piers, but you will be at the Mirror soon,' he retorted to large applause. Too large for my liking – even from my own colleagues.

TUESDAY, 2 APRIL

The *Mirror* went blue for the day today. Literally. We got paid a small fortune by Pepsi to print it on blue paper. In return they gave every reader a free can of their new Pepsi Blue drink. I loved the whole idea, mainly because I knew it would get right up the noses of all those drunken old *Mirror* journalists who love to bang on about ethics and 'quality' when they used to fiddle their expenses with the best of them and write a load of old claptrap most days. It looked weird on the newsstand though, and I don't think we'll be doing it again in a hurry. But no readers complained, apart from one who rang to protest that we'd gone Tory and he was cancelling his order.

WEDNESDAY, 1 MAY

Michael Howard invited me to breakfast this morning at his home in South Eaton Place. I was curious to see how a Home Secretary lives in the permanent shadow of an IRA attack, and the answer is pretty grimly. From the moment I knocked on the door, there seemed to be armed policemen everywhere, inside and outside the house. Some actually live downstairs all the time, apparently. It seemed a bit excessive, but then the IRA don't have me at the top of their hit-list, so who am I to quibble. Howard was casually dressed and as charming as ever. I genuinely like the guy because he understands the difference between being a politician and being a human being, and can have relationships with the media wearing both hats. His very attractive wife Sandra prepared us a lavish cooked breakfast, and they seem a very happy couple, both I thought rather enjoying all the glamour of high office even if it comes at the expense of sharp-shooters in the loo. Howard is worried about what's happening to his party. 'I still think we will win the next election,' he said. 'But we have got to sort out our differences or they will tear the party apart.'

I asked what he thought of Blair. 'All show and no substance,' he said. 'Good brain, and a tough opponent when we debated against each other. But it's superficial and he'll get found out soon.'

I explained that the *Mirror* will be kicking the Tories all over the place what-ever they do or say, and he laughed. 'Oh, I know that. Don't think I've given you eggs and bacon in the belief that I can get the Mirror to say Vote Tory. But I just hope you give us a fair crack of the whip on policy.' I laughed now. 'Michael, the only fair crack of the whip you lot are going to get in the Mirror will be over your backsides. It's going to be war, and we're with the other guys.'

'OK, OK – well, just try not to whip me too hard if you can possibly avoid it.'

WEDNESDAY, 8 MAY

Jane Atkinson, Princess Diana's new PR, rang this morning to say she has persuaded her boss to invite me round for lunch at Kensington Palace.

To say I am mildly excited by this news is the understatement of the century. Diana's the biggest star in the world and I am getting a private audience. *Wow!*

FRIDAY, 10 MAY

Paula and Bob have got divorced. She gets their London house, and he – unbe-lievably – gets Hutchence's home, plus the Kent place he shared with Paula. Very progressive.

I called her and she sounded happy and relieved. 'I can get on with my life now,' she said.

But what will life with Hutchence really be like for her? He's never exactly been one for the longer-lasting snack.

THURSDAY, 16 MAY

Lunch with Diana. A big day; a massive, humungous day, in fact.

I got there ten minutes early, feeling decidedly nervous. The Kensington Palace front door was opened by her beaming butler, Paul Burrell, known to everyone in Fleet Street as Diana's Rock. He walked me up the stairs, chatting cheerfully about the weather and my journey, as if a tabloid editor prowling around Diana's home was a perfectly normal occurrence. He seemed a very nice guy, polite and friendly. I could see instantly why she gets on with him. He said the 'Boss' was running a bit late, joking, 'She'll be furious you are here first!' and invited me to have a drink. 'What does she have?' I asked. 'Water, usually,' he replied, 'but wouldn't you rather have a nice glass of wine? She won't mind in the slightest.' I readily agreed, if only to calm my racing heartbeat.

Burrell then left me alone in the suitably regal sitting room. Diana has a perfectly normal piano covered in perfectly normal family snaps. It's just that this family is the most photographed on the planet. Lots of pictures of her boys, the young heirs, the men who will perhaps kill off, or secure, the very future of the monarchy. To us they are just soap opera stars, semi-real figments of tabloid headlines and the occasional Palace balcony wave. But here they were, her boys, in picture frames, like any other adored sons.

Just sitting in her private room was fascinating. Her magazines lay on the table, from *Vogue* to *Hello!*, and her newspapers – the *Daily Mail* at the top of the pile, obviously, if distressingly. After ten minutes on my own, she swept in, gushing, 'I'm so sorry to have kept you, Piers – I hope Paul has been looking after you alright.' And then came surely one of the most needless requests of all time: 'Would you mind awfully if William joins us for lunch? Only he's on an exeat from Eton and I just thought that given you are a bit younger than most editors, it might be good for both of you get to know each other.'

'I'm sorry but that would be terribly inconvenient,' I replied sternly. Diana blushed slightly and started a stuttering 'Yes, of course, I'm so sorry …' apology, when I burst out laughing.

'Yes, ma'am, I think I can stretch to allowing the future King to join me for lunch.' The absurdity of this conversation held no apparent bounds. But before he joined us, Diana wanted a little chat. 'How's your circulation?' she asked. Bloody rampant, I thought, as she nestled into her sofa, radiating a surprisingly high degree of sexual allure.

'Oh very healthy, ma'am, thanks to you.' She laughed, a tad insincerely. We discussed her mate Fergie. 'Can't you go a bit easier on her?' Diana pleaded, with genuine concern in those extraordinarily big, expressively deep blue eyes.

'Well, she's her own worst enemy,' I replied. 'Look at this morning's front pages – I mean, who the hell goes on Concorde the day after the papers reveal she's £3 million in debt?'

'I know, I know,' sighed the Princess, 'but she means well, she has a big heart. It's not easy for her.' We debated the merits of Fergie, or even Diana herself, emigrating away from the media firestorm. 'Yes, but to where? I've thought about it often, but somebody would find me wherever I went.' And then I saw a flash of real sadness in her face, a desperation almost, to have her anonymity back, but knowing it is gone for ever. I asked what it was like 'being Diana'.

'Oh, God, let's face it, even I have had enough of Diana now – and I *am* Diana.' She screeched with laughter, and I saw her chameleon side. Able to switch so easily from misery to hilarity. 'It's been ridiculous recently, just one thing after another. But I can't stop the press writing about me, can I? You are hardly going to say "Oh, OK then, we'll leave you alone." I would like to have a good break.

'I meet a lot of ordinary people and they are always so kind to me. They shout out things like, "Eh, Di, I know what you're going through, luv," and I laugh and think, "If only you really knew. He's worrying about his allotment or whatever and I've got things like the future of the monarchy on my mind." '

More screeches – she has a great laugh. A really earthy, infectious cackle. Like a Sloaney Barbara Windsor.

William arrived at 1pm, aged thirteen and a half, with braces on his teeth. Tall, shy and clearly a bit bemused to be here, he nodded, rather embarrassed, in my direction. 'Hello, sir,' I said, totally unsure of what to call him. 'Hello,' he replied, preferring not to call me anything.

Jane Atkinson made up the four. We went through to a small but very pleasant little dining room to eat. William asked Diana if she'd seen the portrait of the Queen in yesterday's papers. 'Her hands looked like she'd been in the garden all day, they were all big and dirty,' he laughed. Diana giggled instinctively then stopped herself. 'William, please, don't say that.'

'Sorry, Mummy, but it's true: Granny did look really funny.'

Granny. How odd it sounded. Burrell poured some wine, but not for an indignant William. 'Can I have some wine, Mummy?'

'No, William, whatever are you thinking?'

'But Mummy, I drink it all the time.'

'Erm, no, you don't, actually, and, well, you can't have any.'

'Yes, I can,' he replied with a mischievous but determined grin.

And he did. A small but interesting piece of power play to observe. William knows what he wants, and Diana's a soft touch with her boys. Both facts seem quite good news to me. She had water.

The meal was simple but very nicely prepared: salmon mousse, chicken and veg, ice cream, coffee. Diana ate all of hers, quite normally. If she still suffers from any eating disorder, then she hides it very well.

The conversation moved swiftly to a recent edition of *Have I Got News For You*.

'Oh, Mummy, it was hilarious,' laughed William. 'They had a photo of Mrs Parker-Bowles and a horse's head and asked what the difference was. The answer was that there isn't any!'

Diana absolutely exploded with laughter.

We talked about which is the hottest photo right now.

'Charles and Camilla is still the really big one,' I said. 'followed by you and a new man, and now of course William with his first girlfriend.'

He groaned. So did Diana. Our 'big ones' are the most intimate parts of their personal lives. It was a weird moment. I am the enemy really, but we were getting on well and sort of developing a better understanding of each other as we went along.

Lunch was turning out to be basically a series of front-page exclusive stories – none of which I was allowed to publish, although I did joke that 'I'll save it for my book', a statement that caused Diana to fix me with that stare again, and demand to know if I was carrying a tape recorder.

'No,' I replied truthfully; 'are you?'

We both laughed, neither of us quite knowing what the situation really was.

The lunch was one of the most exhilarating, fascinating and exasperating two hours of my life. I was allowed to ask Diana literally anything I liked, which surprised me, given William's presence. But he is clearly in the loop on most of her bizarre world and, in particular, the various men who come into it from time to time. The *News of the World* had, during my editorship, broken the Will Carling, Oliver Hoare and James Hewitt scoops, so I had a special interest in those. So, unsurprisingly, did Diana.

She is still raging about Julia Carling. 'She's milking it for all she's worth, that woman. Honestly, I haven't seen Will since June '95. He's not the man in black you lot keep going on about. I'm not saying who that is, and you will never guess, but it's not Will.'

William interjected, 'I keep a photo of Julia Carling on my dartboard at Eton.'

This was torture. That was three fantastic scoops in thirty seconds. Diana urged me to tell William the story of what we did to Hewitt in the *Mirror* after he spilled the beans in his ghastly Anna Pasternak book. I dutifully recounted how we hired a white horse, dressed a *Mirror* reporter in full armour and charged Hewitt's home to confront him on allegations of treason with regard to his sleeping with the wife of a future king – an offence still punishable by death.

Diana exploded again: 'It was hysterical, I have never laughed so much.' She clearly has no time for Hewitt now, despite her 'I adored him' TV confessional. 'I knew he was selling stories to the papers, and as for Anna Pasternak, she was clearly seduced by him,' she said.

On the Oliver Hoare fiasco and those cranky phone calls, she said, 'I know

*My first ever meeting with Diana. 'Ah,' she said sarcastically,
'Mr Morgan ... the man who knows me SO well.'*

where it came from. It caused me a lot of damage, didn't it? People thought I was mad.'

'What's been the most upsetting thing you've had to read about yourself?'

'Well, those pictures the other day of my supposed cellulite upset me a lot, actually. It really hurt me. It was too painful, too personal. It's my body everyone was talking about, not just my face. I felt invaded, because they put the cameras deliberately on to my legs.'

Diana's relationship with the paparazzi is obviously complex. She professed to hate them: 'I know most of the paparazzi and their number plates. They think I am stupid but I know where they are. I've had ten years' practice. I would support an anti-stalking bill tomorrow.'

Then she took me to the window and started showing me the various media cars, vans and motorbikes lurking outside.

But when I asked why she doesn't go out of one of the ten other more discreet exits, she exposed her contrary side: 'I want to go out the front like anyone else. Why should I change my life for them?'

'Because it would make your life easier?' I said.

William was equally upset by the constant prying lenses. 'Why do they have to chase my mother around so much – why? It's unfair on her.' I was torn between genuine concern for the young man protecting his mum so gallantly, and a sense of foreboding for him, that one day it will be him, not his mother, who will be chased just as aggressively. How do you explain to a thirteen-year-old boy that he sells papers and therefore he's a valuable commodity to photographers and editors like me?

Diana was recently photographed in full make-up in an operating theatre, watching a heart operation. It sparked not a little controversy. But she was unrepentant: 'That little boy is alive and well and coming to see me at the Palace. The charity got loads of publicity and benefited hugely, and I'd do it again tomorrow. The others were wearing make-up and jewellery, nobody told me I couldn't. I didn't even think about it.'

The rest of the lunch was a random romp through their extraordinary tabloid lives.

'Do you regret doing Panorama?'

'I have no regrets. I wanted to do it, to put my side over. There has been so much rubbish said and written that it was time people knew the truth. But I won't do it again. Once is enough. I have done what I set out to do.'

I mentioned I'd been in contact with her mother.

'Oh, crikey, that sounds dangerous!'

'She's a feisty woman, isn't she?'

William giggled. 'Granny's great fun after a few gin and tonics.'

'Shhh, William,' Diana said, giggling too. 'My mother's been a tremendous source of support to me. She never talks publicly, she's just there for me.'

'And what about William's other granny?'

'I have enormous respect for the Queen, she has been so supportive, you know. People don't see that side of her, but I do, all the time. She's an amazing person.'

'Has she been good over the divorce?'

'Yes, very. I just want it over now, so I can get on with my life. I'm worried about the attacks I will get afterwards.'

'What attacks?'

'I just worry that people will try and knock me down once I am out on my own.'

This seemed unduly paranoid. People adore her.

I asked William how he was enjoying Eton.

'Oh, it's great, thanks.'

'Do the press bother you much?'

'Not the British press, actually. Though the European media can be quite annoying. They sit on the riverbank watching me rowing with their cameras, waiting for me to fall in! There are photographers everywhere if I go out. Normally loads of Japanese tourists taking pictures. All saying: "Where's Prince William?" when I'm standing right next to them.'

'How are the other boys with you?'

'Very nice. Though a boy was expelled this week for taking ecstasy and snuff. Drugs are everywhere and I think they're stupid. I never get tempted.'

'Does Matron take any?' laughed Diana.

'No, Mummy, it gives her hallucinations.'

'What, like imagining you're going to be King?' I said.

They both giggled again.

'Is it true you've got Pamela Anderson posters on your bedroom wall?'

'No! And not Cindy Crawford either. They did both come to tea at the Palace though, and were very nice.'

William was photographed last week at a party at the Hammersmith Palais, where he was mobbed by young girls.

I asked him if he'd had fun. 'Everyone in the press said I was snogging these girls but I wasn't,' he insisted.

Diana laughed. 'One said you stuck your tongue down her throat, William. Did you?'

'No, I did not. Stop it mummy, please, it's embarrassing.'

He'd gone puce. It was a very funny exchange, with a flushed William finally insisting, 'I won't go to any more public parties, it was crazy. People wouldn't leave me alone.'

Diana laughed again. 'All the girls love a nice prince.'

I turned to more serious matters.

'Do you think Charles will become King one day?'

'I think he thinks he will,' replied Diana, 'but I think he would be happier living in Tuscany or Provence, to be honest.'

'And how are you these days – someone told me you've stopped seeing therapists?'

'I have, yes. I stopped when I realised they needed more therapy than I did. I feel stronger now, but I am under so much pressure all the time. People don't know what it's like to be in the public eye, they really don't. Look at poor Michael Barrymore.'

The TV comic has recently been treated in a clinic for booze and drug addiction, and I'd heard rumours that Diana had been secretly comforting him.

'I feel so sorry for Michael; he is so good on TV, so funny. It would be awful if it ends for him. I hope he gets better soon.'

We'd finished our coffee. The lunch was over. Two bizarre hours that had flashed by like some high-octane fireworks display. The Princess took me downstairs and back to the real world, asking me as we walked not to tell James Whitaker, our royal correspondent, too much about our lunch.

'Just throw him a morsel every six months to drive him mad,' she said.

'He's a terrible skier,' said William.

We stepped out into the forecourt. Diana shook my hand, then darted over to speak to my very excited driver. As she shook his hand too, she reached for his ample neck and exclaimed, 'Ooh, what a nice tie – is it from Tie Rack?'

It was. He will never wash it again. What a gal. I sat in the car, and started frantically scribbling notes. I don't want to forget any of this.

TUESDAY, 21 MAY

I wrote to Diana.

> Thanks for a fascinating lunch. I had worried it might be an elaborate plot to get rid of me, especially when you mentioned the worrying word 'arsenic' several times. But it turned out to be an extremely enjoyable and enlightening afternoon. I thought Prince William was extraordinarily mature for his age, very level-headed and adult in his thinking. I also came to the conclusion that if someone with your sense of humour, confidence and personality needs therapy then I may as well book myself in to see Susie Orbach now. I hope you didn't find the experience too awful and that if you got as much out of it as I did then we can repeat the exercise. If only so I can taunt Mr Whitaker even more. The poor man is beside himself – I won't even confirm I met you. Kind regards. Piers.

THURSDAY, 23 MAY

I went to record *Have I Got News For You* tonight, and quite fancied my chances against Hislop and Merton. Despite Kelvin telling me yesterday that my decision to take part was evidence I had 'now gone completely mad'.

When I got to the studio, I was slightly taken aback to be told there will be a 'run-through' two hours before the show started. 'A run through of what?' I asked naively. 'Of the show,' an assistant replied, as if this was perfectly normal. I had assumed, rather like most people, I suspect, that it was recorded live and all the funny lines were ad-libbed. How very silly of me. I went out for the rehearsal and discovered Merton's away and my partner will be Clive Anderson. This was slightly unsettling as he's more aggressive and combative than Merton. And to make things worse, I'd already locked horns with him unsuccessfully at the Press awards.

But hey, he's only a comedian.

We were shown almost everything and I noticed the rest of the panel all making notes as we went along. Then we retired to our dressing rooms for a couple of hours to 'prepare' and were told we could confer if we wanted to. I was stunned. These guys have kept this a pretty tight secret. I'd wondered how they always seemed so brilliant off the cuff, and now I knew. They've been rehearsing the lines for hours. But, like all guests I presume, I was asked not to say too much about what went on behind the scenes to 'preserve the mystique'. Hmmm. I felt terrible, thanks to a lingering flu attack, but pumped myself full of pills and had perked up a bit by the time we went back out for real. The recording took over an hour and a quarter but they trimmed it to half an hour.

It all went quite amusingly as far as I was concerned. I took on Hislop a few times, he and Anderson gave me an entertainingly good kicking, and Angus Deayton just read his autocue. But in the greenroom afterwards some people seemed to think I had got genuinely wound up and angry. I was bemused, I was just having a laugh. But perhaps it didn't come across that way. Hislop came in and said he thought it was a 'fantastic show' and congratulated me for having a go. As did Colin Walsh, the producer, who said it was 'one of the best shows we've ever done'. I left feeling quite pleased with myself and looking forward to watching it tomorrow.

FRIDAY, 24 MAY

HIGNFY was broadcast tonight, and Mum rang the moment it finished to say how hilarious she thought it all was. I thought so too. I'd always wanted to be a memorable guest, and I reckon I've achieved that goal. Other friends called to say how funny it was as well. I swelled with pride at my comic genius. Then I phoned the newsdesk around midnight to ask vainly if there had been any reaction. 'Er, well, one woman just rang to ask where we found such a pillock,' came the reply. I laughed again, a bit nervously.

MONDAY, 27 MAY

A Mr Brian Bostock from the Garrick Club has written to say:

Dear Morgan, can you have ever made a worse decision in your entire life than to appear on *Have I Got News For You?* Why you should wish to appear to the British viewing public as a dullard and a shit, substituting vague tabloid threats for wit and humour, is beyond me. Hislop made you look nasty and foolish. Mirror Group ain't gonna like this, better watch your back again, mate. PS. I'll buy you a Pimms if they ever let you in here again.

Another fan wrote:

Dear Whoever, are tickets on sale for Piers Morgan's suicide yet? If so, please advertise fully to enable full coverage and attendance. Such puerile and childish retaliation has probably never been seen before a British television audience from one in such a position of power. The man is a creep. *Distribute the tickets!*

The TV critics were even kinder. Joe Joseph in *The Times* said:

Piers Morgan's performance was so utterly embarrassing you swore you would never miss another episode of *HIGNFY* again. It was riveting. He was as funny as a flatworm, and dug himself into ever deeper holes like a demon.

I've obviously been a complete disaster, but I am baffled.

Richard and Judy have written to thank me for supporting them in the paper, following all the fuss about them quitting their Liverpool base and bringing their show to London. 'You gave us a fair shake over the last month. It's easier to ride the flak if you know that not all the guns are pointing at you, and not all firing at once ... looking forward to lunch/dinner/drinks when we get down there.' It's amazing how few celebrities ever bother to thank editors or newspapers for helping them, given the vast number of times we do. Whenever they do, I instinctively feel more amenable towards them. It's human nature.

FRIDAY, 31 MAY

A terrible day. Phil Hall called me late in the afternoon to say my friend Chris Blythe, a brilliant *NoW* reporter, had been involved in a serious road accident while on holiday with his new wife Stella in Portugal.

'How bad was it, Phil?' I asked, feeling suddenly sick to the pit of my stomach. 'Piers, I'm very sorry to have to tell you this, but Chris has died.'

I was grateful for the directness. But the news just wiped me away. He was so young, so talented, so entertaining. I tried to carry on working but it all seemed pointless and irrelevant, so I went home early to drink myself into oblivion.

FRIDAY, 14 JUNE

Our legal manager, Charles Collier-Wright, has flown to Los Angeles to inspect Michael Jackson's nose to try and settle our ongoing case with him after we ran a picture of his face and said he was disintegrating. Charles had to stand and watch as our expert surgeon literally prodded and poked the legendary proboscis. The examination confirmed Jacko has had surgery to his nose and chin but concluded that 'although his nose might be regarded as inappropriate from an aesthetic point of view, it appears currently satisfactory from a medical point of view. He does not show any sign of being "hideously disfigured".'

HIGNFY producer Colin Walsh has written to congratulate me. 'With so much flak flying around, most others would have ducked, but you stuck to your guns and it made for an excellent show. I hope you had a good time.' Well yes, I did, actually. But everyone else seems to think I was appalling. Either I am very thick-skinned, or just very thick! Either way I'd better keep my head down and not do anything stupid for a bit.

MONDAY, 17 JUNE

Tonight I had dinner at Shepherds with Peter Mandelson, the svengali PR brain behind Tony Blair. He's an extraordinarily impressive man, immaculate in his attire and manner. He's very direct, and very determined. 'We need the Mirror to help chuck these nasty Tories out of office for at least twenty-five years. You have got to be there for us,' he said, with just a dash of menace in his voice. He was charming and amusing, but only drank water and after less than an hour he just called for the bill and left, which seemed a bit rude. But he said he had to go and vote. Which begged the question, well, why book the table for 9pm, then? He obviously likes being 'mysterious'. But it didn't overly impress me.

WEDNESDAY, 19 JUNE

England are doing well in the European Championships, which is just as well as they're the host nation.

We've drawn Spain in the quarter finals and I want to make the *Mirror* the team's No. 1 cheerleader in Fleet Street.

But I didn't excel myself in morning conference by demanding quotes from famous Spaniards, and when pressed as to who I had in mind, replied, to stifled hilarity, 'Oh, well, Mussolini for a start.'

THURSDAY, 20 JUNE

We got a tip this morning that three of England's Euro '96 soccer heroes, Paul Gascoigne, David Seaman and Ian Walker, were fishing at a trout farm in Maidenhead, and despatched a photographer to record the historic images. Unfortunately, the trio spotted our man Arnie Slater lurking in the reeds with his long lens and phoned the farm's owner, who promptly shut him in by lock-ing the only exit.

Furious Gazza then rowed in to confront Arnie, trying to grab his film through the window of his Ford Mondeo as Seaman and Walker went to work on letting down one of the tyres. Arnie, who felt rather intimidated, decided to flee and suddenly accelerated off, straight through the closed gate – causing considerable damage to his car and nearly breaking both Gazza's legs and the two keepers' hands in the process. The implications if he hadn't narrowly missed those particular limbs don't really bear thinking about.

Gazza had nicked Arnie's phone and rang me to scream abuse about our underhand tactics. 'We've got a fucking big game on Saturday and are trying to relax and all you can do is send these fuckers down to take pictures and try and kill us, you stupid bastard!' I listened to his ranting for a few minutes then politely asked if we could have Arnie's phone back. 'You want his fucking phone back do yer, yer cheeky bastard? Right, you can have it back. Listen to this, you fucking twat.'

I couldn't hear much, apart from a gentle plopping sound, then disconnection.

FRIDAY, 21 JUNE

If England beat Spain, as seems very likely, then we will play Germany in the semi-final.

Most football fans in the country will instantly be thinking – great, we can knock the Krauts out again. Unfortunately, I am not a normal football fan. I am a national newspaper editor with a certain duty of responsibility. The *Mirror's* coverage of England's previous opponents in the tournament so far has grown increasingly hysterical and jingoistic. For Spain, we offered 10 THINGS YOU DIDN'T KNOW ABOUT THE SPANISH, the first being that they introduced syphilis to Britain. The Dutch game was celebrated with a big slab of Edam cheese and the headline GIVE THEM EDAM GOOD THRASHING BOYS. Which even my village pub mates groaned at – never a good sign.

But Germany always brings out the worst xenophobic juices in tabloid editors, and I bounded in to work today full of alarming ideas on how best to set out our stall for the Hun in Monday's paper if we win tomorrow. After much amusing debate I opted for a war-flavoured ensemble of admittedly quite scary crassness, but of a humorous quality I'm sure will appeal to the nation.

Page one will be headlined ACHTUNG! SURRENDER – FOR YOU FRITZ ZE EUROPEAN CHAMPIONSHIPS ARE OVER. It is going to be illustrated by two images of our most warlike heroes, Paul 'Gazza' Gascoigne and Stuart 'Psycho' Pearce, in tin helmets. And I personally have written a troop-rallying speech (borrow-ing freely from Neville Chamberlain and Winston Churchill), full of such inci-sive wit as 'we will fight them on the flanks, fight them in midfield' – although something stopped me from going the full hog and crying 'and we must fight them on the terraces'. The inside pages are full of more Churchillian jingoism. We even had a reporter invading the swimming pool area of Germany's training ground and slamming *Mirror* towels all over the loungers. It is all very, very silly, but does make me laugh.

SUNDAY, 23 JUNE

I played cricket for my village today and top-edged a bouncer on to my temple, third ball, knocking myself straight out and collapsing on the ground, waking after a few seconds in agony and bemusement. I *never* miss-hit a bloody hook shot – this was so embarrassing. I stupidly insisted on batting on, but got clean bowled two balls later and shuffled off the field, still dazed, straight into Dad's car and home, to be swathed in bandages and dosed with painkillers. I managed to make a quick call to the office, where luckily everything was fine.

MONDAY, 24 JUNE

Hmmm. I turned the radio on at 8am as I drove up from Sussex to work and there was some guy from the Simon Wiesenthal Centre condemning this outrageous piece of disgusting journalism … in the *Mirror*.

What? Have I missed something here? Why wasn't he laughing? I switched channels, listening to ever more enraged people calling in to phone-ins venting their spleen, calling for boycotts of the paper, and for me to be fired. This was not going very well, but honestly – where was their sense of humour?

I arrived at the office at 9.20am to find David Montgomery waiting for me. He was half smiling, half grimacing, his preferred method of facially confusing his editors.

'Not your finest hour, Piers.'

'No, David.'

'In fact, possibly your worst.'

'Yes, David.'

'Well, it's tin hat time for us now, ironically, so you had better get apologising. Fast. I'll support you, but for God's sake calm down about this bloody football tournament.'

Monty's never liked or understood sport.

I retreated, slightly shame-faced now – already feeling that slight wave of panicky nausea that only editors who have dropped really big clangers would understand. I needed cheering up, and, right on cue, Kelvin rang. 'Great stuff, man – what are you doing tomorrow?'

I told him our plans. A Spitfire dive-bombing the German training ground in two hours' time, dropping front pages of today's paper over their players – and a tank rolling into Berlin to invade the offices of their biggest tabloid, *Bild*.

Kelvin loved it. 'Hilarious, brilliant – good luck. Go for it.'

This urgent encouragement from the world's most dangerous journalist worried me more than anything else.

I said an abrupt goodbye and sprinted out into the newsroom. 'Kill the fucking Spitfire, for Christ's sake.'

'But it's about to take off, boss, it's going to be great.'

'*Kill the fucking Spitfire!*'

'Yes, boss. Er … and the tank?'

'Yes, and the fucking tank.'

The rest of the day was spent slumped in my chair watching the TV news work itself into a quite staggering degree of foaming indignation. Even Bobby Charlton's called me 'thick'.

TUESDAY, 25 JUNE

Every paper led on my cretinousness today. There was no choice: I was going to have to publicly apologise. I did so, trying not to laugh at the ludicrousness of the whole thing. The BBC did four minutes on my humble mea culpa. Only later did I realise they were showing *Dad's Army* and *'Allo 'Allo* either side of their main bulletin featuring me saying sorry for taking the piss out of the Germans. I arranged for a Harrods hamper peace-offering to be sent to Germany's captain, Jurgen Klinsmann, which he graciously accepted.

Most of their players, ironically, seem to have found the whole thing entirely predictable and rather amusing. We ran the photo on page one with the lame pun, PEAS IN OUR TIME. Because there were frozen peas in the hamper …

An incredible 956 letters of complaint have already come in, an all-time record. Charlie Wilson strolled into my office. 'Right, laddie,' he growled in his rough Glaswegian accent, 'you've fucked this right up, so here's what you're going to do – send every one of these people a personal long letter of apology, and here's the trick. Send them two stamps, one for the cost of the letter they have sent you, one for the cost of any further letter they wish to send.' I have done exactly as he said. This is not a time to start playing hardball with the management.

Michael Parkinson interviewed our football writer, Harry Harris, and sent him back with a handwritten note for me saying: 'Don't let the bastards get you down, about time we had another lunch, you might need a laugh. Hope you're in good repair. Parky.' Nice touch.

WEDNESDAY, 26 JUNE

One of the cricketers I played against on Sunday has written to the *Guardian* detailing my bang on the head. 'Looking rather uncomfortable against the sustained onslaught of our bowlers, Mr Morgan decided that defence was the best form of attack. Unfortunately his technique was not up to it and he top-edged a short ball on to his head. I feel sure his rational view of Euro '96 was affected by this blow.' Cheeky bastard.

Amusingly, *Bild* newspaper has retaliated by printing ten questions for the British including: 1) Why do you drive on the wrong side of the road? 3) Why can't you pull a decent pint of beer? 4) Why do you wear bathing trunks in the sauna? 7) Why can't you beat your former colonies at cricket?

And a German has sent me a postcard saying: 'Achtung! For you Britz ze world cup, ze Ashes und ze Empire alles Kaput! Sieg Heil! Adolf!'

Why do the Germans all find it funny, but the British have all had a collective sense of humour failure? Rather like my appearance on *HIGNFY*, I am baffled.

It was the semi-final tonight and I spent all day in the office crapping myself that there would be a riot and everyone would blame me. To help this nightmare come true, England lost on penalties – and places like Trafalgar Square started erupting nastily.

I was driven home through that area watching all the aggro kicking off and assuming there would be a lot of bad incidents and my position might well become untenable by the morning. I feel awful. This was supposed to have been a bloody joke.

THURSDAY, 27 JUNE

The only reported incident of any significance concerned a young Russian who's been stabbed in Brighton by yobs who thought he was German. He is OK, and it probably would have happened anyway, but I still felt sick about it.

Princess Diana had agreed to pose with some young patients at the Royal Brompton hospital at 3pm for pictures to include in a new *Mirror* book called *Heart of Britain*. I went along to thank her and escape the media furore. 'Well, hello, Mr Morgan,' she said with a huge grin. 'Haven't we been a naughty boy.' Not as much as I'd like to be with you, ma'am, I thought, but kept my disrespectful thoughts to myself. 'Yes, your royal highness, very naughty. Must remember not to take the mickey out of the Germans again.' 'No, indeed,' she giggled. 'Mind you, I'm very grateful to you for knocking me off the front pages.' 'An absolute pleasure and a privilege,' I replied. She was amazing with the children, walking from bed to bed, hugging and cuddling them in a way that made them hug and cuddle her back. She has a special way about her in situations like this, no question. Professor Magdi Yacoub, the surgeon, was with her. 'Look at Diana,' he whispered to me, 'she's like a living saint, isn't she?' And to these kids she was, no question.

FRIDAY, 28 JUNE

Charlie Wilson's double-stamp masterplan has worked. Almost everyone has now written straight back saying how much they appreciate my personal letter, how they have calmed down, and how they will now not cancel their subscription. Charlie is a genius. I am a halfwit.

Jo Brand, tragically, has decided to resign from her weekly *Mirror* column with immediate effect over ACHTUNG SURRENDER.

It's the only bit of good news I've had all week.

SUNDAY, 30 JUNE

The tributes to me in the Sunday papers and weekly magazines are long and spectacularly poisonous. Robert Harris has devoted 1000 words in the *Sunday Times* to the premise that 'A little bit of England died this last week and it wasn't our football: what died was the tradition which a newspaper stood for.' Stephen Glover's asked in the *Spectator*, 'Who is Piers Morgan? An unfunny young man whom the *Mirror*'s management has cruelly miscast.' And John Junor said he felt sorry for me because I am 'so unbelievably stupid'.

Only Dominic Lawson, editor of the *Sunday Telegraph* and former pupil at my old prep school Cumnor House, sprang heroically to my defence: 'That the *Mirror*'s harmless bit of facetiousness should have caused such national outrage demonstrates that the famous English sense of humour has been neutered by the sort of self-lacerating political correctness which we used to think was uniquely German.'

Kelvin rang to cheer me up a bit. 'Look upon all these attacks as badges of honour, matey; just grit your teeth, have a drink and forget about it. They did all this to me, then when I finally went they acclaimed me as a journalistic genius and started giving me awards.'

The last word, though, had to be from Grandpa, showing his old commando colours. He rang in a terrible state. 'Stop bloody apologising to the Hun,' he spluttered; 'they took half my colon out, the bastards.'

TUESDAY, 23 JULY

Paula has had her baby, and she's called Heavenly Hiraani Tiger-Lily Hutchence. God alive.

FRIDAY, 26 JULY

We launched a campaign last week to get Diana her HRH title back. As 100,000 readers have now signed our petition, I wrote formally to the Queen today requesting she do just that.

FRIDAY, 9 AUGUST

A woman called Mandy Allwood is pregnant, with *eight* babies. This is going to be a sensational story whatever happens.

TUESDAY, 13 AUGUST

I have been invited to attend the German–British Forum 1996 awards to receive their annual 'booby prize' for the Least Constructive Contribution to

Anglo–German relations of the year. I declined, but sent David Seymour, our leader writer, to collect it. He told them he did help me on that edition, but that he was 'only obeying orders'.

WEDNESDAY, 14 AUGUST
The Queen's office has replied to my request for an HRH for Diana, saying: 'The Queen has seen your letter and those from your readers you sent with it. The Princess of Wales announced publicly in March that she wished to be known after divorce simply as Diana, Princess of Wales. The decision on future style and title of the Princess was taken after careful consideration and with the agreement of all concerned.'

Like hell it was.

THURSDAY, 12 SEPTEMBER
One of my features executives had the brilliant idea of setting up a fake restaurant called The Paper Bag, and inviting loads of celebrities to an opening night party – to see how many would literally turn up to the opening of a paper bag. It worked superbly, with endless B-grade celebs like model Paula Hamilton and society girl Liz Brewer all strolling down our red carpet straight into our trap. Some took it in good spirit, others sprinted off in shame.

SUNDAY, 15 SEPTEMBER
Had a think-tank for the *Mirror* executives at the Ashdown Park Hotel in East Sussex, and it nearly ended in complete disaster.

I returned from the local nightclub at 3am to find a fracas erupting in the snooker room. A group of German bankers had several of my executives up against a wall and were threatening to punch their lights out. A few of us, all very drunk, moved to help them.

I regret to say that when one of the bankers shouted, 'You started zis!' I shouted back, 'No ve didn't – you invaded Poland!'

I'm not John Cleese and they didn't laugh. In fact, more of them started swinging punches.

But we held our own, and when some staff members arrived to break it up the bankers eventually retreated to their rooms. We all had a last drink, then did the same.

When I went to check out this morning, the girl said the manager wanted to see me 'urgently'.

Shit, I thought. He's going to report us, or he's called the police or something. I could see it now: ACHTUNG, NO SURRENDER! MORGAN AND HIS MIRROR TEAM BRAWL WITH GERMANS. I'd never survive it.

The manager arrived. 'Mr Morgan, I just want to say how terribly sorry I am about what happened last night. We know it was nothing to do with any of your people and have reported some of the other group to the police. Please accept my very sincere apologies.'

Phew.

TUESDAY, 24 SEPTEMBER

A sensational day. Gerry Agar, Paula Yates's best friend, arrived in my office flanked by two of my reporters and clutching a Smartie box full of what appeared to be class A drugs. 'What the hell is that?' I asked, and she explained that Paula's nanny, Anita Debney, found the box under her employer's bed this morning and was so freaked out she wants us to expose it. Paula's in Australia with Hutchence.

I was horrified by both the revelation and the fact that Agar had brought the drugs into my office. 'Look, Gerry, this is obviously shocking and I can understand why Anita and you want to expose it, but you must take these drugs back to where you found them and call the police. Right now.'

Agar looked shocked too. 'Right, OK, I'll do it now. I didn't know what to do, I'm sorry.' She left.

WEDNESDAY, 25 SEPTEMBER

Gerry Agar called to say she had put the Smartie box back where it was found by Anita and called the police, who were now searching the house. Later we discovered that the drug was almost certainly opium, and they had also found a load of hard-core pornographic photos in Paula's bedroom. I called Paula in Australia to tell her what had happened. 'What?' she screamed down the phone. 'Is this some sort of fucking joke?' 'No, Paula, it's not,' I replied. 'And you'd better take it seriously because the cops are stripping your house down and you're going to be in deep shit.' 'Christ, *Christ!*' she shouted, and then the phone went dead. The cops confirmed everything early evening and we did a big splash: OPIUM AND PORN BUST AT PAULA'S HOME.

THURSDAY, 26 SEPTEMBER

Both Anita Debney and Gerry Agar announced they were quitting working for Paula, after giving full statements to the police. Paula has disappeared and won't answer any calls, and the world's media are going mad. Bob Geldof, understandably, has gone straight to court to seek a custody order for his kids – and got one, albeit temporary.

SATURDAY, 28 SEPTEMBER

My Friday night slumber was crudely wrecked by a phone call from a hysterical sounding David Leigh, our deputy news editor, at 2.30am. He has spent months working on a sensational book with a woman called Madame Vasso, Fergie's psychic. We've agreed to pay him £100,000 for the serial rights, even though he basically acquired her through his *Mirror* job, and are due to start running it on Monday. David was desperate because he had just heard that the *Sun* are spoofing their first edition tonight and running all the best bits from the book. He knew this for a fact because his wife, Sue Thompson, is the *Sun*'s news editor and has finally told him, literally as they lay in bed tonight.

One can only imagine the tensions in that household now.

Sue has effectively helped ruin David's great scoop, and their mutually beneficial pay-day. Because there's no way we will pay the same money now. He is almost in tears.

'We'll have to slam it in now!' he shouted. But that was impossible, it was far too late.

'No, mate, we've been fucked and we will have to see how we can salvage something for Monday.'

I feel really sorry for the guy, but I am more upset that we've had a fantastic story wrecked by our rivals.

WEDNESDAY, 2 OCTOBER

To the Labour Party conference in Blackpool, and lunch with the Blairs. It's a *Mirror* tradition for editors and management chiefs to dine with the Labour leader at conference.

I sat next to Cherie and she was very friendly, which was hardly surprising given our front page today, which had a huge gushing photo of her kissing Tony and the cheesy headline NEW LABOUR, NEW PREMIER with another load of positive coverage of his speech inside. It was way over the top, but we're into election year now and I am keeping to my chief cheerleader script. I just hope they remember all this once they get to power.

Cherie had another, more personal reason to be nice to me. We were recently offered some grainy paparazzi photos of her sunbathing topless on holiday, and had turned them down.

She thanked me early in the meal, but it was obviously playing on her mind, and when the pudding was served she leaned over and asked, 'Did you see those pictures yourself?'

I confirmed that I had indeed spied the First Lady's naked breasts.

'Did I ... well, did I look awful or was it OK?'

'You looked fantastic,' I said. 'Shame we couldn't have published them, or you'd have definitely increased the male Labour vote.'

She giggled. 'Oh, don't, Piers, I'd be so embarrassed.'

It was a happy encounter: there's a confident mood among the Labour hierarchy and they know we're a very valuable tool for their election campaign. Blair made a speech saying as much. 'The Mirror's always supported us and we are incredibly grateful to you for that support and never take it for granted.'

FRIDAY, 4 OCTOBER

I think today may go down as my lowest moment as an editor. Bereft of any ideas to put on the front page yesterday, I was told we had a 'borrowed' video of *EastEnders* character Ian Beale getting shot in a tightly embargoed and much hyped forthcoming episode. 'Let's splash on that, then!' I'd cried, with fake enthusiasm. 'Everyone hates the little runt, it might be quite popular.' Nobody had a better idea, so we did under the headline THE ENDER IAN? My circulation manager came to me this afternoon with a big grin. 'Bingo, boss! Went up a hundred thousand copies.' We didn't know whether to laugh or weep. A video grab of a soap character had been our biggest selling cover of the year. I feel repulsion for the public. But not quite as much as I felt towards the *EastEnders* press office, who rang up to complain that we had broken their embargo not to publish before tomorrow. They get the whole front page of a tabloid to promote their show and all they can do is moan about it.

MONDAY, 7 OCTOBER

The nightdesk rang me in the car at 9.30pm tonight saying the *Sun* has got a huge royal story tomorrow – video footage of James Hewitt romping semi-naked with Diana. It was all over five pages and the byline was 'The editor', meaning Stuart Higgins had written it himself. He must have been sure of the veracity of this video to do that. It's midnight now and I feel done in. Coming so soon after the Fergie book leak this is another hammer-blow. I told everyone to ignore the story tonight and see how it develops tomorrow. But *News at Ten* led on the story, with *Sun* logos bursting off the screen. I know exactly how this will turn out for us tomorrow – very painfully.

TUESDAY, 8 OCTOBER

Stuart was all over the morning TV news doing interviews about his great scoop. Couldn't blame him, but it made me puke watching it. We'd been regally stuffed and it hurt like hell. And for their editor to break it all himself reflected even more badly on me. Then came a call from Max Clifford.

'Hello, young man,' he said cheerily. 'I think Christmas might have come early for you today.'

'What do you mean?'

'The Sun video's a hoax. The director's come to me and revealed how they filmed it all with lookalikes.'

'You sure, Max?'

'Absolutely sure. I've seen the whole thing, and you can see stage managers moving around in the background shoving the actors' arms and legs about. It's hilarious.'

I punched the air jubilantly.

Oh *yes, yes, yes!*

I concluded a quick and easy deal with Max – frankly I would have happily paid him £1 million right there and then, but fortunately he was a little more reasonable. Then we ordered the hit on Stuart Higgins – getting a photographer and reporter to track him down at the Tory Party conference in Bournemouth where he'd been boasting and celebrating.

He spotted our team and looked startled, then hit his mobile phone to find out what the hell was going on. Within minutes he had the bad news relayed to him from his own newsdesk, and headed home disconsolate, near to tears, and compiling another 'By the editor' story – only this time a grovelling apology to his readers for being hoaxed.

We went to town in the *Mirror*, splashing FAKE across the front, and revelling in the real story of the video over five pages inside. In less than 24 hours, my mood has gone from abject despair to one of bounteous joy.

A spokesman for Kensington Palace confirmed marvellously: 'The Princess of Wales does not recognise herself or James Hewitt from those photographs.'

I wouldn't like to be in Stuart's shoes when Murdoch calls for a little 'chat' after this. But I'm buzzing, and took the team down to the pub for champagne all night. If there is one thing better than breaking a great scoop, it's exposing a rival's great scoop as a fake.

THURSDAY, 10 OCTOBER
Paula Yates and Bob Geldof have agreed joint custody of their girls. I wonder if this would have happened had those drugs not been found? I doubt it. I'm glad we exposed it. Bob deserves what he has now got.

MONDAY, 14 OCTOBER
A dramatic news day.

Eight-baby mother Mandy Allwood has lost all of them, after controversially selling her story to the *NoW* through Max Clifford, and it was their joint funeral today. Awful.

And Paula Yates flew home to be arrested over the opium bust. Both women provoke similar public reaction, half contempt and half sympathy. I feel more of the latter for both of them. Mandy has become a tragic tabloid icon, caught up in a story that was always going to end tragically, but which, because of its unique human interest appeal, propelled her into a national figure. Yes, she made money out of it, yes, she's got a dodgy boyfriend. But when I saw those eight coffins today and her weeping devastated face behind, I felt nothing but sorrow for her. As for Paula, she is on what appears to be a helter-skelter ride to chaos. From the moment she met Hutchence she has spiralled down into a world of increasingly outrageous behaviour that has made her feel fantastic in the short term, but will surely ruin her in the end. She won't take my calls any more.

She's told police that the drugs must have been planted because they weren't there when she left the country, but nobody believes her.

WEDNESDAY, 16 OCTOBER

I took a call this morning from a 'friend' of Sheryl Kyle, now officially Mrs Gascoigne, saying Sheryl had been beaten up by Gazza. Badly. She had bruises over her face and her arm in a sling and looks a right mess, apparently. He'd attacked her after getting drunk in a restaurant at the Gleneagles Hotel in Scotland. Sheryl's 'friend' said, 'She's in a terrible state, Piers, can you help?'

I suggested that if Sheryl wanted to get back at him then all she had to do was pose for pictures. The 'friend' called back half an hour later. 'OK, she'll do it, but she won't pose, you're going to have to take them like they are paparazzi pictures from the bushes or something.' It was easy to fix, and Sheryl walked straight past our man at the appointed time. In full make-up, I noticed, but still clearly beaten up quite nastily.

We splashed it big. Gazza's going to get caned for this, by the press, the public, and Sheryl's lawyers, I suspect.

THURSDAY, 17 OCTOBER

Some stories are so entertaining you just want to sit back and chuckle for a few hours. Virginia and Peter Bottomley's fourteen-year-old daughter has been suspended from her school for illicit boozing. They are comfortably the most pompous, hectoring and smug couple in politics and I would have paid large amounts of cash to have been there when they found out. When we put the story to their office, they reacted in typical style – immediately calling our chairman Sir Robert Clark to demand he pull it. I can't think of this ever happening before and Sir Robert to his great credit just told them to bugger off, very politely, of course. The Bottomleys claim their daughter is too young to be exposed, but they forget the ruthless way they have recently exploited her in photocalls while on official business. You can't use your kids like that and bleat privacy if they get into trouble. If you want privacy for your children, then don't use them as political tools.

SATURDAY, 19 OCTOBER

Kelvin had a brilliant 50th birthday party in the City tonight, with all the good, bad, ugly, and really appalling characters from his past and present there to salute the great man. Stories abounded about him from all corners. My favourite was from Martin Dunn, former No. 2 on the *Sun*, but also a former editor of the Bizarre column, who once ran a story about Boy George buying a new house. Unfortunately, they pictured the wrong property and the owner, a professor, rang Kelvin in a fury demanding to know what he was going to do about the fact that 2000 screaming transvestites were outside his home. '*Dunn!*' he screamed.

'Come in here now, you fucking halfwit!' Martin sloped into Kelvin's office, his shoulders sunk back in anticipation of his impending thrashing. He saw Kelvin's bulging neck veins, mad staring eyes and half-clenched fist and decided there was no course of action left to him other than to pretend to faint. So he collapsed face down on to the floor, falling convincingly flat and hard. Kelvin ran over, picked Martin up by his left ear, and said calmly, 'You'd better be dead, Dunn, because if you're not you fucking soon will be.'

SUNDAY, 20 OCTOBER

A dull old Sunday today so I sat in front of the box watching Newcastle, incredibly, thrash Manchester United 5–0. It was stunning to watch, and when I called in to the office it was all they were talking about. 'Let's splash it,' I said. 'Erm, we can't do that, it's just a football match,' was the universal response. 'Yes, but it's news, we're all amazed, so the public will all be amazed too.' Most people thought I'd taken leave of my senses but we did it anyway under the headline '5–0'.

MONDAY, 21 OCTOBER

Sales of the *Mirror* rose by 50,000 copies. A quarter of this increase was in Liverpool alone, where apparently it has already become a collector's item. There were also heavy extra sales in places like Newcastle (obviously), North London and Leeds. Rather like with Ian Beale, there's a lot to be said for front pages depicting unpopular institutions getting their comeuppance.

WEDNESDAY, 23 OCTOBER

My radio alarm clock went off at 7.30am and the news mentioned a helicopter crashing after flying back to London from the Bolton/Chelsea match. I wasn't paying much attention, though they said all passengers and crew were believed to have been killed.

A few minutes later my phone went and it was Andy Lines on the newsdesk, a Chelsea fan, saying, 'Piers, I'm really sorry to have to tell you this, but it seems Matthew Harding was on the helicopter that went down.'

One of the best things about being an editor is that you hear all the news before anyone else. But sometimes, like now, you wish you heard it last. I could picture Matthew's cheeky drunken face at the Chelsea/United match chanting 'Who the fuck are Man United?' next to me in the director's box, or warning me never to leave his table at the Savoy until he'd decided lunch was finished.

Matthew was a one-off, and it was shocking to think he was dead at 42. Truly, horribly shocking. I phoned his girlfriend Vicky a few hours later and she was in near hysterics. 'I thought our love would last forever, I was wrong,' she recited to me, from that *Four Weddings* Auden poem. She could hardly speak and I felt guilty ringing her not just to sympathise but to get some quotes for the paper. But Matthew would have wanted a big tribute in the papers: he loved the whole fame thing.

MONDAY, 28 OCTOBER
I've been involved in a tediously long correspondence with Sir Alastair Morton, boss of Eurotunnel, after we claimed the Chunnel had been a specific IRA target, and it reached an amusing denouement today:

> Dear Mr Morgan, I simply will not believe that a person holding your job is as inpenetrably thick as you are representing yourself to be over this point. I consider this correspondence has gone on long enough.

> Dear Sir Alastair, you are an extremely rude little man but since you're now retiring anyway I agree the correspondence should close.

THURSDAY, 31 OCTOBER
Matthew Harding's funeral today in his Sussex village, Ditchling, four miles from mine. I was astonished to see Ken Bates arrive. Everyone knew his view of Matthew, everyone knew he hated the man. I wanted to punch him. Matthew would have enjoyed that enormously. But there was no need for me to provide any drama. Vicky, who'd been very magnanimously invited by Matthew's wife Ruth, walked out of the service in tears when her daughter by him wasn't mentioned though Matthew's other four children were. I understood her anger; it was a crass omission.

WEDNESDAY, 6 NOVEMBER
Sir Alastair Morton wrote again: 'Dear Mr Morgan, a little postscript to our correspondence. I am 6 ft 3.5 in. How tall are you?'
   I replied, 'You're clearly not little then, though I note you don't deny being rude. I am 6 ft 1 in, so you have a couple of inches on me, which must be very satisfying.'

SUNDAY, 10 NOVEMBER
I enjoyed a long, relaxing lunch in Wandsworth and was asleep on the sofa at home when I got a call to say Marje Proops had died. I went straight in to edit a special edition. She was, for all her vanity and sharp behaviour to those that posed any kind of threat to her (particularly women), a genuine Fleet Street legend and someone I came to admire enormously for her amazing devotion to ordinary *Mirror* readers. She knew them better than anyone had ever known them, and I knew she would therefore be hugely missed. I was keen to make sure we got tributes from every great public figure we could. Unfortunately, in the heat of the deadline race, I shouted out 'Have we got a quote from Harold Wilson?' only to be reminded rather quickly that he was dead. 'Well, can't we

get him via Doris Stokes?' I shouted back, rather pathetically. The damage was done. It will doubtless be leaking already. There are several poison pens in the newsroom determined to ensure all my gaffes and cock-ups get faithfully recorded in broadsheet diaries and *Private Eye*. I hate them for it.

THURSDAY, 14 NOVEMBER

Dr Miriam Stoppard, a friend of Marje and someone who had helped her with the column from time to time, came to see me and I knew instantly she would be the perfect replacement. Miriam's very smart, very attractive, hugely successful and has that instinctive feel for people so important in an agony column. She agreed immediately to take over and I know she'll be brilliant.

SUNDAY, 24 NOVEMBER

John Junor has had another go at me for our front page about John Major betraying the families of Dunblane by not banning handguns, ranting: 'What the *Mirror* did was betray the standards of journalistic decency. But what can you expect from an editor who is so politically naive he thinks Harold Wilson is still alive?'

MONDAY, 25 NOVEMBER

An extraordinary day. Around midday the newsdesk told me we'd got a leak of tomorrow's Budget. A real one, documents and everything. I was astonished. Security is so tight around it that I could never remember any paper ever getting a whiff of paperwork. But here it was, sheaves and sheaves of it. The content was actually fairly dull, since the 1p cut in income tax had been heavily trailed. But the impact of us having it before Chancellor Ken Clarke announced it would be unbelievable.

Such was the potential severity of the consequences, I called Monty and Charlie Wilson and we convened a meeting in my office. Opinions were split. Everyone agreed it was a potentially great scoop, but there were obvious concerns. Were the documents genuine? Would financial markets go into turmoil if we published them? Was it responsible to do it anyway, given that the Budget dictates the wellbeing of our readers? This was not an easy call, and the hours were ticking by. We couldn't do anything more to verify the stuff because there wasn't time and our conduit, a freelance journalist called Peter Hounam, had tried unsuccessfully to get more material from his source. Perhaps he was being stitched up? By 6pm we had to do something or the paper would come and go and we'd miss our chance. I was not in favour of just lobbing it in. 'Look, we don't know what we're really dealing with here and we don't have time to find out for sure. I think we should play the good guys and hand it back, not least because it's not that interesting anyway. We'll get loads of publicity anyway and can say we behaved responsibly, which will be a new first.' Everyone agreed – we had little alternative.

I called Christopher Meyer, Major's press spokesman at No. 10.

'Hi, Christopher, do you want your budget back?' He is a man of rare calm in any crisis, but even Meyer was stunned when I explained what we had and what we planned to do, and faxed him a few sheets to prove it. 'Well, that's very decent of you,' he said finally, confirming the documents were genuine.

He agreed that Downing Street would let our man be pictured physically handing it back tonight, and they would issue a statement thanking us. I then called Gordon Brown and alerted him to what we'd got. He was desperate for information from the documents so I told him, on strict condition he didn't tell anyone else. The revelation caused shockwaves through Westminster when it broke around 10pm. And so did the *Sun* when it landed with what looked like an exact précis of what I had told Gordon Brown. I was not amused. Later we were, as expected, formally injuncted by the Government and banned from changing our minds about publishing the details. That, too, had always been likely given the sensitivity of the information.

TUESDAY, 26 NOVEMBER

There has been general praise in the papers for what we did, with the *Guardian* saying I have finally grown up and done the right thing. The leak story led all the news, and raised plenty of gags at Clarke's expense when the Budget debate got going. I am certain now we did the right thing.

WEDNESDAY, 27 NOVEMBER

The atmosphere's changed somewhat now, and everyone has started accusing me of bottling it, fuelled by Peter Hounam, who is telling the world what a gutless disgrace I am. The *Guardian* has revised its earlier view and now agrees I should have published. The hypocritical prats. We had a bit of fun with Major later in the day, running after him with a bath plug to prevent any more leaks, causing him to lose his temper and barge our man out of the way with a short arm jab to the kidneys. Winding up Major is very easy and great fun. He really doesn't like it up him. All this Saint John stuff is rubbish.

THURSDAY, 5 DECEMBER

Had an incredibly entertaining lunch with Fergie at a restaurant in Dorking today. Her autobiography's just come out and she's keen to try and rebuild her rather smashed-up reputation with the media and the public. I'd not met her before and she was absolutely exhausting company – a whirlwind of energy, tormented emotion and quite painful and obvious vulnerability. Her divorce from Prince Andrew five months ago has, she admitted, left her feeling 'very bruised'. She still spoke highly of him. 'He's a lovely man, and a great father. We still see each other all the time.' After a couple of drinks she relaxed a bit, and started laughing and telling gossipy stories. 'Have you heard the one about

Andrew and the navy officer?' she squealed. 'It was a joke that I started to see what happened, and now people tell me about it as if it was true!'

I asked if she was happy. 'I'm OK,' she replied, looking suddenly a bit tearful. She lives her life at a frantic pace, racing around in a terrible hurry without, it seems to me, knowing where she's hurrying to. I felt sorry for her. 'I can't go out with a man without the papers all asking if we're going to get married the next day: it puts such pressure on relationships. It's impossible to be normal. I wish I could turn the clock back, but I can't.' She asked if I could give her an easier time in the *Mirror*. 'I know I've made mistakes,' she said. 'But I have learned my lesson. I just want a fair crack of the whip as I try to put things right again.'

It would have taken a pretty hard-hearted monster to reject her appeal, but that's roughly what I had to be. 'Look, the truth is that if there's a good story about you behaving badly, then it's going to get more coverage than you doing something good for charity. It's just the way it is, and it's not going to change.' She looked very sad. 'I know. I know. I just wish it could be different. But I suppose bad news is always more popular than good news.' She kissed me goodbye. 'I won't be gratuitously unfair,' I said. 'Thank you,' she replied; 'I'm only human you know.'

The Mirror

Monday September 1 1997 · 30p

1961-1997

TUESDAY, 14 JANUARY

Diana has gone to Angola to continue her campaign against landmines, and the first pictures in today were amazing shots of her with a load of laughing local guys with various legs and arms missing, lost to mines. They were very powerful images and there is no doubt Diana is making a difference with this one. Nobody can fail to support her view that these mines have got to be banned.

WEDNESDAY, 15 JANUARY

Just when I thought I'd seen it all, yesterday Diana walked through the live landmines herself, wearing a protective helmet. You've got to hand it to her, this takes balls, whichever way you look at it. The whole world is waking up to this issue entirely because of one headstrong young princess making it her business to highlight it.

WEDNESDAY, 22 JANUARY

Had supper with Gordon Brown at the Commons. Brown's big on aspiration. 'We need more entrepreneurs,' he said, 'more creators. More people with big ideas. I want to encourage that by giving them the right financial environment to take some risks.'

We talked about Diana. 'She's quite a girl, isn't she?' he laughed. 'Perhaps we should make her Foreign Secretary, she seems to get things done!'

He spoke highly of Blair. 'He has a great feel for public opinion. He instinctively knows what people are thinking and where we should be going.' They're a tight team.

MONDAY, 27 JANUARY

Alan Clark has written to thank me for my note of congratulations after he won the Kensington and Chelsea by-election and re-entered Parliament: 'Yes, it was a lovely blow against the establishment. The Tory Party at grass roots is much more democratic, y'know!'

I called him to ask how he thought he'd swung it. 'Well, they made the mistake of lining up all the candidates and asking them to declare any skeletons in their cupboard,' he sniggered. 'And when it got to me I just shrugged my shoulders and said "Where do you want me to start?" '

FRIDAY, 31 JANUARY

The sports department have devised a cunning ruse in the last couple of years to divert attention from their deficiencies in morning conference. If they don't have a story, they simply invent an Arsenal transfer scoop and stick it at the top of their schedule. This will get them off the hook, and depending on the stature of the alleged transfer target, everyone else too. A 'Ronaldo for Arsenal' exclusive is guaranteed to put me in a good mood all day. But they have overplayed their hand recently by naming Paul Ince as our intended new midfield general three times in less than a month.

To stop this nonsense once and for all, I phoned the sports editor, Dave Balmforth, who never played these games himself, and told him we were going to stitch up his worst offending executive, Bob Blair.

Dave was instructed to ring Bob from home first thing in the morning and tell him he was in Milan, where Arsenal chief David Dein had just signed Paul Ince.

Bob came into conference two hours later, looking unbelievably smug, and announced with tremulous excitement the stunning news that, after all his predictions, Ince was finally a Gunners player.

'Do you stake your job and reputation on it, Bob?' I asked.

'Oh, yes, I'd go further than that – I'd stake my life on it.'

'Do you mind if I get a second opinion, Bob?'

He looked slightly nonplussed. 'Er … no, of course. Who from?'

I phoned out to Kerrie, my new personal assistant, and asked her to bring in my special secret guest.

He walked in, and I asked, 'Your full name, please?'

'David Anthony Dein.'

'Your occupation?'

'Vice-chairman of Arsenal Football Club.'

'Thank you, Mr Dein. Are you in Milan?'

'Er, no, I don't think so.'

'Has Paul Ince signed for Arsenal?'

'No.'

'Have you had, or do you have, any intention of signing him for Arsenal?'

'No.'

I turned to a puce Bob Blair.

'Bob, any last words?'

'Yes, I think I'll get my coat.'

WEDNESDAY, 5 FEBRUARY

We were offered a set of photographs of Brian Harvey, the East 17 pop star halfwit, having a fight in the street. The asking price was £10,000, and I agreed on the basis we had little else for the paper worth a light. But an hour later the agency told me the *Sun* had bid £15,000. In other words the agency had decided to start a little auction, the greedy bastards. I didn't want Stuart Higgins beating me on this, so bid £20,000. Fifteen ridiculous minutes of tit-for-tat bidding later, I successfully bought the pictures for – £35,000. At least four times what they were worth.

It was an absurd exercise in editor willy-waving, and I 'won'. I cleared the first five pages for it to justify my decision.

THURSDAY, 6 FEBRUARY

We were absolutely inundated with calls of complaint from readers about the Brian Harvey photos. 'Famine, war and child abuse and you fill the Mirror with this shite about a little prat from a band I've never heard of getting a slap,' was one call that summed up the general mood. At 4pm my circulation manager brought more good news – sales were *down* by 40,000 copies. I spent a bundle of cash buying something that actively drove readers away. Not my finest hour.

WEDNESDAY, 19 FEBRUARY

Kelvin challenged me to squash today and I was quietly confident. I'm 31, reasonably fit, and he's over 50, overweight and losing his hair.

After ten minutes I had to stop and lie down. He'd smashed me all round the court in a frenzy of demented, and highly skilled, strokes – all struck with devastating power. I lay on the floor panting and dizzy. 'You OK, man?' he said. 'Erm, yes, can I just … can I just … rest for a bit.' I started seeing stars and asked for some water. 'Shall I call a nurse?' he cackled. But I wasn't laughing. I really thought I might be dying. Eventually my heart rate calmed down, and I clambered back to my feet. Only for my knees to collapse. 'It's no good, Kelvin, I've had it.' I could tell he was absolutely delighted. This was better than just beating me. He'd reduced me to a pitiful wreck of a human being. I shuffled to the showers, mortified.

FRIDAY, 28 FEBRUARY

Labour crushed the Tories in the Wirral by-election last night, and we revelled in the Tories' misery by doing up Major's hapless crew as the *Dad's Army* boys with the headline WIRRAL ON THE MARCH WITH TONY'S ARMY and the subdeck (referring to the Tories) of '… and Wirral doomed'.

Alastair Campbell rang, chortling away. 'Fucking classic, well done, mate.'

The result suggests Labour are going to walk the election. 'They're on the run,' said a jubilant Alastair.

MONDAY, 3 MARCH

Blair wrote to thank me for the Wirral front page. 'Just a note to say thanks for a wonderful front page and also for all your support. The paper is in great shape and in no small measure due to you. Keep in touch, Tony.' He knows how to play the media. The note was handwritten and sent first-class post the morning after the by-election.

THURSDAY, 6 MARCH

Been having a correspondence with Frances Shand-Kydd again about some story in the *Sunday Mirror* she says is untrue. I always try and persuade her to do an interview in these exchanges because I am sure she will one day, and I am equally sure it will be utterly sensational when she does.

'One day you'll crack and tell the lot, but I accept it may not be in this millennium,' I joked at the end of my last fax.

She was back within half an hour, in a not entirely coherent way: 'Are you a betting man? Pound notes (not Smarties or baked beans or Château '57 vintage). You reckon I'll crack, eh? Well I haven't in this millennium and maybe the same in the next. I'm 61 ... I have three daughters and even though I haven't got an O-level in the Mensa dept I know which one you're on about. I hope we never meet, faxing suffices.'

TUESDAY, 18 MARCH

The *Sun*'s come out for Blair. Doesn't surprise me, but it's bloody annoying because it removes a good commercial edge we might have had in this election. The decision makes big news, and will delight Labour.

TUESDAY, 25 MARCH

Had dinner with Mark Bolland, Prince Charles's bright new aide, at the Savoy Grill and mentioned my amusing contact with Diana's mother. 'Yes, I gather she can be quite lively after lunch,' he said.

WEDNESDAY, 26 MARCH

Tea with Tony Blair at No. 10.

I gave him a present – a *Mirror* front page with the headline MIRROR BACKS MAJOR.

'Just thought out of courtesy you should know first about tomorrow's edition,' I said, straight-faced.

He looked at it for a couple of seconds, then asked rather nervously, 'Erm, that's a joke, I take it?'

'No, afraid not, we had to do something to counter the Sun backing you.'

He looked even more twitchy, and glanced at Alastair for guidance.

I laughed. 'Only kidding. But on a serious point, I hope you won't forget who your friends are in all this cosying up to Murdoch?'

'Piers, I had to court him,' said Blair. 'It is better to be riding the tiger's back than let it rip your throat out. Look what Murdoch did to Kinnock.'

'I understand that, but I don't want the Mirror squeezed in all this,' I replied. 'How did you swing his vote then?'

'Well, I think a meeting I had with him about Europe was the vital one; he wanted to hear that I'm not too pro. But I said no Tory would ever pull out of Europe, whatever they say. We're in it now and always will be.'

This afternoon, Michael Howard had tried to turn the IRA attack on a passenger train line in Cheshire into political capital by accusing Blair of being soft on terrorism – breaching a long-standing agreement that parties stood together in the wake of such incidents.

Howard said Blair had not once voted for the renewal of the Prevention of Terrorism Act. 'His vote and the votes of his party show that you cannot trust Labour to be tough on terrorism.'

Blair was still seething.

'What Howard said about the IRA today was fucking disgusting, frankly, just completely outrageous. Nobody is more determined than me to defeat terrorism, and I'm not going to have him behaving in this reprehensible way.'

I was a bit shocked – I hadn't heard him swear before.

Blair looked tired, and a bit bloated. He was yawning a lot and drinking endless cups of tea. I tried to wake him up a bit. 'You're going to win this election by a bloody landslide, you do realise that?'

'Well, it's too early to be sure, but all the signs are there that Middle England is turning away from the Tories in its droves. Thatcher attacking me, as she's been doing recently, just reminds everyone what they are really like, and will encourage more people to say "enough is enough".'

'Will you be doing an election TV debate?'

'Yes, but I'll only do it with the public. Not Dimbleby or anything like that. And I'll only debate with Major – I'm not having Paddy Ashdown sitting there scowling.'

THURSDAY, 27 MARCH

I went back to interview Blair officially for the *Mirror*. He was very pumped up today, must have had a good night's sleep.

Best line was him vowing to sack any sleazy ministers on the spot.

'I won't be weak on sleaze like the Tories,' he said. 'We have got to be whiter than white if we are to rebuild trust in government.'

I reckon that might just come back to haunt him.

FRIDAY, 28 MARCH

An odd letter from Frances Shand-Kydd:

Dear Piers, now that the interest in William's confirmation has died down. This is just for you … I didn't attend his confirmation because I wasn't invited. I was therefore in a hugely difficult position before and after the service. As, trying to be ever a defender of all my family, whatever I said would (I needn't explain) be so cheated that I couldn't improve on silence. Now we have a general election about which I am a touch joyous as it does mean little space to print stuff on my team. Yum Yum!

She'd obviously been deliberately banned from William's big day – but why, and by whom?

The *Sun*'s front page this morning, on yet another shagging Tory MP, called Piers Merchant, read END OF THE PIERS SHOW.

I sent Murdoch a fax saying, 'Isn't this taking the *Sun/Mirror* rivalry a bit far?' He won't reply, but he'll probably laugh.

WEDNESDAY, 2 APRIL

John Major's launched a ridiculous election campaign theme, billing the party as one for 'Happy Families', branding the family the 'most important institution in our lives'. His brass neck knows no apparent bounds. For a laugh, we did a front page composed of eight of his MPs who've done their bit for the 'family' recently: Mr Toesucker (David Mellor); Mr Randy (Rod Richards); Mr Rampant (Alan Clark); Mr Fiddler (Rupert Allason); Mr Cradle-Snatcher (Piers Merchant); Mr Lovechild (Tim Yeo); Mr Goes-Like-a-Train (Stephen Norris); and Mr Swinger (Jerry Hayes).

It's a bit childish, but bloody funny. And it signals our intent to get stuck into the Tories big time on their most vulnerable issue – sleaze.

THURSDAY, 3 APRIL

We got wind that the Tories are sending a man dressed as a chicken to chase after Blair because he's decided not to engage Major in a live TV debate. So we sent our own guy down in a chicken outfit and he chased the Tory chicken down the road. Great fun. Our man ripped the head off his rival for good measure to give us the joyful headline MAJOR'S HEADLESS CHICKENS.

MONDAY, 7 APRIL

Alan Clark wrote today to join in the latest tedious debate on whether the *Mirror* ain't like wot it used to be:

I want to congratulate you on your spirited defence against all those boring obselete farts who used to edit your paper and are always complaining about your own stewardship. I think you've got one of the most difficult jobs in Fleet Street. It's strange, but readers no longer seem to want political instruction. But there has got to be some kind of ethic, even if subliminal, to which the readers get conditioned and respond. It's very elusive. The *Mail* has it, the *Mail on Sunday* doesn't. Sue Douglas wrecked it at the *Sunday Express* irredeemably by jettisoning it too far abruptly, although to be fair that whole group is probably doomed. Let's meet after the election. I've no idea where we're heading. I do see by the way that my own name and likeness are periodically brought to the attention of your readers.

I replied: 'Yes, you're the only person I know who would see the term Mr Rampant as an accolade. I'm afraid you're all heading down the pan, though I can't see the great people of Kensington going red even under this onslaught for change.'

TUESDAY, 15 APRIL

I went to see Labour's election war rooms at Millbank, and got a guided tour from Gordon Brown and Peter Mandelson. It was a stunningly efficient and impressive set-up, a bit like a political NASA centre. They run it like a newspaper office – there are the 'editors' barking orders from the 'back bench', and teams of 'hacks' writing copy and monitoring TV and other media. Mandelson was particularly pleased with the rapid response desk, where groups of bright young things stood glued to their screens searching for any attack on the party by the opposition, so they could crush it on the spot. 'Major's having a go about crime,' one would suddenly shout, prompting an immediate press released to be bashed out destroying the Tory record on crime.

It's a ruthless machine, with the latest technology to support it. There was something a bit demented about the 200 intensely focused inhabitants of the room. But I left feeling that I had seen the next Government in action, and had a genuine sense that they would make a difference running the country.

'Good, isn't it?' said Brown, basking in his role of general.

Blair leaves them to it down here, content that his work is being done for him. 'Yes,' I replied, 'it's very good. The Tories have had it.' Brown was having none of it. 'I've heard all that before and it didn't win us an election. We've got to win this time, and that means no complacency.' The hours are punishing – Brown hosts his first meetings soon after 7am and they are often still pounding away into the late evening. He doesn't look tired though, just scarily intense.

Later I had lunch at Harrods with Mohammed Al Fayed. He was hilarious company, mixing the latest dirty joke he'd heard with extraordinary claims about newspaper editors being spies, the royal family being full of illegitimate children, and all politicians being crooks. I found it all most entertaining. And behind all the flamboyant bombast there lies a razor-sharp mind.

Towards the end of the meal I asked why he wears clip-on ties. He chuckled. 'So it comes off quickly when a nice girl comes along.'

But it's actually a security thing: his bodyguard told me he's paranoid about being strangled by his own tie.

As he saw me out, he insisted I take the tie as a gift. I'd been warned that he'd thrust presents upon me and wouldn't take too kindly to rejection, so I thanked him very much and took it back to the office. Then I called Harrods, found out what they sell them for, and biked him round a cheque for that amount.

He sent me a fax: 'What a gentleman you are – I was only expecting a fiver in a brown envelope. You will find the clip-on tie will come in handy the next time an ambitious young lady reporter tries to pull you behind the filing cabinets and says "It came off in my hand" – you can say she was talking about the tie.'

THURSDAY, 17 APRIL

A nurse has sent in a heartbreaking letter about her terrible working conditions. We splashed on it in virtually pure text form, which made for a very unusual-looking front page – just the wording of her letter and a small headline saying simply READ THIS AND WEEP … AND THEN GET ANGRY.

As we stared at the finished product, a young, talented and quite cocky Liverpudlian production journalist called Matt Kelly piped up. 'You know, boss, I know it looks a right mess. But it's so bad – it's brilliant.'

Everyone fell about. And I went ahead with the page.

WEDNESDAY, 30 APRIL

We've had a lot of fun tearing into the Tories during the election campaign. Exposing Steven Dorrell's family for employing workers on 66p an hour in Morocco, Michael Heseltine for some minor tax dodge, and so on. Day after day of relentless abuse. The wind has changed, and Labour are going to win big. The only question left, is how big?

Alastair rang. 'It's looking very good, but we can't be complacent. The Mirror's been fantastic, and I won't forget it. But we really need you to get people out to vote. There's a real danger that they will all think it's a foregone conclusion and stay at home. That would be a disaster.'

'How's Tony?' I said.

'Tired, but focused and excited. He has waited a long time for this, we all have. And we're nearly there.'

Our last front page was a picture of Blair pointing straight ahead above a huge throng of cheering people this afternoon, with the headline YOUR COUNTRY NEEDS HIM. And it does.

THURSDAY, 1 MAY

Election Day. My first as an editor, and what a day! It was pretty slow to start, but by late evening it exploded into an orgy of excitement. And when the results began streaming in, it grew increasingly amusing, as Tory legends started toppling like dominoes: Rifkind, Mellor – then Portillo.

When Portillo fell, a huge cheer went up in the *Mirror* newsroom. A lot of my staff are Labour loyalists, and paid-up party members. This was a massive night for them, and they were loving it. We changed the splash throughout the night. The speed we can do this with new technology is incredible – we can whack up a new front page in five minutes on the screen, send it to the print sites by fax and have it running on the presses within twenty minutes. At 1am a jubilant Alastair Campbell rang: 'Come over to the Festival Hall, we're having a big party.'

I cleared the final front, a picture of Tony and Cherie smiling and the headline YES! PRIME MINISTER, and went down to join the fun.

Seconds after I got there, I bumped into Blair's dad.

He hugged me, though we'd never met before. 'Isn't it marvellous?' he said, with tears in his eyes. 'Yes, Mr Blair, it's amazing,' I said.

His son arrived an hour or so later, to be met by a chanting, dancing, partying mob. He got up on a makeshift stage outside as the sun was coming up and the election anthem 'Things Can Only Get Better' belted out on the loudspeakers, and made a dramatic but obviously well-rehearsed speech.

He looked and sounded the business. It was enthralling to be there at what will surely be a pivotal moment in modern Britain's development.

TUESDAY, 6 MAY

To the Treasury, two hours after Gordon Brown had sensationally announced he was ceding interest rate control to the Bank of England. Making it an economic, not a political decision in future. A brave, radical and extraordinary move.

Brown was on ebullient form, as well he might be. 'We had a long time to prepare for this, and I was determined that when we finally got back in we'd be ready and waiting to hit the ground running. It was important to remove political opportunism from the calculations,' he said.

'Yes,' I replied. 'And rather handy for you guys not to be responsible if rates have to rise, of course.'

He laughed. 'Don't be so cynical, Piers.'

Brown's such a clever guy. And everyone in the party's terrified of him, including Blair. He has such a ferocious work ethic, and such a mastery of his brief, that nobody can ever pull the wool over his eyes. 'The key to running a successful government is discipline, and that stems from the Treasury,' he said. 'People always say Labour can't run the economy, and in the past that's sometimes been true. But we will show them we can now, and run it well. And if we get that right then we can really make a difference.'

Got back to the office to find a memo from Kelvin who's been running LiveTV for the Mirror Group, to the management team. 'You will be pleased to know that I won the General Election sweepstake. You may also be disappointed to learn that on Friday I also had a £2000 bet on Michael Heseltine becoming the new Tory leader. The net effect is that Labour have been in power for just five days and I am already £1740 out of pocket.'

WEDNESDAY, 7 MAY

We got a great story today from a patient at the famous Priory clinic, who'd called to say Diana made a secret visit there and opened her heart about her own eating disorders. The informant didn't want money, she just thought others who suffer from this kind of thing should read what the Princess said so they could feel as enthused as she did. It was a bit of a sensitive one, though, so I called Diana's office and explained what we had to Michael Gibbins, her grandly named 'Comptroller', as well as faxing him the full story.

I said I would rather Diana read the copy and let me know if anything was wrong so that we could cover what she said responsibly. He said he would talk to her and call me back.

An hour later Kerrie came over rather excited, which is highly irregular for her, whoever rings, and said, 'I think I've got Princess Diana on the line for you.'

Kerrie always has to qualify this kind of statement because we get so many nutters on the line claiming to be everyone from President Clinton to Queen Victoria. I ran to my office and picked the phone up. It was indeed Diana.

'Hi, how are you?' I said, trying to sound calm.

'I'm fine, thank you, Piers, but I wanted to talk to you about this story you've got. Can we go through it line by line?'

'Of course. Do you mind if I tape this, my shorthand's terribly slow these days?' She laughed. 'No, no, that's OK.'

This is the extraordinary transcript of our call:

Diana: 'Your article suggests I still have a problem when I don't. Why can't we put the tone on it that I am now completely recovered and I am happy to help any other ladies who are distressed or suffering from eating disorders?'

Me: 'Fine, no problem.'

Diana: 'And I didn't relapse. I have had three years clear of it. I was very happy to go around talking about my experience, or I was until this lady made me very unhappy by going to you and talking about it.'

Me: 'I think she was on a high after you left, and wanted to share what you said with others. She is unwell, and only acting in good faith. I think we should be careful about not launching some sort of witch-hunt to expose her as the mole. Nor do I wish to put you off doing it.'

Diana: 'Well, I understand the story is going in whatever, but it would be nice to get it right.'

Me: 'What are you most annoyed about?'

Diana: 'Well, I haven't, as it says here, shared my most intimate secrets with a bunch of total strangers for starters.' [Laughs]

Me: 'Riiiight. Well, that's the first paragraph out of the way. Is this going to be like the Monty Python cheese sketch, where we go through every paragraph, then realise there is nothing accurate in here at all?'

(Diana laughs)

Diana: 'There were thirty young women suffering from bulimia and anorexia. I didn't feel the Priory were supporting their needs, I must say: some of them had been in there for two years. But you had better not say that or I will have everyone from the Priory banging on my door. I didn't reveal anything, I just came there to try and help them.'

Me: 'OK, now you did do this the day before the General Election?'

Diana: 'Yes.'

Me: '… and you did wear a nice cream dress, did you?'

Diana: 'No …'

Me: 'That was just a little joke. Now, we say here you have kept the disease under control since 1995. The assumption being that once you are a bulimic you are always a bulimic.'

Diana: 'I have beaten it, but like any addiction it is about one's head, all the time, just in case. You find that with drug addicts and alcoholics.'

Me: 'Our source told us that you were linking your gym work to controlling your bulimia.'

Diana: 'Well, they asked me why I went to the gym so many times, and I said I went three days a week and didn't think that was obsessive. They also kept asking me about anger and I said, well, aren't they addressing that here, and the answer was no. But it is important for them to understand the anger they feel towards their loved ones – their parents or their husbands. The thing about eating disorders is that people think it's about fitting into a small dress or whatever, but it's not. It's in the head, it's about self-esteem and all that. It's difficult to explain it.'

Me: 'How big a part does anger play?'

Diana: 'A lot. Especially with anorexics, because you are slimming to such a degree, then everyone henpecks you all the time, and if you eat half a potato then the whole family cheers as if it's wonderful, and you are left angry because it is not what you wanted to do at the time.'

Me: 'And your gym work helped you with those feelings?'

Diana: 'Yes, it does. It is great to go for a run or a walk or something to let off all the steam you are feeling.'

Me: 'Is that why I saw thirty women running down Roehampton Lane by the Priory this morning?'

(Diana laughs)

Me: 'You apparently said you were ninety-five per cent over it?'

Diana: 'No, I am clear of it, but like any addiction you know that one day it can come back to haunt you. I said this because they think that once they get out of that place in Roehampton they are as free as a bird, but it is not that easy, and I made that very clear to them. I said the real struggle would come when they went home back into an environment where everyone wanted them to be better suddenly because they had been away in an expensive clinic. When the reality, of course, is that all their emotional crutches fall away when they leave.'

Me: 'Is that because many of the problems they've had are linked to home life?'

Diana: 'Exactly. If there is a lot going wrong in their family lives, then no clinic is going to cure that overnight.'

Me: 'Did you find it distressing?'

Diana: 'Well, I did find it very sad, I must say. They were fifteen to thirty-five years old and some were married with children and felt terrible guilt about being away from home. There was one young girl who had bulimia, and her sister also had bulimia. And it was obvious that she idolised her sister so much that she wanted to follow her path.'

Me: 'You said that going back to bulimia was "not an option" for you. Is that how you feel?'

Diana: 'Yes, it is not an option. I told them that it wasn't great when I had to go back into the environment I used to share with my husband and the royal family, to somewhere like Balmoral or Sandringham. Because I had been unhappy there and the bulimia just got rifer each time I went.'

Me: 'So it's Balmoral's fault, is it? That's a good headline: "Diana is allergic to Balmoral".'

Diana (laughing): 'Well, I love Scotland ... ...*but*. There was a nurse in the Priory who had been struggling in that place for eight months and was dreading going back to work because a) people were going to ask her questions and b) she was going back somewhere she was not particularly happy. And I said to her, why don't you change your job and go to a different hospital, and she said she didn't have the courage to do that yet.'

Me: 'So your advice would be to change the circumstances that caused you to be unhappy?'

Diana: 'Yes. When they are in the clinic, they are all with each other, but when they come out they are immediately vulnerable because their loved ones expect so much.'

Me: 'Where do you feel the Priory is letting them down?'

Diana: 'Well, I have been to a lot of clinics in London, and there are usually fifteen girls or so and they are quite chirpy because they've only been in a few weeks and seemed to be looking forward to coming out, whereas these thirty girls were all, like, how on earth are we going to cope? I could tell it wasn't like the other places and it wasn't right.'

Me: 'You told them that psychotherapists didn't help you, didn't you?'

Diana: 'Yes, that's right. I saw a lot of them, but in the end I concluded that most of them needed more help than I did! I think you are better off talking to someone who has actually been through this, like me, than some therapist who hasn't.'

Me: 'I've had a great idea: what about "Dear Diana" – we get Mirror readers to write direct to you with their problems and you help them.'

Diana: 'God, you'd get all sorts of weirdos writing!'

Me: 'Come on, I'll get you two secretaries to sort the postbag out …'

Diana: 'Well, I want to be paid more than James Whitaker.'

Me: 'I'm not sure I can go that far, to be honest … now you say here that you suddenly woke up one day and thought you'd had enough of everyone treating you like rubbish?'

Diana: Yes, the thing is that when you are vulnerable everyone thinks they can help you, but when you show it as a sign of strength, they get intimidated and anxious and try and squash you back to where you were. And the thing is that as you grow up you have to leave people behind and move on and let go, and people are very frightened by that.'

Me: 'Now what about …'

Diana: 'Can I just say that I never ask people to call me ma'am or Princess?'

Me: 'Well, I thought ordering them all to curtsey was a bit much.'

Diana: 'I would *never* do that.' (Laughs)

Me: 'No, but a little bow of the head never goes amiss, does it? Sorry to be pedantic – but a cream trouser suit and black top?'

Diana: 'Yes. And they gave me a huge bunch of flowers which was so sweet of them.'

Me: 'Would you go back there?'

Diana: 'Well, it's not easy, because once someone has gone to a newspaper then trust has gone.'

Me: 'Well, this girl's intentions were honourable, but we have said you wouldn't like it, and she is mortified by that.'

Diana: 'I understand. But I don't want to be the centre of attention: it's about them, not me. But I won't do anything about it because I can see how this happened. You're getting very good on the Mirror, we've had your campaign against stalking and now this.'

Me: 'I know, I'm becoming a one-man charity here. It's the war on those paparazzi guys that make your life hell that I am keenest on since our lunch.'

Diana: 'It's been a lot better recently, thanks. I've had no fights with them recently and have been remarkably restrained!'

Me: 'Now, it says here you looked stunningly beautiful. Obviously we can't have that …'

Diana: 'No, obviously not.' (Giggles)

Me: '… and much better in real life than on TV, so that will have to come out too.'

(Diana giggles)

Me: 'Is the rest of it OK, then?'

Diana: 'Yes, it's fine, thank you.'

Me: 'Right, well, I will change all this myself, and whack it back to you on the fax.'

Diana: 'Yes, thanks, Piers. Please remember that we have a chance here to help other people.'

Me: 'I can see that. By the way, I spoke to your mother the other day; we have entertaining exchanges of faxes and things.'

Diana: 'Well, she says she hates the media, so be careful.'

Me: 'I will. Mind you, *you* say things like that, but you love us really . . '

Diana (laughing): 'Hmmm, well send it over when you've finished amending it, could you?'

Me: 'Yes, I will. Thanks for all your help. It's important it is right.'

An hour later I faxed all the copy to her office, and Michael Gibbins rang back to say the Princess was 'very happy, and very grateful'. I went over all the headlines with him, and he said he would come back to me if there were any problems.

I had a few drinks tonight to celebrate a great scoop and an extraordinary day.

THURSDAY, 8 MAY

I woke to hear our scoop leading all the news bulletins and it felt great to have done it responsibly, and in a way that Diana can feel comfortable with, rather than just recklessly slamming it all in the paper. Then, at 9am, the radio news said the Princess had issued a statement ferociously attacking the story. I assumed this was some kind of wind-up. But no, a check call to the newsdesk confirmed she had actually said the following:

> The Princess of Wales is deeply disappointed to learn that one of the group of patients whom she visited last week at the Priory has disclosed to the *Daily Mirror* details of private conversations. Her frankness about her own eating disorders, which are long in the past, gives her a unique understanding for those with similar problems. The benefits to patients depend enormously on privacy being respected and it is particularly sad that on this occasion the visit has been sensationalised. The Princess hopes the repercussions do not undermine the positive aspects of this visit or jeopardise any she may make in the future.

I was flabbergasted, absolutely gob-smacked. How could she possibly do this after all that happened yesterday? My mood fluctuated on the drive to work between blind rage, utter bemusement, and rueful revenge.

I toyed with sticking the tape of our conversation on an 0898 phone line under the headline DIANA – WE NAME THE SOURCE. But she knows I won't do that. She knows she's got me over a barrel. If I want any more from her, I will have to play the game by her rules. And if I don't, it's permanent Siberia for me, like so many of her friends and media contacts before. I called her office to demand answers, though, and Michael Gibbins just sighed. 'I'm sorry, Piers, but the Princess thought about it overnight and just didn't want this to signal a free-for-all on these visits being made public. She hopes you understand.'

'Michael,' I replied, 'I don't understand, no. It's a bloody joke. She went through every word with me, laughing and joking throughout. What will she do when I put the tape in the paper?'

'Oh, the Princess doesn't think you will do anything like that now you are getting on so well.'

I'm trapped on Planet Diana, a crazy place where she calls all the shots and is famous enough and important enough to newspapers to get away with it. You have to hand it to the little minx. Even by her standards, this is breathtaking behaviour.

FRIDAY, 9 MAY

A handwritten letter arrived from our new PM. 'Dear Piers, Thanks for your great coverage during the election campaign. You made a really significant contribution to our victory. Well done! Let's meet up soon. Tony.'

His office called later to invite me over on Monday. It feels worryingly intoxicating to be on such matey terms with the new most powerful man in the country.

MONDAY, 12 MAY

I headed off at midday to tea with Blair at No. 10. His grin was even more gigantic than usual.

'Well, hello, Prime Minister,' I laughed.

I am going to have to remind myself not to amble in and say, 'Hi, Tone, mate,' in future.

'How does it feel to be the most powerful man in Britain, then?'

He laughed this time.

'Better than being the most powerful opposition leader, definitely.'

He looked and sounded utterly euphoric.

'It is such a huge relief after all this time in opposition to be able to actually do things at last,' he admitted.

'How did you feel on election night?'

'I couldn't believe what I was seeing on TV. My initial thought was that we'd win by thirty or forty seats. Then Hove went and I realised it was going to be a massacre. I said to someone "We can't have won Hove … we'll be winning Hastings next" – and we did!

'It was all rather anti-climactic after that, particularly after the campaign from hell. Brilliantly run, but a living hell, not really knowing which way it was going. I tried to stay calm on the night and remember that I had important speeches to make whatever happened. And I told others to calm down too. But John Prescott just shouted, "You must be fucking joking! We're murdering them out there … I've waited eighteen years to do this to the Tories!" '

'Talking of which, how did Major take it?'

'Well, he rang to cede the election, which he didn't have to do, and he was pretty gracious about it, actually. I felt sorry for him, he was crucified by his party and there's a hard lesson for us to learn there. If you want to govern you can't spend all your time backbiting and infighting, or the country will just turn round and say thanks and goodbye.'

I told him we'd sent Alastair a pager message saying his flies were undone as the celebration unfurled in Downing Street. He was hugely amused.

We were served our tea in bone china cups.

'Can't we have it in the old socialist mugs we used to get?' I joked.

The tea lady didn't bat an eyelid. 'Of course, sir, I will get you a mug.'

I hurriedly told her I was only joking, but she was having none of it.

We talked about Gordon Brown. 'I keep telling people how he has eighteen times more intellect than Kenneth Clarke,' said Blair. 'He will be as great a Chancellor as Lloyd George, he has a brilliant mind.'

The admiration is total and seems utterly genuine.

'I feel a deep sense of purpose, of responsibility,' he continued. 'We have been given this extraordinary mandate by the electorate and we mustn't fail them. There is so much optimism and enthusiasm, we simply have to drive that through. If I can be remembered for one thing in this first term, I'd like it to be education. If I fail there, I have let everyone down, because that must be the basis of the New Labour Government.'

'Talk me through the new ministers, then.'

'What do you think?'

'Well, the big jobs were all obvious – you have some large beasts there. But I was a bit surprised by Clare Short, Frank Dobson and Tony Banks, to be honest.'

'Well, we needed to give Clare Short a job where we can control her. She is a loose cannon.' He and Alastair, sitting a few feet away, both raised their eyebrows to the ceiling. 'And I thought giving Frank the health job would be good for morale in a difficult position. As for Tony, I took some flak for it but he is an energetic guy and knows a lot about sport.'

'What do you think the Tories will do now?' I asked. 'William Hague's been mooted as a possible leadership contender.'

'I think Hague could be a threat,' said Blair; 'he's young and clever.'

'But he's such a nerd,' I replied, 'and nobody's going to vote for someone who speaks in that ridiculous way.'

Blair shook his head: 'I'm not so sure, he could do well for them.'

I asked what he hoped to achieve in Northern Ireland, an issue Blair cares passionately about.

'Well Prime Minister, nice place you've got here.'
I take tea with Blair days after his 1997 election win.

'It is very difficult,' he conceded. 'The time may have come to take a risk. Politicians have tried for more than twenty years to sort it out and got nowhere.'

Blair looked fit and pumped up, and determined to sort problems and make a difference. It's exciting, genuinely exciting. I believe he can do it. He's got the energy and the brain and the people around him to shake Britain out of the malaise it has sunk into under the Tories, and John Major in particular.

I'd been at No. 10 for 40 minutes when his right-hand woman, Anji Hunter, popped her head round the door and said his next meeting was due. Anji's from Newick too, and I used to work with her brother Johnny at Lloyds. The boys in the Royal Oak wouldn't quite believe this little vignette.

'Well, Piers, I must get back to running the country now, if you don't mind,' Blair said, laughing again as if he still couldn't really believe it himself. He thanked me for all our support as I walked out. 'You made a big difference,' he said. 'Not as big as the Sun,' I replied. He grimaced. 'Now, don't be like that, we were grateful they backed us, but we know who our old friends are.'

TUESDAY, 13 MAY

I sent Peter Mandelson a case of Evian water to congratulate him, with a twist of lime obviously. He wrote today: 'You do realise that my teetotal resolution was only until Tony was through the door of No. 10 ... however, Evian is my favourite and I am *very* grateful to you and the *Mirror* for all you did for us.'

WEDNESDAY, 28 MAY

Extraordinary scenes down at Eton today, where William invited his nanny Tiggy Legge-Bourke rather than his parents to the annual open day. Tiggy, game as ever, was soon pictured smoking and guzzling champagne next to Wills, images that sent his already rather annoyed mother off the dial.

I got a call from Michael Gibbins in Diana's office, who had some 'thoughts from the Princess that she would like you to be aware of'.

I could actually hear her dictating them in the background.

'Erm, the Princess feels deeply hurt and angry that Ms Legge-Bourke would behave this way when she is with William and there are cameras around. It is idiotic behaviour and clearly shows that she is a bad influence on the boys, as the Princess has been privately fearing for some time.'

I asked Michael if these 'thoughts' were being conveyed to other papers and he said he was under instructions to speak to Stuart Higgins at the *Sun* and Richard Kay at the *Daily Mail* but nobody else.

Confident that we'd all have the same line, I splashed on 'SILLY GLASS – Di's fury as Wills phones Tiggy for Eton booze-up'. First editions of the *Sun* and *Mail* were much the same, though the *Sun*'s gone a lot harder than we have. She'd clearly got herself nicely worked up by the time Michael Gibbins called Stuart.

FRIDAY, 30 MAY

Diana's finally lost it. Her views on Tiggy dominated the news all day yesterday, and she was beginning to get a lot of flak for being so unpleasant towards her. Mid-afternoon today, I heard she was going to issue a statement denying saying anything unpleasant about Tiggy, insisting she was 'delighted' that she went to Eton in her place, and blaming an 'employee in her office' for speaking without her consent. For God's sake, I'd *heard* her in the background giving Michael Gibbins specific adjectives to describe Ms Legge-Bourke.

Now she was dumping on him in the most disgusting manner. I rang him, outraged, but was told he will no longer be taking calls from the press. Unbelievable – she's not only dropped him right in it, she's banned him from defending himself. Michael's far too loyal and decent to return the favour, but he must be bitterly hurt inside.

Late tonight I finally got to speak to him on his mobile and he sounded petrified of saying anything. 'This is all bullshit, Michael, don't let her get away with this.' But he just replied sadly, 'Piers, you know what the Princess can be like, you remember that stuff with the clinic. It will blow over, it always does.'

I rang Stuart and Richard and asked what they were doing, and both said they are going to criticise Diana tomorrow. Richard said that William had had a go at Diana about the story, and she had panicked and denied everything – sticking all the blame on Gibbins.

Nobody should treat a good guy like this, it's cowardly and horrible.

I splashed on 'QUEEN OF FIBS – Di carpets top aide for telling the TRUTH on Tiggy'. And inside we gave her the full nine barrels for stitching up Gibbins.

I know she'll freeze me out for a bit now, like she does everyone who ever criticises her. But I don't care. Diana's got to learn that you can't behave like this.

Incredibly, I heard late this afternoon that her mother, Frances Shand-Kydd, has sold an interview to *Hello!* After all those endless protestations that she would never do anything like that.

I faxed her in disbelief, asking if we can have a slice of it for the *Mirror* in advance. She replied, without a trace of embarrassment, 'I can't help, I'm afraid because I have a legal contract with *Hello!* and can't speak to anyone for some time. Before you ask, don't, or I might extend it.'

FRIDAY, 13 JUNE

Fergie invited me to dinner at Mosimann's last night with a couple of her aides, and it turned into a riotous affair. Say what you like about her, Fergie is good fun. She drank like a fish, laughed like Sid James, and got more and more hilariously indiscreet as the evening wore on. I asked how her love life was going, and she squealed with laughter. 'I'm in love,' she said excitedly. 'Blimey,' I replied, 'who's the lucky guy?'

'Well, he's more of a boy really, and he doesn't know yet – it's Tiger Woods!' I fell back in my chair. The pair of them had been photographed at some golf tournament last week, but I'd thought nothing of it. Now she looked like a lovesick puppy. 'He's so gorgeous,' she cooed. 'Do you think I stand a chance with him?'

I can't imagine she does in a million years, but this was not the right moment to say that. 'Well, who knows. He's very focused on his golf, isn't he? I doubt there's much room in his schedule for dating royals.' Fergie roared again. 'Well, I am going to follow him around the courses for a bit and see how I get on.' Poor old Tiger isn't going to know what's hit him.

'How do you know him?' I asked. 'Oh, through Kevin,' she replied. 'Kevin who?' 'Costner, of course.'

Ah yes, silly of me. 'What happened with Sly Stallone?' I asked, trying to douse her ardour. Sly, my favourite celebrity, had begged me during a London stay two years ago to try and fix him a date with Fergie. 'Now there's a real woman,' he'd cackled. 'I've always wanted to bed a royal broad.' I had passed on the interest and was curious to know what happened. 'Oh, he's not my type at all,' she giggled. 'Tiger's much more like it.'

When I asked if she'd seen Diana recently, though, her mood suddenly changed. 'No, she won't talk to me.' I was amazed: 'Why?' 'Because I put in my book that I once caught verrucas after borrowing her shoes.'

'What?'

'Yes, and because I said I thought Charles was an extraordinary man, which he is, by the way. Diana just cut me off. I haven't spoken to her in eight months. She won't take my calls or reply to my letters. And worst of all, she won't even let me see the boys, which is so upsetting. I loved seeing William and Harry, and so did my girls. It's just not fair that they can't see their cousins.' Tears were in her eyes. 'I have tried everything, but she can be so obstinate. I've said how sorry I am, but she won't listen.'

She went to the loo then, I suspected to dry her eyes. When she came back, she changed the subject and started laughing again. She's very jolly hockey sticks, old Fergs, but I do like her. We all staggered into the night woefully inebriated and vowed to do it again soon.

'Don't forget to bring Tiger,' I said; 'he can give me some tips on my putting while he's eating.' She squealed again. God help him.

WEDNESDAY, 18 JUNE

My second son Stanley arrived into the world today. Within two hours a huge parcel of gifts arrived from Fergie. And I mean huge. No wonder she's so skint.

FRIDAY, 20 JUNE

The *Guardian* have dramatically won their Jonathan Aitken case after finding last-minute evidence that he was lying about some flights taken by his wife and daughter. I sent a case of champagne to Alan Rusbridger, who'd told me last week he thought they were going down for £2 million, and he replied: 'Thanks, not many of the lads here have ever tasted it, so it will be quite an experience.'

Great win for press freedom though, and for the *Guardian*'s QC, George Carman. A genius in the courtroom, and a serious drinking partner out of it.

SUNDAY, 13 JULY

Diana's gone on holiday to Fayed's pad in the South of France, with her boys and some of his family. I called Mohammed to try and prise some info out of him. 'No, no, my lips are sealed,' he laughed.

'That's a first,' I said.

'Ha, ha. Look, I just want Diana and the boys to relax. Give them a break, you know.'

MONDAY, 14 JULY

Bizarre scenes today when Diana went out in a small dinghy to talk to the flotilla of journalists and photographers sitting out at sea trying to film her on the beach. She asked how long they were going to be there, complaining she was trying to have a private holiday, and seemed, according to James Whitaker, to be 'rather over-animated'. She ended their little chat by saying, 'I will shock you with what I am going to do next.'

James was bemused. 'I don't know what to make of it. It was all very odd.'

I rang Fayed. 'Does she want us to pull out, Mohammed?'

I then heard him talking to Diana in the background.

'No, no, it's OK,' he replied. Wonder what she's up to?

TUESDAY, 15 JULY

Fashion designer Gianni Versace was shot dead today outside his Miami mansion. A close friend of Diana and Elton John, he appears to have been the victim of some random slaying – possibly because he is gay. He was wearing a pair of his own-brand sandals at the time, prompting us to do a headline BLOWN AWAY IN HIS VERSACE FLIP-FLOPS. Seemed a good idea this afternoon, but rather tasteless now I see it in print at midnight.

THURSDAY, 17 JULY

Charles is throwing a 50th birthday party for Camilla tonight, and, as if by magic, Diana appeared on the beach in St Tropez this morning in a leopard-skin swimsuit.

For half an hour she preened and posed for all she was worth, supplying the press flotilla with amazingly sexy photos.

The message was obvious: 'Happy birthday, Camilla'.

Nobody's going to stick the party pics on page one now: it will all be Diana looking sensational.

Fayed rang later to ask what we were doing. 'We're running great photos on the front page of Diana in that leopard-skin swimsuit as a postcard to Camilla.'

He laughed loudly. 'Great, great, Diana will like that. Can you fax it later for her?'

FRIDAY, 18 JULY

The customer services department daily newsletter recorded today: 'We received a letter to the editor containing excrement. It was posted in Germany and referred to the SAS.'

MONDAY, 28 JULY

To No. 10 today for the first newspaper interview with Blair. He looked like he'd been getting some sleep, and was on sparkling form as we sat in the garden outside drinking tea.

I asked him first about Diana. 'It's important she is allowed to carry on the work that she is doing. She earns a lot of respect around the world for her work on things like landmines and I want that to continue. There are difficult human situations involved, but the royals should not get pulled to pieces like they do. They're a great asset to this country.'

'She's quite a fan of yours too, I hear,' I said.

He glowed happily.

'How's your neighbour getting on, then?'

'Gordon's incredibly important to this Government. We work very closely together and it is a good partnership, which is vital. He has enormous political and intellectual depth. He really is one of the cleverest people in politics in a very long time and we are lucky to have him. I said this last time I saw you, but he is similar to Lloyd George – he has tremendous drive and ability, as well as humanity.'

Blair's throwing a 'Cool Britannia' party at Downing Street on Wednesday for all the new great and good. And me.

I couldn't resist asking him how he could justify having a self-acclaimed drug abuser like Noel Gallagher from Oasis there.

'Well, because we should celebrate great British bands like Oasis ...'

I could see Alastair, sitting next to him, hastily scribbling a note, which he slipped straight to Blair, who paused in mid sentence.

'... though as for his views on drugs, I can assure you this Government will do everything in its power to crack down on drug abuse. Like most parents, it is the thing I worry about most with my children.'

Hilarious.

Blair then took me for a stroll around the No. 10 garden, which was bigger than I'd thought.

'Bet you can't believe this, can you, Tony?'

'No, it is a bit surreal, I must say.'

'Jim Callaghan said that being PM was like being in a choppy ocean: you just get hit by wave after wave until you realise it's always like that and you learn to ride them. Is that how it feels?'

'Yes, I know what he means. It's true there is constant pressure, but it's also bloody exciting. For the first time in my political life I am able to do things rather than just talk about them. I want to make this country a dynamic, innovative, creative place.

'I want people to look back on my time as Prime Minister and judge this government to have been fair, modern and strong. To say that we brought in better teachers into better schools, helped improve the NHS to get people better cancer treatment, better preventative health care. That we improved Britain's standing in the world, and made businesses feel we're on their side. And that we were tough on crime, especially juvenile crime.'

'And how do you think your kids will cope with growing up here?'

'Pretty well, actually. We've explained to them that this is all great fun, but it will end one day and you'll be making your own way in the world then, and I'll still be there for you as your dad, as I am now. But don't get too hung up on all this privilege because one day it won't be here for us.'

'Cherie seems to be blossoming into a fine First Lady.'

'Well, I don't think she has any aspirations or intentions to be a First Lady. But she is being tremendously supportive, while holding down a demanding job of her own and bringing up three kids. I think her job is tougher than mine in many ways, because she can't answer back.'

We had a cup of tea back in his office and I said I'd bumped into his dad on Election night.

'He seemed so ecstatic.'

'Yes, I think it was a mixture of great pride for him in seeing me become Prime Minister, and a sense of his own frustrated ambition being finally realised. I think he would have been a really serious political figure, but his career was thwarted before he got the chance.'

'And how do you think your mother would have been about all this?'

'Oh, I think she would have told me to remember it won't last long and someone else will come along to take over, so make the most of it while you can.'

Back at the office, we decided the stuff he said about the Princess of Wales was the most newsy and splashed on BLAIR: I BACK DIANA. The Palace aren't going to like it very much, but I think he's right to support her.

WEDNESDAY, 30 JULY
Off to the Cool Britannia party at No. 10. After all the hype, it was a rather motley gathering of media luvvies, actors and pop stars – all wondering what on earth they were doing there.

Noel Gallagher told me he'd planned to put a Hitler moustache on the portrait of Maggie Thatcher halfway up the stairs ... but his mother stopped him. 'I had me marker pen and everything ready, but she read me the fucking riot act and said I couldn't let her down like that!'

I saw Eddie Izzard and finally got the chance to ask why everyone laughed when he said the word 'jam' on *Have I Got News For You*, but stayed silent when I said it the week after. 'Ah, well, Piers, it's all in the telling,' he replied, and then gave me several theatrical renditions of the word 'jam' – which did, indeed, make me laugh.

Blair himself revealed he got a bit of a kicking from the Queen in their weekly meeting over his 'I back Diana' splash in the *Mirror*.

'It was a rather uncomfortable meeting,' he said. 'The Queen was not very happy that I had said that.'

'Really?'

'Yes, she was definitely not amused by it. At all. But it was OK in the end.'

As he said this, Blair suddenly realised he had breached the very strict rule that no Prime Minister talks about anything he discusses with the monarch in their weekly meeting. 'God, forget I said that!' he exclaimed. 'I'm not supposed to say a word about those meetings.'

Cherie came over and pleaded with me. 'Don't put in pictures of my cellulite when I go to Italy ... ...*please!* I don't want the Diana treatment, thank you.'

'Do you like Diana?'

'Yes, I do, she is a nice woman. Complicated, but nice. And William is a little charmer – he played with Kathryn all the time when we went to Balmoral.'

'How's it all going?' I asked.

'It's OK so far,' she replied. 'At least Tony works at home now, so he can see the kids in the evenings. Sometimes I just want everyone to piss off, but it's not too bad. I'm very tired, though. Think all the election build-up and all the emotion of winning and coming in here has taken its toll a bit. We need a good break to recharge the batteries.'

As I left I noticed Lenny Henry stumbling around trying to enter some back office. 'You lost?' I asked.

'Yes, it would appear I am.'

I led him to the front door.

WEDNESDAY, 6 AUGUST

James Whitaker has got wind of a fantastic story – Diana and Dodi Fayed, Mohammed's son, are apparently an item after meeting on the holiday. I called Mohammed to ask if it was true, knowing he wouldn't be able to resist telling me if it was.

He was very cagey at first, but finally confirmed it was.

'It is very early stages, Piers, but they seem very happy and are getting on very well.'

'Are you worried there might be a bit of a backlash?'

'No. It is a simple case of two people meeting and falling in love, and if people don't like it then they can go to hell.

'I let them just relax and get on with whatever they wanted in France and they just had fun together. I wanted her to have space and freedom and the boys had a lot of fun with all the watersports. I hope it works out for them. I knew Diana's father Johnny Spencer and we would meet twice a week for tea or lunch with Raine or whatever, and shortly before he died he asked me to keep an eye on his family, so I have tried to do this.'

'Mohammed, how serious is it?'

'I think it is a proper relationship. But please go gently now, let them have some space.'

We splashed it over the first seven pages – this is a massive story.

FRIDAY, 8 AUGUST

It's been Di and Dodi mayhem for two days. A good set of photos of the happy couple sunning themselves on a yacht came out yesterday, but Jason Fraser, self-styled 'King of the Paps', has got a sensational new set of photos of the world's hottest couple kissing in the sea.

We've all been bidding, but I found out this morning that Bridget Rowe's snaffled them for the *Sunday Mirror* for £300,000 – and excluded us from the deal. To make it worse, the *Daily Mail* have got second rights for next Monday. I stormed round to confront Bridget, and we had a screaming row in her office. To no avail.

'Right, fuck you, then,' I shouted, and raced back to my newsroom.

'Get those photos of Di and Dodi from yesterday and turn his head round.'

'*What?*' was the universal reply.

'Look, I've seen the kissing pictures and they're not a million miles away from these. We just need to flip his head round and it will look like he's kissing her.'

'But we can't do that – it's cheating,' said Simon Cosyns.

'No, it's not, we know they kissed, and we know the photos look a bit like these. If the Sunday Mirror want to piss around with us, then we will piss around with them.'

I laid out a front page with the 'new' photo and the headline THE KISS.

David Montgomery came up. 'You can't do that,' he said.

'Why not?'

'Because that's the Sunday Mirror headline and we've spent too much money for you to do it first.'

'What about "Hot lips", then?' I said.

'Yes. Fine.'

He didn't give a monkey's about the head being flipped around.

I called Fayed again.

'I have seen the kiss photos. The Sunday Mirror are running them on Sunday but they are very expensive. Your son's photo was worth five pounds last week and is now worth about five hundred thousand!'

Fayed laughed. 'He's worth it!'

'Are you worried about Dodi getting into the media circus?'

'No, no. He is a big boy and he knows what he is doing. He is used to the movie business. He is very cool, as if he is with an ordinary girlfriend. He says the press are hounding them but he is OK about it. No problem.'

Later, Bruce Grobbelaar walked free from his football match-fixing trial with the *Sun*. Everyone thinks he's guilty but I still let the *Sun* have it for 'smearing soccer and an innocent man'. They are the enemy, after all.

SATURDAY, 9 AUGUST

Frank Bruno invited me to his son's christening today, which seemed a bit odd.

It seemed even odder when I got there and discovered he'd invited 1500 other people. Everyone from Harry Carpenter to pop stars, footballers and journalists.

I asked one mutual friend what was going on. 'Don't know, mate, think Frank's lost it a bit. Apparently he didn't tell Laura until the last minute and she's gone mad about it.'

Bumped into Derek Jameson by the bouncy castles.

'You shouldn't have attacked the Sun over Grob,' he said.

Made me think. Kelvin had said the same thing yesterday on the phone, saying our coverage had made his 'stomach turn'.

I got back home and sent Stuart Higgins a letter apologising. 'Sorry, mate, I was being a prat and a tosser and got a bit carried away.'

SUNDAY, 10 AUGUST

I've been getting loads of stick for switching Dodi's head round, and am beginning to regret it. New technology is a particularly powerful tool for photography, but the ability to manipulate images has never been easier and we have got to resist it. It's a con.

FRIDAY, 15 AUGUST

Press Gazette's front-page headline is PIERS MORGAN: I WAS A TOTAL PRAT AND A COMPLETE TOSSER. Thanks, Stuart.

SUNDAY, 31 AUGUST

Diana is dead. And today has been the most dramatic, emotional and draining day of my career. I still can't really get my head round what has happened.

I got home from a nice, relaxing dinner last night, and had a glass of whisky before heading up to bed.

Around 12.30am the newsdesk rang to say that Diana and Dodi had been involved in some sort of run-in with photographers in Paris and pranged their car. It didn't sound too serious, but I immediately sensed this would be big trouble.

There were bound to be paparazzi chasing them around and everyone's going to think they nearly killed them and start demanding a privacy law again.

I switched on the TV news, and a couple of commentators were already saying just that. By 1am, the news was more serious. Dodi appeared to have been badly hurt and there were reports that Diana might have been injured too.

Their car had crashed in a tunnel being chased by photographers from a hotel. The ultimate nightmare.

I tried to get hold of Mark Bolland, but couldn't.

By 1.30am the first pictures came on screen of the crash scene and the car, a black Mercedes, looked smashed to pieces.

God, what if they've been killed?

It didn't bear thinking about. It was clear now that this was a massive story, so I called the deputy editor Brendon Parsons and asked him to go straight to the office and start preparing a tribute supplement, just in case the worst had happened.

The *Mirror* can only print 48 live pages, so it would have to be a pre-printed section which would then be inserted into the main paper, but that meant it would have to be sent to the printers by 11am – a logistical nightmare.

Brendon dashed in, making sure that other key staff were aware and going in too. I was glued to the TV now: nobody seemed to know what the hell was happening, other than it didn't look good and the consequences might be dreadful.

Faces, and voices were growing more sombre by the minute.

There were wild rumours all over the place – from a multiple pile-up, to some sort of explosion, to the fact that the car may have been driving on the wrong side of the road, a confusion caused by the fact the French drive on the right and the car had flipped right over.

At 2am, the BBC said there were reports that Diana had been seen walking away from the car. I breathed a huge sigh of relief. But the newsdesk warned there were lots of conflicting stories flying around and we shouldn't assume anything yet.

Then came confirmation that Dodi had died.

Brendon was at the office and I pressed the button to do the supplement.

He said more and more staff were arriving in various states of disrepair as it was Saturday night, their normal night off.

I was flying on adrenaline by now, and calling everyone I knew in royal circles to see what the hell they knew. I finally got hold of Mark Bolland, who sounded shocked and said he was also trying to find out, but the word was it was 'very bad'.

Then, around 3.30am I got the call I'd been dreading. Robin Cook, the

Foreign Secretary, had been briefed in Manila by his French counterpart that Diana was dead.

He had put a news embargo on this fact until an official announcement could be prepared, but the Press Association news wire broke the embargo and ran with the story.

I sat back in my sofa, sweating and bursting with tension and an odd excitement that only journalists feel at times like this. This was the single most dramatic news story of my career. Diana, the great icon of our times, was gone. Professionally, I was already gearing up to go to the office and run the team for what will surely be weeks of extraordinary coverage. But as I got in the car, I felt a surge of raw emotion sweep through me too.

I got to the office by 5.45am and there was controlled pandemonium. My picture editor, Ron Morgans, a brilliant veteran operator, immediately led me to a screen where he had photos of Diana lying dead in the back of the car. She looked serene, like she was asleep. There was a trickle of blood running from her lip but otherwise no visible sign of injury. I stared at the screen for minutes, just saying 'fuck me' repeatedly. I had never seen more sensational news images.

Then I realised the enormity of what I was looking at. I ran to the phone and called the boss of the agency who had sent the pictures in. 'Retrieve those fucking photos from everywhere you have sent them right now, or you will be out of business by the end of today.' He sounded panicky. 'What do you mean, why?'

He was a good operator who ran a good business, but he hadn't quite got to grips with this yet. 'Listen, mate, Diana's possibly been killed by the bloody paparazzi and you are trying to flog me pictures of her still warm corpse. Think about it, for fuck's sake.'

'It's too late, they've gone out,' he said, his voice trembling a bit. 'No, it isn't, ring everyone and say there's been a terrible mistake and these photographs are not for publication. They will all understand. Then if I were you, I'd turn your machines off and leave the country until it all blows over. Because if people find out what you were doing they will come and get you.'

He thanked me for the advice and withdrew the pictures.

By 7am, 200 people were in the newsroom, all stunned and quite emotional. As with all these kind of stories, some key people were away or couldn't be raised.

Simon Cosyns is on a family driving holiday through France. That will be a big drawback if he can't be found. He is a brilliant newspaper designer.

Some members of staff amazed me with their attitude. Several senior people called in to ask if they would be 'needed', because they were going on holiday. The answer was no. I don't 'need' people who aren't interested.

The day seemed to pass in a flash. The country seems to have gone into some sort of seismic collective shock. The last editions of the Sunday papers all carried reports of the death, so I opted for a more symbolic front page for our

Monday edition. There were, of course, millions of images of Diana to choose from, but the most striking for me was a black and white portrait of her in a silver tiara, smiling at the camera. Taken by Patrick Demarchelier, her favourite photographer, it encapsulated the free-spirit Princess. The page just had that picture and a black masthead and border with the dates '1961–1997'.

No need for a name on this story.

The media, and tabloid newspapers in particular, have been getting hammered on the airwaves. We are being, as I feared, directly blamed for the accident and the repercussions are going to be unprecedented. People in my office are already talking of us never buying paparazzi photos again.

But I don't care about any of that at the moment. As I sit here now at home, still buzzing with an odd mixture of adrenalin and sadness, all I can think is that we've lost an extraordinary woman today. Someone who was beautiful, complex, funny, inspiring, irrational, and totally unique. There will never be another Diana.

MONDAY, 1 SEPTEMBER

There is a God.

Henri Paul, driver of the Mercedes, was reported in France to have been three times over the drink limit, and going at 121mph. 'Drunk, speeding Fayed driver kills Diana' is a lot better than 'Paparazzi kill Diana'.

The press, desperate to switch the blame from ourselves, have immediately turned our collective turrets on to Henri Paul.

This is going to get uglier and nastier as the days go on.

David English, boss of the Mail newspaper group, sickened me by going on TV and distancing his rags from any blame for anything. 'We never buy paparazzi photos,' he said, straight-faced, in a deliberate and cynical attempt to shift all the attention on to papers like the *Mirror*.

The *Mail*, of course, is one of the biggest buyers of paparazzi pictures in the world. I am stunned by his behaviour. He is a personal hero of mine but this is contemptible.

TUESDAY, 2 SEPTEMBER

The national outpouring of grief is astonishing. More and more flowers are being left outside Kensington Palace and thousands of people are turning up to hold candle-lit vigils all night. I have never seen anything like this in my lifetime for anyone – not even Elvis or Lennon.

Diana, in her death, has proved she was what I always thought she was, the biggest star of the modern world. The TV cameras keep showing all these people sobbing in the street, it's extraordinary. There is a lot of antipathy towards journalists. One of my photographers was physically attacked in the street today, and I got two letters with blood-red hand-prints this morning.

The atmosphere is febrile: people want someone to blame and someone to hate for killing their Princess, and the prime targets at the moment are the press, Fayed and the royal family. In that order.

Some are already speculating that Diana was murdered by the secret services to stop her marrying Dodi. Incredible, but gathering momentum.

The funeral is already building up to be a massive event.

Elton John is going to sing, Earl Spencer's going to talk, and there will be a cast of thousands.

Simon Cosyns finally called in today from the middle of nowhere in France. He has just heard on the car radio the words 'Diana' and *'morte'* and actually crashed his own car into a wall out of shock.

He left his wife and kids with the car and got a taxi to the airport to fly straight back. He is appalled that he's only just found out, but to be honest I am glad we will be getting him fresh and raring because most of the rest of us are shagged out from working eighteen-hour days.

Sales of the paper yesterday were truly staggering. We were up an extra 800,000 on the same day last week. There has never been anything like this.

But it is not making us any money because nobody wants to advertise in these grief-strewn newspapers, and we are using three times the usual amount of newsprint to cope with the bigger papers and unprecedented demand. Diana would have been amused by the irony of us selling so many papers on her death, but losing loads of money at the same time.

WEDNESDAY, 3 SEPTEMBER

Late in the afternoon I got a call from the Lord Chamberlain, formally inviting me to the funeral. I was surprised and immediately asked if this had been cleared by the Spencer family. He assured me that it had, and that there had been a firm decision to invite the editors of every newspaper.

I have accepted the invitation, because it seems churlish not to, and I will be effectively representing the paper and our readers. But the thought of going up there to Westminster Abbey on Saturday given all the abuse we've been getting is unnerving.

The royals, too, are coming in for fearful stick, because they haven't lowered the Buckingham Palace flag yet and are still at Balmoral. I spoke to Mark Bolland, and he admitted the royals are all 'like frightened rabbits in headlights'.

'I've been trying to tell them about the flag and stuff, but they are in shock and don't know what the hell to do. There is a genuine mounting concern that their safety might be in jeopardy down here. Some people were trying to get over the walls into the palaces last night, and it wasn't to say thank you.'

Mark is a cool, clever guy, but even he sounds concerned as to how this will now play out.

'This is a very worrying situation, and slightly out of control. People are blaming you lot, but they are also buying into this theory that Diana and Dodi were murdered by British intelligence. It's crazy, but what can you do?'

'Mark, I think the best thing the Queen can do is lower that bloody flag, then come back and address the nation on TV.'

'We're trying to sort that. Protocol says the flag is only lowered if the Queen dies, but sod protocol, frankly.'

Our front page tonight read YOUR PEOPLE ARE SUFFERING, SPEAK TO US MA'AM. There are several other splashes saying the same thing in other papers. The royals have got to pull themselves together.

THURSDAY, 4 SEPTEMBER

They have. Mark rang first thing to say the flag was coming down, and the Queen was coming back. Charles was also going to come out with the boys at Balmoral and meet some local people and read some of the messages on the flowers.

'Make sure he's tactile,' I said.

'What do you mean?'

'I mean he should hold their hands or something. People don't want to see those boys treated in some formal stuffy way at the moment, it would be disastrous.'

Mark concurred.

An hour later, I was watching the appallingly sad scene when the TV closed in on Charles clutching Harry's hand in a tender and gentle way as they walked among the bouquets.

That was the picture everyone wanted to see.

We cleared the front page for it, under the headline IN SAFE HANDS. Later in the day, it was confirmed that the Queen will address the nation on TV. I've never known her react to the newspapers like this, she must be in complete turmoil, poor woman.

Tony Blair is going on *The Frost Programme* on Sunday and Mandelson rang to discuss it with me. 'I was talking to him this morning about what this has to do with legislation, because you can't legislate for things like this. But the press have a responsibility to make sound editorial judgements about how to handle celebrities and public figures. The problem is that if the press say they will sort it out through the PCC, then the public won't wear it.'

I said it would be pretty helpful if the Prime Minister said he was aware there had already been a groundswell for change among papers, because there had – with Diana in particular.

Mandelson was not sure. 'But it doesn't look like anyone was moving away from paparazzi, does it?'

'No, but she was on the phone a lot to people like Richard Kay and me, and it was getting better.'

'I have no doubt about that. People don't want this at all. The public don't understand why the press have to destroy people and tear them apart.'

At 2pm, Earl Spencer called me. 'Hello, Mr Morgan, I am ringing on behalf of my mother to ask all tabloid editors not to attend the funeral service.'

He was polite, but firm. I could sense the rage simmering in his voice.

'OK, but can I just say that when I received the invitation from the Lord Chamberlain yesterday I specifically said I would only accept if it had been expressly approved by you and your family, and I was assured it had been and that the invitation was from the family.'

'I don't wish to be rude, Mr Morgan, but it would just be preferred if you showed our request respect.'

Basic human decency dictates that you don't argue with someone who has just lost their sister.

'It goes without saying that we will respect your wishes. Could you please pass my personal condolences to your mother, as we have always got on well? Thank you.'

'I will, thank you.'

I put the phone down and called Stuart Higgins at the *Sun*, who said the same thing had happened to him, and Paul Dacre at the *Mail*. We've definitely been set up here.

FRIDAY, 5 SEPTEMBER

The broadsheets all ran with TABLOID EDITORS BANNED FROM FUNERAL.

In mid afternoon news broke that Mother Teresa had died in Calcutta. Normally she would get on every front page and have huge pullout tributes to her inside. But today she was an afterthought, tucked away on page 21. It will be a great Trivial Pursuit question in years to come: On what page did the *Mirror* cover Mother Teresa's death in 1997?

SATURDAY, 6 SEPTEMBER

We decided to do a first-ever special lunchtime edition of the *Mirror* in London to cover the funeral. So I went in early and sat watching it on a big screen with a few colleagues in the newsroom. The whole thing was incredibly stirring and very emotional.

Maybe it's because we're all overly tired and stressed, but from the moment Diana's gun-carriage came into view and several people in the crowd started wailing and throwing roses, I could feel myself welling up and had to go back into my office to calm down.

There were so many poignant moments, most notably those poor boys having to march down the Mall behind their dead mother. Apparently Prince Philip insisted they do this. I don't know how they handled it.

Elton John's haunting re-worked rendition of 'Candle in the Wind (Goodbye England's Rose)' reduced most of the congregation, and our newsroom, to silent tears. But it was Earl Spencer's thumping tirade from the pulpit that really got to me.

And not because I don't like the guy, but because I found myself oddly agreeing with him. The more he spoke of Diana being hunted, the more I nodded and felt a weird empathy with him.

If this was my sister, I'd have felt and said the same. And after the way the royals treated Diana when she was alive, they really have no right to object to Spencer settling a few scores with them now he's got the world watching.

Diana would have revelled in it, that's for sure.

We ran off the funeral edition and I went home to Wandsworth to a lunch party. As I walked through the door, the tears came again and I just sat crying in a chair, totally physically and emotionally exhausted, as everyone looked on in bemusement.

I have never reacted to any story like this, but then there has never been anyone in my professional life like Diana – and I guess part of my distress is also to do with the fact that there never will be again. We have lost an extraordinary creature from public life. And like millions of others in this country and around the world, I have found it all just terribly upsetting.

As Diana's hearse headed up to Althorp, where she is to be buried on a small island, I was suddenly struck by the irony of thousands of flashbulbs going off. The public, so outraged by paparazzi photographers all week, thought nothing of taking souvenir snaps of Diana's coffin themselves.

MONDAY, 8 SEPTEMBER
There is no sign of the mourning abating. Kensington Palace now has a pile of flowers heading back towards the high street, and there are swarms of people still milling around looking for some sort of answers to what happened. The conspiracy theories are still raging, and most people now seem to just assume that there was something other than an accident about her death.

Late in the afternoon Earl Spencer released photographs of himself on Diana's burial plot, which was covered in a carpet of flowers. Quite why he needed to be in the picture, only he knows.

TUESDAY, 9 SEPTEMBER
Paul Burrell's brother has spoken out about the terrible sadness of Diana's most trusted servant. 'Nobody will ever know how close Paul was to Diana, and he will never say.'

I hope the royals look after him. They have a bad track record in dispensing with servants when they have served their use.

THURSDAY, 11 SEPTEMBER
Diana's bodyguard, Trevor Rees-Jones, is still recovering after surviving the crash. But his injuries are so severe that the doctors have decided he can't be told Diana is dead yet. What a story he will have if he can remember what happened.

TUESDAY, 16 SEPTEMBER

He does remember. I had a brief chat with Fayed today and he said that Rees-Jones is awake, and having flashbacks of the crash.

'Can we have the first interview?'

Fayed was anxious. 'He needs to tell us what happened first, that is the most important thing. Then perhaps he can talk to you. But we must be careful Piers, he is in a very bad way.'

Sales of the paper collapsed yesterday as I tried to run the Diana story into a third week. Britain has got a grip at last and gone back to work.

FRIDAY, 19 SEPTEMBER

Victor Lewis-Smith has been banned from writing his column during the last fortnight, because I knew anything he wrote in the week Diana was killed would be inevitably utterly tasteless and inappropriate.

Today I thought it was safe to let him back, and his opening line was: 'The things some people will do to get a sneak preview of the Versace 1998 collection …'

SUNDAY, 28 SEPTEMBER

Dinner with the new Home Secretary, Jack Straw, in Brighton to kick off the first Labour Party conference since they swept to power. He was in ebullient form, as they all are at the moment while the honeymoon lingers long.

I like Straw because he's got a sense of humour, and a shrewd legal brain, and doesn't seem to take press criticism too seriously. As the wine flowed, I asked him what he plans to do about Myra Hindley, as he has to make a formal decision soon about whether she will ever be released from prison.

He smirked. 'Well, officially I fully intend to afford her the same rights as any other prisoner in Britain … but unofficially if you think I'm going down as the Home Secretary that released Myra Hindley, then you must be fucking joking!'

We all laughed, but I'm not sure Lord Longford would be quite so amused.

Later, I bumped into Mandelson on the seafront, and he's desperately hoping to win a seat on Labour's National Executive Committee. I think he deserves his chance after all he's done to make the party electable – and I told him we will say so in tomorrow's paper. He was in the middle of thanking me when his phone rang and he exclaimed theatrically, 'Tony, how are you?'

He winced at me, as if to suggest it's rather irritating of the Prime Minister to bother him like this. 'Yes, yes, I think you have to go big on why we may not be the biggest, but we can be the best.'

I realised they were discussing the big speech for Wednesday – Blair's first as Prime Minister.

Mandelson was being remarkably indiscreet, but then I guess what's the point of being so close to the chair of power if you can't show a few people that you are occasionally?

TUESDAY, 30 SEPTEMBER

Blair's speech electrified the audience. He gave his 'not the biggest, but the best' rhetoric the full Tony, all raised fists and slightly evangelical delivery. I can see Blair doing one of those US preacher-style tours one day – the ones that end with 'I have sinned – now give me your cash, O believers.'

Later we had lunch with him and Cherie, our annual *Mirror* conference tradition.

It was all going quite well until the issue came up of Blair's pay rise, or lack of it. The *Mirror* had run a campaign to stop him and the Cabinet awarding themselves big salary hikes, and they had eventually backed down.

'It's alright for you,' Cherie said. 'But we have had to give up our house in Islington and we can't make any investments. The pay rise would just bring the Cabinet in line with jobs of similar importance.'

'That may be true,' I said, 'but I don't think the average Mirror reader expects their first Labour Prime Minister in eighteen years to be filling his boots quite so quickly.'

Cherie scowled at me.

'Oh, come on, then,' I said, 'if you're that hard up, let me help.'

I tossed a £20 note across the table. 'Get the kids something nice for Christmas.'

Blair smiled thinly, Cherie's scowl got deeper, Montgomery's face went puce. Campbell laughed.

MONDAY, 6 OCTOBER

Mandelson lost his NEC bid, but sent me a letter of thanks anyway:

'Piers, I hope that one day, in the distant future, I will be able to stand by you in the way you stood by me last week. Peter.'

SATURDAY, 1 NOVEMBER

Alan Partridge, the genius comic creation of Steve Coogan, has been interviewed in *Radio Times* and when asked, 'Who do you most admire?' responded:

'Piers Morgan. A man who hasn't let his physical appearance impede his lifetime quest for the truth.'

I'm taking it at face value, as an enormous compliment. Just as Alan would himself.

THURSDAY, 6 NOVEMBER

Blair had another Cool Britannia party last night, which was livened up a bit by Harry Enfield getting very drunk, telling Mandelson he was 'bloody ghastly' and then marching over to Blair shouting, 'Tony, you've got to sack Mandelson, he's an awful little man.'

You have to love him.

Went to the Oxford Union tonight to debate whether the libel laws should be changed. I was with Max Clifford and Alan Rusbridger, and we were up against four libel QCs.

The Union President helped us enormously by pointing out that when the lawyers replied to their invitations, all of them had indicated they didn't mind which side they argued for. A revelation which was met with jeers and catcalls.

I went for a cheap but effective jugular assault.

'Let me introduce you to my opponents,' I said. 'The millionaire Nigel Tait, the multi-millionaires James Price and Andrew Caldecott, and the multi-multi-millionaire Charles Gray.'

The point was obvious, especially to a bunch of hard-up students.

And by the time I had pointed out that Elton John got awarded £750,000 tax free after a paper accused him of sucking prawns, while the Yorkshire Ripper's victims got £6000, it was game over.

Amusing night.

FRIDAY, 14 NOVEMBER
I called James Whitaker into my office today and said I thought it was time he gave up royal reporting.

'It's never going to be the same, James, you've been the best for a long time now, but after Diana it will never be the same. I think you should give it up. Do a weekly column for us or something, take it easy, you've worked so hard – it's time to enjoy a more leisurely working life.'

To my amazement, he burst into tears.

Not because he was upset at my decision – he agreed with me. But because he suddenly knew it was all over. That Diana was really gone, and the world he loved reporting on so much was finished in the way he knew it.

'I never realised how much I would miss her,' he said. 'Yes, me too, James,' I replied, 'me too.'

It was strangely a very poignant moment. I think all those royal hacks fell a little bit in love with Diana.

THURSDAY, 20 NOVEMBER
Jack Straw announced today that Myra Hindley will end her days behind bars. I could have told her that last month.

SATURDAY, 22 NOVEMBER
Michael Hutchence committed suicide today, found hanging in a hotel room in Australia. The Paula nightmare goes on. Poor girl. This will destroy her.

MONDAY, 24 NOVEMBER
Earl Spencer's divorce battle with his wife has kicked off in a South African court, and today we heard sensational claims that he confessed to having twelve

affairs while she was being treated in a clinic for various addictions. He also admitted being 'vicious, cruel and bullying'.

So all the time he was pontificating about my ill-treatment of her while she was sick, he was allegedly cheating on her with a dozen women. Unbelievable.

TUESDAY, 2 DECEMBER

Spencer's settled his divorce to avoid any more horrific headlines coming out.

Game, set and match, Victoria.

It's nearly Christmas, so we did a splash with an old photo of him dressed as Santa Claus and the headline HO HO HO.

My glee is unconfined.

THURSDAY, 11 DECEMBER

I was part of history today in a very weird and rather uncomfortable way. Blair had asked me to go and see him at No. 10 for a chat along with some of my political team before everyone disappears for the festive season.

When we arrived, we were taken in – very unusually – through a back door.

'What's going on?' I asked. 'Look down the corridor,' came the cryptic reply.

And so I did, and there were Martin McGuinness and Gerry Adams – making the first official visit by Sinn Fein to Downing Street.

There were hordes of media everywhere, and a distinctly tense atmosphere inside.

We were taken to wait outside Blair's office, which afforded a view straight down the long red carpet to the famous black door. And there they were, McGuinness and Adams, waiting with Blair to go out for their historic handshake. It was an amazing moment. And reminded me once again of Blair's real achievement in Northern Ireland. He has worked so hard to get to this point, rarely getting the credit he deserves. It must stick in his craw to be doing this with these men, but he will do it to force on the peace process. And that's what men of character and leadership do.

The door flew open and a hundred flashbulbs exploded for the handshake.

Ten minutes later, Blair was back in his office, striding towards me to shake *my* hand. 'Erm, got any rubber gloves, Prime Minister?'

He laughed. 'God, those two are nothing. Some of the other world leaders I've had in here recently, from some of the African states for instance, make them look like choirboys.'

Blair was on good form. 'We are getting somewhere with Ireland, slowly but surely. And McGuinness and Adams are playing their part in that. It's no good constantly looking back to the past, that was then and this is now.'

SUNDAY, 14 DECEMBER

Just when Paula Yates thought her life couldn't get any worse, Hughie Green –

that very irritating old bloke who used to present *Opportunity Knocks* in the '70s – has revealed he is her *father*.

MONDAY, 15 DECEMBER

We had a tip-off last week that William Straw, Jack's seventeen-year-old son, was into the drugs scene at a pub near the family's London home in Clapham.

I sent two of our top investigative reporters, Dawn Alford and Tanith Carey, to take a look last night. And sure enough, they found young William with a group of mates. Dawn and Tanith began drinking with them, and after some chatter about raves and drugs generally, William eventually offered to sell Dawn some cannabis.

'I'll get some at tens,' he said, implying he could get ten joints for £10. It was not the language of someone unacquainted with the drug world.

Ten minutes later, he was back with the dope and the transaction took place. 'It's good strong hash,' he said.

Today we mulled over the legal implications of what had happened.

'He's only seventeen, and therefore a minor in the eyes of the law,' said Martin. 'And the PCC for that matter.'

'But his dad's the Home Secretary for goodness' sake,' I replied, 'and he is breaking the law.'

'I know,' said Martin, 'but this is still a very difficult one because of his age.'

FRIDAY, 19 DECEMBER

One of William Straw's pub mates rang Dawn today to say there was a big party this Saturday night, where there would be 'plenty of drugs'.

'It's a spliff party,' he said. 'But there'll be harder stuff too.' He confirmed that William was going to be there.

We held another meeting.

'If we know that the law is going to be broken again, then we ought to expose this now before we allow it to happen,' said Martin, ever the lawyer.

'But how?' I replied. 'He's too young to expose.'

'Well, then we should tell Jack Straw and let him deal with it.'

'Yes, I don't think we have any choice, do we?'

Dawn wasn't happy, and I felt for her. It would have been a cracking story. But it is the right decision, I feel sure of that.

SATURDAY, 20 DECEMBER

I called Jack Straw at about 6pm. He was in his ministerial car.

'Hi, Jack, it's Piers Morgan.'

'Hi, Piers, just been to the Blackburn game, we beat West Ham three nil.'

'Oh, well done. Look, I'm afraid I have some rather bad news.'

'Right – OK.'

'Your son William is into drugs.'

'I see. Well, he is sitting next to me now. How do you know this?'

'Because he sold one of my reporters cannabis last weekend.'

'Right.'

'And we believe he is on his way to another party tonight where there will be harder drugs available.'

'I see. What do you intend to do?'

He sounded shocked, almost in disbelief.

'Well, we have thought about this a lot and decided that he is too young to expose in the paper, so we are not going to publish the story. But I thought you should know what happened, so you can deal with it as his father. And there is a possibility that our source, who is a freelance journalist, will try and go somewhere else with the tip.'

'Well, I am very grateful to you, Piers. Thank you very much. I will speak to William now and get to the bottom of all this.'

'All I would ask, Jack, is that if you decide to make this public, then you let me know.'

'Of course, I understand.'

SUNDAY, 21 DECEMBER

Jack Straw rang me at home. 'I've had a long series of chats with William since we spoke, and he has confirmed what you told me. It has obviously been a hell of a shock and we are still coming to terms with it all to be honest. I don't think we will be saying anything at this stage, but we are still talking it over as a family, and I will let you know if we decide to do so.'

I thanked him for calling. 'I know this is bloody tough, Jack. I appreciate you ringing.'

'Well, you have been fair to me.'

MONDAY, 22 DECEMBER

I was at Lord Rothermere's Christmas drinks party at Claridge's when I bumped into Alastair.

'Quite a weekend,' I said.

'Yes, not easy,' he replied. He looked a bit shifty, avoiding my eyes.

'Alastair, what's going on?'

'OK, look you may as well know, Jack's taken William to a police station this evening.'

'*What?* He can't have, he said he'd tell me if he did anything like that.'

'Well, he has thought about it, taken legal advice, and really he had no choice. He's the Home Secretary and you have told him about a crime that had been committed. He has a duty to report it.'

My mind was racing.

'But the cops leak like sieves, they will be straight on the phone to the Sun.'

'I doubt it, but I admit it's a possibility.'
'We weren't going to run it.'
'No, I know.'
'But we'll have to now.'

TUESDAY, 23 DECEMBER

I phoned Straw from my car first thing.

'I'm sorry, Piers, but I had no alternative. I took William to Kensington police station last night and he made a full and frank statement, admitting what he had done.'

'Was he arrested?'

'Yes, that's automatic.'

'Jack, we will have to run the story now – I can't take the chance of it leaking to a rival and someone thinking we suppressed it for some dodgy reason.'

'Well, you must do what you have to do, Piers.'

'I won't name him, though.'

'Thank you.'

I talked to Martin and he was adamant about the naming, 'He is seventeen, we can't.'

'But what if the Sun does?'

'They won't.'

We laid out a splash, CABINET MINISTER'S SON SELLS DRUGS TO MIRROR. It's 24 December tomorrow, normally the quietest news day imaginable. Happy Christmas everyone ...

WEDNESDAY, 24 DECEMBER

Meltdown over our story. Nobody knows who it is, and speculation is out of control very quickly. Any minister with a teenage child is under suspicion. It's chaos.

MONDAY, 29 DECEMBER

Dawn Alford went to make a statement to the police today, and promptly got arrested. It's a travesty – they still haven't collected the offending drugs, despite our repeated offers, but now seem more interested in targeting our reporter than the young villain.

And while Dawn's face is now being splashed everywhere, he still remains anonymous. After the way we tried to play it, it stinks.

I drew up a front page: IS IT FAIR MR STRAW? Everyone in Fleet Street now knows who the minister is, and they will know what we are doing.

Doesn't stop some of them calling Dawn a 'honeytrap', though, and suggesting she lured him into selling the drugs by fluttering her eyelids and wiggling her cleavage. Which is bloody insulting, considering she's been heading up our Sorted investigations column for two years.

I rang Straw to complain at 9pm and he said he knew nothing about the arrest. 'It's out of my hands, Piers,' he said.

I've just heard that the Attorney General has granted an injunction preventing anyone naming the boy or his father. It's a total farce.

THURSDAY, 1 JANUARY

Straw gave us some quotes to use anonymously. 'I want to talk about this in public, but I can't legally.'

I feel for him: he's had a week of shit now, and it's not going away.

FRIDAY, 2 JANUARY

Scottish papers, not covered by the injunction, have revealed Straw's name. And, under mounting pressure, the High Court lifted the English injunction late afternoon and he finally went public.

'Of course I have been embarrassed by this; any parent would be, given the information I received.'

Dawn had her charges dropped. And the story that was never supposed to be published has led the news for a week. Amazing.

The Mirror

Monday July 13 1998

www.mirror.co.uk

30p

DIANA AND RAINE

Our shared love for one man - her father, my husband

WORLD EXCLUSIVE – PAGES 15, 16 & 17

Arsenal win the World Cup

By LORRAINE FISHER

TWO Arsenal heroes clinched France's first World Cup triumph last night.

Gunners' midfielders Patrick Vieira and Emmanuel Petit combined to score the late goal which killed off holders Brazil's hopes and gave France a sensational 3-0 victory.

When the pair joined in lifting the Jules Rimet trophy they were celebrating a unique treble — the Premiership, FA Cup and now the World Cup.

The Arsenal team-mates sealed their hat-trick with a spectacular goal as hot favourites Brazil desperately piled on the pressure.

Vieira, brought on as a substitute, held off two Brazilians, spotted Petit charging through the midfield and slid him a left foot ball. Petit collected it on the edge of the area and slammed it into the net. All North London yelled "Magnifique".

SEE MIRROR SPORT

MAGNIFIQUE: Arsenal's Emmanuel Petit celebrates his goal with Patrick Vieira

1998

MONDAY, 5 JANUARY

Kelvin's been appointed deputy chief executive of the Mirror Group and is now in charge of the national papers. He's my boss again. Gulp.

TUESDAY, 6 JANUARY

I rang Frances Shand-Kydd to see how she was.

'Well, it's kind of you to ask. I get some sleep now, and it is good to have got Christmas and New Year out of the way. They were very hard times indeed.'

I asked how the public were reacting to Diana being buried at Althorp.

'Half the letters I get say how lovely it is that she is buried on that island and we can come and see her, and the other half say how disgusted they are that we are doing this and how awful it is to do this. All we can do is see what happens in the first year and assess things after that. I guess one of the problems is that the memorials to people like Kennedy and Marilyn are free to the public. But we have a lot of costs, and surely people don't expect us to be out of pocket. And it is my son's home and he needs to ensure he can have some privacy from the public.'

It is a terrible dilemma for them, I can see that. And they will never win.

TUESDAY, 13 JANUARY

Benjamin Pell, a very strange guy who has peddled me a few stories in the past, rang me this morning with an extraordinary offer. 'I've got all Elton John's bank statements,' he squealed in a high-pitched voice.

I knew immediately where he would have got them. His nickname in Fleet Street is 'Benji the Binman'. He goes around nicking rubbish from outside celebrities' houses, or the offices of their lawyers and accountants. Loads of papers buy his stuff, despite the seriously unethical way he acquires it.

He arrived later with sackfuls of Elton's documents, which he'd 'found' outside the office of Elton's manager, John Reid. It was amazing stuff. Extraordinary detail of Elton's lavish spending, letters exposing an ongoing feud with Richard Branson over Diana, and most damaging of all, notes from his accountants warning he was running out of cash.

Benji never charges much for these things, he's slightly potty and just does it for a laugh. So we did a quick deal and ran the Branson story as a splash. Let's see what happens.

MONDAY, 19 JANUARY

Had dinner with Kelvin. He wants us to stick it to Labour.

'They are the Government now, and their decisions are directly affecting your readers' lives. It doesn't make any sense to suck up to them any more.'

'No, but Montgomery always wants me to.'

'Fuck Montgomery, I'm running the papers now.'

WEDNESDAY, 21 JANUARY

Stephen Byers has been asked on a visit to a school what 8 times 7 is, and he said 54.

We splashed it, with a leader savaging his idiocy. Kelvin loved it.

THURSDAY, 22 JANUARY

Alastair phoned. 'Has there been a change in the atmosphere the way you did the Byers stuff. We're concerned. Well, I'm not especially, but others are. A lot of people here were pretty bothered about what you did to Jack Straw, but I wasn't. And on the Byers thing I have no problem either. But is there a change in agenda going on?'

I assured him there wasn't. 'Look, Straw was a great news story, and Byers can't do simple arithmetic. It's not an agenda issue, it's called being a newspaper.'

'Yeah, that's what I said.'

SUNDAY, 25 JANUARY

Kelvin's being a nightmare. He keeps calling the newsdesk and barking orders, ringing the back bench and changing headlines, and generally poking his nose in everywhere without any recourse to me. It's undermining me at every turn and is getting worse.

This morning he came up and bollocked the picture desk for missing something, giving them the full eye-bulging rage he used to unleash at the *Sun*, and saying they were all facing the sack.

I spent today drinking too much and working myself into a rage. It can't go on like this. I called Kelvin at 4pm. 'I can't accept you treating me like this, I'm sorry. I am the editor and you are undermining me every day. If you don't want me as editor, that's fine. Just give me a cheque and I'll go.'

He exploded: 'Perhaps I fucking will. Fucking come and fucking see me first thing in the morning.' And slammed the phone down.

I assume he's going to fire me.

MONDAY, 26 JANUARY

I was outside Kelvin's office at 8.30am. He was talking to Roger Eastoe when he saw me. 'Come in, man.'

I walked in and started to speak when he burst out laughing and said, 'Look, you're right, I'm wrong, I'm sorry.'

I couldn't believe what I was hearing.

'I just can't stop myself. All those years at the Sun and Live TV, I've been free to roam around shouting at people, and I've forgotten that I can't do it any more. But I've thought about it and I know I have to let you edit: it won't happen again.'

I went back upstairs with a new spring in my step.

We ran another load of stuff from Benjamin Pell today, centring on Elton's 'cash crisis'.

John Reid, Elton's manager, called, sounding rather distressed.

'Two stories from my office in two weeks, this is a problem for me. What axe is being ground here? This creates a major problem for me about confidentiality. I have got to find out who the source is. Someone stole this stuff and gave it you, and Elton's going mad about this.'

I said I couldn't reveal the source, but did tease him a bit by adding, 'But I can say it's so good I've even got the handwritten memo from your hotel room at the Ritz in Paris saying "Call Piers Morgan".'

There was silence.

'You have to stop this or Elton will fire me. I am warning you not to carry on.'

WEDNESDAY, 28 JANUARY

John Reid took out an injunction today banning us from any more revelations.

But we've got another big story on the go. Robin Cook has fired his secretary Anne Bullen for being 'impossible to work with', and she has now spilled the beans to us about her life with him.

Best story is how Cook upset Princess Diana by keeping her waiting for fifteen minutes when she went to talk to him at the Foreign Office about landmines. Cook took the extraordinary decision this morning to release private correspondence from Diana, which he said confirmed she wasn't upset at all.

I called Diana's office aide Jackie to ask if this was right. 'Look, he did keep her waiting fifteen minutes, and when the Princess came back here she commented on it, and obviously wasn't happy about it. But the meeting itself went well and that's what really matters.'

Kelvin rang and I asked him how he thought we should respond to Cook in light of this 'confusion'.

He dictated me a statement off the top of his head: 'The Mirror supports Tony Blair. We don't support a nasty little despot treating his secretary in this disgraceful manner. We will expose nastiness wherever it is, and if the Labour Party want to view us as their in-house paper on issues like this they are gravely mistaken.'

I toned it down a bit, but I can see our treatment towards Labour might be a little less deferential as long as Kelvin's around.

THURSDAY, 5 FEBRUARY

Blair's threatening to impose stricter privacy laws to shackle the press, and Kelvin's having none of it. 'Do a splash telling him to keep his fucking tanks off our fucking lawn,' he shouted down the phone. It's so funny hearing a *Mirror* manager talk about Blair and his team like this after years of being effectively ordered to toady to them. I did the front page up, minus the swearing, and it looked great. This is going to be amusing while it lasts.

MONDAY, 9 FEBRUARY

Kelvin's putting the heat on for a big scoop. 'We've got to lead the news, create waves,' he said. And I agree with him.

I rang Frances Shand-Kydd to see if she would do an interview. 'No, Piers, I can't. You know I can't. It's too private and too upsetting.'

TUESDAY, 10 FEBRUARY

Spoke to Mark Bolland about Charles and Camilla today. Their relationship's had to be kept out of public view again since Diana died, for fear of a backlash.

But Mark says they are planning to test the waters again soon. 'The strategy really is a bit of softly softly, test the public reaction. Will it lead to marriage? Who knows. They both want to keep it private. I don't think they do want to get married, to be honest. Having spent years being hunted and not being able to see each other publicly, they can now do that and it is very different. I think before Diana died the mood was softening anyway. But that obviously put things back a bit. He was happy to be seen having a party for her. The policy was to be honest and not furtive or deceitful. Diana's death meant that Camilla disappeared for six months. It was very hard. She doesn't want a public role though. So to some extent it has given her the excuse to go private again. Charles had so many feelings, he was so traumatised he was lost, and his main priority was his kids, to be honest.'

'How often do they see each other now?'

'Well, a lot less than they used to, because it is so hard to be seen together since what happened.'

'What's Camilla like?'

'Oh, she's sharp, straightforward, funny – very quick-witted. No long, boring jokes, good one-liners are more her forte. She is nice and warm. Without her he would not be able to cope at all, she is his best friend and integral to his life. They are fifty and have been together for so long, they're each other's best friends. They have a very strong relationship. He is basically a one-woman man, but he married the wrong one, I guess.'

All fascinating stuff from a young man who has been more responsible than anyone for making the public accept Charles and Camilla. The royals should put Mark in charge of all their PR, but they won't. There are too many factions in the various palaces with too many vested interests. They will force him out one day, because they will see he is too influential.

WEDNESDAY, 11 FEBRUARY

Having failed with Frances Shand-Kydd, I turned to another more likely target. Mohammed Al Fayed has been itching to go public about the crash and the royals. He's a hurt, deeply distressed man.

But his spokesman, Michael Cole, has been keeping a lid on him, fearing understandably that any public outburst might turn the public against him.

I heard yesterday that Cole was out of the country, so picked the phone up and seized my chance.

'Mohammed, you should go public and say what you want to say. People need to hear you.'

He needed no encouragement. 'Come round now, then.' I dropped everything and dashed round to Harrods.

I spent two hours with him, and it was as utterly explosive as I thought it would be. He said the crash was 'no accident', suggested Diana and Dodi had been murdered by British security people, tore into the royals, and generally vented his wrath.

THURSDAY, 12 FEBRUARY

Our splash this morning is leading all the news.

'Fan-fucking-tastic, matey' was Kelvin's professional and considered opinion.

Then Frances Shand-Kydd rang, in tears.

'I remember you telling me that my son made your mother cry when he banned you from Diana's funeral, and I can tell you that what you printed from Fayed made me cry today a lot so maybe that is one–all. You never told me you were in touch with him as you tried to persuade me to do an interview, and I don't like that. Fayed has never asked to speak to me, ever.'

'He's not an evil man,' I said. 'He lost a child in that crash too.'

'I don't know. You gutted me. Gutted me. Because you never told me what else you were doing. You betrayed me. It made me cry a lot. It is commercial for you, but to me I am just one pence in the big money game. You are just trying to sell papers.'

She was sobbing uncontrollably now and I felt very uncomfortable.

'Frances, do you not think he has the right to talk about his dead son? Mohammed cried in the interview, he is as upset as you are, I assure you.'

'Who cares about the boys in all this, Piers? *Who?* Tell your mother I cry too. The trust I had in you has gone. I spoke to you the day before you did this and you didn't tell me what else you were doing.'

I tried to explain, truthfully, that I hadn't spoken to Fayed until after our phone call.

But she didn't want to hear it.

'Newspapers rang at midnight to ask me about Fayed saying my daughter was murdered. And I thought, "Piers Morgan, you bastard, you never told me about this." Ask your mother if you should have told me.'

I tried to calm her down. 'Frances, I have a lot of sympathy for you, you have had a hellish life ...'

She interrupted me: 'No, I haven't, I have had a great life. But when people let me down I tell them. And you have.'

The call ended soon afterwards and I went for a drink. On my own.

I feel desperately sorry for her, yet at the same time I don't like the way she and her family have treated Fayed, and I certainly believe he is entitled to his opinion on how his own son died.

SATURDAY, 14 FEBRUARY

I spoke to Michael Cole, who is understandably very upset about the interview – and the torrent of abuse now raining down on Fayed from rival papers.

'This is precisely why I didn't want him doing it, Piers. You went behind my back and caught him at a vulnerable moment.'

'But he wanted to do this, Michael, and he would have done it soon whether you wanted him to or not. We both know that.'

'Yes, well, that's as may be, but it has made me look impotent.'

WEDNESDAY, 18 FEBRUARY

Kelvin's legendary patience has run out with our off-stone times and Jon Moorhead and Matt Kelly, my production chiefs, received a memo: 'For the umpteenth time you were late last night. I have tried to be friendly about it but you appear unable to carry out the simplest of commands. From now on the off-stone time will be 8pm. Every time you fail to hit it I will remove another 30 minutes. If we end up going off stone at 3pm in the afternoon, you will be removed!'

FRIDAY, 20 FEBRUARY

Michael Cole resigned today. 'He was a good man, but he wouldn't let me speak out,' said Mohammed when I called. 'The public have a right to know the truth.'

I was sorry for Cole, but knew there was an even bigger scoop to land: Trevor Rees-Jones.

'Trevor would be an incredible interview, Mohammed. The whole world would want to hear what he can remember.'

'Yes, and they will. As soon as he is ready. It won't be long.'

TUESDAY, 24 FEBRUARY

I took Kelvin to tea with Blair at No. 10 this afternoon. He'd had a busy day with Iraq, after the UN announced a promising new weapons inspection agreement with Saddam Hussein, and a new row over the Dome.

Kelvin was slightly less 'get your fucking tanks off our lawn' and rather more 'it's very good of you to spare the time to see me, Prime Minister', which made me laugh.

He's never quite the same beast outside his caged newsrooms.

He did, though, stress our new independence.

'It hasn't done either of us any good, all this arse-licking,' he told Blair. 'We should be more critical now you're running the country, because our readers will be more critical now your decisions affect their lives and their wallets.'

Blair agreed. 'I think that's right, and it is healthy for the Mirror to take us to task from time to time. But it would be rather unhelpful if the Mirror started to treat us like the Mail.'

Kelvin showed me his thank-you note afterwards saying: 'Dear Prime Minister, Millennium in the morning, Saddam in the afternoon, tabloid tosspots for tea ... nice meeting you.'

Fayed called in the evening to say Rees-Jones was fit enough to talk to me. 'But Piers, you must go easy on him, he has been through a terrible thing and if he gets too upset you must stop, OK?'

I rang Kelvin. 'Looks like we've got the bodyguard.'

'Fuck me, matey, that's sensational. Let me know how it goes.'

What I love about working for Kelvin is that the bollockings come and go at the same rate as the excitement, humour and praise where it's due. It creates an atmosphere of passion and danger, and out of that comes great papers.

WEDNESDAY, 25 FEBRUARY

I can't sleep. This is going to be the biggest interview I have ever done. Rees-Jones is the sole survivor of the crash that killed Diana – the biggest single news story of my career. If he talks frankly, it will lead the news around the world for days.

I got to Harrods, and Fayed was waiting to lead me up to a room where the interview would take place. Again he stressed. 'Be careful with him, he is fragile. Please be gentle.'

Then he was there, tall but frail, and his face pretty badly scarred. 'Hi, I'm Trevor.'

Fayed introduced us and left the room.

Two of his other top security men, Paul Handley-Greaves and John McNamara, stayed with us.

I placed two tape recorders on the table, and said that if he felt uncomfortable about anything he should say so and I would move on. And if he wanted to stop, I would stop. We spoke for about thirty minutes. Every second was electrifying. He said he was getting flashbacks of more and more stuff.

Most sensationally, he now remembered hearing Diana's voice after the crash, calling out Dodi's name. A former paratrooper, Rees-Jones is a tough man. But he was close to tears several times. I sensed he feels very guilty too for not preventing the crash. He was the bodyguard, they died on his watch.

I went back to the office in an over-excited haze, and headed straight to Kelvin's office.

'It's beyond sensational. This is it, the big one.'

We discussed how to promote it. 'I think we should do a TV advert with him, and use Saturday's paper to blurb it. Just announce we have him. Then run it all next week.'

Kelvin immediately agreed, and started barking orders down the phone to various commercial managers. God, it's good to see decisions taken so fast.

SATURDAY, 28 FEBRUARY

We laid out a big splash, I SURVIVED, with a sensational photo of Rees-Jones's battered, haunted face. The pages 2 and 3 spread was headlined HELLO ... I'M TREVOR. And that was the only quote I used; the rest was me talking about my amazing meeting with the man everyone wanted to meet. Together with a photo of Trevor and me sitting in between my two tape-recorders, for authenticity. It was a huge puff for Monday's paper, but I knew today's would sell like hot cakes anyway, so we would have two bites at this before we really got going.

Late afternoon though, I heard that Rees-Jones had hired a couple of lawyers in his home town of Oswestry, who were trying to get him out of our deal.

We had no contract with him, so legally no hold. But Fayed was his boss and I couldn't believe he'd walk away from him now.

At 6.20pm, Rees-Jones issued a statement saying he'd received no money for the interview, and that he had been forced to go into hiding since we boasted an 'exclusive'. The implication was clear to my rivals – he was still up for a transfer. Shit. I waited a while before calling his 'representatives'.

At 8.30pm I spoke to a man called Ian Lucas, who was clearly revelling in his new-found power.

'Ah, Mr Morgan, I wondered when you'd call. I've had all your rivals on. You're not in a strong position, are you?'

I could almost hear his smirk.

'No, Mr Lucas, I'm not. Other than that I have done a powerful interview with Trevor, with his consent, and he is still employed by Mr Fayed, who has also given me his consent. And I don't think the public will think too kindly of your client making millions out of talking about a crash he was employed to try and stop happening. Do you?'

It was a hard thing to say, but a necessary one if I was to save this scoop.

I went on, 'I sent every word to Mr Fayed for approval given the obvious sensitivity involved, and assumed Trevor had read it too. If that is not the case, I will happily send you the material too. I will also confirm he didn't get paid, split any syndication money fifty-fifty with you, and pay your costs up to ten thousand pounds.'

Lucas seems happy with what he's heard.

SUNDAY, 1 MARCH

A long, difficult day. Lucas rang early on to say the *Sun* had offered him £250,000 for Trevor to jump ship, and media groups from all round the world were queuing up to match it.

'You won't dare do that,' I said. It was time for the cosy gloves to come off.

'I will let you know,' he said.

At 6pm he rang back and said Trevor was staying with us and Fayed.

He couldn't resist a little taunt about my poetic prose. 'Isn't this copy just a little Mills and Boon?' Cheeky sod. But I wanted him to feel big and important until it was over.

Trevor signed off every word of it and faxed it back. I think the headline for tomorrow morning is one of the most dramatic in modern tabloid history: I HEARD DIANA CALL OUT FOR DODI AFTER THE CRASH.

MONDAY, 2 MARCH

Kelvin burst on to the newsroom floor like a madman and marched to the terrified newsdesk.

'*That is ... the ... greatest ... fucking ... paper ... ever ... printed!*' he screamed jubilantly. And everyone relaxed, and laughed, and even cheered.

FRIDAY, 6 MARCH

The Trevor interview has run all week, every word signed off by him personally. And we have sold, so far, an extra 1.5 million newspapers. The biggest increase with a scoop anyone can remember in Fleet Street history.

'Been a pleasure working with you, Mr Lucas.'

'Well, I am sorry we had to be so tough,' he replied.

I tried very hard not to laugh. 'No, no, fully understand.'

WEDNESDAY, 18 MARCH

Dinner at Montgomery's, with Alastair.

He was fascinating about the royals after Diana died.

'They just lost it completely,' he said. 'Didn't know what the hell to do. We had to basically take charge of everything. They ended up pretty much doing whatever we told them to. Quite amazing. If we hadn't stepped in I dread to think what might have happened. There was a real air of republicanism gathering momentum.'

I congratulated him on Blair's speech the morning after Diana died. 'He really hit a nerve, captured the public mood perfectly with all that People's Princess stuff.'

'Yes, I did, didn't I?' Alastair smirked back.

THURSDAY, 19 MARCH

Interviewed Blair at No. 10 today. And he talked for the first time about Diana's death. 'I felt then, and I feel now, a deep sense of personal loss. Diana was a remarkable individual, once met never forgotten. She was contributing an awful lot to this country and I am sure would have carried on doing so. It was, and remains, a tragedy for everyone.'

'Many people think that without your guidance, Prime Minister, the monarchy might have sunk under the pressure of those extraordinary weeks after her death.'

I was referring directly to what Alastair had said last night.

'We just had to keep a focus on the royal family, which was going through enormous grief at the time. We all had to try and keep our nerve. In a situation like that, there are no rules or training. You do what you instinctively think is right, and I am very proud of my team and the work they did.'

We walked around the garden at the back of Downing Street for part of the interview.

'Can you still really believe this is home?' I asked.

'Not really, no, but then it isn't a home in the conventional sense. It's a Tardis, full of vast rooms and offices. And once inside here you are pretty cocooned. I miss walking down the street and saying hello to people. That's the biggest change, the lack of freedom to just be normal.'

Euan had been beaten up by a few yobs at school last week, and I asked him if this kind of thing worried him.

'Of course it does, he's my son. And he gets stick because I am the Prime Minister and that's not easy for him. But he also gets a lot of good things to compensate. I remind the kids of that constantly.'

'Talking of kids, what did you make of the Jack Straw saga?'

'I think he handled it very well, actually. He told me what he planned to do about it and I agreed with him. He had to act strictly within the law, which he did. But like all parents, I thought: there but for the grace of God … It is really worrying to think of how prevalent drugs are now.'

FRIDAY, 27 MARCH

Dinner at David Montgomery's house again tonight, with Ken Bates, the Chelsea chairman. It descended, predictably, into a full-scale rant about Matthew Harding.

'Just let it go, Ken,' I finally said. 'The guy's dead, for God's sake.'

'Why should I? He tried to ruin my life, and I won't change my view just because he's dead. I won't be a hypocrite.'

No, I thought, but you will continue to be a heartless bastard.

As we traded insults, Ken's wife started crying. 'Oh, stop it, please stop it!' she said.

'Well, Matthew is dead and not here to defend himself, so I'm afraid I will have to do it for him,' I said.

The row continued even as I left in my car, with Mrs Bates sticking her head in through the open window, still weeping, pleading with me to 'understand Ken'.

Oh, I understand him alright.

THURSDAY, 2 APRIL

James Hewitt's fiancée, an Italian woman called Anna Ferretti, came to us a few days ago trying to sell some of Diana's old love letters to the man known throughout Fleet Street now as simply 'The Cad'. They were the originals, and she'd taken them from the safe of his Devon home.

In one of them Diana even begged Hewitt to 'please burn all my letters' because she knew they were dangerous in the wrong hands.

There was no way we could ever publish them. But I did see a good opportunity to get them out of Hewitt's clutches and returned to Diana's estate.

We set up a trap in which we promised Ferretti £150,000 if she handed over all the letters. She was greedy and eager, and went back to get them all from the safe.

We then handed them back to Kensington Palace yesterday – where a grateful Michael Gibbins thanked us profusely – and revealed the whole story in today's paper.

Obviously we had a read of them before we sent them back. I mean, what human being wouldn't have?

There's no doubt though that Diana loved him deeply, and was genuinely concerned he'd die in action. There's also no doubt that Hewitt would sell them as soon as he got a decent offer. They're safer at the Palace.

Just to really annoy him, we've also got Ms Ferretti's views on his prowess in bed. 'I wouldn't say he was a hopeless lover, but I used him as an egg-timer,' she said.

MONDAY, 6 APRIL

Anthea Turner, the squeaky-clean TV star, wrecked her halo image six months ago by leaving her husband Peter Powell for a married man called Grant Bovey.

Today, Bovey ditched her and went back to his wife, Della, leaving Anthea heartbroken.

I've been speaking to all three of them on and off for months now, and the reactions today were curious. Della didn't even seem that pleased to have won him back when I rang. 'I am a reasonably happy person. That sounds pathetic, so I will have to think of something better, won't I? I do feel satisfaction, but I don't want to get at Anthea. What has happened, happened and Grant has realised he has made a mistake and is coming back home. I am glad he is back. We have had a little blip in our relationship but you know, it's OK now.'

'Della, forgive me for asking this – but can you trust him?'

'Bloody hell. I don't know. It's a bit early for questions like that. The kids don't know yet, they are going to have to read about it in the papers. Peter Powell has my utmost sympathy in all this and has been very kind to me all the way. He's a great guy.'

'Anthea put everything on red and it has come up black, hasn't it?'

'Yes, I suppose it has. But I didn't want any of this to happen in the first place.'

'You must feel pleased you have stood up to a glamorous TV presenter and won back your man?'

'Yes, I am, I suppose. Everything has worked out in the end. I don't hatch plots, smoke fags and drink coffee. Things just happened.'

'Do you have a large pair of nutcrackers for Grant if he does it again?'

'Hmmm. Yes.'

Later I spoke to Grant.

'Della's delighted, Anthea's devastated. How do you feel?'

'It has been a difficult time.'

'Most wives will admire Della for fighting for her man and winning.'

'I was surprised at the way she coped with a terrible situation, yes.'

'It must have been hard to have told Anthea this?'

'It was, yes. I had feelings for Anthea or I would not have put myself or my family through this.'

'Have those feelings ended?

'I would rather not comment on that.'

'Della says she has forgiven you.'

'Good … that's a relief. I am glad she left the door open or it could have all been very different. I have gone back to the family and everything that's involved with it.'

'Peter was a very good friend of yours. Do you feel guilty?'

'We're getting into areas I would rather not discuss. He was a good friend of mine and an incredibly likeable man. He felt it was in her best interests to let her go and see what happened. He will think I have let Anthea down big time, I guess.'

'Anthea's gambled it all on you and lost.'

'Yes, I suppose she has, yeah. I feel very bad about that. I hope Anthea finds happiness and I am able to sort my own life out. We both found the future rather hard.'

Bizarre conversations, really. I doubt this is the end of this saga by any means.

I rang Peter Powell to see if he wanted to say anything.

'No, Piers, I think what is called for is some dignified silence, don't you?'

Such a nice guy. He must be hating all this.

WEDNESDAY, 8 APRIL

George Michael's been caught in a public loo in Los Angeles trying to have sex with an undercover policeman. It's not quite as good as Hugh and the Hooker, but it's pretty hilarious all the same. Problem is that most of our older readers will be revolted by it, so we tried to reflect that by doing a fairly serious splash headlined GEORGE'S SHAME and detailing his various misdemeanours. The *Sun*, when it dropped later, was funnier: ZIP ME UP BEFORE YOU GO-GO.

THURSDAY, 9 APRIL

A fax arrived from David Yelland, an ex-*Sun* colleague now at the *New York Daily Post*, addressed to me and Kelvin, saying: 'Dear lads, it appears from your front page this morning that you have forgotten how to write a headline. As an old editor mate of mine used to say, it was about as much use as a chocolate fire-guard. I felt so perturbed I had to write and pass on my concerns. The *Sun*'s splash was a stroke of genius. Raise your game, lads, raise your game. The world is watching and growing concerned. DY.'

Cheeky bastard.

Kelvin and I concurred that he must be on some form of medication.

TUESDAY, 12 MAY

Richard Desmond, owner of *OK!* magazine, is upset because our City Slickers have called him a 'porn publisher' in their column. It seems a fair enough description, given that he owns a huge stable of porn mags including *Asian Babes*. But he is livid:

> It may be a bit of fun but we will both need each other over the next 30 years and those words 'Porn Publisher' do not reflect well on my publish-ing company and the people within it. If you want to carry on getting stuff from *OK!* like the Boveys etc will you please not call me a pornographer and exchange it for publisher or businessman. Pornography is illegal in this country and my company is certainly very legal!

I replied:

> My apologies for the Slicker boys, they are very naughty and frankly a public flogging is too good for them. I hugely admire your success with *OK!*, and will have a word with them to ensure that if they plan to insult you in future they do so in a more respectful way.

Bit odd, though: I mean, anyone that publishes titles like *Asian Babes* has to admit to being a porn baron – don't they? Why be embarrassed by it?

THURSDAY, 14 MAY

Bill Clinton's coming to town next week and Kevin Maguire, our political editor, had the good idea of asking him to write an article for the *Mirror* urging the people of Ulster to vote 'Yes' in the historic poll on the Irish settlement this Friday. He put it to Alastair Campbell, who said it was a great idea, but the great man didn't have time to knock it out himself, so could Kevin write it for Clinton and they'd get it signed off by him? Maguire transported himself into the mind of the President, sent it to Campbell, who sent it on to Clinton's spin doctor Mike McCurry, who gave us the thumbs-up. 'My trip was one of the high-points of my presidency and my life,' sighed Clinton/Maguire. 'Most of all, I remembered the faces of the school children. I hope all of those voting on Friday will have the children of Northern Ireland in mind when they choose … What dreams will those children realise if you seize the chance for peace and vote "Yes"?' We laid it all out as a big *Mirror* exclusive and I congratulated Kevin on a clever idea, well executed.

Then the *Sun* dropped at 9pm with the headline PRESIDENT WRITES FOR THE SUN – SAY YES TO PEACE. It was *our* article, written by *my* political editor. I phoned Campbell and screamed at him, 'What the fuck are you doing, you devious little turd?'

He pretended he didn't know what I was talking about.

'Honestly, I've no idea how they got it,' he simpered.

I carried on shouting. 'Yeah, right, you lying slimeball.'

More profanities spilled from my lips until he silenced me with the immortal confession: 'OK, Piers, I did it – but please understand that I did it for peace.'

I couldn't believe what I was hearing. 'For peace, for *peace*? You treacherous bastard, Campbell, you'll have no peace from us now, that's for sure.' I was shaking with blind rage. How could he do this to us, his supposed great newspaper friend? Then I remembered that Rupert Murdoch was in town. And it all fell into place.

I chucked Clinton's article out of the paper, and the next day's TV news led on 'the *Sun*'s great scoop'. They've been in power less than a month and already stiffed us to help the *Sun*.

FRIDAY, 15 MAY

Frank Sinatra died last night and I told the team I wanted the best coverage of any paper. 'Just clear the adverts and go mad. He was the greatest.'

They did a terrific job, and we just had the front page left to do. It's always a tricky decision to choose the picture for a legend who has died. Do you go for a recent image, or one of them in their prime? I always prefer the latter: let the public remember them as they should be remembered.

I opted for a photo of Sinatra from his Capitol Records days, arguably his best musically, in a smart blue suit and trilby. Below it I ran my favourite, and now very appropriate, Sinatra quote: 'YOU GOTTA LOVE LIVING BABY, 'COS DYING'S A PAIN IN THE ASS.'

When the other papers dropped, it was obvious that we'd creamed them.

THURSDAY, 28 MAY

There are suggestions in the papers that German media firm Axel Springer are going to buy the *Mirror*. So Kelvin sent round some useful phrases for us all the memorise:

1) When do I have to vacate the room? *Bis wann muss ich das Zimmer raumen?*
2) May I use your phone? *Kann ich lhr Telefon benutzen?*
3) Is this the road to Munich? *Ist dies die Strasse nach Munchen?*
4) Can I have a receipt? *Kann ich eine Quittung bekommen?*
5) Achtung! Surrender ... er, Piers can help with that one when they sack him.

WEDNESDAY, 3 JUNE

Stuart Higgins 'resigned' today, and David Yelland has been appointed *Sun* editor. This should be fun ...

MONDAY, 8 JUNE

Lots of weird rumours swept the building that Kelvin was quitting. It sounded absurd to me, given that things were going so well.

Eventually I called and asked him direct.

'Absolute bollocks,' he insisted. 'Honestly, I'd tell you if was true.'

I repeated this categoric denial confidently to the back bench.

An hour later it was formally announced that he's leaving to run Talk Radio. He rang, apologetic, but cackling, 'Sorry, matey, but I couldn't say anything earlier. You can't trust journalists, can you?'

It will be a massive loss to the *Mirror*. Kelvin and I had developed a great working relationship recently and I have felt inspired to work harder, and be more creative, than I have done for years.

FRIDAY, 19 JUNE

I got an odd call from El Vino, the famous Fleet Street bar, today, asking if I really wanted so much wine.

'What wine?' I said.

'The wine you ordered by fax. Only it's the fourth case in two weeks and it seems a bit unusual as you haven't ordered from us before.'

'I don't know what on earth you're talking about, sorry.'

They faxed me my supposed 'order letter' and it was a fake. Some cheeky sod has been ordering loads of wine from El Vino and passing himself off as me.

I called the police, and a trap was set. Sure enough, the villain turned up at El Vino claiming to be my driver.

'Got Mr Morgan's wine?' he said. Seconds later the cuffs were applied.

They must have thought I had a serious booze problem.

SUNDAY, 5 JULY

Liz Murdoch threw a huge party last night at her new home in Kingston, Surrey. There were dozens of stars and the hospitality was impressively lavish.

Celebrities may have abounded, but there was only one superstar, and we all felt the same. Jack Nicholson radiates the kind of celebrity fever that only he, Diana and Muhammad Ali have infected a party with, and in the flesh he didn't disappoint. He sat next to Fergie, a table away from mine, and all I could hear was The Joker's wicked laugh filling the air, and everyone roaring with laughter. Not because they were fawning to a big star, but because he is just naturally very, very funny. Later, the marquee had virtually emptied and I was talking to the Duchess – who couldn't stop raving about Jack – when in he stumbled, very pissed, shirt open to his navel, sweating like the proverbial pig and still wearing those shades. 'Where's that chick Ulrika?' he cried.

Ms Jonsson was nowhere to be seen, but I suspected she wouldn't be that hard for Jack to locate later. I asked Fergie how I could get him to talk to me. 'Just tell him you're something interesting like a bank robber,' she said; 'don't tell him you're a journalist, for God's sake.'

I walked over to a clearly disorientated Nicholson. 'Hey, Jack!'

He peered up, dejected to find me standing before him, not Ulrika.

'Yeah?'

I swallowed deeply. 'Fergie says if I tell you I'm a bank robber, you'll talk to me.' Silence.

'She said that?' More silence. 'Well, you know what they say about bank robbers?'

I was about to get my own pearl of Jack magic and could barely contain my excitement. 'No.'

More silence, then that huge grin lit up the marquee. 'You never catch a good one. See ya later, pal.'

MONDAY, 6 JULY

Richard Branson's sold his new autobiography to the *Sun* to serialise, after I thought we had it in the bag. I've been spitting blood about it, because he's incredibly popular and his story will definitely sell loads of papers. I let his right-hand man Will Whitehorn know my feelings in no uncertain terms last night. Today Branson faxed me himself:

> Will tells me your reaction to being told that you had not won the rights to serialise my autobiography was to say you had been 'stitched up', that it was 'incredibly important to the *Mirror*', and that you 'are not going to take this lying down'. Subsequently I have been told by others that you are planning to enact some sort of revenge on me for this decision.
>
> Soon after we put the autobiography up for sale I realised I could end up with more enemies than friends. I had the publishers of two papers and

the editors of five ring me personally to try and persuade me that their particular paper was the right one. Although you and I didn't speak I knew how keen you were and was tempted with the bid you put up. But with outside shareholders owning 50 per cent of Virgin Books we decided that the correct way was to make a judgement on pure commercial grounds.

I appreciate that you might be disappointed but I'm not sure what I've done to warrant the kind of reaction to our decision (if true). We've had a good, if not particularly close, relationship with the *Mirror* since you've been editor and I see no reason why it can't be developed over the coming years.

I thought long and hard about a response. Part of me wants to run a damning exposé of the real Branson to vent my wrath and spoil the *Sun*'s exclusive. But the truth is that I like and admire the guy, and there wouldn't be much to expose anyway.

I wrote back:

In answer to your fax, I would say:

1) I do feel we got stitched up because we were definitely given a guarantee we'd got the book the night before it suddenly disappeared from our grasp.
2) It was incredibly important to the *Mirror* because, as I'm sure you can imagine, I want to give the *Sun*'s new editor a good kicking and this would have helped.
3) I am not going to take this lying down because a) it's uncomfortable editing from that position and b) you would think less of me if I simply shrugged my shoulders and said: 'Oh well, better luck next time.'
4) I have no idea who thinks I am planning to 'enact some revenge' although I can imagine my friends at the *Sun* telling you that. The truth is that we will defend our commercial position in the same way you would if British Airways had just done you up like a kipper.

However, I am sure my fury can be comfortably allayed by a month in Necker, permanent lifetime upgrades for all my friends and family to the Caribbean (and my secretary as well), free Virgin pension, unlimited CDs and a personal assurance I will never have to travel on one of your trains. Alternatively you can take me out for a lavish dinner and give me something else for the *Mirror*.

Piers.

TUESDAY, 7 JULY

Met Victor Blank, the Mirror Group's new chairman, today. Seems a very charming and intelligent guy. Got a reputation for being pretty ruthless in business though. Be interesting to see how he gets on with Montgomery.

WEDNESDAY, 8 JULY

Branson called this morning. 'Let me buy you dinner.'

Later in the evening, we heard the *Sun* had some big exclusive that Prince William was going to meet Camilla for the first time. I rang Sandy Henney in the Palace press office. She sounded jittery, and said she'd have to put me on hold. Which she did, for 45 minutes, occasionally coming back on the line to say she was still trying to find out what was going on. I knew exactly what was going on. She'd agreed to give the *Sun* the scoop and was keeping me at bay until they told her it was too late for us to get it in our first edition.

'What *exactly* are you asking me?' she kept saying, presumably so she could say afterwards that I didn't have the right story.

I held the presses, and when she eventually confirmed the story past 10pm, we crashed it straight into the first edition.

I then shouted abuse at her for five minutes and said I would make it my personal business to return the 'favour'. She's totally out of her depth there. You can't behave like this if you work for the royals.

MONDAY, 13 JULY

France won the World Cup last night, and their third and last goal against Brazil was scored by Emmanuel Petit, from a pass by Patrick Vieira. Two Arsenal boys making history.

I called the circulation department.

'Can we do a special run just for North London?'

'Erm, well, yes, probably. Why?'

'Never you mind, just an idea.'

I went to the back bench and got them to put the picture of Petit and Vieira on a front page lay-out. Then inserted the headline ARSENAL WIN THE WORLD CUP.

Everyone looked at me like I'd gone stark raving bonkers.

'It's OK, it's only going to North London,' I explained.

The circulation manager still wasn't happy.

'But some copies will slip into places like Tottenham and West Ham ... that would be a disaster.'

'Oh, I don't know, it will be quite funny.'

Forty thousand copies of the special edition went out. It has been a shocking, and glorious, abuse of my position.

MONDAY, 27 JULY

Tea with Gordon Brown at the Treasury. He's just got back from addressing Murdoch's News International hierarchy in Sun Valley – where he made it clear we will not rule out entry into the euro.

'That must have gone down well,' I laughed.

'Well, it would be crazy to say we're never going in. It's not going to happen in the near future, but if you asked me if I thought we'd still be out of it in ten years' time I'd say that is very unlikely. It's inevitable we will join the euro at some stage, but it has to be when it is in the economic interests of this country. I won't gamble.'

Peter Mandelson is tipped to get a top Cabinet job today, and I'd been told that Gordon broke the good news to him personally yesterday afternoon.

'Peter is an able man and would be an asset in any Cabinet,' was all he'd say, with a smile that suggested a rather different thought pattern.

FRIDAY, 28 AUGUST

I've been having trouble with some weird virus that won't go away, and eventually went into hospital today for an exploratory investigation to see what it might be. I woke from the op in the recovery room feeling very groggy.

'Hello, Mr Morgan. Feeling better?' said some doctor standing over me.

I groaned.

'We hope you don't mind, but we took some photographs of you lying naked to sell to the Sun.'

He and his colleagues fell about laughing.

Honestly, the level of invasion of privacy in this country is out of control.

MONDAY, 7 SEPTEMBER

Rupert Murdoch is trying to buy Manchester United. Kelvin told me that he'd first had the chance years ago, when it would have cost him just £10 million. Now Sky are poised to bid nearly £600 million.

The consequences for the *Mirror* are obvious and awful.

The *Sun* would get all the access they need to Britain's biggest club and we'd get squeezed out.

'We've got to stop this somehow,' I said in conference, to general agreement.

I did up a front page of Murdoch pointing his finger, coloured his face bright red, added a couple of horns, made his ears like Spock from *Star Trek* and did a splash: 'RED DEVIL – Will the only man in Britain who thinks Rupert Murdoch should own Manchester United please raise his right index finger now ...'

WEDNESDAY, 9 SEPTEMBER

Sky gave a press conference today to discuss their acquisition of Manchester United. When I saw the line-up on TV, a mischievous thought came to me. I called in the news editor and said: 'Right, their chief executive Mark Booth's going to take questions, by the look of it. He's a big chunky American who I bet knows nothing about football. If we get the chance, ask him who plays left back for United.'

The instructions were instantly forwarded to our man at the conference. We then watched in the office as questions started and our guy got his chance.

'Mr Booth, I'm from the Daily Mirror. Can you tell me who plays left back for Manchester United, please?'

Vic Wakeling, the brilliant boss of Sky Sports, and a diehard Red who could tell you who played left back in the 1910 Cup Final, looked horrified sitting next to his boss. He realised this was potential disaster.

Booth looked bemused, then quizzical, then eventually spluttered. 'Er, I'll pass that on. The football side and naming players is not my area of expertise.'

The room exploded with laughter, as did our newsroom. This wasn't a car crash moment, it was a full M5 pile-up.

Wakeling, who took the question on as requested, just said wearily: 'Sir Alex names the team.' We'd ruined their whole day. Our man pursued Booth afterwards and got him to confess that he's never even seen United play. I cleared the front page for our question and his answer with a big photo of him. The imagery is devastating. Big fat Yank who knows nothing about football wants to buy United. Not good.

Later Booth revealed that Murdoch had liked our 'Red Devil' page.

'He chuckled about it, signed it and gave it to me to hang on my wall.'

I reckon Booth will be hanging next to it soon.

FRIDAY, 11 SEPTEMBER

The long-awaited Kenneth Starr report into Bill Clinton's affair with White House intern Monica Lewinsky was published today and was utterly sensational. My favourite bits involved their imaginative use of a cigar during their 'I did not have sex with that woman' encounters, and the revelation that Monica gave Bill oral pleasure while he spoke to congressmen on the phone. What a guy.

MONDAY, 14 SEPTEMBER

Had dinner tonight with Richard Branson at his favourite restaurant, a great little Greek place called Halepi, in Notting Hill.

He was a bit diffident to start with, and seemed tired and distracted. I'd heard he could be quite shy in one-to-one situations, which seems extraordinary given his showmanship, but I saw that side of him tonight, definitely.

After a couple of drinks he relaxed, though, and I felt emboldened enough to make a dramatic proposal.

'Why don't you buy the Mirror?'

He nearly choked on his kebab.

'Er ... well ... why should I do that?'

'Because you're a stinking rich left-wing entrepreneur – and the Mirror needs someone like you to compete properly. You'd also have a ball owning a newspaper, it's made for someone like you.'

'But the other papers would start attacking Virgin brands if I bought the Mirror. We do lots of deals with the press and they would all stop.'

'Well, we still carry adverts and promotions for Sky.'

He thought for a second.

'Yes, good point. But wouldn't they go after me personally?'

'No chance, all the owners look after each other. That's the beauty of being a newspaper owner.'

'How much would it cost me?'

'Bugger all, the share price is ridiculously low at the moment. You could buy it and sell it in three years' time if you wanted to and make a lot of money. Now's the time – these chances don't come very often.'

'OK, you've got me interested.'

I left the restaurant on a high. Branson was definitely nibbling, and he would be a brilliant *Mirror* owner. He's got the money, likes taking risks, wouldn't be afraid to take on the Government.

TUESDAY, 15 SEPTEMBER

Will Whitehorn called.

'You've got him going with this Mirror idea. But I don't think he should do it. Virgin would get hammered everywhere if he ran a paper.'

'No it wouldn't, Will,' I stressed again. 'It doesn't work like that.'

'It did with Maxwell.'

'Only after he died, and then Richard's not going to have to worry too much, is he?'

'Well, I am going to tell him not to do it. Just thought you should know.'

'OK, I respect that, but it's a big opportunity.'

WEDNESDAY, 16 SEPTEMBER

A reader writes: 'Dear Mr Morgan, you trot out the same old trash week after week, it's an insult to anyone with six brain cells. You are a brown-nosed, jumped-up shit who should be fucked with a telegraph pole on a regular basis. Yours sincerely, Michael Flahety, Walsall.'

The really abusive ones always include their name and address.

SATURDAY, 19 SEPTEMBER

Ian Botham invited me and my sports editor, Des Kelly, to dinner at Bibendum last night to discuss the renewal of his contract.

We found him guzzling champagne in the oyster bar. 'Right boys, let's have a bit more of this, then we'll get stuck into some good wine.'

Half an hour later he'd ordered four *magnums*.

At 3am, after six hours of hilarious anecdotes and £700 worth of booze, Botham pulled out a piece of paper and got me to sign it.

His lawyer, Naynesh Desai, called this afternoon. 'Very generous of you, Piers, doubling Ian's deal like that.'

TUESDAY, 22 SEPTEMBER

I submitted my expense claim for £760 for dinner with Botham, with a note explaining I'd promised him a slap-up meal when we renewed his contract.

Roger Eastoe, my hard-working and likeable MD, sent a memo up: 'I sincerely hope you won't be making too many promises like this in the future to other contributors. It must be a pleasure having dinner with you, it's a great pity we haven't got round to it yet.'

Wait until he sees the new Botham contract …

FRIDAY, 25 SEPTEMBER

We ran a story last week about Prince Harry scoring two goals at Eton against a rival school. The headmaster, John Lewis, has written to complain that we have breached the agreement not to do this kind of thing.

> This has all the makings of a wedge with a very thick end. It's not that the story was hostile or that intrusive. But if that story is OK, then what story is not? I don't want Harry's arrival at Eton to mark the start of a new season of what antipodeans call 'open slather' – especially at a time when some hard and necessary lessons about infringing privacy appear to have been learned.

I liked his approach, and replied in the same spirit. But made what I thought were a few pertinent points:

> If we'd revealed Harry had a girlfriend or was caught behind the bike sheds having a crafty fag, then I'd understand the concern. But saying he's the new Gary Lineker doesn't seem too offensive, especially as his goals were watched by a large crowd of strangers who would all have gone straight home and told everyone.

This debate will run and run. There's a fine line between protecting those boys, and over-protecting them.

SUNDAY, 27 SEPTEMBER

I'm up at the Labour Party conference in Blackpool. Now Brendon has moved to the Sunday Mirror as editor, Tina Weaver is my new deputy. Tina rang to say we'd got a story about Cherie allegedly getting free clothes from the trendy designer Burberry. I told her to put it to Fiona Millar, Alastair's partner and Cherie's 'fixer', which she did, only to get a volley of abuse.

'Look, I am telling you this story is not true. Are you calling the Prime Minister's wife a liar?'

Half an hour later I got a fax from Alastair:

1) We get plagued by companies claiming to be suppliers of free clothes to Cherie. 2) If she denies it, you can be assured it is not true. 3) Her

view of your paper is already very low because of the way, gratuitously, you involved Euan in a story which had nothing to do with him, illustrated by an agency picture every editor agreed not to use when it was taken some time ago.

Then David Montgomery called to say he had been 'personally assured' the story was untrue, and we were to pull it.

MONDAY, 28 SEPTEMBER

Extraordinary scenes at the *Mirror* stand inside the conference centre when Cherie stormed up and started shouting, 'Your staff called me a liar yesterday – it's disgraceful.' And stayed there ranting away for a few minutes to our startled staff.

WEDNESDAY, 30 SEPTEMBER

Lunch with the Blairs in the Imperial Hotel, Blackpool. It was already a rather tense atmosphere, with Cherie still fuming about our 'treachery'.

I didn't endear myself any more to her by asking, 'So, Cherie, if hypothetically Tony had a fling with a Downing Street intern, do you think you could stand by him like Hillary has Bill?'

It was deliberately provocative, I suppose, and she took dreadful offence – scowling at me, and saying, 'I hardly think that is an appropriate question.'

Things went from bad to worse.

To my astonishment, David Montgomery changed his usual Chief Executive script to launch what can only be described as a scathing attack on the *Mirror*, accusing us of being 'backward-looking, cynical and negative'. I could hardly believe what I was hearing. Particularly as our front page this morning could only be described as very positive.

Alastair nodded away throughout it all, in a way that suggested he knew in advance what Montgomery was going to say. Blair himself just looked rather taken aback and uncomfortable. It was like being at a family Christmas when a mad uncle suddenly tells everyone exactly what he really thinks of them. Lots of looking at the floor and ceiling.

When Montgomery had finished, I just turned to him and asked, 'Did Alastair write that for you, David?' Which merely added to the appalling atmosphere. I was absolutely raging by the time he and the Blairs had gone. What the hell did he think he was doing, dumping on his own papers in front of the Prime Minister. To me it seemed such a serious matter that I spent the afternoon considering my position. Montgomery, alerted to this by someone, rang to explain that he had only been 'trying to start a useful debate'. I said it had not been the right time or place to do that and I was very upset by the public criticism. Montgomery doesn't do confrontation very well, and just started stammering and stuttering until I said I had to go. By evening everyone was talking about it at Conference and I was even getting calls asking if I'm going to resign. Whatever possessed him?

THURSDAY, 1 OCTOBER

Launch party for Murdoch's new merged TV company, BSkyB, at Battersea power station. It was not a great success, mainly because none of the screens worked properly when the big switch-on came. Matthew Freud, who organised it all, took it rather badly, drinking very quickly and very heavily to numb the shock of his cock-up, then slumping into a corner with his head in his heads, gurgling, 'I'm fucking finished.'

Liz Murdoch dragged me over to her dad to force him to talk to me for the first time since I quit. 'Hi, Piers, how are you?' he said, amiably. We chatted for a few minutes and there was no trace of bitterness – nor offers of any jobs, it has to be said. There were, though, plenty of hacks around to ensure that the encounter gets reported, which might just give Montgomery something to think about next time he wants to humiliate me in front of Blair.

FRIDAY, 2 OCTOBER

The *Mail* have overtaken our circulation. It's not rocket science, they just have four times as much money to spend on promotions.

But Paul Dacre is undeniably a very good editor, and I dropped him a line to congratulate him and warn that we'd be back on top soon.

'What a nice letter, your surrender is gracefully accepted,' he replied. 'As for your determination to get ahead of us again – even in his last demented days in the bunker, Hitler dreamed of his 1000-year Reich!'

WEDNESDAY, 7 OCTOBER

Victor Lewis-Smith politely declined my invitation to come to a lunch for all my columnists at the Mirabelle next month. 'I can't think of anything better than sitting down between James Whitaker and Tony Parsons and discussing philosophy. Sadly I was knocked down and killed last week and therefore am unable to attend.'

TUESDAY, 27 OCTOBER

Ron Davies, a Cabinet minister, has quit after a curious late-night incident on Clapham Common involving a young gay man. All the papers have had a field day.

Mandelson rang to urge restraint.

'Nobody knows the truth yet at Number Ten. Unless you were there, you won't. The public will be more sympathetic than you lot about him.'

'Why doesn't he just tell the truth?' I asked.

His reply was fascinating. 'Why does he need to?'

I paused for this to sink in, and he hurriedly added, 'He shouldn't lie, I agree. If he hadn't resigned, he would have been in a better position. Being a minister requires consistently high quality of judgement and behaviour above and beyond being an MP.

'He was screwed up by what happened to him as a kid and people will feel sorry for him as a result. I think this will end with it going away and nobody knowing the full truth.

'People will think he was a stupid clot who fucked up and paid the price. He has lost his seat in the Cabinet for God's sake – it's a disaster for him.

'I think if you have a lapse of judgement you leave the Cabinet, if you break the law you have to leave Parliament. Have a heart with him, he is deeply, deeply embarrassed and bruised. Don't cross that line into hounding the guy unnecessarily. Can you imagine what he's going through, terrible.'

Mandelson was outed on *Newsnight* as being gay by Matthew Parris last week, and he's still seething.

'I don't want to talk about Parris. People who are gay should be treated the same as if they were straight. We don't ask straight MPs about their sexuality for the sake of it. If you are Gordon Brown trailing around with a floozy on your arm orchestrated by Charlie Whelan for the cameras then fair enough, but why otherwise? My private life is my private life until or if it ever impinges on my public duties – then I will discuss it.'

I laughed. 'You're not the third man in the Ron story, then?'

'No, darling.'

Alastair called later to endorse the 'leave off Ron' sentiment.

'Focus groups are telling us that the press should leave the guy alone,' he said, 'but my real anger is towards the police for leaking it. Nobody knows what's true. There are only so many times you can ask a guy what the truth is, with him saying he won't lay himself open. He said he was a victim of crime, made a huge lapse of judgement and it has cost him his job. And I think he wants to spare himself having to reveal every spit and fart of his sexuality to the public.'

'Well,' I replied, 'I think the public are getting fed up with political sex scandals and don't really care any more.'

He laughed: 'I fucking hope so, because we've got some fucking belters coming down the track ... The tragic thing is we had him hidden away and it was very hard to talk to him on the phone because his twelve-year-old daughter was there with him and I really felt for him. I ended up feeling very, very sorry for him; he is a very sad, lonely kind of guy. I think Diana has changed a lot of this – changed the way the public view this kind of hounding, whatever the person has done.'

FRIDAY, 13 NOVEMBER

A big night – Charles's 50th birthday party at Buckingham Palace.

I was standing with David Yelland when Prince Philip loomed into sight and marched towards us. He got within a few feet, scrawled his eyes up to read our name-tags, looked none the wiser and barked, 'Who are you, then?' in that brusque, bloody rude way we've all come to know and love.

'Well, sir,' I replied, 'I'm afraid you are currently surrounded by the tabloid press.' He stared at me as though I had literally just informed him I'd like the fried corgi for tea, please. A defiant disgust radiated from every craggy nostril, and he said not a word before turning abruptly to his left and marching off as fast as he'd arrived.

As he passed Colin Myler, who's been editing of the *Sunday Mirror* while Brendon's been on leave, Philip looked back at me and sneered, 'God, you just can't tell from the outside, can you?'

His son was much nicer. Given all the crap I've thrown at him over the years, Charles was remarkably friendly, and utterly charming. I wished him a very happy birthday and he said he's really pleased about his new official website, 'which is getting thousands of … what do you call them? "Hits"?' 'That's excellent, sir. We're getting just as big a response to our own unofficial Camilla website.'

He looked bemused. 'Your what, sorry?'

'Oh, we set up a tribute site to Mrs Parker-Bowles on the Mirror, sir, and it's proving rather popular.'

He laughed, still vaguely incredulous.

'Is it? Good, good.'

'Yes, sir, we have invited readers to pay their own tributes to her, and some are even being quite complimentary.'

Charles looked at me in bewilderment, then thanked me again and shuffled off for his next meaningless exchange with someone he'd rather shoot himself than talk to.

Right behind him came his grandmother, the Queen Mother, who is absolutely tiny and moves very, very slowly – like a little shrew walking through a sea of treacle.

She was surrounded by an extensive fawning entourage, and just seemed to be flicking that famous grin and handwave at anyone she passed, without saying much.

I decide to engage her in conversation, on the basis that it might be the last chance I ever get. 'Good evening, your majesty,' I said, as her aides rushed to create a human barrier against this tabloid monster.

'I am Piers Morgan, editor of the Daily Mirror, and it is a great pleasure to meet you.' She shook my hand and replied: 'Ah, the Daily Mirror, we always had it in the nursery. Charles loved Pip, Squeak and Wilfred, you see.'

I had no idea what she was talking about. 'Yes of course, ma'am, very popular, old Pip, Squeak and Wilfred.'

A voice from behind whispered, 'It was a cartoon strip, years ago.' 'We don't carry it any more, sadly,' I said, now more comfortable with the conversational thread.

'Oh, that's a pity,' she replied. 'It was very amusing. Charles used to laugh and laugh.'

She is an amazing old bird, frail of body but sharp as razor blades in the mind. And when she fixes you with that glare, as she did when I repeated my line about Camilla's website, you can see the blue-blooded steel flashing behind the procession-line veneer.

Later, I stopped the Queen as she walked past, and introduced myself. She stared at me with a slightly unnerving look.

'Oh, yes, how do you do?' she said. 'Are you enjoying the party?' Her eyes bored into me with a mixture of irritation and pity.

'Yes, your majesty, it's a marvellous occasion. And very nice of you to honour Prince Charles in such a lovely way.'

She couldn't have looked less keen on prolonging this encounter if I'd shouted 'Vive la république' at her. 'Yes, it's all gone very well, hasn't it?' Silence. An embarrassingly long silence. And then she moved on, unsmiling and ice-cold. She has none of the warmth of her mother or son, but is not quite as rude as her husband. As I left, I nipped into the cloakroom and nicked some loo paper. There wasn't a lot left. I reckon I wasn't the first to take a little souvenir home.

MONDAY, 21 DECEMBER

I was preparing to leave the office to head off for the *Mirror* executives' Christmas party, when my political team said there were rumours of a 'huge' scandal on Peter Mandelson about to break in the *Guardian*.

I called his aide, Benjamin Wegg-Prosser, to find out what was going. He said he would call back, but in fact Mandelson did himself.

By now I knew it involved a story from Paul Routledge's new book, about Mandelson borrowing over £378,000 from fellow minister Geoffrey Robinson to buy a house.

I called Paul and he was furious, claiming the *Guardian* had 'nicked' his manuscript.

This was a matter for another day. By any yardstick the home loan revelation was sensational. But Mandelson was either oblivious to what was engulfing him, or in denial.

'There's no story, no scandal,' he insisted robotically. And then talked me through every detail of the story for half an hour. I was stunned by what I was hearing.

'But Peter, that's a huge amount of money – what were you thinking?'

'Geoffrey is a friend, there is nothing wrong in a friend lending you money.'

'But he's a fellow minister and you haven't declared it.'

'I have done nothing improper.'

Wegg-Prosser rang back a few minutes later.

'All OK?'

'Not really, Ben. This stinks. Out of interest, did Peter declare the loan to the building society when he applied for the mortgage?'

There was a brief silence. 'I'm sure he did. It's all completely above board.'

'Well if he didn't, that's an offence.'

'Right, OK. I will get back to you.'

Later Wegg-Prosser admitted there were possible 'doubts' about the answer to the question I'd asked. If he didn't declare it, he's gone. Even if he did, he's probably gone.

What a fool.

We wiped out the first three pages for the scandal, slapped 'world exclusive' all over it, and had everything the *Guardian* had for nothing.

I then went to the Apollonia Taverna off Tottenham Court Road to get regally drunk on retsina, throw a few plates and practise my belly-dancing. At 3.30am, I was dancing on a table with several colleagues, singing Abba songs, and sweating neat ouzo. At that point my deputy editor Tina tapped me on the shoulder and asked, 'Piers, aren't you seeing Blair in the morning?'

Christ, yes, I was. In six hours to be precise.

I could barely speak or walk. This was going to be interesting. Tina got me a cab and I went straight home.

TUESDAY, 22 DECEMBER

I woke feeling horrendous. A headache from Hades, and severe nausea. Not the best conditions to meet the Prime Minister.

My driver was appalled by the sight that greeted him.

'Bleeding hell, mate, how bad do *you* look?'

'Number Ten, please, quickly – and quietly.'

I lay back in my seat with stars still flashing in my eyes and a debilitating dizziness refusing to relent.

I was also trying hard to resist the overwhelming urge to vomit.

Alastair met me at the door. 'Christ, what's happened to you?'

'Oh, just gone down with bloody flu.'

'Great, come to infect us all with it, have you?'

I couldn't even laugh, but my excuse seemed to have worked.

Blair looked even worse than me when I went into his office. He'd obviously been up most of the night with this Mandelson business.

'Not great, is it?' I remarked, referring to Mandelson, not my appearance.

'No. It's not.'

I thought Blair was going to cry. Campbell, too, seemed in a bad way. Mandelson is one of their top guys, a New Labour architect, a great mate, teetering on the verge of professional and personal collapse.

'Can he survive?'

Campbell shook his head. 'Hard to say at the moment, but it's a massive blow.'

'Did you know about the loan?'

'No, we didn't,' said Blair firmly. And I believed him.

'But didn't his house seem a bit grand for someone on his money?'

Mandelson quits the Cabinet after that home loan scandal.
The architect of New Labour brought down, ironically, by a house.

'I've only been there once,' Blair replied, 'and it didn't seem unusually lavish or anything. Just can't understand it.'

I switched the conversation to Iraq – we've been bombing Saddam with the Americans for the past few days in what looks suspiciously like a clever way of Clinton diverting attention from Monica Lewinsky.

'You know, people ask what the most difficult thing about being Prime Minister is, and until now I haven't really known the answer. But I can say in all honesty that taking the decision to send the RAF into battle has been the worst moment for me. I couldn't sleep the night it happened, I was just worried sick.'

The mention of the word 'sick' was unhelpful.

My stomach was making worrying gurgling noises.

We tried to chat about other things, but I could see that he and Alastair were only thinking about Mandelson, and my insides were thinking only of a clearout.

'I can see you guys have got more important things to worry about – let's talk another time.'

I hid the real reason for my need to exit fast, and went straight back home to bed. Mandelson could wait until this afternoon. When I finally got to the office, I was told that Mandelson had not declared the loan on his mortgage application form.

WEDNESDAY, 23 DECEMBER

Mandelson resigned today, and called me an hour after the announcement.

'Tony is shocked,' he said. 'I called him last night to tell him and he said, "Don't rush it, think how you feel overnight and let me know." And I felt the same way. You have to do what you think is right, or you can't live with yourself. Anyway, have a nice Christmas.'

He sounded half dead. This is his life, his dream. I feel sorry for him. But he has been incredibly stupid.

Blair himself called later, with a plea. 'Hi, Piers, I just wanted to phone and ask that you treat Peter OK tomorrow.

'Last night he had come to the view to go. Despite all the attacks on him he does think of the party and the Government, and he concluded it was a breach of faith with the people.

'Then we spoke again this morning. I have been so busy with Iraq but even if he has done nothing wrong, you can't end up in a situation where ordinary people feel let down. That is always the most important thing. The most vital thing is that people don't think we are like the last lot, frankly.'

'How are you feeling about it, Prime Minister?'

'I just feel really sad for him. I know all the good stuff he has done. And even though some of the sums of money are huge, we all know he could earn a lot more outside politics. But the fact is that he has been one of the people without whom the Labour Party would not have been rebuilt and New Labour would not exist. People who know him well know a different side to the public image. He knew he had to go. It is a bloody tragedy, to be honest.'

'How do you think he will get over it?'

'I would like Peter to rebuild from this. It was a silly thing to do. Foolish. It wasn't illegal, but he should have said at the time he was doing this. Everyone's going to kick Geoffrey, but what's he supposed to have done wrong? I think there's a bit in this that people just don't like a rich, successful bloke.

'This was a moment of madness by Peter but not bad enough for me to think he can't give public service again. I attended a business seminar last week where he was bloody dazzling, and that was the view of everyone there.'

'Do you think it's damaged your Government badly?'

'I don't know what you think, but I think that although the public will be pretty horrified by what's happened, they will think the penalty has been paid. They know that people do wrong things, but they only resent it if they don't have to pay the penalty they have to pay. It is important that these things are dealt with quickly, unlike the Tories.'

There was a big, unspoken question, of course, so I asked it. 'Would you have sacked him if he hadn't resigned?'

Blair paused. 'Well, it never got to that stage, so I would rather not answer that.'

Campbell, listening in, said, 'I could tell from the TV yesterday where he was going.' Blair agreed. 'Yes, I could too.'

I tried to lighten the mood. 'You can relax about people thinking you're like the last lot, by the way: my brother thinks you're a lot worse.'

Campbell retorted: 'But he's a scumbag, and we are going to get the IRA to decommission some of their weapons on him.'

I laughed, then added, 'He also said, Tony, that if you could get rid of Campbell as well it would really make his Christmas.'

Blair laughed, but not very convincingly.

'Well, Peter will remain a friend of mine. That is for sure.'

'Who will replace him?'

'Steve Byers. He's a good guy. Alan Milburn is taking over from him at the Treasury, and John Denham is going to Health as Frank Dobson's No.2.'

Campbell interrupted: 'Er, we haven't actually announced that yet. You haven't told Frank Dobson yet.'

Blair sighed. 'Oh, right, sorry.'

THURSDAY, 24 DECEMBER

Great card from Alan Clark. 'Jadedly I survey the rubble ... Happy Christmas, love Alan and Jane.'

THURSDAY, 21 JANUARY
Tea with Gordon Brown at the Treasury. He's still smarting after having to lose his trusted aide Charlie Whelan in a row over whether he leaked some story about Government plans on the euro.

'He became the story because certain people made sure he became the story,' Gordon growled, his eyes flashing with fury.

SUNDAY, 24 JANUARY
High excitement today when Kofi Annan, United Nations Secretary-General, met my man in New York, Andy Lines, at a reception.

'Aaaahhh … the Daily Mirror, yes. Your editor is Piers Morgan, isn't he?'

Andy was, understandably, shocked.

Then Kofi laughed: 'Actually, I have to be honest and say I have never heard of him, but my PA man told me to mention his name to you. Is the Mirror an English magazine?'

Crushing.

MONDAY, 25 JANUARY
Grant Bovey has, predictably, dumped Della and is back with Anthea. But not before he had sold his MY LOVE FOR DELLA story to *OK!* magazine.

I had dinner tonight with Grant and Anthea at the Belvedere.

'Grant, I hope you don't mind me saying this, but do you realise you behaved like a complete dick?'

He laughed. 'Yes, I do.'

Not much you can say to that, really. He's a bit smarmy, and cheesy, and greedy, but Anthea loves him, and he clearly loves her too.

TUESDAY, 26 JANUARY
A fascinating day. David Montgomery 'resigned' this morning after losing a long and bitter power struggle with Victor Blank, who was knighted in the New Year's honours list. Monty may be a cold fish, but I always rather liked him. His trouble

was that he was brilliant at cost-cutting, but never worked out a way to sell more papers at the same time as spending less money. Mainly for the reason that there isn't a way, I suspect. But he helped rescue the Mirror Group after Maxwell died, and that should not be forgotten as everyone inevitably dances on his grave now.

We've been serialising the rest of Paul Routledge's Mandelson book, which is pretty scathing. Paul hates everything his subject stands for, and the feeling is mutual.

I rang Mandelson today to check he wasn't too offended.

He was.

'I am fine, thanks, despite your efforts.'

'What efforts?'

'You know how you described me and what you did to me. You were engaging in what you might call showbusiness. The language you used to describe me was extremely snide. Considering when we had that cup of tea at last year's party conference you said I was the only one of these cunts who you had time for or trusted, how you could think I could transform my moral standards and integrity in a few months to become someone not a million miles from Jonathan Aitken beggars belief.'

I said we were just running a perfectly legitimate story, and it was his own behaviour that was to blame. He snorted with derision. 'You were playing politics with me, and using me to settle scores with the party and the Prime Minister, people you're in a fight with. I am just not into all this personality stuff at all. You edit your paper how you like, but I only care about being an MP.'

This was all laughable. Mandelson's the king of personality politics.

'Hang on, you can't come out with all this garbage and expect me just to take it,' I snapped back.

But he did, clearly, and launched into a ferocious monologue. 'You have a vendetta against the Labour Party and I am the latest victim. I have lost my job, my home, over half my income, my prospects. The only things I have discovered are my sense of stability and humanity. I am becoming a human being again out of all this, and I have a really strong group of friends. I had taken them for granted and ignored them, but they have all come back to me at a time of real crisis in my life and given me support when I didn't deserve it. I will never cease being a human being again in my future career.

'I really don't want to have it spoiled by arguments and rows about semantics. What you did in relation to the Routledge book was a vicious hatchet job, for the sake of a feud and a war which you chose to take part in. You were acting as someone who wanted to take sides in a very unpleasant battle. The tone of your serialisation created the impression you were taking sides in the little war-with-Brown camp, etcetera. It was very partisan and your people got caught up in it. I didn't deserve it. You also ran a page of disgusting homophobia from that book. You regard politics and life as showbiz, I don't.'

I suggested that if his postbag is anything like ours has been, then perhaps he should take a look in his own backyard to see who is really responsible for the plight he's now in.

'Nonsense,' he blasted back. 'I have had less than a dozen letters saying good riddance to bad rubbish, you've had your comeuppance, you're a sick pervert, thank God you've gone, etcetera. But most of the letters have been very supportive. Fifteen hundred in all, saying thanks for doing the decent thing in resigning. The others said you shouldn't have given in to the media, they think they call the shots and run everything in this country. I told them all I should have resigned because I made a mistake, and it is time someone in politics acted properly. If I hadn't gone, I'd have been besmirched by the media.'

'Perhaps all politicians should have setbacks, it makes you look at yourself differently. But it was such a waste, all the work I had done was going to be wasted. But now I just want to repay that loan, and I have had many people offer to pay it for me, to help me out.'

I couldn't believe what I was hearing. 'Isn't that precisely how you got into trouble to start with, Peter?'

'No. It was imprudent to accept such a large sum of money but it was not the crime of the century. Geoffrey was a decent, generous man.' He sounded robotic now.

'Well, how can we start to repair our relations?'

'I would just like you to be fair to me in the future and not keep calling me "shamed". I don't like being called "Mandy", because it has now taken on very anti-gay homophobic connotations, and we all know what that nickname is about. And as I am now a very impoverished ex-Minister, you can now take me out for a very expensive luxury meal somewhere, and my only sorrow will be that Mr David Montgomery is not there to sign the expenses.'

At least we ended with a laugh. But God, what an extraordinary conversation. He seems ravaged by the loss of office. I wonder if I'd be like that, if it ever happens to me? These jobs are so all-consuming.

Alastair rang an hour later trying to persuade me to help them out in their disastrous Welsh election debacle. Alun Michael, who took over from Ron 'moment of madness' Davies as Welsh Secretary last October, is heading for humiliating defeat against popular local choice Rhodri Morgan in the first ever Welsh General Election in May. 'I am down on my knees, hands together, a blank cheque in one of them, and begging you to do something special for us in Wales for Alun Michael,' Alastair pleaded.

'He may not be the most charismatic guy, but he is good at his job,' he went on. 'Rhodri Morgan is good with his one-liners, but you could not imagine him running the country in a month of Sundays.'

I said we'd have a look at it. Then I told him about Mandelson.

'I know, he is not in a good way. The more he tries to keep his head down the more people are trying to find out what he's up to. I don't know what he will do now, to be honest. He has had his entire life taken off him.'

I asked if he knew Charles and Camilla were going to pose for their first official picture tonight, coming out of a theatre.

'Really? I'd heard they might. Is it on then?'

'Yes – two hundred and fifty snappers, eleven pm, the whole deal. Only rules apparently are no kissing, touching or handshakes.'

Campbell whistled. 'Fucking hell, I'd better see what bad news I can slip out today, then. Maybe now's the time to reveal my secret Swiss bank account …'

Charlie Whelan called just before I went home.

'Mandelson was trying to get me for ages. The bastard.'

God, they're all trying to kill each other. The New Labour bubble is bursting internally. It's frightening to watch.

I spoke to Montgomery late tonight. He said he felt 'sad but philosophical'. His wife Sophie was less so when she came on the phone: 'I can't believe what a bastard Victor's been.'

WEDNESDAY, 27 JANUARY

Fayed's birthday, and I'd recently stood him up for lunch. I sent him a note, apologising and congratulating him.

He faxed back: 'You want to see me then you cancel. Don't you love me any more? Today of all days I want to be happy so please don't play hard to get. If you still care about me then call my secretary and make a firm date. And remember, with age comes wisdom.'

THURSDAY, 28 JANUARY

My godfather Simon, a successful and allegedly well-connected man-about-town, has been urging me for ages to become a member of the Groucho Club. Eventually I bowed to his pressure and filled in an application form. Today I got my response. Rejection. In fact, they not only said they didn't want me as a member now, as there was an eighteen-month waiting list, but they also stressed, 'We don't think it would be appropriate in your case for you to reapply.'

MONDAY, 1 FEBRUARY

Glenn Hoddle has been sacked as England manager for claiming disabled people are being punished for sins they committed in a previous life.

It was a stupid thing to say, obviously. But when I spoke to him today, he revealed his mother actually works with the disabled, and he visits her at the school quite often.

'Why didn't you say that, Glenn?' I said. 'It would have helped you enormously.'

'No, I couldn't do that to my mum or the people she helps. It wouldn't have been right.'

Then he got quite tearful as he told me how his young daughter had written to the BBC complaining about the way her dad was being treated.

'She said it was pathetic, and I felt so proud of her. It made me cry.'

He's a complicated guy, Hoddle. Very inarticulate, hence all the 'them things' stuff. But a great coach, and a good man, I suspect, underneath all this nonsense. I felt sorry for him, but nobody else seems to want to.

I've being having a few run-ins with Alan Rusbridger lately, so offered to take him to the Ivy for a kiss-and-make-up dinner. He had caviar and champagne, I had sausage and mash and the house red. Broadsheet socialists, eh?

TUESDAY, 2 FEBRUARY

James Hewitt has been given back his Diana letters by Kensington Palace. I am totally bemused. Why?

WEDNESDAY, 3 FEBRUARY

Had an entertaining dinner with Robin Cook at the Howard Hotel tonight. We discussed the succession of the Labour Party, should Blair fall under a bus.

'Presumably Gordon would be a shoo-in,' I said, knowing Cookie would internally explode at such a thought.

'Oh, no, no, no, I don't think it would be a foregone conclusion at all. There would be lots of strong candidates.'

'Blunkett?'

'Britain's not ready for a blind Prime Minister.'

'Straw?'

'Or a deaf one.' He laughed.

I rattled through most of the other candidates, who were all dismissed in similar brusque fashion. I'd deliberately left one name out.

'So ... let me think ... that doesn't seem to leave anyone ...'

Cook looked desperate.

'Oh, wait a minute ... hang on – of course. You, Robin! You'd be perfect.'

He flushed with pride, and relief.

'Well, it would be totally inappropriate for me to say such a thing, of course, and I am very happy in the job I am doing ...'

'Of course,' I said. We ordered another bottle of wine.

Funny thing is that Cook's probably the cleverest man in the Cabinet, and is a master of all the briefs thrown at him. He also has, I think, a genuine streak of principle about him.

He'd probably make a rather good Prime Minister, but it will never happen.

FRIDAY, 5 FEBRUARY

Syd Young, one of the *Mirror*'s most legendary reporters, retired today after 38 years on the paper. He had a huge bash at the Ivy, with a star-studded cast including Campbell and Annie Robinson.

Given that the room was packed with loads of ex-*Mirror* hacks who spend all their time boozily bemoaning the fact it ain't like what it used to be, I dug out the paper from the day Syd joined and read out the stories.

'Ladies and gentlemen, the first three pages were devoted to a house fire in which nobody died, but three stars of the Carry On movies were guests. Page five was an exclusive on Charlie Drake quitting showbiz because he's exhausted. Page nine was an interview with Zsa Zsa Gabor. There was a nice scantily-clad woman on page eleven, a twelve and thirteen centre spread on the Mirror's TV awards, three pages of sport and a back page lead on Princess Margaret learning to swim.'

I paused for effect, as the room had now been rendered virtually silent through appalled shock.

'I must say, I can quite see why they called them the glory days of crusading, campaigning, investigative journalism.'

To be fair, they did all laugh. But I'd nailed them, once and for all.

All this bullshit about the *Mirror*'s 'glory days' has to stop. It was 24 pages of cheap-as-chips trivial rubbish most days.

THURSDAY, 25 FEBRUARY

We offered £50,000 reward today for anyone who provides us with information leading to the arrest and conviction of any of the thugs who killed Stephen Lawrence. The phone lines were red hot all day, but mostly from white racists threatening to torch Canary Wharf and kill all the journalists. I usually laugh off this kind of nonsense, but there was one call that sent the security guys a bit twitchy, from Combat 18. They are a well-known far-right group known for extreme views and even more extreme violence. Their threat, if it is indeed from them, is specific and reveals details of where I live, what time I go to work, and so on. They are also rather specific about what parts of my neck they are going to slice into ribbons. It's designed to shake me up, and to be perfectly honest it's worked. The head of the *Mirror* security team recommends I have a couple of bodyguards at home for a bit, until things calm down. I resisted at first, but then remembered it's not just my safety we're talking about here, it's Marion and the boys too. So reluctantly, I have agreed. The two men are here at the house now, both ex-SAS and impressively mean-looking specimens.

FRIDAY, 26 FEBRUARY

No sign of my assailants as I leave home, which is almost a pity, because I'd quite like them to try it on now my back-up is in place. I swept into Canary Wharf with my guards liaising with the *Mirror* security boys on walkie-talkies next to me in the car. It's all very *Hawaii 5-O*, and I have to confess rather exciting.

SATURDAY, 27 FEBRUARY

Marion has been told not to leave the house without telling the bodyguards, but wants to get her hair done, so my driver has gone over and escorted her, with her armed protection team, to Toni and Guy in Wimbledon, where they lurk menacingly in the shadows as she has a blow-dry. This is getting ridiculous.

SUNDAY, 28 FEBRUARY

They are nice blokes, but their mere presence in the house is now becoming very irritating. For the first time I realise how oppressive it must be to live with this kind of thing constantly in your life. A lot of former Northern Ireland and Home Secretaries have guards for life. Just sitting there, watching your every move. You can't have an argument about even the telly without thinking they're listening. I used to think it must be terribly dull doing 24-hour surveillance on someone, but now I think it must be riveting – the ultimate reality TV show. Just watching people living their lives.

MONDAY, 1 MARCH

Enough. I would genuinely rather have my throat slashed by Combat 18 than this. I tell them it's nothing personal, and it's not because they're not nice guys, but they have got to go. They don't seem too surprised.

MONDAY, 8 MARCH

Alastair faxed me to inform me of the following:

> The *Chosun Daily*, which you will be aware is one of Korea's leading papers, has just published a survey of 503 people consisting of 251 MPs and 252 university students. They were asked to name 'an ideal role model for Korean political leadership for the 21st century'. The results were:
> 1) Blair – 35.1%
> 2) Mandela 9.9%
> 3) Clinton 6%
> 4) Thatcher 5.8%.
> Of those who voted for TB, 22% did so because he was 'clean and fresh', 19% because they 'admired his vision for the future' and 14.8% because they liked his 'will to implement reform policies'. Knowing as I do your interest in world affairs I thought you'd like this.

THURSDAY, 18 MARCH

Rod Hull, of Emu fame, has died falling off his roof while trying to fix his TV aerial so he could watch the Manchester United game. Everyone burst out laughing in conference, which is probably how most of Britain reacted. Meaning that Rod, ironically, got his biggest laugh at his darkest moment.

TUESDAY, 23 MARCH

Spencer, aged five and a half, sang at the Royal Albert Hall tonight.

Oh, alright, he sang with 1000 other kids for a school charity thing. But it still sounds good.

Sinatra, the Beatles, Clapton, Morgan.

WEDNESDAY, 24 MARCH

We sent the bombers in against Milosevic tonight, and there was almost as much violence at the UK *Press Gazette* awards.

An altercation between a *Mail* reporter and some of my lot ended with Lloyd Embley, the most mild-mannered of production journalists, getting a blood-splattered shirt and police being called.

To round off the evening, we gave the Team Reporting award that we'd won for Omagh to Don Mackay, a rough, tough news reporter, for safe keeping – and he promptly dropped it, smashing it to pieces.

SUNDAY, 11 APRIL

Fayed's had Michael Jackson, an old mate of his, round Harrods for a midnight shopping flit – spending over £1 million on more trinkets he'll never use.

It gave me a barmy idea.

'Mohammed, Michael's not given a British newspaper interview for at least twenty years – reckon you can swing it for me?'

'Of course,' replied Fayed, chuckling. 'Michael's a nice guy, and my friend, and he will do it for me.'

I know he's powerful, but I don't think even Mohammed can pull this one off. Jackson doesn't do British tabloids, full stop. And he employs a whole army of minders at Sony to ensure hacks never get near him. The nearest was Peter Willis, who before he became one of my features executives was the *Sun*'s official Jacko correspondent on his UK tour back in 1990, and revealed such gems as JACKO IN AIDS SCARE (because he'd kissed the Blarney Stone), and JACKO HIT BY FLYING CHEESEBURGER (thrown by Mr Peter Willis).

But Fayed's got me into places no one's been before, so who knows?

MONDAY, 12 APRIL

Fayed rang at 10am. 'OK, Michael will call you a bit later, it's all fine.' I was stunned. 'Seriously? That's amazing, Mohammed. How did you persuade him?'

Fayed chuckled again. 'I just said I had a good friend of mine who wanted to speak to him.'

I put the phone down and waited. At midday, Kerrie popped her head round my door with the immortal words, 'Erm, there's some bloke saying he's Michael Jackson on the phone, but I think he's probably a nutter.'

I laughed. 'No, no, amazingly I think it really might be him. Stick him on.' And it was indeed the King of Pop.

What a bizarre 40 minutes then followed.

He cried twice, once when I asked him about the child abuse stories: 'I love children, if it wasn't for them I would throw the towel in and I'd kill myself.'

And the other when I brought up Diana.

'I had a concert on the day the news broke, and my doctor woke me up to tell me Diana was dead. I literally collapsed, I fainted. He had to give me smelling salts to revive me and I cancelled my show because I simply could not perform. I just broke down. I wept and wept for weeks afterwards.'

He told me that he and Diana talked often on the phone. 'She felt hunted in the way I've felt hunted. Trapped, if you like. You can't talk about that to your neighbour, because how would they ever understand? No normal person could possibly understand, could they?

'I've had that attention since I was a kid, whereas Diana had it suddenly thrust upon her at the age of nineteen. I've had it all my life, so I had the experience to tell her how to handle it.

'I just said to her, "Rise above it all." I'd tell her how I would go on stage sometimes in the worst pain – either emotionally, or physically with something like a toothache – and I would put whatever it was out of my mind and perform.

'I'd say, "Be strong and be determined, and nobody can hurt you. Only you can hurt yourself – so be defiant." I think she appreciated it and got something from my words. I think I was able to comfort her.

'I adored Diana. We talked so many times, much more than people realised. When I heard about the paparazzi chasing her, I just thought how lucky I was that it had never happened to me, because I've been chased the same way so many times and you always wonder.

'Diana's death was the saddest I've ever felt – it reminded me of when Kennedy died. It broke my heart so much, I just cried and cried.'

What was fascinating about Jackson was how he could switch from sobbing about Diana to a totally different mood and tone of voice, seemingly at the drop of a hat.

When he told me how Fayed had shown him round Fulham, I said, 'You should buy Manchester United.'

'I'd love to get involved with one of the big teams if it was right to do so. How much are they?' he asked.

'Six hundred million.'

'Dollars or pounds?'

'Pounds.'

There was a long pause.

'That's interesting, very interesting.'

'Manchester United and Michael Jackson – could be a perfect union.'

He laughed. 'I'll have a think about that. It sounds intriguing. I'm astounded by how much I enjoyed the soccer, that's for sure.'

'Are you still living your life as a recluse, Michael?'

'Well, I've started going out again, thanks to my friend Elizabeth Taylor. Every Thursday we go to the movies together. She is godmother to my son Prince and we get on so well. I said I could get Warner Brothers to put aside a studio just for us every week to watch films in private, but she forces me out. She's the only person who can get me out in public.

'We walk in, sit down, watch our film and walk out. And every time we leave, the audience all stand up and applaud us. It's funny. The last one we saw was "Patch Adams", which we loved. It was so touching, it made me cry.'

I couldn't remember ever being quite so excited speaking to anyone. Since Diana's death Jackson is indisputably the biggest star in the world. And unlike Diana, he never talked to the press.

I could hear Fayed in the background, chuckling again as we said goodbye. He loves all this mischief.

I called him later. 'Did he know that I edit a tabloid paper?' I said.

'Of course, of course. I said you were a good friend of mine.' And he chuckled again.

WEDNESDAY, 14 APRIL

David Puttnam invited me last night to the 30 Club, a sinister-sounding organisation that actually isn't that sinister, but consists of senior media figures getting together every month for a big black-tie dinner at Claridge's to hear a speaker, swap gossip, do a few deals and get pissed.

The star turn was Conrad Black, owner of the Telegraph Group, and a man who loves the sound of his own voice even more than I do. And I mean *loves* it.

He spoke for nearly an hour in a grating Canadian motonone about the threat of a federal Europe and why we should be in the North American Free Trade Agreement (unspoken answer: because it would make Conrad Black much richer, I suspect).

He stared out from the lectern, a bear of a man with small, unsmiling eyes and a ferocious demeanour which made me laugh. It's all Chatham House rules, which is just as well, as he berated most of his interrogators with dismissive, haughty arrogance. He is a man who doesn't just think he's right about everything – he knows it. Afterwards I joined a small group having a post-dinner whisky with him. He treated me like something trapped on his shoe until I said I'd been a Murdoch editor for two years. Then he was fascinated by my every word. I gave him a few stories about my old boss and he loved it, revelling in every snippet of revelation about Murdoch's personality, leadership and human side.

He had no interest in me at all, but as the conduit of inside information about his obvious hero, I was the object of his rapt attention. As he drank more, he relaxed and became quite amusing himself – telling great stories about Kissinger and Clinton and all his other powerful mates. It was shameless name-dropping, but entertaining nonetheless. Black's an odd guy. Impressive on one level, but more boastful and shallow than Murdoch could ever be.

MONDAY, 26 APRIL

It was a quiet Monday until just after lunch, when news began to filter through that Jill Dando, the BBC TV presenter, had been involved in some sort of shooting incident. It seemed too far-fetched to be credible and I didn't give it much thought until the newsdesk raced into my office and confirmed she had been shot dead. Everyone was stunned. She seemed such an inoffensive, uncontroversial, likeable person. Who the hell would want to shoot her?

As we planned the paper, Peter Willis suddenly pointed out a rather appalling problem. The cover of this weekend's *Look* magazine had a big photo of Jill, with an interview about her forthcoming marriage to gynaecologist Alan Farthing, with the headline WHY I'M LOOKING FORWARD TO A BRIGHT FUTURE, BY JILL DANDO. I stared at it in a slight panic. Over a million copies of the magazine had already been printed. But we'd have to pulp them and take the huge financial hit that would involve. I'd always feared something like this might happen one day, but until now it never has. I had to shout the immortal movie line 'Stop the presses!', and dump the interview. It would cost us at least £200,000, but there was nothing we could do.

By mid-afternoon, people had started coming out and laying flowers at the scene of Jill's murder outside her house in Fulham, south-west London. There was a slight parallel with Princess Diana here. They looked quite similar, lived alone in the same part of town, attracted a lot of male admirers, and had both now been killed in dramatic and terrible circumstances. And as with Diana, the reaction from the public was enormous, and genuinely grief-stricken. Early signs are that Jill was killed by some stalker-style nutter, but, given that she put a lot of bad guys in jail during her time presenting *Crimewatch*, it may be more sinister than that. Whoever did it was a hitman, capable of cold-blooded execution with one shot.

TUESDAY, 27 APRIL

Sales of all the papers yesterday were huge. This was the biggest news story circulation-wise since Diana's death, though not quite in that league. Jill's home town are now publicly calling her 'our Diana', and the scale of mourning is really extraordinary, given that she was really just a rather nice TV presenter. Even the Queen has expressed her 'shock and sadness'. Amazing.

SATURDAY, 1 MAY

I am so fed up with not winning any awards this year, I decided to run a special *Mirror* poll this morning on which is the best newspaper in Fleet Street. We won, but rather worryingly with only 70 per cent of the vote. The *Sun* got 8 per cent, despite me informing readers that it's 'edited by an alien and read by the lowest form of human life in Britain'; the *Guardian* 6.5 per cent, after I described it as 'generally reviled by everyone with a brain cell in the country'; the *Mail*

5 per cent, after I generously paid tribute to it as 'a right-wing, sexist, racist and misogynist paper that never breaks news stories but just steals them'; and even the *Financial Times* scraped 0.5 per cent.

WEDNESDAY, 5 MAY

Had lunch today with Jack Straw at the People's Palace restaurant overlooking the Thames. It was our first encounter since we exposed his son, and he was not exactly brimming with the camaraderie we enjoyed before. 'I want to put all that behind us,' he said quickly. I started to proffer my apologies but he cut me off in mid-stream. 'Look, I know how it all happened, and he was a stupid boy for getting involved with a bad lot. I am OK about it, really. It was my wife who took it very badly. She was very, very upset and still is.'

I asked how William was doing. 'He's fine, hopefully it will be a shot in the arm for him.' We both laughed at the rather unfortunate choice of phrase.

'Well, I think we probably did him a favour in the end,' I said. 'He was getting more and more involved and it could have been a lot worse.'

'Yes, I know,' replied Straw. 'I don't think "doing him a favour" is quite how I would describe it, but he seems fine now.'

THURSDAY, 6 MAY

Peter Willis had a brilliant idea a few weeks ago to do a *Mirror* awards ceremony, with the neat twist of getting celebrities to give gongs to ordinary people who have done extraordinary things.

It's all come together amazingly fast, and today we had the judging panel meeting for the Pride of Britain awards at Richard Branson's house in Holland Park. Diana's butler Paul Burrell, Miriam Stoppard, Spice Girl Mel B and Richard himself were the panellists.

I had a quiet word with Burrell.

'How are you, Paul?'

'Oh, OK – day to day still, you know. I've just been in America where I met Bill Clinton and Tom Hanks, which was good fun. But I still think about her all the time.'

'Well, you were always there for her, her most loyal aide. Never forget that. You were the only one she never sacked!'

He laughed. 'Not through lack of her trying!'

FRIDAY, 7 MAY

Paul McCartney has replied to my invitation to present an animal-loving award in memory of Linda at the inaugural Pride of Britain awards. He suggested someone he would like to get it, Juliet Gellately, who founded the anti-vivisection group VIVA.

He said he may be able to attend in person: 'I'll let you know nearer the time, if that's OK. But either way I'd like to thank you once again from me, the kids *and* Linda for this very touching tribute.'

It would be fantastic if he came.

THURSDAY, 20 MAY

The first Pride of Britain awards took place at the Dorchester today, and what a turn-out!

My top table had the Blairs, Queen Noor of Jordan, Michael Owen, and Richard Branson. And all around me were superstars like Lennox Lewis, Cilla Black, etc, etc. I made a speech saying I'd given Peter Willis firm instructions that he was to get 'a Prime Minister, a Queen and at least one member of the Beatles' to attend, and that 'two out of three wasn't bad.'

Everyone laughed, but only a tiny handful of us knew that there was still a remote possibility Macca might come. As the meal started, though, and the minutes ticked by, I assumed he couldn't face it and had stayed at home.

Cherie was on good form, making Owen blush by telling him her daughter Kathryn had his photo on her wall. Owen, just eighteen, barely said a word – though he did ask what he should say when he received his award. 'Oh, just say you won't have the Sun in the house,' I said. He thought I was serious. 'Erm, I'm not sure I can do that.' 'Why not?' I said, adding, 'Nobody in Liverpool has the Sun in their house.' 'No, I know,' he replied, half-smiling. 'But I don't want to cause any trouble.'

Cherie stopped my fun. 'Don't be so mean, Piers. Stop teasing Michael.' I laughed. 'Cherie, *you* don't have the Sun in the house, do you?' She flashed that steely look she reserves for my more contemptible remarks. 'I don't comment on things like that,' she said firmly. 'And nor should Michael have to.' Realising the game was up, I carefully briefed the young footballer on what he might want to say and who he might want to thank. He listened intently and spent the next hour rehearsing his lines under his breath. Only to then walk up, say 'thanks very much' and go and sit back down again.

Queen Noor was delightful, radiant and charming. But quite serious. Just when I was beginning to sink in a complex debate about Jordan's place in the world peace effort, I heard a commotion in the corner of the room, a flurry of flashbulbs went off, and everyone's heads darted round to see what was happening. And there he was: Paul McCartney, wearing a smart black suit and trainers, looking shy and ambling towards our table with a fixed, nervous grin on his face. It was his first public appearance since Linda died, and the place was going wild with people clapping and cheering. There are stars and superstars, and then there are legends. And Macca's one of the biggest names in the world.

I stood up and introduced him to the table. Michael Owen, a Liverpudlian through and through, looked like he'd pass out with excitement. I wasn't much more controlled myself.

'Thanks for coming, Paul,' I said, breathlessly. 'No problem, it's a pleasure,' he said, looking terrified. 'Can't be easy, though,' I said. 'No, it's not, feels quite strange, actually, but I had to do it some time.'

He sat next to me and started picking at his food, his eyes darting around the room. Cilla loosened him up by giving him a big kiss and hug. 'Oh, Paul, darling, I'm so glad you came.' He seemed relieved to have such an old mate nearby. When the awards started, the atmosphere got steadily more electric and moving. Helen Rollason, the very sick BBC sports presenter, had everyone in tears with a speech that might well be her last. And as the incredible stories of courage came one after another, emotions ran higher and higher.

Barbara Windsor made everyone laugh when she said, 'Piers Morgan asked me to come up and do one of my famous giggles to stop everyone crying, but I can't – it's all too emotional,' and started blubbing again!

One of the most memorable moments came when Heather Mills, the model who lost her leg in a car accident, presented an award to a young girl who'd lost both legs to meningitis. Heather, looking very buxom and sexy in a tight top, made a fantastic, rousing speech. McCartney leaned over at one stage and asked, 'Who's that?'

'That's Heather Mills.'

'Who's she?'

I told him Heather's story and he looked back at her.

'She's quite a girl, isn't she?' he said. I noticed then a striking resemblance to Linda, not just physically, but in the strong-willed, independent way she spoke. Later he asked me some more questions about her, and I said Heather had founded a charity for people around the world who've lost limbs to things like landmines, and perhaps he'd like to help her out. 'Yes, might just do that,' he replied. 'I like the way she talks, she's a gutsy girl.'

Macca later presented an award in Linda's memory to an animal rights campaigner and made a brilliant speech.

'I've been crying all year and now I come here!' he joked.

A brilliant, unforgettable day.

WEDNESDAY, 26 MAY

I can never normally stomach watching a football match that doesn't involve Arsenal, but the Champions' League final is different, especially when your chairman is a Manchester United season-ticket holder like Victor, who invites you to go with him on a private jet.

Also on the flight to Barcelona were Alastair Campbell and his son Rory, Blair's fundraiser Lord Levy, and John Monks, the union leader. It amused me to see the cream of British socialism all lapping up their champagne on the private jet. Campbell regaled us with a bizarre story about how Rory advises Sir Alex Ferguson on football.

'No, seriously,' he exclaimed when I raised an eyebrow of suspicion. 'Alex believes you can get a lot from a child's eye view of how players are performing. So he'll often ask Rory what he thinks.' Rory, a nice lad, confirmed he was indeed an unpaid United scout. Quite bizarre to think of Tony Blair's spindoctor's twelve-year-old son telling Fergie, 'Beckham's a bit off at the moment, I'd drop him if I were you.'

The game was very dull until the last five minutes, when United scored twice to beat a shattered Bayern Munich team, who just collapsed on to the turf face down like they'd been shot.

'Don't you love seeing Germans like that?' said Alastair.

THURSDAY, 27 MAY

The *Sun* ran a photo of Sophie Rhys-Jones topless on Tuesday – taken by someone who worked with her on Chris Tarrant's Capital Radio show – just three weeks before her wedding to Prince Edward, and there's been a complete meltdown of fury. We've had a lot of fun at Yelland's expense – running a 'Beam the Alien Back to Planet Tharg' campaign, doing him up as a *Who Wants To Be A Millionaire?* contestant with the question 'Who is the most stupid man in Britain: a) David Yelland b) David Yelland c) David Yelland d) David Yelland?'.

He's saying sorry every ten minutes and looks shot to pieces. I don't think he'll last long.

FRIDAY, 11 JUNE

Alan Clark's been ill and I sent him a note saying he couldn't die yet because Hague is still Tory leader.

'I loved your message on my card – thanks,' he replied. 'Tony B wrote at once, in his own hand. Nothing from the Nerd, though: keeping his fingers crossed I suppose. I've still got my own hair and the surgeon told Jane, "Biologically he's thirty to forty years old." Best to all my mates at the *Mirror*.'

SUNDAY, 20 JUNE

Sophie and Edward married yesterday, and he became Earl of Wessex. Charlotte rang me from Newick.

'He's always been an Earl.'

'What do you mean?'

'His name is Edward Anthony Richard Louis.'

She was right, and we splashed on this rather amusing fact.

FRIDAY, 25 JUNE

Greg Dyke's been appointed Director-General of the BBC, which strikes me as a bloody good idea. Anything's better than Birt.

Dyke's been forced to sell all his media shares, so I sent a fiver to help out a bit. He replied, 'Thanks for the cheque, instead of cashing it I've decided to frame it as who knows what a Piers Morgan signature might be worth in ten years. I can cope with the financial burden!'

MONDAY, 28 JUNE
Rupert Murdoch married his 31-year-old Chinese girlfriend, Wendy Deng, at the weekend, and I decided to mark the occasion with a *Mirror* headline competition.

We had 3000 entries by first post, and did up sixteen of them as *Mirror* front pages. Some were clever – IT'S BEASTY AND THE BEAUT and DING DENG MARRY ME ON SKY. Others were a bit sneering – IN SICKNESS AND IN WEALTH and DENG DOES HER BIT FOR AGE CONCERN. And a few were just predictably racist and offensive: WOK A BRIDE, and RUPERT'S CHINESE TAKEAWAY.

Not sure if he will laugh when he sees it. In fact the more I look at the page today, the less funny I find it myself. Why do I do these things? I can never beat him, so why wind him up?

WEDNESDAY, 30 JUNE
Manchester United have pulled out of the FA Cup to play in some ridiculous World Club Championship in Brazil. It's a total disgrace, and they are as much to blame for it as the Government and FA are for asking them to play in it. We launched a campaign to stop them today, to make them play in the Cup. Because without them defending their title, it is meaningless.

SATURDAY, 3 JULY
Janet Street-Porter has been made editor of the *Independent on Sunday*. Prompting Kelvin, her former boss at Live TV, to comment that she 'couldn't edit a bus ticket'.

TUESDAY, 6 JULY
Rosie Boycott's been letting her diarist stick it to me in the *Express* for months, and I finally responded yesterday with an invented little news story saying EXPRESS EDITOR FACES THE AXE.

She's taken it well, sending a legal letter claiming the report was 'devastating, professionally and personally', demanding £10,000 in damages, and, unbelievably, the right to choose her own picture to accompany a grovelling apology.

I laughed out loud. For several minutes.

MONDAY, 12 JULY
Our FA Cup campaign's really struck a nerve, and all sorts of politicians, celebrities and soccer idols have backed us.

David Beckham was the first United player to break ranks today: 'I hope we play in it. We'd rather play in the FA Cup, definitely.'

WEDNESDAY, 14 JULY

Sir Alex Ferguson's been getting more and more wound up as the campaign's gone on, and he finally snapped when *Mirror* reporters got to him at a champagne reception in Manchester.

'Tell your editor Morgan to fuck off back to Highbury and stagnate,' he shouted.

FRIDAY, 16 JULY

We jumped the unsuspecting United chairman, Martin Edwards, at Sydney airport and got him to pose with our 'Save the FA Cup' baseball cap. When he twigged, he went mad. 'Oh, I see, you've set me up there, haven't you? I'll be in trouble if you publish that – that picture's off the record.'

TUESDAY, 3 AUGUST

Went to Chequers for the first time today for tea with Blair. An extraordinary place, stuck out in the middle of the countryside and so hard to find that the locals are apparently quite used to having to direct people like Boris Yeltsin.

I took Tina, my deputy, and we got the full-blown charm offensive for two hours, with Blair even pouring the tea. He's always more relaxed when Campbell's not around doing his hand signals, sighing or interrupting with his own views on life.

'Do you fancy a look round the old Cabinet war rooms?' he asked. And we strolled up to where Churchill made all those 'fight them on the beaches' speeches. As we did, we passed a wall of photographs of every Prime Minister who has served this century.

As we looked at them, Blair urged, 'Go on then, Piers, see how many you can name.'

I stared intently at the grainy black-and-white images and realised it was a game of two halves.

The right half did itself – Maggie, Major, Wilson and so on were all instantly recognisable, obviously.

But the other half, the early half, was a little more tricky. I mean, who in the world actually knows what Sir Henry Campbell-Bannerman or Andrew Bonar Law looked like? Blair sensed my discomfort. 'Come on, you're the editor of the Mirror, you must be able to name a few Prime Ministers.'

The glint in his eye was almost satanic. I looked again at the wall, then calmly delivered the names of every single one – moving from face to face, studying them for a few seconds, then answering correctly. Only Arthur Balfour (Conservative, 1902) didn't look suddenly very familiar.

Blair was stunned. 'Crikey, I take it all back.' Tina looked completely bemused, knowing I know bugger all about politics, and that I'd pulled some rabbit out of the hat here but having no idea what it was.

I sent Blair a fax later that afternoon. 'Dear Tony, to put you out of your misery, they had all signed their photos in small writing at the bottom. I just couldn't read Balfour's.'

THURSDAY, 5 AUGUST

There is still no plan for a Diana memorial, which is a complete disgrace. So we started a campaign for one yesterday, and 50,000 people called our hotline to support it.

Today we had a hilarious splash – photos inside Sandringham of all the Queen's stone memorials for her dead corgis.

'They do it for dogs, but not Diana,' said the leader.

Late in the afternoon, it was confirmed that we have merged as a company with Trinity, the biggest regional publishers in the country. This will be my third management team in just four years. And people wonder why the *Mirror*'s been struggling.

MONDAY, 9 AUGUST

Charles Kennedy was appointed leader of the Liberal Democrats today. I got horrendously drunk with him at Wimbledon once, and he seemed a top bloke. If he gets the Lib Dem ganders up, there is no reason why they can't quite quickly replace the Tories as the real opposition.

WEDNESDAY, 11 AUGUST

It was the eclipse today, and naturally we didn't miss the chance to fill the paper with '*Sun* eclipsed' gags.

At the appointed time we all filed out on to the streets of Canary Wharf with our paper glasses. It went very dark very quickly, and felt genuinely eerie.

MONDAY, 16 AUGUST

Our Diana memorial campaign has now been backed by 100,000 readers, a record for any phone poll we've ever run.

TUESDAY, 7 SEPTEMBER

Alan Clark died today. I rang Alastair, an old mate of his, to see if he would write a tribute, and he instantly agreed. 'He was the acceptable face of the Conservatives,' he said. 'Yes, and a bloody laugh too,' I replied.

Life will be slightly less amusing now.

I did a page one blurb saying, 'Farewell to the only Tory the *Mirror*'s ever loved.' He'd have laughed at that.

WEDNESDAY, 8 SEPTEMBER

Heard today that Paul McCartney is romancing Heather Mills. They apparently met up after the Pride of Britain awards, and he made a big donation to her land-mine charity. I'm pleased for him; he deserves a bit of happiness. Funny to have been the conduit for their first meeting, though.

WEDNESDAY, 15 SEPTEMBER

I was caught speeding in Colchester visiting Charlotte last month, and have recruited a lawyer to help out, because I was doing 58mph in a 30mph area and might get a ban despite a clean licence.

It turns out my brief is Gary Herbert, better known as the little guy who cried on the podium when the giant Searle brothers won Olympic rowing gold medals.

He rang after the hearing.

'Didn't go brilliantly, I'm afraid.'

'Go on.'

'Well, they banned you for twenty-eight days, fined you five hundred and forty pounds, and the chief magistrate even made a little speech about public figures having to set a better example.'

I was appalled. 'Christ almighty. Didn't you start blubbing again, Gary, to try and help me a bit?'

He laughed. 'Piers, the way she was talking made me think she would have been rather tempted to bring back hanging for you if she'd been allowed to! And by the way, the only reason I cried on the podium was that Chris Searle was standing on my foot.'

Later my newsdesk informed me that David Ginola had been caught doing 59mph in a 30mph zone in London – and got away with three points and a £200 fine.

I ordered an immediate leader tearing into the inequities of speeding laws in this country ... until I was reminded that I had only last week ordered a leader demanding stiffer sentences for those who 'recklessly speed through towns'.

TUESDAY, 21 SEPTEMBER

I've finally persuaded Blair to be interviewed by Paul Routledge, our political commentator and scourge of New Labour. I escorted him down to No. 10 to make sure he wasn't immolated on the spot.

It was an amusing encounter, Blair giving it the full charm offensive and Routers melting before my eyes to such an extent that he even asked for some autographs for his grandchildren at the end.

But the interview was thought-provoking and good for both sides.

Paul gave him a hard time over Kosovo. He has a deep knowledge and love of the Balkans, having travelled there for over 30 years.

And there was an interesting clash over Saddam Hussein.

'If we don't contain him the world's at risk,' Blair insisted.

'That's nonsense,' retorted Paul. 'Where's he going to invade – Canada?'

'It's not nonsense, Paul. If he was allowed to develop nuclear weapons, which he was …'

'But he hasn't been.'

'Only because we stopped him, Paul. He has used chemical and biological weapons, he was developing nuclear weapons, and I think you can guarantee that a man like Saddam would use a nuclear device if he could develop it.'

Fascinating stuff, watching these two finally jousting like this.

I particularly enjoyed Campbell squirming when Blair jibed, 'I'll say this about Alastair – he makes a good cup of tea.'

'What was the last thing that made you laugh out loud?' was Paul's last question.

'The thought of being interviewed by you, Paul.'

As we were leaving, Campbell asked me to wait a minute. I could tell from the smirk on his face that they had something good for me.

'Ask him about Diana,' he whispered.

'Prime Minister, anything I should know about Diana?'

Blair laughed. 'Yes, there is actually, Piers. I thought you'd like to be the first to know that there is going to be a permanent memorial to her.'

Campbell winked.

'Blimey, it worked then.'

'Yes, well, it's important to honour someone who was so dear to the people of this country, and who did so much good in her life.'

Since we were on a roll, I asked him whether he'd told United to get back in the FA Cup yet.

'That's more difficult. I think they should play in the Cup like most people, but it's not easy to sort it now.'

Tony Banks has recently been sacked as Sports Minister, and his replacement Kate Hoey has been vociferous in her demands for United to play.

'Banks was a halfwit,' I said.

'No, he wasn't,' said Blair.

'Yes, he was. And you must have agreed or he wouldn't have been moved on. He should never have let it get this far. The FA Cup will never recover.'

Campbell obviously agreed. As he walked me out afterwards, he said, 'Alex is trying everything to get them back in. But the first team will have to go to Brazil and he doesn't want to play a bunch of kids in case they get murdered ten–nil and lose all their confidence.'

'That's better than not playing at all, isn't it?' I asked.

'Yes, it probably is, I agree. We're working on it.'

WEDNESDAY, 29 SEPTEMBER

The *Mirror* party has been the highlight of Labour conference for a few years now, and this year we excelled ourselves by persuading Boy George to re-form

Culture Club and play on the pier at Bournemouth for us. The spectacle of Peter Mandelson grooving around the dance floor to 'Karma Chameleon' will live long in the memory.

FRIDAY, 1 OCTOBER
We were offered photographs today inside Prince William's bedroom at Eton by some sneaky little ex-pupil who's recently left. They were reassuringly typical of any teenage lad's school bedroom, with supermodels and sporting icons sharing wall space. But my eyes alighted on one particular image showing a well-known poster of a man smoking a giant spliff and the headline, DON'T DRINK AND DRIVE, HAVE A SMOKE AND FLY.

My immediate thought was, 'Fantastic – Wills is a drugs fiend,' and I began to prepare a dramatic front page in my mind to that effect. Then we began to talk about it in the office, and suffered a surprising outbreak of fair play. He's only seventeen after all, this kind of poster adorns many a seventeen-year-old's bedroom without the occupant necessarily taking drugs, and the pictures had effectively been stolen. It would breach the PCC code to publish them, no question of that. And the public interest defence that we are exposing criminal behaviour by the future King would get us laughed out of the country. Nope, this wasn't going to happen.

I rang Mark Bolland to tell him the bad news that we had the pictures, but the good news was that we weren't going to run them. In fact, we were going to expose the boy who tried to sell them to us as a disgusting rat. 'But I want William to know what we've done,' I said. After all, there's never any point being a good Samaritan in this kind of situation without a) the person knowing, and b) them feeling they owe you one.

Mark called back later to say the Prince was 'relieved and grateful' for our restraint.

TUESDAY, 5 OCTOBER
There was an appalling train crash today at Paddington, with a whole first-class carriage burned out altogether. At least 80 people are feared dead, though nobody can really tell. These stories are nightmares for newspapers, because we all want a death toll in the headline and it is usually impossible to be sure. When the papers dropped tonight, some said '80 dead', like us, others went for much lower or higher figures. Makes us look ridiculous.

I popped in to Paul Burrell's book launch at Asprey's tonight: he's written tips on how to be a good butler. We had a chat, and he thanked me for supporting Diana's memory with our campaign.

'The establishment just want to forget her,' he said, sadly. 'That must never be allowed to happen.'

WEDNESDAY, 6 OCTOBER
Alex Ferguson has got off after speeding on the hard shoulder by claiming he

had urgent diarrhoea and was dashing to the loo. This was all confirmed by … United's own club doctor. What a joke.

Feeling mischievous, I told Kerrie to buy some Imodium – then sent it to Ferguson with a note saying, 'Dear Alex, we Gooners have known you've been full of crap for years, now we've got the proof. Love, Piers.'

THURSDAY, 7 OCTOBER

Alex Ferguson's PA rang this morning. 'I have never been so offended in my life,' she wailed.

What? Working for him?

'I'm chucking this in the bin – it's disgusting.'

'Hang on a second,' I replied. 'That is my property and I must insist you give it to Sir Alex or I will take immediate legal action against you.'

Pause.

'Oh, for goodness' sake, this is ridiculous.'

'Yes, it is, now just give my present to your boss, please, and we can avoid any unnecessary court battle.'

SUNDAY, 10 OCTOBER

Today the family celebrated the eightieth birthday of our amazing Grand-mère Margot Barber at a barn in Berkshire. Every one of her four children, nineteen grandchildren and sixteen great-grandchildren turned out to salute the remarkable woman without whom none of us would, quite literally, be here.

'Remember, darlings,' she often says, 'one day you're the cock of the walk, the next a feather duster.'

Her other favourite saying was addressed to her war hero brother John by a Covent Garden flower-seller: 'Life ain't much, but it's all yer got, so stick a geranium in yer 'at and be 'appy.'

MONDAY, 11 OCTOBER

High drama in the newsroom today when Gerald Corbett, the boss of Railtrack, came in to defend himself and his company over the Paddington crash.

Visibly stressed from the moment he arrived, Corbett got increasingly angry as a group of us quizzed him in my office.

He finally blew when I asked him if he was concerned about corporate manslaughter charges being brought, which seemed a perfectly reasonable question to ask.

'I find that question deeply offensive,' he raged. 'I can't believe you asked me that. God. I give you forty minutes of my time and you do that to me. I'm sorry, but I'm leaving.'

And that was it, he stormed out – photographed by waiting *Mirror* snappers as he did so.

TUESDAY, 12 OCTOBER

Fergie is 40, and I persuaded her to do a big interview with us. We met at the Berkeley Hotel in Knightsbridge, and she bustled in at 100mph as usual, full of hugs, kisses, gushes and questions about my family.

'Blimey, you're on time,' I said.

'Oh, do shut up, Piers.'

She's had a rough couple of years, losing Diana at a time when they weren't speaking, and her mum last year in a car crash in Argentina.

The rift with Diana still hurts. 'She hadn't talked to me for a year before she died. We'd had three longish periods when we fell out in the twenty-five years we knew each other, and this was unfortunately one of them. She didn't like some stuff in my book, but it was all so silly. Diana would have come back to me, I know that, but she never got the chance and now I miss her so much.'

Her eyes filled with tears. Diana had an unpleasant streak in her that caused her to freeze out endless friends and family on a whim. I wonder if she ever stopped to think of the pain she caused.

What of Charles? 'I've always adored him, but he doesn't have time for me.'

And Philip? 'He's entitled to his opinion, what can I do about it – go and hit him on the head?'

Fergie's had some terrible press.

'What's been the worst thing you've ever read about yourself?' I asked her at one stage.

'Oh, when eighty-two per cent of Sun readers said they would rather sleep with a goat than me.'

I laughed, but she didn't. 'It made me cry all day. It was so hurtful, so nasty, so unnecessary. Everyone told me to ignore it, but you don't, do you? It's like when they call me Duchess of Pork. I just burst into tears when I saw that headline.'

She has an amazingly good relationship with Andrew. 'We're the happiest divorced couple in the world. He is always there for me. And so's the Queen. She's an amazing lady.'

But not so amazing that she lets Fergie join the royals at Christmas. She has to slum it in a Sandringham outhouse with her kids, which seems totally outrageous.

'Well, it's sad, but that's the way it has to be I suppose. The thing that upsets me most is I hardly see William and Harry any more, and the girls miss them terribly – they were all so close.'

Fergie's back in credit now, after tireless work for Weightwatchers and Wedgwood china, and I admire her a lot for clearing her debts.

THURSDAY, 14 OCTOBER

Mandelson's back! He's been appointed Northern Ireland Secretary in Blair's reshuffle, and Mo Mowlam's been cast into the political ether, to her fury. This is going to be interesting …

WEDNESDAY, 20 OCTOBER

Nobody's apologising for Paddington, and we did the front page up today as a railway station announcement board with the message: 'Attention all passengers: we regret to inform you that the next train you board from any platform in Britain may misread a badly-sited signal, run a red light and kill you. In the old days British Rail would apologise for any inconvenience this may cause, but now nobody apologises because none of the people who make millions from our privatised rail system and none of the politicians entrusted with guaranteeing your safety is prepared to take the blame. Sorry!'

By midday I'd received two notes of congratulations – from Maurice *and* Charles Saatchi, separately. I am thinking of selling them some more of our 'art'.

Jane Clark wrote to thank me for some photos I sent of Alan in more amusing moments. 'I'm so glad you enjoyed the fact none of you knew he'd died until I'd given him a private funeral,' she said, 'I know he'd have been proud of me for that!'

THURSDAY, 21 OCTOBER

It's the annual Booker Prize, which has always struck me as a particularly ghastly literary event.

Someone on the staff had the bright idea of sending a former Booker Prize winning book, *The Elected Member* by Bernice Rubens, to a load of publishers as a bare manuscript with the title changed.

Predictably it was rejected by all seventeen publishers we sent it to. The funniest response came from Little Brown, who published it originally and have reprinted it nine times. 'It would be a tough one to sell,' they said.

THURSDAY, 28 OCTOBER

Had lunch at the Royal Lancaster Hotel with Manchester United chairman Martin Edwards to try and resolve the crisis. But he seemed more interested in asking me why he kept being exposed for having affairs. 'I mean, what's this country coming to if a man can't have the odd jump now and again?'

He obviously loathes Ferguson as much as Ferguson loathes him. 'Alex always likes to make out that I haven't let him buy the best players. But we've only turned down three of his requests in my time – including Batistuta and Desailly. And that's because their personal terms were so outrageous.

'I get a hard time from the fans because I have made a lot of money here, but I've turned this club into the biggest business in world football and we've won everything in the process. What's their problem?'

'Perhaps they don't think you're a real fan,' I said.

'Really? Well, I have followed United for forty years and can tell you the name of every player who has ever played in a Cup Final for us. Go on, test me.'

I did, and he could. Edwards may be a rather displeasing little man personally. But he loves his football and United would not be anything like the club they are without him.

WEDNESDAY, 17 NOVEMBER

I got a call from Max Clifford saying he had a dynamite, but 'not nasty', one-fact story on Cherie Blair and wants an equally dynamite cheque for it. I heard the fact, and instantly agreed a fee with Max not massively far from £50,000.

Cherie is pregnant, at 45. This will mean the first baby ever born at No. 10. Max came to us with this scoop because he has calculated that a) Downing Street won't mind the *Mirror* breaking it, and b) we will treat it sensitively.

THURSDAY, 18 NOVEMBER

The two immediate problems with sensational one-fact stories are absolute secrecy and confirmation. I set up a special office on a different floor from the newsroom and despatched a team of writers and production staff to prepare a special edition – I wanted every single cough and spit of this extraordinary state of Downing Street domestic affairs. Meanwhile, the rest of the staff carried on with a normal edition obliviously.

At 12.45pm, I rang Alastair. If anyone knew the story was true, it would be him. He'd promised me when I came to the *Mirror* that he would *never* tell me a lie, though he's already broken that promise over that Clinton article by Kevin Maguire.

I said one word to him: 'Stork?'

He burst out laughing. The story's obviously true. Or he'd have replied in one of his three usual ways: 'Bollocks,' 'Not that old chestnut,' or 'Print that, my friend, and you'll sleep with the fishes.'

Usually I would go to the subject of such a sensitive story much later, an hour or so before publication at most, to stop them leaking it or getting an injunction. But this was such a hot one that I had to know early if it was true, and I had to trust Alastair.

I also told him that if the three months' 'safe' pregnancy time gap had not yet elapsed, I wouldn't publish the story until it had. Pleasantly surprised that I was apparently behaving so responsibly, he agreed the story would be a *Mirror* scoop and he said he'd get a quote from the Blairs. But only after he'd been to the dentist.

Alastair finally got round to telling the Prime Minister at 5.30pm. Blair was pretty relaxed about us having it as an exclusive, and it all seemed to be going pretty swimmingly. I had eleven pages of the paper devoted to every conceivable nuance of this one-fact story, and prepared for the bombshell to rock Britain.

Then, at 8pm, Alastair rang to warn me that Rebekah Wade, who's just been made deputy editor at the *Sun* had got wind of it too. This struck me as extremely unlikely unless someone at No. 10 had deliberately told her.

But he denied it: 'It hasn't come from here. Rebekah got word that Cherie was seriously ill and phoned her at the Number Ten flat and put it to her. Cherie didn't think she could lie, so felt compelled to tell her the truth. I'm really sorry, but we can't lie to papers about stuff like this.'

I didn't believe a word of it and exploded, 'You lie about stuff like this all the fucking time. If you lot have blown our exclusive, then I will find it very hard to forgive you.' Alastair was indignant. 'These things happen, for fuck's sake – we can't stop it.'

I waited to see what the *Sun* had in its first edition, if anything. Their deadline's around 7.45pm, so it might have been too late and there was a possibility our scoop might have been preserved.

At 9pm, I discovered it filled their entire front page, with the words SUN WORLD EXCLUSIVE emblazoned all over it. I called Alastair with the good news. Sensing my complete apoplexy, he said he would get the Prime Minister on the phone to explain what happened and corroborate his story.

Minutes later, Blair called.

'Piers, hi, Alastair wanted me to call you, because he didn't think you would take it from him. The Sun have phoned up and Rebekah has spoken to Cherie, and they had some story about her being very ill or something, and she has spoken to them and confirmed she is not ill, but pregnant. You must believe me when I say to you I really didn't want this news to come out like this, never mind exclusive to the Mirror. I am only doing this because I don't want you thinking we have been playing politics with our baby, because I would never do that or allow anyone to do that.'

I replied, 'Well, I can't pretend I am not a bit disappointed, Prime Minister, given that I went to Alastair early on today to avoid precisely this happening.'

'Look, I am just concerned and anxious that with Alastair's past relationship with you, you don't think he rang them up. There are more important things, frankly, than who gets what story when.'

'Well, it's quite important to us, to be honest.'

'Yes, well, it is just unfortunate that Rebekah got straight through to Cherie and said she heard she had been very ill and had gone to hospital and all the rest of it. And Cherie, rightly or wrongly, thought she had to tell the truth. I personally, having talked this over with Cherie, think we should put out a statement, and if you want me to say it was following enquires from the Mirror or whatever, I would be perfectly happy to do that.'

Campbell came on to the line.

'Piers, I am really sorry about this … I really am.'

'Oh, that's OK,' I said, trying very hard to control my feelings of complete rage. 'I must try ringing the flat direct myself next time, and bypass you, Alastair. Seems to work better, doesn't it.'

Blair sighed. 'Yeah, well. Hmm.'

Campbell said, 'I will say that following enquiries from the Daily Mirror, I can confirm Cherie is pregnant.'

A meaningless sop. The damage is done and we've been shafted.

Blair had sounded embarrassed. Now he went on the attack, sensing possible political problems.

'Piers, the thing I am really concerned about is that you know you did not get this story from us, and I will be really angry if people suggest you did. We wanted to keep it secret until all the various tests have been completed.'

'Well, Prime Minister, I thought I might put out a statement saying I've heard of some ways of keeping Ken Livingstone and his battle to be Mayor off the front page, but this is ridiculous.'

'Yes, exactly.'

It was time to calm down a little. He is the Prime Minister after all, and we were talking about his baby.

'So how does it feel, then?'

'It's a very strange thing at my age, I can tell you. I hate to think what the fallout will be.'

'Well I think sales in Pampers might go through the roof. Was it too much Chianti in Tuscany, then?'

He laughed.

'No, no, nothing like that, I assure you.'

I congratulated him, and he apologised once more.

Then I put the phone down and screamed abuse at the wall.

THURSDAY, 25 NOVEMBER

Spencer came in to the newsroom today with his classmates, and produced an eight-page special edition of the *Mirror* during the day. Highlight was when a fax rumbled through from Tony Blair saying, 'I understand your son and some of his friends are taking a look around the *Mirror* today. I hope they enjoy themselves very much. If you are planning to hand over the job of running the paper to them, I have no doubt they will make an excellent job of it. Yours ever, Tony.' The kids thought it was amusing, but the teachers were shell-shocked and vaguely appalled that the Prime Minister has the time or inclination to do this kind of thing.

MONDAY, 29 NOVEMBER

I phoned Fiona Millar on the pretext of something else and casually said after a few minutes, 'What a laugh all that pregnancy stuff was. I don't blame Cherie for telling Rebekah she was pregnant because she was so annoyed we had the story exclusively. I can see now how annoying it must have been for her.'

Fiona swallowed the bait. 'Oh, I'm so glad you see it that way, Piers. Cherie just felt she had no choice: she didn't want her pregnancy used as some commercial tool, so she gave the story to Rebekah as well.'

'Thank you, Fiona,' I said, 'now I know what really happened.' Then I slammed the phone down.

TUESDAY, 30 NOVEMBER

Victoria Beckham's been taking a fearful hammering in the *Mail* for her thin appearance, even being dubbed 'Skeletal Spice'.

I rang Caroline McAteer, her PR, today to offer my assistance in repelling the misogynists of Kensington.

She got Victoria to call me.

'This is all fucking bollocks,' was her opening line. 'They ran a photo of me last week saying I look great. But that was taken at midday in the sun, this one is all shaded and distorted. I know I am incredibly fit and healthy, but what bothers me is that all the young kids will see this and think that's how they want to look. I felt so angry this morning, people will think that's how Posh Spice looks. To call me Skeletal Spice is really malicious. It reduced me and mum to tears this morning. It winds her up, because like any parent she hates people saying this stuff about her daughter.'

'Well, I am here to help you fight back,' I said.

'Thank you so much. This is the first time anyone's given me the chance to respond to something like this. Normally no paper is going to print the other side of another paper's story. My mum cooks my dinner every day and she is helping me so much and you think – oh, for God's sake, leave her be. Don't upset her by printing this crap.'

'Are you slimmer than normal?'

'The truth is that when I had Brooklyn I lost a load of weight afterwards. I haven't been down the gym once. He was a difficult baby, didn't sleep. Very, very active all the time. And I am the same – even if I have a weekend off, I am always on the phone sorting stuff and talking to people. I am all over the place and always have to be busy. So many people have come up to me and said they lost a load of weight after they had a baby. My mum went down to six stone after she had me. It obviously runs in the family. I guess I weigh about seven and a half stone, which is about a stone less than a year ago. But I am very busy now. They are so full of shit.'

'What does David think?'

'David won his game last night, and he asked me what was in the papers, and I said they were having a go at me. Everyone's so nice to him at the moment, I call him Goldenballs. So they take it out on me.'

'What do you call him again?'

'Goldenballs.' (Laughs loudly.)

'I see. He's a bit of a star in the bedroom as well, then?'

'Of course he is. But I'm not here to talk about that. A few weeks ago, someone accused me of having anorexia, and that's like saying I've got some awful life-threatening disease. My mum actually rang up the editor and had a go at him about it. She said it was bang out of order. She got an apology but then two weeks ago they did it again.'

'I think you look great … I can't believe you're still mucking about with that footballer.'

'Ha, ha.'

Into the lion's den ... I give the unofficial Queen, Victoria Beckham, a tour of the Mirror newsroom.

'I'm serious – imagine David with brains, and that's what I'm offering you.'

'Oh, do behave, Morgan!'

'What did you eat today, anyway?'

'I had two bowls of sugar puffs, two chicken kievs with potatoes and veg and then some cod and veg, and then my mum will have cooked dinner for me when I get back. And I swear on my life that's what I've eaten. Is this going on the front page, then? I hope so …'

'I'll see how you behave. Any keep-fit routines with David you want to share with me?'

Victoria emits an extended filthy cackle.

'None I want to tell you about. Use your imagination, sunshine. David thinks I look great. You should ring the Chinese restaurant I'm at every night and ask them about my appetite.'

'Lots of prawn goldenballs, then.'

'Very funny.'

'What did you have at the Ivy with Elton the other night?'

'Swordfish.'

'And you didn't nip out the back to chuck it all up?'

'God no, I couldn't do that. I couldn't waste the money. I'm too tight. Eat an expensive dinner, then throw it up: what a shocking waste.'

'You are known to be a bit thrifty, aren't you?'

'Oh, yes, and always will be.'

'Must have been a bit of a night though – all those stars, and you.'

'It was. I still get a bit starstruck around famous people. And I was sitting there with my sister at a table with Elton John, George Michael, Richard E. Grant, Hugh Grant, Liz Hurley and we're like, "Oh, my God. This is so bizarre." '

'Yes, but they are all thinking, "Oh, my God, it's Posh Spice." '

'No, they're not, are they?'

'Of course they are.'

We both laughed.

'Does all this Skeletal Spice stuff really annoy you?' I asked.

'Yes, I do feel frustrated, because people do actually believe this rubbish. There must be more important things to worry about in the world.'

'Not sure there are, actually.'

'Well, how stupid is that, Piers, honestly!'

Gordon Brown's planning a dinner party at No. 11 for me and a few celebrity friends who I think he and Sarah might enjoy meeting. I'd mentioned this to Victoria before, and she reminded me of it now.

'Is that thing at Downing Street still on? I hope so, sounds a real laugh. Not that I'm very political, or anything. But it would be nice to see what it's like in there … What's going to be your front-page headline, then?'

'Erm, it will be "Phwoar, we would" – something like that.'

'Yeah, perfect.'

'But only if David signs for Arsenal, OK?'

'You tell him ... I'd love him to. It's nearer the shops.'

FRIDAY, 3 DECEMBER

Victoria's doing her own TV show called *Victoria's Secrets*, and has come to interview me at the *Mirror*.

We had a good laugh.

She had a go at me for doing her David as a dartboard when he got sent off in the World Cup, and for running endless 'rubbish stories' about them.

'Look,' I responded, 'you are the new royal family. And you should be thanking me for all the attention we give you. In twenty years' time, when you and David are doing Snow White in panto, I'm going to get this tape and remind you of how great your life was right now, so stop moaning.'

I took her on a guided tour of the newsroom, and the whole place shuddered to a halt. Quite amazing.

FRIDAY, 10 DECEMBER

Had another Christmas lunch for my columnists at the Mirabelle today. In trooped legend after legend – Alan Sugar, Carol Vorderman, Jonathan Ross, Miriam Stoppard, Tony Parsons.

I made a suitably scathing speech, and they all got suitably scathingly drunk.

Worst offender was Ross, who, on being told the cigars were free, called over the waiter with the case and helped himself to handfuls of Monte Cristos – stuffing them all into his various pockets.

'Cheers, Piers, great fucking party, mate,' he cried to general hilarity as he staggered out with his £1245 haul.

My menu's littered with touching messages:

'What did happen to the gorgeous young showbiz reporter from the *Sun* ... now a fat git ego-in-chief? Love, Carol.'

'Worst fucking food I've ever tasted – great cigars though, Jonathan.'

'Bollocks, you Southern tosser, Brian Reade.'

I bet Cudlipp never had to put up with this. But I guess you reap what you sow.

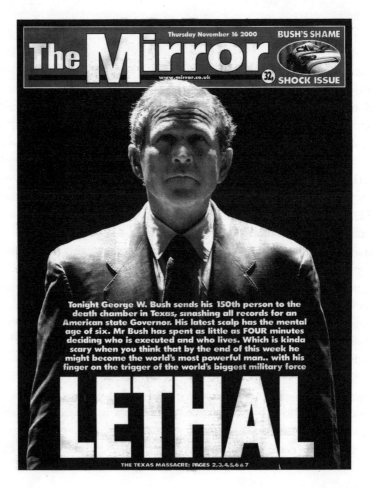

The Mirror

Thursday November 16 2000

www.mirror.co.uk

32p

BUSH'S SHAME

SHOCK ISSUE

Tonight George W. Bush sends his 150th person to the death chamber in Texas, smashing all records for an American state Governor. His latest scalp has the mental age of six. Mr Bush has spent as little as FOUR minutes deciding who is executed and who lives. Which is kinda scary when you think that by the end of this week he might become the world's most powerful man.. with his finger on the trigger of the world's biggest military force

LETHAL

THE TEXAS MASSACRE: PAGES 2, 3, 4, 5, 6 & 7

2000

SATURDAY, 1 JANUARY

The Millennium Dome was opened on Millennium Eve with a huge party. I was invited, but couldn't think of anything worse in the entire world than spending the dawn of the next 1000 years with a bunch of politicians.

I heard today that all the editors who did make the effort got left for hours at Stratford station with a plastic cup of warm wine. That will be the end of the Dome, then.

TUESDAY, 11 JANUARY

With shocking predictability, Martin Edwards – chairman of Manchester United – has been caught by our undercover reporters whilst on the tour in Rio enjoying the pleasures of local hookers. I don't think it's so much that he can't help it, more that he loves it so much and is so rich that he doesn't actually care about being caught.

THURSDAY, 13 JANUARY

Ian Brady has complained to the PCC about us printing a photo of him under the headline THE FAT HUNGER STRIKER. Incredibly we also heard today that Yorkshire Ripper Peter Sutcliffe is doing the same over a photo we ran of him last year.

Two of Britain's most depraved and appalling serial killers taking us to task for invasion of privacy. Happy days.

MONDAY, 17 JANUARY

I've been dabbling a bit in the stock market and bought shares today in a company called Viglen Technology, one of Alan Sugar's companies. Our 'City Slicker' columnists, Anil Bhoyrul and James Hipwell, have tipped them several times since the start of the year, and both my broker and my uncle have also recommended them to me recently, so they sound a good bet.

TUESDAY, 18 JANUARY

The share price of Viglen rocketed this morning, and apparently it was entirely down to a story the City Slickers ran in their column today, saying Viglen are launching an internet business. I had no idea they were running the story until late last night when the first edition dropped. I didn't read their column before publication – hardly ever do. (Most daily editors rarely see more than 50 per cent of their paper before the first edition is printed, whatever they claim; there just isn't time.) Spoke to my broker, who reassured me that he had no problem with what had happened, and it was just an unfortunate coincidence. But he warned me to be more careful in future about this potential conflict between my share-buying and the Slickers column. 'It's just not worth any aggro, is it?' he said.

I've never given it any thought before, but now it seems blindingly obvious. Coincidence or not, I feel rather uneasy about this. I can see how it might look to the outside world.

WEDNESDAY, 19 JANUARY

A bizarre fax from Alastair this morning, saying, 'Tabloids are about pictures, mate. And the *Sun* and *Star* are right. BRITNEY BRIT-NEY!'

Last week he was seen at a Britney Spears concert. He appears to have developed a rather unhealthy obsession with the young lady.

SUNDAY, 23 JANUARY

A small piece appeared in the *Sunday Business* newspaper today saying the Financial Services Authority were having a look at trading in Viglen shares to see if anyone had been 'insider dealing'. It leapt off the page. I am now seriously uneasy. I was a bloody fool to be buying shares without checking what they were tipping in their column.

MONDAY, 24 JANUARY

Had lunch with the boss of MI5 today, Stephen Lander, at his HQ on the Embankment. I knew from his cuttings that he was one of the key intelligence figures in successfully foiling a string of IRA attacks in recent years, which is why he's now got this job.

He was very matter-of-fact about what his organisation does.

'Look, forget all the myths and James Bond tales. We are a disciplined intelligence agency, and our job is not to go around assassinating people or tapping everyone's phones illegally. Our main job is to find out what bad people are up to and prevent them doing it.'

I asked who the biggest threat to Britain was. 'France,' he replied, to my astonishment.

'They have some very dangerous terrorists, mainly of Algerian descent, and given the proximity to our border they represent a very serious and present danger. But there are many other terrorist organisations out there, and we have to keep tabs on all of them.'

'Do you keep tabs on people like me, then?'

He laughed. 'Piers, I could read all your emails this afternoon if I wanted to.'

I think he was joking. I hope he was!

'You must be a top target though, Stephen. How do you and your family deal with that?'

He told a great story by way of response. 'My teenage son was walking around Hammersmith a while ago when he thought someone was following him. I'd told him to call me if anything like this happened, so he did and I called the police who sent a unit straight round. But the guy had gone. I arranged for my son to have an alarm device in case he got worried again. A few weeks later, he was back in the same area and the same man started following him. He really panicked now, and activated the alarm. The police charged down there and caught the guy.'

Lander paused for effect.

'After five hours grilling him at a station, they were satisfied that he wasn't Carlos the Jackal ... but a harmless gay guy who'd just taken a fancy to my son.'

He burst out laughing. And so did I.

Lander's an impressive man – calm, very bright, and extremely focused. And with a sense of humour.

I felt a bit safer after lunch than I had before, knowing someone like him is running MI5.

THURSDAY, 27 JANUARY

A big useless lump called Julius Francis is fighting Mike Tyson this weekend, and odds on the British boxer lasting even one round are pretty long. But watching him give a press conference full of the usual 'I'll whup Tyson's butt' bravado, an amusing idea flashed into my head. I called his promoter, Frank Warren. 'Frank, how much would it cost me to sponsor Julius for this fight, with logos on his clothing?' I could tell Frank was rather surprised. 'Are you serious?' he said. 'Yes, very,' I replied, 'but there are very specific parts of his anatomy that we wish to sponsor.' 'Riiiight,' said Frank; 'like what?' 'Well, the back of his shorts and the soles of his boots.' There was a pause as the penny dropped.

Frank's a smart cookie.

'What, so when Tyson bangs him over, everyone sees the Mirror logo, right?'

I laughed. 'Yes, that's about the gist of it.'

Frank thought it was hilarious, and I could tell that sponsors were not exactly queuing up to back our boy, because he promised he'd talk to Julius and come back to me. An hour later he was back. 'He says he'll do it for twenty thousand.'

SATURDAY, 29 JANUARY

Julius Francis was knocked over five times in two rounds, and kept falling on to his hands and knees in such a way that the viewers watching on TV were shown regular large images of his backside and the soles of his feet – all sporting large red-and-white *Mirror* logos. What made it even funnier was that the fight was being screened on Sky, owned by Murdoch. So we were getting unbelievable publicity on our biggest rival's network. I sat watching it all happen at home with tears of laughter rolling down my face.

MONDAY, 31 JANUARY

We did a special front page today, showing our hero flat on his face under the headline PRIDE IN DE-FEET. Alastair faxed me: 'What's the point of sponsoring the back of a boxer's shorts if he spends most of the fight sitting on them?'

I replied: 'I know you're a halfwit, but surely even you can see that Julius kept falling forward, thereby revealing our logo to the world. Now we're in the mood for sponsoring heroic failures, how about Tony's teeth for the next election?'

Frank Warren called later in the day, still chuckling. 'Got your money's worth, then?'

TUESDAY, 1 FEBRUARY

I saw a headhunting firm in secret this morning. They'd approached me about the vacant managing director's job at Arsenal Football Club. But they couldn't afford me. Tragically.

At 7pm I came back from a management meeting to find a message from a reporter called Suzy Jagger on the *Telegraph*'s City desk.

'Did you buy shares in Viglen Technology through Kyte Securities on 17 January?' it read.

I froze to the spot.

'You OK?' asked Kerrie.

'Well, I'm not sure, to be honest. I bought some bloody shares a few weeks ago, and I think it's about to crash around my ears.'

I called Suzy Jagger back, admitted buying the shares, and explained how and why.

Better to be open and up front in situations like this.

Then I called the *Mirror* lawyers and talked them through it all.

When the *Telegraph* dropped at 11pm, there was just a small, balanced story on a left-hand inside page. I wasn't too worried when I saw it: if they'd really thought I'd done something awful, it would have been on the front.

WEDNESDAY, 2 FEBRUARY

Shit. The *Sun* have splashed on the story in their later editions, and done a leader article demanding I resign. This has provoked meltdown at our place, understandably.

I was called down to see Deputy Chief Executive John Allwood and company secretary Paul Vickers, and asked to reveal all my share dealings since I'd been *Mirror* editor. This wasn't difficult as I'd only dealt about twenty times in six years, and made hardly any money on anything. And I had never bought any shares before a Slickers tip before.

I told them the circumstances behind the Viglen purchase and they seemed satisfied. I also explained that both my broker and one of my cousins who occasionally trades with him had bought Viglen shares a few weeks before I did. And that my uncle had also recommended them only last week.

Viglen's share price has crashed back down again, and I haven't sold any as it has done so. But Trinity Mirror is getting besieged with calls. And I can see how it all looks– bloody awful.

THURSDAY, 3 FEBRUARY

The PCC have said they are formally investigating me to see if I have broken the Code of Conduct in relation to financial journalism. Even more worryingly, the Department of Trade and Industry have separately announced they are investigating whether I have broken the insider dealing law.

I checked exactly what that is on the internet, and just saw the words: 'maximum sentence of seven years in prison'.

Christ alive, what the hell have I got myself into here?

FRIDAY, 4 FEBRUARY

The board have cleared me of any wrongdoing after studying all the tapes between me and Anthony Laiker, and reading emails between me and Anil. They can see that while I may have been naive and silly, I am not a crook.

I sold the Viglen shares today and gave all the proceeds to charity. I don't care if some people think, wrongly, that this is some admission of guilt. I don't care if I never see another share again in my life, frankly. The papers are still full of my 'scandal', though interestingly hardly any of the TV news networks are running with it.

SUNDAY, 6 FEBRUARY

Some little runt from *Sunday Business* kept banging on my door this morning, despite being repeatedly told I wasn't going to say anything. Eventually I called his boss Jeff Randall, because I know him, and said, 'Look, Jeff, he can do it all day, but I am not allowed to talk about this, so there's little point.'

He seemed to understand, and pulled his dog off.

Must say it's not very pleasant being on the receiving end, though.

TUESDAY, 8 FEBRUARY

Pride of Britain judging panel meeting at Branson's house again. Probably the very last thing I felt like doing, hosting a panel full of celebrities and trying to be both in charge and entertaining.

But Branson was very nice. 'You OK? Seem to be copping a lot of flak on this shares thing. Don't worry about it, it will all blow over.'

He's a genuinely nice guy.

It was a top line-up, including Trevor McDonald, Mo Mowlam and Victoria Beckham, who greeted me with the words, 'Who's been a naughty boy, then?'

I did my best to be upbeat. But my heart wasn't in it. I just want this shares thing to go away.

Had a date for dinner booked with the new Lord Rothermere, owner of the *Daily Mail*, tonight, but assumed he would cancel it in light of the 'scandal', and pre-empted that call by ringing his office to say I would quite understand. 'Oh, no, no, Mr Morgan, Lord Rothermere is looking forward to it. Pont de la Tour, eight o' clock.'

Well, fair play to the man.

Dinner was great fun, and he couldn't have been more charming.

I met his dad, Vere Harmsworth, a few times and he was a wonderful character. Exactly what you want in a proprietor – intelligent, charming, courageous, mischievous, in love with newspapers, and with billions of pounds in his pocket.

His son and heir Jonathan is like a chip off the old block.

'Thanks for keeping the date,' I said.

'Why wouldn't I?' he laughed.

He was very sympathetic about my plight. 'Fleet Street loves tearing into its own. But it seems to be blowing over already.'

We talked about newspapers. 'I love them,' he said, 'always have done. Growing up with my father, it would have been impossible not to.'

Vere had an extraordinarily close relationship with his editor, David English: they even died within a few months of each other. Everyone's wondering if Jonathan will have the same with Paul Dacre.

'I hope so, I really do,' he said. 'Paul's a brilliant editor. But there's a big age gap between us. He's teaching me the ropes, though, and I hope I can be a help to him and not a hindrance.'

We had a couple of bottles of wine, talked indiscreetly about various journalistic legends, and had a very nice time.

'Perhaps we'll work together one day,' he said as we left, around midnight.

'Well, I might need a job, the way things are going,' I replied.

We both laughed, him more easily than me.

I'd work for him tomorrow, though. It says a lot about him that he had dinner with me in a high-profile restaurant despite all the flak I'm getting.

THURSDAY, 10 FEBRUARY

Alun Michael quit the Welsh Assembly today after losing a vote of no confidence – and Rhodri Morgan has taken over. The man of whom Alastair told me last January, 'Rhodri is good with his one-liners, but you could not imagine him running the country in a month of Sundays.'

Well, he is now, Alastair.

Later *Press Gazette* drops with a piece about me pulling rank over that *Sunday Business* reporter and pleading with his editor to make him go away. I emerge as a hypocritical twat.

FRIDAY, 11 FEBRUARY

Craig MacKenzie, Kelvin's brother and the *Mirror*'s Irish editor, sent me a note from Ireland today:

> Remember what President Teddy Roosevelt said at the Sorbonne in 1910: 'It's not the critic who counts, not the man who points out how the strong man stumbled, or where the doer of deeds could have done better. The credit belongs to the man who is actually in the arena; whose face is marred by the dust and the sweat and the blood; who strives valiantly, who errs and comes up short again and again; who knows the great enthusiasms, the great devotions, and spends himself in a worthy cause; who at the best, knows in the end the triumph of high achievement, and who, at worst, if he fails, at least fails while daring greatly; so that his place shall never be with those cold and timid souls who know neither victory or defeat.'

That's all very well, but dear old Teddy never bought shares in Viglen, did he?

TUESDAY, 15 FEBRUARY

Les Hinton cancelled dinner with me tonight. It was supposed to have been, ironically, at the Pont de la Tour.

A letter from Lord Rothermere arrived in the afternoon post, saying, 'It was good to finally meet you after learning so much about you. I now know why the *Mirror* is doing so well. I enjoyed our conversation and hope it will be the first of many and that we will both grow old and successful in the business we love.'

The reactions of both men to my plight speak volumes.

THURSDAY, 17 FEBRUARY

Anthony Laiker's been fired by his company, Kyte Securities. For no apparent reason other than that his name has been caught up in this 'scandal'. He's a good, straight guy, who did absolutely nothing wrong, and I am completely distraught for him. Where will all this end?

FRIDAY, 18 FEBRUARY

It's got worse. Anil Bhoyrul and James Hipwell were fired by the company today. A decision I was not allowed to play any part in, but everyone will think I did – to save my own scrawny neck.

I can sense a frostiness among some of the staff, and there are even rumours that some senior journalists are planning a vote of no confidence in me. I let it be known that if that is true, then those who feel that way should come and tell me themselves – and I will resign. If I've lost my staff, then I have lost everything as an editor. It's a miserable time. I'm spending hours each day locked away in my office, trying to work a way through this, fending off calls from gnashing reporters, and trying hard not to walk away. I even drafted a resignation note on my computer today, but deleted it when John Howard, the circulation manager, suddenly came into my office and I pressed the wrong button in a panic. Hopeless.

SUNDAY, 20 FEBRUARY
Several Labour MPs, including Frank Field and some woman I've never heard of called Fiona McTaggart, have called for me to be sacked. As a result, Victor Chandler's offering 6–4 on me going. Quite fancy a dip at that, actually.

SUNDAY, 27 FEBRUARY
I've fled to Spain for a week with the boys to try and escape the mayhem.

But there is, of course, no escape. The *Mail on Sunday* ran a prominent story implying I've stashed away £5 million in some slush fund for my share-dealing, and naming loads of stocks they've found in this strange account that must be mine. Many of which were tipped in the *Mirror*.

It's all nonsense. I've invested a total of less than £100,000 on shares in my life, and never dealt in any of these companies. But I can tell all bets are off now, and Fleet Street wants to nail me as the new Nick Leeson, regardless of the truth. The scale of lawless inaccuracy in the reporting is frightening – if we are like this with our own, what the hell are we doing to other public figures?

MONDAY, 28 FEBRUARY
Robin Cook left a message with Kerrie today, saying, 'Don't let the buggers get you down.' He's the only politician to have bothered, and I won't forget it.

TUESDAY, 29 FEBRUARY
Murdoch kindly helped me out when asked about the Slickers scandal at a News Corp meeting today.

'I'd have fired an editor in that position,' he said. 'But it doesn't matter whether he stays or goes now, because his credibility is so damaged that he is hurting the paper.'

But I got an incredibly nice letter from Brian Hitchen, former editor of the *Sunday Express* and *Daily Star*, which lifted my mood.

'I don't know the ins and out of this story and I don't care. What I do know is you're the best editor of the *Daily Mirror* in 35 years. So no matter what muck other editors throw, hang in there. Everything eventually blows over and goes away, however unbearable it may seem now. Keep your chin up and tell the opposition to go to hell.'

WEDNESDAY, 1 MARCH
Dominic Lawson took me to lunch near the Wharf today, and we spoke fully and frankly about the Slickers affair. He's a former City editor of the *Financial Times*, and his verdict – 'it's a load of trumped-up nonsense, don't worry' – cheered me enormously.

Later I got a message from a friend who works at the Financial Services Authority. 'Did you know you were sitting at the next table to my boss, Howard Davies, today?'

He runs the FSA. And would have heard everything.

THURSDAY, 2 MARCH
Philip Graf, the chief executive, wrote to me today following a board meeting.

'This has been a very serious set of circumstances for the company and you: we cannot afford another one.'

I replied, thanking him and the board for their support and accepting I'd been a stupid arse.

'I made a number of misjudgements, and with hindsight I'm incredulous I didn't see any warning signs about the Slickers column or my own share dealings.'

And incredulous is the right word – how could I have been so fucking *stupid*?

James Hewitt has been asked by the *Mail* for his reaction to my little difficulty. 'Isn't it marvellous?' he was reported to have 'chortled'.

FRIDAY, 3 MARCH
Had my first meeting with a lawyer from Clifford Chance, Jeremy Sandelson, who is going to act for me in the DTI investigation. He is bright and amusing, but direct. 'Piers, it seems from everything you have told me that you have not broken the law. But I must tell you that the fact you bought Viglen shares the day before your paper tipped them doesn't *look* good, and there has to be a chance that you might be prosecuted for insider dealing, albeit a very small one. The DTI have unlimited powers to investigate this, and unlimited time. So you have got to tell me everything that might be relevant.'

I liked him. I don't want some bullshitter now, I want someone who is going to talk to me straight. I know I'm still in trouble here. Potentially very, very big trouble.

MONDAY, 13 MARCH
Anil Bhoyrul sent me a goodbye note, so I returned the favour. 'I'm sorry the column had to end the way it did. You brought a lot of energy and creativity to

the newsroom, and on a personal note I shall miss having you around to cheer up all those dull days when nothing's happening. But as my grandmother always says: "One day you're the cock of the walk, the next you're a feather duster." So if I need any cleaning doing, I'll give you a call.'

I feel sorry for him, genuinely.

THURSDAY, 16 MARCH

Matthew Wright's got wind that Madonna's pregnant, and we had pictures of her leaving a Harley Street clinic which seemed to prove it. I called her notoriously unhelpful PR woman, Liz Rosenberg, in New York and she denied it.

I asked if she was sure.

'Piers, listen to me. Madonna. Is. Not. Pregnant. OK?'

I don't believe her, I've never believed a word she says, and I instructed Matthew to write the story, but to qualify it slightly as 'rumour' rather than 'fact'.

SATURDAY, 18 MARCH

A hilarious apology in the *Financial Times* under the headline SIR ALAN SUGAR: 'Sir Alan Sugar has pointed out to us, and we accept, that he is not a friend of Piers Morgan, editor of the *Mirror*, and had nothing to do with Mr Morgan's decision to purchase shares in Viglen Technology. We are happy to confirm that we were not suggesting otherwise.'

It's true, I hardly know him, really, but it seems a bit harsh all the same.

SUNDAY, 19 MARCH

Went to my first Arsenal match today since the scandal broke – I've not had the time or the will until now. But nothing would keep me away from the Spurs match at Highbury.

As I arrived at the ground, a group of lads clocked me and one shouted, 'Got any tips, Piers, mate?'

I ignored them, silent shame burning inside me.

'You greedy wanker,' shouted another.

Sun readers, I expect, who've read a month of poisonous front-page bile about what a flash, spivvy, crooked sod I am.

I took my usual seat, and a guy I vaguely know came over to offer his sympathy. 'We were talking about it in the pub last night and decided that not only don't we understand it, we don't care either. Fill your boots, mate, everyone else is.'

It was nice of him to come over, but I feel even more humiliated now. Everyone thinks I'm guilty.

As I left the ground, another cry of 'Any tips, Piers?' went up.

'Yes,' I said. 'Sell Tottenham.'

They all laughed. Right. Humour seems to be the way out of this, then.

MONDAY, 20 MARCH

The *Sun*'s website breaks the news that Madonna *is* pregnant. I called Liz Rosenberg. 'I couldn't say anything, you know what it's like.'

TUESDAY, 21 MARCH

It was the Budget today, and Gordon Brown rang me as usual to see what I thought. He does that with most editors, and it of course has the disarming effect of putting you on the spot.

It's quite hard to say, 'Well, it was crap, Gordon,' when he's growling down the phone at you. And you can't say, 'It was great,' and then print the opposite. He's a canny one, Mr Brown.

The theme of this year's Budget was health, and we'd done up Brown in cartoon form as a surgeon injecting life into the NHS.

The caricature was quite sinister.

'How are you, Piers?' he asked.

'Fine thanks, Gordon. Have you got any share tips for me?'

'Ha, ha. Buy Labour. What do you think of the health stuff, then?'

'Well, we're doing you up as a doctor curing the country of all known ills. Trouble is that the cartoon looks a bit like Joseph Mengele ...'

He laughed nervously.

'Oh, dear. Well, so long as it's not like Harold Shipman – that would be really serious!'

WEDNESDAY, 22 MARCH

It was the Press Gazette awards at the Hilton last night, and I disgraced myself: there's no other way of putting it.

The butt of sneering stares and 'tuts' all night, I drank myself into a raging stupor and started reeling around the bar, picking arguments with all my tormentors.

Finally I alighted on Les Hinton, and unloaded all my bile on him.

'You think it's alright to fuck with me and my family do you, Les, you prick?'

Everyone backed off as he tried to calm me down. 'It's just business, Piers, not personal.'

'Of course it's personal. We'll see how you like it when I come after you and your family and whack the lot of you, won't we?'

It was Sonny Corleone without the brains or the charm.

I was led away by a colleague, only to run straight into the *Sun* executive team, who I greeted with another stream of drunken invective.

Then one of the *Sun* lot, quite understandably, threw a punch at me, which missed, and all hell broke out – with journalists from the *Mirror* and *Sun* trading shoves, slaps, kicks and abuse.

My head was swirling, I was out of control. All the simmering anger I'd felt for the last six weeks was spilling out in ghastly fashion. I'd 'gone'.

THURSDAY, 23 MARCH

I spent the day in bed being sick and feeling sorry for myself.

My behaviour at the Press awards was just appalling, and everyone's gossiping about it, apparently.

I am seriously thinking of resigning. Every week's bringing ridiculous new 'revelations' about me, shares, the Slickers … There's no end to it, and I'm spending every bloody weekend sitting by the phone waiting for the inevitable call from a Sunday paper with their latest 'bombshell'. I'm being regularly doorstepped outside my houses in London and Sussex by reporters and even TV crews.

The kids are getting unsettled by all the attention, but there's nothing I can do about it. I can't sue or go to the PCC without looking like a pathetic hypocrite. I learned that lesson from the Sheryl Gascoigne episode.

I've lost a stone in weight since the story broke, hardly eat, and am drinking far too much.

Last night's behaviour was a culmination of all this, and I've had enough.

FRIDAY, 31 MARCH

Marco Pierre White's getting married to his lovely fiancée Mati in a week, and they invited Marion and me to his restaurant, the Mirabelle, for dinner tonight to 'celebrate the marriage and your survival'. Typically generous of him, though I'm definitely not out of the woods yet, and still feel terrible.

The meal took a turn for the absurd about halfway through when Marco suddenly said, 'Right, I think it's time for something special.'

And I heard him ordering a bottle of Château Margaux, which even I know is expensive.

We drank it quickly, and moved on to a Château Lafite of equally impressive and distant vintage.

Then a bottle of Mouton Rothschild from 1945. It was getting very, very silly. We were swigging some of the greatest wines ever made here like it was Ribena.

Another bottle arrived …

It was all utterly, fantastically delicious. As good as you always hoped this kind of stuff would be if only you could afford it.

Then Marco announced, 'Something *really* special.'

A slightly cobwebbed bottle of Château d'Yquem arrived, dated 1911.

'One of the best wines ever made,' Marco purred, and slurred.

'Marco,' I said. 'How much does all this stuff cost?'

He laughed. 'Piers, you don't want or need to know. I am getting married, and you have had a hard time, and we are celebrating. You can't put a price on that.'

'Come on, I'm dying to know. It must be unbelievably expensive.'

Marco laughed again. 'Actually, I'm curious myself.' He called a waiter over. 'Can you print me off a bill, please?'

'But Marco, it is your restaurant.'

'Yes, I know that, but just print me off a bill, please.'

It came back five minutes later. Food: £260. Wine: £26,000.

I blinked and read it again.

Yes, £26,000. The d'Yquem alone was £11,000.

Marco fell about laughing. 'Fancy going Dutch?'

I asked him to sign each bottle so I could take them home as souvenirs. He signed the d'Yquem '£1500 a sip – love Marco!'

Then he and I had two glasses of cognac from 1900.

We staggered home laden with bottles.

SATURDAY, 1 APRIL

Woke up with no hangover. No wonder all those emperors could go into battle after a night on the lash if the wine was that good all the time.

My parents came for lunch today, and I noticed there was a good two inches left in the d'Yquem bottle, so I poured it into a glass for my father.

'Here you are, Dad, nice bit of plonk, this – have a try.'

He swigged it down in one. 'Mmm. Very nice.'

'So it should be: that was two thousand pounds' worth.'

TUESDAY, 4 APRIL

Fayed's not happy after I cancelled a lunch date at the last minute. 'This is becoming a habit of yours,' he wrote angrily. 'It would have been decent of you to give me notice of your cancellation rather than just call on the day. I have thousands of people to see. C'est la vie!'

I replied: 'My humble, abject apologies. Unfortunately my routine, mundane day job occasionally ruins the best-laid plans, even for meeting personal heroes such as yourself. I presume you want me to be Fulham manager, in which case, for £1 million a year, a nice big Aston Martin, yacht in the Bahamas and a free licence to sign the whole Arsenal first team, I'm yours and can start Monday.'

FRIDAY, 7 APRIL

Marco's wedding at the Belvedere restaurant. What do you give a man who can spend £26,000 on a meal?

I opted for something no money can buy – a special genuine printed edition of the *Daily Mirror* with four pages about him, Mati and their wedding. Three hundred copies arrived after the speeches, and were handed out to all the guests. He loved it, as I knew he would.

Michael Winner was best man, and managed to drop the pudding, a towering six-foot profiterole. To his intense embarrassment and our intense amusement.

MONDAY, 10 APRIL

Lunch with Blair at No. 10. The first contact since the shares scandal broke. My chances of hanging on must have been deemed fairly high by his advisers for him to be seeing me again now.

'Everything OK, now?' he said. 'Yes, all OK, thanks,' I replied.

Though it isn't yet. One of his own government departments haven't finished their investigation yet and could conceivably still sling me in jail.

But this wasn't the time or place to discuss that.

We had a convivial chat, and I asked how he thought he was doing.

'Quite well, I think. But I'd like to make faster progress. It's been harder to repair the damage caused by the Tories than I anticipated.'

I got back to the office to learn that Kate Winslet, having indicated she would come to our Pride of Britain awards tomorrow, is now saying she can't. Someone had got hold of her mobile phone number – I never like to ask how – so I rang her.

A voice answered and sounded a bit like Kate, but said she wasn't and she would take a message. 'OK, well this is Piers Morgan from the Mirror and I'd like to talk to her about Pride of Britain.'

I was sure it was her.

Half an hour later, Kerrie said, 'Kate Winslet's on the phone.'

'Hello,' she said, sounding a bit taken aback. 'How did you get my number, I've only just changed it. You've got to tell me, *please*. I am so worried now; if the press get my number, then I have to change it.'

'Relax Kate, I won't be giving it to anyone. I thought it was you when I called before, actually.'

'No, it was my assistant.'

'You sure?'

'Well, fairly sure, yes, she's black.'

She laughed loudly.

'OK, well, look, I'm really sorry, but I can't come to Pride of Britain because at the moment I am supposed to be filming. I'm really sorry. I am still trying to sort it, but it's not looking good. I am pregnant and I forgot to deal with this until it was too late.'

I wasn't giving up easily.

'But that is exactly why we want you to present to this foster mum with six hundred and fifty kids. Come on, you can do it … we'll be forever in your debt.'

'Yes, you bloody will be!'

'I told your assistant that the bad news was you'd have to sit next to the Prime Minister, the good news was I'd be on the other side.'

'Ha, ha! I'd quite like to meet Tony Blair, actually. But that would mean I'd have to be on really good behaviour and I wouldn't be able to say fuck.'

'You could sort your damehood out …'

'Yes, I could, couldn't I? I will definitely try and sort it out. But I still want to know who gave you my number. It must be someone I know.'

'My lips are sealed: sorry.'

'Oh, please …'

'I'll tell you if you come to the lunch.'

'That's terrible.'

'Look, Kate you don't get to be editor of the Mirror without being a fairly despicable human being.'

'No, I guess you don't … you awful man.'

'Look on the bright side – at least we haven't delved into your wild sex and drugs past yet.'

'That's because I've never taken any fucking drugs. I am so boring.'

'It will happen. Some scandal will occur, then you'll get caught, blame the media and next time I try and ring you, you will slam the phone down and tell me to piss off.'

'It won't happen to me because I am being a mum. Talking of which, what's the dress code for this, because I don't fit into any of my clothes.'

'Look, you're only competing with June Whitfield and Diana Ross, so I wouldn't worry too much. It's not BAFTA, darling. But remember, if you want to get on the front page, then don't wear black, because we only put colour photos on the front.'

'I'll wear black, then. Ha, ha! Listen, you wicked, awful man, I will try, OK?'

'We have a deal, then?'

'Not yet.'

'What do you want then, a holiday for your parents in the Bahamas, then you'll present to the foster mum?'

'Oh, do be quiet.'

'Would it be better or worse if I got Richard Branson to call your producer?'

'Worse, definitely. It's better if I try. They like me and trust me.'

'We all do … my staff are bashing down the door to get to the phone right now. Now let me give you my mobile, if only so I can tell people you carry my number around on your phone.'

'Oh, God, you are so fucking cheap, Morgan. If I do this, you will have to be so fucking nice to me in your paper.'

'We already are.'

'I know.'

'But this will be ten times as saccharine with extra syrup, OK?'

I put the phone down and laughed. She's such a nice, natural and unaffected girl – unlike most of her profession, in my experience.

We've tried to reduce the time Blair speaks at Pride of Britain tomorrow, to stop him banging on for hours. But the suggestion has provoked anger at No. 10.

Alastair faxed to ask sarcastically, 'Can you please explain to me what, in the 60 seconds the Prime Minister is allowed to speak, is the single point you want covered?'

TUESDAY, 11 APRIL

Pride of Britain awards at the Hilton Hotel today. One of the highlights was the appearance of a young Gurkha widow who lost her husband in Kosovo. She'd flown from the Himalayas for the first time with her children to receive an award from Michael Caine.

The poor woman burst into tears when TV news footage was shown of a mine exploding in Kosovo – she thought, wrongly, that it was the moment her husband died. We hadn't thought of that and should have done.

Caine spent most of the time in tears. 'This is unbearable,' he said. 'I've never experienced anything so moving.'

Blair was pretty chuffed, too. 'I've always wanted to meet Michael Caine and Diana Ross,' he said as he sat down at the top table.

I'd put myself next to Arsene Wenger, who arrived twenty minutes late – and looked horrified to see who else he was sitting with.

'My God, I had no idea I would be with the Prime Minister and all these superstars,' he whispered to me. 'I feel so embarrassed to be so late.'

'Oh, don't worry about it, Arsene,' I laughed. 'You're God's representative on earth, so you have nothing to worry about.'

We spent most of the next hour discussing tactics, transfers and trophies. Pure bliss. He's charming, intelligent, and totally obsessed by football – so didn't mind me yapping on about who I thought should play left midfield.

WEDNESDAY, 12 APRIL

Richard Desmond sent me a note congratulating us on Pride of Britain. Inevitably, the last line read: 'Could you make me happy, Piers, and publish our Fantasy Channel listings, it means so much. Please, Piers.'

THURSDAY, 13 APRIL

Paul Burrell wrote to thank me for Pride of Britain: 'Keep up the good work in continuing to champion those causes which need highlighting. The *Mirror*'s voice remains strong out there, on the factory floor, where people are the priority!'

SATURDAY, 15 APRIL

A long, handwritten letter from Kate Winslet:

Dear Piers, Please accept my humble apologies for not being able to attend the Pride of Britain awards. I *honestly* tried my best in getting the powers-that-be at work to alter the schedule for that day, but with only five days to go before Day 1 of filming I think they were nervous that there wouldn't be another occasion to rehearse at our locations. I'm pleased to say I caught some of the ceremony on TV, and it was certainly very moving. As far as I'm concerned, all award ceremonys [sic] apart from this one should be banished. Look, I'd love to write to that extraordinary woman and send her some signed photos etc. Maybe you could give me her details.

Let's really try and make it happen next year. Let me know about two months in advance (!) as the more notice I have the more I'll be able to schedule it in. Take care, best wishes Kate. xxx.

WEDNESDAY, 19 APRIL

In Barbados for a fortnight to try and recharge my shattered batteries. Spotted a poem today on a local shop wall, called 'No giving up!' with the refrain, 'I'm going to *win!*'

Very cheesy, but it made me smile and feel a bit cheerier, so I bought it.

WEDNESDAY, 3 MAY

The *Mirror* declared 'Vote Tory' on the front page today. Only because we think Steve Norris would be the best Mayor of London, and can't stomach the thought of Ken Livingstone.

Everyone's horrified in the newsroom, they're all pretty much left of Tony Benn around here. But I reminded them that the *Mirror* has said 'Vote Tory' before – at the 1929 General Election.

WEDNESDAY, 10 MAY

The PCC published their official adjudication into the City Slicker share-dealing affair today, and they completely trashed me, saying I had 'fallen short of the high professional standards demanded by the code'. A long and damning statement.

They've also referred the adjudication back to my chief executive, only the second time this ultimate sanction has ever happened. There was an almost comical moment on Sky when the presenter asked the reporter outside the PCC HQ who the other offender was.

'Erm, well, it was Mr Morgan again, actually, for invading the privacy of Countess Spencer.'

I feel wretched, but my bosses have made it clear they're going to stand by me, so I'm just going to have to pull myself together and get on with it.

I ran the whole adjudication, although we weren't obliged to. Only later did I realise that it was so long, and so dense, that nobody would actually bother to read it.

Curiously, despite wall-to-wall coverage on TV today, we have not had a single complaint about me to the newsdesk. In fact, we have hardly had a complaint about the Slickers scandal at all since it started. Odd. But strangely comforting.

SATURDAY, 13 MAY

I took Spencer and his class, complete with siblings and parents and teachers, to the Millennium Dome today, to test my theory that it's actually rather good.

With almost no exceptions, they loved it. This has become a white elephant probably because all those editors were kept waiting at Stratford station on 31 December drinking warm wine.

WEDNESDAY, 17 MAY

I went to the UEFA Cup Final in Copenhagen to see Arsenal play Galatasaray. We lost a dismal match on penalties, but that scarcely seemed relevant because of the appalling violence before, during and after the game.

I have seen crowd trouble at football matches before, but nothing like this. I could sense the mounting tension during the day as English fans drank themselves stupid just yards from Turkish fans. It was the first encounter between supporters from these countries since two Leeds fans were stabbed to death in Turkey. And I spotted quite a few Leeds shirts among the Arsenal fans.

There were skirmishes all day, but full-scale rioting broke out after the game, and I was caught right in the middle of it with Martin Cruddace.

At one stage we were pushed up against a wall by riot police as bottles, chairs and glasses all hurtled past us. Anything that could be thrown was being thrown. Local people who'd been happily serving us all afternoon now cowered in terror as hooligans smashed up the main square. It was scary, and thoroughly sickening.

I called the back bench around 11pm and they could hear it all going off in the background. 'Er … are you OK, out there?' said Jon Moorhead. 'No, not really. It's bloody frightening, actually. I'll call you when we get through it.'

We eventually did, but both felt mentally and physically pounded.

I don't care who started this; Arsenal fans were out of control, and I was disgusted by their behaviour.

THURSDAY, 18 MAY

I arrived back in the office chastened and angry. Through the day, a load of riot pictures came in, and we ran them with a leader saying the culprits should be banned from the club and sacked if they have jobs.

TUESDAY, 23 MAY

Arsenal have moved swiftly to ban the Copenhagen hooligans for life, and some of them have been sacked from their jobs as well.

WEDNESDAY, 24 MAY

Rebekah was made editor of the *NoW* today. I rang to congratulate her. 'Well done, you're the second youngest editor of the NoW in the last ten years.'

'Hmmm, but the youngest this Millennium,' she replied.

It's brilliant news though, and I am thrilled for her. She'll be a star.

THURSDAY, 8 JUNE

Had lunch with Jeff Bezos, the owner of Amazon, today at the Lanesborough. An extraordinary character. Worth several billion now, fizzing with creative force, and ever so slightly barking. He kept throwing back his head and exploding with laughter in a sort of Sid James-times-twenty way.

He confidently predicted the imminent demise of print newspapers.

'Everyone will be reading their papers on flexible computers in five years' time,' he declared, with another cavernous cackle.

'Rubbish,' I said.

He cackled again.

'Well, you would say that, wouldn't you, Mr Editor?'

He was very entertaining, and explained the success of Amazon very simply. 'Delivery. We deliver stuff quickly, and are reliable. We offer good prices, and we are aiming to stock pretty much anything people want, but ultimately our selling point is delivery. That's what people know about Amazon. We deliver.'

He's right, that's all they do really. Deliver. But then that's all any business has to do, so long as the product is what people want.

TUESDAY, 27 JUNE

I've been trying to devise a new showbiz column to replace Matthew Wright, who's quitting after five years.

I suggested a female replacement to Richard Wallace, the showbiz editor.

'Why not three?' he said. 'We could call them "The 3am Girls", and capitalise on the ladette culture out there.'

It's a brilliant idea.

Today we unleashed The 3am Girls on an unsuspecting nation.

THURSDAY, 6 JULY

Euan Blair was arrested last night for getting completely pissed and ending up face down and gurgling in Leicester Square, while celebrating finishing his GCSEs with a few mates.

He gave a false name at the police station, and said he was eighteen when in fact he's sixteen.

I felt sorry for him, but it's quite reassuring to discover he's just like any other kid of his age.

I spoke to Alastair, who confided, 'The worst thing is that Cherie's away at the moment, so Tony was in charge. She's gone bonkers at him. Quite funny, though.'

Earl Spencer, my bitter enemy for so long, came to our monthly lunch today as the star guest. I was flabbergasted that he'd actually come, after all our history. But pleased, too. Feuds are great fun, but they should always come to an end before somebody dies or you both go mad. He was charming, but combative. Making no apology, really, for the way he'd behaved. Mind you, nor did I.

'I did what I thought was right to protect my family, and my sister in particular. I may have made a few mistakes along the way, but that's the way it is.'

We went over a few of our battles, and I began to see his point of view in a more sympathetic light. When I was younger, the truth is that I didn't really give a stuff about people like him so long as we got our story.

'We went over the top sometimes, especially with Diana,' I conceded.

I took him on a guided tour of the newsroom afterwards, to general astonishment. Most amusing moment of the day was his failure to recognise Carol Vorderman. To her visible dismay. Very funny.

MONDAY, 10 JULY

A handwritten letter from my new friend Earl Spencer:

Dear Piers, Many thanks for an interesting and enjoyable lunch. A varied guest list, the airing of many subjects, and the *Mirror*'s hospitality all made for a justifiably long session at the table. I feel bad not remembering Carol Vorderman. Still, she looks a lot better now than I can ever remember her looking in *Countdown*. There again, being next to Richard Whiteley should make anyone look good … Yours, Charles.

TUESDAY, 25 JULY

A sensational story broke just after 3pm, when reports came in that Concorde had crashed on take-off in Paris. My mind began racing with the possibilities of who might have been on board. Tickets cost at least £6000, so everyone on it would have been definitely rich and probably well known in their field.

'Christ,' I said loudly on the back bench, 'this is it, the big one. Murdoch, Naomi Campbell, Schumacher, who knows who was on it? But this is going to be huge.' Controlled panic swept the newsroom. I quickly agreed to requests for at least twelve journalists and photographers to fly to Paris as soon as possible. We'd want news reporters, feature writers, columnists and snappers out there. The story will run for days, if not weeks. I called advertising and asked for the first nineteen pages to be cleared immediately. This is normally not a problem on big tragedies, because most advertisers don't want to be in those papers anyway. I also requested an up-paging of at least eight pages to do justice to the story.

Then, just as I was starting to really pump with adrenaline, a news 'snap' flashed up on the Press Association wire service, saying the plane had been chartered to a German tourist firm. '*What?*' I shouted. 'Is this just a load of bloody Germans?' Even as I said it, I knew it was a terrible thing to say. But people often say terrible things in newsrooms on days like this. The newsdesk scrabbled for information, but PA beat them to it, confirming minutes later that they were indeed all 'bloody Germans', and in fact were all German pensioners on their way to join a cruise ship. None of them were believed to be remotely famous.

I sat back in my chair and groaned. 'Oh, for fuck's sake, a hundred old Germans. It's not a story.' A few people looked at me in vague disgust. One was bold enough to say, 'I think it's still a story, boss, to be honest, even if Naomi Campbell hasn't died.' I knew I was being an unfeeling, heartless bastard, displaying the worst kind of tabloid emotions. But I couldn't disguise my deflation.

From being one of the biggest news stories ever, I could see this was now going to be a tragic event, but nothing like as big. 'Just do the first seven pages and get on with it,' I said, before heading to a Canary Wharf bar to meet a potential new recruit to the paper as planned.

It's only now, as I sit having a Jack Daniel's and watching the grief-stricken relatives on TV, that I can see my behaviour was appalling – beyond contempt, really. But every other paper has downgraded the story to just a few pages, too. So even if they didn't say it in such a crass way, every editor thought the same as me. Doesn't excuse my reaction, though. It's quite chilling to sit back at times like this and see how desensitised I've become after a few years of editing tabloid papers. I don't like it.

FRIDAY, 28 JULY
We were offered a dodgy transcript of a phone conversation between James Hewitt and Anna Ferretti today.

My attention was drawn to a moment when she asks, 'If you don't win the case, will you kill Piers Morgan?'

Hewitt replies, 'Maybe. I don't know, I don't know.'

In another call, he expands on his thoughts, saying he knows a 'Nicaraguan hitman' who can take me out for £20,000!

God almighty.

I hurriedly leaked all this to the *Telegraph* diary, so at least everyone will know who did it if some bloke from South America guns me down in Soho.

TUESDAY, 22 AUGUST
Arsenal's first home game of the season today against Liverpool, and I discovered in rather brutal fashion how the pen isn't always mightier than the sword. It was a night match, and as I walked away from the ground afterwards, I was stopped in my tracks by an enraged and very large Arsenal fan screaming abuse at me. 'You got me fucking fired and banned, you *cunt!*' he kept shouting, as he

pinned me up against a wall. Yep – one of those hooligans we exposed in May. It seemed a good idea at the time, but I am beginning to regret that particular investigation. Because these guys are going to be reminding me of it every time I go to Arsenal for the rest of my life. Great work, Piers.

THURSDAY, 31 AUGUST

To Charing Cross police station, taking Martin with me, where I was quizzed under caution by two senior Scotland Yard detectives about Hewitt and those bloody Diana love letters.

'Never mind me,' was my opening line. 'Why aren't you taking action against Hewitt under the 1361 Act of Treason, which renders him liable to death by hanging for having an affair with the wife of a future Crown?'

The two detectives stifled laughs.

'We are not intending to look at the Act of Treason just at the moment, Mr Morgan.'

I then read a prepared statement and refused to answer any more questions. Martin and I left feeling pretty pleased with ourselves.

There was really no way back for them after the prospect of Hewitt being hanged loomed into the equation.

THURSDAY, 14 SEPTEMBER

John Redwood called me today. I thought about it for a bit, then decided there was absolutely nothing in the entire world that I wanted to discuss with John Redwood, so didn't call him back.

SUNDAY, 17 SEPTEMBER

Paula Yates has killed herself. The saga that amused a nation, and filled so much newspaper space, has become a tragedy of epic proportions. I sat in my office remembering all those conversations I used to have with her – she was clever, funny, flirtatious, mischievous. And yet fatally flawed by her desire to be a rock chick and to be Hutchence's babe. She'd have been so much better off staying with Geldof.

TUESDAY, 26 SEPTEMBER

Labour conference time again in Brighton. Couldn't be arsed to watch Blair's speech in the main hall. It's always boiling hot, and there's this terrible collective compulsion to clap every word he says, when I often have no wish to.

So I watched it on TV in my room, and was so glad I did because I was able to spot quite early on that he was sweating rather badly. And wearing a blue shirt, which is always a recipe for disaster.

Sure enough, as the lights got hotter, so did the Prime Minister, until by the end he was like that poor guy Aaron in *Broadcast News*, just drowning in a sea of perspiration. Bloody funny.

'Got any share tips for me laddie?' The Chancellor
and I share a pint after the shares scandal.

WEDNESDAY, 27 SEPTEMBER

Lunch with Blair was dominated by sweat jokes. Not sure he was overly amused, really, but everyone else was. 'I should have worn a white shirt,' he admitted. 'I could feel myself go, but there was nothing I could do.'

FRIDAY, 13 OCTOBER

The *Telegraph* diary called to ask my reaction to the revelation that my village bonfire society were going to burn an effigy of me on the stake at this year's big night.

Now, Sussex village bonfires are huge affairs, and Newick has one of the biggest and best. They only burn really appalling people, like Saddam or the local policeman if he's had a run on drink-drive arrests.

Surely they weren't going to do me? I rang a few locals quickly. It was OK, just their little idea of joke.

'The village is still behind you,' one of them said, laughing. 'About a hundred yards behind you, but still there.'

TUESDAY, 31 OCTOBER

Interviewed Blair at No. 10 today. When I arrived in his office, I spotted one of those ghastly singing fish you get everywhere now. The ones that move about and sing 'Don't Worry, Be Happy' incessantly.

'Come on, let's have a photo of you and Billy,' I said.

'No, no,' shouted Alastair, racing over to block our snapper.

'Oh, come on, it's funny, it can be Tony's message to the nation: "Don't worry, be happy".'

Alastair backed off for a second and my photographer whipped a quick photo of the PM and Billy.

Back at the office, Campbell tried to pull it. 'It makes him look ridiculous,' he bleated.

'No, it doesn't, it makes him look normal.'

We ran it anyway, all over the front page.

FRIDAY, 10 NOVEMBER

The *Mail on Sunday* rang today, saying they had a load of my Viglen-related emails.

'It's the smoking gun everyone's been waiting for, isn't it, Mr Morgan?' the reporter said proudly.

Not really, mate, I thought, the company and the investigating authorities have had all these since February.

'No comment, sorry.'

WEDNESDAY, 15 NOVEMBER

George Bush looks like he's heading into the White House, and someone had the bright idea of checking his execution record as Governor of Texas. It turned out that in just five years, he has personally ordered the killing of 164 people, including one man recently who had a mental age of six. It was an all-time record for any governor in American state history.

'He's lethal, isn't he?' said Simon Cosyns.

Bingo.

'Find me a sinister photo of him, Si, and do a front page with the headline "Lethal".'

We had another break when we discovered that pictures and names of every one of his execution victims could be found on the internet, complete with full details of their age, sex, crime, and even their last meal.

'Run them all,' I said. 'Every single one, take three spreads if we have to.'

When Simon had finished, it all looked tremendously powerful. You'd read this and think, 'This guy's dangerous.' I had a leader done saying just that, and how worrying this was for world peace.

After re-reading all the detail, though, I couldn't decide what was most disturbing – Bush's trigger-happy behaviour, or the fact that 70 per cent of all those executed chose a Big Mac and large fries as their last meal.

THURSDAY, 23 NOVEMBER

We've been offered some paparazzi photographs of Jeremy Clarkson kissing a woman who is not his wife in his car. They're quite fruity, and since he's such a sexist pig on TV there's a bit of justification in having a little pop at him. He also does a column in the *Sun*, which he signed up for after virtually promising me he'd do it in the *Mirror*. So I hardly owe him any favours.

But we've always got on pretty well, so I called him anyway, to say what we had and suggest he made a joke of it.

'It's ridiculous,' he said. 'That's just a producer friend of mine who I work with.'

'Well, a very good friend, judging by these pictures, Jeremy.'

'They can't show anything, we didn't do anything.'

'Jeremy, you're snogging her face off.'

Silence.

'Look, Piers, I'm going to tell you something now. I'm not capable of having an affair.'

'I see.'

'You can ask my wife. I'm not physically capable. I'm telling you this so you can see how ridiculous these pictures are.'

'Right. OK. Well, that certainly puts a new light on them. Thank you.'

'So you won't run them, then?'

'Well, if we don't, these guys will just take them somewhere else. You're only kissing her, Jeremy, just make a joke out of it and we'll go along with it.'

He sounded crestfallen.

'OK, well if you're going to do it anyway, please just don't say I am having some sort of affair, because I'm not.'

'No, no, just a quick romp in your car.'

'It's not a romp.'

'Sorry, snog.'

'Whatever.'

We put the pictures on pages one and three, with jokey headlines about him getting into top gear, etc. The copy went easy, just taking the mickey really. He shouldn't be too upset, other papers would have gone much harder.

MONDAY, 11 DECEMBER
My third son Bertie was born today.

FRIDAY, 15 DECEMBER
We ran photos on page one yesterday of Cherie Blair in fancy dress as a punk, which are due to be screened in a BBC show called *Before They Were Famous*. Unfortunately, it's not her. And No. 10 is jubilant.

'Ha, ha, ha! You halfwits,' was Campbell's generous comment on the phone.

'Well, it's obviously a BBC plot to destabilise New Labour,' I said.

Later I got a formal fax from him, demanding an apology. 'I don't know what BBC spindoctor persuaded you that the person on page one and three is Cherie, but it is not.'

He wants a donation to a charity of her choice, too.

TUESDAY, 19 DECEMBER
I was interviewed by the DTI today. Four hours of intense, gruelling 'fact-checking'.

Under oath.

The guys doing it were polite, but ruthlessly methodical. They had every relevant email, tapes of every conversation with my broker, every other document that might possibly pertain to my purchase of Viglen shares.

I was startled by the sheer volume of stuff they had. And by the inadvertent hilarity of some of the questioning.

At one stage I was confronted with a letter from Kerrie to our florists, Molly Blooms, in which I'd ordered flowers for Mum's birthday in July and signed it, for a laugh, Piers, Marion, Spencer, Stanley and Viglen.

The DTI boys clearly thought this was some secret code for my share-dealing ring. I was crestfallen to have to disappoint them. So much more glamorous and exciting their way.

My lawyer, Jeremy Sandelson, had told me not to say too much.

'If the answer to a question is "no", then just say "no". Don't volunteer unnecessary material.'

It was good advice, which of course I completely ignored – banging on about all sorts of things that had nothing to do with the question.

It was part nerves, part bravado. I found it an unsettling experience. And the process is not over yet: they warned me it could take some time to make any decision. Some time? It's been nearly a year already. A year of relentless press attacks, jibes in the street, loss of confidence, loss of weight.

I wonder if the people who run the DTI have any idea how debilitating it is to be 'under investigation' for so long.

WEDNESDAY, 20 DECEMBER

The 3am Girls ran a nudge-nudge, wink-wink piece yesterday about Amanda Holden being offered a lift home from a party by her producer Andy Harries.

Les Dennis is not happy. 'Dear Piers,' he wrote today:

> Amanda and I are very strong and will not be rocked by such salacious and vindictive gossip. It seems she cannot be seen out in public without your 'girls' suggesting there is something furtive and underhand going on. Andy's a valued friend of ours and it's a sad reflection on our times if [when] a man is chivalrous and offers a woman a lift home it is reported as something sordid. Finally, I take exception to being given patronising advice from your staff. I am not a victim and can make my own mind up about the future of my marriage. I was not sitting sadly at home, I was working. As it is, we now feel like prisoners in our own home again.

I rather admire him for writing to me like that.

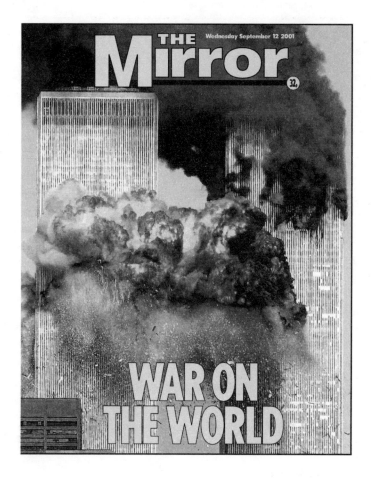

2001

TUESDAY, 2 JANUARY

George Carman, the great barrister, died today. He was a wonderful character who loved the pure theatre of the courtroom. He also loved the theatre of life. I regularly bumped into him in smart hotel bars, where he'd be holding court over a bottle of fine champagne with several usually very beautiful trainee lawyers. 'A very naughty boy,' was how most of his colleagues described him.

I remember giving him a lift home with some *Mirror* colleagues once after a particularly spicy night on the sauce.

'So, George, who would you most like to find in the witness box?' I asked.

'Oh, Piers, that's easy,' he replied with a slight slur; 'a journalist. They are always convinced they know more than I do, and are therefore relatively simple to disintegrate.'

'I see. Can you narrow that down at all?'

'Yes, Piers, I can. I would say that tabloid editors are an especially pleasing sight in the box because their arrogance tends to know no bounds, their knowledge of the law is never as great as they think, they can't stop talking, and they can't help trying to take me on, which usually adds up to complete disaster.'

'I think I know where this is going, but I'll ask anyway. Is there one person in the world you would like to see there that you haven't seen before?'

Pause, for dramatic effect. Intake of breath.

'Yes, Piers, I think I can narrow it down for you. I am talking to him right now.'

FRIDAY, 12 JANUARY

After much wooing, we've hired astrologer Jonathan Cainer from the *Express*. We pay him hardly anything, but he gets to keep the revenue from his daily phone lines. I'd always wondered why anybody would want to be an astrologer. 'I reckon we'll make two million from them in our first year,' he said.

I'm in the wrong game here.

Kelvin once sacked an astrologer after he'd caught him re-running old horoscopes, by writing a letter starting: 'As you will already know …'

WEDNESDAY, 17 JANUARY

Mum graduated with a BA honours in fine art today, making her officially more intelligent than her four children – none of whom got a degree. We took her to lunch at the Ivy to celebrate, and I arranged for us to be 'papped' by Kent Gavin, Royal Photographer of the Decade, as we left. She loved it. I am so proud of her.

I got back to the office to learn that Paul Burrell was sensationally arrested yesterday, for allegedly nicking loads of stuff from Diana. I can't believe he would do that in a million years. What's in his head is worth millions if he ever needed the money – why would he need to steal anything? But the police are clearly going for him big time, and it must be with the backing of the royals. Our headline was DI BUTLER ARRESTED. His trial will be sensational.

I rang Mark Bolland at the Palace.

'You guys are mad, Mark. Burrell could say anything in that stand.'

'I know, I know,' he replied despondently. 'It's a mess.'

'Well, end it now, before it's too late.'

'We can't, the police are running the case now.'

A cornered Burrell could be a very dangerous beast. I tried to call him to offer support, but couldn't get hold of him, so I left a message with his brother Graham to say I didn't believe a word of it.

THURSDAY, 18 JANUARY

A letter arrived from a Mrs Di Butler from Wales, complaining quite seriously that our front-page headline yesterday has made her life hell, because all the neighbours think it's her who has been nicking Diana's possessions. I looked at Kerrie and we both just slowly shook our heads.

FRIDAY, 19 JANUARY

Fiona Phillips wrote to thank me for lunch yesterday. 'I thoroughly enjoyed meeting you, despite your patronising and irritating behaviour. In fact you're just the kind of man I'm attracted to.'

MONDAY, 22 JANUARY

Mandelson's in deep trouble again, for allegedly putting pressure on the Home Office to try and fix a passport for an Indian tycoon called Srichand Hinduja – after he and his brother helped bankroll the Millennium Dome. It's all a bit complicated, and seems to rest on who remembers what. But the media scent his blood again and he's fighting to save his career.

By coincidence I had lunch at No. 10 today with Blair and my parliamentary team. He seemed pretty rattled and distracted by the Mandelson scandal, as well he might. It will damage him hugely if his mate has to quit again. 'He's done nothing wrong as far as I can see,' he said. 'But because it's Peter he attracts more headlines than anyone else.' Alastair was adamant he was not going to have to resign. 'He didn't make any calls himself, he's sure about that. So it's not a problem.' No. 10 later brief to this effect, standing firmly by Mandelson.

TUESDAY, 23 JANUARY

Mandelson *did* apparently make a call to Home Office minister Mike O'Brien. He says he 'forgot' and the call was completely 'innocent'. But Alastair's furious. 'Downing Street misled journalists yesterday because Peter told us he didn't make a call,' he said when I rang for an update. 'It has made us look like fucking liars.'

'You *are* fucking liars,' I said.

'No, we're fucking *not*,' he lied.

'Well, you'd better get your story straight before Prime Minister's Questions.'

'Yes, well, it would help if people told us the fucking truth. We had ministers out there defending him yesterday, and they were misleading the Commons and the public. It's ridiculous.'

He sounds incandescent, as angry as I've known him.

Simon Cosyns came in with a brilliant idea for a front page – putting Mandelson's head on that famous memory advert: 'IQ of 145 and can't remember?'

It says it all – Mandelson's too clever not to have remembered this call. At least, that's what most people are going to think.

WEDNESDAY, 24 JANUARY

Mandelson quit today, insisting perversely that he had done nothing improper, but conceding he had phoned the Home Office contrary to his initial denials. To general hilarity, he denounced the media, and said: 'I want to remove myself from the countless stories of controversy, feuds and division and all the rest.' Most of which have been sparked by him, of course. This will be the end of him; nobody can come back from two ministerial resignations. Not even him.

FRIDAY, 26 JANUARY

I've been called to another interview with the DTI next month. Rather worryingly, this development leads to a flurry of calls from journalists asking about it. Given that the DTI has not to my knowledge leaked anything about this case to anyone, I am mystified. But someone suggested today that people might be listening to my mobile phone messages. Apparently if you don't change the standard security code that every phone comes with, then anyone can call your number and, if you don't answer, tap in the standard four digit code to hear all your messages. I'll change mine just in case, but it makes me wonder how many public figures and celebrities are aware of this little trick.

TUESDAY, 30 JANUARY

We revealed today that Naomi Campbell is attending Narcotics Anonymous to treat her cocaine addiction. In an effort to be fair to her, we didn't go for the jugular, as we could have done, and wrote a very positive piece about how brave she was being, and how good it was that she was having treatment. But on legal advice from Martin we blanked out the faces of the other NA attendees, and didn't say whereabouts in the world it was.

Matthew Freud called this morning to ask if we'd be interested in a response from Naomi, if he could fix it. 'Of course, we'd love it. You can see we've been sympathetic, Matthew, and if she talked to us we'd be even more so.'

He said he'd see what he could do, but was 'pretty hopeful'.

THURSDAY, 1 FEBRUARY

Naomi was initially keen to talk, apparently, but has now decided to sue us. Matthew sounds exasperated. 'I tried,' he said, 'but she won't listen.'

'Well, it's up to her,' I said. 'But how she can expect to win a privacy case when we're talking about her addiction to cocaine? It's illegal, for Christ's sake.'

Matthew sighed. 'Yes, not the greatest case really, is it …'

WEDNESDAY, 7 FEBRUARY

The PCC threw a very glamorous party at Somerset House tonight to celebrate their tenth anniversary. Charles, William and even Camilla turned up to confront their tormentors over champagne and canapés.

I spotted William being led away to have a quiet word with Rebekah and Liz Murdoch and went to his rescue.

'Want me to save you from these dreadful harpies, sir?'

He laughed. 'Ah, Piers, hello, how are you?'

'Fine thanks, but I'm worried for your safety with those two, especially that flame-haired monster.'

'No, I'm sure I will survive,' he replied as Rebekah tried to muscle me away.

Guy Black, the very clever and charming director of the PCC, materialised out of nowhere. 'You see what I have to put up with now, William?' he said.

Tried to talk to Prince Andrew, but he couldn't hide either his boredom or irritation at having to be in the same room as us. He gave monosyllabic answers to everything I said, even when I tried to discuss golf. 'Yes, I like it.'

Either he's a crashingly rude bore, or he's thick, or – more probably – he just loathes us so much he can't be arsed. Chip off his dad's block, though, definitely.

Charles was thoroughly charming, as ever.

'You have a brother in the army, don't you?' he said, as he shook my hand. Which would have been slightly more impressive if I hadn't seen one of his aides whisper that very fact in his ear two seconds earlier.

'Yes, sir – Royal Regiment of Wales. He met you recently, actually.'

'Yes, I think I remember now,' he replied, which was probably untrue, but Jeremy will be chuffed.

Camilla sidled up to say hello.

'We're from the same neck of the woods,' I told her.

'Really? Good God, where?'

'Well I'm from Newick and you were brought up in Plumpton, two miles away, weren't you?'

'Yes, yes, I was. How funny. Do you get down there much?'

'Yes, all the time. If you ever fancy a drink in the Royal Oak, I'm sure the locals would be only too pleased to see you.'

'How kind of you. I'll bear that in mind.' She laughed, a good earthy laugh.

Her sister Annabel Elliott was with her. 'I think you know my sister,' I said, to even more horrified eyes. 'Her husband's a lieutenant colonel and has worked with your husband.' In fact, Annabel's husband has stayed at Charlotte and Patrick's house, where he was appalled to see a photo of me on the side as he came down to breakfast. 'God, what's he doing there?'

'He's my brother,' said Charlotte, laughing. He was rather taken aback.

Poor William was being stalked all evening by that ghastly creature Lady Victoria Hervey. 'Need some help in giving her the slip, sir?' I asked as he scurried past with her in hot pursuit.

'No, no, I'm fine – but thanks for your continued concern, Piers. I'll let you know if I need assistance.'

Later I heard him say to *Coronation Street* star John Savident, 'You're in EastEnders, aren't you?'

On learning he was the Street's butcher, William said: 'Oh, right, sorry. Well, why don't you introduce organic bacon to your shop – the bacon from the Duchy of Cornwall's great.'

William still blushes quite easily when he meets people, but he's already displaying all the different charms of both his parents.

It was a successful night. The more we meet these people, the more human they become, and the harder it will be to treat them inhumanly. That's the theory anyway, and I think it's right.

TUESDAY, 13 FEBRUARY

Fayed's furious with my leader supporting the royals after the PCC party, which ran alongside one backing Blair.

'What dreadful arse-licking to the royal family and the Government,' he wrote by fax. 'Take my advice and don't suck up to these idiots any more – in case you lose your balls altogether.'

I replied, 'I just can't stop myself – it's like when I keep writing leaders supporting dodgy billionaire shopkeepers who want passports. I know it's wrong, but I just feel this overwhelming urge to do it.'

THURSDAY, 15 FEBRUARY

Mandelson came to the monthly lunch today. He seemed angry and bitter about having to quit again. 'I did nothing wrong,' he said. 'But the media wanted my head on a plate and unfortunately Tony let them have it. I asked him if he was going to ruin my entire career over one lapse in memory that didn't change the story, and he said unfortunately he had no choice. And I thought, well, yes, you do, actually. You don't have to do this.'

It's still not entirely clear what he actually did wrong, and I feel a tinge of pity for him. Politics is his life and I can't imagine what the hell he will do without a front-line role.

TUESDAY, 20 FEBRUARY

An exhausting day. It was my formal DTI interview at their HQ in Victoria Street, and I was grilled for over five hours under oath by the 'investigative' arm of the department rather than the fact-checkers. They played loads more tapes between me and my broker, dating back months before I bought the Viglen shares.

It's now more than a year since this investigation started, and I'd forgotten most of what I was listening to. They seem to expect me to have a forensic memory for all this stuff, but I don't. 'We'll be in touch,' they said. But they warned it could be 'some time' before any decision is reached. Some time? How much longer do they need for God's sake?

MONDAY, 5 MARCH

Michael Jackson's back in Britain to speak at the Oxford Union, so I faxed Fayed. 'Dear Mohammed, if you don't ask you don't get – any chance of persuading our mate Michael Jackson to give me another phone interview?'

He faxed back: 'Dear Piers, why is it you only ever contact me when you want something? Regardless of this I will endeavour to seduce him for you.'

I replied: 'For the same reason that you only contact me when *you* want something. I've learned from the master. See what you can do, there may even be a Harrods hamper in it for you … '

FRIDAY, 9 MARCH

We've got a story that Paul McCartney had a blazing row with Heather Mills in a London restaurant, supposedly because of her plans to go to India and help the victims of the Gujarat earthquake. Heather was said to be so furious with him that she stormed out of the place. We put the usual call in to Geoff Baker, his PR, and heard nothing back. But our information was good, so I stuck the story on to pages one and seven and headed down to the pub for a quick drink. As I was walking in, my mobile went and a familiar voice said, 'Hey, Piers, it's Paul here. Paul McCartney.'

I always assume these kind of cod calls to me are wind-ups, but this definitely sounded like the genuine article. 'Look, man, I know you guys have a job to do, but I'm after a favour here. It's true that Heather and I had a row in a restaurant and things got a bit out of hand. But it's not been easy for her being with me, with all the crap that comes with it, and I'm just appealing to you as a Beatles fan to give us a break here. If every time we have an argument you guys splash it across the papers, then our relationship won't survive and, you know, I'd like it to.'

I was stunned. And to be honest, I felt uncomfortable about even having put him in this position. 'Look, Paul, I really appreciate you calling. I know how hard it must be to do this, and it says a lot about you that you've done it. To be honest with you, I do want to give you guys a break and I'm going to pull the story even if it enrages my staff.'

He sounded incredibly grateful. 'Thanks, mate, it means a lot to me, you know. Heather's a great kid, but we just need some time to sort ourselves out a bit, if you know what I mean.' I told him that other papers may not be so help-ful if they hear about the story. 'No, well, if I have to call them all, then that's what I'll do,' he replied.

'I'll want two tickets to your next show though,' I joked. Well, half-joked anyway.

'Yeah, of course, you can come backstage and fly on my plane if you just do this,' he laughed back.

I really felt for him. He'd been totally devoted to Linda, and when he lost her thought he'd never find love again. Now he has a chance, and we've been doing all we can to bugger it up for him. 'Paul, I don't want anything in return. There are times when even tabloid editors find a sense of humanity in their dark souls, you know.' He laughed again. 'Yeah, well, I appreciate it. Thanks.'

I ran back to the office and told them to ditch the story, fending off the predictable protests with a shoo of my hand. 'Look, if Paul McCartney can demean himself enough to ring someone like me and ask for a rare act of kind-ness, then the least I can do is give him one.' It would set a terrible precedent, of course, and I was certain the story of the restaurant row would pop up somewhere else. But right then, as I pulled the story, I knew it was the right thing to do.

What's happening to me? Am I going soft in my old age – or just develop-ing a conscience?

Rupert Murdoch was 70 today. The *Guardian* asked me for a tribute:

> Happy birthday, Mr Murdoch. You remain a handsome, powerful and brilliant newspaper genius. Which makes it all the more baffling why you continue to employ the current editor of the *Sun*. Still, nothing £1m and a nice new Ferrari couldn't tempt me to resolve for you. Love, Piers Morgan.

The worrying thing is that he looks younger now than when I worked for him.

MONDAY, 12 MARCH

I've got a brand-new Arsenal credit card, which I used for the first time in the Ivy tonight, only for the manager who processed my bill – a West Ham fan – to gleefully return it to me and say loudly, so everyone around me could hear, 'I'm terribly sorry, Mr Morgan but your card has been *rejected*.' I was mortified. Later I discovered the whole Bank of Scotland credit card system had collapsed. But the damage was done.

WEDNESDAY, 28 MARCH

Sometimes someone comes up with a headline that's so good, you just have to sit back and applaud. A story broke today that pigswill is to be banned after fears that foot-and-mouth came from infected meat used in a Chinese restaurant.

SHEEP AND SOW SAUCE was our splash. Take a bow, Mr Jon Moorhead.

MONDAY, 9 APRIL

The Pride of Britain award winners were all invited to a dinner tonight at the Cumberland Hotel in Marble Arch on the eve of the big day, but it descended into appalling and very sad scenes.

Michael and Sara Payne, parents of the murdered schoolgirl Sarah, were there and the former drank very heavily, very quickly. Problems started when Carol Vorderman, presenter of the show, introduced everyone and Michael stood behind her pulling faces, slurring insults about her cleavage and exposing his own chest. When several people tried to calm him down, he swung a wild punch which failed to land, and then had to be physically dragged out, screaming 'You're all cunts' at the other shocked and upset guests.

Minutes later a glass window at the side of the room was kicked in by Michael from outside in the street, prompting several of the children to become hysterical and an elderly woman to start having palpitations.

An ambulance was called, and the police soon arrived too. But Michael had done a runner by this time and there was no point in pursuing it. Some people were appalled by his behaviour, others amused. I just felt desperately sorry for him.

TUESDAY, 10 APRIL

Sat next to Geri Halliwell at the Pride of Britain awards. She was quite entertaining, though slightly self-obsessed in that rather dreary way that most pop stars are. She looked slimmer than she has done for a while, and told me it was all down to some amazing new diet and fitness regime she's on.

She kept flirting with Tony Blair, admitting to me when he turned away at one stage: 'I really fancy him, you know – don't you think he's really sexy?' I had to admit I didn't, actually, and I've rarely met any woman other than Geri who thinks he is, for that matter.

Cherie was over as soon as she got the chance, and started badgering Geri to help with her charities.

THURSDAY, 12 APRIL

Having been back in the editor's chair for less than a year Colin Myler's been fired from the *Sunday Mirror* after collapsing the trial of Leeds players Lee Bowyer and Jonathan Woodgate with an article that was deemed 'seriously prejudicial' while the jury were out.

I've recommended Tina, and she has got the job. She'll be brilliant; she's one of the best journalists I've ever worked with. I've appointed my sports editor Des Kelly as my new deputy. A surprise choice, but I think he's got flair and management skills.

THURSDAY, 19 APRIL

Robin Cook was the star guest at our monthly lunch today, and the papers were all carrying leaks of a speech he was giving tonight in which he was to declare chicken tikka masala the new national dish of Britain.

To test his commitment to this, we abandoned the usual menu and ordered a dozen chicken tikka masalas to be delivered instead.

He loved it.

SUNDAY, 6 MAY

The *Sunday Business* says the DTI have cleared me and the Slickers. Invented rubbish again. Unfortunately. The lawless and woeful reporting by many of the broadsheets on my 'scandal' is genuinely disturbing.

WEDNESDAY, 16 MAY

Amazing scenes on TV this evening. John Prescott punched a yob who threw an egg at him. A right hook right on to his hooter. The bloke reeled back stunned as Prezza had to be held back from following through with more blows.

Any other member of the Cabinet who did this would have had to resign immediately. But this appears to have enhanced his reputation rather than damaged it. I think Blair keeps him there as a sort of useful idiot. And he's right to. He's the perfect deputy for him.

THURSDAY, 24 MAY

Fergie arrived an hour late for today's monthly lunch, full of apologies. I'd expected nothing less. I love her to bits, but organisationally she's a disaster area. She sat next to Davina McCall and the pair of them soon bonded, comparing in ever more graphic detail the problems they've had in their lives.

At one stage I actually heard Davina tell our royal guest, 'I kept several grams of cocaine in my handbag at the height of my drug problem.' To which the Duchess replied, 'I know all about addictions, I've suffered lots of eating disorders.'

Later I took Fergie on a tour of the newsroom, including the *Sunday Mirror* floor where I spied their top columnist Carole Malone, who had absolutely trashed Fergie last week.

'Shhhh,' I said, as I led our party slowly and quietly up behind Carole, who was on the phone.

I tapped her on the shoulder. 'Carole, I've got a friend who'd like a word.' She turned, and nearly self-combusted.

'Oh, my *God!*'

Her face turned puce, and we all fell about as Fergie remonstrated with her about her hatchet job. There's nothing so disarming for a columnist than having to meet your victims.

SATURDAY, 26 MAY

Played for the Newick 1st XI today in our annual grudge match against Ringmer.

Things kicked off as usual when they ran out our best batsman as he backed up at the bowler's end – the worst example of bad sportsmanship any cricketer can perpetrate, in my view.

We collapsed after that, and by the time I got out there, the temperature was rising to fairly dangerous levels.

'You lot were always fucking cheats, glad to see nothing's changed,' I said as I took guard.

'Please watch your language, or we will have to report you,' said one of the umpires.

'I couldn't give a toss,' I said. 'I don't play much league cricket anyway, so you can hardly ban me. This lot have cheated today and you've let it happen.'

'Well, if they appeal we are obliged to give it out.'

This was, sadly, true.

'Their captain could have withdrawn the appeal, though, couldn't he?' I observed, throwing a filthy look at Ringmer's skipper – who promptly snapped.

'I'm not being lectured to about morality like this by a multi-million pound international fraudster like you, you prick.'

I had to laugh. Great line.

WEDNESDAY, 6 JUNE

It's Election Day tomorrow, thank God. Can't remember a more tedious, one-sided affair in modern political history. To relieve the boredom, I sent a global email to all the staff offering a bottle of champagne to anyone who came up with the best splash headline for the big day.

Winner was night editor Lloyd Embley, who just put a photo of Hague looking even smugger than usual on a front-page layout, and the headline X MARKS THE CLOT.

Brilliant.

*I give Fergie a guided tour of the Mirror newsroom
and she finds an appropriate headline.*

THURSDAY, 7 JUNE

Labour won by another huge landslide, and they all look particularly pleased with themselves, despite having had no opponents worth a light to fight. I decided to make a point of this, rather than being overly celebratory. WHAT ARE YOU LOT LOOKING SO SMUG ABOUT? GET BACK TO WORK was our splash today, above smirking pictures of Brown, Blair, Prescott and Cook.

Inside, we did a big leader article claiming the Tories were now so hopeless we'd decided the *Mirror* was going to be the official leader of the opposition instead.

'We'll be watching, Tony, and we'll be more critical.'

Can't say he hasn't been warned now, anyway.

WEDNESDAY, 13 JUNE

I took the plunge and had laser surgery on my eyes today. I've always suffered from mild short-sightedness, and have spent the last twenty years stumbling around trying to find contact lenses or repairing broken glasses.

I'd read an article about Tiger Woods having this operation just before he won all the Majors, and figured that if the world's greatest golfer was prepared to take the risk of ending his career at 21, then it must be pretty safe.

I chose a surgeon called Keith Williams, who'd done Richard Branson's eyes recently, as well as a lot of professional sportsmen's. He's a softly spoken guy with a very reassuring manner, who does about a dozen of these operations a day in his Harley Street clinic, at £3000 a pop. That's £36,000 a day, or £180,000 a week. Or, gulp, just under £10 million a year ...

'It only takes a few minutes,' he said. And it did. The procedure sounds utterly ghastly – the corneal flap is cut back, the cornea is zapped to the correct shape by the laser, the flap is resealed, and that's it. All over in three minutes, with just a few anaesthetic drops to help. I'd been warned you could smell burning, but I didn't smell, or feel, anything. It was like having a tooth removed at the dentist after a jab – you have a vague sense of something going on, but no pain at all.

I was given some goggles to wear, and told to sit in the waiting room for twenty minutes. As I did, I suddenly realised I could read the posters on the wall, right down to the tiniest words. Amazing.

I got back to Martin's flat and watched TV for a bit. Never has Deirdre Barlow's face seemed so hideously clear to me.

THURSDAY, 14 JUNE

I can see! Nothing can adequately describe how I felt this morning when I woke up and could see the door of my bedroom. I ran to the window and looked out across London. My long sight was piercing, quite extraordinarily good. Keith had told me I could expect 20/10 sight, which is even better than 20/20. 'You'll be able to fly fighter jets,' he laughed.

My near sight was perfect too: I could read the papers for the first time without aid. This is the nearest thing to a miracle I've ever experienced. I chucked my contact lenses into the bin, and then my glasses.

WEDNESDAY, 27 JUNE

Chris Evans has been having an ongoing public ding-dong with his bosses at Virgin Radio – taking days off 'sick', then being seen buying a load of booze.

He rang my mobile tonight, and said he'd been banned from doing his show tomorrow and had been offered £3 million to walk away. He sounded angry and upset.

'I've been ill, but they won't believe me,' he said. 'By talking to you now like this, they'll probably fire me.'

He ranted for half an hour, and it was all great copy. But how was I going to file it? I was on a day off, not at home, and didn't fancy doing it over the phone.

So I found an internet café on the Fulham Road, plonked myself down with my notes and started sending it all in by email – as a few people looked at me and possibly thought, 'Nah – can't be the editor of the Mirror.'

All quite exciting.

MONDAY, 2 JULY

A loner called Barry George was convicted today of killing Jill Dando. None of the reporters covering the case think he did it, a very worrying sign.

My suspicion has always been that it was a Serbian hitman exacting revenge for her fronting an appeal for Kosovan refugees on *Crimewatch*. During the case, an intelligence report was read out saying that Arkan, the infamous Serbian warlord, had ordered the execution after a TV station run by Milosevic's daughters was bombed by the allies. So there was motive, and an easy target guaranteed to generate a lot of headlines.

Much more likely, I reckon, than some weirdo loner like Barry George behaving like Michael Corleone.

TUESDAY, 3 JULY

There's been a lot of speculation that Sol Campbell, captain of Totttenham, will join Arsenal. But I confidently declared in morning conference, 'Sol Campbell won't sign for Arsenal in a million light years, and I'll take any bets you like on it.'

At 3pm, Sol Campbell signed for Arsenal.

I sent Duncan, one of the picture desk guys, straight to Highbury to buy the first Campbell shirt – which he did. And I wore it all afternoon in the newsroom.

SATURDAY, 7 JULY

Played cricket today in Newick and did something nasty to my back in the nets. Got home in agony, but assume it's a pulled muscle or something.

SATURDAY, 4 AUGUST

My back's not felt right for several weeks, and when I got up off a chair in Sussex this afternoon I suddenly felt an unbelievable searing pain shoot through my right leg. I fell to the floor and just lay there, having these acute stabbing sensations for the next half an hour, as the boys watched in a mixture of horror and amusement.

Peter Estcourt, our marvellously relaxed GP, arrived, took one look at me, and promptly burst out laughing.

He reckoned it was possibly a slipped disc which was rubbing against my sciatic nerve and provoking this intense discomfort. I have never experienced anything like it.

WEDNESDAY, 8 AUGUST

I had an MRI scan today. It confirmed a slipped disc, which explains why I have been hobbling around the newsroom like a 90-year-old man with chronic gout, to general amusement. The specialist says there is not much I can do other than take it easy and let it recover naturally.

MONDAY, 13 AUGUST

Jaap Stam, a Manchester United defender, has written a book that everyone's ignored because he's not Beckham or Keane. But one of my sports guys brought it to me last Friday and said, 'Have a read of this.' Half an hour later I bought it for just £15,000, at least two noughts less than Beckham's.

It's sensational.

Stam accuses Ferguson of illegally approaching him before signing him to United, and ordering his players to dive in European games; calls the Neville brothers 'busy little cunts'; says United were wrong to pull out of the FA Cup; claims Beckham's 'no mastermind'; and so on. It's the longest suicide note in modern British football history.

We ran the tapping-up stuff today, and Fergie went bonkers, causing Stam to realise he may have slipped up and try to can the rest of the serialisation.

'Bollocks,' was the message I relayed to his agent. 'I'm an Arsenal fan and he's going to be out of Old Trafford by the end of the week, which means we will win the League.'

FRIDAY, 17 AUGUST

Angus Deayton has lost his battle to have us censured by the PCC over a 3am Girls' story alleging he behaved like a prima donna on a trip to Paris for a party organised by Mel Smith and Griff Rhys-Jones.

I had tried in vain to sort out his gripe through his very good and long-suffering lawyer, Gerrard Tyrrell, but he wanted to take it all the way – and now he's lost.

What really annoyed him, apparently, was our 3am Girls saying he is a short-arse who lies about his height.

Anyway, the PCC have sent him packing, and Britain's 'funniest man' has shown the world how unfunny he can be away from his beloved autocue.

SUNDAY, 19 AUGUST
Matthew Freud married Liz Murdoch at their beautiful house next to Blenheim Palace yesterday. It was a fantastic laugh from start to finish.

As we all entered the marquee, I found my seat and spotted Rupert walking towards me.

'It's your lucky day, Mr Murdoch,' I joked, 'you're sitting next to me.'

He managed a laugh, just. 'Yeah, well, I'd probably have more fun there, that's for sure,' he growled as he marched on to the enlarged family top table.

The speeches were hilarious. Clement Freud, Matthew's dad, took the chance to plug his new book and hoped the Murdoch union with his family would 'boost sales'. Rupert admitted he'd had his doubts about Matthew at first, but was now delighted to have him as a son-in-law.

The groom then insisted on singing a karaoke version of some Isley Brothers' song – because he'd promised Liz he'd do that if she married him.

Afterwards, I got completely hammered in a tent with the Murdoch brothers. (I always get completely pissed whenever I see them, and can't work out if this is a good or bad thing.) But at least I didn't get as pissed as Harry Enfield, who nearly provoked Ross Kemp, Rebekah's boyfriend, into beating him up, with a long, drunken diatribe about how Murdoch papers had debased society.

I love Harry, he really doesn't give a shit.

More drama came when my friend Angus Deayton walked past the 'tabloid corner' we had created and reacted rather badly to our piss-taking catcalls – along the lines of 'Hi, shorty,' and 'You only sing when you're winning.'

'Why don't you all just fuck off,' he shouted, very, very unhappily.

I'd done a special four-page edition of the *Mirror* with photos and headlines about Liz and Matthew, which arrived at midnight. Five minutes later, so did Rebekah's special edition of the *Sun*. We raced to Murdoch for his verdict.

'Think mine's better, don't you, Mr Murdoch?'

He looked at me and shook his head.

TUESDAY, 21 AUGUST
I saw another specialist about my back today, because it is still incredibly painful.

'How long have you been like this?' he asked.

'Oh, about six weeks. Why, is it serious?'

'Well, if you don't have an operation to remove the slipped part of your disc in the next week, then you could end up partially paralysed from the waist down. Is that serious enough for you?'

'*What?*'

'Yes, what's happening is that the slipped disc is continuing to irritate the sciatic nerve, and that is killing off other nerves in your foot and leg. It needs to be taken out, or you could be in trouble.'

'Right, I see. When can I have the operation, then?'

'How about tomorrow?'

'Yes – right, OK.'

I was shocked.

The specialist watched me stumble out of his office in obvious physical torment.

'Don't worry, I had another newspaper editor in here, lying on his back, screaming in pain. You're not as bad as that yet.'

WEDNESDAY, 22 AUGUST

I had the operation at the Wellington Hospital today and it all went pretty well, though I've almost certainly permanently lost a few nerves in my right foot.

'You'll be able to run,' said my specialist, 'but only in a way that makes everyone think you are a hundred and eight years old.'

I've never exactly been Linford Christie, so this is not a massive blow.

THURSDAY, 23 AUGUST

Victor Blank popped in to the hospital today with a bowl of home-made stewed apple. He's a decent man, civilised and proper in the way he conducts himself and his businesses. We are lucky to have him as our chairman.

MONDAY, 27 AUGUST

Jaap Stam has been sold for £18 million to Lazio. 'The commotion over my book hasn't done me many favours,' he said, with commendable understatement.

I rang David Dein at Arsenal from Sussex, where I'm slowly recovering, and we had a good laugh about it. 'Piers, if you've got any other books by Roy Keane or Paul Scholes like that, please run them immediately!'

WEDNESDAY, 5 SEPTEMBER

A phone message from Mo Mowlam is sent on by email: 'Tell Piers I hope he gets well soon … and that he's still a wanker!'

The back's getting there, but I can still barely walk and the specialist says I can't go back to work for another month. So I might as well stay down here in Sussex. Which ironically means I will now be rendered paralysed anyway – from boredom.

MONDAY, 10 SEPTEMBER

Still in a fair amount of discomfort, and still hardly able to walk. There is a big Arsenal European game on TV tomorrow night, but you only get it if you have OnDigital and I don't. Kerrie has made a few calls and sorted it for me, as ever.

TUESDAY, 11 SEPTEMBER

Two engineers arrived this morning to install OnDigital for me in time for the match.

I lay on the sofa as Grande prepared a nice pizza for our lunch.

Just after 2pm, the newsdesk called and said the World Trade Center had been hit by a plane. I switched to Sky and saw a smallish plume of smoke coming out of one of the twin towers. Just seemed like a tragic accident. 'Keep an eye on it, but it looks like a light aircraft to me, which is a tragedy but not a huge story over here.'

I carried on watching and about twenty minutes later the presenter Kay Burley said we were watching footage of the plane actually hitting the tower from Fox News.

Only we weren't. She very quickly realised this was *live*, and we had just seen a second plane hit the *other* tower.

I called the newsdesk.

'We saw it – we saw it! That was a big plane, this isn't an accident, it can't be.'

I looked back at the screen. A huge ball of flame was coming out of the second tower, and Sky were already speculating about terrorism.

Dad came in to see how I was.

'Terrorists have bombed the World Trade Center with hijacked planes,' I said, hardly able to believe what was happening.

We both watched in horror.

Then one of the OnDigital engineers asked if he could switch channels to test the football output.

'No, no, can't you see – the twin towers have been hit. Thousands of people work in there.'

The guy turned, said, 'Oh yeah, right,' then got back to his work.

My phone started to ring and then carried on doing so every 30 seconds.

'Dad, this is Bin Laden, it has to be. He's tried to take those towers out before.'

I conveyed my thoughts to the newsdesk, and they said others were saying the same thing on TV.

It seemed that Al Qaeda, Bin Laden's terrorist organisation, had struck the big one.

Grande arrived with my pizza. 'Sorry, I've got to go,' I said, and hobbled slowly upstairs to find a suit.

The back would stand it, I'd had ten days to recover.

I stumbled to the car and drove at high speed to Canary Wharf with the in-car TV on with live reports.

The newsdesk called again. 'The Pentagon's been hit by another plane.'

'Fuck, what's happening here. Is this fucking Armageddon?'

Nobody knew: this was an ongoing news event of epically awful proportions and none of us knew how it would end.

I got lost three times on my journey, the last time when the newsdesk called and said, 'The towers are collapsing.' At one stage I was actually driving the wrong way round the M25 – towards Heathrow, not east London.

I stopped the car so I could see the TV pictures, and there they were, those famous symbols of American economic power, disintegrating before my eyes.

It was appalling to watch.

The phone rang. It was Mum. 'What are you doing, Piers? You shouldn't be driving,' she shouted.

'Mum, this is the biggest news story of my lifetime, I'm not missing this.'

'Well it's ridiculous to risk permanently harming yourself like this, just stupid.' My mother doesn't get angry very often, but she had a point.

'Look, it's OK, I'll sit down when I get to the office.'

'*You're going to Canary Wharf?* What if they attack that too?'

I hadn't thought of that. I worked halfway up the UK equivalent of the World Trade Center. And this incident was obviously far from over.

I put the phone down and called the newsdesk.

'Are we being evacuated?'

'No, the TV are saying we are, but we're not yet.'

Since the IRA bombed the Wharf, we've had a proper plan in place for producing the paper in the event of evacuation, and I actioned it. I finally got to the office about 4pm to find controlled mayhem.

It's at times like this that you look to your big players to take charge. And in Jon Moorhead and Simon Cosyns we have the best tabloid production team in Fleet Street.

The pair of them were drawing pages like hungry hyenas.

I called an immediate conference and went through everything we knew.

Three planes had crashed, two into the towers and one into the Pentagon. A fourth had crashed into a field with American military jets in hot pursuit. The towers were gone, crumbled to a layer of powdery dust now covering most of the tip of Manhattan. The Pentagon was burning.

It was just unbelievable horror. Fifty thousand people work in those towers, and nobody was sure how many were dead, but it would definitely be in the thousands.

It was one of those news days when only one image would make every front page – that of both towers drenched in a fireball of flame. We wiped the front for it, with the simple headline WAR ON THE WORLD.

At 8pm I noticed the Arsenal match was running on one of the TV screens in the newsroom. I'd forgotten all about it.

'Turn it up a bit,' I said.

'Piers, I don't think this is the right time to be watching football, do you?' said Jon, quietly.

I felt suddenly very embarrassed. 'No, you're right. Thanks.'

Every editor needs a few people around him to tell him he's being an arse from time to time.

We didn't go off stone until after midnight, but it was a fantastic team effort and the paper looked superb. The *Mirror*'s always the best on the big ones, and everyone knows it.

I thanked everyone, and went home exhausted. My back suddenly felt a bit painful and I realised adrenaline had got me through. It had been less than two weeks since the operation.

I watched American TV news until 3am, then fell asleep.

WEDNESDAY, 12 SEPTEMBER

Woke at 5.30am, wide awake and not feeling remotely tired. Got dressed and went to a local café for breakfast and a read of all the papers. We looked and read brilliantly well. Given our meagre resources compared to some of our rivals, it never ceases to amaze me how strong we can be on big stories.

I called the newsdesk at 8am to find out what was developing.

They'd just had an ironic reader on, saying, 'Why didn't you lead on Posh Spice this morning? I'm very disappointed, you normally always fuck it up.' Made me laugh.

The scenes from New York are repellent. The south-west tip of Manhattan's just gone. They're calling the hole that was once the towers 'Ground Zero'.

Anyone who has ever been to that part of New York will know how devastating the damage is from the overhead shots. Almost a square mile has disappeared. Terrifying.

There seems little doubt it's Bin Laden now. And also little doubt that the Americans will be bombing the crap out of Afghanistan pretty soon.

President Bush looked and sounded completely stunned today – close to tears and almost foaming with anger. He is not the kind of man to take this lightly. 'We will crush this new, deadly enemy,' he said ominously.

The team were really pumping today – we did a 36-page pull-out on the disaster, as well as a huge main paper. The sheer logistics of doing this kind of thing are mind-boggling.

The weirdest thing about this is that there are no pictures of anyone covered in blood, or any dead bodies. Everyone either survived intact, or got pulverised. Freakish.

Got to bed at 2am, still not tired.

THURSDAY, 13 SEPTEMBER

Woke at 5am again with a start, and sat bolt upright, sweating. I was sure I'd heard a huge explosion outside – like a nuclear bomb had gone off. But it was a nightmare of sorts. Weird. Couldn't get back to sleep, so went back to my café and read the papers again. We'd creamed everyone with our pull-out. Just looked like we'd tried harder.

Sales of all papers are through the roof. We were up 423,000 on day one alone. Interestingly, still only half the increase we saw the day after Diana died. Confirming my view that her death will remain the biggest single news event of my lifetime.

An amazing photograph came in today of a New York fireman going *up* the towers after the planes had struck – wide-eyed, frightened. I rang Andy Lines, our man over there, and told him to drop everything and find that guy if he is still alive.

Everyone looked a bit fried today, most of them are getting about as much sleep as me, and we're a bit tetchy with each other. Lots of 'No, you fucked up page thirteen, you twat,' going on. And the smoking room is jam-packed all the time.

Spencer wants me to have a parachute in my office. I revealed this in conference to laughter, but it seems a pretty good idea to me. The images of all those people jumping to their deaths are beyond haunting. For £500 a pop, army surplus, we could ensure everyone who jumped would probably live.

As we finished conference, a largish jet was spotted heading straight towards the tower. We all froze. Then remembered that City Airport is right next door to us, and these smaller planes come over us all the time. Not comforting, though. We are an obvious target.

I spoke to someone in Gordon Brown's camp today, who said they deliberately stopped the evacuation of Canary Wharf to avoid scenes of panic sweeping the world's TV screens. 'All the planes were grounded anyway, so there was no real risk,' said my source. Hmm.

FRIDAY, 14 SEPTEMBER

Andy found the fireman. He'd traced his station from the number on his helmet, gone down there and gently asked if the man in the photo had made it. 'Sure, Mike's upstairs asleep,' came the reply. Andy went up and found Mike Kehoe lying on the floor. He woke to tell us his amazing story of incredible heroism. 'I just did my job,' he said. Yeah, right.

Sales of all papers have been huge. But we are leading the way: tabloid-reading people turn to the *Mirror* at times like this – they believe us more than the *Sun*.

Iain Duncan Smith has been appointed leader of the Conservative Party, which seems utterly irrelevant in the scheme of things. My only knowledge of this guy is that I appeared on *Question Time* with him once, and he was crashingly dull. How the Tories have gone for him over the charismatic Ken Clarke is beyond any sensible human being. They are just self-imploding, slowly but surely.

SUNDAY, 16 SEPTEMBER

I'm now very tired. Can't sleep at all, and keep having the same nightmare about a bomb going off. It seems so utterly real.

Bush is playing to type now – saying he wants Bin Laden's 'head on a platter'. Our leader article today urged a note of caution. These are scary times, and it worries me that we have this trigger-happy Texan in charge of our response. It really does.

MONDAY, 17 SEPTEMBER

Bush is out of control. 'There's an old poster out West that said: "Wanted, dead or alive" – Bin Laden's the prime suspect and I want justice.' He thinks he's John Wayne.

WEDNESDAY, 19 SEPTEMBER

A representative of Stelios Haji-Ioannou, the billionaire Greek who runs Easyjet, has written to complain about a story linking him to Dannii Minogue. 'It's totally untrue. And even more lamentable is the fact that one of your photographers door-stepped Stelios on his way to a restaurant.'

I am not overly sympathetic. 'What's rather more lamentable is that you choose to bother us with such nonsense in a week like this,' I replied. 'I like Stelios and have enjoyed some marvellous hospitality from him at the Grand Prix. But there are honestly more important things to worry about right now than whether or not he's having it away with Dannii bloody Minogue.'

Stelios himself then emailed. 'Piers, I agree with you there are more important things. I was only annoyed because it was repeated in the Sunday Times as fact. Hopefully we won't have to spend any more time on this now. See you soon!'

We have done a broadsheet-sized pull-out today, with 6000 words by Tony Parsons. It looks absolutely stunning, and Tony's words moved a lot of people to tears. On his day I think he's the best populist writer in the country. He just hits the nerve.

THURSDAY, 20 SEPTEMBER

Matthew Freud emailed this morning. 'Thanks for coming, not causing *too* much trouble, the paper and the flowers. How weird is it doing an important thing like editing a newspaper at a time like this? How will you cope with the inevitable return to trivia?' Made me think. Perhaps we will never return to 'inevitable trivia'. I am loving editing the paper through this extraordinary story. It's what journalism is all about, bringing a dramatic, fast-moving world event to a mass audience in a way that informs, explains and inspires opinion. Celebrities are back in the box they belong in. But for how long?

Late tonight there were amazing scenes from Tony Blair's visit to New York. He is indisputably brilliant in situations like this, having a real empathy for people suffering. Diana had it, and he has it. If it's an act, then it's a good one. He got a standing ovation from Congress. They love him over there.

MONDAY, 24 SEPTEMBER

Still can't sleep. And *still* keep hearing bombs go off. My local café has my two cheese and tomato rolls ready for me now the moment I arrive in the morning. I think they assume I am a sort of loner weirdo.

Bin Laden made a public statement today, vowing to 'crush the infidels'. This is shaping up to be a holy war – Islamic fundamentalists against the crusading Christians, Bush and Blair. I am, like most people, very worried about where this is all going.

WEDNESDAY, 26 SEPTEMBER

Finally managed to sleep, only for the phone to ring at 7.15am. Must be serious, I thought. I'd told the newsdesk not to wake me up on pain of testicular removal.

'Really sorry to bother you, Piers, but Patsy Kensit has just called and wants you to call her urgently.'

'Don't be ridiculous,' I replied, annoyed that they'd woken me for such an obvious wind-up. 'I don't even know Patsy bloody Kensit.'

But the desk was adamant. 'No, no, it definitely sounded like her and she said she really needs to talk to you as soon as possible.'

I rallied quickly. Hey, if a celebrity sex symbol wants me urgently at 7.15am, who am I to argue. I had a quick shower to wake up, then called the number she'd left, still confidently predicting to myself that it was a prank.

But it sure sounded like Patsy when she answered the phone. So I decided to assume it was her.

'Hi, Patsy, it's Piers Morgan, how can I help?'

I then heard one of the more bizarre statements of my career.

'Oh, thanks so much for calling back, Piers. I just want to tell you about my secret affair with Ally McCoist.'

'Er ... um ... right, I see. OK, well, fire away by all means.'

What on earth was this all about?

Patsy then described in extraordinary detail how she had been seeing the Scottish footballer on the quiet since her divorce from Liam Gallagher. I had no idea why she was telling me, but was obviously very grateful for this early, quite spectacular contribution to tomorrow's paper. She said she had to tell me all this because she believed they were spotted at a hotel together and the story was about to break.

She thinks going public will force Ally to leave his wife and three kids, and put the seal on their relationship. Wreck it more like, is my guess, but anyway.

I got my notepad out and started scribbling. 'We've known each other ten years,' she sighed, with a slight slur to her voice. 'Ally's a fantastic guy and there was always a spark between us. But nothing happened until I split up from Liam, and Ally started working more in London. We inevitably began seeing each other more and more, and we are both in love with each other. His marriage has been rocky for a long time.'

I asked if she was worried people would perceive her as a marriage-wrecker. 'I'm not, I'm not,' she insisted. 'It's nothing like that. He was going to leave his wife anyway. This is not some silly fling, we really love each other. I've never felt like this about anyone. Ally's in bits about it all, because he loves his kids, and when he got married he thought it would be for life. But it's been bad for a while. Who knows what will happen now? Ally's got to sit down with his wife and sort things out one way or another.'

I asked how we could prove what she's saying is actually true. 'He might deny it all, and we'll be left in deep shit then.'

She thought for a bit, then gave me specific times and places she'd recently been with him.

'He spent five hours at my home in Bayswater on Tuesday, and then we went to the Marriott Hotel at County Hall and spent the night together. We arrived and left separately, so nobody would see us. He stays there whenever he's filming the Premiership. But I am sure some of the staff recognised me and knew what was going on. And that's why I am talking to you now. Don't quote me directly though, just say it's from a friend of Patsy's.'

After our 25-minute conversation, Patsy eventually said she had to go, and hung up. She sounded completely out of it throughout, like she'd been up drinking all night or something. The whole experience was utterly bizarre. But I called the newsdesk back and told them not to worry too much about their list for morning conference. They were equally stunned when I told them what she'd told me.

THURSDAY, 27 SEPTEMBER

As I expected, Ally McCoist wasn't quite as keen as Ms Kensit to get this story into the public domain. In an anguished scene outside his home in Glasgow, he admitted the affair, but said, 'I have been a complete fool. The only thing that matters now is Allison and the three boys.'

I called Patsy to relay the bad news. 'He's said what? That can't be true.' I told her that unfortunately it was.

'Bastard,' she said.

Two hours later her agent put out a statement saying, 'Patsy Kensit is entirely focused on her sons and her work, and her friendship with Ally McCoist is over.'

And that was that.

Some more amusement later, when it emerged that a sneaky TV crew's been caught trying to film Prince William at university, and it turned out to be working for Prince Edward's Ardent Productions company.

I rang Mark Bolland to see how this had gone down with Charles.

'Not very well, as you can imagine,' he laughed.

'What did he say about it?'

'Oh, well, he called Edward a fucking idiot, if you really want to know.'

TUESDAY, 2 OCTOBER

Blair made an extraordinary speech at the Labour conference today – almost messianic in its zeal.

He basically vowed to rid the world of all its problems – from Afghanistan to Rwanda, to Israel and Northern Ireland, global warming, the starving, the dispossessed, the poor – everything and everybody.

Delegates were drooling afterwards, but I thought it was faintly ridiculous and told Alastair.

'Mate, you can't save the world.'

'Why not? Someone has to.'

I asked Christopher Hitchens what he thought of Blair's conference speech.

'Well, it didn't make me want to kneel down and take his massive member in my mouth, that's for sure,' came the reply.

THURSDAY, 4 OCTOBER

As I drove back from Brighton, Alastair rang for the traditional post mortem on the lunch. He said he understood the more sceptical tone we've been adopting. But added, 'When all the rightwing hawks in Washington start saying we have to go after Saddam, that's when we're going to need you on our side, when we're trying to restrain them.'

FRIDAY, 5 OCTOBER

Our *M* magazine has inadvertently rehashed the story of Stelios dating Dannii Minogue and he emailed again: 'It will soon enter popular culture as a fact and because it's not true, I can't begin to imagine how one day it will backfire. Sorry to trouble you again but I am trying very, very hard to keep my private life … well, private.'

SUNDAY, 7 OCTOBER

Jon Moorhead called me at 2am to say we had started bombing Afghanistan. The war has begun. I put Dannii Minogue to the back of my mind, hard though it was.

MONDAY, 8 OCTOBER

Gary Jones called from his satellite phone on the frontline in Afghanistan, and I could actually hear bullets flying over his head.

'You alright, mate?'

'Erm, yes, I think so,' he chuckled nervously. Sounded bloody terrifying to me. We're just pounding them relentlessly, raining huge bombs down on a rocky terrain.

TUESDAY, 9 OCTOBER

A government adviser called Jo Moore has had to issue a grovelling apology after it was revealed she sent an email during the 9/11 attack saying, 'This is a very good day to get out anything we want to bury.' The sheer scale of crassness and shameless opportunism shown by Ms Moore defies belief, but nobody seems too surprised by anything New Labour's spin machine does any more.

WEDNESDAY, 10 OCTOBER

Have I Got News For You want me back, and are offering £1000. I responded: 'I'd love to come and torment your humourless collection of social misfits again, but I'm afraid you'll need to add a nought to the fee. I'm sure the ratings will justify it.'

They declined my suggestion, saying 'Everyone gets the same.'

'Not everyone gets the same abuse, though,' I said. 'It's danger money.'

THURSDAY, 11 OCTOBER

The bombing goes on, loads of civilians are getting killed, and it all seems rather pointless. Bin Laden's obviously in hiding, probably with most of his top henchmen, so all we're doing is smashing a lot of rocks up and destroying the odd innocent family in the process. Which is all whipping up more of the anti-west sentiment that caused 9/11 in the first place. I decided to make a point with page one tonight. RUBBLE REDUCED TO MORE RUBBLE was the splash: 'Is this relentless bombing actually getting us anywhere nearer to catching Bin Laden or is it playing into his hands?' It's provocative, but I think the time has come to start really questioning what we are doing out there.

FRIDAY, 12 OCTOBER

Mike Moore, our senior foreign photographer, and Wayne Francis, a news reporter, have found a way to go behind Taliban lines and actually meet members of Al Qaeda. It's a trip fraught with obvious danger, but Mike is a very experienced warzone photographer and he is desperate to do it.

I eventually agreed because they are on the ground and only they can really assess the risk. But I stayed up most of the night to hear they had got back safely. They did, and have some incredible material.

Their bravery is amazing.

TUESDAY, 16 OCTOBER

Great. Now media companies in America are being targeted with anthrax. So we have to face the risk at Canary Wharf of being hit by planes, bombed and now poisoned.

THURSDAY, 18 OCTOBER

Mohammed Al Fayed was star guest at our monthly lunch today – with Kirsty Gallacher, Ulrika Jonsson and David Mellor, who thanked me again for exposing his affair with Lady Cobham.

Fayed was on top form, and put it down to the bronze energy bracelet he was wearing, and which are all the rage, apparently. I must have looked interested, because he biked one round to me this evening with a note saying, 'It will have a tremendous effect on your nether regions and activate you sexually, but be warned – don't exercise it too much or you'll end up in a wheelchair. I hope the size is adequate but I can send you a smaller one if required ...' He clearly doesn't just wear it on his wrist.

'Thanks,' I wrote back, 'it will clearly refresh the parts other bangles don't reach. Don't worry about my libido though – I'm half your age and twice as potent.'

TUESDAY, 23 OCTOBER

To Belfast to make a speech at the Society of Editors conference. I used September 11 as my theme, saying it had 'redefined tabloid newspapers':

> We all saw big sales increases through July and August thanks to *Big Brother*, the most inane television ever made. I remember sitting in my office one night as bidding for interviews with various occupants of the BB house reached ridiculous proportions, thinking: has it really come to this?
>
> Is my journalistic career going to depend on whether I can persuade some halfwit from Wales called Helen to take my company's £250,000 and reveal in sizzlingly tedious detail that she's even more stupid than we first feared?

I explained how I'd detected a new hunger for serious news that had at first been driven by fear after 9/11, but was now born out of real interest. 'I hear secretaries talking about anthrax and Al Qaeda, not EastEnders,' I said.

·And I reminded them of the great defence of tabloid journalism by former *Mirror* editor Sylvester Bolam: 'The *Mirror*'s a sensational paper, but sensationalism doesn't mean the distortion of truth. It means the vivid and dramatic presentation of events so as to give them a forceful impact on the mind of the reader.'

I genuinely believe we're on to something here. And so did most of the delegates.

Bill Deedes held a very funny Q and A later. I asked him whether it was true standards in Fleet Street were worse than they had ever been. 'Oh, well. I have been working in Fleet Street for most of the last century, and I can honestly say that in my opinion standards are about as bad as they have always been.'

WEDNESDAY, 24 OCTOBER

A leaked minute from a secret Labour fringe conference has come into our possession, which reveals former No. 10 spindoctor Lance Price confessing they deliberately leaked the 2001 election date to the *Sun* because winning their favour at the *Mirror*'s expense was a price worth paying.

The exact admission went as follows:

Q: 'The Sun had consistently said the election would be in May, and had to be bought off for the fact it wasn't going to be, so the only way to do that was to give them the story exclusively, right?'

Price: 'I think that is almost entirely correct, yes. The problem we had was with the Mirror, which rightly felt mightily aggrieved by the whole thing, and we had a considerable task on our hands trying to mollify them. They were never going to be a Conservative paper, but they were not as helpful to us in the campaign as they might have been. Having the Sun on board was a sufficiently important prize to take that risk.'

I shook with anger when I read this. Here was the hard proof that they had stitched us up, and evidence of the appalling way they take us for granted. I called Campbell and shouted abuse at him for a few minutes. He didn't even try and defend it. He just said Lance was 'not quite right about it'. Bullshit.

I splashed the story under the headline A SPIN TOO FAR, and wrote a ferocious leader tearing into the treacherous lot of them.

FRIDAY, 26 OCTOBER

We splashed TODAY IS A VERY GOOD DAY TO BURY ALAN MILBURN today after NHS waiting lists were all exposed as a sham.

Milburn, recently made Health Secretary rang, laughing. 'Hi, it's Alan here. I'm still alive.'

He was calm, assured, and spent some considerable time explaining what he planned to do about this problem. I was impressed. Any politician that can make that call in that way after we've screamed for his head all over page one is a serious, clever operator.

SATURDAY, 27 OCTOBER

Philip Graf emailed me this morning: 'I'm going on a two-week holiday: do me a favour and don't buy any shares.'

I was sitting bored on the back bench at lunchtime when a mad thought came to me. 'Get me John Pilger's number,' I shouted. Who better to cement our new brand of journalism than the great radical ex-*Mirror* legend himself?

I rang him, and he sounded immediately sceptical – not surprisingly, given that we've spent the last few years slagging each other off in print.

'Look John, there's no agenda here. You know what we've been doing, I know you'd write a great piece for us, and your return would be great for the paper.'

He said he'd think about it and call back. Five minutes later he did. 'OK, I will do it, but I want absolute control over my copy, and the right to make all cuts myself.'

'Great, John – you can write up to fifteen hundred words and I'll pay you a pound a word.'

SUNDAY, 28 OCTOBER

Pilger's article arrived and was as brilliant as I'd hoped. I did a quick word count and chuckled. He'd filed almost exactly 1500 words. I did it up as a big splash: 'THIS WAR'S A FRAUD – John Pilger, back in the *Mirror* for the first time in 15 years, delivers his devastating verdict on the conflict.'

MONDAY, 29 OCTOBER

We ran a pretty fierce leader to go with the Pilger piece today, attacking Blair for not dealing with Al Qaeda the way he dealt with the IRA – by diplomacy not bombs.

Alastair rang, furious. 'What the fuck are you doing?'

'Being your conscience,' I said.

'The situation is hardly comparable,' he countered. 'Northern Ireland is part of the United Kingdom and thus our law enforcement agencies were on the same side in the battle with the IRA. The Taliban are part and parcel of the Bin Laden network.

'On a general point you continue to put the odd line in here and there that you support the Prime Minister in his aims and objectives, yet it's clear that you've taken the decision that virtually every piece of coverage should be pointed in the opposite direction.

'That's obviously a judgement for you to make but I think you'd be hard pushed to say you've given us much of a hearing.

'Your readers have a right to hear what their Government is saying, not just what you think about it.

'Real progress is being made with our campaign objectives.'

I suggested Blair do an interview with us.

TUESDAY, 30 OCTOBER

George Galloway wrote today:

> Dear Mr Morgan, we've had our differences but I am honour-bound to congratulate you on the breath-taking brilliance of your *Daily Mirror*.

Both journalistically and politically it is a thing of beauty, which should be a joy for you forever. A return to the great days – but in a modern suit!

Blair did his *Mirror* interview and assured us Bin Laden would be caught. He was a bit testy with the team, apparently.

WEDNESDAY, 7 NOVEMBER

Concorde flew back into service today, after the French air crash threatened to finish it forever.

Every editor was invited but most felt duty-bound to pass it to a reporter. I felt no such sense of duty and snaffled it myself. I mean, what's the point of being editor if you can't grab all the best freebies?

Fortunately the *Independent*'s Simon Kelner is of the same mentality as me (though I'm slimmer, obviously), so I had a mate to play with.

It was my first supersonic Concorde flight, though I'd been on it once before, taking part in a bizarre subsonic Radio One mid-air golf competition with Suggs from Madness. (We tried to putt a ball down the gangway, hoping it would qualify as the longest putt ever, since the ball would technically have travelled more than 6000 yards when it reached the glass 'hole', but Norris McWhirter was having none of it.)

My God, supersonic's a fantastic experience. We got to 1350 mph, 57,000 ft, and minus 63 degrees outside. It was, I imagine, like being in space, only brighter, obviously.

Take-off was like something on an Alton Towers roller coaster. You taxi normally for a bit, then this roar starts and you feel you're being sucked into the air, the G-force smashing you back in your seat.

The plane rockets into the skies. And the landing is equally dramatic, as you feel another rush of power that would knock you clean off your feet.

In the middle of all this you burst through the sound barrier – experiencing a low-grade yet curiously enjoyable thud in your stomach. Mach 2: I recommend it. It really is thrilling.

Concorde is not big. The seats have no more leg-room than normal business class. And there are just two either side of the gangway. But the luxury is incredible.

There are cashmere-covered pillows and blankets, 'spa-like' bathrooms, rich blue pinstriped carpets, and lambswool curtains. And a menu of caviar, lobster, smoked salmon, truffles, quails' eggs – all washed down with 1986 Krug, Puligny-Montrachet 1993, and a pleasing Château Pichon-Longueville Comtesse de Lalande 1988 Grand Cru Classé. A wine only the *Mirror*'s James Whitaker could ever know how to pronounce, let alone drink.

OK, the plastic cutlery was a disappointment. I know the safety reasons behind it, but you just can't spoon that caviar up in quite the same way as you can with mother of pearl.

One BA executive summed it up by saying: 'The new Concorde is a balanced mixture between the newest Aston Martin car and the Ivy restaurant. And you are likely to see the same faces in all three.'

The pilot, Mike Bannister, came down to chat later and told me how as he taxied at Heathrow, ground engineers and pilots cheered him on. Then an American voice came over his radio from a pilot waiting behind him shouting, 'Go, Concorde, go.'

'I'm not ashamed to say a tear came to my eye,' he said.

Sting flitted down the aisle to greet everyone, and I was amused by the ghastly levels of sycophancy among my journalist colleagues.

'Watch this,' I told Kelner. 'I'll get him to serve *us* champagne.'

I called a waitress over and asked her to bring over a nice bottle of Krug.

'Hey, Sting, how about doing the honours?' I said.

He laughed.

'Yeah, OK, why not?'

As he poured Simon and me glasses of Krug, the on-flight photographer snapped away. This will go down well in my newsroom, I thought.

BA boss Rod Eddington was in typically feisty form. 'What do you make of all these American stars like Bruce Willis refusing to fly since 9/11?' I asked him.

'They're gutless cowards,' he snapped. 'They want everyone to see their movies and think how big and brave they are. But at the first sign of trouble they cower under their beds like gutless cowards. It's pathetic.'

As he moved on, a BA press officer said nervously, 'You won't quote him on that, will you?'

'Why not? He said it,' I replied.

We arrived at 9.08am in New York, 1 hour and 22 minutes before we'd left London. I felt like I'd had a comfy car ride from London to Brighton, not a 6000-mile flight. No jet lag, no weary legs, no nothing.

New York's mayor Rudy Giuliani boarded the plane to make a fairly revolting speech about his city being the 'capital of the world', and urging us all to 'spend as much as possible'.

Just don't get it, some of these Yanks, do they? It was too brash, too cocky and too grasping. And a bit too old New York too. A simple 'thanks' would have done.

As we filed off the plane he was waiting to shake all our hands.

As he shook mine his eyes had already moved on to David Frost. So I refused to let go. Eventually he looked back.

'Hi, Mr Giuliani, was a bit worried you were ignoring me there.'

He looked like he wanted to murder me.

'Right, well, hello.'

Just one thought marred an otherwise special day. There wasn't one Muslim on board, or a single black face.

I'm sure this was an oversight. But it jarred with me that on this symbolic day, nobody thought about how this might look to those already feeling marginalised by September 11.

Many of the first editions of the papers carried photos of me and Sting. The *Daily Sport* captioned theirs: 'Sting serves champagne to an unknown passenger.'

THURSDAY, 8 NOVEMBER

Met Sting at the Concorde departure lounge. 'Hey, you've made me famous,' he said, clutching the front page of the *International Herald Tribune*.

Yes, the world's most serious and boring newspaper had indeed chosen that one picture to illustrate the momentous day.

I got Sting to sign it. He did two speech bubbles. Him saying: 'More champagne, sir?' and me saying, 'Just get on with it, Sting.'

He found it all very funny.

TUESDAY, 13 NOVEMBER

The Northern Alliance have taken charge in Afghanistan and are brutalising the Taliban in a horrific manner. A shocking image came in of a Taliban fighter stripped naked and being shot by five Alliance operatives. I did it on the front with the headline OUR 'FRIENDS' TAKE OVER. We're getting more and more attitudinal on the front, and people are really taking to it. The *Mirror*'s becoming the focal point for people who don't like the way this whole fatuously named 'war on terror' is going.

WEDNESDAY, 14 NOVEMBER

Paddy Ashdown's not happy that we didn't use his first-person piece on Afghanistan yesterday. 'I am pretty (understatement here) grumpy that having bust a gut to get you the piece you didn't use it. Last time you cut it to ribbons, now you don't use it at all. Despite saying it was exactly what you wanted. What happened? Very Grumpy of Yeovil.' I didn't have the heart to tell him it was too boring.

SUNDAY, 18 NOVEMBER

The *Sunday Times* says I have been cleared by the DTI. Complete invented rubbish, yet again – by the same reporter who said last year I was going to be prosecuted. I wish it *was* bloody true, I've had enough of this incessant uncertainty.

MONDAY, 19 NOVEMBER

Martin's quit to go to Schillings, a top entertainment law firm. It's a good move for him, but I am incredulous we're letting him go. He's the best libel lawyer I have seen, and a great friend when it really matters.

TUESDAY, 20 NOVEMBER

Richard and Judy did an interview for us to plug their move to Channel 4 with their magazine show, which we agreed they could have copy approval on. This is a hidden shame for most papers, that has grown in recent years to be an epidemic. We need celebrity interviews, but they don't trust us, so the only way they'll do it is if we let them 'approve' the copy, and sometimes the headlines and photographs too. Every tabloid does it, and it has always stuck in my gullet, because it is effectively censorship. But today it tipped over the edge into ludicrous farce. Jenny Johnston did the chat and wrote a pretty positive interview up, bordering on mild sycophancy. It was sent to Richard and Judy for their 'approval', and then came back four hours later with over 800 words changed.

Almost all of it had been changed, turning it into a virtual press release, with the pair of them adding whole sentences of praise about themselves. Now I happen to like Richard and Judy, and it's not their fault for trying it on, given all the agreements we'd made. But something inside me just flipped today and I decided to run the interview before and after, showing the unapproved and approved versions. We also ran a scathing leader article attacking this nonsense, and declared a permanent ban on copy approval. It will cause mayhem tomorrow, but this has been brewing for years and papers have to make a stand or we'll lose every last vestige of credibility.

Later, news breaks that Murdoch is to be a father again, at 70. You've got to hand it to the old devil.

WEDNESDAY, 21 NOVEMBER

Channel 4 went predictably mad, accusing us of betraying them, threatening to withdraw all future co-operation with the *Mirror* and generally throwing their toys out of the pram. But at 4pm, Richard Madeley called me. 'Piers, I won't pretend that Judy and I weren't bloody furious and upset when we saw what you'd done to us this morning. But having thought about it a bit, we think you were right and we were wrong, and I just want you to know that.'

I was shocked. 'Right, well, that's very good of you, Richard. I just flipped when I saw all the changes, to be honest. It could have been any celebrity, because they all do it, but unfortunately it was you guys.'

He laughed. 'Look, I was a newspaper journalist and I know how pathetic we looked today. It won't happen again, that's for sure. Sorry for being such luvvies, I hope we can still be mates.'

'Of course you will, it's big of you to call and say this.' And it was.

Later, the 3am Girls tell me that Mick Jagger's spindoctor Bernard Doherty has issued a statement denying our story about his client dating Amanda de Cadenet – forgetting to mention that he actively encouraged us to do it in the first place. I told the girls to run the tape of him urging us to publish yesterday.

This time Doherty rang, pleading with me to pull our story about his duplicity. 'Sorry, mate, you shouldn't play games with us like this. Especially not at a time when celebrities aren't as important as they would like us all to think they are.'

TUESDAY, 27 NOVEMBER

Our man in Los Angeles interviewed Kate Winslet last week in a 'round robin' with other journalists.

She's now complained to the PCC about misrepresentation because we put the tag 'exclusive' on it. Unbelievable. Our cheeky but very talented Liverpudlian deputy picture editor Greg Bennett shook his head. 'She's disappeared up her arse, that girl.'

So I did a page lead headlined KATE WINSLET DISAPPEARS UP HER ARSE – and a leader saying, 'Sorry Kate, we're so unbelievably bloody sorry, Oh God, we're incredibly, embarrassingly, sickeningly sorry.' My war on celebrities continues. Sad to see her behaving like that though. It gets to them all in the end.

WEDNESDAY, 28 NOVEMBER

We've taken out adverts in the trade press showing a fake letter from me to all celebrities saying:

> The *Mirror* is delighted to offer full interview and photo approval, as often as you like, and as long as you like, on any day of the week. You may flatter yourselves to your hearts' content, and even take advantage of Air-head, our unique facial retouching service to smooth away those unsightly blemishes. For full details, please contact: The Advertising Department, MGN Ltd, Canary Wharf, who will be happy to supply a price list.

THURSDAY, 29 NOVEMBER

Because Blair had been understandably too busy at the Labour conference to attend our usual *Mirror* lunch, we had it today instead at Downing Street. I sat between Cherie and Fiona Millar. 'Ah,' I joked, 'the *real* Axis of Evil.' They actually laughed, which amazed me.

'So, Piers, why are you being so ridiculous about the war?' Blair said, before the starters had even arrived.

'*Me* being ridiculous? How about looking in the mirror, Prime Minister?' I retorted.

This early exchange set the scene for the most fractious encounter I've ever had with him. The other managers and editors kept out of it as I went toe-to-toe with him over the way Labour had treated the *Mirror*.

I was still simmering with rage about that Lance Price memo about the 2001 election.

'Do you feel ashamed that you leaked the election date to the Sun?' I asked, my voice rising a little above the comfort zone.

'We didn't,' he hit back, his own voice louder than usual.

'Sorry, Tony, but yes, you did,' I retorted. I reached into my pocket to pull out Lance Price's memo, and read out the confession.

'Well, that's a matter for Lance,' he said, squirming.

'No, it's not – he was acting for you,' I said. 'And don't tell me you didn't know what was happening.'

'I didn't.'

'Sorry, but do you really expect me to believe the Number Ten press office did all this without you knowing?'

'Yes. I am the Prime Minister and I don't lie.'

I was fuming, and even toyed with walking out. But you can't, can you?

The subject was changed and we moved on.

Cherie and Fiona, perhaps realising things were getting a bit out of hand, went on a massive charm offensive, fluttering their eyelids and stroking my ego at every opportunity. They can both be quite charming. When they want to be.

I calmed down after a while and got Blair to sign the menu. 'Must be the first time you've laid out the silver service for the Mirror,' I said; 'I want a souvenir of this.'

Campbell scrawled his name too, then Cherie wrote: 'To my new best friend Piers, love Cherie.' And Fiona added: 'Mine too!'

I'll stick it on the loo wall.

When lunch finished, Cherie went off and brought down Leo to say hello.

'He's been speaking French to President Chirac today,' she said.

'Has he?' I replied. 'What a clever little boy.'

FRIDAY, 7 DECEMBER

My Christmas card arrived from the printers today, depicting a photo of Cherie fiddling with my tie as Tony looked on at the Pride of Britain awards, and the headline BLAIR GETS A GRIP ON WAR WOBBLERS, with speech bubbles from him saying, 'Tighter, Cherie, tighter.' Her saying, 'I'll stiffen your resolve.' And me saying, 'Easy, tiger, I'm not the Taliban.'

WEDNESDAY, 12 DECEMBER

Marco Pierre White's 40th birthday party last night, and it lived up to every expectation. He'd invited 40 people from all walks of his life to share the momentous occasion over a stunning meal in the private room of his Mirabelle restaurant.

What do you get a man like Marco for his birthday? The answer in my case was an Arsenal shirt (he's a fan) signed in an Islington bookmakers yesterday by 1971 superstar Charlie George, for £50 cash. And a genuine Taliban whip, taken off the streets of Kabul by one of my foreign reporters. The meal was enlivened by the quite disgusting behaviour of *Times* food critic Jonathan Meades, who arrived late and already very drunk from a long lunch at Le Gavroche, and groped Michael Winner – to the latter's horror. He had an equally drunk girlfriend with him, and the pair of them instantly started abusing each other and other guests at our table with admirable abandon, while tucking into Marco's feast of fine wines and a menu of the best lobster, caviar and oysters. At one stage, Meades tumbled to the floor and lay there gurgling, shouting, 'What are you lot fucking staring at?' as we gawped in collective horror. Marco saw what was happening and was not amused. 'He is showing no respect,' he said grimly. And in Marco's book that's as bad as it can possibly get.

But we were then distracted by two other late arrivals – Madonna and hubbie Guy Ritchie. She is tiny, like a little china doll. And sat wearing a tweed cap at Marco's table, drinking water. Guy's certainly come on in life since I last saw him, when he was a barman at a mate's bar in Fulham called Joe's Brasserie. At 11pm, the cabaret arrived in the form of Bernard Manning, and much amusement ensued. He started by peering at Madonna, who he didn't seem to recognise at all, and sneered, 'Who the fuck do you think you are – Lester Piggott's sister?' She didn't know whether to laugh or be horrified, but Guy was in hysterics next to her, so she forced a smile. That smile grew thinner and thinner as the jokes got worse and worse. From Freddie Mercury and AIDS to gags about Pakistanis, Jews, the Irish, French and Bin Laden – it was a full frontal assault. All delivered with the usual extreme profanity. Marco was crying with laughter, as was Guy. But Madonna was stony-faced after a few minutes and didn't find it remotely funny.

Jonathan Meades meanwhile began to heckle and jeer before finally standing up, shouting, 'This is a fucking disgrace, we're leaving,' to a round of applause. He then staggered out to the loo, threw up, and returned shouting more obscenities.

The table fell quiet. 'I think it may just be time to go home, Jonathan,' I ventured. 'Fucking right,' he shouted, 'this has been a repulsive party.' And they finally stormed out for good, to more applause.

After Manning wrapped up his act, I walked over to Madonna and asked how she'd found his performance. 'Well, I didn't really understand any of it,' she said, looking rather shell-shocked. 'And the bits I did understand didn't seem massively funny.' Guy, still laughing, interrupted, 'Oh, come on, he was hilarious.' I mentioned my old connection with Guy and he then seemed rather less amused. 'Yeah, yeah, I did work there for a bit,' he said, before sliding away to talk to someone about his new life rather than his old pint-pulling days.

Everyone was now hideously drunk, apart from the Ritchies. Later, Madonna came over to my table to talk to Nicola Formby, TV critic A. A. Gill's partner. I couldn't let the moment go. 'I used to stalk you,' I announced. 'You did *what?*' she said. 'I used to stalk you, around Cannes and places like that. I was a reporter on the Sun.' Her face froze in disgust. 'Well, I hope you got off on it,' she finally replied. 'Well, I never fancied you, actually, but I did once get a photo with you that we ran under the headline "Who's that with Piers Morgan?" ' Madonna was now disgusted. Then Guy arrived. 'Hi, mate,' I slurred. 'Do us a favour for old time's sake and get me a beer, can you?' He, too, looked disgusted. 'Get it yourself, you cheeky bastard.'

Nicola, seeing the situation deteriorating, led them away to Mr Gill, who promptly started obsequiously smarming and guffawing for all he was worth. 'Get your tongue out of her arse, Gill, for God's sake,' I shouted.

He hurled a napkin at me. 'Oh, piss off, Morgan.'

I was ruining his big moment.

Madonna left soon afterwards. It was a genuinely hysterical evening.

THURSDAY, 13 DECEMBER

I called Marco to thank him for one of the all-time great nights. He was fuming about Meades. 'He was drunk, rude and obnoxious. He embarrassed everyone, humiliated himself, and frankly I never want to see the horrible little man again.'

Then he paused. 'Great party, though, wasn't it!'

Marco will be secretly thrilled it all kicked off so spectacularly.

WEDNESDAY, 19 DECEMBER

I wrote a conciliatory letter to Blair at Victor's behest, suggesting we try and move on from that frosty lunch, and saying that despite our differences over what's happening in Afghanistan the *Mirror* would obviously support him as much as we could in the general 'war on terror'.

Today he replied in an unusually terse way.

Dear Piers, thank you for your kind words of support in relation to the war on terrorism. I have to be blunt, I don't think you could argue that that view has been borne out by your coverage and I do think there is a difference between critical support, including hard-hitting criticism, and negative propaganda which, rightly or wrongly, I felt the paper was pushing. On the *Sun*, of course you are in a battle with them and I understand the sensitivity about claims of special favour to them. But it would be unfortunate if a mistaken view about leaking an election date coloured your coverage of me and the Government. In the end, I have to deal with all the media and you would be surprised at the numbers of other papers who complain that we give too much to the *Mirror*! But that's life. Ultimately what is printed is for you to decide and the worst thing any politician can do is get a thin skin about the press. So we should keep in touch so that at least if you are having a go, it's on the basis of what we are doing, not what others may think we are doing!

THURSDAY, 20 DECEMBER

It's the annual What The Papers Say awards tomorrow. We've got to be in with a chance of something this year – by common consent our coverage since 9/11 has been pretty outstanding. But tabloids hardly ever get anything at this event, so I am not holding my breath.

FRIDAY, 21 DECEMBER

We won!

When they announced we were the Newspaper of the Year, I nearly fell off my chair.

We've done it. We've scooped the big one at last. The citation said: 'In the years when people start writing the history of the events of 2001, the *Mirror* will stand out as a shining example of journalism at its best.'

I suddenly felt a surge of real pride for the *Mirror* staff. After all the share-dealing crap, the endless management changes since Maxwell died, the constant stresses of working for a PLC in a rocky market, they had earned this big time.

To make it even sweeter, tonight was the office Christmas party.

I got back to the newsroom to cheers and applause. 'Champagne on me,' I said, and headed off to the nearest bar to get completely hammered.

How sweet it feels.

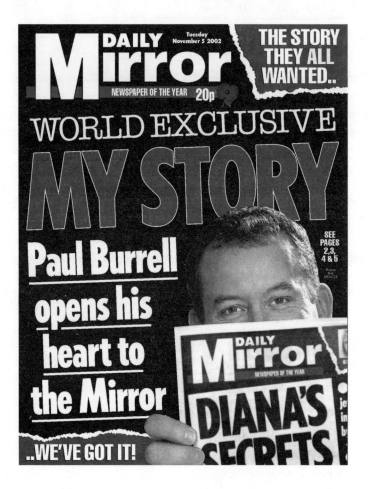

TUESDAY, 1 JANUARY

Sarah Brown had a baby girl very prematurely three days ago. Everyone's been worried about her because she weighed just 2 lb 4 oz, but she seems to be doing well.

I sent some flowers, and Gordon handwrote a reply today thanking me: 'Once again we have attempted a surprise in a quiet run of news days!! Jennifer is getting stronger every day. See you soon, all the best for 2002, Gordon.'

FRIDAY, 4 JANUARY

Mandelson emailed to say we've called him 'shamed' again in Scurra (the *Mirror* diary) and could we please not do that.

I replied: 'Sorry, I will try and stop them doing that, always assuming you don't re-offend, obviously. Had quite a frosty lunch with Tone recently. He seems to be taking life and himself a bit too seriously these days, needs to lighten up.'

'Well, he's been working very hard recently. Also, I wonder if you realise the effect having his main supporter in the press having a go at him has. Shouldn't be thin-skinned, but imagine if the bombardment was reversed.'

'I suppose the answer to that is that it's always been one-way traffic, culminating in that Lance Price confession that the *Sun* was deliberately leaked the 7 June election date – a decision No. 10 knew would upset us, but judged that our fury was a "price worth paying to buy off the *Sun*". I've been unbelievably supportive to TB and his crew for six years here and got virtually bugger all back. Murdoch's cronies have been courted so hard everyone's forgotten who their real media friend was. But that's not why I was critical of the war strategy. I think we spoke for most people in Britain.'

Mandelson admitted: 'The relationship with the *Sun* is a fairly grim thing, I accept. I doubt the folk at No. 10 really enjoy the *Sun* but ...'

MONDAY, 7 JANUARY

Gordon and Sarah Brown's baby Jennifer has died after a tragically short ten-day life. I am devastated for them; they had both looked so happy. A photograph of them driving away from the hospital came in, and there was a newsroom debate about whether we should use it. I decided that we should. This is a news event, albeit a desperately sad one, involving a couple I know well and like very much. These are always the most difficult calls for editors. But I suspect there will be no complaint from the Browns.

MONDAY, 14 JANUARY

Cherie Blair was one of the guests at this year's Pride of Britain panel meeting at Richard Branson's house and arrived late, with a face like thunder. Her black mood was not helped when I did my usual speech about 'Look, although obviously we want the best candidates to win, we also need to think about what will make the best television, too.' Cherie was enraged. 'No, we will judge on merit, not looks, Piers.' Christ alive, loosen up, girl, for goodness' sake.

Branson wasn't overly impressed by all the Special Branch cops trawling his house beforehand, either. 'Who do they think I am – Bin Laden?' he joked.

THURSDAY, 17 JANUARY

Dale Winton called me today to say he loved me and thinks I am 'incredibly talented and very handsome'. I feel a little unnerved.

SUNDAY, 20 JANUARY

Shocking photos have come out of Guantanamo Bay in Cuba, where the Americans are holding terror 'suspects' they've picked up off the streets in Afghanistan.

They show inmates hooded and shackled in obvious breach of the Geneva Convention on human rights. What makes it all the more extraordinary is that they have been posted on the official Pentagon website.

We splashed on WHAT THE HELL ARE YOU DOING IN OUR NAME, MR BLAIR?

It's time to raise the ante a bit over what our supposedly caring, sharing Labour Government is up to.

MONDAY, 21 JANUARY

Had a row with Alastair about our front page today.

'You should be behind us on this terror stuff, not sticking the boot in. It doesn't look good for the Mirror to be so unsupportive.'

'Look,' I said, 'we are not just a Labour propaganda organ any more, so get used to it. You are doing some dodgy stuff in this war on terror, and we are not going to ignore it.'

'So you're saying you're not a Labour paper any more – is that right?'

'No, I'm saying we're not the brown-nosing Pravda sheet we were when you were our political editor.'

'Well, you should be.'

THURSDAY, 24 JANUARY

Labour have been squabbling with the Tories over some 94-year-old woman called Rose who was allegedly treated badly in a hospital. I got Brian Reade, our most acerbic columnist, to write a pretty devastating exposé of what happened to his own mother in an NHS hospital, and ran a leader blaming Labour for the current appalling state of the health service.

An angry fax arrived from Alastair:

> You said on the phone the other day that the *Mirror* is no longer a Labour paper. That could not be clearer from the fact that you so willingly take the Tory line on events in the Commons yesterday. Duncan Smith got his facts wrong, not having bothered to check. The family might feel very strongly about the state in which they found their mother, but, as the hospital explained, this was despite their care efforts, not because of them … so no scandal, just a little smokescreen whipped up by the Tories once they realised Duncan Smith's efforts had backfired. If we had mounted an attack on the flimsy evidence he had, we'd have rightly been monstered.
>
> What Brian Reade's mother suffered was obviously bad. But my point is that there are good things happening in the NHS every day and they get no publicity. You have repeatedly told me you will be happy to show good things going on, but you never do. Many of your readers work in the NHS and many others get good treatment from it. I believe they will think it is right to expose things when they go badly in the NHS, but wrong to go along with the Tories when they seek to undermine it based on inaccurate personal information.

I replied:

> Dear Director, as the *Mirror*'s 'no longer a Labour paper' (hilarious misquote from A. Campbell) then I no longer have to put up with your ridiculous attempts to treat me as some form of extension of your *Pravda*-sponsored department. I'm sure the *Sunday People* will be available for your press releases, though, squeezed in between Jordan's tits and the kinky sex spread.

Mandelson's not happy either. 'Can't we leave all the homophobic stuff – "princess of darkness" – to the *Sun* where it started and belongs. Mandy and all?'

Routledge calls him these things just to wind him up, which it always does.

MONDAY, 28 JANUARY

A postcard arrived this morning with a picture of a tiny baby on the front and the caption: 'Jennifer – the first picture – sleeping, one hour old.' It was from the Browns. On the back was a printed note saying: 'We are both grateful for the message of sympathy and support you sent to us about Jennifer, we will treasure your thoughts and thank you for thinking of us.' Sarah added a personal note of thanks underneath. I felt so sad for them again. Just such an awful thing to have happened.

TUESDAY, 29 JANUARY

Had dinner with Geoff Hoon at the Commons tonight. I asked him what the chances were of a hijacked plane crashing into Canary Wharf.

'Well, it would take a jumbo loaded with fuel about four minutes to get to you from Heathrow or Gatwick.'

'Right, but you have RAF jets on permanent stand-by, presumably.'

'Yes, but by the time the hijack had happened and all the relevant people had been informed and made the decision to shoot it down, it would be too late.'

'Right. Who makes the call to shoot it down, then?'

'Well, in America Bush has ceded power down to two major-generals, so it would be a military not a political decision. But here it would have to be authorised by Tony Blair.'

'He's never going to order a passenger plane to be shot down over London, is he?'

'Well, let's hope we never have to find out.'

We all feel vulnerable at Canary Wharf, to planes and bombs. We're such an obvious target.

Hoon was reasonably affable company, though like his fellow ex-lawyer Straw he talks in that legalese way that can grate after a while. Every word is thought about for several seconds to assess the potential hazards.

I told him my brother said the army boys had a new nickname for him – 'Buff'.

'Why "Buff"?' he said, looking bemused.

'Buff-Hoon,' I replied.

He was not amused.

FRIDAY, 1 FEBRUARY

Went to a leaving party for the *Sun* picture desk legend Glenn Goodey last night, one of the really nice guys of our profession. Yelland was there, but lurked in the corner most of the time, looking friendless and awkward.

Kelvin emailed me this morning about it. 'That was the first time I'd detected so much hostility to a *Sun* editor since the bad old days when I was in loo-cabin No. 3 at Wapping once and heard two reporters discussing in some length what a dick I was.'

SATURDAY, 9 FEBRUARY

Princess Margaret died today, the second royal to die in my editing career, and like Diana she died on a Saturday, thus rendering all our carefully honed supplements completely useless.

SUNDAY, 10 FEBRUARY

Marion and I have been having a few problems, and I've been staying on and off with Martin Cruddace in his Clerkenwell flat. It may be an old cliché, but you really do find out who your friends are when you suffer a bit of domestic upheaval. And he's been fantastic. We had a laugh about the Naomi trial, which starts tomorrow. He cleared the original drugs story for publication as the *Mirror* legal manager, and now he's gone to her law firm Schillings. Talk about divided loyalties!

MONDAY, 11 FEBRUARY

The Naomi trial started today, and she flounced into court wearing a smart grey pin-stripe suit, loads of make-up, and enough expensive perfume to turn the room into a temporary boudoir. The judge, Justice Morland, looked suitably entranced. Must make a nice change from all the ugly rapists and murderers he normally gets to deal with.

When Naomi sidled up to the witness box and tried to find her documents, Justice was off his chair faster than Vanessa Feltz with a Big Mac voucher. 'Oh, do let me help you with that,' he cooed, embarrassingly.

She spoke in a weird pseudo Manhattan-meets-Knightsbridge voice – a world away from her Streatham roots. And tried her best to come over as a coy, demure, much-maligned young woman.

Our QC, Desmond Browne, did a pretty good job exposing her as a compulsive liar, and the whole case as a nonsense. She readily admitted she's a drug addict, and that we were perfectly entitled to expose her *and* say she was having treatment. Only the picture was a gross invasion, even though we blanked most of it out.

'I felt shocked, angry, betrayed and violated by the article,' she said, her voice trembling.

I bet she did. Now everyone knew she was a coke abuser, after years of her insisting she never took drugs.

As she left the stand I threw her a little wink. She snorted and threw her head back.

Desmond thought we'd done pretty well.

TUESDAY, 12 FEBRUARY

Overnight, Desmond had found a load of inconsistencies in Naomi's statements from yesterday, and today he threw them back at her one by one, until it was obvious to everyone she'd been telling porkies indiscriminately under oath.

He also showed a video we'd acquired of her attacking a woman on a plane for trying to photograph her asleep. As she snarled and swore in a much more credible Sarf London alleycat voice, I could see the blinkers fall off Justice Morland. She wasn't quite the demure young thing he may have thought.

I was impressed. He's not theatrical like George Carman, but Desmond is a very clever, methodical barrister and had slowly dissected his victim like a rat in a biology lab at school.

Naomi left the stand, predictably, in tears. A last plea for mercy.

It was my turn next.

It's a long old walk to the witness stand. Not in distance, but in what you're thinking as you go. One mistake up there, and I could be fucked. I was going up against Andrew Caldecott, one of the top QCs in Britain.

But I'd prepared a few little soundbites to grab the headlines, which is half the battle in these cases.

'If you are voluntarily going into Hannibal Lecter's cage, then eventually you are going to be nibbled around the back of the neck,' I said in response to why I thought she deserved no real privacy. Cue fevered note-taking by the hacks below. This was fun.

I was on a £50 bet to ask Justice Morland for help with my documents, but Desmond pleaded with me not to do it.

'It will backfire on us, and we're doing well,' he said.

I spent three hours ducking and diving with Caldecott, but he never landed a killer punch.

'It's going well,' said Desmond, 'very well.'

WEDNESDAY, 13 FEBRUARY

The papers are all full of 'Hannibal Lecter and nibbling neck' headlines. My strategy worked.

Caldecott came out fighting today, and introduced a new line of attack – claiming we had been racist in describing Naomi as a chocolate soldier in a column last year by Sue Carroll. We hadn't at all – we'd used a well-known phrase to ridicule her after she paraded naked for an anti-fur campaign, and was then seen wearing a fur a few months later.

But Naomi played the race card because she was losing.

'This is pathetic and offensive,' I said, and stared over at Naomi, who was curled up in a little ball trying to look all frail and innocent. This from a girl who had dated Mike Tyson. 'Are you saying that the term "chocolate" is racist? When I have a cup of hot chocolate at night am I being racist? This is ridiculous.'

Even as I said that, I realised it was a stupid thing to say. But too late.

THURSDAY, 14 FEBRUARY

Desmond summed up our case superbly. I cannot see how we can lose this. Naomi's been shown up for what she is – a lying, moaning hypocrite. It was a perfectly reasonable privacy case to fight, and I have a certain sympathy with celebrities attending any of these 'anonymous' addiction centres wanting privacy. But she is the worst person to fight it. People just don't believe, or like her.

FRIDAY, 15 FEBRUARY

Caldecott gave me the full barrels in his own summing up, saying I had a 'touch of the Bill Clintons' about me, which I presume alluded to my honesty on the stand. He also criticised me for 'intellectual poverty', which was a posh lawyer's way of saying I'm thick. Cheeky sod. But he won't get much of a show in tomorrow's papers because it's Friday today, everyone's lost interest in the case anyway, and Saturday's papers will be full of lighter lifestyle fare. When I saw the first editions, this was confirmed: he barely got a mention. We'll hear the final verdict in a few weeks' time.

THURSDAY, 21 FEBRUARY

Fascinating monthly lunch today – with everyone from Tony Benn to Michael Winner, Alan Milburn to Sophie Raworth, the Israeli ambassador to Mary Nightingale. I asked the ambassador, a former top military man, if it was the ex-military guys in the current administration pushing to go harder on the Palestinians.

'No, the opposite,' he said. 'Those who have experienced war at first hand do all they can to stop it. Those who have never experienced it are much more aggressive.' He seemed a wise and intelligent man.

I gave Milburn a bit of a noisy going-over about the NHS, and to his credit he gave as good as he got.

'Goodbye, you *bastard!*' he fake snarled as he left. Everyone was impressed by him, though. Lots of 'I didn't think he'd be as smart as he is' comments afterwards.

FRIDAY, 22 FEBRUARY

I've spent the last month working on a big appeal for Barnardo's in the *Mirror*, one of the pegs being that Cherie Blair is their president this year. Nick Lloyd, former *Express* editor turned PR man, has been doing the planning with me, and we've thrown a lot of good ideas around in several lengthy meetings.

But today he dropped a bombshell out of the blue:

I am very sorry, but the Barnardo's situation has completely changed. Despite prior agreement with Cherie, there have been lengthy toings and froings with No. 10 about the plans. As you know Cherie and Rebekah Wade are very good friends and now Cherie has decided she wants to do the appeal with her at the *News of the World*. Despite lengthy protestations from me and Barnardo's, we will therefore have to withdraw from participation with the *Mirror*. I am very, very embarrassed and can only thank you for all your help and generosity of spirit which was much appreciated. Barnardo's are also embarrassed, but they feel they cannot fall out with their new president. I owe you a large lunch. Nick.

I was trembling with rage by the end. Not at Nick, but with Cherie. What *is* her problem? I called Fiona Millar and screamed at her for about twenty minutes. Having lived with Campbell for years, I imagine she is quite used to this kind of treatment, and just dismissed my view with a 'Well, I'm sorry, but it's entirely Cherie's decision.'

Further probing revealed some extraordinary insights into why this has happened. 'She's not been very happy about the way you've been having a go at Stephen Byers, to be honest,' said Fiona in that clipped, schoolmistress voice I've grown to find extremely irritating. We've been hammering Byers since the Jo Moore 'burying bad news' affair, which he has been particularly disingenuous about in a transparent attempt to save his own skin.

'Stephen Byers!' I exclaimed. 'Is this some sort of bloody joke? You've pulled a huge campaign for kids because we've had a go at a lying scumbag minister?'

Then I gave up and slammed the phone down.

TUESDAY, 26 FEBRUARY

An exhausting day. It was my formal DTI interview at their HQ in Victoria Street, and I was grilled for over five hours under oath by the 'investigative' arm of the department rather than the fact-checkers. They played loads more tapes between me and my broker, dating back months before I bought the Viglen shares.

It's now more than a year since this investigation started, and I'd forgotten most of what I was listening to. They seem to expect me to have a forensic memory for all this stuff, but I don't.

'We'll be in touch,' they said. But they warned it could be 'some time' before any decision is reached.

Some time? How much longer do they need, for God's sake?

WEDNESDAY, 27 FEBRUARY

Spike Milligan died today, and I preferred to dwell on his humour, rather than the lack of it he displayed when I was on the *News of the World*. My favourite joke when I was a young lad was, 'What does a hypochondriac have written on his tombstone?' Answer: 'Told you I was ill.' It was a gag Spike had used as well, so I did up the front page as a giant tombstone with those words on it. Everyone had a laugh when they saw it, and that indisputably would have been the way he would have wanted it. Assuming we didn't publish a picture of someone else to go with it.

SUNDAY, 3 MARCH

Blair made some ominous noises today about us needing to 'deal with Saddam Hussein'. He says Iraq has 'the capability and intention to use weapons of mass destruction'. It's being spun by No. 10 as the 'second phase in the war on terror'. I remembered what Alastair said at last year's party conference – about us needing to help them restrain Bush from attacking Iraq. The position seems to have shifted somewhat. But we haven't dealt with Bin Laden yet, and he seems far more dangerous to me.

MONDAY, 4 MARCH

Byers has kept his job, with Blair refusing to buckle to media pressure as he did with Mandelson.

I sent the latter an email:

> You were well and truly done over in this business. Blair lost his bottle: how he can stand by Byers and not you when Byers is so obviously lying on a different scale to your memory lapse is beyond me.
>
> You were just too big, too famous, and too controversial to ever survive normal Cabinet affairs. But you'll be back running the country in a couple of years – London Mayor maybe?

He replied: 'Byers is the chief beneficiary of what happened to me. It cannot be allowed to happen again.'

TUESDAY, 5 MARCH

A very moving Pride of Britain awards, thanks mainly to the appearance of Mike Kehoe, the hero fireman Andy Lines had found alive after 9/11, and some of his colleagues from New York. He sat on the top table next to Blair, feeling rather bemused by all the attention. A genuinely modest man.

The night was slightly marred by Michael Barrymore. Pissed before the awards started, he greeted most celebrity presenters with the words, 'What the fuck is that wanker doing up on stage?' Later he accosted Judy Finnegan and put his hand up her dress, before heading off to the loos to openly snort cocaine without even closing the cubicle door. I approached him at one stage, and he just hugged me, slobbering drunken kisses on my cheeks. I felt sorry for him. The guy's right on the edge.

THURSDAY, 7 MARCH

I did a photo shoot at the Savoy Grill today to go with an interview I've done with *Vogue*. To my delight, I am described as a 'model' in their schedule for the day. It took hours, though, and I was pretty sure I looked a right prat by the end. No wonder Naomi gets so agitated by her life.

FRIDAY, 8 MARCH

Gordon Brown sent me a note:

> My congratulations on your success with the outstanding and inspirational Pride of Britain. Many who saw the TV programme told me how

very moved they were, often to tears, by the stories of courage. You have created not just an annual event but a national institution. A people's honours list! Well done.

SATURDAY, 9 MARCH

We ran a front page yesterday on Blair's trip to Texas to rubber-stamp an Iraq war, with them both mocked up in stetsons and the headline HOWDY POODLE.

Another letter arrived from George Galloway this afternoon, asking for an original colour photo of the page so he can frame it. 'You are excelling even the old *Daily Mirror*, one of the greats,' he enthused.

Not sure I feel too comfortable about this. If George loves our coverage so much perhaps I'm going too far ...

MONDAY, 11 MARCH

I've tried to poach Matt, the brilliant *Telegraph* pocket cartoonist, offering unfathomably large sums of money. He wrote back today declining, but adding charmingly, 'I'm afraid I'd only squander it on food and heating ...'

There are lots of people who think they are geniuses in Fleet Street. He actually is one.

WEDNESDAY, 20 MARCH

Last night was the best night of my career. I hoped we'd win a few awards at the Press Gazette awards given the great stuff we've done since 9/11, but never in my wildest dreams did I think we'd walk off with all three of the big ones – Newspaper of the Year, the Cudlipp award and Team Reporting of the Year.

But we did, and pandemonium ensued as I led the team on a little conga around the stage to general revulsion from our rivals.

I've bought a flat in Fulham, near the boys, and got back around 4am feeling drunk, but totally elated. The last six months have been the most satisfying period of my professional life.

THURSDAY, 21 MARCH

William Cash, writer and mate of Liz Hurley, sent me a note today:

I bumped into Alastair Campbell at a party and asked what he thought of the *Mirror*. 'I can't understand why Morgan wants to make it a non-Labour paper,' he snarled, to which I replied, 'Perhaps he just doesn't like being controlled – most editors don't, at least not by someone who doesn't own them.' To which he said: 'Some people like to be controlled. Or need to be!'

TUESDAY, 26 MARCH

Halle Berry, Denzel Washington and Sidney Poitier all won Oscars yesterday in an amazing night for black actors. I decided to make a point of this, and splashed on their celebratory pictures under the Martin Luther King quote: 'I have a dream that my children will one day live in a nation where they will not be judged by the colour of their skin but by the content of their character.'

Some people thought it was a bit tokenist and saccharine, but a black female member of staff who I had never really spoken to before knocked on my door and thanked me, with tears in her eyes.

Had drinks with Blair in his flat at No. 11 tonight. Just the two of us, in a clear-the-air meeting set up by Lord Levy, who's a good friend of Victor's.

'Fancy a beer?' he said, sounding a bit like Alan Partridge. Never really had Blair down as a big beer drinker, to be honest.

He came back with a silver tankard and a can of foaming bitter from the fridge. Definitely Partridge.

We sat on opposite sofas swigging our beer.

'What's the problem between us?' he asked.

'Nothing really, other than I don't agree with your foreign policy and I don't want us to suck up to the Government too much.'

'OK, but it seems to me that it's getting a bit personal at the moment.'

'Honestly, Tony, I have no issues with you and never have had, we've always got on well. But Alastair's always got it into his head that we are the enemy, and that doesn't help.'

'No, I realise there's a problem there.'

Levy will have communicated our corporate concerns about Campbell.

I told him that I found Alastair increasingly difficult to deal with. 'He's a big problem. He gets up feeling angry, goes for one of his runs which make him tired and angrier, reads the papers and starts foaming at the mouth, and by the time he's got to you he's absolutely flying with rage and telling you the Mirror are a bunch of treacherous infidels. Whereas you're cool about it all, know the papers don't matter that much – and just want a nice, quiet breakfast.'

Blair laughed. 'Well, it's not quite that bad.'

'OK, but you get my point. I like him, but it's not helpful to you that Alastair bullies all the press, and tells you constantly they're all out to get you.'

'No, I know. He has done a great job for me, but he perhaps needs to calm down a bit sometimes.'

We had another pint and Euan came in to say hello.

'Hi, Euan, me and your father are just having a few beers before hitting Leicester Square, if you fancy joining us ...'

He semi-smiled. Must have been a bit bruising for him, all that. Nice lad, though.

'I got it in the neck from Cherie for that,' said Blair. 'She was away and I was in charge – she was not amused! But you have to let the kids try and lead as normal a life as possible. It's not easy for them living here.'

'Talking of Cherie, why has she got it in for the Mirror so much?'

'Oh, it's not just you guys, I think she finds a lot of the press coverage just so negative and upsetting. It's difficult for her, trying to juggle a job and a family here with all the nonsense that goes on.'

'I understand that, but it doesn't help you that she is always at war with the papers. And I don't really understand what I or the Mirror have done to her, frankly. It seems crazy that a Labour Prime Minister's wife hates the Mirror and its editor.'

'I agree. Look, I'll talk to her. Perhaps you should have tea together or something.'

I asked how he got on with Bush.

'Very well; he's not as stupid as people think, you know. I know you're not a fan, but his country's still reeling from 9/11 and we have to be there to help them.'

'You can't go bombing everyone, though.'

'Well, no, obviously we can't do that. But we have got to root out these terrorists and tackle this issue head on. Because they're intent on destroying the whole Western way of life.'

'But shouldn't we be going after Bin Laden, not Saddam? Iraq isn't the threat it once was, surely?'

'Yes, I think it is. Saddam has used WMD before on his own people, and won't hesitate to use them again. We have to deal with him as well as Bin Laden.'

It was a bit odd, chewing the fat over a few beers with him like this. But it reminded me that he's a decent bloke. We talked for an hour and a half, the longest one-to-one I've had ever had with him.

'It's right that the Mirror should be more critical of us now we're in power,' he said. 'I understand that. All I ask is for fairness. If we do something good, and we are actually making real progress in areas of health and education, for example, then I hope you will say so.'

As I walked down Downing Street afterwards I felt rather privileged to have had such a meeting. It's sometimes easy to forget that I am in an exceptionally fortunate position to enjoy such access to people like this.

WEDNESDAY, 27 MARCH

Can you bloody believe it – Naomi's won. Admittedly the judge has only given her £3500, so it's a Pyrrhic victory. But the headlines will still be NAOMI BEATS MIRROR. It's pathetic.

Our headline is JUDGE GIVES LYING DRUG ABUSER £3500, which sums up the farce.

I tossed the TV news another well-rehearsed soundbite: 'One of her colleagues said supermodels did not get out of bed for less than ten thousand pounds – she hasn't even got enough to pull back the bedclothes.'

We will appeal, but costs are already past £200,000 – this is going to be a long and expensive fight now.

SATURDAY, 30 MARCH

My 37th birthday, and I was looking forward to a splendid night's entertainment in the fleshpots of London when a phone call came through mid-afternoon saying the Queen Mother had died. I wish I could say my first reaction was to bow my head and pay silent tribute to Her Majesty for all she'd done for this country in her amazing life, before racing to the newsroom to start work on Monday's paper.

But all I could think of was that she had died on a Saturday. Every single royal who has died in my lifetime – Diana, Margaret and now the Queen Mother – died on a Saturday. Which means a third beautifully crafted supplement disappearing into the bin. The number of hours that goes into these things can't be overstated – thousands over the years, constantly updating and revising. All gone, because the Sundays have enough time to do their own, that they too will have carefully worked on for decades.

A sad day, though; she was a wonderful old bird. 'Never explain, never complain, and never speak in public,' she used to say. And that's how she got away with a constant £4 million overdraft and extravagant lunch parties every day, yet the public still loved her.

THURSDAY, 4 APRIL

Mandelson emailed:

> TB was really happy about the discussion you had with him. You have an effect, probably greater than you realise. Power is all the more powerful when used selectively.

I replied:

> Yes, I thought it was about the best chat I've had with him. Frank, honest and productive. Probably because Alastair was nowhere to be seen. TB seems to understand that what we are doing is not disloyalty, it's journalism. Hence the renewed credibility, awards and strong sales. I said I didn't want to be the *Mail*, just criticising everything for the sake of it. I want to whack the Government around and keep them on their toes, but support on key policy when it matters, if we think they're right. When we back Labour now it carries much more weight than when people thought we were *Pravda*.

SUNDAY, 7 APRIL

Blair's in Texas to support Bush on his plans to go to 'deal with Saddam', and saying it's not a question of 'if' we attack him, but 'when'. The rhetoric is being seriously ratcheted up here, and I don't like it. We did a cartoon splash of Bush as a gunslinger sitting astride Blair as his yapping poodle. Harsh, but fair. We just seem to be heading inexorably into war here, and it's dangerous and wrong.

TUESDAY, 9 APRIL

I was invited to the Queen Mother's funeral today, and got there early after someone told me the seats were allocated pretty much on a first come, first served basis.

They were, and I found myself sitting less than twenty yards from the Queen and the coffin.

Felt a bit strange, really. Like I was intruding. But I looked all around me, and saw all these other people who had no right to be there either, and relaxed. This, like so much of the royals' lives, was not a private occasion, but a public event.

It was a solemn, very traditional affair, and not especially moving as a result. There was none of the supercharged emotion of Diana's funeral. Just a quiet affection and appreciation for a thoroughly admirable life of duty and service to her country.

Charles looked really upset. I suspect he was closer to his grandmother than his mother in many ways.

WEDNESDAY, 10 APRIL

Breakfast with Gordon Brown at the Treasury.

'Ah, Piers, come in, I've got something for you.'

He pulled out a small tape from his desk.

God, what was it? Blair being spanked by a dominatrix?

'This is a recording of Liam Fox saying he wants to kill off the NHS and make everyone pay for treatment.'

'Right, where's that from, then?'

'A meeting of Tory members. We, ahem, infiltrated it.'

It wasn't exactly Watergate, but it was a good story, and I was grateful to have it.

'You keep saying we don't help you, so I thought you might like it for the Mirror.'

Gordon seemed a bit nervous, as if he was being rather naughty.

'No, definitely,' I said. 'This is great, thanks. We'll splash it tomorrow.'

I told him we were planning a secret relaunch in a week, including a price war with Murdoch.

'Is that wise?' he observed, raising one of those bushy eyebrows.

'It is if we match him penny for penny, up and down. But if we blink, he'll kill us. I believe we are stronger than the Sun all round now and if we are the same price we will beat them.'

'Well, good luck. If you need any more help, let me know.'

Later on, Jeremy emailed in horror: 'It is with disbelief that I see your mug hovering only a few rows back from Her Majesty and Family. The Queen Mother must be turning in her grave.'

Had dinner at Mo Mowlam's place tonight, which was great fun. She blames Mandelson for wrecking her career by putting pressure on Blair to give him her Northern Ireland job.

'He was spreading his usual poison everywhere, telling everyone I was mad and so on. He wanted my job and he's got it. But I will never forgive him. What made it worse for me was that despite it all I took time to show him the ropes over there and introduce him and Reinaldo to people. And I've heard nothing from him again. He just used me, and moved on.'

Mo, to my surprise, has no protection now.

'They won't give me anyone, because they say I am not at risk. But everyone who has done that job is at risk. It worries me.'

THURSDAY, 11 APRIL
Lunch with Mandelson at the Four Seasons in Canary Wharf. I told him about Mo.

'Well, I'm sorry she feels that way. Mo thinks everyone was out to get her, but the truth is that she had gone as far as she could in Northern Ireland and it needed some fresh impetus.'

'Did you knife her, then?'

'Oh, Piers, p-l-ease. I don't knife anybody.'

And with that he carved expertly into his chicken.

TUESDAY, 16 APRIL
We relaunched the *Mirror* today, bringing back the 'Daily' to the title and dropping the red masthead altogether. I've been wanting to do this for ages, to try and move us into a new marketplace away from the *Sun* and *Star*. We don't have the money to compete with Murdoch and Rothermere in their markets, but a slightly more serious, radical and campaigning left-wing paper might just let us stand alone, like the *Guardian* in the broadsheet market – immune from purely commercial attacks based on greater resource. Our new motto is 'Think again', and we have a whole TV ad campaign to support it, testing people's views on big issues like the fire strike, oil prices and Iraq. It is very different, very expensive and very challenging. But will it work? Or are my bosses going to look at my contract in six months' time and 'think again'?

Kelvin emailed me. 'Good luck, it's the right decision. I raised it with the board at the *Mirror* four years ago, but it was met with hostility and fear – shows you what dimwits ran the place.'

WEDNESDAY, 17 APRIL
As part of the relaunch, I've got to make some savings, and one obvious target is Alan Sugar's fee for his column – which he donates to charity, anyway. I explained that money's tight and asked if he'd consider taking a drop in salary to

£20,000, given that he doesn't keep it. 'You can either storm off in a fit of legendary Alan Sugar businesslike pique, in the belief I am a conniving Gooner editor trying to scam you, *or* accept I am telling the truth.'

I expected Vesuvius to erupt and I was right.

'You must think I'm getting soft in my old age. I'm not. You pay idiots like Matthew Norman hundreds of thousands of pounds to write a load of crap, but want me to do it for nothing. Stick your £20k up your arse, I'm leaving.'

I called his bluff. 'You wouldn't expect me to pay Ledley King (great, but at the back) as much as Thierry Henry (star striker, up front). But consider my offer firmly implanted between my butt cheeks. Thanks for all your work for the *Mirror*, I'm genuinely sorry about this.'

THURSDAY, 18 APRIL

'I think you may have to sit down for this one.' Richard Wallace, my new news supremo, had flown into my office looking even more pleased with himself than usual, and I could tell from the wicked grin on his face that this was a big one.

'You'll genuinely never guess who Ulrika's having it away with now.' Well, there's a challenge, I thought. 'Um … Gazza?'

'Nope.'

'Blair?'

'Nope.'

'Barrymore?'

'That's absurd.'

He paused for effect. 'Sven.'

I gasped, audibly. '*What*? Not *the* Sven?'

'I'm afraid so, yes.'

It was right up there with Elvis dead and David Icke's 'disciple of our Lord' infamous performance on Wogan for knock-me-down-with-a-feather quality. 'Bloody hell,' I laughed. 'This is going to bring a rather rapid end to our Serious News agenda, isn't it?' For a one-fact sensation, this was a quite spectacularly massive big of gossip.

I called Ulrika's agent Melanie Cantor myself, and just put it to her straight. Most of my reporters hate doing this any earlier than about 9pm, in case the agent runs to another paper. But I always think if the editor calls directly and stresses the exclusivity of the story, then it takes an agent bent on commercial suicide to stitch that editor up. So I called Melanie, and said one word: 'Sven?'

She laughed. 'Sorry?'

I laughed too. 'You probably will be, yes. Come on, then, is it true?'

Melanie danced round the houses for a few minutes before ascertaining that we clearly did know everything and that it was all coming out, whether she liked it or not. She said she'd talk to Ulrika and call me back, which she did half an hour later.

There was something about her cheery manner which suggested her client was not entirely averse to this information emerging. Melanie confirmed the affair, said it was a 'serious relationship, not a silly fling', and added that Ulrika expects Sven to leave his long-time girlfriend Nancy Dell'Olio for her.

Blimey.

I relayed the good news to Richard. This one's going to put the old leopard in the pigeon coop, that's for sure.

Every bone in my tabloid body told me to wipe out the front for it. But I was determined to maintain our more serious approach, so did a big half-page blurb on it instead, splashing on something else – to my back bench's astonishment.

SUNDAY, 21 APRIL

I've written an article for the *Independent on Sunday* about the Sven/Ulrika story, in which I respond to all the usual snooty broadsheet sneers about intrusion, etc, by recording how big each broadsheet's coverage has been of this 'non-story'. The *Telegraph* wins with an extraordinary 10,584 words, *The Times* comes second with 8653, and the *Guardian* third with an impressive 6793. Argument over, I'm afraid.

Alan Sugar rang later to say he'll stay on. My Bay of Pigs crisis with him is over. And I'm glad, because I do really like the man – he makes me laugh.

Melanie Cantor rang me in the afternoon to say Ulrika's furious with Sven, because he won't take her calls and it looks like he's freezing her out.

'She says he's a spineless little toad and a liar.'

I attribute this all to 'close friends of Ulrika'.

MONDAY, 22 APRIL

Melanie called again to say Sven's phoned Ulrika and asked her to hang on a bit.

'She's said she will, but not for long.'

Later Stuart Higgins, now a PR man, rang on behalf of Sven to find out what Ulrika was telling me.

You couldn't make this up.

TUESDAY, 23 APRIL

Dominic Lawson and I played chess at an Italian restaurant in Canary Wharf. The significance being that as well as both being newspaper editors we were both chess champions at Cumnor House prep school. It was a tight struggle for an hour, then I lost concentration (and a pawn), and Dominic moved slowly but inexorably in for the kill until I finally surrendered.

WEDNESDAY, 24 APRIL

Sven took Nancy to the Arsenal game tonight, and I watched in amusement as she stood up and took the cheers of the crowd. Looks like it's all over for Ulrika now.

THURSDAY, 25 APRIL

The royals held a party for media people at Windsor Castle, and a very jolly affair it turned out to be, too. They all appeared through a large door panel, like a family of ghosts. The Queen was on more cheery form than when we'd last met at Charles's 50th, so I tried to at least make her laugh to avoid that ice-cold stare again. 'Do you have any inside information on Beckham's foot, ma'am?' She laughed, I think genuinely. 'No, but I realise it is very important for the country.'

Then she surprised me by adding, 'I don't know enough about stress fractures to go into any detail, but I do know he is not doing the right things to get it fixed,' she said, referring to Zara's jockey boyfriend.

'You mean he shouldn't be driving his car?' I said, remembering Beckham's prang in his Mercedes last week.

'Yes,' she replied, smiling. I asked if she knew any good physios who could perhaps assist his progress.

'I do, actually. My granddaughter Zara has just qualified. She helped to get Richard's leg fixed,' she said, referring to Zara's jockey boyfriend.

Buckingham Palace traditionally frowns on individuals publishing details of their private conversations with members of the royal family, so I wasn't going to do anything. But word spread I'd got some Beckham quotes from Her Majesty, and being journalists they all wanted to file it. Eventually a Palace spokesman consented, on condition I shared them with my rivals.

Later on, I joined the Queen's group again to hear her respond to a question asking if she enjoyed her recent garden party at the Castle by saying, 'Well, would you enjoy twelve thousand people trampling around *your* garden?' Then she roared with laughter. I may have been a little hasty about her last time.

MONDAY, 29 APRIL

We were lined up to do an exclusive interview with Mikhail Gorbachev, with the help of former Tory Minister Norman Lamont – but the deal's collapsed at the last minute because Gorbachev suddenly demanded $70,000. An embarrassed Lord Lamont wrote to apologise: 'I entirely understand your frustration and irritation at how this has been handled and I have written to the Russians to add my voice of protest. The ridiculous request for $70,000 came out of the blue at the very end and was obviously unacceptable.'

A reader sent me a cutting about Ulrika declaring she'll name secret celebrity lovers in her new autobiography, and had scrawled on the top, 'I'm not surprised, she's had more pricks than a second-hand dartboard.'

TUESDAY, 30 APRIL

Nicola Formby, A. A. Gill's other half, has begged me to step in at the last minute and do the monthly 'Lunch with …' feature she writes for *Tatler* magazine, after Sven pulled out at the last minute over the Ulrika storm.

She said we could go anywhere, so I opted for the Mirabelle, one of my favourite restaurants. The meal was fine, and we had a good laugh. Until near the end, when she suddenly produced an envelope, started to blush slightly, and said: 'Erm, if I said this contained naked photos of me, what would you say?'

I felt rather bemused. This was obviously some sort of gag, but I couldn't work out what it was yet. 'Well, I'd probably say, can I have a look?' I laughed, and reached over to take the envelope. She encouraged me to take it, feigning mock horror.

I assumed there was nothing inside, or at the very least photos of Ms Formby fully clothed. But to my amazement there were twenty-odd pictures of her completely starkers on a very ornate bed, prancing for all she's worth like one of those readers' wives in *Escort* magazine.

It was my turn to blush.

'They were taken in a suite at the Burj Al Arab hotel in Dubai,' she explained matter-of-factly.

In one of the shots I saw A. A. Gill in some sort of weird smoking jacket, looking on proudly as his missus strutted her stuff. 'Oh, and the photographer who took them is over there in the corner taking photos of you looking at them.' I looked round and sure enough, there was this weird-looking bloke leering at me and pinging away on his camera.

I started to feel uncomfortable. I mean, these weren't just accidental glimpses of nudity that had slipped into a batch of otherwise tasteful bikini shots on the beach. These were porn shots, to be perfectly frank. You could see everything, and the poses were explicit. Ms Formby sprawled here, Ms Formby's legs akimbo there, Ms Formby thrusting her bottom everywhere. She obviously thinks she's an absolute sex kitten, but I fear the mists of time have taken their toll a little too much for her to pull off the Jordan gig.

I was truly at a loss as to what to say. 'Erm, well, Nicola, you look … er, great. Really nice. Thank you for showing them to me. Does Adrian know you're doing this?' She assured me he did.

Perhaps they're just into some kinky swinging thing with their B-grade celebrity pals. But I was genuinely embarrassed, for me, and for her. Then she suddenly stared me in the eye and asked, 'Are you a good lover?'

It was a car crash moment. And a few minutes later I checked my watch and, in time-honoured tabloid fashion, made my excuses and left.

WEDNESDAY, 1 MAY

A postcard arrived first post from Nicola Formby. 'Still can't believe I showed you those photos … what am I worth? Thank you for doing lunch, I really enjoyed it.' Bizarre. Utterly bizarre.

Blair did a tub-thumping interview with Brian Reade today, saying the *Mirror*'s been wrong about everything. We splashed it, and put an off-the-cuff quote from Campbell on the front as well: 'Your poll on us was bent and Pilger's articles are a load of bollocks.'

Pilger's very unhappy about this:

For me, Piers, good faith was broken today. Where was the serious journalism you promised? Where were the tough questions to Blair, why let him lump me into the 'ultra left', and why run Campbell's puerile comment on the front? Either you want serious journalism or you don't. Your response is important.

I replied:

John, I think you're over-reacting a bit. You had two pages to tear into Blair yesterday, he's entitled to have his say back. It's not 'stunt journalism' to illuminate the Prime Minister's spokesman as a foul-mouthed yob who says ICM polls are 'bent' and that you are 'talking bollocks'. I'm sorry if you don't like what I did, but if you feel you can't write for us any more, I understand.

He'll calm down. I admire his passion, though, even if his ego is enormous. Later I get another much more conciliatory email, just asking to be consulted on stuff that involves him, which is fair enough.

SATURDAY, 4 MAY

Gary Farrow, an old mate who works for Sony, married the *Sun* columnist Jane Moore today in a lavish bash at Claridge's. It was an extraordinary guest list, half celebrity, half tabloid journalist. And we'd all been slotted in together, to mutual discomfort until enough alcohol had flowed.

I sat next to Nick Faldo, and expected a crashing bore banging on about his four iron. But he couldn't have been nicer, and seemed to have mellowed very well in his old age. Perhaps his gorgeous new wife Valerie has helped calm him down. Barbara Windsor was on the table too, with her boyfriend Scott, who looks ridiculously young. But they laughed a lot and seemed very happy.

The amusement was somewhat tarnished, though, when a PR woman sitting with us called Sue Brealy, who was heavily fortified, started laying into me for 'stitching up Mr Motivator' on an interview four years ago. I had no idea what she was talking about, and tried to explain this wasn't really the right time for this kind of discussion, but she was having none of it.

'You are a bloody stitch-up merchant,' she slurred. 'It was a disgrace and you should be ashamed of yourself.'

Even Faldo felt sorry for me. 'God, do you get that everywhere you go?'

'Yes, mate, it's not like you walking around like some god being fawned over. I just get abuse.'

There was an electric moment before the speeches when Kelvin walked across the room, his every move being watched by a steely-eyed Elton John. They hadn't seen each other since the *Sun* paid Elton £1 million and gave him a front-page apology for those false rent-boy stories.

Time hasn't diluted Elton's anger. But he cooled down enough to play 'Your Song' for the happy couple before leaving.

I got into more trouble in the bar afterwards, when Jeremy Clarkson and his wife laid into me for those pictures we ran of him kissing his producer.

'Oh, come on, let's move on, can't we?' I said. 'If you don't want to get in the papers for that kind of thing, then don't kiss women in cars,' I said.

'It wasn't what it seemed,' he said fiercely.

I looked at him and then his wife. And decided life was just too short for this kind of feud.

'OK, look, I'm sorry we did those pictures, Jeremy assured me it was perfectly innocent, Francie, and I'm sure it was now. If it upset you, as it clearly did, then I am sorry.'

Clarkson looked amazed. 'Right, well – thank you. It's a bit late in the day, but better late than never, I guess. Let's put it behind us, shall we?'

We shook hands I and went home.

THURSDAY, 9 MAY

Every former editor of the *Sun*'s infamous Bizarre showbiz column met up tonight for a twentieth anniversary party, and much hilarity was had when Kelvin got up to make the speech, and promptly got loudly booed and jeered. 'I always knew you lot were a bunch of miserable bastards,' he sighed.

Later, Peter Stringfellow arrived with a phalanx of his lapdancers. 'Just a little gesture to say thanks for all the publicity over the years, guys,' he laughed. Typical Stringy.

SATURDAY, 11 MAY

The *Express* has run a whole-page feature on me headlined IT'S BIN MORGAN, MAD MULLAH OF THE MIRROR. It says I'm a useless failure, who since my separation from my wife now spends 'hours of loneliness and frustration' on my own, plotting a 'dangerous obsession to be seen as a success'. It included a nice big picture of me and Marion to go with it.

A few friends rang, furious at the piece and offering to help exact retribution. But I couldn't help laughing. It is so vile and offensive that it's funny. Richard Desmond thinks he'll get to me like this, but he never will.

MONDAY, 20 MAY

I called Mandelson to congratulate him on a good performance on *Off The Record*.

'Still think you should be wary of the overly forced grin. Either laugh or snarl – you are the Prince of Darkness, after all.'

He laughed: 'I try and avoid bitter. Think I am succeeding. My protection officer suggested I smile more, and I told him it's important to ensure you are smiling rather than grinning.'

FRIDAY, 24 MAY

A tetchy note from Jonathan Ross. 'I gave the not-very-hilarious *Thunderpants* two stars, but someone changed it to four in the paper. Presumably just a mistake, but an irritating one, especially if it gets used on some poster or publicity. Please make sure it doesn't happen again or I'm off.' Despite his rather impertinent threat, I am inclined to agree with him.

SATURDAY, 25 MAY

George Michael's done an anti-war song called 'Shoot the Dog' and wants to use our HOWDY POODLE front page as the cover – and to do an interview with me about it all.

'Can you fly over to my place in the South of France?' he said.

'Er, well, not really, George, I'm a bit busy editing the paper these days.'

'Oh, OK. Well, I'll be at my London studio in a couple of days – how about you come over for lunch or something?'

I agreed.

MONDAY, 27 MAY

Off to west London to see George Michael. He was on great form, fortified, I suspect, by a few of his beloved joints. We spent a couple of hours listening to his new album and swapping old stories about celebrities and newspapers.

My all time great clanger involved George.

I was editing the *Sun*'s Bizarre column when I got a tip that George had impregnated a young German fan during a tour there, and she was now chasing him for maintenance through the German embassy in London.

His record company confirmed they had received official correspondence to this effect, and Andy Coulson was sent to Frankfurt immediately to try and find the girl.

I wrote up the story, and Martin Dunn, the deputy editor – Kelvin was away – thought it was so sensational we'd spoof the first edition, running a different story for a few minutes, and splash it after that. Our rivals would get the 'spoof' and not realise we had a big story until it was too late.

I went home basking in my own glory, until the phone suddenly went at 10pm. It was Andy in Frankfurt. 'Mate, we've got a problem. The baby exists, but the girl's only fourteen, and would have been twelve when she got pregnant. Her mum says the father's a local skinhead, and she must have made up the George stuff because she's obsessed with him.'

I listened in horror.

'Right, OK, I'd better call Martin.'

I made the dreaded call.

'Martin, it's Piers. I'm sorry, but we've been sold a pup here.'

I explained the story. He was very good about it, and dashed off to ditch it and replace the spoof edition.

About 100,000 copies had gone out with the story, though, to places like Cornwall. It was too late to call them back. All I could do was pray George never saw it.

We got away with it, and never heard a word from his people.

As I told him this story now, he laughed out loud. 'I've got that fucking front page on my loo wall: "George Michael's Secret Lovechild". Obviously in light of what you may now know about me, it was never going to be that likely, was it?'

He'd known all along.

'Why didn't you complain?'

'Well, my PR people thought it was great – proved I had sex with women!'

Later in the evening, I went to the Picture Editor awards, where we were Newspaper of the Year yet again. Blair was presenting the awards and I persuaded him to take a photo of me and my team celebrating.

Say what you like about the man, he's got a sense of humour.

WEDNESDAY, 29 MAY

Had lunch with the BBC Breakfast News duo Sophie Raworth and Jeremy Bowen in my favourite Italian restaurant at Canary Wharf today. I never normally drink at lunchtime, but it was a quiet day and nothing much was going on, so we had a bottle of wine. And then another … and by 6pm we were all completely hammered. I rang Kerrie. 'I'm shorry, can you bring down my briefcase because I can't walk straight.' She laughed: 'You naughty boy.' Where would I be without her?

THURSDAY, 30 MAY

Sophie sent me an email at 04.59 from work: 'My head feels like it's stuffed with cotton wool, one too many grappas maybe … going to be an interesting programme … roll on 9am.'

FRIDAY, 31 MAY

Steve Bing, Liz Hurley's billionaire American ex-lover, is suing us for millions for calling him Bing Laden for dumping her after making her pregnant.

Today I was forced to spend ten hours giving a deposition to his legendary lawyer Marty Singer – who'd flown in from Hollywood to do it.

Things got more and more heated as it went on, mainly because I was totally bored and could only amuse myself by taking the piss out of him – which made him even more laborious.

Eventually he shouted, 'Mr Morgan, if you persist in behaving this way, then we will just have to fly over to Malibu and do it all there.'

Excellent!

'Great, when can we go?'

THURSDAY, 6 JUNE

Tatler has come out with Nicola Formby's interview. She calls me 'boyishly good-looking, unexpectedly neat, mischievous, confident, flirtatious, boisterous and fearless'. Then admits showing me her naked pictures.

There is clearly something going on here, I'm just not sure what it is. And nor am I sure I want to know.

MONDAY, 10 JUNE

Had dinner with the Home Secretary David Blunkett at Rules.

I tried revving him up about a leadership battle.

'If this war on terror goes pear-shaped, as it seems to be, then Gordon might make a move,' I said.

Pause.

'And he might be looking for a brilliant Chancellor.'

Blunkett leaned forward. 'Well, perhaps you can remember me if you have that particular conversation with him in the future.'

I was surprised. I'd expected to be stonewalled.

We got a bit pissed after that. Blunkett's amusing company.

TUESDAY, 11 JUNE

Murdoch's given an interview to the *FT* in which he says, 'I don't know what they're doing at Trinity Mirror. You have a bright editor who needs a newspaper boss.' Asked if he'd have me back, he says, 'No. He burned too many bridges.' I was asked for my reaction by the *Guardian* and said, 'Mr Murdoch sounds like a newspaper boss in desperate need of a bright editor.'

Then, rather than leaving it there, which would have been quite an amusing riposte, I got overexcited and continued, 'He couldn't afford me anyway. The only way I'd want to go back to News International is to buy it. And judging by the News share price and Murdoch's advancing years, that can only be a matter of time. As for burning my bridges, I've incinerated most of them, I agree, but there are still a few News International bridges that need a good arson attack, and I look forward to lighting the matches in due course.'

I read these comments later on the website and realised I had come across as a) stupendously arrogant, b) needlessly insulting, c) possibly career-wreckingly stupid.

Matthew Freud rang: 'The first bit was funny, but why did you have to go and say all the rest of it? Rupert was being flattering about you.'

'Matthew, you have to say that, he's family. I don't have to worry what he thinks about me any more.' But I do, of course.

WEDNESDAY, 12 JUNE

I've instructed the 3am Girls to launch a campaign to find the 100 Most

Irritating People In Britain. A man called John from Brighton sent his entry today: 'The most hated twat in Britain is Piers Morgan, closely followed by you three pointless parasites. Why don't you find something useful to do with your lives?'

Everyone's gunning for Alastair over a row about whether Blair tried to muscle in on the Queen Mother's funeral arrangements, which I think sounds ridiculous. So I went on TV and said so, actually defending him.

THURSDAY, 13 JUNE

A fax first thing from Alastair: 'I know Government relations are not in a great state, and we both have our views on the way relations have developed with you, but I wanted to say thanks for what you said about me personally last night.'

I replied: 'It was a slip of the tongue and I've been kicking myself ever since. My standing in the journalistic community has now collapsed.'

MONDAY, 17 JUNE

It seems like every Government minister is lining up to attack the press at the moment, which seems like political suicide to me.

I asked Mandelson this morning if Downing Street has finally gone mad. He replied:

> No, they haven't (yet). But as I always said to people in Northern Ireland, you have to put yourself into the others' shoes and see it from their point of view. You need to understand that a) the right are out to destroy the Government, b) the press has become histrionic in a way that happened to Major (but with more justification then), and c) there's an unjustified insistence that Downing Street cannot and should not be believed on anything. They saw what happened to Major and they don't want to be killed. It's a very interesting time for politics at the moment. The Tories think they're on the brink of turning the whole press against the Government and it cannot survive that. This may be true. But in which case, sooner or later, it will be time to take sides, and you need to see round this corner. As for the Government, they need to think very carefully about the position they have got into. It is not sustainable, so they have to reassess by autumn. Sermon over …

I replied:

> Well, the reason you guys are copping it now is because you sucked up to the playground bullies, treated your mates like shit, stamped on everyone who got in your way, and generally behaved like a super-arrogant, hectoring, lecturing, dictator. This is the inevitable payback. But if the Government now sucks up to its bruised mates, scorns the scornful

bullies, and learns some quick humility, pays rigid attention to things that are actually important and starts to govern for the people, then it may not be too late for the 'left' media to give them their due as a bunch of rather talented and well-intentioned politicians.

TUESDAY, 18 JUNE
Mandelson emailed again, he must be bored:

> There's more chitchat about the *Mirror* amongst the chatterati than you might realise – what's happening, where's it going, what does it all mean. That's why it's good for you to leaven the mix more over your TB and Government broadsides. I know how you feel about the sucking up, to the *Sun* and *Mail*, for obvious reasons, I resent it too. Nobody ever stood up for me against these bullies, over Europe, my private life etc. But ranting is not a substitute for argument. You're right to depart from *Pravda* style, it's worked. Now it should go up a gear and be more refined. By the way, I can't resist it. Exactly the same proportion as think politicians don't tell the truth also distrust newspapers.

I laughed out loud. 'Don't think I will take lectures in ranting from someone who made that "I'm not a quitter" speech on election night.'

'No, it was reasonably and rationally expressed, but slightly loudly because of the emotion I felt and because I was being shouted down by the Scargillites from the floor. That's my excuse and I am sticking to it.'

I told him:

> *Pravda* failed for us and so will *Pravda* (reversed) in the long run. 70 per cent whack and 30 per cent support is about right. And as for lying journalists, all I would say is that we *know* we're hypocritical, pious, sanctimonious scumbags and I for one have no trouble admitting it.

Later in the day, Cherie got into hot water for expressing apparent sympathy for the Palestinians. I asked Mandelson: 'CHERIE – SHOULD SHE PUT A CORK IN IT?'

He replied:

> It's true that many young Palestinians feel hopeless and are queuing up to volunteer for these acts of slaughter. But there are many other older Palestinians who are manipulating them, recruiting them, training them, deploying them, and using them to murder young and old alike. She didn't mis-speak but she did under-speak, in my view.

Mandelson has many flaws, but he is an astute political thinker. I can always see why Blair values him.

FRIDAY, 21 JUNE

Philip Graf came into my office mid-afternoon and told me an extraordinary story of how Cherie Blair sat next to him at a newspaper industry dinner in Scotland last night and spent half an hour demanding he sack me.

Even Philip, one of the most mild-mannered guys you could ever wish to meet, was pretty appalled by how she'd behaved. And to my relief he said, 'I told her that you were a very good editor and she was wrong about you as a person too.'

But it wasn't a throwaway line, he added; it was a relentless attack on my character, banging on about my 'lack of moral compass' personally and professionally.

As Philip regaled the story, I could feel the blood starting to burn inside me. How dare she do this? Who the *hell* does she think she is?

I called Alastair to tell him the good news. He just sighed for about five seconds as he took in what I had said.

'Christ, that's all we fucking need.'

'Does Tony know what she's done?'

'Of course he fucking doesn't,' replied a clearly angry Alastair. 'He'll be furious about this. Especially after you and he sorted things out over that drink. I'll talk to him.'

Just in case he conveniently forgot, I fired off a fax to Blair himself:

Prime Minister, if you are curious as to why the relationship between the *Mirror* and No. 10 is still, unnecessarily, more than a little fractious – perhaps this might enlighten you. Cherie told my boss last night that I was an immoral little crook trying to get you turfed out of Downing Street and that I should be sacked. It is hardly surprising that I am not subsequently enthused with a warm feeling of camaraderie towards you guys. This is depressing, because you and I seem to get along fine, and after our very cordial last meeting I thought we understood our relative positions much better. I also think the *Mirror* has been more than fair to the Government in recent weeks. I bring this to your attention because I suspect you are not fully aware of this kind of thing going on.

I mentioned Cherie's bizarre behaviour to Sarah Brown when she got in touch about her new charity book. 'Sorry to hear you are still not thought of by everyone as a delightful human being,' she joked. It's no secret that she and Cherie loathe each other.

Still fuming, I emailed Mandelson to tell him what had happened:

Cherie sat next to Philip Graf last night and spent the entire time telling him I was an immoral crook trying to get her husband kicked out and that I should be fired. You might care to mention Cherie's nasty vindictive invective next time you see TB, in case he's curious why the *Mirror* isn't as sycophantic as it might be.

He replied: 'She didn't convert Philip then? (Only joking).'
I was not in the mood for laughing:

Peter, she's not doing him any favours at all. I wouldn't mind but when I see her she's all over me like a ghastly rash, cooing and bringing down the bloody baby for more cooing. I can't stand her hypocrisy in dealing with the media. Tony sat next to Victor and could not have been more charming. After the more supportive stance we adopted this week I expected more than his wife pissing all over me to my boss. And I bet he doesn't realise a thing.

Mandelson replied: 'I love your emails. I honestly don't think it would have occurred to Tony to express a view at all. It doesn't go that deep with him. I will mention, though.'

England's World Cup games are all starting at 7am, which makes our paper immediately old news. Today's the big Brazil match and I have got round the problem by doing an entirely blank page apart from a small headline in the middle saying THIS PAGE HAS BEEN CANCELLED. NOTHING ELSE MATTERS. And a small England flag.

SATURDAY, 22 JUNE

Our front page yesterday has been sent back to me with a note written on it from a D. Clark of Portsmouth, saying: 'Tell that to the starving millions in Africa, the thousands in the Middle East and all over Asia who are blowing themselves up, or the countless homeless and jobless throughout the world. Print one less *Mirror* from tomorrow.'

SUNDAY, 23 JUNE

The *Mail on Sunday* says the DTI are hampered in their investigation because a load of emails between me and Anil have 'disappeared'. Truth is … there weren't any more. But nobody's going to believe it.

SUNDAY, 30 JUNE

George Michael's getting twitchy about his interview in which he poured his heart out about everything from Iraq to his rampant sex life.

Piers, we both know the sex stuff was an aside even if it was great tabloid fodder, and perhaps a little brave/foolish of me. But it would be a shame if England being beaten by Brazil in the World Cup relegates the impor- tant Day One stuff to the inside of the paper, and the sex stuff on Day Two then gets stuck all over the front page. The pair of us might be doing something really important here and I never thought I would ever be saying anything remotely like this to a tabloid editor, so I hope my trust in you is justified. Without copy approval I am totally at your mercy and that's something I would only do in an extremely urgent situation (and by that I don't mean there's a new Gareth Gates single on the way!). I'm not worried about Day Two in itself, 'My torrid night with Sheffield Wednesday' would be fine by me. George. PS. Don't get any ideas, I've never been to Sheffield.

I reassured him:

One word, George, *relax*. We're doing 'George on the war' over the front and four pages tonight, more than we even gave Kissinger. Day Two is 'George on the paw' (any paw he can get his hands on by the sound of it, especially in Sheffield apparently) … just my little joke obviously. But it will be the agreed Day Two, very amusing fare. So go down the pool, try not to overdo the spliffs, and have a good laugh at he-man Robbie Williams pawing Rachel Hunter for £200,000 in the *News of the World*.

He replied, 'If only I had some not to overdo …'

TUESDAY, 2 JULY

George was thrilled. 'Great piece, Piers, thanks. As for your suggestion of MP status, I'm not sure I would go down that well in Goring, are you?'

THURSDAY, 4 JULY

We've wiped out the front page for a headline MOURN ON THE FOURTH OF JULY over a devastating article by John Pilger, saying America's now killed twice as many people as died on 9/11 and has become the world's No. 1 rogue state.

Alastair Campbell sent me a fax wishing me a 'Happy US Independence Day' and enclosing copies of our two leader articles immediately after the 9/11 atrocity demanding that Britain help America find the culprits.

FRIDAY, 5 JULY

Our Independence Day front page has gone down well in the States, with the Murdoch-owned *New York Post* running a story about some of our US investors being furious with us. Someone called Tom Shrager, managing director of the financial house Tweedy Browne, says he called my bosses to complain, and thinks I am a disgrace.

How ironic it is that this American banker thinks his money gives him the right to dictate editorial policy at a British newspaper. It's not a long way ideologically from George Bush trying to force his nation's 'values' on countries like Afghanistan.

I issued a statement saying we'll carry on running Pilger's stuff. I expect more trouble. But this is a fight every journalist in Britain will agree with me over. Pilger himself is thrilled: 'Today's front page was a *Mirror* classic. There's a popular stirring and you have caught the mood.'

WEDNESDAY, 10 JULY

Breakfast with Gordon Brown.

'Blunkett wants to be your Chancellor,' I said as he poured the tea.

He laughed.

'Well, I am not the Prime Minister, Piers, so that is not possible, is it? Biscuit?'

SATURDAY, 13 JULY

George Michael has attacked Murdoch on TV after his papers all laid into him following my interview, and we've done a leader article applauding his courage. He emailed: 'Thanks for supporting me. They didn't use some of the heavier stuff I used in Rupertslagathon, but I think I made myself clear. Now if I could just find the bleach and the belly ring … love, Britney.'

MONDAY, 15 JULY

Petronella Wyatt, daughter of my late old 'mate' Woodrow, came to my office today to interview me for the *Spectator*. She bounced in full of the joys of summer, wearing a low-cut top with her impressive breasts covered in sparkly paint of some sort. It was everywhere, making her cleavage dazzle like a Catherine wheel on a dark bonfire night. Quite odd, but each to their own.

I spent a few minutes exchanging pleasantries before saying suddenly, 'Ask me about Cherie Blair.' She looked puzzled.

'Erm, OK, what about Cherie Blair?' I then told her the story of her demand for my head on a plate, and added a few juicy quotes to go with it. 'She's caused a lot of problems between Tony and the media, she's too aggressive, and loves to bestow her patronage, then remove it on a whim. But she isn't going to get me fired, however hard she tries. But I told Tony I'd appreciate it if he stopped his missus from trying all the time.'

I gave it the full nine yards, expunging my fury with every insult. Then my door suddenly opened and it was Kerrie, saying she'd 'got Mrs Blair on the line'. I looked at Petronella and she obviously thought this was a rather lame wind-up. But Kerrie stressed it really was the Prime Minister's wife on the phone.

We all fell about laughing. 'Tell her I'll call back when I've finished the interview,' I eventually said.

Petronella seemed appalled by this and said I should take the call. Must have remembered all those times her dad ran to the phone when Major called. We spent another half an hour chatting before the interview wrapped up and

Petronella scuttled away, hardly able to believe her luck. It's going to be a rather interesting interview now, and we both know it.

I shut the door and dialled the number Cherie had left for me. She came on all melodramatic.

'Piers, I am ringing to offer you an olive branch.'

'Well, that's very nice of you, Cherie, but I'd really rather snap it over your head, to be perfectly honest, after what you've been doing.'

She snapped back, 'It's not how you've been told, but if you are going to be like this, then let's forget it.'

'No, no, I'm all ears. What did you have in mind, then?'

'Well, let's have lunch at Hakkasan on Monday and try and put this behind us.'

I'm amazed: Hakkasan is an ultra-trendy, very popular Chinese restaurant bang in the middle of town, and there couldn't be a more public place for our kiss-and-make-up meeting if she tried. 'OK,' I replied; 'sounds good to me, I'll see you there.'

I called Petronella later to ask when the interview is running. 'Either this week or the week after, depending how fast I can do it,' she said.

Meaning either before or after my lunch. Hilarious.

TUESDAY, 16 JULY

Gordon Brown made a tremendous pre-Budget speech yesterday, that many believed signalled the start of his charge to No. 10. At the same time, a brilliant picture of a large elephant tossing a baby elephant with its trunk came in. So I splashed on that picture, with an inset of Brown towering over Blair in the Commons, and the headline PACK YOUR TRUNK TONY, I'M IN CHARGE. It was only when I looked at it this morning that I realised it was a ridiculous page that didn't work on any level at all, other than in my weird little mind. It's embarrassing.

One of our showbiz reporters, James Scott, later brought in a good little story about Blair's aide Anji Hunter having an affair with Sky News political editor Adam Boulton. Neither's a household name, but it's a good page lead, given that they are both married. Except that Anji's a mate from Newick, and I know her husband Nick well, and my little brother Rupert has house-sat for them from time to time – and, well, it's just not worth all the aggro for the sake of a page nine lead, to be honest.

I called Anji to tell her I was killing the story, and she was suitably grateful, whilst aware that it will almost certainly pop up somewhere else anyway.

My decision to spike it went down badly with a few of my staff. But I really don't care. All editors look after their mates, whatever they are prepared to say in public. And I will never publish anything that ruins the atmosphere for me in the village, because that's the one place where I can find peace from all this mayhem. I sent out a global email to all staff saying:

Following my clarion call last week for more scoops, James Scott came up with a good one about Anji Hunter. Unfortunately she lives in my village, has known me since I was 3 ft 6 in, and drinks in my local pub, so she is therefore, tragically, protected from *Daily Mirror* exposés of all aspects of her life bar, possibly, having an affair with Osama Bin Laden. All reporters are hereby granted official permission not to turn over regular drinking partners or neighbours unless they want to.

Rebekah married Ross Kemp last month in Las Vegas and it's their wedding party tomorrow night. He's a great guy, much brighter and more amusing than Grant Mitchell.

I emailed Les Hinton to try and head off the inevitable drunken row between us ensuing. 'Dear Les, try and behave yourself on Wednesday night. You know what you're like when you've had a few. I'll be in the corner burning bridges.'

He replied: 'I'll leave you in peace – after all, wasn't it Napoleon who said you should never interrupt an enemy when he's making a mistake?'

WEDNESDAY, 17 JULY

The party was fantastic fun, and I even managed to avoid insulting Les, which was a massive step forward.

THURSDAY, 18 JULY

I was woken at 8am by a flurry of text messages from journalist mates. The *Spectator* interview has come out early and was leading Sky News with the headline CHERIE TRIED TO GET ME SACKED SAYS MIRROR EDITOR. Roger Alton, the *Observer* editor, emailed me: 'Christ, mate, this is fucking sensational – XXX-rated.'

When I got to the office, there was a message from the newsdesk: 'Mrs Blair's office rang at 7.15am to cancel your lunch. We asked if she wanted to re-arrange and were told that would not be necessary.'

Later the story came up in the No. 10 lobby briefing and the Government spokesman said: 'We live in a free country. Newspapers and newspaper editors are perfectly entitled to write and say what they want. I have never heard Mrs Blair express a view about a newspaper editor ...'

The assembled press laughed out loud at that particular claim, apparently.

MONDAY, 22 JULY

David Mellor's lawyers have written to point out that now Antonia de Sancha has admitted in an interview with the *Indie* last week that he never actually wore that Chelsea shirt in bed with her, or sucked her toes, could we please delete all reference to these allegations from our files.

Oh, I don't think so, on balance. Sorry, Dave.

TUESDAY, 23 JULY

Ollie Picton-Jones rang from the Paris fashion show to say, 'Bumped into George Michael and he was sitting there with Donatella Versace, Puff Daddy and Liz Hurley telling them all what a great paper the Mirror is … don't think Liz was entirely convinced, but hey, he tried.'

THURSDAY, 25 JULY

Michael Howard came to lunch today and we laid into him about Duncan Smith.

'He's got the charisma of a drugged aardvark,' I said.

'Well, charisma isn't everything, you know. Liverpool fans like me thought Bill Shankly was the greatest, most charismatic manager ever – but Bob Paisley, who had none of Shankly's charisma, won all the big trophies.'

'The only thing Duncan Smith's going to win is a place on the dole queue, Michael, and we both know it.'

He smiled and poured himself a glass of water.

FRIDAY, 9 AUGUST

George Michael emailed me in a state of some distress:

> I am shocked and depressed by the entire media's willingness to spread Murdoch's shit internationally, which is fucking my airplay everywhere. I know that a lot of these journalists share my views on Bush and Blair, but enjoy kicking George Michael more.
>
> In retrospect I think I will be vindicated but that's not much consolation right now. In all honesty, Piers, I have paid a heavy price for talking to you, but I don't regret it because you presented the argument beautifully and we should both be proud of what we tried to achieve. What the fuck is a hit single compared to the shit we are trying to prevent? Keep it up, patience will see the *Mirror* establish itself in a new light and your bravery on this issue is remarkable. George. PS. It could have been worse, I quite like that picture of my head in a toilet, they could have used a bad one, now *that* would have ruined my week!

MONDAY, 12 AUGUST

My flat's sprung a bad leak from a cracked communal soil pipe, so I've been forced to decamp up to the One Aldwych hotel while it is repaired and redecorated, which will be a few weeks at least. Luckily it's all on insurance so I'm

living a life of unadulterated luxury in this fabulous place for absolutely nothing. Richard Harris lived permantely at the Savoy and I can see why now. Saves a lot of aggro.

FRIDAY, 16 AUGUST

I've been taunting Alan Sugar about all the halfwits now running Spurs, and he finally responded: 'I know, it's like watching the mother-in-law drive my Ferrari over a cliff.'

SATURDAY, 17 AUGUST

The bodies of two missing schoolgirls, Holly Wells and Jessica Chapman, were found today after a two-week hunt since they disappeared from near their school in Soham, Cambridgeshire. It's a story that has gripped the nation and dominated the news every day, fuelled by a painfully evocative photo of them both smiling in Manchester United shirts hours before they vanished. Someone raised an interesting point today, though. Would we all have been quite so gripped if they had been two black girls? I think the answer, and it is a shameful one, is no.

SUNDAY, 25 AUGUST

I got a family cricket team together last year to take on the village, and they sneaked a Pakistani ringer in to smash a century and beat us. Never one to take that kind of thing lightly, I turned up this year with four West Indies test batsmen, Alvin Kallicharran, Richie Richardson, Sherwin Campbell and Stuart Williams, Phil Tufnell to bowl, and Frank Bruno to watch. I was quietly confident, on and off the field.

We batted first, and Richie – eighteen test centuries – was caught for ten, off Tim Gill, one of village cricket's worst-ever trundlers.

Then it poured with rain, and we had to scrap the game after just an hour.

I took the legends back to my place for a party, and Tuffers in particular embraced the festivities with great gusto. At midnight, having had his first pint at midday, he careered upstairs to be met by Grande on the landing.

'Hello, madam, and who might you be?'

'Who are *you*, more to the point, young man?' Grande barked back.

Tuffers, wearing his Middlesex sweater, stood to attention and saluted.

'Madam, I am Philip Tufnell, Middlesex and England.'

She eyed this drunken, shambling 'athlete'.

'Well, I am very pleased for you: now please turn that racket down, I can't sleep.'

MONDAY, 26 AUGUST

John Pilger wrote a brilliant piece today attacking Blair and Bush for planning to attack Saddam – saying it's a war 'based on lies'. He says he doesn't believe Iraq has WMD, and the United Nations weapons inspectors have found nothing so far. Nobody understands the urgency for this conflict, but Bush seems determined to do it, and Blair equally determined to help him.

FRIDAY, 6 SEPTEMBER

Jonathan Ross is having a lot of trouble with the *Daily Mail* over his marriage, and wants my advice:

> Do you think it's worth me complaining to the PCC over the *Mail*'s treatment of the Ross family saga? I've always felt that the less you say the sooner it dies down and the damage has already been done. But the character assassinations they seem to run on Jane wherever possible have really fucked me off.
>
> And at best the only 'proof' they have to shore up their interpretation of events would be inadmissible in any court, so what do you think?
>
> Obviously any pursuant story that comes out of this will come to you, but I am asking you first as someone who knows his way around these things, is it worth it or will it just make the shit storm kick off again?

I thought carefully about my response. Jonathan's a good guy and I can tell he is really hurt by all the stuff on his marriage. But going to war with the *Mail* will just make it worse.

'My heart says get the filthy bastards, my head says forget it,' I said. 'The PCC would fudge that kind of complaint, the *Mail* will unleash a dossier of investigative shit in revenge and you'd end up feeling it wasn't worth it.'

TUESDAY, 10 SEPTEMBER

It's the first anniversary of 9/11 tomorrow and we decided to make a big point about the 'war on terror', taking an image of the burning World Trade Center and asking, 'How many more flames are we about to fan?' It's provocative, but entirely justified. If we go into Iraq, we are going to whip up even more anti-west sentiment, encourage even more retaliation. There has to be a better way to go after the terrorists then bombing countries that supposedly harbour them.

SATURDAY, 14 SEPTEMBER

Driving back from the Charlton/Arsenal match I tuned into Talksport and heard 'Kelvin from Kent' dumping all over his team, and adamantly insisting to the polite presenter that the final score was 4–0 not 3–0. I laughed. It had to be …

I confronted 'Kelvin of Kent' and he admitted it. 'Trouble was that I left the ground as the fourth goal went in and didn't see it had been disallowed!'

MONDAY, 16 SEPTEMBER

Right, I've had enough of this Iraq nonsense. Bush made yet another of his dumb John Wayne speeches today, so we stuck his head all over the front page with a headline saying LOOK AT DUBYA, HE JUST CAN'T WAIT TO GO HUNTIN',

SHOOTIN', BOMBIN' AND KILLING IRAQUIS … TONY, THIS IS WRONG. If nobody else is going to stand up to our Government over this, then we will.

TUESDAY, 17 SEPTEMBER
Nelson Mandela has piled into Bush, telling him to stop being such a 'bully' and cancel any plan to attack Iraq. More significantly, the French are making strong similar noises too, suggesting the United Nations might be splitting in two over this issue.

WEDNESDAY, 18 SEPTEMBER
Rosie Boycott threw a small dinner party tonight for Charles Kennedy, the Lib Dem leader, and I sat next to him.

He insisted on drinking half glasses of wine, as if making some point about all the boozing rumours.

By the tenth half glass, I had to laugh. So what if he likes a drink, anyway? He's a nice guy, if a bit too timid.

'You should be ripping into Blair over Iraq,' I said.

'I am,' he replied.

'Well, with all due respect, you're just slapping him gently on the back. Get out there, beat your chest a bit, and start really going for him. The whole country will be behind you.'

Rosie enthusiastically agreed. 'I've been saying this for ages.'

But he wasn't sure. 'I have to tread carefully. I am not a natural chest beater, I'm afraid.'

And there lies the problem for the Lib Dems. They could make much faster progress if they just made more noise.

MONDAY, 23 SEPTEMBER
A letter comes out of the blue from someone called Sarah in Dorking, who says, 'Darling Piers, thank you with all my heart for all you do. I love you. I am overwhelmed by your integrity and kindness. Thank you.' No idea who she is or what she's on about, but hey, who cares? Particularly as in the same postbag comes a scrap of paper with the words: 'I've seen you on *Question Time*. I find you one of the biggest bores that I have ever seen. You're a creep.'

TUESDAY, 24 SEPTEMBER
Blair published his long-awaited dossier on Iraq today, which he claimed justified war. We turned up the heat this morning with a splash saying OK TONY, PROVE IT, and he called me down for a cup of tea in the afternoon at No. 10 to have a 'little chat' about it.

He didn't muck about.

'You are perfectly entitled to your view, but Saddam is a very dangerous man, Piers, and we have got to stop him before he does something very nasty.'

'Well, I'm not so sure, Prime Minister. People I know in the army say he's a bit of a dead duck militarily after the last Gulf War, and it's better the devil you know in terms of regional stability. We've contained him pretty well for the last decade, why not keep on containing him? Surely a new war will just make things worse out there at a time when we should be building bridges with Muslims, not killing more of them?'

He was adamant. 'All the intelligence says he has got weapons of mass destruction and won't hesitate to use them. And after 9/11, we cannot take any chances. The Middle East will never be stable as long as he is in power, and his people will never be safe.'

I told him I wasn't convinced by the dossier, and nor did I think most of our readers would be either.

'Well, it is important that people understand the threat he poses, a threat I believe it would be reckless and dangerous to ignore. I hope at least you present both sides to the argument fairly.'

Blair seems almost messianic in his zeal over Iraq. I hope to hell he knows what he's doing.

I went back to the office and canvassed opinion on the dossier. Nobody was remotely convinced.

We splashed on: 'We asked Blair to prove the case for an attack on Iraq. Did he succeed? NO PRIME MINISTER.'

The tea and cakes charm offensive hasn't worked very well for him, then.

Philip Graf resigned today. He's a good man, perhaps too nice for the national tabloid war, and I will miss him.

SATURDAY, 28 SEPTEMBER

Sophie Raworth and Jeremy Bowen are leaving the *BBC Breakfast* sofa – so I said I'd buy them lunch at the Ivy yesterday to celebrate.

We all knew after our last encounter what this might mean, so had all booked the afternoon off work.

It was a spectacularly memorable afternoon. Sometimes there is no rational reason why you get on with people almost as soon as you meet them – and despite hardly knowing Jeremy and Sophie, we all hit it off hilariously well.

Having got very drunk very quickly, we then just carried on drinking as everyone else left, then watched all the pre-theatre crowd come in at 5pm – and carried on drinking.

I vaguely remember Nigella Lawson coming over to say hello.

I definitely remember Emma Noble and her agent joining us from a nearby table, then Adam Faith and his very, very young companion, and Emma's husband James Major who arrived at 8pm, just as we were all singing Faith's big hit 'Someone Else's Baby' in the bar and making a hell of a racket.

'Erm, Mr Morgan, perhaps it may be time to move on … ,' suggested one of the Ivy waiters ever so politely.

We tried, but Jeremy fell over. 'Can you carry me to a taxi?' he slurred. So we did.

Over one last glass of champagne 'for the road', I said to James, 'Your old man should be back in front-line politics you know. People liked and trusted him.'

'I don't think that's going to happen,' he laughed.

We all headed up to Teatro, Leslie Ash and Lee Chapman's club, for yet another drink, but then I remembered I had to go to my 3am girl Eva Simpson's leaving party.

So I hailed one of those rickshaw things you get in Soho and a man ran me down to Brown's nightclub, where I fell out on to the street, picked myself up and marched to the front of the queue, slurring, 'I'm Piers Morgan, let me in.'

I only know this because the rest of the queue were so disgusted they told everyone at the party what an arse I was.

By now blindly pissed, I picked a verbal fight with a barman, then a near physical fight with two perfectly pleasant PR guys from Freuds, before finally falling over on the dance floor and being led to the exit for a cab home by concerned colleagues.

I got back at 2am and my phone rang.

'Edwina Currie's revealed a four-year affair with John Major,' said Jon, breathless with excitement. 'It's in her book which the Times are serialising, they spoofed it all.'

'But I've just been with his son, James Major,' I said, breathless from alcohol. 'He never mentioned it.'

'You sound completely pissed,' he replied.

'I am, but that's still true. Well, just nick it all … I'm going to sleep.'

Sophie sent me an email this afternoon entitled 'Black Holes':

Now then, a few things bemusing me today. 1) Why do I have your mum's mobile number in my phone? 2) Why did my dad call me from Portugal and sing Adam Faith songs on my voicemail? 3) Why didn't James Major tell us about his dad? 4) How the hell did I get so drunk? 5) Why didn't I have a hangover?

I'd forgotten we'd called my mother, and Sophie's dad, and I think we even tried to get Adam to serenade Jeremy's new baby.

MONDAY, 30 SEPTEMBER

We got hold of Major's sister over the weekend, who said of her brother's affair, 'At least it wasn't Ann Widdecombe.' We all laughed so I did up that quote as a splash this morning.

Maurice Saatchi emailed first thing: 'Everyone is talking about your front page today, congratulations.' He's nice like that – always dropping little notes when he sees something he likes.

Early in the evening, I got a call from Blair's new right-hand woman, Sally Morgan. She was very distressed, pleading with me not to run a story about her decision to send her son to a private school.

'I'm sorry Sally, but it's hypocritical, given your position, and you know it. We won't tear you to pieces, because I feel for you as a parent myself. But it is a legitimate story – you know what people like Alastair will be thinking of you doing this, they'll be furious.'

'But my son doesn't deserve this.'

'No, he doesn't. But that's why I will never go into politics, frankly – if you work for a Government that has a policy of urging voters to choose state schools and denouncing private education, you can't then send your kids to private school and not expect some flak for it.'

I spoke to Alastair later. I was right, he *was* furious. 'It's like when Tony sent his kids to a school right across London – it smacks of elitism, and Labour voters don't like it.'

TUESDAY, 1 OCTOBER

A riotous dinner at the Labour Party conference with Mandelson, Christopher Hitchens, Matthew Norman and Conor.

After Mandelson left we had hatched a serious plot for Hitchens to jump Bill Clinton during his big speech here in Blackpool tomorrow. He has always believed him to be a war criminal for the way he bombed Iraq to get Monica off the headlines.

The plan was for him to scream, 'I am Christopher Hitchens from the Daily Mirror and I accuse you of being a *murderer!*' He would then run out of the conference hall to a waiting car, head straight to the local airstrip and flee in a helicopter. I even called the newsdesk to get them to hire one for us.

WEDNESDAY, 2 OCTOBER

Hitchens is still up for it. But I have had slight second thoughts. Which is why he will always be a braver journalist than me.

GQ magazine have made me the 7th Most Powerful Man in Britain, squeezed in between Rupert Murdoch and Greg Dyke. Farcical, but hey – I'll take it.

The annual Blair lunch went ahead, but without Cherie, who apparently said 'I'm not sitting anywhere near that bloody man' – referring to me. I tried to control my distress.

Blair was half an hour late, and stayed just twenty minutes before telling us he had to 'go and see Bill'. He was distracted and uninterested, and bordering on the rude. Which is not like him, but I suspect he's starting to feel the heat over Iraq.

Alastair got very overexcited as he told us how he'd gone for a Big Mac with Big Bill.

'We were just walking down the promenade, as you do, and he said he fancied a McDonalds. You can imagine all these local guys' faces when in walks the President …'

'And then they see you, Alastair, a double thrill,' I interrupted.

'Yes … oh, fuck off, Morgan.'

When they'd gone, I suggested to Victor and Tina that we go and wait by the exit of the Imperial Hotel, because everyone will have gone to the hall already and we'll get to see Clinton close up.

The plan worked very amusingly.

He and Blair swept down the stairs, and Tina and I shouted, 'Hello Mr President!' which made him stop and come over to shake our hands. Tina's first, naturally.

Then mine. I couldn't think of what to say, so I just gripped his hand and said, 'Well done, Bill, well done.'

'Thanks, buddy,' he replied, neither of us really sure what the hell I was congratulating him about.

Cherie slithered past next, and didn't say a word.

At a party later, Andrew Marr came up to me and said my meeting with Clinton had been flashed up on the lunchtime news – the BBC were filming at the time.

'What did you say to him?' he asked.

'I said well done.'

'For what?'

'For everything, Andrew, for everything.'

Clinton's speech was genuinely amazing. He has the power to captivate an audience that I have only seen matched by Mandela, and the former RUC chief Ronnie Flanagan – who spoke without notes for 45 minutes at the Society of Editors dinner last year and was mesmerisingly powerful.

As we came out, Frank Dobson grabbed me and shouted, 'Fooking brilliant, wasn't he – fooking brilliant!' with a wild look in his eye.

Most of the female delegates just looked like they'd had some weird virtual sex experience with him.

THURSDAY, 3 OCTOBER

Mandelson thanked me for dinner, and for running an article by him in today's paper supporting Blair. Now he's worried about how it will play with Gordon Brown.

'Trouble is that GB thinks anything I write, especially in his fiefdom of the Mirror, is some sort of declaration of war on him and I don't want to get into that sort of skirmishing with him.'

He asked how lunch with Blair went. 'Well, he turned up an hour late and stayed twenty minutes,' I said. 'Perfectly pleasant while he was actually there, but not very useful to either camp, given the brevity. It's a shame, because I think we've got the paper back on a more even keel now. Anyway, good to see you getting hugged by Clinton – I'm going to book him and Ronnie Flanagan for my funeral.'

'I'll carry the wreath,' he replied.

MONDAY, 7 OCTOBER

Jeremy Bowen finally recovered enough to thank me for lunch. 'I fell asleep afterwards and woke up in Morocco, got back yesterday. What a day. Have dim flicker somewhere of Adam Faith inviting me for lunch … and did John Major's daughter-in-law know about Edwina? Let's do it again if my liver transplant kicks in.'

TUESDAY, 8 OCTOBER

James Whitaker wants me to let him spend eight weeks at the rugby World Cup in Australia. 'If you let me extol the virtues of Malaysia Airlines first class travel in my column, they will upgrade me to first class.'

I declined his suggestion.

He responded: 'Your comments are noted. You've done me a favour, really, because I had budgeted to spend £10,000 out there and television does the job pretty well.'

WEDNESDAY, 9 OCTOBER

We ran some fascinating letters by the man charged with the Soham murders, Ian Huntley, today, about his girlfriend Maxine Carr, his life in prison and his thoughts on his trial.

Newspapers often run letters from notorious killers, and the reason is simple. Most of them have sharp reporters who send cod letters to these people in jail. Men like Huntley have loads of 'pen-pals', and plenty of time to keep up the correspondence. What they don't know is 'Letitia from Eastbourne' is more likely to be 'Dennis from the *Sun*'.

THURSDAY, 10 OCTOBER

Hilarious front page in the *Daily Sport* this morning showing Nell McAndrew in bodice and suspenders with a fake apology next to it, saying, 'Sorry, folks. We were going to bring you a collection of front page exclusives this morning analysing the grim political situation in Iraq, looming war in Ireland and various intrigues from the Tory party conference. But then we saw this photo of Nell's panties and got sort of distracted. Erm … more photos inside.'

MONDAY, 14 OCTOBER

I'm in La Manga, the famous Spanish golf resort, for an annual long weekend with my village cricket mates.

News flashed through this morning that we've won our Naomi appeal. So I put my clubs away and spent the day giving gloating phone interviews to all and sundry.

I couldn't be happier.

Martin's technically lost this case twice now, once on each side, though he didn't actually work for Naomi's law firm Schillings on the appeal.

I rang to congratulate him on what might be a legal first.

FRIDAY, 18 OCTOBER

After weeks of legal argument, the Paul Burrell trial finally kicked off today, and was as sensational as I expected.

Today's evidence contained a lot of juicy stuff about Diana flogging dresses and using the profits as petty cash, and other royal gossip. This will go on for weeks, and can only be damaging to the royal family. They must be mad allowing Burrell to potentially take the stand. Cornered and desperate, he might say anything, and he knows the lot because he was there.

There's also no way he stole Diana's stuff, anyone who knows him knows that. He could make more money from what's in his mind than he ever could from a few of her trinkets.

Our reporter at the trial is Steve Dennis, who has worked on Burrell as a contact for years. 'Anything could happen, to be honest,' he said. 'Paul is very angry and upset and feels he has nothing to lose now.'

MONDAY, 21 OCTOBER

The Steve Bing case has been rumbling on for ages now, and I'm bored with it. He seems ready to settle, and we just want to get rid of it.

Bing's lawyer, Marty Singer, had a drink with our new legal manager, Marcus Partington, last night and asked for a million dollars and a front-page apology. Marcus laughed and offered an apology inside with no money.

Today we got the suggested wording of the apology, and a more obsequious and sickening diatribe of self-congratulatory twaddle I have rarely read. Marcus and I began laughing so much, in fact, that I spotted a chance to turn this thing to our advantage in spectacular style.

'Why don't we stick this rubbish all over the front page?'

Marcus was temporarily stunned.

'Why the hell do you want to do that?'

'Because if we really lay it on with a trowel, everyone will know we're taking the piss – apart from Bing and that idiot Marty Singer, because they are Americans and won't understand irony or sarcasm.'

Marcus, always up for a laugh if we can get away with it, said it was worth a go. So we ran a front-page headline, A HUMBLE AND SINCERE APOLOGY TO MR STEVE BING, PHILANTHROPIST AND HUMANITARIAN, and further grovelling in nauseous, gut-wrenching detail on page nine – together with a piece on page eight by Kevin O'Sullivan headlined WHY AMERICANS DON'T UNDERSTAND IRONY OR SARCASM.

It worked beautifully. Bing and Marty thought we were sincere and had completely capitulated, while everyone in Britain knew it was a gag. I did an interview for Radio 4 in which the presenter Nick Clarke and I had a great laugh, without ever actually laughing.

TUESDAY, 22 OCTOBER

Well, nearly everyone. Alan Sugar's bemused. 'Er, I just read the paper – what's all this with Steve Bing? Why'd you give him a full page? Even if you were wrong, normally all papers just give you a postage stamp apology. This has to be a first. Which lawyer did he use? I would like to know for the future.'

Well, he is a Spurs fan.

Marty Singer was on Radio 4 today, insisting, 'Our response to Mr Morgan's comments yesterday is that this was an unprecedented apology, and this is a very serious and not humorous matter. If you're telling me that in England the wording of this apology would be read as humorous then I'm sorry, but I see nothing funny about it.' Marvellous.

THURSDAY, 24 OCTOBER

Will Carling was the star of this month's Chairman's Lunch, which given the presence of Peter Mandelson was quite an achievement. For one of Britain's biggest 'loverats', he was surprisingly nice, and not overly bitter, which surprised me.

But I had to clear up one amazing story I was told about him. A very, very big sporting legend assured me that it was true. Apparently, when Carling played a rugby match with Harlequins during his 'friendship' with Diana, he rejected her phone call urging him to come round the Palace, because he was 'having a few beers with the lads'. Allegedly, an hour later a motorbike courier arrived with a gift-wrapped box which, when Carling opened it, contained what appeared to be pubic hair. With a note from the Princess saying she hoped that might accelerate the process of his arrival. I put it to Carling, who nearly choked on his asparagus. 'Erm, who … that's not true. No, no, definitely not.' His face had gone purple, his eyes looked suddenly rather glazed, and he was having difficulty breathing. 'What a shame,' I said, 'what a great story for the grandchildren that would have been.' 'Yes,' he burbled, 'shame it's definitely not true. Definitely.' He spent the rest of the lunch fending off a fairly relentless barrage from me about his lovelife, but took it all in good spirits.

Mandelson emailed me afterwards to say, 'Thanks for lunch and for not picking on me – glad Will was there. I told Victor on the way out that you were now on such ebullient and unstoppable form that he wouldn't be able to fire you even if he wanted to – he looked quizzical!'

SUNDAY, 27 OCTOBER

Lunch at Rebekah and Ross's. Mark Bolland was there, and as the wine flowed I had a quiet chat with him about Burrell.

'Mark, this is very dangerous. If he takes the stand anything could happen.'

'I know, I know, the whole thing is crazy. We tried to broker a secret meeting between the Prince and Paul a few months ago, but unbelievably the Prince fell off his horse playing polo and had to go to hospital instead of attending the meeting. I'm sure if they had met, this would have been resolved. But after that the police kept insisting they had hard evidence that Paul had sold stuff he'd taken. But that seems like complete bollocks now.'

'Mark, it's never too late. The royals can stop this trial whenever they want.'

'They can't interfere with a legal process.'

'No, but Burrell knows everything, and if he starts coming out with it in the witness box he could bring down the bloody monarchy.'

'Well, it could be very damaging, I agree.'

FRIDAY, 1 NOVEMBER

Had the day off in Sussex. Just after midday, Tina rang asking if I would mind if she got Steve Dennis to make an offer to Paul Burrell for the *Sunday Mirror*.

'Why?' I said.

'Don't you know? Burrell's just been cleared – the Queen said she remembered him saying he would take Diana's stuff for sake-keeping.'

'*What?* Nobody's bloody told me. I want Burrell's story, so, no you can't have Steve, sorry.'

I was hopping mad, not with Tina, who was just doing her job quickly and efficiently as usual, but with my deputy editor Des Kelly – who hadn't bothered to call me with this bombshell news.

'Des, has Burrell been cleared?' I shouted down the phone.

'Er, yeah, he has. We're doing it as a splash and spread inside.'

'Well, first of all, why did nobody call me, and secondly, it's an unbelievable story and we should be clearing at least four spreads for it. And more importantly, how much have we offered him for his story?'

'Er, have I missed something here? Nobody really cares what some old queenie butler has to say, do they?'

'Of course they fucking do, Christ almighty! He knows everything.'

This was a waste of time. Des has been a mistake as my deputy. He was a good sports editor, but I don't rate his news sense at all. He lives with Carol Vorderman, who he pulled at a *Mirror* Christmas party, and is so paranoid he refuses to even tell me where they go on holiday or leave a hotel number.

I killed the call and rang Conor on the newsdesk. 'Get Steve Dennis to call me now, we have got to get Burrell.'

Conor knew immediately the importance of this moment.

Steve called two minutes later, breathless with excitement.

'Boss, it's mayhem down here, but I've spoken to Paul and we're in with a good shout. Leave it to me.'

'Steve, mate, this is the big one. We have got to get him, OK? Do whatever it takes.'

Steve's a brilliant, tenacious reporter: I wish we had more like him. He's spent five years befriending Burrell, and now we will see if he can pull it off. The big problem he has is that Richard Kay on the *Mail* is so close to Burrell from when Diana was alive that Paul's even godfather to his child.

SUNDAY, 3 NOVEMBER

Burrell's lawyer appeared on *Breakfast with Frost*, with a smiling Richard Kay next to him. Shit. He's in there, and we're never going to get him out. Spoke to Steve. 'Piers, it's not over yet. Paul hasn't made his mind up, and that lawyer's not the one doing the deal, he's got an agent called Dave Warwick.'

'What's he like?'

'Big, northern, not very used to stuff this big. And has a big ego. He's already loving all the attention.'

I rang Mr Warwick.

'Dave, I want Paul's story.'

'Join the rest of the world, Mr Morgan!' he chortled.

It was time to tease that ego.

'But I want you too.'

'What do you mean?'

'I see you as an integral part of this. I see you on the TV news selling this interview for us, morning, noon and night. You give it to us, and Dave Warwick's going to be a big star by the end of the week.'

He laughed. 'Well, that sounds good to me.'

We chatted for another ten minutes and got on pretty well. I can tell he's not going to be overly impressed by the normal Fleet Street bullyboy tactics.

'I'll do what's best for Paul Burrell, and for Dave Warwick,' he said, deploying that amusingly egocentric footballer trait of talking about himself in the third person. 'And that's not necessarily selling to the highest bidder. It will be where we feel most comfortable.'

MONDAY, 4 NOVEMBER

Steve rang first thing. 'I've spoken to Paul again and he wants to do it with us, but he's obviously got the Mail going mad at him and I'm worried that they will offer him so much money he'll have no choice but to go with them. We've got to work on Dave Warwick!'

I rang Dave Warwick.

'Piers, I won't kid you, I've had four hundred offers from around the world.'

'OK, Dave, I understand how hard this is. But I just want to tell you what our offer is. I will pay you three hundred thousand. But for that, Paul can say whatever he wants. Literally. There will be no pressure for him to say anything at all. The Mail and the others will want every spit and cough of life with Diana. I am just offering him the space to say what he wants about what happened to him.'

'Let me get this straight – Paul can say what he likes, and you won't push him for more?'

'That's right. He can come in, say "Hello" and bugger off again if he wants. But I think he will say more than that, and we will publish every word of what he feels comfortable saying.'

'That's very interesting,' he replied. 'Because I'm getting a bit fed up with the Mail and others trying to bully me.'

'Dave, come with us and nobody will bully anyone. It will be published on your terms with full copy, photo, and headline approval. You will have complete control. I know we're not the highest bidder, but Paul needs to get his message to the masses of this country. That's what Diana would have wanted I'm sure.'

'You're right there.'

Dave is a working class lad from the North, like Paul. This was going to help us enormously.

'I'll call you back.'

Two long hours went by, then he called.

'OK, I've told Paul what you said and he wants to go with you. I want this nice and easy, so I'm sending you one sheet of paper with a few of our requirements, sign it and send it back and we're in business.'

The fax, when it arrived, was laughably short and legally pointless. We could wriggle out of it at any stage if we wanted to. But this was a deal done on trust, and oddly I trusted Dave Warwick to deliver more than any agent I had ever dealt with before.

I signed it and sent it back.

He rang ten minutes later. 'Thanks. The Mail have just offered a million, and the NoW say they'll go to two million. But don't worry, we're with you now.'

Incredible, we'd got it with the lowest bid in Britain.

I rang Steve. 'You're a genius, this is all down to you, mate.'

I stuck out a suitably gloating statement, and reports flooded in of mass suicides in the *Mail* newsroom. We'd legged them over on this one, quite beautifully. Steve is now encamped in a hotel with a *Mirror* team and has already started the interviews. There is no time to lose.

On page three tonight we had a bit of fun with Ian Hislop, who has been insufferably smug over the demise of Angus Deayton, and really stuck the knife into him on *HIGNFY* after he was fired last week. We've offered £50 for any scandal on the 'moon-faced little midget'. Doubt we'll get anything, but it will be a good laugh trying.

TUESDAY, 5 NOVEMBER

Burrell, as I thought, has given us utterly sensational material. Steve rang to say, 'He's pouring it out, everything. He's angry and determined to have his say and settle his scores. It's going to be amazing.' At 6pm I sat down to read the first instalment and was stunned by how explosive it was. The most incredible revelation was the detail of the three-hour meeting he had with the Queen, where he told her he would be keeping some of Diana's stuff to protect it.

The pair of them stood for the entire time in one of the Palace rooms, and Her Majesty told him at the end, 'Be careful, Paul; nobody has ever been as close to a member of my family as you were to Diana. There are powers at work in this country about which we have no knowledge.'

Christ almighty.

This was going to be the biggest bargain in the history of buy-ups.

WEDNESDAY, 6 NOVEMBER

Burrell led all the news all day long, and me and Dave Warwick popped up everywhere plugging it. Big Dave's loving it, and good luck to him. Day Two is just as powerful, with Burrell dumping all over the Spencers. And the material is so strong it will run at least for the rest of this week and probably into next week too.

We sold an extra 400,000 copies yesterday, and it seems everyone's reading it.

Paul Gilfeather, one of our political team, sent me an email saying, 'Bumped into Michael Foot just now who said he'd bought the *Mirror* for the first time in years today – because he loves the Burrell story.'

The BBC lunchtime news had Jennie Bond saying the Palace were dismissing Burrell's claims, saying the meeting with the Queen had been 'nearer three minutes than three hours'.

The same line ran on the Press Association wire.

I rang Penny Russell-Smith, the Queen's press secretary.

'This is outrageous and I'm not having it. Put out a correction on PA or you guys will regret it. Paul is not in the mood to be dicked around.'

'What do you mean by that?' Penny asked.

'I mean he can say a lot more than he intends to, including stuff about all you lot, so I would tread carefully.'

She rang back fifteen minutes later to say PA were putting out a 'clarification'.

'What does it say?'

'It says that the meeting lasted up to an hour and a half, that is all our records can establish.'

'Sorry, no good. I will accept "at least an hour and a half", but not "up to".'

Ten minutes later, a clarification of the clarification ran on PA – an unprecedented climbdown by the Palace. They are terrified.

THURSDAY, 7 NOVEMBER

Burrell's getting viciously kicked around by the *Mail* and *Sun* now, which is rankly hypocritical. But I've been guilty of similar stuff myself. If you don't get the big story, then you have to trash it as best you can. It's the law of the Fleet Street jungle.

FRIDAY, 8 NOVEMBER

The Hislop campaign's been going well, with all sorts of accusations ranging from a weird obsession with tangerines to a chronic piles problem that needed lasering. No idea if any of this stuff is true, but we keep putting little teasers in anyway – just like he does with *Private Eye* when he's not sure if something's true or not.

Everyone's fascinated by why we're doing it, and most think it's about either my appearance on *HIGNFY* or stuff he's done in the *Eye* about my private life or share-dealing.

But it's simpler than that.

I'm just doing it for fun. He is, after all, the editor of a piss-taking magazine and the presenter of a piss-taking TV show. Yet nobody dares take the piss out of him.

Spencer was in the same class at school as Hislop's son William for a couple of years, and I was thus able to observe at first hand what a sly little sod Hislop is. He'd be all friendly to my face, then dump all over me behind my back and in his rag.

Hislop finally reacted today, telling the *Standard* diary, 'I'm longing to see Morgan's dossier on me, and so are my lawyers.'

His lawyers? How amusingly touchy.

THURSDAY, 14 NOVEMBER

To Norwich for *Question Time*, and as soon as I saw the name William Shawcross on the panel I knew it was all going to kick off over Burrell. He's an arch monarchist, and sure enough let me have it big time for being disrespectful of the royal family and so on.

Just when he started being really insufferably pompous about the tabloids, I reminded him, and the audience, that he was Murdoch's very sycophantic official biographer. He exploded with indignant rage and actually tried to order me from the studio. All most amusing.

He was still simmering away afterwards over dinner, so I wound him up a bit more just for fun. Dimbleby chuckled away; he loves a bit of mischief.

FRIDAY, 15 NOVEMBER

Despite our scoop, the bookmaker Paddy Power is offering odds of 8–1 in their annual 'Dole Derby' that I will be sacked.

I'm in there with Saddam, Alex Ferguson and the Pope.

TUESDAY, 19 NOVEMBER

I am negotiating with my new buddy Will Carling to do an interview in the *Mirror*. He wants a guarantee that there will be 'no photos of Ali, Julia or Diana, and particularly not that one of Ali crying as she holds Henry'. I agreed to Diana because that's so historical now, and the crying one because it was a *Sun* picture, so we can't use it anyway, but insisted on small photos of Ali and Julia. He agreed.

WEDNESDAY, 20 NOVEMBER

We sent our new New York man, Richard Wallace, on to the streets today armed with a children's map of the world, and asking the first hundred people who passed by where Iraq was.

Eighty per cent had no idea; eight of them thought it was in France, five in Mongolia, six in South Africa, and one in India.

Even more worryingly, ten per cent didn't know where *America* was.

A Mr Jordan Rios insisted, 'Us Americans aren't all as dumb as you think we are.' As he pointed to Nicaragua.

THURSDAY, 21 NOVEMBER

Little brother Rupert (who is 6 ft 3 in and unfortunately inherited most of the good looks in the family) invited me down to his new Soho nightclub tonight, and to my amazement kicked Westlife off the top table to make way for me and my aged village mates to swig free champagne. A small, yet extremely pleasing moment.

MONDAY, 25 NOVEMBER

Jeremy emailed from Cyprus to say:

> Looks like we may be involved in some live action out here next March. We are rather well placed for operations in the Middle East. The good news is that we are in range of your mucker Saddam's ballistic missile arsenal so we'll get war medals in Cyprus for 'speeding glum heroes up the line' (Siegfried Sassoon, 1917) whilst sipping brandy sours as we gaze wistfully out over the Eastern Mediterranean.

FRIDAY, 29 NOVEMBER

I hosted a Q and A interview with Phil Tufnell tonight at a cricket dinner for the Warwickshire Pilgrims touring club in Coventry, one of my favourite collections of human beings in the world – if for all the wrong reasons. I did the same thing with him last week at Lords, and he was sober and hilariously funny.

But tonight Tuffers got pissed. He was knocking back a few pints in the bar before the meal, then got stuck into loads of wine at the table. When the dinner ran on a bit and he started necking flaming sambucas and doing throat-cutting signs, saying, 'Let's get going, mate, I'm getting wasted here,' I knew I was in trouble.

By the time we got on stage, I'd lost him completely.

'So Phil, what do you think of the current Australian team?'

'Bunch of fucking poofs.'

And so on. It was like Ollie Reed on *Aspel* and George Best on *Wogan* rolled into one.

We reeled through 40 minutes of drunken abuse, Tuffers tumbling off his stool at various stages. Half the audience thought it was hysterical, some of the older members didn't.

When we finished, he slurred: 'Why didn't you let me speak more, mate?'

'Because you can't,' I replied, accurately.

SUNDAY, 1 DECEMBER

An extraordinary story has broken involving Cherie Blair and Fleet Street's most notorious conman, Peter Foster. He's been having it away with Cherie's wacko 'guru', Carole Caplin, and has used the link to worm his way into Cherie's email inbox and advise her about buying some flats in Bristol. The suggestion being that she's used a crook to give her financial advice.

It's all very entertaining, with Cherie calling him a 'star' in the emails and talking about them being on the 'same wavelength'.

I am speechless with joy. So much for Cherie's fabled moral compass. It seems to have gone off the radar a bit. Downing Street are denying Foster helped her buy the flats, but that's obvious nonsense when you read the emails.

TUESDAY, 3 DECEMBER

Hislop came to Canary Wharf today to sign copies of the new *Private Eye* annual, and it seemed churlish not to afford him a nice welcome. I despatched a group of twenty staff from all departments armed with large placards saying 'Gnome, go home' to confront him inside the tower. We were helped by amused bystanders and local office workers who joined in the chanting.

Hislop tried to laugh it off by sneering to passers-by, 'Is that it? Paaaatheeeetic.' But it was obvious he was a very unhappy bunny.

FRIDAY, 6 DECEMBER

Cherie's finally been forced into confessing that Foster did indeed advise her on the flats, and I can't resist doing a front page saying 'MISSING: ONE MORAL COMPASS. If found, please return to the PM's wife.' Nobody will get it, apart from me and a few journalists, but I've waited months for this joyous moment. What goes around comes around.

MONDAY, 9 DECEMBER

We tore into the Blairs over Cheriegate today, splashing on QUESTION OF TRUST, and revealing a poll that shows 58 per cent of the public think Labour's now the party of sleaze.

'Gnome, go home.' Mirror *staff ambush a very unamused*
Ian Hislop as he signs books at Canary Wharf.

Mandelson was outraged: 'Your paper today and its leader is so extreme and personal and so unjustified that I just cannot find the words. It just smacks of vengeance.'

I expressed surprise that he'd be so supportive of the Blairs, given the way they dumped him.

'Well, they weren't very loyal to me, no, but as TB has said, if he and others knew then what he knew subsequently about the sequence of events, then my resignation would not have happened. Cherie's guilty of misplaced loyalty and poor judgement, not a crime against humanity.'

'Peter, frankly I'm pleased she's getting her comeuppance after what she did to me. Particularly the way she stressed my lack of moral compass when she demanded my sacking from my bosses.'

'Piers, however much you may or may not be justified in your strong dislike of her, this shouldn't mean all perspective goes out of the window.'

He has a point. Perhaps I need to cool down a bit.

TUESDAY, 10 DECEMBER

Cherie gave an extraordinary press conference, where she started weeping and wailing about her poor little boy going to university. It was cringe-making stuff and completely, perhaps deliberately, missed the point.

WEDNESDAY, 11 DECEMBER

Mandelson's still raging: 'Your front page yesterday went too far and today's does too. You are the Great Editor, so you may be right, but from the inside it looks too much like a personal vendetta.'

'Well, I don't forget people who try to get me sacked,' I replied. 'It doesn't dictate my agenda about them in the paper, but human nature says it doesn't help either. I warned Tony many times that her treatment of the press would come back to haunt him.'

We have a new chief executive. I'd suggested to Victor recently that what we really needed was 'a younger female version of Michael Grade'.

'I think you'll be happy,' he said. 'It's Sly Bailey from IPC.'

This will be interesting. I've only met her once, and she's all bangles, boobs and blonde hair. Quite fun, though.

THURSDAY, 12 DECEMBER

I've now been staying at the One Aldwych for four months. The redecoration of the flat has turned into a total nightmare.

A reptile called Wayne from Tooting took £5000 up front to do the repair work … and disappeared. I eventually tracked him down, threatened him with exposure in the paper and the police, and he didn't care. 'Do what you like, mate.'

One Aldwych is probably the best hotel in the world, but now *I've had enough.* I've had enough of their huge pillows, their fresh strawberries for break-fast, their movies, their vodka tonics, their brilliant service … *all of it.* I want my bloody flat back.

To try and sweat some of this stir-crazy madness out of my head, I went down to the gym for the first time since I've been here.

I had a swim in their amazing Roman-style pool, on my own, and then strolled into the small but well-equipped gym itself for a work-out. It was empty apart from some old guy pedalling on a cycling machine at the back and reading a paper. I found a running machine and started jogging. Being inordinately unfit ever since my back operation, I was soon struggling. But the old man in front seemed to be speeding up if anything, which made my lumbering, wheez-ing performance all the more embarrassing.

Then he turned his head a touch, and bugger me – it was Rupert Murdoch.

He hadn't spotted me, but I was now in a terrible dilemma. I could hardly stop running after five minutes without humiliating myself, but I couldn't run much longer without the same result. Did I talk to him? Or walk out?

Would he think, God forbid, that I had deliberately come down here after stalking him for weeks to find where and when he worked out? I bet some people do that.

We were the only two people in that room and I just kept on running for ten and then twelve minutes, nearly killing myself, as he just calmly kept plodding and flicking the pages of the *Financial Times.*

It suddenly felt so farcical I nearly burst out laughing. I should have just gone over and said hello, but something stopped me. Then his trainer appeared and took him off to do a bit of kick-boxing. He didn't look round and I don't think he saw me. I was very relieved not to have to run any more, though, and lay down for a break.

I showered and went out to find my driver.

'You won't believe who's just come out of there,' he said, chortling.

'I will, actually – Rupert Murdoch, right?'

'Yeah,' said Martin, 'he came out, opened the boot of his car, took out a copy of the Mirror and the Sun, a notebook and some pens, and walked off to that coffee shop over there.'

Very amusing: it was clearly time for his morning exam-marking.

We've had some eclectic line-ups for our monthly lunches, but nothing quite like today. Cleo Rocos, Ken Clarke, Ann Widdecombe, Dale Winton, Alan Rusbridger, Chris Gent from Vodafone, Harry Enfield and Simon Kelner were just a few of the twenty-odd guests.

Tragically, James Hewitt was supposed to be coming too, but didn't turn up.

Sly Bailey did, though, and I managed to impress her instantly by tipping my red wine all over the table during the first course.

Harry and I had great fun teasing Widdecombe about drugs, and Dale blew me kisses.

Cheriegate got more interesting, with the *Scotsman* claiming documents relating to Peter Foster's lawyers were faxed to Cherie at her flat, apparent hard evidence that she has been lying about her relationship with him. Caplin insists she had them faxed over, but Cherie never saw them. Nobody believes her.

I emailed Mandelson: 'This is now a farce, nobody's going to believe a thing Cherie says now. She's terminally damaged, and it's not personal, it's her own extraordinary behaviour.'

He fired straight back: 'No, Piers, I'm afraid you're wrong. The media are being fed scraps by Foster and his people to encourage you to draw precisely that conclusion. You'll never believe anything Cherie says, because that's the decision you took some time ago. You've decided she's a liar and that's that. So if Carole obtained papers that Cherie never saw, you're simply not going to believe her. It's a shame, but there it is.'

I wasn't having that.

'I'm afraid you're wrong, Peter. This latest stuff stinks. I know you're trying to help her, but if she refuses to be honest, she's beyond even your skills.'

'Piers, I am not trying to help her either way, but I do not think it is reasonable to swallow the self-interested snippets from a conman to entrap Cherie further in order to help him fight deportation. You may think she's a compulsive liar (and on that we disagree), but I would back her against Peter Foster any day.'

'Peter, you are more loyal to them than they were to you when it mattered. This mess is entirely of Cherie's own making and she's getting the full hairdryer treatment because she's treated the press with utter contempt for years. For God's sake, Peter Foster at the heart of Downing Street, it beggars belief.'

'But Piers, Foster was never at the heart of Downing Street, he was at the heart of Carole Caplin. The Blairs have never met him. He passed in and out of Cherie's life in a matter of weeks, but during that period sowed the seeds we see now. No doubt Cherie dearly wishes Carole had never fallen in love with a conman. But accidents happen. Having said that, I couldn't help saying to Cherie this week that I wish I'd been given the chance to defend myself during my own "scandal" and make a statement for myself like she did before I was thrown out of the top floor window. But I can't rewind the film.'

THURSDAY, 19 DECEMBER

Bush was banging on again about the need to 'deal with Saddam'. He sounds stupid and dangerous. We did a front page with a warning sign over Bush's head saying: 'There is a lunatic with weapons of mass destruction "ramping up" for a war that will imperil the whole world. STOP HIM.'

I don't know if we are making any difference to anything with this stuff, but I am going to keep it going. I don't believe the British public want a war with Iraq, and nor do they want to see our Prime Minister sucking up to this President all the time in such a toe-curling way.

FRIDAY, 20 DECEMBER

Edwina Currie was guest speaker at the *What The Papers Say* awards today and bombed like I've never seen even a lead balloon bomb.

Highlights included bizarre references to Russian peasant proverbs, an ill-advised attack on the press for not unearthing her relationship with John Major, and an astonishing exhortation for 'people such as Paul Burrell to keep their mouths shut'.

The speech was greeted with near silence. It was hilariously embarrassing.

It was our Christmas staff party tonight in a bar at Canary Wharf. I'd promised everyone a 'world famous star who has straddled three decades at the top'. They all assumed it was George Michael and got rather over-excited. So you can imagine their reaction when Tony Blackburn emerged from the shadows, fresh from winning *I'm a Celebrity Get Me Out of Here*.

He tried to win over the audience with a series of rather lame gags and stunts, but drunken hacks are a notoriously cynical audience, and eventually he just dropped to the floor and started writhing like a dead fly to some dreadful disco song.

I regret to say that Tony was soon surrounded by a baying mob, all throwing kicks and punches at him. Playfully, but there was still a bit of an edge to the work.

'I'll get my coat, I think,' he said, looking rather hurt.

MONDAY, 23 DECEMBER

An American reader called Ben Merchant sent a delightful email:

Dear English dumbfucks, your paper has gone loony! I realize most Englishmen have crooked teeth, bad breath, are ugly as my poop, and are jealous of the USA but your latest trash article is over the top. You are racist hatemongers and your piece of shit country would be nothing without us. How many times have we saved your dumb asses? We should have let Hitler kill all you dumb fucking losers. After Bush turns Iraq into a parking lot you'll realise how stupid your opinions are. Now pull your dick out of your ass and kindly eat shit, from *all Americans*.

Obviously he has made me completely change my view on the war.

2003

WEDNESDAY, 8 JANUARY

Steve Dennis came to see me. 'Paul wants me to help him do a book.'

'OK, good idea.'

'Yes, but I will need to have some time off to do it. Like six months.'

I didn't have much choice. I have seen this coming, and Steve and I both know it will be a massive bestseller, making him so much money that his *Mirror* contract will seem a rather trifling irrelevance.

I agreed a secret sabbatical.

'It will be incredible,' he said; 'much better than the interview we did when he was acquitted.'

FRIDAY, 10 JANUARY

Kate Winslet's done a photo shoot with *GQ* which is so hideously airbrushed she looks a completely different woman.

Every magazine does this now, though none of their editors ever admit it. Until now. I called Dylan Jones, *GQ* editor, to confront him over his traversty of photojournalism.

'Yep, all airbrushed, you're quite right.'

'What? You're confessing?'

'Of course, we can hardly deny it, can we? Kate had approval over the pictures, and various parts of her body were improved, including her stomach and legs. I don't think we've gone too far – she looks magnificent.'

Good old Dylan, he reminds me of myself sometimes. Which ought to worry him a bit …

MONDAY, 13 JANUARY

Tragedy. David Yelland has 'resigned'. He's going back to school at Harvard University, the little lamb. I toyed with running eight pages on the rise and fall of The Mekon, but opted instead for two paragraphs on page two. I then reached into my desk drawer for my Yelland voodoo doll, complete with pins to insert, and tossed it into the bin. He's gone, it's over.

Even better news came later when Rebekah was made the new editor of the *Sun*. She will be brilliant, and we'll have great fun trying to out-fox each other.

WEDNESDAY, 15 JANUARY

Andy Coulson's been made editor of the *News of the World*. It's so weird, seeing two such close friends reach the top. He, too, will be a great editor. He's got the drive, like Rebekah.

A few of my staff seemed to be concerned that our relationship with the *Sun* will be all sweetness and light now my mate's in charge over there, and aren't happy about it. So I sent out a global email:

> Just so there is no doubt about my reaction to the appointment of a new *Sun* editor, I expect us to *pulverise* them with journalistic brilliance. Mediocrity is not an option, and I'm sure you all share my determination to send another *Sun* editor back to school as soon as possible. But this will be strictly business, not personal, so when we've destroyed them with great papers I have no problem with you buying our rivals a drink and consoling them.

Peter Willis poured scorn, quite rightly, on my rhetoric: 'You really should do one of those inspirational management books based on your go-get-'em emails.'

THURSDAY, 16 JANUARY

TV star Matthew Kelly was arrested last night for offences he's supposed to have committed 30 years ago. The story broke late, but we held the presses and got it into the first edition. But the *Sun* missed it. I know this is because their off-stone time is an hour earlier than ours, unfortunately due to the fact they sell so many more copies, but sent Rebekah a taunting email anyway. 'Don't worry about bottling it first time last night – you'll get more decisive as the years go on. This daily lark is hard to get the hang of at first …'

'*Excuse me*,' she replied, 'but when you get a print run of four million you might understand why we had to go off before the story broke.'

'I know about those, thanks,' I responded. 'I had a print run of five million on the *News of the World* before you shrank it to four million.'

'Oh, *please*,' is her considered reaction.

I'm only teasing, and there will be no war like there was with The Mekon, but anything I can do to slightly dent her considerable confidence is fair game, I reckon. And she'll be thinking just the same about me.

FRIDAY, 17 JANUARY

We've persuaded Christopher Hitchens, in my view one of the world's best columnists, to join our new, more serious paper on an exclusive basis and I suggested he might like to model himself on Maximus from *Gladiator* and 'unleash hell'.

He replied, 'He was a good egg in his way but I turn always to Odysseus on Nausicaa's island, where at the wedding the couple are introduced as "a great joy to their friends and a great grief to their enemies". Sic semper.'

I am going to have my work cut out keeping up with this cerebral mass.

MONDAY, 20 JANUARY

It's bleedingly obvious to everyone now that we are going to go to war with Iraq. Yet absolutely nobody I speak to, either at work or in my village pub, thinks it's a good idea. The United Nations weapons inspectors haven't found anything so far, we've contained Saddam pretty well for a decade or more, and bombing Baghdad just seems completely pointless – and more linked to America's desire for revenge after 9/11 and the need to grab Iraq's oil reserves in case the House of Saud collapses as many fear it might.

It is hard to escape the feeling that we're being railroaded into this by the Americans for reasons that are not in Britain's national interest.

If the inspectors had found hard evidence of these weapons of mass destruction Bush and Blair keep blathering on about, I might feel differently. But they haven't.

I've been working myself into a lather about this for a while now, and decided this morning it was time to do something about it. I cleared the whole front page for a picture of a British soldier and the headline: YOU ARE NOT POWERLESS, YOU DO HAVE A VOTE, NO WAR. And we include a petition to fill in, saying: 'Mr Blair, I hereby register my opposition to any war with Iraq not justified by unequivocal UN evidence.'

Our message to Blair is simple, I think. Show us these weapons, demonstrate the threat from Saddam is real and present, get the United Nations to support new military action, and we'll back you. But otherwise, think very, very hard about this.

Be interesting to see how the public react.

TUESDAY, 21 JANUARY

Falklands hero Simon Weston has backed our petition, saying, 'This war is wrong. There's no proof, no heart for this one, no belief.' It's strong stuff, coming from a man like him. We've also been inundated with calls and emails from readers. I think we've struck a nerve.

Alastair launched his charity run tonight at the House of Lords. Blair popped in briefly and shook my hand, but seemed less than keen on being seen being nice to me. Alastair's already conveyed No. 10's general thoughts: 'What the fuck is this stupid campaign all about?'

You're on message or not with this Government: no deviance is tolerated. Or an icy chill descends upon you.

Derry Irvine, the absurd Lord Chancellor, floated around in his Cardinal Wolsey gear, looking and sounding utterly ridiculous. I reckon he is personally costing Blair a thousand votes every time he is seen or heard in public. He is the antithesis of everything a Labour Government should stand for.

WEDNESDAY, 22 JANUARY

We've had 15,000 petitions back by first post; incredible. This is going to be massive, and I see a real opportunity here for the *Mirror* to become the anti-Iraq war paper and give a voice to the millions who clearly agree with me. But it will get sticky and nasty with Downing Street and the right-wing media. Just the way I like it.

SUNDAY, 26 JANUARY

We've beamed the NO WAR front page on to the House of Commons, thanks to a cunning film device first used by *FHM* magazine in a similar stunt, only they used Gail Porter's bottom. We did it very late at night, and only for a few seconds. As a photo, it worked a treat. I'm right up for this campaign now, it's got legs and reason and power.

MONDAY, 27 JANUARY

Bush has told the world he's 'ready for war' at the same time that the United Nations weapons inspectors are begging for more time to finish their work. What *is* the hurry, for God's sake?

But then we knew what we'd get with Bush – we can hardly complain now he's behaving exactly to type. It doesn't excuse Blair, though. I just can't understand what the hell he thinks he's doing, supporting this nonsense. And nor can most of his Cabinet and party.

TUESDAY, 28 JANUARY

John Pilger rang this morning, determined to write a 'defining' attack on Blair for his refusal to stop Bush going to war. It was classic Pilger, tub-thumping, damning both statistically and historically, and written superbly. He has headlined his piece 'Blood on his hands'. And I like that idea.

Minutes later we had wiped out the front page for a photo of Blair with mocked up blood-red hands and the headline BLOOD ON HIS HANDS.

It's very provocative. But it's also right. He is going to kill a lot of innocent people very soon, if he doesn't stop and think about it.

WEDNESDAY, 29 JANUARY

Victor rang later, a bit perturbed by our front page. 'Don't get too personal,' he cautioned.

MONDAY, 3 FEBRUARY

Branson has gone back on his agreement to do my new *Tabloid Tales* BBC1 series, in which I grill celebrities about their life in the headlines, which is bloody annoying because he'd be great, and it's quite late in the day.

'I'm hopeless at saying "no" face-to-face,' he wrote. 'But now I haven't got you standing next to me I've plucked up the courage! I'm really sorry, but I've had a few calls from people approached by your researchers in a very negative way, concentrating solely on leading questions about media manipulation and special relationships that resulted in a picture of Richard Branson that even I didn't recognise!'

THURSDAY, 6 FEBRUARY

Liz Murdoch emailed to say, 'One of your paps jumped over me last night, bashing my head with his lenses, to get a better shot of Chris Evans and Billie. I was impressed by his athleticism even if I had a sore head.'

I replied, 'Don't know whether to sack or promote him … by the way I found myself running behind your dad in the One Aldwych gym the other morning, just me and him pounding away (him for a bit longer than me, I might add). I was going to say hello and ruin his day when his trainer arrived to take him boxing. All very amusing.'

She emailed back, 'I'm sure dad jogged longer than you on purpose. He does that kind of thing.'

I bet he does, too.

We've been getting dozens of celebrities to sign our petition, and today landed a really big fish – Dustin Hoffman. 'The Mirror's campaign is excellent, I applaud you,' he said, to general awestruck disbelief in the newsroom.

FRIDAY, 7 FEBRUARY

Marion's gone on a charity bike ride to Laos in Vietnam, so I've got the boys for ten days, which is great for them because it means lots of pizza, sweets and Coke. She'd assured me it was safe out there. But today I was flicking through the news files and suddenly saw TOURIST CYCLISTS KILLED BY LAOS BANDITS.

Ten people have died in a shoot-out, including two western cyclists.

I immediately called the emergency number for her group, and thankfully it wasn't them. But half the people on the trip wanted to come straight home, and who can blame them.

'You keep going, dear,' I joked.

And to my surprise and admiration, she's going to.

News broke tonight that Derry Irvine's getting a twelve per cent pay rise.

That's another, oooh, 100,000 votes gone, Tony.

MONDAY, 10 FEBRUARY

Catherine Zeta-Jones is suing *Hello!* magazine for 'invasion of privacy' because they sneaked into her wedding to Michael Douglas and grabbed some pictures

– after she'd sold exclusive rights to the rival *OK!* magazine for £1 million. What a farce.

I remember her when she was a nice, bright, amusing girl who'd just made it big in *Darling Buds of May*.

What the hell has she become?

TUESDAY, 11 FEBRUARY

We ran a photo of GMTV star Fiona Phillips without her make-up today, walking along the street. It's always a cheap shot doing that to female TV stars, because they always wear make-up on screen, so always look very different without it, like every woman.

She emailed me in the afternoon:

> Pathetic Fiona squeals like a baby about privacy after appearing in the *Mirror* looking like Pauline Fowler after a long day at the launderette. 'I feel violated,' she sobbed; 'it was a truly gut-wrenching experience, like a Peeping Tom had been present.' 'Ah, diddums,' replied Justice Lindsay, 'that's what all the girls say when that old c*** Piers Morgan tries it on …'

Hilarious. Think I might hire her as a columnist, actually. Anyone that can laugh at herself in such an amusing way must be worth employing.

WEDNESDAY, 12 FEBRUARY

Amazing scenes today as tanks rolled into Heathrow after a 'specific threat' to down an airliner. The timing is very suspicious, if you ask me. Just when Blair needs to scare the life out of us to justify his dreadful war, we see our major airport turned into a military battleground. Unsurprisingly, nothing happens. But the pictures will have worked everyone into a terrified state.

THURSDAY, 13 FEBRUARY

We'd invited Liz Hurley to one of our monthly lunches.

Her assistant, Miss Sara Woodhatch, responded today: 'Elizabeth [sic] says the *Mirror* is too mean about her for her to feel comfortable having lunch with its editor and chairman! She thanks you for the invitation, though.'

MONDAY, 17 FEBRUARY

The anti-war march on Saturday was the biggest in British history. And there were *Mirror* banners everywhere, thanks to my fantastic PR executive Sarah Vaughan-Brown and her team. I emailed Jeremy in Cyprus. '1.7 million people marched on London, biggest demo ever. Are they *all* wrong?'

'Yes, all of them. I've never heard such an utter load of horse shit in my life. In any case, as one top general said to me earlier this week, "The train has already left the station." '

And I suspect it has.

David Beckham was sporting a big gash above his eye after Alex Ferguson kicked a boot at him after they lost to Arsenal in the Cup on Saturday. Victoria's PR, Caroline McAteer, said David was furious: 'He's sick of being treated like that.' He's not going to stay at United much longer.

TUESDAY, 18 FEBRUARY

Interviewed Victoria Beckham for *Tabloid Tales* today at a recording studio in Chiswick. She was on great form. I suggested that it was time David quit United and joined Arsenal. Their house is near our training ground, and I know she loathes Manchester.

'Oh, I'd love that,' she said. 'I'm sick of the way Alex Ferguson treats us. He kicked that boot right at him, for God's sake – what way is that to behave towards one of your best players? It's disgusting. Can't you run a story saying Arsenal want him?'

The interview itself was brilliant. She's a natural and gave me some great lines.

Me: 'Have you seen Footballers' Wives, then?'

VB: 'Yes. My hairdresser has started calling me Beaujolais.'

She was very relaxed until we got round to the latest rumours that David's been a naughty boy. 'He'd never be unfaithful to me,' she said sternly. 'These girls just make up this stuff, it's pathetic.'

Her mum, who was watching, agreed: 'It's all lies.'

I remembered a time when Posh was rumoured to have given Becks a whack when a paper ran an alleged kiss-and-tell.

'Yeah, I did. I punched and kicked him. It turned out it wasn't true, but he'd put himself in a position where this girl could say these things, and I was really upset. He wouldn't dare cheat on me – he knows what I'd do to him.'

I got a taste of it myself when she whacked me over the head with a copy of our *Look* magazine for saying she'd spent £20,000 on Brooklyn's nursery.

'Don't be so bloody stupid – behave yourself!' she screeched, as I dived for cover.

She was particularly entertaining about her fabled, but very obvious, boob job.

'I've got fake eyelashes,' she said, coquettishly.

'Anything else that's not entirely genuine you want to admit to?' I asked.

'Yes … my nails.'

Her noticeably impressive new breasts told their own story.

Caroline McAteer got a text from David Beckham while we spoke that said, 'He's a c**t,' which apparently was a reference to Sir Alex Ferguson. We all burst out laughing.

Caroline later emailed me to say, 'Victoria's concerned about camera angles, said she'd rather re-do the interview if she looks dodgy.' 'Do it again?' I replied incredulously. 'Is that some sort of joke?' 'Look, she needs to see how she looks,' said Caroline, 'to reassure her.'

'Yes, OK' I relented, 'but I can't do it again, it would be like asking da Vinci to repaint Mona Lisa. And anyway she looked as fit as a butcher's dog to me.'

And she did, actually. People always criticise her looks, but in the flesh she is very pretty and nowhere near as bony as you think.

MONDAY, 24 FEBRUARY

Sophie Raworth emailed from the BBC newsroom to say, 'Want a funny story? Just had to run into the studio during the one o'clock news with no make-up on and hair in need of washing to take over from Anna Ford halfway through the news 'cos her voice had gone. Hysterical!'

And when I saw the video, it was.

TUESDAY, 25 FEBRUARY

Jeremy emailed me his new joke: 'Going to war without France is rather like going deer hunting without an accordion, all you do is leave behind a lot of noisy luggage.'

WEDNESDAY, 26 FEBRUARY

Interviewed Anthea Turner today for *Tabloid Tales*, and it turned out to be quite an emotional experience for her. As we analysed how the media had built her up and destroyed her, tears started flooding down her face. And I felt genuinely sorry for her. She's not Adolf Hitler, she's just a nice, bit cheesy, TV presenter who had an affair. And for that we collectively dragged her through the mill until she was effectively dead. She looked a broken woman in front of me today, and I felt bad about that.

The *Daily Sport* did a full-page leader article on me today, illustrated by a big picture of Saddam reading the *Mirror*. It was great stuff. 'Piers Morgan, this poncey public schoolboy, is doing Saddam's dirty work for him. Morgan may be a colossus among monkeys, but he is a pygmy among Brits.'

THURSDAY, 27 FEBRUARY

Had dinner at Liz Murdoch and Matthew Freud's vast Notting Hill mansion tonight. They gave us Beluga caviar and Château Margaux 1960-something, which was revoltingly decadent, but bloody delicious. I got increasingly vocal as the £500 bottles slipped down, and got into a very intense discussion with Liz about her dad, in which I said that the one thing that really upset me when I left the *NoW* was his belief that I'd gone to Hayman Island knowing I was going to the *Mirror* and had therefore done it to nick all his secret plans. 'That's just bull-shit,' I ranted. 'I didn't know for sure what was happening.'

Liz listened patiently, as she probably has to with millions of people haranguing her about her father. 'Hmm, well, that's not what he thought and I doubt he'll change his mind,' she said. 'He rarely does!'

FRIDAY, 28 FEBRUARY

I emailed Liz to thank her for a fantastic night, which it was, and added, 'In case I didn't make myself clear, *I did not bloody well know I had the* Mirror *job when I went to Hayman Island.*'

She emailed back: 'I will spread the word about Hayman. Maybe. It's a better story the other way ...'

She's right. It is.

MONDAY, 3 MARCH

To the Pride of Britain awards at the Hilton in Park Lane. Mum and Charlotte came for the first time.

Sat next to Blair, as usual, and asked him how the battle for a second UN resolution was going. Britain and America put a new draft resolution forward to the UN Security Council last week, which, if passed, would effectively endorse immediate military action against Saddam for failure to co-operate with the weapons inspectors.

'Very well. We're nearly there. I don't think there will be a problem.'

'But what if there is? What if you don't get it?'

'Well, we will have to cross that bridge when we come to it, but I am very confident we will. We want to do this with the UN, and we will do it with the UN.'

He was pretty frosty with me. Our anti-war campaign has not helped him.

'I understand you don't agree with me,' he said, 'but I hope you respect that I am doing what I think is right. I think some of your coverage has been a bit unfair and hysterical at times.'

'Well, war's a serious business, Tony. A lot of people are going to die.'

He seemed tense, but very, very confident the UN resolution would come through and validate any military action. I hope so, for his sake. Because going to war without the UN would be a disaster for a Labour Prime Minister.

Paul McCartney came with his wife Heather, for the first time since I played Cupid to them at the same event in 1999. We had a good time over lunch, and Heather decided to take the mickey out of me on stage.

'I can't believe that someone like Piers Morgan's involved in such a worthy event,' she sneered. To virtual silence.

Even I expected a rousing round of applause, but nothing came. Just a quiet murmuring of discontent and a few tuts. Heather looked stunned by the reaction. She obviously thought this gag was a real vote-winner. But these awards are genuinely emotional, and this kind of cutting piss-taking doesn't really go on. I didn't mind at all, in fact I laughed out loud. But Mum was furious – and marched over to remonstrate with her afterwards. 'I want a word with you, madam,' she said to a startled Lady McCartney. 'How dare you talk about my son like that.' Sir Paul intervened to try and calm things down, but Mum was having none of it, not even from an ex-Beatle. 'Sorry, Paul, she was completely out of order saying that.'

Mum and Charlotte had a great day other than that, and I later found them drinking champagne with Des Lynam.

'What have you been talking about?' I asked nervously.

'Sex,' said Des, smirking.

'What? Seriously?' I stuttered.

'Yes, I didn't know your sister was a sex therapist, we've been having a marvellous conversation.'

I flashed a glance at a rather tipsy Charlotte, who winked and laughed.

She's not a sex therapist, obviously.

But Des thought she was, and that meant she and Mum have had one of their heart-throbs talking just how they want him to for twenty minutes.

TUESDAY, 4 MARCH

We forgot to invite Alan Sugar to Pride of Britain for the third year running, and he's understandably not very amused:

> Oh dear, didn't you get an invite? Bloody hell, I told my secretary to send you one, you're on the list, oh, isn't Sugar on the list? What's that ... you did send him one, didn't you, oh dear, must have got lost in the post ... Piers, in keeping with my ongoing passion for ultra efficiency, I have pre-empted what you would say when I asked why you didn't invite me to the Pride of Britain awards. It's not rocket science, it's what you've said for the last three years. I would have come as it was a Monday night.

I couldn't believe we'd forgotten again and sent back a long grovelling apology. He replied:

> It's OK, but your excuses get more sincere every year and I just like hearing them. I am going to compile them all and have them mounted in a collage to put on your wall. On the Richter scale of bullshitters you are very low. The first rule is always remember what you have said before. It's a bad memory that lets most people down (El Tel Venables ...) It's my impeccable memory that allows me to be high up on the scale.

WEDNESDAY, 5 MARCH

Had a most entertaining dinner at No. 11 tonight with the Browns. They don't use the No. 10 flat to live in, but they do enjoy taking people up there for drinks. It's all been kept exactly as previous Prime Ministers decorated it, so you have Norma and John Major's kitchen and dining room (very, *very* boring as you'd expect), and the Thatcher bathroom. I couldn't resist this one, and posed for a photo on my mobile phone, sitting on Maggie's loo. The seat down, and trousers up, I hasten to add. Sarah Brown tried to stop me, then just laughed and accepted it was something I had to do.

After a fun dinner, Gordon took us on a tour of the building and we all ended up in the Cabinet room. I sat in Blair's chair and shouted across the table, 'Oi, Brown, you're fired.' He took my imbecility well. But he got rather agitated when I tried to get into Blair's private office next door. 'No, no, you mustn't go in there,' he cried. 'Why not?' I replied. 'It'll be yours soon, anyway.'

We finished up with a few whiskies in the flat. Brown was relaxed and jovial. The public never see this side of him, which is a great shame because he is incredibly charming when his political antennae are down. The Brown camp don't openly trash their neighbours, but there's always an undercurrent of tension there. One person who they are quite happy to trash, though, is Mandelson. 'He's the kind of guy who uses you until you're no longer useful to him, and then just ups and leaves,' said Sue Nye, Brown's long-time adviser, ruefully. She should know, he lived with her for a while on his way up in Westminster. Brown nodded. 'Peter's a clever guy, but he can't stop plotting and creating problems for everyone.'

I asked Brown if he thought the UN would pass the second resolution. 'Yes, we're pretty confident they will.'

Nobody seems certain, though.

THURSDAY, 6 MARCH
Right, well, France, Germany and Russia have all now threatened to veto any UN resolution approving war on Iraq.

And Hans Blix, the chief weapons inspector, says Iraq is disarming and he must be allowed to stay out there. But the American war machine is in place, and they can't retreat now. Blair is going to get fucked here, if he's not very careful.

SUNDAY, 9 MARCH
Clare Short's laid into Blair and said she will quit the Cabinet if we go to war without the UN. Good for her: thank God one of these spineless Labour ministers is prepared to say in public what most of them have been saying in private.

MONDAY, 10 MARCH
Sly Bailey has fired Mark Haysom, our MD.

In response to the obvious follow-up question, she said, 'Piers's job is safe. The entire market has suffered throughout the war. I don't make reactive decisions, I make decisive decisions.'

Sounded like the dreaded vote of confidence to me. I sense I might become a 'decisive decision' sooner rather than later. Sly likes to be the centre of attention, and I am a rather large obstacle to that.

She also wants to take the paper back downmarket again, which is dispiriting to say the least. One of the biggest problems I've had editing the *Mirror* is the constant change in management teams, with all their different views on where the paper should be going, and how it should be pitched. It just creates inevitable inconsistency and confuses the readers.

Jonathan Ross's agent, Addison Creswell, a man I would literally cross continents to avoid, informed me that unless we give his client a 50 per cent pay rise to £150k a year for his film column, then he'll be off.

I told Addison to shove his request up his arse, and awaited the usual climb-down. But no, he actually meant it, and Jonathan has formally resigned!

I sent him an email: 'Thanks for everything, I will have to console myself with the thought that I may never have to deal with Addison "JR won't do it any more for a penny less than fucking ton-fifty grand" Cresswell again. It's been a gas, but that's showbiz.'

To my amazement, Jonathan rang to admit it was *his* idea to demand all that money. 'To be honest, mate, I don't need the money and it's a bit of bind doing it every week, so if you were prepared to pay me a ridiculous sum like that then I'd carry on, but I kind of knew you wouldn't.'

I laughed. You have to admire the honesty. 'Addison's still a wanker,' I said. 'Yes, I know,' he replied. 'But unfortunately I like him and he's a very useful wanker.'

Blair hasn't sacked Clare Short, as perhaps he should, because he daren't. Too many people agree with her. We did a wipe-out front page calling her a WEAPON OF MS DESTRUCTION. I'm full of admiration for her. When push came to shove, she has acted on principle.

TUESDAY, 11 MARCH

I was called to give evidence to the Culture and Media Select Committee this afternoon, chaired by Gerald Kaufman. It was the pointless exercise I assumed it would be.

'What exactly is the need to bring us down here for our ritual bollocking when tabloid standards have self-evidently improved in the last few years?' I asked.

But Gerald had me where he wanted me, and treated me like some sort of convict on day release. I amused myself by lambasting the broadsheets' hypocrisy, defending us against charges of being 'hydra-headed monsters going round gobbling people up', and got away with a few whacks against Gerald whenever I could, to his visible annoyance.

Later Rebekah excelled herself by virtually admitting she's been illegally paying policemen for information. I called her to thank her for dropping the tabloid baton at the last minute. She apologised: 'That's why I should never be seen or heard in public.'

Alan Rusbridger emailed me to say, 'Simon Hoggart's sketch says the clash between you and GK was like a bouncy castle pitted against an airbag. Outrageous stunt. Once you went, the temperature fell about 1000 degrees, even the sketch writers fell asleep.'

THURSDAY, 13 MARCH

Had lunch today with David Blunkett at the Goring Hotel. He was on good form as usual, full of gossip and intrigue. I asked him how Blair was coping with the constant threat of an Al Qaeda hit.

'He deals with it pretty well, considering that every day I read intelligence reports suggesting he is the second biggest target after Bush in the world. He must read them too, and that can't be easy on anyone. There was a specific assassination threat against him recently, suggesting Al Qaeda would kill him at a public event. And then I realised I was going to be sitting next to him at it. That was rather a long day, I can tell you ...'

I brought up the recent scare at Heathrow when he ordered soldiers and tanks to patrol the airport, and suggested it was a rather handy device to frighten the public into supporting a war they don't want.

He was angry I'd even suggested it. 'I was very angry about that. I agreed that we should have some military presence at Heathrow, because there was a specific threat to bring down a plane. But I didn't know that tanks were going to be used – it was a terrible image and I told John Stevens to remove them.'

As for the war itself, he insisted he was 'right behind the Prime Minister', and gave me all the usual platitudes about WMD, and what a threat Saddam was, etc.

'I don't think he's a danger at all,' I said. 'He's just a sad old tyrant eking out his last miserable years. Why cause mayhem by blowing up Iraq?'

Blunkett tutted. 'I understand your view, but you're wrong, I'm afraid.'

'I'm not wrong, you guys are,' I retorted. 'It's monstrous, frankly.'

That word hung around my mind as I went back to the office.

'Get me a picture of Blair looking demented, please,' I asked.

You can actually tap the words 'Blair' and 'demented' into our picture library now, and a load of suitably mad images will come up. Such is the power of modern technology.

I put one particularly bonkers one all over the front with the words: 'PRIME MONSTER – Drag us into this war without the UN, Tony, and that's how history will judge you. For God's sake, man, DON'T DO IT.'

I know it's way over the top, and pretty personal. But this *is* personal now. Blair's determined to do this, and he's got to be stopped somehow before it's too late.

FRIDAY, 14 MARCH

Victor rang early in the morning and was very unhappy. 'This is wrong, Piers. You know I never normally say that, but this front page is too personal and too unpleasant. We can't, as a Labour-supporting newspaper, call the Prime Minister a monster like this.'

'But he's going to kill thousands of innocent people illegally, Victor,' I replied.

'The argument about the merits of this war are there to be debated. But we should not be descending to this kind of thing.'

I suspected Victor had had a call from someone at No. 10. Probably his big mate Michael Levy.

He sounded agitated, which was unlike him. But I respect his opinion.

SUNDAY, 16 MARCH

A nervous email arrived from my man on the front line, Tom Newton-Dunn, saying everyone he meets in the British services 'loathes the *Mirror*'. He said, 'One young marine actually asked me if he would be spat at when he got home because of all the anti-war invective the *Mirror*'s whipped up against an "illegal" invasion.'

MONDAY, 17 MARCH

The UN have not passed a second resolution. So that's that, then. Blair either backs down or goes to war, as our front page tonight said, 'illegally, unethically and unstoppably'. I think we all know the answer. But tomorrow is the big Commons vote, and at least we'll see who is prepared to stand up against this madness.

TUESDAY, 18 MARCH

Clare Short has done the most ridiculous U-turn in history and backed the war *without* the UN just a week after she said she would quit if that happened. It is scarcely credible that she has done this, and I am utterly appalled. She says she's been assured by Blair that she will have a key role to play in shaping the future of Iraq after any conflict. Bollocks. They wouldn't need our help if we weren't about to blow them to pieces. We have done a big picture of her on page one with the headline 'REVOLTING ... cometh the hour, cometh the coward'. And lacerated her in the leader.

Had a long meeting with Victor and Sly in the afternoon about how we would cover the war.

'You must be careful, Piers,' Victor said forcefully. 'When our troops go in, the public will rally behind them, whatever they thought of the political argument to go to war.'

'I know that, Victor, but I refuse to go all gung-ho just because the bombing starts. It would be rankly hypocritical.'

'I agree, but don't be too critical either while it is actually going on. Play it straight.' Wise words – wonder if I will be able to heed them in the heat of the battle.

It was the press awards tonight, and the *Guardian*'s brilliant cartoonist Steve Bell won an award and held it aloft to the audience, before saying: 'I'd just like to say ... fuck the war.' Everyone cheered.

WEDNESDAY/THURSDAY, 19/20 MARCH

I have booked myself into the Four Seasons Hotel at Canary Wharf, so I can be nearby if the action kicks off.

The phone rang at 2.41am. It was Jon Moorhead, informing me, 'It's started.' I expected to hear about some horrific 'Shock and Awe' strike on Baghdad that we'd been told would reduce the city to ashes in hours. But it sounded even more dramatic. Jon, normally a bastion of calm amid a sea of newsroom hysteria, was beside himself.

'Um, well they appear to have tried to assassinate Saddam.'

There was no real need for me to go back to the office. It was now 3am, there would be only a few hundred thousand copies left to print ... and yet how could I not go back? If a direct strike on Saddam doesn't get you racing to your desk, then tabloid editing is not your bag.

I arrived to find controlled pandemonium, a small group of perhaps 30 people changing pages, cajoling the printers to keep going, urging the circulation crew to get extra vans to send late papers. We got two more editions out, the last one accurately labelled '6am Special', with a live picture of a Baghdad building in flames, and extraordinary pictures of George Bush having his hair combed before declaring war. My team were amazing – fast, accurate, ruthlessly professional. I returned to the hotel bursting with pride at a job well done – and with fury at what's unfurling in Iraq. We've done it – Britain's actually gone to war unlawfully.

THURSDAY, 20 MARCH

I got the lifeless, war-less, first-edition *Mirror* at the hotel in the morning, a totally deflating antidote to my adrenaline-surged torso. But a quick stop at the nearby newsagent, and there it was: 6am Special – DAWN ATTACK. We'd beaten everyone with that late edition. It had been worth the effort, it always is. The immediate problem for the *Mirror*, though, is how to cover the war, given our strong 'anti' position and the fact that our armed forces are now risking their lives. It is a dilemma facing most of the country, and was illuminated rather graphically when I appeared on *Question Time* tonight, and got loudly cheered and booed for just walking on. Clearly the *Mirror*'s anti-war position is now cemented in the public psyche, but how that plays for us remains to be seen. The audience seemed to rather enjoy me repeatedly asking Peter Hain to back Clare Short when he would evidently, as he'd made clear to me before in the greenroom, rather impale himself on a rusty skewer. 'How do you defend the indefensible?' he said afterwards.

William Hague called me a Saddam apologist, which got him cheap laughs and a rather pleasing crescendo of appalled gasps and boos. Can't blame him, though: at the last election, we did put his head all over page one with the headline X MARKS THE CLOT. Backstage, he was surprisingly friendly. When I asked what he missed least about losing his job, he said the on-message shackles that went with it: 'It was very nice this morning, when Conservative Central Office rang to give me my Question Time briefing notes, to say "No, thanks – I'll say what I really think,"' he said, with a mischievous smirk. I'd buy shares in a Hague comeback if I were allowed to.

FRIDAY, 21 MARCH

Overnight, twelve British troops were killed in a helicopter crash. The brutal, uncompromising and often quite hideous reality of warfare is now kicking in big time. Our forces are attacking Baghdad and Basra with sustained ferocity – all captured on TV in a way that is quickly turning this war into a unique reality show, beamed minute by ugly minute into millions of sitting rooms.

Around 6pm the giant screen in our newsroom suddenly exploded into what looked like Sydney Harbour on New Year's Eve. The staff rushed to see what was happening, as a Sky TV presenter informed us that it was the start of 'Shock and Awe'. It was truly shocking, and truly awful. And yet surreal. As hundreds of cruise missiles rained down on Baghdad, a few of my staff whooped and hollered as if watching a big catherine wheel doing its stuff. They didn't mean to be insensitive, it was an instinctive reaction to what they were watching. But they were quickly shhh'd into silence. Anton Antonowicz, our man in Baghdad, filed a stunning report on the 'mother of all bombings' raining down over his head. Our cameraman Mike Moore, who was there in 1998 for the last blitz, says this is bigger than anything he's ever seen. I fear for both of them – who knows what will happen next?

SATURDAY, 22 MARCH

At lunchtime I got a text message saying that ITN reporter Terry Lloyd was missing, feared dead, with his crew. This is going to be a very dangerous war for journalists. The ground attack is already huge and rapid, and there are an unprecedented 4000 hacks embedded with the soldiers. I can't imagine how the ITN staff are feeling: if it was one of my *Mirror* people I would be completely pole-axed. News organisations are families; we work, play, argue and – very rarely, thankfully – mourn together.

SUNDAY, 23 MARCH

Sunday, normally a day of rest and alcohol. But not in wartime. I got up early to do the paper review on *Breakfast with Frost* with the *Mail*'s foreign correspondent, Ann Leslie. Frost asked me whether there would be any change in the *Mirror*'s position now the war has started. I replied confidently, 'I think you can rally behind the armed forces who are bravely giving their lives – and we have seen that today – whilst continuing our position, unhypocritically saying that we didn't agree with this last week and we don't agree with it now.' Nobody seemed to find this an illogical argument.

Later I had lunch at the Four Seasons, where I have been living all week, and will do for a few weeks longer, I suspect. My brief moment of convivial relaxation was interrupted by a bizarre encounter with a grim-faced man from Essex who stopped me as I went to the loo and said, 'I saw you on Question Time and wanted to say something to you.' 'Oh, yes,' I replied, my chest instinctively puffing up with pride as I awaited the inevitable rather embarrassing torrent of praise, 'fire away.'

He stared violently into my eyes: '*You are a bloody disgrace.*' Temporarily startled, I followed my new friend outside and asked him to repeat what he'd said. '*You are a bloody disgrace and a fucking traitor,*' he happily obliged, as his wife pleaded, 'Oh not again, it's my birthday, for God's sake.' After two weeks of little sleep, and a few too many adrenaline surges, I unburdened myself on to my verbal assailant with an equally tart character assessment. 'Why don't you fuck off, you prick?'

He took it well. 'How fucking dare you talk to me like that?' he screamed, by now puce with rage. '*I know,*' I shouted back, '*bloody disgraceful, isn't it?*'

I went in to the office to calm down.

New angles on the war have been pouring in every hour. American soldiers have been captured and paraded on TV, prompting fury from George Bush. The same Mr Bush who thinks it's OK to parade Afghan PoWs in hoods and shackles on the Pentagon website. The hypocrisy of this ludicrously named 'War on Terror' knows no bounds.

An RAF Tornado's been shot down by an American Patriot missile, and British military chiefs are enraged. Why is it *always* the bloody Americans that commit these friendly fire acts?

Tom Newton-Dunn filed an astonishing piece of reportage after being told to keep his 'fucking head down' as Iraqi snipers attacked from roofs in the town of Al Faw. I spoke to him, and he was high on adrenaline and fear. 'Boss, it's bloody terrifying,' he admitted with admirable candour. We gave a spread to the latest peace march, but I can sense from the lukewarm response it got that the public mood is already shifting. The question is, how fast?

Clare Short's mother says she should have quit, which amused.

And Elton John told our 3am Girls that he thinks the war's disgraceful, but it won't stop him throwing his Oscars party. What a trouper.

MONDAY, 24 MARCH

Jeremy emailed me his latest joke: 'You know the world's going crazy when the best rapper in the world is a white guy, the best golfer black, the Swiss hold the America's Cup, France accuses the US of arrogance, and Germany doesn't want to go to war.'

A reader also sent me a great quote that he'd found in a book about the Second World War:

Why, of course the people don't want war. That is understood. But, after all, it is the leaders of the country who determine the policy and it is always a simple matter to drag the people along, whether it is a democracy or a fascist dictatorship, or a parliament, or a communist dictatorship. Voice or no voice, the people can always be brought to the bidding of the leaders. That is easy. All you have to do is tell them they are being attacked and denounce the peacemakers for lack of patriotism and exposing the country to danger.

No, it's not Alastair Campbell. It was Hermann Goering at the Nuremberg trials. I sent it to my brother, who responded:

Goering was just a fat drug-addled old Fascist by then with nothing to look forward to other than the hangman's noose – his own 'defence' turned out to be one of the best mini-cabarets of all time. But if you want a quote, then try this: 1) 'He knows no details, has only got half the picture in his mind, talks absurdities and makes my blood boil to listen to his nonsense.' Field Marshal Alan Brooke on Churchill, 1942.

Late tonight the filmmaker Michael Moore outraged Hollywood's elite by mentioning something so trivial as the war at the Oscars – but heavily pregnant Catherine Zeta-Jones calmed things down by getting up on stage and shrieking her 'oggy, oggy' love for Michael, Dylan and Swansea, looking staggeringly pleased with herself. Ugh!

TUESDAY, 25 MARCH

Brian Reade emailed me. 'I just want to say that in the nine years I have worked here, and the 30-odd years I've been reading it, I've never felt so proud of the *Mirror*. When you look at that Wapping rag's Stalinist line, imposed by an American hawk who thinks the price of oil is a reason to go to war, you realise why you wanted to work for this paper instead. Keep it up, don't falter, stick a big cigar in your mouth, it's your finest hour.' I was very cheered by it. My bunker feels a lonely place at the moment.

Anton rang to say he could actually hear American howitzers outside Baghdad. But he can't see in front of his nose because of a weird, thick orange sandstorm that's engulfed the city. I asked him how he was feeling. He said he was nervous, excited, frightened, dirty. He's an astonishingly brave man who has been to many warzones, but I could tell this one's really worrying him. Nobody knows what Saddam will do, but most people fear something very, very nasty. 'If you want to come out, Anton, at any time, don't ask – just do it. But you are doing some incredible journalism in there.' He won't come out, he's one of the bravest guys I've ever worked with.

Basra is said to be uprising, but there's little evidence to support it. I detect more Allied propaganda, which I'm sure is very useful to undermining the Iraqi morale – but does nothing to help the trust between the media and the army chiefs. The two institutions, I fear, are not and never will be compatible bed-fellows in time of war.

Ex-SAS man Andy McNab wrote a brilliant piece for us about the difference between British and American soldiers. 'They've got the gear, we've done the practice,' is his conclusion. Tom Newton-Dunn quoted a marine in a trench outside Basra as saying, 'If Basra's taken, as I keep hearing from Qatar, then why the fuck are we all still sitting out here in the mud and rain?'

Dubya appeared on TV, smirking. He always smirks. And it always irks. Without Blair he'd be buried, PR-wise, on this war. Our Prime Minister has become his mouthpiece, an eloquent articulator of America's unjustified foreign policy. Oh, and Arsenal stuffed Chelsea 3–1 in the FA Cup. I barely notice. Important evidence that even I, sometimes, can accept there are more important things in life than football.

WEDNESDAY, 26 MARCH

Baghdad's marketplace was 'accidentally' hit by American smart bombs, killing fourteen civilians. Bush appeared on TV hours later, smirking again and glad-handing howling US soldiers. I wanted to punch the screen. Blair would never do that, he seems at least to understand that wars are serious things, not a rolling election rally. We did a split front page showing a bereft Iraqi woman amid the market devastation, and Bush celebrating with the headline HE LOVES IT.

I know it's provocative, and harsh. But sod it – he doesn't seem to care about what he's doing, so why should we worry about being fair to him? Later in the afternoon, I got some odd and very disturbing sales figures for the day before. About 60,000 readers seem to have disappeared. And the opinion polls are swinging wildly, too – from anti to pro war. These two facts, I imagine, are connected.

THURSDAY, 27 MARCH

Anita 'Bodyshop' Roddick emailed me to say, 'Your front page today will go down I think in media history as the best.' Blimey, didn't think it was quite in that league, but very nice of her to say so.

Victor thought it was OTT, though. He's very twitchy about our critical front pages. 'Our boys are risking their lives, we have to be supportive,' he said. 'The readers won't like it.'

Al Jazeera, the Arabic TV station, ran a quite horrific photo of a young boy with half his head blown away. It is utterly gut-wrenching, and no British media organisation has gone near it. But the Arab world is seeing this image every ten minutes, all day long, and you can only begin to imagine the fury it is causing.

FRIDAY, 28 MARCH

I heard someone on radio making the valid point that if we'd had all these 24-hour TV cameras at the Somme or in Dresden, we might never have won the world wars, as the public would have been horrified. But I think having the endless frontline footage is helping Bush and Blair – it's making people more patriotic, because they can see the soldiers being shot at. By way of distraction, we offered our readers the classic tabloid tale of Emma Noble's affair behind James Major's back. It didn't get on to page one – another casualty of war …

SUNDAY, 30 MARCH

My birthday. But not much time to think about that. The British marines pushed hard into Basra, and the images that have emerged could be straight out of a Vietnam photo gallery – combat troops trudging and fighting in sludge and grime. They called it Operation James, after 007, and a picture of Mr Newton-Dunn duly arrived of him in dark glasses, scarf and combat trousers standing in front of a mural of Saddam. His sense of humour amid the flying bullets is amazing. A few rainy doorsteps in Scunthorpe will sort our 'special agent hero' out when he returns.

MONDAY, 31 MARCH

Late tonight a car full of women and children was blown to pieces at a check-point by American troops. Seven die. I can understand the anxiety of all Allied forces at these checkpoints following a suicide bombing incident. But the American inexperience in this kind of situation is worrying. They are too trigger-happy, too gung-ho, too nervy. They need to cool down and take a lead from the British in Basra.

Tom Newton-Dunn wrote a hilarious diary from his trench, notable for more evidence that he is indeed 'going native' and starting to revel in the stinking, starving, macho world of sleep-deprived heroism on the front line. His reporting, though, is a constantly brilliant reflection on the reality of being with the commandos on the front line. He concedes, 'It's a 360 degree world of apparent confusion and chaos, and to be honest I've got no idea what's going on.' Anton Antonowicz filed an equally compelling report from Baghdad, describing what it's like to be bombed: 'Each blast, each explosion, sends a tremor through your body. It seems as though your mouth, your ears, your lungs are filled with the force of them.'

We also carried a piece by Mo Mowlam, saying if we want to win this war quickly, then we have to bomb harder. And she's anti-war! No wonder everyone's getting confused about what to think.

TUESDAY, 1 APRIL

Scurra, our *Mirror* diary, asked today who wrote this: 'Our armies do not come into your cities as conquerors or enemies, but as liberators. Your wealth has been

stripped of you by unjust men, the people of Baghdad shall flourish under institutions which are in consonance with their sacred laws.' The answer was
General F. S. Maude, commander of the British forces in Iraq in 1917. It
reminded me of the last time I heard President Bush explaining that going to
war with Saddam would make the world a safer place. That was in 1991, and it
didn't, did it?

British marines have swapped their helmets for their famous green berets in
Basra. A small, but massively symbolic step – sending a message of friendship,
not hostility, to the terrified local people who only remember the way we let
them down last time. We did a big page three leader article praising them, but it
won't cut much ice with the small, but significant body of *Mirror* readers
who've become wrongly convinced that we are anti the forces because we refuse
to buckle and say we now support the war.

Sales may be terrible, but I won't back down completely, because it is too
important. If we temporarily lose some readers on this point of principle, that is
a price we will have to pay. If I'd just turned round on day one of the war and
gone all gung-ho like the *Sun*, then the paper's credibility would be in ruins.
Anton filed his own diary from Baghdad. He is such a powerful writer, truly one
of the best in Fleet Street. I spoke to him and he sounded tired and edgy. There
are less than 30 English-speaking journalists there and he is one of them.

Liz Hurley popped up to lambast the press for invading her privacy. I
thought of Anton risking his life as she preens herself in her mansion – and
chuckled at her absurdity and utter irrelevance.

Later in the day, my circulation manager John Howard brought some more
bad news. Sales have fallen off a cliff this week, absolutely crashed. And he's a
desperate man. 'Piers, I know you're anti this war. But we just can't go on
attacking it while our boys are under fire. It's suicide.' I looked at the figures and
gulped. It's unbelievable: at least 80,000 readers have buggered off. I thought
about this carefully, then wrote an urgent email to Sly Bailey.

> We have a problem, and it's my fault. I'm afraid I misjudged the way our
> readers would respond to the start of the war, and our line has clearly been
> too confrontational and too critical for many of them. We need to be more
> news led, less attitudinal, without abandoning our line (which I still believe
> is right), but without ramming it down people's throats either. I am very
> sorry about this, it means we'll drop below 2 million for the month and that
> is desperately unfortunate. I am sending this email to show you how much
> I care about this situation and how bitterly disappointed I am that this
> should happen. The fall off was very fast and hard to predict given the OK
> build-up. But it's done now and I will just have to get those readers back as
> fast as I can. One thing I won't be doing is sitting here defiantly telling
> myself how I'm right and they are all wrong. The readers are never wrong.
> Editors, as I'm afraid you have just experienced, can be.

Sly called me down and we talked it over. She was understanding and supportive. But understandably rather unnerved by the scale of losses. So was I. 'Sly,
this isn't just a blip, this is a bloody disaster.'

I trudged disconsolately back to the office and called Victor. 'You were right
and I was wrong,' I admitted. 'I was a total arse, in fact, and should have listened
to you properly and done what you suggested. Short of having to call Alex
Ferguson to tell him what a great team he's got, I can think of few more humiliating calls than this.'

Victor was his usual self, reassuringly calm and cheery. He'd be good in the
trenches. But I felt terrible by the end of the day. This is an impending catastro-
phe and that usually means only one thing – the exit door.

WEDNESDAY, 2 APRIL

Alan Milburn has kindly sent me an unutterably tedious pamphlet about his
bold vision for ridding the world of all known diseases. 'I know Iraq is dominating everyone's thoughts – and your coverage – but I thought you might like to
see how money is being spent on the NHS. It would be good to have a chat
soon.' I try and read it, but my brain recedes after a few minutes into a semi-
comatose state. I write back:

> Thanks for your note. I got to page 8 and then felt my eyelids compress-
> ing in a quite worrying way. Perhaps we can wait until the war's over
> before discussing this further. In the meantime I will take your
> pamphlet home tonight as I've been having trouble sleeping and it
> might do the trick.

The Americans are going mad for Private Jessica Lynch, a 19-year-old US PoW
who's been saved by a daring special forces rescue operation. I am thrilled for
her. Not least because of the inevitable movie/TV series/book/video/coffee
advert deals that now loom large and lucratively for her and her family. I see
Spielberg, Hanks, Scarlett Johansson. And a *lot* of schmaltz.

Our own poll, conducted by ICM, was interesting – support for the war is
falling, and four times as many people trust reporters on war as they do George
Bush. Andy McNab assured me the war is going very well now, fast and efficient, and he should know.

But I can't work out what's happening. Either Saddam's storing up his
alleged weapons of mass destruction for one big bang, or he really is the ageing
old tyrant with no army and no meaningful weapons that I thought he was. Soon
we shall know. Britain's surge of patriotism was sealed with England's rout of
Turkey in the European Championships. Private Wayne Rooney was the star,
and I predict the full Jessica Lynch treatment for him too.

THURSDAY, 3 APRIL

Richard Wallace emailed me from New York: 'Keep your chin up, we fight to the death.'

Still nothing from Saddam. What *is* he playing at? Where *are* his Republican Guard? The war is progressing so fast and so easily that almost every armchair pundit who confidently predicted this would be Vietnam 2 is now running for the hills. Tony Blair met some service wives today, and promised to bring their men home. He is having a good war, no question. He's stuck to his guns, literally, and has been serious, sober and statesmanlike. I may not have agreed with him, but there's no denying he is a brilliant politician.

Tara Palmer-Tompkinson laid into the 3am Girls on her LBC radio show this afternoon, calling them 'Absolute mingers who write a load of nonsense and should wear bags over their horrific heads when they go out.' Then she added, 'But Piers Morgan's still handsome, I've heard he's an absolute stallion and goes like a trooper!' I was slightly disconcerted by this tribute. How does she know?

I decided today that we would do a different, lighter, page three for the first time since the war started. Jon Moorhead was not happy and sent an email to a few senior execs, saying:

As you dandle your grandchildren on your knee, telling them the story of how you covered the outbreak of the west's catastrophic 100-year war against Islam, and they ask, 'Tell us, granddad, what were you doing when the imperial forces stormed the gates of Baghdad?' you will always be able to answer, 'I was doing Britney Spears on page 3.'

Very good.

FRIDAY, 4 APRIL

A relatively quiet day, until the TV screens suddenly erupted with video footage of Saddam going on a walkabout in downtown Baghdad. It was astonishing stuff – he was even kissing babies. You can't help thinking he must know something we don't – but what the hell is it?

Other pictures came in, of two female suicide bombers defiantly declaring their martyrdom before doing their terrible business. It was a shocking spectacle. Most of us in Britain can barely comprehend the suicide bomber problem. But we need to if we are ever to solve the root cause of all this mayhem – Palestine.

Anton filed an awful story of an Iraqi man who has lost his daughter to a bomb and who said, 'A shell came as she stood by the dressing-room. Nadia had a PhD in psychology, she was thirty-three and very clever. Everyone said I had a fabulous daughter. She spent all her time studying, she didn't care about enjoying herself. Me? I am just a lorry driver, a simple man.' Anton described it as the saddest story he had ever reported and begged me to read it all. I did, and just wanted to shut my office door and cry for the poor man.

SUNDAY, 6 APRIL

The BBC's John Simpson was bombed by the Americans and finally got the headline attention he's clearly been hoping for, having been stuck out in Northern Iraq after his Baghdad visa was rejected. He may be a rather pompous and self-promoting man, but he is undeniably a quite superb and fearless journalist. His report was electrifying – he is wounded himself and the camera was splattered with blood. But he reported what he had experienced in graphic and compelling detail, barely able to contain his rage at the Americans for targeting his convoy. We also learned of a British helicopter pilot shot at, predictably now, by the Americans – he jumped out of his chopper and punched one of the offending US marines. 'When was the last time you saw a fucking Iraqi in a helicopter?' he shouted. His commanding officer, when grilled about this incident, admitted, 'I'm afraid it would be an RAF kind of thing to do. These guys are not known for tolerating fools gladly.'

Colonel Chris Vernon, army spokesman and a close second to BBC 'Scud Stud' Rageh Omaar as the *Mirror* office heart-throb, announced later today that we've won the war. Bit prematurely, I think. He's certainly won the hearts of a thousand panting women. My sister told me he's been sent 300 pairs of knickers already.

A terrible photo came in of a little boy called Ali Ismaeel Abbas, who has lost his arms and most of his family to a bomb. He pleaded for new hands and said he will commit suicide if he can't have any. It is an image that will haunt this conflict.

Tom Newton-Dunn sent in his own contribution to the day's photo library – a picture of him sitting on Saddam's lavatory. You have to laugh, the tinker.

MONDAY, 7 APRIL

A new comedy star has emerged in the shape of Iraq's Minister for Information, Mohammed Saeed Al-Sahaf. His daily briefings have been genuinely hysterical, but now his performances are reaching BAFTA standard. He reassured us this afternoon that his army had 'retaken the airport' and were 'slaughtering' American infidels all over the place. He also said that no US tanks are in the city, even when we can see them behind him on television rumbling down the high street.

TUESDAY, 8 APRIL

I spent last night in my hotel room watching early rushes of some of my *Tabloid Tales* series.

I emailed Mandelson this morning to say he's come across very well, which he does, but will rate a lot worse than Victoria Beckham, because he's a politician. 'Let's wait and see, shall we … can I have a look at it, so I can warn my mother what to expect?' You have to admire the attempt. 'No,' I replied. 'Of course you can't. But I think both our mothers can watch it safely and ring their little charges at the end to say "There, that wasn't so bad, was it?" '

The Americans bombed the hotel where all the journalists are staying in Baghdad this morning. My first thought, obviously, was for Anton and Mike Moore. A quick call established that they were OK.

But Anton is furious at what's happened. The journalists who've been killed are people he has spent four hellish weeks with. And everyone, *everyone*, knew it was the media hotel.

Mirror readers inundated us with calls about little Ali, so we have launched a front-page appeal for him and all the children of Iraq sacrificed at the altar of 'regime change'.

WEDNESDAY, 9 APRIL

The day of 'liberty'. Quite extraordinary scenes in Baghdad as the Americans just rolled in and took over with barely a rusty old AK-16 raised in anger. Saddam and his army have been defeated without turning up for the fight. It's like Arsenal playing Manchester United for the title – and Sir Alex and his boys just not getting on the team bus for the match. None of it makes any sense. But obviously I, like everyone, am thrilled and relieved it seems to be over so easily. A symbolic statue of Saddam was duly demolished with the help of an American armoured car. But not before a Marine had draped a Stars and Stripes flag on to the despot's head. The exact same flag, it later turned out, that flew on the Pentagon on 9/11.

Suggesting that the American troops think what they are really doing out there is avenging 9/11.

The TV was full of jubilant Iraqis dancing in the streets. But we'd probably get a bit of that if Tony Blair's regime got overthrown. How the wider population feel about this 'liberation', we will see in the next few months. I am sure the warmongers will gloat and taunt those of us who were against this conflict. Let them have their day. I am glad Saddam's gone, but I'd be just as glad if most of the equally repellent regimes in the Middle East and Africa were gone, frankly. Britain still has 300 trading arrangements with Zimbabwe, so please don't tell me we did all this just to unseat a bad guy. We did it primarily to show the world how powerful America is, and how they will deal with the new world order of terrorism and any states who sponsor it. But I personally won't be sleeping any easier tonight just because Saddam Hussein's gone. He was never going to bomb me here in London. But the number of those that will want to has just risen rather dramatically.

Our official monthly ABC sales figures have come out and revealed the scale of the hammering we've suffered. I know what's coming next – endless media 'think' pieces pissing all over us for being morons. And all because we were right about the war.

I emailed Mandelson, urging him to make Blair realise that 'the *Mirror* will be back in line with Labour a bit more once the war's finished. If we were having our euro debate now, then we'd be in the *Sun*'s position and they would be in ours. It's important to remember that.'

He replied:

You don't get noticed by being the same, I realise that. But this leads to some difficult judgement calls for you. The mistake you've made is allowing the impression to grow, through Routledge in particular, that you're just out to get Blair. Re the euro, the battle is on and it's being lost by those who favour entry.

THURSDAY, 10 APRIL

Hilarious letter popped up in the *Independent* from David Yelland, saying how disgraceful I am for supposedly 'humiliating' poor Blair and Bush over Iraq, and talking of his 'profound sadness' over my stupidity. He gave his address as 'Harvard Business School, Massachusetts.' A *school*, for God's sake.

David 'Banksy' Banks, former *Mirror* editor, wrote a very kind letter to say:

I'm prouder of the *Mirror* over the last three months than in any of the 30 years I've been associated with it. Although I reluctantly concluded in the end that invasion was inevitable, your determination to stick by your guns and speak up for what the majority of decent Brits think on the issue of Iraq is the most admirable position the *Mirror*'s taken in my adult memory. I'll stop now, I'm getting hormonal again.

I was really touched.

MONDAY, 14 APRIL

A curious package arrived from New York containing a front page of the *Sun*. I was slightly bemused, as it carried my head superimposed on to the now famous photograph of Saddam's statue tumbling down. There was a headline saying 'MIRROR MIRROR ON THE FALL … the *Sun* is the greatest of them all.' And a second headline, up by the masthead, saying: 'ANOTHER SHADY REGIME IS SET TO TOPPLE – see pages 2–98.'

All terribly amusing. But hang on, what was this scrawled across the middle? A handwritten signature. Closer examination confirmed my first analysis: Rupert Murdoch. This was obviously a wind-up.

But then I checked the envelope and it had been Fedexed from News America in Manhattan, Murdoch's company address. I rang Rebekah Wade asking what on earth it was all about. She burst out laughing, and confirmed that Murdoch rang up specifically requesting the page be drawn up by the *Sun*'s finest production operatives, had it flown to New York for him to personally autograph, then flew it back to me at Canary Wharf.

You'd think he might have more pressing things to concentrate his mind in his global empire than going to so much trouble to take the piss out of me. But it's a splendid piece of journalistic memorabilia whichever way you look at it, and I have already sent it off to be framed for the loo wall. I emailed Liz

Murdoch to tell her what her father had done. She replied, 'That's pretty funny … somewhat complimentary in an odd sort of way … and pretty damn rude!'

TUESDAY, 15 APRIL

Had dinner tonight with the leader of the House of Commons, John Reid, at his very plush home in Westminster, with his wife Carine, Margaret McDonagh and Waheed Ali. As I sat having a welcome drink on a large sofa, Reid suddenly said, 'That's where David English died.' I sat up with a start. 'What? The Mail editor?' Reid nodded. 'Yes, this was his old home, and he had a serious stroke right here and then died in hospital.' Reid was on good form all night. He gave up drinking ten years ago, but doesn't mind everyone else piling in. By 11pm he was on his electric piano singing 'Wind Beneath My Wings' in a rather fetching falsetto. There's more to Dr Reid than meets the eye.

I got up and had a bash at 'Let It Be', just about the only thing I can remember how to play, but couldn't get past the first few bars, so we all just sang the chorus repeatedly. I like Reid. He's a no-nonsense, bruising old pro. Very loyal to Blair, and utterly determined to sell the Government's record in a better light. 'We're doing a pretty good job, but the constant media abuse and negativity means nobody realises it,' he said.

THURSDAY, 17 APRIL

Tina O'Brien and Bruno Langley, who play Sarah Platt and Todd Grimshaw in *Coronation Street*, and are real-life lovers, have written me a furious letter complaining about paparazzi photos being taken without their permission:

> We accept our roles may prompt interest in us as a couple, but we have never courted publicity and are keen to keep our off-screen relationship as private as possible. We have recently had to suffer gross invasions into our private lives and will not hesitate to go to the PCC to stop the paparazzi harassing and pursuing us.

I replied:

> Dear Tina and Bruno, thanks for your fascinating letter. I can assure you that you will enjoy a much less distressing relationship with the papers if you take yourselves ever so slightly less seriously and lighten up a bit. For what it's worth, I think you're both terrific young actors and I promise you there is one thing worse than being photographed at the height of your fame and that's not being photographed when everybody's lost interest.

TUESDAY, 22 APRIL

A Mr Kazuya Endo, deputy director of the Japan Information and Cultural Centre, complains that we have used the word 'Japs' again. 'Even if this is a shortened version of "Japanese" due to space limitations, it can sound like a racial slur and, as such, is offensive to Japanese people.' Fair enough.

TUESDAY, 29 APRIL

My *Tabloid Tales* series started on BBC1 tonight with the Posh programme, amid some hilariously damning previews. My favourite was the *Standard*, which said, 'The programme-makers have had a chuckle, turning Morgan into a self-important comic character – Piers Brent, long-lost brother of David from *The Office*.' Most of the texts I get refer to my hair rather than my interviewing skills. 'You've got a right dodgy mullet there,' was about the gist of it. Knew I shouldn't have bowed to pressure to have hairspray.

WEDNESDAY, 30 APRIL

Fiona Phillips emailed me. 'You smug old bastard, is there nothing you're not good at? You'd have a great career in television if only people liked you. I can give you some coaching if you like, I know how much you admire my professionalism ...'

THURSDAY, 1 MAY

Sat next to British Airways boss Rod Eddington at the monthly lunch today, and he revealed some of the hidden reasons Concorde had to be axed.

'Look, we lost about forty of our most regular Concorde fliers in the World Trade Center disaster. And after that our top dozen or so corporate clients decided it was too big a security risk and switched from Concorde accounts to normal first-class Jumbos and stuff.

'I'm talking about clients spending millions a year.

'Add the fact that a lot of other people stopped flying altogether, and you can see that it became very quickly a financial disaster to run.'

I asked him if money was the only factor in his decision.

'No, no, it was getting old anyway, and the parts were costing a fortune because nobody makes them any more. It would have stopped soon, regardless of 9/11.'

'Why don't you give it to Branson?'

'Because he can't afford to run it, it's all bluff. And anyway, I don't think our Concorde staff would work for him, they're all very loyal BA people. So he'd have nobody to fly it even if he could afford it.'

FRIDAY, 2 MAY

We've run a big interview with Fayed about his decision to quit Britain because the taxman is hounding him so much. He was delighted. 'Dear Piers, thank God for an editor with balls! I have many friends willing to back me privately but it takes real courage to do what you have done and I thank you from the bottom of my heart.'

Steve Dennis came to see me. 'We've done a deal with Penguin for the book.'

'How rich are you, then?'

'Erm, well, I've done OK out of it.'

'Come on, how much? Tell me or you're fired.'

A joke, obviously.

He told me what he and Burrell were getting.

'Fuck my boots,' I replied. 'I'm in the wrong job.'

MONDAY, 5 MAY

Arsenal failed to win the League, and Sugar sent me a typically heartfelt message of sympathy: 'I'm sure you will know by now how genuinely sad I feel that Arsenal didn't win the Championship. You can surely feel the emotion coming through your screen.'

My old City Slicker friend Anil Bhoyrul wrote to me out of the blue, apologising for the endless bile he's been churning out about me in the *Sunday Express* under various pseudonyms:

> Nothing would make me happier than not having to write all this stuff, but then nobody else pays me £6k a month. I don't sit at home thinking 'how can I fuck Piers this week?' – the thinking behind that column comes as you can guess from people above me. It is those people who have issues with you, Piers, not me. I have no scores to settle with you. What happened in 2000 happened. My memories are of the two best years of my working life with you and I will always be grateful for that. The *Mirror* these days is fucking great. For the first time in my life I am reading it every day, something I never did even when I worked there.

THURSDAY, 8 MAY

Victor said my job is 'safe for the moment' at the AGM, prompting everyone to start speculating on quite why he felt the need to qualify that support – not least of all me. He called to apologise later, saying he didn't mean it the way it sounded. I suspect that's true, but the damage is done and all the headlines surround that 'at the moment' line.

Philip Graf summed it up in an email that said: 'Oh dear, I hope that isn't the dreaded vote of confidence. Hang on in there.'

Later I appeared on Andrew Neil's live *This Week* politics show and got five seconds into my 'The trouble with Tony Blair is ...' speech when there was a huge explosion and all the power cut out. I sat there with Andrew, Michael Portillo and Diane Abbott, laughing nervously and wondering what the hell was going to happen next. The answer was nothing. They couldn't get the power back on, the whole of Westminster had gone down, and since the show was live, that was it for the night. I called my mother, who I knew was watching at home, to reassure her that we hadn't been terminated by Al Qaeda. She said they were running *Dr Finlay's Casebook* now, which she likes anyway, so not to worry.

FRIDAY, 9 MAY

Sarah Brown has written a book on public figures and their mentors. I chose Kelvin, and penned a short adulatory tribute to the great man, paying homage to this 'raging, cackling, mischievous, monstrous, brilliant genius'. I sent him a copy of it this afternoon, saying, 'I don't know what came over me … I think alcohol played a large part in this and would like to retract it all, obviously.'

He replied: 'Have you gone mad? That's the only flattering thing written about me for almost 40 years of being in the game. I have no idea what this book's about, but I suspect if your offering is anything to go by they won't sell many.' He'll be quietly pleased, though.

Simon Cosyns quit today to go back to the *Sun*. That's all I need right now. My No. 3 defecting to the enemy. I sent him home in a blind fury, and would have happily thrown him off the top of the tower if I'd had the chance.

TUESDAY, 13 MAY

Took Alastair to the refurbished Savoy Grill for lunch. He was on ebullient form.

'We won the war, and did it quickly,' he said. 'And when we find all the WMD and mass graves and so on, then people will understand why we had to do it.'

'What if you don't?' I asked.

He looked affronted. 'Oh, come on, you don't seriously think we won't find anything. Saddam's been developing WMD for years. And anyway, you can see by the reaction in Iraq that they are all delighted he's gone.'

Alastair was pumped up with victory radiance. It glowed off him. And I found myself strangely muted.

'Yes, well, I guess it's turned out well for you in the end. Tony had a good war, I'll give him that. Much better than Bush.'

'Yes, well he was better advised. The Americans have a different view of it all, and a different way of doing things. You have to understand that.'

We both tried to order the steak and kidney pie, but when it came it had no pastry, just a thin coating. 'Where's the crust?' Alastair berated the waiter.

'Gone, sir. It's a pudding now, not a pie.'

'Well, we want the old pie back,' we choroused.

'Sorry, sir, it's gone.'

Madness.

I asked Alastair how Blair felt now. 'Relieved, I think, and tired. It's been exhausting, but we're over the worst now and he can relax a bit.'

'And you?'

'I don't know what I'll do, to be honest. I was going to go a while ago, before Anji resigned, but Tony persuaded me to stay on for Iraq. He knew it would be a huge political fireball and he was right. But I fluctuate between wanting to go now, and thinking that I will never get as big a buzz from anything else.'

We discussed my Mandelson show. 'Yes, it was interesting. I agree with you he was right to be sacked first time, but not the second, with hindsight.'

'Could you have him back again?'

'I don't think so, no. Everyone would just slate Tony for taking a risk again. But if Tony ever stood down, and Gordon took over leading the party, for argument's sake, then he'd be mad not to give Peter something.'

'Would Gordon make a good leader?'

'Yes, he would. But he's a bloody good Chancellor at the moment and Tony's going nowhere.'

We exchanged the usual jibes about football, then called it a day.

I asked Mandelson what he thought of the show. 'Well, everyone said I looked very handsome, so that is something. My criticism is over the choice of other interviewees, who were the worst possible assassins. It's not acceptable for Trevor Kavanagh to call me a congenital liar. Rich coming from him. I am not, and I think the viewers should have been told by someone other than me that these people are self-interested, self-obsessed wankers who would not recognise the truth if it hit them in the face. But apart from that, fifty per cent of the people volunteering a view thought I came out of it well, so onwards and upwards, or at least forwards.'

I then told him about my meeting. 'I had lunch with Alastair today, who said he agreed with my summary that you were done in fairly the first time, but unfairly the second time. He also said, intriguingly, that were Gordon ever to get the top job he'd be mad not to have you back. Interesting coming from him.'

He wasn't happy.

'If AC thinks GB should bring me back, that means TB won't in the meantime. Very interesting.'

Phil Tufnell's won *I'm a Celebrity* … and is trying to flog his life story for a six-figure sum. I remembered a great autobiography he did a few years ago, and we quietly bought serialisation rights this morning for £10,000. It's got everything you'd want – sex, drugs, booze. And all for a pittance. I did a big page one blurb: 'MY STORY – Tuffers in his own amazing words!' A good day's work.

WEDNESDAY, 21 MAY

Mandelson has piled into Brown and Blair for dithering on the euro. He's bang on about this, and I sent an email saying, 'Fantastic stuff today. You are so right.'

He replied rather dolefully, 'I wish your email had arrived yesterday when I was feeling at my most kicked and lowest with dishonesty spilling out from every direction. They want to shut me up but I have written again in the *Guardian* today. Anything you can do to support.'

I wrote a full leader article calling on Blair and Brown to bang their heads together and put their differences behind them, for the sake of party unity, likening them to Lennon and McCartney, and Mandelson to Brian Epstein. Together, it all sort of works, divided it splits into acrimony and mayhem. These guys could conquer the world political stage if they just stopped trying to kill each other all the time.

THURSDAY, 22 MAY

Mandelson was on first thing:

> Interesting paper today and excellent leader. Why don't you help bring about what you advocate? How can I, as Oonagh says in her intro, have deepened my bitter feud with the Chancellor with an interview I did months ago? You talk about a deadly rift, but when Gordon reads this sort of thing, isn't it just going to make the animosity all the deeper? I do not harbour these feelings about him actually or against him, but when the stereotypical writing kicks in like this, it makes it almost impossible to repair.

I replied:

> Gordon can either keep sucking up to Murdoch or he can realise that actually if he does the right thing on the euro, gives TB the legacy he wants, he still might be king. And if he was really clever he'd have you back as Foreign Secretary or something.

Mandelson responded tersely:

> GB is doing as much damage to himself as I am to myself. And TB is simply not achieving as much as he could and should be because of what all of us are doing to each other. We are at a Rubicon in my view. We either recognise this and draw back or step over a cliff. Can you help?

'Yes,' I said, 'I can.'

FRIDAY, 23 MAY

Brown's apoplectic with Mandelson, and his people briefed us the usual poison. They will never stop, on either side.

THURSDAY, 29 MAY

Jonathan Aitken and Ken Livingstone were the star guests of our monthly lunch. The latter was calm, amusing, and clearly revelling in his mayoral job. I also think he's doing a bloody good job, and told him so.

'Yes, well, perhaps I have turned out to be not quite the loony monster everyone feared,' he laughed. And he hasn't, that's the truth.

Aitken was fascinating. His hands shook quite a lot, a sign perhaps of the trauma that going to prison must have caused him. But I found him genuinely remorseful, yet with no bitterness and a total acceptance of his failings.

'Look, what I did was wrong. I let my arrogance get the better of me. It was stupid and I paid the price.'

He was very interesting about the drugs problem in jails. 'It's a vicious cycle. People come in who may have taken cannabis before, but that is actually quite rare inside because it stays in the blood stream for a month, so you will almost certainly be caught in a random test.

'But cocaine and ecstasy disappear after thirty-six hours, so there is always loads of class A stuff around. If they do a line or two of cocaine then they often drink twelve pints of water to make sure if they do get tested in that small window, their urine for the sample is clear.

'Drug barons support this situation by swamping the prisons with very cheap coke and ecstasy, the prisoners get hooked on it, and then when they get released they are met by the same dealers, only the price has rocketed.

'They need the stuff, so they have to go thieving to pay for it. They get caught eventually, and go back inside and it all starts again.'

I would make Aitken prisons minister tomorrow.

Got back to the office to find a letter from *Mail* editor Paul Dacre, now back at the helm after a heart operation. 'I take two months off and you still lose circulation,' he started with typical modesty. 'On the health front, my doctors say I will have more energy than before, so you'd better watch out.'

I can't think of anything to say by response other than: 'Dear Paul, fuck – you're still alive. Piers'

He'll like that. Brutal, to the point, totally devoid of any compassion. Very *Daily Mail*.

TUESDAY, 3 JUNE

Prince William threw a birthday drinks party tonight at St James's Palace for a few editors. Or rather, he was ordered to, when he would almost certainly rather spend the night in a cage full of ravenous hyenas. Whenever editors get together in a confined area like this, it is always an amusing clash of gigantic egos. Nobody wants to lose face or concede that any other editor is more important or distinguished than he or she is. So as we waited for William to appear, our motley group of ten or so editors circled each other like basking sharks, swapping jibes. When he eventually arrived, we were told that he would meet us in little groups, but I quickly noticed the first group was the broadsheet one, led by the *Telegraph*'s Charles Moore.

Well I wasn't having that. So I just walked over and joined in their chat, to Moore's splendidly lofty horror. I had the advantage of actually knowing the young Prince, and more importantly knowing that he has a good sense of humour.

'Hi, William, need saving from these dreadful broadsheet reptiles?' I said. He burst out laughing. 'Ah, Piers, wondered how long it would take you. No, I'm fine, thank you.' A few minutes later, we were able to talk on our own for a bit. I took the chance to mention Paul Burrell. 'You guys should close him down before you regret it,' I said. He looked a bit bemused. 'What do you mean? He's already done his interview with you, it's too late.' 'Oh, come off it, William, that was just the tip of the iceberg, and you know it. Paul feels very aggrieved by the way he's been treated. Why have none of you bothered to contact him and just say sorry, or see how he is?'

William looked suddenly very serious. 'I have wanted to, several times, but I am not allowed to.' I asked if he thought his mother would have made the call anyway. He nodded. 'Yes, probably.'

I obviously know that Burrell is doing his book with Steve Dennis. But I've always felt that if the royals took him back in, he might can it.

'William, if he does a book or something, then all sorts of stuff will come out. But it's not too late, you could stop him by bringing him back into the fold.'

'What do you mean?'

'I mean employ him again, here at the Palace or something. He was incredibly loyal to your mother, and would never have betrayed her. He didn't say a word about her for five years after she died, despite huge offers to do so. Millions, literally. But you guys then kicked him in the teeth.'

William recoiled. 'The police misled us,' he said defensively. 'They said he'd been selling the stuff.'

'Yes, they did,' I replied. 'But you must have known in your heart that he wouldn't have let your mother down?'

He didn't respond for a few seconds. Then he nodded: 'I hear you, I do.'

We were then joined by several other editors and I decided to lighten the mood by congratulating him on the size of his huge feet, which had been on show in the recent official birthday photos. 'Thanks,' he said, 'and can I congratulate you on your six-pack, Piers ... or should I say keg.'

Cue much fawning hilarity from my rivals. 'Very droll, your royal highness, very droll. Some of us have to work for a living, you know.' As the champagne flowed, I thought it might be appropriate to record this historic event, and pinged a sneaky picture of William meeting Andy Coulson on my mobile phone. William wheeled round. 'Hey, what are you doing, Morgan?' 'Just sneaking a paparazzi photo of you with the gutter press, sir,' I replied. He laughed, so I took the bull by the horns. 'Come on, how about a souvenir photo with all of us?' Some of the editors feigned mock horror at this request, but I could tell they were all secretly longing to have a picture. 'We can use my mobile if you like.' William looked at his aides, who didn't know quite what to say. 'Relax, it won't be published, and nobody's going to get hurt, are they?' William laughed. 'Oh, OK then.'

So we then all lined up on, and by, the sofa as Prince Charles' new adviser, Sir Michael Peat took several snaps of us on my phone. After the first one I moved from standing at the back to kneeling at the front beside him. 'Just think at least one of us should be showing some proper deference,' I explained. It was all very funny, and he played along superbly well. William seems a top lad, bright and confident and up for a laugh.

WEDNESDAY, 4 JUNE
Steve Dennis came to see me.

'Think you'd better know some of the stuff in the book before you see the Penguin people and agree serialisation,' he said.

'Go on, then.'

'There's a letter.'

'Right.'

'Handwritten by Diana.'

'I'm listening.'

'Eight months before she died.'

'Yep.'

'Predicting that she'd be killed in a car crash.'

'*What?* Who by?'

'We can't say that, we are putting the letter in the book, but the name will have to be blank.'

'OK, but who is it then?'

'I don't really want to say.'

'I'm still your boss, and I need to know.'

'OK. Prince Charles.'

THURSDAY, 5 JUNE
Got a worrying phone call from Frank Bruno today. He sounded barking mad, making no sense at all. I've heard lots of sad rumours about his mental demise, but it was really shocking to hear it for myself. I want to help him, but what can anyone do?

Spoke to Steve Purdew, a mate who owns a load of health clubs like Henlow Grange, about it, because he knows Frank well.

'Mate, he's gone, I can't get through to him. It's terrible.'

Later in the day, we got wind that British Telecom had done a deal with the *Sun* to slash the price of their paper by 6p to promote some new deal BT are running. We were hoping to land this business, which will add around 100,000 to the day's sale. In fact I even called the BT boss Ben Verwaayen to try and twist his arm. To be fair, he did make a few calls and rang later to say had he known a bit earlier, he might have been able to swing it our way. But as I sat furious in my office, another idea sprang into my head and I called Charles Dunstone, boss of BTs biggest rival, Carphone Warehouse.

'Charlie,' I said, 'how do you fancy helping us fuck the *Sun* at the same time as you fuck BT?' He laughed, and asked how. 'Simple,' I replied. 'Pay for us to cut the price of the Mirror by 12p this Friday, and I'll give you half the front page and all of page three to plug whatever you like.' I then explained the background in more detail. He laughed again. 'OK, sounds good to me, I'll get back to you.' And he did, showing the speed and decisiveness that's made him around £800 million. Within a couple of hours it was all agreed.

FRIDAY, 6 JUNE

The *Sun* only found out what we were doing at midnight, far too late to change their own deal – and they were locked into the 6p price anyway, because of BT's promotion. The BT guys have gone apeshit, calling all my commercial people, swearing blue murder. But Charles Dunstone is delighted, sending me an email saying, 'It's fantastic, the other guys must be feeling sick. Thanks for thinking of us, it's a great coup.'

Penguin's top brass came to see me in the afternoon about the Burrell book. I agreed to pay £500,000. It's probably worth double that, but their options are limited given that my reporter has written it.

Secrecy is paramount, though. Just a handful of people are going to know.

THURSDAY, 12 JUNE

Alan Milburn resigned today, which was a genuine shock. All the usual rumours swirled around about secret affairs, a drink problem, etc. Nobody ever believes a minister can just quit without being forced to. But when he called me, he sounded like he'd just had enough. 'I've got a young family and I'm just fed up with never seeing them,' he said.

'No lovechild we don't know about, then?'

'God, no, I wouldn't have time,' he laughed. 'I am going to genuinely spend more time with my family, and if people don't want to believe that, then that's up to them. The grind of a job like this is pretty devastating to family life. And I have just reached the point in my life where I don't want it any more. My relationship won't survive if I don't do this now.'

I wished him well. Ever since he came into the bearpit of our monthly lunch and gave as good as he got, I'd changed my mind about Milburn and come to like him. And he was one of the few ministers to call regularly and ask for ideas, and then actually act on some of them.

He'll be back, I am sure of that. He's too ambitious and too talented.

Lots of rumours that David Beckham's going to Barcelona. But when I called Caroline McAteer to ask if it was true, she said, 'I'd think more Real Madrid, if I were you.' I told the sports desk to lead the back on Becks for Real. When the other papers dropped, they had all gone with Barcelona. But why would he go there when he can go to Real? Nobody does that. And Caroline wouldn't steer me that way if it wasn't true. The sports desk aren't convinced though, and are worried, understandably, that their editor may have cocked it up again.

WEDNESDAY, 18 JUNE
David Beckham signed tonight for Real Madrid. I don't know who was more pleased – him, or me.

FRIDAY, 20 JUNE
Had a great dinner party at my flat tonight, starring the two greatest spin doctors in modern British history – Mandelson and Mark Bolland – together with Mark's partner PCC Director Guy Black, Rebekah and Ross, and my news editor Conor Hanna and his girlfriend Joanne. It was a raucous, amusing evening. Mark is obviously pretty cheesed off with the way he was treated in the end by Charles. He did so much to rehabilitate our future King, and to make the public accept his relationship with Camilla. Only to be kicked out by a bunch of suits. Mandelson's story is not, of course, very different.

FRIDAY, 27 JUNE
Campbell's gone to war with the BBC over a *Today* programme claim that he 'sexed up' the government's Iraq war dossier, inserting bogus claims about Saddam unleashing WMD within 45 minutes. The reporter, Andrew Gilligan, changed his claim after his first broadcast, but Campbell's gone for the jugular anyway – even though hardly anybody heard it. I called him tonight. 'What on earth are you doing this for?'

He sounded indignant and angry. 'Because they got it wrong and they have refused to apologise, and the BBC's been doing this for too long.'

'Alastair, mate, this is madness. You can't win a war with the BBC – the public will always be on their side against a government. And they're not that biased, it's nonsense to say that.'

'They fucking are, and I'm not having them smear me like this.'

'But Alastair, you're not important. All this will do is make everyone focus on Iraq again just when you've had a chance to go back to a domestic agenda. And that's not going to be good for Tony. This is personal, and you should rise above it.'

'It is personal, yes. But they are effectively saying I deliberately inserted false claims, knowing they were false, to justify the war. And that is a disgrace.'

'But no one heard it, and no one really cares. Now everyone will pile in, and you are bound to get a load of crap over it. All the media will jump in behind the Beeb.'

He sounded vaguely demented. 'I don't care, they are going to apologise.'

The first rule of being a spindoctor is never become the story. Alastair has lost his marbles.

FRIDAY, 4 JULY

I went to David Frost's annual summer garden party for the first time last night. I'd only got about ten yards inside when I bumped into Alastair chatting conspiratorially to General Mike Jackson. The pair of them rounded on me. 'Now here's someone who needs reconstructing, General,' snarled Campbell; 'have you met Piers Morgan, the anti-war editor?' Jackson eyed me with that craggy ravaged face of his. 'No, haven't had the dubious pleasure. You must be very proud of yourself,' he growled.

I wasn't going to just stand taking this crap. 'Not as proud as you must be of waging an illegal war, General. What are you doing with Alastair, just getting your orders to go and bomb Iran and Syria as well?'

He genuinely looked like he wanted to punch my lights out. Then he cackled. 'What would you possibly know about war?' he said.

'Well, General, I do know we haven't found any WMD yet, and forgive me but I thought that was why we did it in the first place.'

'Listen to me, Morgan,' he snapped back loudly. 'Let me explain. It's very simple. Bad guy got slotted, OK? What's your problem, for God's sake?'

'My problem, General, is that there are lots of bad guys out there and we can't just march into all their countries slotting them or the world will end.'

His eyes screwed up. 'What a load of typically sanctimonious left-wing bollocks. Saddam Hussein was a tyrant and the world is a safer place now he's gone.'

I told him my brother's in the army, and is just as deluded as he is about Iraq. 'Is he? Good man. He must be ashamed to have a brother like you.' I laughed. 'No, no, General, I'd say he is very fortunate, actually. I can point out the error of his ways.'

We carried on exchanging barbs and jibes for about twenty minutes. He's actually good fun, and didn't seem to mind me giving him a bit of stick back. We agreed to have lunch soon so he can 'enlighten' me further.

It was a very nice, if bizarre, event – the great and the good all circling one another in a pretty little central London square, with no obvious connections other than they are all famous and know David Frost. I found Linford Christie lurking by a tree on his own at one stage. 'Hi, Linford, what are you doing here, mate?' I said. 'Don't really know, just got invited. So I thought I'd come down,' he replied.

SUNDAY, 6 JULY

I've always wanted to take part in the famous, and very competitive, River Café quiz, and Miriam Stoppard arranged for me to get a *Mirror* table tonight to take on the finest brains in Britain. Everyone was there, from Stephen Fry to John Mortimer, Jeremy Paxman to Nick Hornby. You can have who you like on your table of six, and I've pulled off a masterstroke by persuading *Who Wants To Be a Millionaire?* winner Judith Keppel to come along. Her arrival sparked a mild storm of interest, concern and fury. Judith turned out to be a charming, vivacious and unbelievably clever woman.

We did exceptionally well, mainly because anything Judith couldn't answer was answered by one of my other big-brained team members – Guy Black. Towards the end we nearly got shafted when the wrong answer was given out to a question. I raced over to register a formal complaint, rather vocally. Everyone seemed appalled. You just don't do that kind of thing at the River Café quiz, apparently.

Well sod that, I'm afraid: I'd come here to win. The answer was eventually changed, enabling us to come a close second to Hornby's team. Since his sister Gill does the questions, I claimed a moral victory.

Bumped into Stephen Fry after it had finished – I hadn't encountered him since he said on Radio Four that 'the new definition of "countryside" is the murder of Piers Morgan.' A great line, admittedly, but I pretended to be still deeply hurt as I confronted him about it. 'Oh, God, I'm sorry, it was only a little joke,' he babbled, as I stood angrily telling him I was going to exact terrible revenge.

'I really am awfully sorry,' he squirmed. Then I laughed. 'Relax, mate, it was funny. But I am going to have to get you to write it down on a piece of paper so I can frame it for the loo wall.' He looked relieved that this was to be his only punishment, and agreed to my request.

THURSDAY, 10 JULY

Nelson Mandela was in town to make an AIDS speech at Westminster City Hall, and I'd been invited to a reception afterwards. I'd never met the great man, and always wanted to obviously, so I headed down there for 3pm. He took five minutes to shuffle to the stage with his walking stick, and seemed very frail. But once there, he made one of the most amazing speeches I've ever heard – short, blistering and utterly inspiring. Most of it was a clarion call to world leaders to fight AIDS, which he said is now claiming more lives than 'the sum total of all wars, famines, floods and deadly other diseases'.

But he also had a whack at Bush and Blair over Iraq, making his disgust at their actions very apparent. I joined the standing ovation at the end, breathless with awe for a man who more than lives up to his legend. At the reception afterwards, there were 200 people at twenty pre-allotted tables waiting to meet the great man. I was on Table 19 and realised I was never going to get near him. I called over the Red Cross PR woman and explained that I had to get back to edit the paper and was there any way I could move up the queue a bit. She had a quick word with her bosses, and I was suddenly ushered straight towards Mandela. Two seats were set up for us, and I sat down on my own next to him. I couldn't believe it.

'Mr Mandela, this is Piers Morgan, editor of the Mirror newspaper which opposed the Iraq war,' said the Red Cross boss. Mandela shook my hand and eyed me carefully. 'That's good to hear.' I congratulated him on his speech and said we were going to lead the paper on his comments about Blair. 'Well, he and Bush have made a bad mistake in Iraq. All the Americans want is the oil, and your Prime Minister has become the US Foreign Minister. You must tell your readers this. It has got to be exposed.' I was staggered by his frankness, but then I guess Mandela doesn't have to worry about his p's and q's too much at this stage of his life. We talked a bit about AIDS, and I told him we did a front-page special edition on the issue, but got ridiculed for it.

'It is the biggest threat mankind has faced,' he said. 'Don't worry what people say, you must continue to press for world leaders to take more action. The drugs to fight AIDS just aren't getting to the people suffering from the disease.'

Richard Young, the legendary photographer, had by now appeared from the shadows to start taking pictures of me and Mandela. I could see the loo wall getting cleared already. I asked if we could pose together for the famous Mandela 'two-shot'. He looked bemused. 'What do you mean, young man?' 'You know, the one where we both give cheesy smiles to the camera as we shake hands. You have to do that for everyone you ever meet.' He chuckled, a big earthy chuckle. 'OK, let's do it, then.'

We posed, very cheesily. Everyone laughed. 'Now, Mr Mandela, I wonder if I could ask you the really big question,' I said, looking as serious as I could. 'And what is that?' he replied.

'Well, do you think that right now … you or David Beckham is more famous?' He burst out laughing. 'Ah, Beckham. He is very famous now. I think he is more famous than me, definitely.'

My seven-minute audience was over, and I said goodbye. 'Goodbye, young man, and please keep fighting in your paper.'

I was halfway back to the office when Jon Moorhead, who used to design my Bizarre column on the *Sun* all those years ago, complete with endless shots of me with stars, called from the back bench where Richard Young had already sent in his snaps.

'God, man, you've done Mandela. You can retire now.'

And that's almost how I feel. I can't imagine meeting anyone else in my lifetime more impressive or more inspiring.

FRIDAY, 11 JULY

Had dinner tonight with Ian Botham at his brilliant lawyer Naynesh Desai's place in Hampstead. Beefy came straight from a 'long lunch' with his bank manager, which was a rather worrying sign. But he was on top form – until former England fast bowler Devon Malcolm arrived to join us, anyway. Trouble flared when I asked Devon to select his all-time greatest England team. It was all OK until he got to the all-rounder slot and chose Alec Stewart. Mr Botham was not amused. 'Alec Stewart … *Alec bloody Stewart*. How many test wickets did he fucking get, eh?'

Devon chuckled mischievously. 'Sorry, Beefy, mate, but you're not in my team.' Now Dev's a big lad, but that didn't deter Ian from putting his head in an instant armlock. Eventually he released him, but Devon still refused to pick him in his team. Furious Beefy marched off to the loo, but stumbled as he re-entered the sitting room, fell on his face and slid ten feet into a fishtank.

MONDAY, 14 JULY
We ran the results of our big Iraq poll today, splashing on the fact that 66 per cent of the public think Blair misled them over the war. But a small majority still think he was right to take action.

Mandelson, inevitably, latched on to that point. 'Your poll is brilliant, having just seen it. After months of all this stuff in the media, a majority still think Blair's right over Iraq. Are they stupid or what?'

A few minutes later, Campbell also emailed me, using almost identical language: 'Interesting poll ... after months of biased, one-sided, anti-TB propaganda on Iraq and weeks of it led by the BBC, a majority still think he did the right thing. You spindoctors just can't tell it straight can you ...'

Oh, ho, ho.

I read both emails again and replied to Campbell first:

'I just got exactly the same email from Mandelson. You spindoctors only have yourselves to talk to these days obviously.'

'How are sales?' he sneered back.

'Booming now the fickle public have realised I was right all along. Surprised you're still there. Surely it's time you became Sir Alex's official lickspittle defendant of all his crimes against humanity. You've had enough practice with TB and his murderous rampage around the globe.'

'Will you never learn about pride before a fall?' he jibed.

I then emailed Mandelson: 'Alastair just sent exactly the same message – clear evidence that the world's two most lethal spin merchants are back working in cahoots to save TB.'

'And a good thing too,' he replied. 'Great minds think alike. So let's agree that if we set fire to the house everyone might get incinerated as a result.'

TUESDAY, 15 JULY
I interviewed Fergie today for a Channel 4 series I am presenting on fame. She was incredibly nervous, and terrified of dropping a clanger. She seemed more vulnerable than last time I'd seen her, though she's lost a fair bit of weight and looked great. After twenty minutes of gentle probing about the pressures of fame, she said she had to stop, and looked close to tears.

She'd just finished telling me how when all the toe-sucking scandals broke, mothers at her girls' school actually crossed the road to avoid talking to her.

'It was very upsetting,' she said in a hushed voice. And tears had sprung up again in her eyes.

'I'm sorry, people don't know how cruel they are when they do that kind of thing. I can't go on, you've got enough now haven't you?'

I really felt for her. She's got her life back on track and is making lots of money. But underneath, the scars of her brutalising treatment by the media have never healed, and probably never will. Fergie-baiting was a sport to us, but it nearly ruined this fun-loving, confident and inherently nice woman.

FRIDAY, 18 JULY

A sensational news day. I was lying in bed watching TV when they suddenly flashed up that Dr David Kelly, the Iraq expert who was exposed last week as the source of Andrew Gilligan's claim that the Government 'sexed up' their Iraq war dossier, had gone missing.

I felt the hairs on my back shooting up. Was he dead? Had he killed himself, or been killed?

God, this was going to be huge. And potentially disastrous for Blair.

I called the newsdesk to find out what we knew. The word was that Kelly hadn't been seen since going for a walk yesterday, and police feared he was dead.

I raced into the office. This was about as dramatic as politics could ever get.

At 11am, a body was found. And at 2pm it was confirmed as Kelly's. He had almost certainly killed himself. An appalling tragedy for him and his family.

The repercussions are going to be massive. Blair was apparently 'very rattled' on his flight home tonight. And he looked terrible when he disembarked. He knows how serious this is.

SATURDAY, 2 AUGUST

To Ian Botham's box for the Test Match, and the day was hugely enlivened by the first public appearance of freed jailbird Jeffrey Archer. He's been stripped of his MCC membership, so can't go to the Lords pavilion as usual. As a protest, *Daily Mail* sportswriter Ian Wooldridge asked Botham if he could bring the shamed lord into his box for the day. Beefy, always keen to protest at the MCC, immediately agreed.

Archer looked slimmer than the last time, and his rhetoric was just as bombastic as ever, but his eyes looked duller, his demeanour a touch less confident. His hands were shaking slightly and I could tell he was finding this quite an ordeal under all the bravado.

Around tea, my mobile phone started firing off with messages from various Sunday paper editors. I had been clocked by the TV cameras guffawing with Archer.

Neil Wallis at the *News of the World* texted to ask if I could save them a lot of time and money by asking my new chum who he's sleeping with at the moment. I'd had a few too many Pimms by then, so went over and asked the question.

Archer smirked, a little wearily. 'No comment.'

MONDAY, 4 AUGUST

A reader called Mr Sparks from Derby has written, giving me a points rating on the *Mirror*'s top team:

Paul Routledge – 0/10 – So extreme.

Brian Reade – 1.5/10 – Can't make up his mind.

John Pilger – 2/10 – I'm alright, Jack, leave it to the others.

Tony Parsons – 4/10 – Neither here nor there.

Sue Carroll – 8/10 – Best columnist you have.

James Whitaker – 7/10 – A bit snooty, but could be worse.

Fiona Parker (letters editor) – 1/10 – I'd like to give her more but she only publishes letters her boss wants her to publish.

Piers Morgan – 0/10 – You are lucky to get zero.

TUESDAY, 5 AUGUST

Our royal reporter Jane Kerr has spotted an advertisement on a Buckingham Palace website for a footman's job. It seems an opportunity too good to miss. Apply for the job and see how far we get. Either we get caught straight away, in which case we'll just let it drop. Or we get the job and actually stick a *Mirror* reporter inside the Palace for a bit. Jane, lovely though she is, would not make an obvious footman, so we scoured the newsroom and alighted on Ryan Parry, a young and very keen trainee who only a few weeks ago did a very good exposé of security at Wimbledon. He'd be perfect, and when we suggested it to him, he jumped at the chance. We decided to declare his real name on the application form, give his genuine CV, bar his job at the *Mirror*, and provide real references. A proper security check will root him out that way, and we can't be accused of too much subterfuge. Be fun to see what happens.

WEDNESDAY, 6 AUGUST

I've reluctantly had to ask Victor Lewis-Smith to 'step down' from his weekly column, because we need to save more money and he's an expensive, if superlative, luxury.

He took it hilariously well:

I understand that newspapers are businesses like any other, and when cuts have to be made it makes sense to axe a few well-paid columnists rather than swathes of foot soldiers. You see, even as my gibbet is being constructed, I'm thinking of others. What a fine and noble human being I am. I really admired your anti-war stance. And it was great to see those articles by Pilger reach a mass audience, even if the price we now have to pay is wall-to-wall coverage of Kylie's arse.

Victor is a one-off. When we caught him rehashing old gags he'd used several times before, he argued, 'Look, when Sinatra sang My Way, did all the crowd ask for their money back because they'd heard it before?'

THURSDAY, 7 AUGUST

No. 10 have formally complained that we've run photos of Leo Blair swimming in the sea with his parents on holiday. 'At a time when security issues are paramount, it is particularly unhelpful,' wrote Ms Anne Shevas from the press office. I replied:

> Dear Anne, thank you for your latest hectoring 'advisory'. It's absurd to demand privacy while swimming in a public ocean with complete strangers floating next to you. I also think it's pretty rich given the recent exclusive *Marie Claire* photographs of Mrs Blair on her marital bed and having lipstick tenderly applied by Ms Carole Caplin. As for the laughable alleged security risk, everyone in the western world knows the Blairs are staying at Cliff Richard's villa. Anyway, always happy to receive more 'advisories' so keep in touch. Love Piers.

I don't anticipate a response.

FRIDAY, 8 AUGUST

To round off the farce, I heard today that Alastair Campbell is planning to holiday in the South of France with Rebekah and a few other friends. I sent an urgent fax. 'Dear Alastair, Could you please give me a personal written assurance that you will not be in the South of France at the start of September as I will be there then and would rather staple my eyelids to the floor of my château than have to meet up with you.'

FRIDAY, 15 AUGUST

Christopher Hitchens emailed Conor and me a life statement: 'The four most overrated things in life are champagne, lobster, anal sex and picnics.'

FRIDAY, 29 AUGUST

Alastair's resigned. It doesn't surprise me. He stayed too long, but only because Blair begged him to. I've had my ups and downs with him, but he's not a bad guy and I'll quite miss him, in a strange way. I gave him one last present with tonight's paper, a splash saying THE MOST POWERFUL MAN IN BRITAIN QUITS. He'll love it.

MONDAY, 1 SEPTEMBER

I did a little piece to camera sticking up for Michael Barrymore for an Edinburgh Festival debate about celebrity scandals.

I got a handwritten note from him today, saying:

> I have had many trials and tribulations to deal with in my life, none more so than in the last two years. It would be easy to point the finger at

everyone else, but as you have proved so many times in your career you 'ain't everyone else'. And because of that my head does not feel so heavy and the days are getting brighter. If at any time in the future you would like my support I can but only offer it whole-heartedly. Extra good luck with whatever you do in your career, as I rebuild mine. Michael.

I do feel sorry for him. Barrymore's been sold out by so many family and friends it's a miracle he hasn't topped himself.

TUESDAY, 2 SEPTEMBER
I won the Editor of the Year award at the *GQ* awards tonight. Mainly because I'm a mate of Dylan Jones, I suspect.

But hey, who's complaining?

I assumed I'd get roundly booed off stage by the rock star audience, but to my surprise I was pretty well received. The *Mirror*'s Iraq war stance has made us very popular with celebrities.

MONDAY, 8 SEPTEMBER
Victor and I threw a dinner party at the Mirabelle tonight for Ian Botham to celebrate him signing a new five-year contract with the *Mirror*.

We assembled a tremendous guest list – Parky, David Frost, Rory Bremner, and a load of cricket legends including Shane Warne, Wasim Akram, Bob Willis and Clive Lloyd.

We'd exposed Warney for sending naughty text messages to a Hampshire girl last summer, which cost him the vice-captaincy of Australia. But he took it well and was fantastic company tonight. 'Mate, I was an accident waiting to happen with those bloody text messages.'

He doesn't eat anything but pizza. So we got him a pizza.

FRIDAY, 12 SEPTEMBER
Geoff Hoon has sent a threatening letter saying if we persist in saying he misled MPs over the war, he'll 'consider other options open to me'. A bit more nibbling and I reckon he'll sue, then we can ask him in court a simple question: 'Mr Hoon, do you think on balance you misled the public about WMD?'

The *Telegraph* ran a feature on leading media figures, giving their tips for how to get to the top. Most, as I thought they would, taking themselves far too seriously. My entry simply said: 'Sleep with the editor. It may be a cliché, but it worked for me at the *Sun*, though Kelvin complained about my stubble.'

SATURDAY, 20 SEPTEMBER
Ryan Parry has landed that job at the Palace and starts work this week as a footman!

SUNDAY, 21 SEPTEMBER

Mandelson emailed in another tizzy this morning:

> Dear Piers, another Saturday briefing from GB's mates, further stories in the *Mirror* and the *Mail* attacking me. Whatever your desire to do in Blair, and use of the newspaper for this purpose, can you please tell your guys to leave me out of the propaganda war?

I replied:

> Peter, I do wish you'd stop claiming I want to do in Tony Blair. I don't. But perhaps one of the reasons why he has no relationship with us at the moment is because everyone keeps telling him I do. He was wrong on Iraq but we are a Labour paper and want him to win the next election.

Mandelson responded:

> Piers, I love you lots but you really cannot get away with that. Do you read your own paper??? It is full of bile about Tony from start to finish. Its attacks on him and anyone closely associated with him – mainly but not only over Iraq – are so extreme and hysterical that they seem to come from a frame of mind that is unbalanced in its attitude to him and New Labour. Tony is not being told you hate him. He just reads the paper and is frankly amazed by it. And, I am afraid, he has given up worrying about something that he seems totally unable to do anything about.

The truth, I suspect, is that Blair doesn't worry much about the papers because he knows most of it doesn't matter. But people like Peter and Alastair rant at him all day long about the *Mirror* being 'traitors', so he sort of feels he has to go along with it.

MONDAY, 22 SEPTEMBER

Frank Bruno was sectioned today. Very, very sad. I called his mobile as soon as I heard the news, and he answered it. 'Frank, it's Piers Morgan, are you OK?'

'Yes, man, yes, I'm …' Then his wife Laura grabbed the phone and told me he couldn't talk any more. She'll be selling her story again soon.

TUESDAY, 30 SEPTEMBER

Down to the Labour Party conference at Bournemouth, and my diary is surprisingly empty this year. It seems the Iraq war has severed virtually all my links with the Government. Though, ironically, I have never been more popular with the rank-and-file down here. So I've spent my time fending off tuts and furrowed brows from the Cabinet – and receiving hugs of gratitude from beer-sodden delegates. Quite odd.

Conference really bores me now. It's always the same people going to the same parties coming out with the same crap. I really find the world of politics so crashingly dull at the moment. Boring people, boring conferences, boring elections. The only sport to be had this year has been to see how the Blairs treated me. There was word they were going to cancel our annual *Mirror* conference lunch tomorrow, but I think they realised it would only fuel a BLAIR SNUBS MIRROR OVER IRAQ headline, so they opted to sup with the devil. I was chatting with Victor about the lunch in his suite after Blair's speech when my phone rang, and it was him.

'Prime Minister, it's been so long …' Victor's eyebrows shot through the ceiling. He laughed.

'Well, I thought it was time to bury the hatchet a bit and move on, don't you?'

'Yes, definitely. I was just saying that to Victor, actually. We liked your speech, sounded a bit more like the old Blair, if you don't mind me saying so.'

'Well, thanks, it has been a tough time, but I think we are through the worst of it now. It's important that you and I have a better relationship, though.'

'Look, I agree. The Iraq thing got a bit personal on both sides. But that's because we totally disagreed about it and both felt passionately that we were right. I still think I was, and you still think you are, and that's not going to change. But I detect that the voters would rather like both of us to get back to things they really care about, like schools and hospitals.'

'Yes, I think you're right about that!' Laughs.

At least lunch will be more civilised now.

'I'm bringing John Reid in case you get out of hand,' he said.

WEDNESDAY, 1 OCTOBER

After all that, probably had our most cordial lunch ever with Blair today. 'Bruiser' Reid eagerly laid into me every time I got, in his words, 'impertinent', we kept the war chat to a minimum, Cherie wasn't there, and a rather nice time was had by all.

Conor rang in the afternoon to say we had photos of Jeremy Clarkson groping a woman in an alleyway running down the side of the Connaught Hotel in Mayfair.

She was Elaine Bedel, the same woman he'd been caught kissing two years ago, when he assured me mysteriously that he 'wasn't capable of having an affair'.

'He wants to talk to you,' Conor said. 'He told Nicola Methven [our TV editor] that you regretted doing this to him last time, and he's begging to speak to you. Says he was just saying goodnight to her.'

'What do you think?'

'Boss, he's bang to rights. His arms are all over her, it's in an alleyway, and the photographer says he followed them there and they were canoodling for several minutes. If we don't want it, the guy wants to go to the Mail.'

'OK, well, in that case I don't want to talk to him. Just tell him I can't keep bailing him out with the same woman, it's ridiculous. I believed him last time, and he was obviously lying then.'

Conor rang back half an hour later.

'He's begging us not to run it. Says we hurt him last time, and this is all totally innocent. And he wants you to call him. But he's lying, these pictures aren't innocent.'

'Well run it then. If he's going to be that stupid, that's his problem.'

TUESDAY, 7 OCTOBER

Kent Gavin, our legendary royal photographer, retired today and we threw a big party for him at Arsenal Stadium – he's a bigger fan than me.

There were many great stories, but nothing to quite beat the time he photographed Doris Day in her eighth-floor Manhattan apartment.

Kent was left with the superstar's beloved pet dog while she answered the phone, and started throwing a little ball around for it to fetch.

All went well until he slightly over-threw it, the dog raced to fetch it, and Kent suddenly realised to his horror that the window was open.

End of Doris Day's dog.

When she came back into the room, a shocked Kent said, 'I'm terribly sorry, but there's been a dreadful accident – your dog has fallen out of the window.'

'*What?*' shrieked Doris, and she then ran sobbing to the lift. Minutes later she was cradling her dead, mangled pet in her arms on the street.

And what was his killer doing? 'I thought I may as well take a few pictures while I was there,' he confessed. Next day's *Daily Mirror* carried WORLD EXCLUSIVE: DORIS DAY WEEPS FOR DEAD DOG. (Pictures by Kent Gavin.)

FRIDAY, 10 OCTOBER

Emailed Mandelson, saying:

We had a good lunch with TB – think the air's been cleared, the ice defrosted, and we can all move on now. Wouldn't say we are quite back to foaming pints in the private sitting room again, but it was good to sort out the unnecessary frisson of mutual angst. Any feedback from your end?

He replied:

The feedback is as follows: Liked the lunch. Liked you. Feels warm towards a lot of what you are doing. Hopes/thinks that things will get better but is confused by the lack of evidence that the treatment of the Government and the paper's political coverage is any different.

My feeling is slightly different. I think that the problem with the *Mirror* is not that it is pro or anti the Government (I think a bit of distance and independence is a good thing) but that its political coverage is unsophisticated. Paul Routledge is a big noise and is not useless from your point of view. But the noise is too loud and dominant and not balanced by more intelligent political analysis and coverage. Essentially, you need a new political editor to bring quality and to balance Paul. Until you get this I don't think you will be in the place you want to be in … Peter

FRIDAY, 17 OCTOBER

Sarah and Gordon Brown's new baby was born, a boy called John, weighing 8 lb 1 oz. I sent a huge bunch of flowers the instant the story appeared on the news wires. You've got to be fast and first, or your floral tribute gets lost in the lorry-loads as the day wears on. Sarah sent me a text message, saying, 'They were lovely, and first.' Job done!

We are due to serialise Burrell's book on Monday, and I've set up a secret production team to lay it out today in a bunker on the twentieth floor.

When I told them about the letter, there was general controlled hysteria.

SUNDAY, 19 OCTOBER

A long, tense day. I can never relax when there's a big one coming, and I sense this is going to be massive. Mid-afternoon was the danger point, when we had to alert the trade to our increased print run. We were printing 30 per cent more papers than usual, a huge increase, and alarm bells instantly rang all round Fleet Street as our rivals wondered what the hell we were up to.

At 6pm, Rebekah sent me a text demanding information.

'It's a free CD,' I said. But she didn't buy it.

At 8pm, I was casually watching Sky when they suddenly flashed up that Tony Blair been taken to hospital with a heart scare.

I wish I could say my first thought was for the PM's health, but it wasn't – it was for my great scoop disappearing out of the news window.

It was too late to pull it, but we had to splash on Blair now, surely.

At least Rebekah was thrown off the scent when I sent a text saying, 'That was our exclusive.'

An hour passed before we heard that Blair was OK and it was some fairly mundane, easily treatable problem. David Blaine was also ending his stint in a box by Tower Bridge tonight, so there was plenty of convincing stuff for the spoof edition.

The headline in the real Diana edition was THEY'RE PLANNING AN 'ACCI-DENT' IN MY CAR SO CHARLES CAN MARRY AGAIN. In fact, the letter says 'Charles is planning an "accident" in my car so he can marry again', but Burrell has insisted we alter the wording so Charles is not branded an assassin.

MONDAY, 20 OCTOBER

Sarah Vaughan-Brown, our star PR, had been up since 4am hitting all the TV stations with our story. By the time I woke at 6am, they were all leading on Diana's letter. Blair's heart problem had been relegated to a lowly second item.

I faxed him a note when I got to the office: 'Dear Prime Minister, can you please stop trying to wreck our big royal scoops ... seriously, glad things are OK. I was going to send flowers but I saw Kew Gardens arrive this morning at No. 10 and assumed Rebekah had got there first.'

Day two of Burrell is hilarious – a note from Prince Philip to Diana saying: 'I can't imagine anyone in their right mind leaving you for Camilla.' I read day three tonight, too, and it's a fantastic letter from Earl Spencer calling Diana a nutter, deceitful and manipulative.

Sales are huge. Burrell has done it for us again.

Richard Branson emailed me: 'Dear Piers, just to say many congratulations – What a coup! I thought brilliant exclusives like this were a thing of the past, but you've proved everybody wrong.'

TUESDAY, 21 OCTOBER

Andrew Gilligan replied to a note I sent him commiserating with his lot:

> Thanks Piers, it really helps having your support. What's kept me going is knowing that no matter how hard the Government PR machine and all its journalistic poodles and toadies try, the public know the truth when they see it. I'd be interested in talking about a job. I don't think the BBC are going to can me, but doing any kind of original or enterprising work is going to get even more difficult here now than it has been.

WEDNESDAY, 22 OCTOBER

As I showered this morning, I reflected on my awful lot in life. This afternoon I was going to have to spend at least two hours in a penthouse suite with Jordan, interviewing her for *Tabloid Tales*. The things you have to do as a tabloid editor these days ...

Kerrie bade me on my way with a cheery, but firm, 'Behave yourself.' I think she was genuinely concerned for my physical safety.

Jordan's a very strange creature. In the flesh she looked tiny, with very slim legs – but those stupendously large, gravity-defying breasts dominating the whole vista, like Canary Wharf dominates east London.

She's a very sexually frank and mischievous little devil. From the moment I arrived, she was off like an extra in a Carry On movie – rattling off double-entendres faster than Barbara Windsor on speed.

'Ooh, while you're down there,' she cackled at the sound man.

'So, Piers, you seen the bed yet, mate? It's a right big 'un – but then I guess you'd know all about those, eh, mate?'

And so on.

All very entertaining.

By an odd coincidence, she's just moved into the next village along from Newick and has started going to my local tandoori and pub.

'You stalking me?' I asked.

'Of course,' she cackled back. 'I'd love to get my hands on your prawn madras.'

The interview took nearly three hours, and she was surprisingly funny, searingly honest, and constantly trying to embarrass me with her sexual jibes.

Plunge below what I would call the Frank Skinner comedy bar, and she can be repulsively coarse. But keep it at Carry On, and she can be bloody amusing.

The poor sound man was singled out for special treatment.

'I know what you're doing, you dirty bastard,' she said as he tried to make her microphone come back to life (the breasts had knocked all the life out of it, I suspect). 'Now, get your face out of my tits right now. Ha, ha, ha.'

Poor bloke looked mortified. 'No, I'm not … honestly.'

'Course you are, all blokes are the same,' she laughed.

And it was hard *not* to gawp at them. They are Britain's most famous breasts, after all.

One exchange summed up the afternoon:

Jordan: 'I'm not fat or anything.'

Me: 'No, you're quite fit, if you don't mind me saying so.'

Jordan: 'I'm not, honestly, you know when you bend over [and she does], look, I'll show you …'

Everything, and I mean everything, starts to tumble out.

Me: 'Oh, please! Put it away …'

Jordan: 'Oh my God! Did you see that? That is disgusting.'

Me: 'This is BBC1, for God's sake, not Playboy Channel. Keep it away.'

As I wound up the chat, she asked, 'Fancy a pizza, then, Piers?'

I looked at her for signs of another 'joke'.

'Come on, let's go and have a Sloppy Giuseppe,' she leered, licking her lips, I guess in her mind seductively.

'Now, Jordan, that's a lovely offer, but tragically I have got to get back to work.'

She looked bemused.

'Suppose I'll just have to amuse myself, then.'

Which I'm sure she did.

THURSDAY, 23 OCTOBER

I've been invited on to Concorde's last ever flight tomorrow, from New York to London, and as before I decided this was definitely a job for the editor.

I arrived at the hotel tonight, and the first thing I saw was Jeremy Clarkson. Right, this is going to be interesting.

FRIDAY, 24 OCTOBER

Woke hideously early at 5am. The flight leaves at 7am.

Met Simon Kelner in the foyer. 'Clarkson's looking for you. He says you're a little shit and he's going to punch your lights out.'

Great.

I got on the plane to find Kelner and I were sitting in the seat behind Clarkson.

He came down spitting bile. 'Oh, fucking hell, I've got a cunt sitting behind me.'

'Yes,' I replied, 'and looks like I've got one in front of me, too.'

Twenty minutes into the flight he made some other derogatory remark.

'Jeremy, if you want to hit me as you've been threatening to, then just get on with it.'

'You are a fucking cunt,' he said, loud enough for all the surrounding journalists like Matthew Parris and Valerie Grove to hear.

'So you say. Come on, then, big man – show me what you've got.'

He eyed me with raw hatred and said nothing. But ten minutes later he turned round and tipped a large glass of water over my trousers.

'Oh, thank you Jeremy, that's really nice of you. If I get that, what's your wife going to get – a case of Evian?'

I thought he was going to hit me then, but he turned round and never spoke again.

Word spread of the 'incident', though, and Jodie Kidd came down with her video camera. 'I'd like to photograph your wet patch,' she said.

Well, since she asked nicely.

I sent Joan Collins a note saying it was traditional for the biggest star on the plane to serve me champagne and could she come down and do the honours.

A note came back. 'I'd love to, but only when I've finished my food and you've dried yourself.'

As my driver Martin took me home afterwards, the phone rang and it was Clarkson. I let him speak on the loudspeaker so Martin could enjoy the moment too.

'Look, this is ridiculous. I don't want a feud with you, this is all getting very silly.'

'I agree, Jeremy, but you're the one chucking water over me and threatening to beat me up. You're also the one who keeps getting photographed kissing and groping the same woman and blaming me.'

'It's not what you think. But let's put it behind us. Please.'

'Sure, mate, whatever you want.'

I'd have respected him more if he'd rung to say 'there's plenty more coming your way, you turd'. This was the worst kind of cowardly grovelling.

MONDAY, 27 OCTOBER

Blair sent a note back. 'Sorry about the timing. I also feel Mr Blaine may be aggrieved. But I assure you it wasn't planned! Thanks for writing, much appreciated.'

Always handwritten, his letters, which never fails to impress.

TUESDAY, 28 OCTOBER

Private Eye has done a spoof Diana letter, saying, 'The *Mirror* is a great paper and Piers Moron is honestly *really dishy*! Yah! After they have fixed my brakes so I die in a car accident I hope you will dish the dirt in the *Daily Moron* and fill your boots, Lots of love, Diana. PS After I die take anything you want and hide it under your bed.' Amusing.

WEDNESDAY, 29 OCTOBER

We got a late tip off that Paul McCartney's wife Heather has had their baby. One of our reporters on our sister paper, the *Daily Record* in Scotland, phoned Macca's brother Mike, who apparently confirmed, 'Yeah, it's a boy, everyone's celebrating.'

We changed the front page and are running the headline IT'S A BOY.

THURSDAY, 30 OCTOBER

It was a girl.

Just as we were cracking the champagne open to celebrate our great scoop, a snap dropped on the Press Association news wire. 'Paul McCartney's wife Heather has had a baby. A girl called Beatrice.'

Balls. I started laughing – what else could you do?

Then the phones started going off ten to the dozen, all media organisations wanting a comment on our terrible clanger. I decide to make it all a big joke, demanding photographic evidence of the child's sex and standing by our story until we see it.

But the truth is that we've been completely stuffed and it's always totally, horribly embarrassing. I confessed to Radio 4: 'Trouble is that all babies look the same from the waist up, so there was clearly some misunderstanding.'

MONDAY, 3 NOVEMBER

Ryan Parry has been under cover at the Palace for six weeks now and has been so impressive as a footman that he's been allowed to serve the Queen breakfast and walk the corgis. The access he's getting is unbelievable. Matt Kelly, my features editor who's been running the story, said that Ryan could take a gun into the Palace if we wanted him too. 'He hasn't been frisked or had his bags checked since he started,' said Matt, 'it's appalling, really.'

It's tempting to have him pictured with a machine gun by Her Majesty's bedroom, but that would be a step too far.

President Bush is staying at the Palace later this month, and Matt and I agreed it would be the perfect time for Ryan to pull out.

'Serve Dubya his bedtime cocoa and then leave,' Matt laughed.

If this all comes off it will be one of the biggest scoops ever.

TUESDAY, 4 NOVEMBER

Jack Straw has written to apologise for not coming to the party tomorrow, but claims he never got an invite. He clearly thinks this was deliberate, because he added, 'We are very careful with all our invitations and if it had been received here we would have had a record ...'

WEDNESDAY, 5 NOVEMBER

We officially launched our centenary celebrations today with a big party at the Science Museum.

Blair was the guest speaker, and turned up looking tired and stressed.

I started my own speech by saying, 'I'd like to thank the Prime Minister for staying alive long enough to attend this evening.'

He smiled wanly.

When he came to speak, he spoke without notes, and was all over the place. Rambling and incoherent at times. It was embarrassing. I have never seen him like this.

He also made a couple of digs at the *Mirror*'s stance on Iraq and was generally exuding an air of not wanting to be there. No problem with that, but why turn up, then?

Blair was the talk of the party afterwards. Everyone asking the same thing: 'What's the matter with him? Is he seriously ill? Is he about to quit?'

To compound his misery, Gordon Brown flitted about for a couple of hours looking on top form. The contrast in imagery was striking.

MONDAY, 10 NOVEMBER

The DTI grilled me for eight hours in Croydon today. Two hard-nosed ex-coppers, now running the legal arm of the department. They were polite, but incredibly detailed. And I had to go through every spit and cough of the whole saga again. It's been nearly four years now.

'We're sorry it's taken so long,' they said, 'but these investigations are always time-consuming.'

Why, though?

I had a chat with the chief investigative guy afterwards, who was surprisingly candid.

'Look, Mr Morgan, the focus of our investigation is now on whether prior knowledge of a share tip in a paper constitutes insider dealing. In your case, I can say we have found no evidence that you had any prior knowledge of a tip.

I asked Jeremy, my lawyer, what he thought as we left.

'Well that was very odd,' he said. 'And very encouraging.'

TUESDAY, 11 NOVEMBER

I was invited to Seaford House, a prestigious military HQ, to debate against Michael Portillo in a motion entitled 'This house believes the world is a safer place since the war on Iraq'. The audience was composed of high-ranking military men and senior diplomats.

I won the debate easily, which says all you need to know about this conflict.

SUNDAY, 16 NOVEMBER

Went to the premiere of Richard Curtis's new movie, *Love Actually*, tonight, and bumped into Earl Spencer on the staircase.

Talk about bad timing.

'Ah, hi there, how are you?' I said nervously.

He smiled, surprisingly warmly.

'I'm fine, thank you, Piers.'

Our mutual mate Harry Enfield was with him. 'Piers likes me, Charles, he really likes me.'

'I wish I could get him to like me,' said the good Earl.

'I do like you,' I protested.

A bizarre encounter.

MONDAY, 17 NOVEMBER

George Bush arrives at Buckingham Palace tomorrow, and Ryan Parry's all set to spring his exposé on an unsuspecting world. He came in this morning with all his finished copy. It was just astonishing stuff – he's been waiting regularly on the Queen and Prince Philip, had unfettered access to almost everywhere in the Palace, taken loads of photos of the royal bedrooms – and, pricelessly, snatched Her Majesty's breakfast table complete with Tupperware, yes, *Tupperware*, pots. It is all massively intrusive, obviously. But, on the other hand, we are only able to photograph it because of a genuinely terrible security lapse. Ryan could have been a terrorist, no question. And if he had been, then our leading royals could be dead already. It's a disgrace.

We've set up a secret production team in a remote room down on the management floor. It has a special code to enter, and always has someone on the door to stop anyone wandering in to have a peek. It is imperative we keep this quiet. Ryan's safety depends on it.

TUESDAY, 18 NOVEMBER

A day of unbearable bloody tension. I can honestly say I have never known anything quite like it. Ryan went to work as normal, and the production team carried on laying out all his material in the secret bunker. Security was massively important – one false move or word now, and Ryan could have been fried while he was still inside. The ultimate nightmare for any undercover reporter. We watched Bush and his huge entourage arrive at Heathrow and then speed off to Buckingham Palace. As they swept through the gates, Ryan was preparing to serve the party drinks and lay chocolates on their beds. Unbelievable. I had told him not to use his mobile because I was sure the secret service would catch him straight away with all their sophisticated kit. But around 7pm we started getting text messages from him. 'I've just seen the Queen kiss the President,' was the first one.

'Tell him to keep fucking texting,' I shouted. 'This is sensational stuff.'

'Where are you?' we asked Ryan.

'Behind a curtain watching them all having drinks,' he replied. 'I'll keep texting copy until it gets too difficult.'

He sent over a load more messages for half an hour and then they stopped coming.

'Where's he gone? What's happened?' I said, slight panic rising in my voice.

'He'll be OK,' said Matt Kelly. 'He said he'd have to finish his shift and then he'd walk out and call us. That should be around 8.30pm. He can't text any more because it's too risky.'

By 9pm, I was seriously concerned. 'Where is he, for fuck's sake? He might be in deep shit here.'

Everyone was getting a bit jittery now.

We'd sent both the dummy first edition, and the real edition with thirteen pages of Ryan's investigation. There was no way back now – we were into the abyss.

I decided to go home and wait for news there.

Sly Bailey rang, and I said it was all OK, apart from the fact that Ryan had disappeared off radar.

'He'll be OK, won't he?' she said.

'Yes, of course, Sly, of course he will,' I replied.

Then I put the phone down and stared out across the river, bloody crapping it.

This wasn't as bad as that long night when Mike Moore and Wayne Francis went to meet Al Qaeda in Afghanistan. But it was pretty close.

Ryan's fate was out of my hands, and anyone else's. He's an incredibly cool customer for his age and experience, but he was taking on the supposedly greatest security team in the world single-handed.

By 9.30pm, an hour after he was due out, I was certain he'd been caught, probably with that mobile phone.

I was ringing the bunker every ten minutes. 'No news, boss, we'll call you – he'll be fine, don't worry.'

Don't worry? He could be dead, for Christ's sake. If they thought he was a terrorist, a twitchy American secret serviceman might just have decided not to take any chances.

I felt sick with worry.

My greatest scoop as an editor. Ryan Parry, a Mirror undercover reporter, on the Buckingham Palace balcony as a footman.

Finally, a few minutes after 10pm, I got the call. 'The Eagle has landed.'

Ryan, cool as you like, had packed all his kit, and walked casually out of the Palace, making sure he was videotaped as he did by our team outside.

I called him.

'You OK, mate?'

'Yes, thanks, Piers, all went fine. I left the chocolates on their beds, then finished my shift and left, no problem.'

'Why were you late out?'

'It just dragged on a bit – I guess it gets busy when the President comes to stay. And I could hardly say I had to nip off early to file my story …'

'Well, congratulations, Ryan, this is one of the greatest scoops ever.'

'Cheers, boss. Mind if I go and have a drink now?'

What a good idea.

I poured myself a large Jack Daniel's and called Sly. 'Ryan's out, everything's gone like clockwork. We'll break the news about 5am and wait for the fireworks to commence.'

WEDNESDAY, 19 NOVEMBER

Sarah Vaughan-Brown is unfortunately away, so her deputy Chris Wade did the calls. I woke after a couple of hours of restless tossing and turning, and called him.

'Are they biting, Chris?'

'Oh, yes, I think you could say they are all quite excited,' he laughed.

It was 6am, and I turned on the news to enjoy that sublime moment of seeing your scoop suddenly storm the screens like an Exocet missile.

BREAKING NEWS, flashed Sky: MIRROR JOURNALIST WORKS UNDERCOVER AT PALACE.

BREAKING NEWS – SECURITY SCANDAL AT PALACE, said the BBC.

BREAKING NEWS – MIRROR INTRUDER EXPOSES PALACE SECURITY, roared ITN.

This was liquid nitrogen and I was loving every second. But there was still one big hurdle to negotiate. I was booked to do the Radio 4 *Today* programme live at 7.10am with John Humphries. There was still time for me to cock it all up by saying the wrong thing, or for Humphries to tear into me about invasion of privacy and unnecessary intrusion. He sets the mood for everyone else on this kind of thing.

As it was, he was a pussycat, and clearly thought it was a cracking story – particularly the Tupperware photos.

As he said goodbye with a 'Congratulations on a great scoop, Mr Morgan,' and another chuckle, I knew we were home and dry.

I called Chris and told him to line up all the usual TV news crews in my office. 'Just get the Burrell ones to come back,' I laughed.

We are leading all the news again for the second time in a month. Life doesn't get any better than this.

THURSDAY, 20 NOVEMBER

Mike Molloy, a former editor of the *Mirror*, sent a lovely note this morning: 'This morning's splash story was one of the greatest pieces of popular journalism I have ever seen. The Burrell stuff was white hot but this was even better.'

My joy was slightly tempered by another letter addressed to 'Mr Piers Morgan RIP', and saying, 'Stop printing anti-BNP stories with immediate effect or we will murder you and your family you filthy lying Marxist scum.' It's from the 'Aryan Martyrs Brigade', whoever they are.

SATURDAY, 22 NOVEMBER

Ryan got served with a formal injunction at his Limehouse flat today, by two officials on behalf of 'The Attorney General and Queen Elizabeth II'.

As they left, one of them turned back and said, 'Oh, and by the way, mate, bloody well done!'

TUESDAY, 25 NOVEMBER

I wrote to Earl Spencer asking if, in light of our convivial encounter, he fancied appearing in *Tabloid Tales*, but pointing out that if he'd rather be impaled on an armadillo's arse, then I would fully understand.

A reply came back from his assistant saying they'd 'very much like to take the armadillo option'.

A ridiculous fax arrived later from David Hill in the No. 10 press office, saying Jacques Chirac had inadvertently invaded the privacy of little Leo Blair by showing off a signed photo of the lad that the Blairs gave him:

> This was a personal gift and was not intended as a photo opportunity, but unfortunately President Chirac was not aware of this and showed it off to some media. The Prime Minister would like you to know his policy on publishing pictures of Leo has not changed.

This is bordering on the farcical now. If you don't want Leo in the papers, Tony, then perhaps don't give big cuddly pictures of him to world leaders just before they address the British media. And anyway, who cares? Honestly, who cares whether a kid of four has his privacy invaded, because he sure as hell doesn't, does he?

MONDAY, 1 DECEMBER

Tea with Blair before the recess. 'I know you're pissed off with me over Iraq,' I said, 'but we had our position and you had yours. It shouldn't contaminate our relationship permanently.'

'No, no, of course not, Piers. It's important we get things back on to a more even keel.'

He looked tired and bored, and yawned a few times.

2004

SATURDAY, 3 JANUARY

I've taken the boys to Tenerife for a New Year break. This afternoon I went to retrieve the older two from the table tennis room and found Spencer locked in mortal ping-pong combat with a middle-aged man who clearly wasn't enjoying having an 11-year-old kid smash him all over the place. When Spencer eventually won, the guy came over to say hello. I suddenly realised it was Huw Edwards, newsreader on the *Six O'Clock News*. I don't know who was more surprised. 'Good God, man, was that your lad humiliating me?' he wheezed.

'I'm afraid so, Huw. Just count yourself fortunate it wasn't his younger brother.'

MONDAY, 5 JANUARY

My first day back in the office after Christmas, and I wanted to make a big splash. Ever since we serialised Paul Burrell's book, with that dynamite letter from Diana predicting her accident, I have been thinking about how to reveal the blanked-out name. It seemed preposterous to tell the world that Prince Charles planned to murder his ex-wife. But then it wasn't us saying it, it was Diana. And at the end of the day, she *did* die almost exactly how she had feared she would – and just eight months after writing the letter.

Today we got our reason to publish. Burrell has been asked to hand over all his evidence, including the letter, to the investigating authorities. This means others will know the name, and it will inevitably leak. I called Conor and a few other execs in and we debated the ramifications. Nobody thought I'd actually do it, and all put it down to too much sunshine on my head in Tenerife. But I reckoned if we did a leader saying the claim was obvious nonsense, we could get away with it. Charles was hardly going to sue over claims by his dead wife, was he? Marcus agreed there was a certain warped logic to my stance. Burrell was the only problem: he'd point blank refused to let us do it before, and he certainly wasn't going to agree now the dust had settled. But he's made millions from that book so far, and I think we're entitled to call the shots a bit.

He went potty when Steve Dennis told him this afternoon, making all sorts of veiled threats. But Steve will calm him down, he always does.

I did a front page saying IT WAS CHARLES. And went home to watch the mayhem commence.

TUESDAY, 6 JANUARY

The TV news were all clearing the decks for our story, and I was fuelling it with plenty of 'Obviously it's not credible it was Charles, but it's amazing that Diana would write that' interviews. And it was, by any yardstick.

Steve Dennis rang: 'Paul says he'll never talk to you again.'

'Right. Does he mean it?'

'Well, for a week I should think, yes.'

We both laughed. We like Burrell, but we both know he's prone to the odd – how shall I put this? – 'hissy-fit'.

He was very naive to think the name would never come out. You can't tell any journalist something that incredible and expect it to remain a secret. We just can't help ourselves.

THURSDAY, 8 JANUARY

I'd been invited on to the *Queen Mary* today for its big launch down in Southampton. But thought on balance that the royals might not be overly delighted to find me strolling across the gangplank, so gave it a miss.

TUESDAY, 20 JANUARY

Tony Blair's had many 'big weeks', but this is a really big one. If he loses the student top-up fees vote a week today, and Lord Hutton criticises him in his report on David Kelly's death, then that could be curtains for him. It's as big as that. I went to see him at lunchtime today, and it was obvious he's really feeling the heat. He looked knackered, and very down. 'It's too close to call,' he admitted on the fees vote. 'But we have got to win it because otherwise we'll just be going backwards and the universities will never have enough money.'

'We will back you on this, Prime Minister,' I said. 'It's just the kind of issue I've been looking for to support you on.' He seemed very grateful. 'Thank you, that would be really helpful.'

As for Hutton, he was guarded but obviously very edgy. 'Look, I don't think I will be heavily criticised, but if I am, then I will just have to deal with it.'

'But it would be pretty serious if you're in any way blamed for what happened, or called a liar, wouldn't it?'

'Yes, it would, of course it would.'

He lowered his head for a moment. He looked a beaten man.

'Prime Minister, I hope you don't mind me saying this, but I think you need to cheer up a bit.'

He looked back up, a bit stunned. 'What do you mean?'

'I mean you look bloody miserable, to be honest, and everyone is reading defeat into your demeanour. I know exactly how you're feeling because I've been there myself. But you're going to have to buck up a bit.' I laughed: this was an outrageous way to talk to the most powerful man in the country, but someone has to say it, and I get the feeling nobody does since Campbell rode off into the sunset.

'Right, well, thanks for that, Piers.' He looked (understandably) a bit put out.

'Look, I don't mean to be rude or personal. But a lot of people have said to me you look like you've had enough, and perhaps you have. But if you haven't, then I think you need to fight back a bit, smile more, and get out there looking like you're going to win the top-up fees vote, survive Hutton unscathed, and go on to win the next election. And I speak as someone who will whack you all over the place if you get hammered by Hutton.'

Blair smiled. 'OK, well, I get the message.'

'And as for Iraq, why don't you accept publicly that there were no WMD, say sorry, and try and move on. Until you do, the public will think you've gone potty and are in some sort of weird denial.'

He smiled. 'We don't know for sure what happened to the WMD, and until we know, I am certainly not going to start apologising.'

'Well, I think you should just say, "Sorry, everyone, but the intelligence I relied on wasn't right." It doesn't mean you lied, just means you were misled by people who should have known.'

He looked thoughtful. 'Well, let's wait and see, shall we?'

As I left, Sally Morgan said, 'Thanks, he needed that.'

I'd been a bit full-on, but why not? I get the feeling there's no one there to do it any more.

THURSDAY, 22 JANUARY

Sarah Brown invited me round to her No. 10 flat to see baby John. I've always liked Sarah. Her brother Sean spent a few months working on the *Sun* before quitting, finding MacKenzie's 'quirky' management style impossible to handle. 'Oi, you dangerous fucking intellectual, write something the fucking readers can understand next time,' was about the gist of it.

The death of Sarah's baby Jennifer was obviously a hammerblow, and every time I've seen her since, Sarah's eyes looked sad and empty. But today she looked great, and her eyes were sparkling again. John's a great little chap, built like a prop forward and bursting with good health. We sat in the kitchen having a coffee, and she told me how the public helped her overcome her ghastly grief. 'I had twelve thousand letters,' she said, still staggered by the response. 'And many from people who'd suffered the same thing, or worse. They were so kind and supportive, and just told me to keep trying for another baby and not to give up.' Sarah replied to every letter, enclosing a card with Jennifer's tiny face on it. Now, as she cuddled John, she looked over the worst.

We talked about Cherie.

'When did you last see her?'

She laughed. 'We don't see or speak to each other if she can possibly help it.'

The more I see of the Browns and the Blairs, the more I feel that their mutual antipathy is not some media invention, it's real. The men just about tolerate each other; the women don't even achieve that advanced stage of camaraderie.

TUESDAY, 27 JANUARY

Andy Coulson's birthday party at a restaurant in Balham. I was sitting opposite Rebekah, and around 8pm I got a phone call from Guy Black, now Michael Howard's PR man, asking if I knew that the *Sun* had a full leak of the Hutton report. I didn't, but across the table I could see Rebekah talking manically into her phone and realised it was probably true. She was making notes on to what looked like part of a transcript, or extracts from a manuscript, perhaps.

Then I looked a bit closer as she poured some wine and saw the word 'Hutton' and a load of quotes underneath. This was the leaked stuff, hot off the press, sitting there right in front of me. All I had to do was get my hands on it, run out of the restaurant and file it to my newsdesk, and we would just about catch the first edition.

I bided my time, the clock ticking fast. Eventually Rebekah sat back and started talking to the person on her left. I looked around quickly, and nobody was paying much attention. So I suddenly swooped, lurching across the table and making a desperate grab for the notes. Rebekah, her senses as acute as you'd expect from a *Sun* editor, saw me coming and responded with stunning speed – snatching the paperwork literally out of my hand. Other guests watched in astonishment as an unseemly tug-of-war struggle then erupted between the pair of us. 'Give me that,' she said firmly. 'Bollocks,' I shouted back. 'You've nicked it, anyway, so why can't I?'

But her grip was firmer and I felt the crucial notes slip from my fingers. No one was quite sure what the hell was going on, or what we were fighting over. But I knew that those few seconds had just dictated how the next few days will go for both our papers. Had my plan worked, we would have shared the glory of the scoop with the *Sun*. As it is, they have had it away and we will be playing catch-up. On such cliffhangers are editing careers sometimes made and broken ...

Rebekah spent the rest of the evening smirking at me, and I could hardly blame her.

On a happier note, Blair scraped through on top-up fees by a few votes.

*We were lovely children, honestly ... me with fellow
tabloid editors, Rebekah Wade and Andy Coulson.*

WEDNESDAY, 28 JANUARY

Hutton's cleared everyone in the Government of doing anything wrong at all – and blamed it all on the BBC. I think it's a complete stinking whitewash. But Alastair Campbell immediately appeared to address the nation from some fancy Government building, and started banging on about being completely exonerated – and effectively calling for BBC bosses Greg Dyke and Gavyn Davies to resign. It was a shocking performance, totally lacking in any grace or dignity. Alastair's conveniently forgotten that if he hadn't gone to war with the BBC in the first place, then none of this would have happened and David Kelly would almost certainly still be alive. Fact.

I hoped nobody from the BBC would resign, but Davies has quickly fallen on his sword. And Dyke's rumoured to be 'considering his position'. We have done a thunderous attack on Hutton and the Government, and urge the BBC to stand firm. But I fear the worst here.

THURSDAY, 29 JANUARY

Dyke's been forced to go too, and Campbell's gloating is reaching epic proportions. He and Blair sold the public this war with a dossier of bullshit, but it's only the media who rightly exposed this who are having to quit. Mum rang, and said very uncharacteristically, 'Campbell is making my skin crawl.' Middle England is hating his behaviour, and it will damage Blair enormously.

MONDAY, 2 FEBRUARY

Back to Richard Branson's house for the annual Pride of Britain awards judging session today. Panellists included Gary Lineker, Carol Vorderman, Fiona Phillips and Eamonn Holmes from GMTV, Heather Mills-McCartney and Sir John Stevens, head of the Metropolitan Police. Just for amusement, I started proceedings by saying, 'Sir John, this might be terribly inappropriate given the occasion, but on the basis that I'm not going to get a better chance to find out, I wonder if I could ask you the big question. Did Prince Charles kill Diana?'

Branson laughed, as he always does at my terrible gags. Lineker looked gobsmacked, Fiona titterered, Heather tutted and Sir John just gave me a wry half-smile and said, 'Well now, Piers, you wouldn't expect me to comment on an ongoing investigation now, would you?' He's a top bloke, straight to deal with, and a good leader.

Lady McCartney was her usual feisty self. She'd really done her research, and offered a string of well-informed observations that put a lot of previous panellists to shame. Funniest moment came when she launched into a lengthy diatribe about cannabis and drugs in general, ending with the memorable declaration, 'There are no drugs in the McCartney house, that I can tell you!' 'Well, that must make a change,' I laughed. Heather didn't. 'Very funny, Piers. But I'm serious.'

TUESDAY, 3 FEBRUARY

Morning coffee with Gordon Brown at the Treasury. I told him how disgusted I was by Alastair's conduct.

'I know, I know,' he said. 'We should not have been seen gloating like that, or demanding people resign. We should have been relieved that we got the result we got, and moved on. Because it could have been very different.'

One of Gordon's closest aides, Sue Nye, is Gavyn Davies's wife. So it will have had a big impact on his world.

'I wish Alastair would just shut up sometimes,' he growled. 'He's become the story too many times. It doesn't help Tony at all.'

We talked about baby John. 'He's a wonderful little chap,' cooed Gordon, his whole face lighting up.

FRIDAY, 13 FEBRUARY

Had a lively exchange with Mandelson this morning. Told him I'd had a really good chat with the PM recently, but said, 'Big question is: How the fuck is Tony going to win back everyone's trust after this Iraq debacle?'

'When he is allowed to speak to the people without the usual filter being interposed,' he replied. 'And when he is allowed to do so on issues that really interest people. You are wrong on Iraq, as history and the development of the country and its wider effect in the Middle East will show (but not for some time yet).'

I laughed. 'Well, continue your lonely, blinkered, obstinate head-in-the-sand fight then. But it reminds me of General Custer's last words to his men on the brow of the hill: "Don't worry, chaps, they'll never hit us from ..."'

'I hope it is neither blinkered nor lonely,' he said. 'But I realise that other points of view can get a bit inconvenient when there's a war on.'

'Yes,' I snapped back, 'but who is going to believe him next time he tries to argue the case for war? Apart from you, of course. Honesty is the best way, then he can move on.'

Mandelson was having none of it. 'But what is honesty in this context? That the intelligence was not real (untrue)? That no one thought Saddam had both battlefield and strategic weapons (untrue)? That battlefield munitions don't count as WMD (untrue)? That Saddam had no UN resolutions to comply with (untrue)? That France, Germany and the rest believed there was nothing to worry about (untrue)? That we know for sure that there are no WMD (untrue)? That we know where they've gone (untrue)?

'I could go on, but you have assembled a prism through which you view all these things and all I am saying is that the world is not as certain as you portray it.'

I replied in kind: 'Peter, trust me. If Tony doesn't admit very soon that the intelligence was wrong and there were clearly no WMDs in Iraq, then he will be fucked. We didn't wage war for the "development of the country" or "the wider effect in the Middle East''. We waged it quite specifically because he had WMDs and could unleash them on us in forty-five minutes. *That was wrong – admit it.*'

He didn't agree. 'I don't think it would be a good idea for him to say that. I understand the passion you have on this subject, but there is room for another view, you know. The fact is that WMD and international terrorism are not some strange preoccupation of a distracted Prime Minister.'

MONDAY, 16 FEBRUARY

I went to the BAFTAs party last night as a guest of Liz Murdoch. Sat next to Mr Carphone Warehouse, Charles Dunstone, who was charming and seems totally unaffected by his amazing success and wealth. A very sexy young lady in silver slithered her way past me several times, having to literally squeeze through as my chair was blocking the way through. 'Do you think she's trying to send me some signal?' I joked with Liz. 'She's too young for you, Grandpa,' came the kind reply. It was only when I picked up the papers this morning that I realised it was Scarlett Johansson.

TUESDAY, 17 FEBRUARY

I'm on a party roll, and went to the Brit awards tonight for the first time in years, and sat next to Alicia Keys, the American superstar singer. I introduced myself as a 'BBC TV presenter', which I thought might impress her more than 'scum-bag tabloid editor intent on trashing your life'. She was great fun for an American, and enthusiastically embraced my suggestion that she blow me kisses every time the cameras panned on to our table. 'You English are so funny,' she said, as she puckered up for the third time. Sadly she neglected to fulfil her promise to dedicate her Brit award to me on stage.

I bumped into Yasmin Le Bon later, who works out at the same health club as me – Diana's old gym, The Harbour Club in Chelsea. 'I time my visits to coincide with yours, and wait until you get on that step machine before getting on to the one behind,' I joked. Well, semi-joked anyway. She looks amazing for her age, and all the rumours about her marriage to Simon being rocky appeared to be nonsense when I saw her nervously and proudly cheering him on as Duran Duran performed a bit later on.

WEDNESDAY, 18 FEBRUARY

A letter arrived from Sarah Brown, thanking me for sending baby John an Arsenal outfit. She also, hilariously, enclosed a photo of John in his dad's arms – watching Arsenal playing on TV.

I couldn't imagine Cherie doing something like this in a million light years. I must have sent her a dozen notes, cards and bunches of flowers over the years, and have never had a single acknowledgement.

SUNDAY, 22 FEBRUARY

I woke up this morning after a heinous party at Martin Cruddace's house, feeling sick as a dog and with the headache from hell.

Things didn't improve as the day wore on, and I threw up three times between 4pm and 6pm. This wouldn't have been so bad if I wasn't supposed to be having dinner with George Michael. Gary Farrow and Jane Moore had invited him to their house in Battersea with me and Rebekah, so he could unburden himself to the tabloid enemy in a controlled environment in the lead-up to the release of his new album.

It turned out to be one of the most hilarious evenings of my life. And one of the most sober, as even the whiff of alcohol early on had me retching. George, who I knew from my recent dealings with him can be somewhat indiscreet, decided to give us the full nine yards of confession. And by the end, Rebekah and I were sitting there, open-mouthed in shock, as Gary hung his head in his hands and prayed it was a nightmare he'd wake up from. Among George's more entertaining revelations (and there were so many you'd have to demolish most of the Amazon rain forest to print them all) were the following:

1) 'I've slept with about five hundred men in the seven years I've been with Kenny, including loads of male prostitutes. Kenny doesn't mind.'

2) 'One French hooker tried to blackmail me recently because I forgot to pay him.'

3) 'I've had a few threesomes too – with women and men. I can still have sex with women, but Kenny doesn't like me doing that.'

4) 'Rod Stewart's the meanest man in the world – I went to his birthday party in Beverley Hills once, and I swear he served us Dairylea cheese quarters for the starter. I told Elton and he was sure it was, too.'

And on and on it went, with George loving the horror he was provoking. He's clearly reached the stage in his life where he doesn't give a toss about what people think. As he put it, 'If I admit I do this kind of thing, then people can hardly expose me for it, can they?' He was incredibly funny all night, and searingly, uncomfortably honest. He also became the first celebrity to ever render me completely speechless by asking, 'Come on, Piers, I bet you've fancied experimenting with a man ...' I sat bolt upright and spluttered back, 'I most certainly have not, George' in my most military voice. Just when it couldn't get any more surreal, Gary took a phone call and said, 'George, it's Elton for you.' I got home still feeling nauseous. But what a night.

MONDAY, 1 MARCH

The newsdesk rang me just as I got home tonight to say the *Sun* were rumoured to be splashing on the footballer Stan Collymore being caught 'dogging' in a car park. Now I like to think I'm a fairly well-rounded man of the world. But this was a pastime that had not even crossed my worldly bows.

'What the hell is "dogging" when it's at home?'

'Erm, it's when you go to a dimly lit car park and have sex with complete strangers.'

'Well, that used to happen all the time in my village,' I replied.

'Yes, but not without at least having had a drink with them first, perhaps. We're talking complete strangers, as in they haven't met before they start having sex over the bonnet.'

'I see. Right. Well, we'd better get hold of Collymore and splash it, then. With an explanatory note for our older readers, perhaps.'

THURSDAY, 11 MARCH

A terrible day, both for the appalling news that broke and the inept way I handled it.

We'd landed a big exclusive interview with one of the British guys released after two years from Camp X-Ray at Guantanamo Bay last week. He's bright, articulate, and was completely innocent by common agreement.

I thought it was a very important story and would flash round the world.

To justify the hefty £40,000 price tag, I cleared the first seven pages for his account of life inside Guantanamo Bay. A bit over the top, maybe, but it was fantastic stuff.

Then in mid-afternoon, news came in that Madrid has been bombed – ten explosions on four trains in three stations. At least 59 people were killed, and it was complete carnage down there. But the general view was it was an ETA attack, and therefore a localised terrorist incident, like the IRA would be to London.

This clouded my judgement, and I kept the Camp X-Ray interview where it was and stuck the bombing up by the masthead and on a spread back in the paper.

It was only when it became clearer that Al Qaeda had probably done it that I realised how bad our paper's news values looked in the first edition.

I split page one after that, still obstinately sticking to our big scoop, when the sensible thing would have been to ditch it altogether. But we were sharing it with a TV network and would lose the exclusivity if we held it a day … and … Oh, sod it. Nobody's going to feel sorry for this guy on a day when Al Qaeda have done something so appalling – regardless of his innocence. As I sit here watching the news at midnight, I know I've really fucked this up big time.

And I can never remember me doing that on a big news story. It's a bad, bad feeling.

FRIDAY, 12 MARCH

We were inundated with furious calls all day – especially from readers who got the first edition. I felt even worse, if that was possible. I can't blame anyone else, it was my call and I got it terribly wrong.

Ali Abbas, the 12-year-old Iraqi boy who we helped get new arms after he touched the hearts of the nation, came into the newsroom today. He was a cheery little chap, and proudly showed me his new arms. It felt quite emotional watching him play with them. We really had taken this bombed, maimed kid from the fires of hell and made his life better.

'Which team do you support then, Ali?' I asked. His translator relayed the question for me. 'Manchester,' he grinned. I groaned theatrically. 'No, no, you must support Arsenal.' He giggled and replied, mimicking me, 'No, no, Manchester.' When I shook his new hand to say goodbye, he crushed me deliberately and giggled again. The little tinker.

MONDAY, 15 MARCH

Pride of Britain awards today, and one of the great joys of being *Mirror* editor is I get to host the top table and have who I like on it. So I had the Blairs to the right of me, through duty really, and Rachel Stevens – recently voted the world's most beautiful woman – to the left. The Prime Minister arrived at the back door of the Hilton Hotel looking tired and stressed, and I wasn't surprised. The Spanish kicked out their own PM last night, José Maria Aznar, in the aftermath of the Madrid bombings. The man who beat him, José Luis Rodriguez Zapatero, swept in on a ticket of pulling Spanish troops out of Iraq, and blasted Bush and Blair for the 'disaster' of the war. The implications of all this are obvious. Prime Ministers and Presidents who backed this war all now run the risk of getting beaten at elections by anti-war candidates, particularly if Al Qaeda decide to help out a bit by bombing their major cities just before polling day.

Blair was cordial, as ever. But looked awful, and seemed very distracted. At least he said hello: Cherie just bustled past me without a word. Euan came too, with his rather striking girlfriend. But we were told very clearly that they and Cherie would be leaving for the theatre soon after proceedings start.

You have to hand it to her.

Cherie finally did speak to me – to ask if I could get a photo of Euan with Michael Owen, one of his Liverpool heroes.

'Of course, Cherie, it would be a pleasure,' I said.

I went over to Michael. 'Sorry, mate, but Cherie Blair wants to know if you'll do a pic with her son Euan.' 'Yeah, no problem,' he said. I took Euan over and introduced him and the pictures were done. Cherie was suitably grateful, with the usual dig in there, of course.

'Thank you, Piers, nice to see you can do something nice for me occasionally.'

'I am here to serve, you know that, Cherie,' I replied. But the generosity was not reciprocated. When our photographers tried to get a photo of the Blairs with Ali Abbas, they were refused permission. His twitchy aides could see the potential damage of that image. Blair and his victim.

Not as good a vote-winner as Euan and Michael.

I took the Blairs through to the top table, and we had the meal. Blair admitted he was 'shocked' by what happened to the Spanish premier, but said, 'I don't think the public would react like that here. I think they would turn against the terrorists, not the Government in a similar situation.' He's probably right, but I bet that's what José Aznar thought.

I tried to make a joke of it. 'You know what's going to happen ... Bin Laden's going to blow up Canary Wharf, and as I tumble to the ground I'll be shouting, "Guys, I was on *your* side." ' Blair stared ahead blankly; Cherie just tutted.

Rachel Stevens laughed, though, so I turned to her and chatted about pop music, a much safer area for me.

A few minutes later, Jason Donovan came over and introduced himself to Blair. 'I just want to say, Tony, that I think you're doing a fantastic job, mate, and I hope you keep going.'

'You revolting toady, Donovan,' I said. But Jason went on, 'No, I'm serious. You've had a really rough time over all the Iraq business, but we Australians are right behind you, mate.'

As he wandered off, I told Blair, 'Well, at least Jason's with you. If you could get Kylie's vote as well, you might survive.' He did laugh, just.

'Are you seriously worried, Tony?' I said. 'Because you look it.'

'Yes, I am. It's a very tough time.'

'Well, look, we've had our differences on Iraq, but I still want you to fight and win the election. And if we can do anything to help, let me know.'

He thanked me, then his eyes disappeared again. He's in a bad way, a really bad way. He looked half dead.

Rachel had to leave, tragically, to present her award, but I engineered Jodie Kidd to be her replacement, and she sat with me and Branson, swigging champagne and giggling.

The three of us then retired to the Zeta bar downstairs for the party, and guzzled our way through four bottles of Cristal. Well, what else can you drink with supermodels?

I had a drink with Jason Donovan as well. As we chatted, a drunken TV reporter came and sat next to me and placed her hand directly on to my genitals.

I leaned over to Jason, who had seen what happened and was hysterical with laughter. 'What did you used to do when this happened?'

'Well, enjoy it usually, mate, to be honest. But in this case I think ignore it might be a better idea.'

The lady concerned was paralytically drunk and making her intentions gruesomely and luridly obvious, both physically and verbally.

'Sorry, love, I'm with Jodie Kidd,' I stuttered finally. 'But my friend Jason would love to talk to you.'

He groaned. 'Nooooo way, mate!'

But I'd gone, and her hand moved on.

The Pride of Britain team had a big suite for the night and we all retired up there for a full-blown drinking session until 5am.

I stumbled into the morning light feeling ghastly. But probably still better than Tony Blair.

TUESDAY, 16 MARCH

I woke at 10am with a monumental hangover. Too bad to even think about going to work. Particularly as tonight it was the Press Gazette awards. It was the most sober I'd ever been at this event. I sat at one of our four *Mirror* tables sweating neat Jack Daniel's, sipping water, and watching a bunch of broadsheet journalists going up to get their obligatory awards for boring journalism, and making terrible speeches.

One guy from the *Telegraph* rambled on so long he even got jeered by his own table, a new first. We had lots of nominations, but won hardly anything. Despite waging what I truly believe was the most powerful and justified newspaper campaign ever.

But I was in too distressed a state to make my usual vocal protests. When the awards finished, I walked past my old friend Jeremy Clarkson, who spat out his usual bile in my direction. I laughed at him. 'Come on then, big boy, let's see if your fists are up to all the talk.' He just grimaced, fixed me with a wild-eyed stare, and stumbled off to get another drink. I saw Andy Coulson have his own minor skirmish with him a little later – and all the signs were that poor Jeremy had been slightly overdosing on the free booze.

His mood wasn't helped when he failed to win the Motoring Correspondent of the Year award, and had to suffer the double indignity of watching his former *Top Gear* presenter mate Quentin Willson get it instead. Clarkson took it well, though, repeatedly shouting 'Cunt!' at the top of his voice as Quentin received his trophy on stage.

Around 11.30pm, I was chatting to Jane Moore and *News of the World* executive Judy McGuire in the main dining area when Clarkson suddenly reeled into view, marched over to me and put his arm round my shoulder. 'Let's stop all this silliness, shall we?' he slurred, his eyes still worryingly demented. 'Sure, Jeremy,' I replied. 'No problem.'

Then I spied his wife Frances staring at me a few tables away, as if I was the devil incarnate. 'Why does your wife always blame me for everything you do?' I asked. Clarkson spontaneously erupted.

'How dare you fucking attack my wife?' he raged. 'How fucking *dare* you, you cunt.' Jane and Judy were stunned by his change in demeanour and tried to calm him down. But he'd gone. And just punched me straight in the head as hard as he could. Fortunately, that wasn't very hard. But it still hurt, and I was slightly stunned. Before I could say anything he threw another right hook, smashing a ring on one of his fingers into my forehead. Never did like jewellery on a man. 'You fucking *cunt*!' he screamed. The whole room had come to a sudden halt, and hordes of yelping journalists started running over to watch the scrap. It reminded me of my old comprehensive school playground, when a fight would start and word would spread like wildfire: 'Bundle! Bundle!'

I wanted to punch him back, and usually would have done without a moment's hesitation.

But I was stone-cold sober and all I could see were members of the press just waiting to record the moment I finally lost it. Instead I pushed him away, which just provoked him into trying to headbutt me. He missed. 'That all you got, you prick?' I sneered, borrowing the phrase from Muhammad Ali when George Foreman ran out of steam in the Rumble in the Jungle. Clarkson was pulled away by a few *Sun* colleagues as he prepared to show me a bit more.

I, too, was now being held back by *Mirror* men. It was a ghastly, unedifying, but hilarious-for-everyone-else scene. I considered my options and concluded that going home was the best one. It was definitely the water talking.

Sitting in a taxi minutes later, I nursed my bruises and reflected on the irony of being finally thumped at the press awards on the only occasion I have attended them sober and remained sober. As I tried to get to sleep, text messages started flooding in from concerned journalists and fellow editors. Rebekah's was the most encouraging. 'Ross is going to kill him,' she said. I'd like to see Big Jeremy taking on Grant Mitchell, I must say.

WEDNESDAY, 17 MARCH
I woke up with another throbbing head, but this time it had nothing to do with alcohol. I looked in the mirror and could see a big weal stuck into my forehead where his ring had connected.

Fleet Street was overdosing with joy about the incident, and I had to turn my phone off to avoid the incessant inquests. I eventually put it back on and spoke to Gary Farrow. 'Want the good news, mate? Clarkson's going to Barbados next week, same time as you, isn't it?' Yes, it is.

There was general amazement that I hadn't clocked him one back. And admiration from most parts, though my features editor Matt Kelly was not impressed. 'Sorry, boss, but you just bottled it, didn't you?' Perhaps I did. But it's a marathon, not a sprint. I owe Mr Clarkson one.

THURSDAY, 18 MARCH
Rachel Stevens was back at my side today for our monthly *Mirror* lunch, and across the table was Zoe Lucker from *Footballers' Wives*. I was on a £5 bet from the newsdesk to get them talking about lesbian sex before pudding.

'Zoe,' I said, as the main course arrived. 'You killed your husband in the last episode I saw, and it was a huge ratings success. So what you need now is a dramatic new storyline, don't you?'

She agreed.

'And Rachel, you'd like a part in the show, wouldn't you?'

Rachel nodded. 'Yes, it would be great fun.'

'Right, well, I think I've worked it out. You're in such turmoil about what happened, Zoe, that you turn to a female friend for comfort. Rachel. And, well, one thing leads to another …'

Zoe exploded. 'What? Me and Rachel would be lesbians?'

'Yep.'

Rachel giggled. 'You're a naughty man, Mr Morgan.'

'Yep.' And five pounds richer.

I got Rachel to sign one of the sexy picture postcards she gives to fans with the words: 'My place, 4pm, love Rachel.' Above it Zoe scrawled: 'After me, darling, love Zoe.'

The newsdesk were suitably disgusted.

MONDAY, 29 MARCH

I'm in Barbados for the Test match with a few village mates and at 7am this morning my phone went and a familiar voice said, 'Hi, mate, Beefy here. I hear it's your birthday tomorrow, so I thought you might want to come on my yacht and have a party.' I relayed the news to my friends. To say they were excited about spending the day sailing with their hero Ian Botham is the understatement of the Millennium. One of them, Oxford brain and obsessive opening batsman Sam Carter, started to convulse with excitement and had to have a cold shower to calm down.

Tonight we warmed up by going to a party at Jodie Kidd's house, Holder's Hill, an amazing, sprawling home on the West Coast. It was a stunning evening of jazz, reggae and opera – in the most incredible setting I've ever seen in the Caribbean.

We met up with Jodie, and my friends duly got their cameras out for the ultimate holiday snaps with the supermodel for the lads back home. She looked sensational, about 7 ft tall in her high heels, and dripping in jewels. She was also a mischievous little madam, and great fun. As the beers flowed, I stood watching and listening to the music, when she suddenly appeared in front of me and started to, well, for want of a better word, 'snog' me in front of my appalled mates.

I was not quite sure what she was doing, but came up with a rapid response, just in case it was some elaborate wind-up. 'Kidd, I've told you before not to do that in public. Now get me a beer.' My mates were now in stupors of horror and bewilderment. But Jodie just shrieked with laughter, and dutifully trotted off to get my beer. I remain bemused, but, hey, if a supermodel wants to kiss me in front of my friends, then who am I to complain?

Later she tried to persuade us to go to a club with her, but we had to get up early for Beefy's boat, so we declined. I saw her heading off instead with England fast bowler Simon Jones, who didn't look quite so determined to resist her very numerous charms, it has to be said.

TUESDAY, 30 MARCH

We boarded the Botham yacht at 7am. He'd been lent it for the entire six-week Caribbean tour by a Welsh tycoon called Stan Thomas. It was 80 ft long, and a beautiful racing boat with a four-strong crew. My village mates lounged back on the deck sipping pints of vodka cranberries – Ian's idea of a 'warm-up' – genuinely thinking they'd died and gone to heaven. It was a magical day, racing up the rough Atlantic east coast in the morning – then drifting slowly back down the tranquil west coast in the afternoon, mooring off the famous Sandy Lane hotel for lunch.

In the evening, Sarah Botham – Ian and his wife Kathy's daughter – joined us with a few of her Sky Television mates and more merriment ensued. Beefy had arranged for me to have a big cake, and a card signed by all the crew. My lasting memory, though, was lying on the deck at 10pm, both of us very, very drunk and gurgling incoherently, choosing our all-time great world cricket team. He resolutely refused to pick everybody else's two certainties – Don Bradman and Garry Sobers – because they were 'massively over-rated'. He did, though, pick himself, naturally. He and his lovely family have become great friends. This was an amazing birthday.

SUNDAY, 4 APRIL

David Beckham's been accused of having an affair in Madrid with a very attractive, rather Sloaney assistant called Rebecca Loos. The *News of the World* have got hold of text messages between them which are pretty lurid and certainly put a bit of a shadow over Saint Becks's halo. It all looks pretty convincing. But when I called Caroline McAteer, she said it was all rubbish, and Victoria didn't believe a word of it. 'Caroline,' I said. 'It's got to be true. Be careful you don't get duped here into denying something that has happened, or nobody will believe you again.' For the first time I could remember, Caroline hesitated. 'Well, I don't think it's true, and Victoria doesn't believe it, but I guess you can never be sure, can you?'

WEDNESDAY, 7 APRIL

A long heart-to-heart with Gordon Brown at the Treasury this morning. He seemed more restless than usual, as if he knows his time has come if he's ever going to go for it. The mutterings that Blair must go are getting louder by the day, and Brown's always been the only viable option. But will he knife his boss? I'm not so sure. He'd love to be Prime Minister, but I'm not sure he actually has it in him to be the Blair executioner. He's too decent, whatever people say. Brown is appalled by what's happening in Iraq, and has been notable for his silence on the matter. 'We need to get back to a domestic agenda,' he said. 'But how can we, when every day carries all this terrible stuff from Baghdad? It's very damaging to us.'

'If you broke ranks to attack Blair on Iraq, you'd finish him,' I said, mischievously. Brown never normally rises to my bait when I do this kind of thing. 'I don't want to finish Tony,' he laughed. 'You are awful, Piers. But it is undeniable that he is getting very personally damaged by Iraq, and that is a problem for the Government and the party. It's a question of trust, and not finding those weapons has caused us big problems, because that's why we went to war.'

I told Gordon I was going to see him again tonight at Claridge's for a big black-tie marketing dinner.

'Well, don't ask me about wanting the job next door or bloody Iraq,' he sighed.

'Of course not, Gordon.'

At 10pm, the questions started and I put my hand up.

'Erm, Chancellor, can I just ask two things? The first is that when I saw you this morning you seemed to have no curtains in your sitting room, and I wondered if this was because you've started the process of moving in next door?

'And secondly, could you tell me if you think with hindsight it was a good idea to go to war with Iraq, because you seem to have been rather quiet on the matter of late?'

He looked at me and smiled. Like a KGB spy smiles just before he injects you with cyanide.

Then he made a quick joke about curtains and ignored the Iraq question altogether.

As I got a taxi home later, I got a text message from him. 'Sorry for not answering your question …'

THURSDAY, 8 APRIL

Disturbing news. I am David Beckham's lover's cousin. Yes, Rebecca Loos is a distant relative through my uncle's wife – and I apparently danced with her at a family wedding in Madrid once. Unfortunately, she is away at some hideaway with the *NoW* and there's no chance of retrieving anything for the *Mirror*. It really does come to something when your own family flog their stories to a rival paper.

FRIDAY, 9 APRIL

I was sent a scrap of paper today in the post with the handwritten note: 'I was born in Hull, I spent last night in Hull Royal Infirmary. I have an 18-inch long penis.' I looked at Kerrie and we both dissolved into giggles.

MONDAY, 19 APRIL

My interview with Tara Palmer-Tompkinson for *Tabloid Tales* went out last week, and she wrote to thank me today: 'I am very grateful for you involving me in your fabulous portrayal of my eccentric, weird and adventurous life. You could have had me for breakfast … actually I'm quite tasty!'

TUESDAY, 20 APRIL

Everyone's had their say on Beckham, and today Miriam Stoppard had hers. To everyone's astonishment in conference, she banged the table suddenly and declared, 'David Beckham is a total *shit*.' Everyone burst out laughing and applauding. It was a classic moment. I haven't heard Miriam swear in all the years I've worked with her, and she'd even warned me once about my own foul language after a particularly blue conference.

I think if Beckham's lost Miriam, then he's had it, frankly. A more tolerant and kindly soul would be hard to find.

WEDNESDAY, 21 APRIL

I had dinner at the Ivy tonight with Moray MacLellan, chief executive of our ad agency M&C Saatchi, and always amusing company. Sitting two tables away was Richard Desmond with his wife Janet and Waheed Ali. I couldn't help shouting over, 'You shouldn't be wasting time with this lot, Richard, you should be going Tory in the Express.' I meant it, too. The few remaining readers the *Express* has are all diehard Tories, and it makes commercial sense to play to them, not to the disillusioned Labour ranks. He laughed in that way that always suggests he'd rather break my legs.

We exchanged some more lively banter after that, with him banging on about our 'fucking terrible' sales figures, and me responding with a generous character assassination of his 'useless fucking editors'.

I never feel entirely comfortable with Desmond, though. Which is, I suspect, how he wants you to feel.

THURSDAY, 22 APRIL

The front page of the *Daily Express* declared this morning that they are going Tory again. It was far too late when I saw Desmond last night for this to be anything to do with our conversation, so just has to be one of the weirdest coincidences imaginable.

I emailed him:

> When I shouted 'You should go Tory' last night, I had absolutely *no* idea that was exactly what you were doing. I burst out laughing this morning. Hilarious coincidence. Anyway, good fun joshing with you again – and you made a good call today for the *Express*, no question. Most of your readers are right of Attila the Hun, and proud of it. See you soon, Piers.

He replied quickly, as he always does, that he was grateful, and that he'll tell *Express* editor Peter Hill what I said.

'Do, yes,' I added, 'and congratulate him on his sales performance – he's making me look a genius ...'

Seconds later he fired back:

Janet has worked out your business strategy. You attack, attack, attack, so the opponent does not get the chance of getting a word in to remind you that your sales slump is the opposite of our sales increase. And Peter is the finest editor the *Daily Express* has ever had.

Leslie Phillips came in for our monthly lunch today, and was an absolute hoot. He's worked with every actress who matters, and probably slept with most of them, too. He's 80 this week so we gave him a big cake, and he was so thrilled he finally relented to my request for the best and worst leading ladies he'd ever had. 'Oh, my God, what a difficult question,' he said, with a huge smirk on his face. 'The best, and most beautiful, was definitely Kay Kendall. She was magical in every way.'

'Leslie, did you ever … you know … ,' I had to ask.

'No, no – I mean, don't get me wrong, I would have loved to. But she was married to my great friend Rex Harrison, so it was impossible. But she was amazing.'

'And the worst?'

'I couldn't possibly … no, really … oh, alright then. Susannah York. Dreadful woman, and I'm not the only one that thought that, trust me.'

FRIDAY, 23 APRIL

Leslie Ash has been badly hurt in an incident at her new flat in Fulham. Varying reports suggested her ribs were broken, possibly her neck, and she was covered in bruises.

Everyone instantly assumed Lee Chapman had whacked her, the unfortunate consequence of his track record. But her agent Neil Reading, an old mate of mine and a straight guy, said, 'I know what you'll all be thinking. but it was a genuine accident. Leslie and Lee were having passionate sex late last night after a party and Leslie just fell out of bed on to a side cupboard and hurt herself.'

'What? You don't expect anyone to actually believe that, Neil, do you?'

'Well, it's the truth, honestly. I've spoken to them both.'

Later I spoke myself to Leslie and Lee, who I see regularly at the Harbour Club. In fact Leslie and I share the same brilliant personal trainer, Wendy Spence.

They were both adamant that this is what indeed had happened, and laughed and joked about the absurdity of getting so hurt having sex. Perhaps it was exactly as they said it was, in which case I feel desperately sorry for them. Because nobody's going to believe it.

SATURDAY, 24 APRIL

Saw Lee Chapman in the gym today, and he thanked me for doing the story straight. 'That's OK,' I replied. 'If you both say that's what happened, then that's fine by me.'

'It was,' he said. 'And I'm going to sue the papers that have been doubting it. I never hit her, it's ridiculous.'

Another regular in the gym told me Lee had been kick-boxing a big punch-bag that morning – and all the women had watched in horror. Not his best move.

I don't really know what to believe, to be honest.

There's no doubt they've had some fiery moments when they've had a few. And there's no doubt they love each other, I've seen them together loads of times.

I sent Blair a note today. 'Dear Prime Minister, feel free to ignore this, but at Arsenal, whenever the team is under the cosh a bit, the cry goes up from the crowd, "Attack, attack. Attack, attack, attack." Seems to work for us. Why don't you try it? Piers. PS. I believe they try it at Newcastle, too, but with slightly less success. You'll need to look in the mirror and see Thierry Henry staring back – not a player like LuaLua.'

SUNDAY, 25 APRIL
Arsenal won the Premiership today at Tottenham. And I was there with Dad to watch it as a guest of Alan Sugar. I am sure there are more pleasurable things in the world than this, but offhand I can't think of them.

TUESDAY, 27 APRIL
We've been working on a potentially big story for weeks, involving photographs of British troops apparantly abusing Iraqui civilians in Basra last summer …

EPILOGUE 1

THURSDAY, 27 MAY

A very bizarre start to the day. I've hurriedly appointed Martin as my employment lawyer, and as the two of us walked down Dean Street in Soho, a people carrier screeched to a halt beside us, and Cherie Blair's head poked out of the back. This was all I needed in my darkest hour.

'Hello!' she shouted, that Grand Canyon mouth flashing a giant overexcited grin. 'How are *you!*'

I laughed. 'Oh, fine thanks, Cherie, just been fired of course, but otherwise fine.'

'Yes, we're still celebrating!' she replied.

I introduced Martin to her as Naomi Campbell's lawyer, which he was for her appeal against the *Mirror*. 'Oh, I am so pleased you won that case,' she said to him, like he was some sort of moral caped crusader. 'It was so wrong what the Mirror did, well done, you.' I let the moment hang for a little, then said: 'Oh, sorry, I forgot to mention that Martin was also the head of the Mirror legal team when we published the original story and personally approved it in my office.'

Her face dropped like a stone.

'Anyway, Tony and I were talking about you this morning, and we both agreed you must still come to dinner in a couple of weeks.'

I'd forgotten that we were supposed to be having yet another 'clearing the air' encounter in a few weeks' time.

'Oh, don't worry, you don't have to bother any more.'

'No, no,' she said firmly. 'You must come.'

I'd heard they did the same when David Yelland left the *Sun*, then Tony pulled out at the last minute to attend to some 'urgent business'.

The thought of dinner solus with Cherie was not something I'd relish. But it seemed churlish to refuse, even given our history together. 'OK, well, that's very kind of you, thanks.'

'OK, great, see you, then,' she cried – and the people carrier screeched off again.

I looked at Martin, who was in fits.

WEDNESDAY, 2 JUNE

I've been having a relaxing week on holiday in Cyprus with Jeremy, now back at his normal base after his two-month stint in Iraq. Mum, and Charlotte and her family, are here too. As also, by a weird coincidence, are the Queen's Lancashire Regiment.

When we landed, Jeremy rang on his mobile to say, 'Keep your head down quick, a hundred QLR boys are coming into the airport right now to fly off for an exercise.'

'Is this a joke, Jeremy?'

'No, it bloody isn't – hide, quick. They'll beat the shit out of you.'

I was on my way at high speed to the loo when he rang back in hysterics. He'd been watching from the sidelines. The QLR were *not* at the airport.

Coming out of a waterpark in Fissouri on the third day of the holiday, an Iraqi man suddenly came up and hugged me. 'Thank you, sir, for everything you tried to do for my country and for my people.' He was almost in tears. Jeremy was stunned.

'My God, he actually means that, doesn't he?' he finally said. We travelled back in near silence. I was genuinely moved, and Jeremy was genuinely perplexed.

WEDNESDAY, 9 JUNE

I was preparing to drive to Gatwick to fly out to Ellis Watson's stag party in Madrid when the phone rang about 4pm, and it was Marion saying a letter had arrived by registered post from the Department of Trade and Industry.

I froze to the spot. This was it. The DTI's investigation into my 'insider dealing' has been going on for almost four and a half years now.

Four and half years of varying degrees of torment waiting for this one piece of paper. I felt sudden, terrible nausea. The ramifications of being prosecuted now wouldn't bear thinking about. Jobless and facing a criminal trial. Christ. How the mighty ...

'You'd better open it,' I told her.

Marion started reading the contents out loud. Every word the potential shuddering of the guillotine.

Eventually, four or five paragraphs of historical legalese down, we got to the only bit that mattered.

'And so we have decided ... not to prosecute.'

I had to grab on to the table. My legs had gone rather wobbly. I am in the clear, off the hook. There will be no trial, no jail, no humiliation.

I asked Marion to read it again, to be sure.

Oddly, it felt rather anti-climactic. I didn't even feel that happy. Just a weird kind of powerful relief flooded through me. This bloody thing has been hanging over me for so long, and has caused such upset.

I phoned Mum, who burst into tears for the second time in three weeks. I was more pleased for her than me. Nobody wants their son to be labelled a crook, do they?

Later, at the airport, I learned that both the Slicker boys are facing prosecution. So Trinity Mirror, roundly ridiculed at the time for standing by me, have been vindicated in their stance after all.

The phone rang, and it was Victor. He sounded relieved, like me. After all, he'd stuck his neck out big time for me when it all happened. I thanked him, again, for what he did. Felt a bit odd, given that he's part of the board that has just sacked me, but I wouldn't have edited the last four years without his courage under fire in those first few months of 2000. He and Philip Graf both backed me when weaker managers would have thrown in the towel. One thing's for sure, the stag party was now going to be *very* celebratory.

THURSDAY, 10 JUNE

At 2pm I was lying face down in a bullring on the outskirts of Madrid, with a very aggressive one-year-old bull bearing down on me. Six months ago, we'd been told on arrival, a Spanish guy on a stag party died in the same situation when a horn gored his intestines.

I lay, curled into a protective ball, as this panting, snarling beast tried to repeat the exercise. It was absolutely bloody terrifying. And all I could think of as I struggled to fend it off was, 'Fuck me, I survive all that mayhem for all those years, then get killed by a bull.'

Fortunately Ellis and Andy raced over to drag it off. Sounds funny writing it now. But it most definitely wasn't at the time.

THURSDAY, 17 JUNE

Richard Wallace has been appointed editor of the *Mirror*. I am delighted, because he's a great guy and a good friend.

It also means Des won't be getting the job, which is equally pleasing. He was the only senior *Mirror* executive not to bother calling me after I was fired, and his girlfriend Carol Vorderman was the only *Mirror* columnist not to either.

Sinead, Des's lovely PA , sent me an email this morning saying she was really sorry to have to tell me this, but my tickets for the Royal Box at Wimbledon next week were being withdrawn because I am no longer editor of the *Mirror*.

I made some enquiries, because this amused me a lot, and discovered that a Ms Carole Hewitt had called the office, and explained the situation to Conor. 'Oh, don't worry,' he'd said, 'Richard Wallace doesn't like tennis. He won't mind Piers having the tickets at all.'

Ms Hewitt said she would have to ask her boss, the chairman of the All-England Club. Mutterings could be heard and then she returned: 'I'm terribly sorry, but the tickets are for the holder of the office of editor, and not for the individual. So Mr Morgan won't be able to come.'

Marvellous stuff. The sheer scale of this arrogance and pomposity knows no bounds.

I never went to the Royal Box in all the ten years they've invited me, anyway, apart from the time I blagged Mum and Grande in. I find tennis a crashing bore, and the officials of the All-England Club even less interesting. But the fact that they have gone to such lengths to *un*-invite me has made my day.

FRIDAY, 18 JUNE

The end of my first proper week living normal civilian life on my own, and I think I've made quite a good fist of it. I got the car MoT'd and serviced without the help of my driver, I sent my first letters for ten years and discovered that stamps these days are self-adhesive; I shopped for my own food at Sainsbury's and got very excited by a 3-for-2 deal on Special K. I forgot the congestion charge exists, and got an £80 fine. My mobile phone packed up and I got a new one, then spent a tortured five hours trying to transfer the numbers.

I even managed to buy and set up a new computer and printer, and actually got it to work. And I found out that there is an amazing newfangled thing called broadband which makes my system as fast as the one at the *Mirror*. I only had to call Kerrie about ten times.

Most striking of all, this week I realised the sheer unadulterated pleasure of waking up with no air-conditioned office to go to, having the freedom to go for a walk in the sunshine whenever I like, take lunch with the phone turned off, go to the cinema in the afternoon, have a siesta.

Bertie had an official 'Taking daddy to school' day today. But we did it, unofficially, earlier this week. And had a picnic on the common when he'd finished, too. I don't know who enjoyed it more, me or him. Life is full of very simple delights; I just never had time to sample much of them before.

WEDNESDAY, 23 JUNE

Yesterday was to have been my day at the Royal Box at Wimbledon. I scoured the broadsheets to see who had turned up. And who should I find on the guest list, but Boris Yeltsin. The *ex*-holder of the office of President of Russia.

THURSDAY, 24 JUNE

No. 10 rang to confirm dinner next week. I am amazed. But assume they'll just be shoving me at the end of some dreary table of European MPs or something.

WEDNESDAY, 30 JUNE

A memorable, extraordinary evening.

I got back three hours ago from Downing Street and dementedly entered it all into my diary for fear I would forget a single word. And now, as I sit back and read it all, I remain rather stunned.

I'd turned up at No. 10, as requested, at 6.50pm, feeling decidedly strange to be going back in there as a 'civilian'. The policeman, who I'd met a few times on previous visits, theatrically asked for proof of my ID, then laughed and said, 'Have a good night, Mr Morgan,' when I showed him my driving licence.

I walked up to the famous No. 10 door, and got a warm welcome from the guy who opened it. I've always made a point of being nice to those poor blokes, it must be one of the world's most boring jobs – opening that door at least 1000 times a day, mostly to very dull people. 'They've been on the phone asking for you, Mr Morgan, just sit over there and they'll be straight down,' he said.

I plonked myself in one of the nondescript sofas around the main lobby area. A door sprang open and Jonathan 'chief of staff' Powell flew past. 'Hi,' he said, looking startled to see me.

'Hi, how are you?' I replied. But he was too busy to tell me, instead he just flicked his arm up dramatically and marched on to whatever terribly important meeting he'd got next.

Alastair, for all his faults, would have always stopped for a chat.

Sally Morgan arrived, Blair's right-hand woman. 'I'll be right back to take you up,' she said, looking harassed as usual. That poor woman is worked to the bone.

A few minutes later, she was back, and led me up into the Blairs' flat – No. 11, not No. 10 since they swapped with the Browns.

The main hall was littered with Leo's toy train set, sprawling everywhere. The little chap wasn't around, but this was a big piece of kit, and allowed little room for free adult movement. I tiptoed through it into the Blair sitting room. Sally left me alone, which gave me time to see all the photos again. Three of Blair and Clinton, one with Chirac, one with Bush. Lots of the kids, and a few of Tony and Cherie. Most had little messages written on.

There was a big white phone with what seemed like a hundred fast-dial buttons on it. Presumably one of them is the nuke one. I resisted the temptation to have a little play.

Sally, who'd been pretty frosty with me since the *Mirror* had exposed the fact she was sending her son to private school, returned with glasses of white and red wine, letting me choose. I took the white, which was very nice. We exchanged idle 'so what are you doing now' chitchat before Cherie joined us. She's such a strange cove. It occurred to me that we loathe each other in the rather superficial way that people who don't really know each other dislike each other because of various assumed slights.

But tonight she immediately radiated bonhomie.

'Would you like some champagne?' she smiled.

'What are we celebrating?'

'Well, Kathryn and Nicky have finished their exams ... and you've been sacked, of course. So there's lots to celebrate!'

And then Tony arrived, barefoot, and in a casual shirt and ankle-length chinos. He looked considerably healthier and happier than the last few times I'd seen him.

'Hi, Piers, how are things?'

'Well, not bad, thanks, Prime Minister – Cherie and I are just toasting my departure with champagne.'

He laughed: 'Oh, we celebrated your sacking ages ago!' He lounged back in a big chair, one leg strewn across the side.

He immediately wanted to talk about Iraq, our great point of disagreement for so long now. It was like he wanted to make a point of it with me.

'You know, I still feel very deeply about it. It's all very well, some people saying we should move on now there's been a handover and so on, but I can't do that. It was the biggest call of my Premiership and I don't want people judging it as a terrible mistake. I really believe it was right. When I talk to the Arab leaders, it is clear the strategic importance of Iraq is massive to all of them. And Saddam had to go.'

'Yes, but why didn't we find the WMD?'

'I just don't know. It is baffling. He had the stuff and it must be there somewhere, it must be. But we haven't found any, and that has been a huge problem.'

'I bet you wake up every morning hoping to see CNN reporting a chemical weapon find in Baghdad.'

'Yes,' he half-smiled. 'It has been a bit like that. But regardless of the WMD issue, I want to see it through now, to prove that we have made Iraq a better place than it was.'

'It's not, though, is it? It's worse. My brother Jeremy's just been out there and he says it's chaos. And he was a big supporter of the war. He believed we'd find loads of WMD, and even now he thinks it was justified to get rid of Saddam. But I can tell he's very disillusioned by what he found out there.

'He says we are viewed as aggressive occupiers, not liberators – particularly the Americans, who are just hopeless peacekeepers, apparently. He went on patrol with one American officer the other day who he says made John Wayne seem like a choirboy.'

Blair nodded. 'They are different to us, that's obvious. They view things differently, and they operate in a different way on the ground. But it is a lot better us being there with them than the Americans going it alone.'

'Really?'

'You know, Piers, when things got really hot for me politically here, and it looked like we wouldn't get the second UN resolution, Bush rang me and said: "If you want us to go in alone, Tony, and join up later on, then we will do that. I understand your problems." It was an incredible offer, but I thought that it would just be totally wrong to do that. We either supported them or we didn't.'

This struck me as a fairly sensational admission.

'It can't help you that Bush always sounds so bloody thick, though, can it?'

Cherie raised her eyebrows to the ceiling at that.

But Blair said, 'It's a funny thing. He is not stupid, he's really not. He made some brilliant off-the-cuff interjections at the NATO meeting this week, for instance, comments that stopped everyone in their tracks.

'But he's not very good at the TV soundbite stuff, and that gives a misleading impression. It's obviously harder to have a Republican rather than Democrat President when you are a Labour Prime Minister. But believe me, Bush listens to us and he acts on what we say. That has been more important than ever since Iraq.'

'Would have been a lot easier to have a benevolent kind of Republican President like Reagan, wouldn't it? Rather than some red-neck Texan who most Britons despise.'

Cherie snorted. 'The left hated Reagan too, you know.'

'Yes,' I said, 'but he didn't sound so dumb, and the left only hated him because he loved Maggie so much.'

We moved on to newspapers. Blair banged on yet again about the *Mail*, so I reminded him, yet again, that more *Mail* readers voted for him second time than first time. He seemed surprised at this, but I've personally told him this three times before.

Cherie loved it. 'See, I told you. They don't matter, darling.'

Blair was more sanguine. 'If I was a Tory, they'd love me and support me all the way.'

'You virtually are,' I said, joking.

'No,' said Cherie, very serious suddenly. 'We are *socialists*.' She was not joking. I reached for another glass of wine and turned the conversation back to Iraq.

I had seen Blair when he was scrapping for that second UN resolution to back military action, and he was incredibly confident he would get it. Then it slipped away at the last minute.

'Was that the most difficult moment you've faced as Prime Minister, when you realised you'd have to choose between America and the UN?'

'Yes, well it was very hard, obviously. I really thought we would get that second resolution, the United Nations would back military action and public opinion would then move with us. But once we failed to get it, I believed it to be the right thing to go with America, and try and act as some restraint, if I could, where it was necessary. It would have been much worse if America had had to go it alone.'

Cherie agreed. 'Tony worked so hard to get the second resolution. It was a nightmare time, and some countries were not being straight with us.'

She got up off the sofa.

'Anyway, shall we have dinner?'

I followed after her into a small, but rather elegant dining room – and saw just three place settings. It was going to be just the three of us after all. God!

The table was laid out with full silver service, cut glass and bone china. I've never been so spoiled at No. 10 before.

'So what are you going to do now, then?' Blair asked, pouring some wine out.

'Nothing for a while, it's quite liberating doing nothing, actually. Not being on call all the time, not going to a tower block every day.'

Blair seemed fascinated by my new life of leisure, asking what hours I'd been doing at the *Mirror* and how I'd handled that.

'It's like your job,' I said. 'You're always on call, you can never really relax.'

He looked rather wistful, 'Yes, people don't realise how relentless it is. You get used to it, but you can never leave the job alone. But I always know that if I get kicked out of here, then I'll be fine, I'll just go off and do other things.'

The simmering tensions between No. 10 and No. 11 have been obvious for ages to anyone who's visited both camps. The truth is that Brown believes Blair welched on his deal to stand aside after two election triumphs. A deal offered not once, as many assume, but several times.

But Brown has never once been openly disloyal to me about Blair.

'You know, despite everything you might think, Gordon has never criticised you to me in any of our many private meetings. Even when I've tried to wind him up a bit, he never has.'

Cherie nearly spluttered into her wine, and Blair seemed staggered.

'Well,' he said after a few long seconds, 'I'm glad to hear that. It's the people around him that cause most of the trouble, I think. Gordon is an amazing politician. The three cleverest people I've met in politics are Alastair, Peter and Gordon. I am lucky to have had them all to talk to over the years.'

Then he added, 'But I have never relied on any of them. I am the one who has to make the call in the end.'

'What do you think of Alastair's roadshow – looks like he wants everyone to think he was the boss after all?'

Blair looked me straight in the eye and quite deliberately said, 'Alastair likes to make out he ran the show, and he was and is a great guy who was very helpful to me. But the truth is that I never ever ran any policy by him. Ever. I might have asked how something would play out in the press, but never how to formulate policy.'

What an extraordinary thing for him to say about his closest political ally.

The elaborate and very tasty seafood salad was finished, and three fine steaks arrived for the main course.

Emboldened by the whole bottle of fine red wine Tony and I had now consumed between us – the first time I'd seen him drink that much – I turned to Cherie and said, 'So, come on, then, why *do* you hate me so much?'

She blushed slightly, and Blair said immediately, 'Cherie doesn't hate you, Piers, it's all been exaggerated.'

'But I know she does, and I can see in her face she's just dying to tell me why. Come on, it doesn't matter now, I've gone – and I am just curious.'

She sighed. 'It started with that feature you ran about my bad skin.'

I quickly racked my brains and couldn't think what the hell she was talking about.

'What feature? Honestly, I have never heard this before.'

She grimaced disbelievingly. 'You know the one I'm talking about. You did this whole thing about celebrities with terrible skin, and put me next to Victoria Beckham. Now that girl has got awful skin – I'm sorry, but she has. I have always been known for having very good skin for my age. I mean, look at my skin – it's good isn't it?'

I peered at the First Lady's cheekbones and conceded, 'Yes, not bad, actually. Sorry about that.'

I didn't know what else to say.

Blair laughed nervously. 'See, Piers, it was all about Cherie's skin!' The absurdity of this revelation made us both laugh out loud.

I moved on to the next 'misunderstanding'.

'And what about the time you rang up Rebekah and gave her our exclusive story of your pregnancy?'

'That's rubbish,' she said firmly. 'I was told the story was coming out on the Press Association wire, and we had to say something because Rebekah got wind of it and thought I was seriously ill.' Blair nodded his agreement, adding: 'We were at Charlie Falconer's party and we got a call saying Rebekah had it too.'

I still believe this is all complete baloney. But you know what? It really doesn't matter any more.

'And you know, Piers, while we're at it, I just want to say I never leaked the election date to the Sun that time, that just wasn't true either,' said Blair.

'Oh, come off it,' I laughed. 'You must remember that Lance Price confession – do you honestly expect me to believe you didn't know your own press office leaked that date to the Sun?'

'Yes, because that is the truth. I didn't.'

I asked if Cherie regretted the whole Fostergate business.

She reacted angrily. 'I only met Peter Foster for a few minutes. He tried to invent emails that I was supposed to have sent him, but we were able to prove from our own logs I had not sent them.'

'What I never understood about Fostergate was that everyone in Fleet Street knew what a conman he is: he's notorious for it. Yet nobody around you guys warned you.'

Blair interrupted, 'I never met the man at all.'

The persistent distancing from troublesome stories, it seemed, was becoming something of a theme of the dinner.

Blair smiled, and poured some more wine.

I was getting a bit pissed. And I think he was, too, though Cherie was on the water now.

'I must say, Piers,' said Blair earnestly, 'that I hate the scale of intrusion into the lives of public figures now. I mean, look at what's happening to David Beckham. All that stuff about him having an affair. We should be behind him, not pulling him to pieces.'

I nearly choked on my steak.

'Come off it, Tony. Beckham's courted the press more than anyone for years. You can't sell your wedding for a million and expect privacy on your marriage, surely.'

'I think you are still entitled to a degree of privacy, yes.'

Sensing the tone of the evening had turned a tad confrontational, I commented on how well Blair looked.

'Yes, I feel a lot better than I did, I must say. It's been a tough couple of months. I was terrible at your Pride of Britain awards. The Madrid train bombings had just happened, and I was as low as I can remember then.'

'Did you consider packing it in?'

'Well, I couldn't see any light at the end of the tunnel and I was very down about it.'

'Not any more, though,' said Cherie, firmly.

'No, now I feel a lot better. Iraq is slowly getting sorted out and I feel we are finally making inroads into things like health and crime.'

'What do you hope your legacy will be?'

'I hope my legacy will be that we made a difference and really revolutionised Britain into a modern country.'

'Well, if I were you, I'd fight a third election, win easily because Howard's hopeless, then hand over to Gordon just before the euro referendum, and at the precise moment Bush tells you he wants to go to war in Iran.'

Cherie burst out laughing. 'Oh, wouldn't that be great,' she giggled.

Blair laughed too. 'Iran, yes … well, I haven't declared war on anywhere for a year now, so I am getting withdrawal symptoms.'

'Yes, you really are Bomber Blair, aren't you?'

He raised his eyebrows and tutted.

'Talking of bombers, what do you make of Clinton's autobiography?'

'It's so long, isn't it? Rather hard going,' said Cherie.

'All political memoirs are boring, aren't they?' said Blair.

'Yours won't be, darling,' she replied quickly.

Then the door flew open, and Euan and his sister Kathryn appeared, to say hello.

After dinner, Tony suggested he and I go back to the sitting room for a final drink before he watched the end of the Portugal semi-final with Euan.

He poured a couple of whiskies.

'You should go into TV full time, you could be the new Parky – I was saying that to someone the other day.'

It was, of course, the usual great Blair flattery, hitting the target right where I wanted to be hit.

'That's very kind of you to say so, but I think I've got a bit of work to do yet. It's a totally different medium to newspapers. And it's all so narcissistic. When I did Tabloid Tales, more people commented on my hair than the interviews.'

'I don't think you'll struggle too hard with narcissism,' he laughed. 'But I think you interview very well. I know Peter thought that when you did him. The other thing I would say, though, is that you mustn't lose your opinions. People respect the fact that you take a view on issues and stick to your guns. I always told people that although I didn't always agree with you, I did admire the way you went for it, and put your case over. You should do something that plays to those strengths. I think that's important.'

It was time for a bit of humble pie.

'Well since we're burying all hatchets tonight, I'd like to say how sorry I am that things got so personally fractious over Iraq, because it seemed to poison the whole Mirror/Government relationship. I don't regret the stance we took, or the conviction we had. But I do think we got too personally abusive from time to time, and I'm sorry for that.'

'Well, I thought you went over the top a few times, and said so to Victor. But I never thought it was a personal thing against me, actually. We always got on pretty well, and Alastair thought the same about you too, funnily enough.'

It felt strange talking like this with the Prime Minister. But then I guess I've known him now for more than eleven years, and we've had a lot of contact in that time. I wouldn't say we're friends, but we've certainly spent a lot of time in each other's company. And I like the man, always have done.

But now it's over and we both sort of know it. He walked me slowly to the door, and Cherie suddenly rushed up unprompted to show me Leo's latest school photo. Not sure why, really, but I made the appropriate noises of approval.

We've cleared the air a bit tonight, no question. Cherie's hopefully realised I am not quite the monster she assumed. And I've had a better insight into her complex character, too, and can see she's maybe not the harridan I feared, either. Prickly, yes; difficult, most certainly. But a victim of her position, too, and the restrictions it has placed on her life and career. And when she relaxes, she can actually be quite fun.

Blair opened the door to let me out, shook me warmly by the hand, and said: 'Keep in touch, call me if you think of anything that might be useful to me. I appreciate your opinion, I really do.'

I think he may even have meant it too, amazingly. I get the feeling he really misses having Alastair around.

I walked out into the street and down towards the Commons to get a cab.

What a strange night. People will never believe me.

EPILOGUE 2

MONDAY, 19 JULY

Richard Wallace made Conor his deputy today. And Ellis has been promoted to managing director. Martin, meanwhile, has moved to a lucrative new job running the legal arm of Betfair, the online gambling firm. That party in my flat the night I got fired sparked quite a change in everyone's fortunes.

WEDNESDAY, 21 JULY

Ross Kemp's 40th birthday party, and my first real outing since my sacking to an event where the great and good will be gathered. Rebekah organised a typically fabulous bash in the middle of Battersea Park. Gordon Brown was there, and came straight up to ask how I was.

'I tried to call you a couple of times on your mobile, but I guess the company took it back, did they?' he said.

I laughed: 'Er, no, Gordon, they didn't actually. It's the same one I've always had and it's been on all the time.' We both knew he hadn't tried to call me. Sarah, his wife, had miraculously managed to get through several times, after all.

I also knew he had sent the new *Mirror* editor, Richard Wallace, a handwritten fax of congratulations within an hour of his appointment – something he'd done to me in 1995.

But I understood. Politics is about priorities.

As I chatted with him, a woman suddenly poked through between us, put her arms round us both and exclaimed, 'Ah, my two favourite men!'

It was Cherie.

I did a mock introduction. 'Gordon, this is Cherie, your neighbour; Cherie, this is Gordon.'

She giggled, he grimaced.

'Thanks for a lovely dinner, Cherie,' I said.

Gordon's eyes squinted darkly at this revelation.

'Oh, I enjoyed it very much,' she said, flashing a huge grin at the Chancellor.

Later in the evening I saw David Blunkett being surrounded by a bevy of beauties, so I sidled up next to him and whispered in his ear, 'Got any good gear on you, mate?'

He spluttered with indignation. 'What? *What?* Who is this? What gear?'

'You know what I mean, mate, come on, some of that good coke or Es will do nicely.'

Blunkett spluttered again. 'Who *is* this?'

'It's Piers, Home Secretary. How are you?'

He rocked back. 'Morgan, you bastard, I thought we'd got rid of you.'

Even later I ended up in a side room with Greg Dyke in a group we called 'Media Martyrs'.

Sir John Stevens, the Met police chief, joined us, and took me aside to say something fascinating. 'There are going to be a lot of court cases early next year involving allegations against British soldiers in Iraq. Just thought you'd like to know. I've seen the paperwork.'

FRIDAY, 23 JULY

Mandelson's been nominated by Tony Blair to be our next European Commissioner, which means he'll have to quit Parliament and move to Brussels. It looks a shoo-in. I am curiously chuffed for him, and he'll be great out there.

Jeremy called tonight to tell me about an extraordinary evening he'd recently had with General Mike Jackson.

Apparently he said that I should have given the MoD more time to inspect the photos, up to a month if necessary, then this 'disaster could have been avoided'. He claimed to have known immediately they were fakes – 'no man pisses like that'. Of course he didn't say that at the time.

The general didn't understand why I'd stood my ground so long, saying I should have caved in a week before I was sacked.

Jeremy tried to lighten the mood by saying I was now looking for a career in MI5, because 'employees don't get sacked when they are duped there'.

The general was not amused, accusing Jeremy of being 'very ungrown-up', and then launching into a full attack on the media, saying we were all out of control, unaccountable and doing anything we liked to sell papers, with no sense of responsibility. Same sort of stuff he'd given me when I met him last summer at David Frost's summer party.

Jeremy tried to defend me, saying I felt a duty to provide some form of opposition to an omnipotent Government.

The general exploded. 'How arrogant – I'm sorry, Jeremy, but how arrogant! Your brother, a tabloid editor, thinking he's the opposition to the Government – who does he think he is?'

Jeremy agreed I was indeed arrogant, but that it went with the job. 'One editor's ego is not worth the life of a British soldier,' Jackson replied, echoing the QLR quote that finished me off.

Then Jeremy mentioned I had just dined with the Prime Minister.

The general erupted again. 'Good God, has Tony Blair got nothing better to do than cavort with a sacked, disgraced editor?'

As Jeremy said, 'Fair point.'

SATURDAY, 24 JULY

To Ian Botham's box at Lords for the test match, and I bumped straight into Lord Archer again.

'*Aha!*' he squealed, with obvious delight. 'I was hoping you'd be here. Last year there was a disgraced peer in this box, this year there's a disgraced Piers.'

THURSDAY, 19 AUGUST

I'd written a note to the Blairs thanking them for dinner and saying I thought we had cleared the air a bit.

A handwritten letter arrived today from 'The office of Cherie Booth, QC'.

'Dear Piers, thank you for your kind letter. I too felt we had cleared the air and hope we can now get our relationship off to a new and much better footing. Keep in touch, love Cherie.'

It is the first time she has *ever* written to me.

MONDAY, 18 OCTOBER

So there I was, having a quiet curry at a fancy Indian restaurant called the Painted Heron in Cheyne Walk, when I heard a familiar voice two tables away.

James bloody Hewitt!

I hadn't seen the old rogue since that hotel meeting on the *News of the World*.

All I knew for a fact was that a) he wants to kill me, and b) I hadn't been in the same room as him since I discovered this.

Half an hour later he got up to go to the loo, spied me, and exclaimed, 'Well well, well, Piers Morgan!'

We eyed each other for a few seconds.

Then he ambled over, sat down and spent the next hour chatting like we were great old friends.

'Sorry about what happened to you,' he said.

'No, you're not,' I laughed.

'No, I'm not – you're right!'

We chatted through our various scrapes.

'I never got paid for that bloody Anna Pasternak book,' he said.

'Yes you did – I saw your bank statements,' I replied.

'Did you? Fuck. OK, well I never was very good at hiding things from the press.'

'You were wrong about those letters,' I said. 'We didn't put your fiancée up to it, she was trying to stitch you and flog them.'

'Really? Well, I was never really sure about that, either way. How interesting.'

'Talking of interesting, what the hell did you say to the Palace to make them give them back to you?'

'Aha! Wouldn't you like to know.'

'Yes, I would.'

'Well, let's just say I put a bit of pressure on.'

The mind boggles.

'I bet you read them, didn't you?'

'Of course I did.'

He laughed. 'God, you're bastards.'

'Well, takes one to respect one,' I replied.

We sank a bottle of wine, and the restaurant emptied. It was totally surreal.

'Well, I'd better be off now. Great seeing you again,' he said.

We swapped phone numbers.

'Be good to have dinner sometime.'

'Sure,' I said. 'Why not?'

WEDNESDAY, 20 OCTOBER

Peter Mandelson's leaving do, at an advertising agency building off Oxford Street.

It was a weird night. All sorts of disparate people turning up to say goodbye to one of the great characters of modern politics.

Bumped straight into Alastair, looking a bit lonely.

'You alright?' I asked.

'Yeah, guess so – you?'

'Yes. Bit odd on the outside, isn't it?'

'Very. It's funny, but I find all the things that pay well bore me stupid.'

He looks fed up.

Saw Gavyn Davies at the other end of the smallish room.

'I haven't spoken to Alastair since it all happened,' he said.

'Well, why don't we go and beat him up. You're too rich to worry about the repercussions and I'm unemployed – it's the perfect time.'

'He'd hurt me,' laughed Gavyn. 'He's much fitter than I am.'

Sue Nye, his wife, was there too – and we were joined by Sally Morgan and Anji Hunter.

'You all just coming to make sure he's going?' I said, talking about Mandelson.

'I'm the only representative he invited from the "other side",' laughed Sue, referring to the Brown camp.

Mandelson himself flitted about like a gadfly, then made a fairly self-congratulatory speech to about 100 people – including Geoff Hoon, who just stared at me with those dreary eyes.

The speech could have been subbed down to 'Tony owes it all to me.' Which he probably does, in a funny way. Anyway, I heckled him a bit to try and bring some levity to the self-congratulation.

As he finished talking, Cherie grabbed me and planted a smacker on both cheeks.

'How's my best friend?' she giggled, to astonishment from everyone around me.

'Oh, missing you terribly,' I laughed.

'Is your personal life sorted out now, I'm worried about you,' she said. 'It's really important you get that sorted out.'

'Don't worry Cherie, my moral compass is slowly coming back on track. To be honest, I've given up hoping you will leave Tony for me.'

'Oooh, you naughty boy! You're far too young for me, and I'm far too old for you.'

'You're never too old, Cherie, we both know our feud was down to sexual tension.'

I thought Anji, Sue and Sally were going to die of shock.

Cherie cackled.

'We've got similar senses of humour really, haven't we?'

'So how's your husband now?'

'He's *great*. It's all going to be fine now.'

'Thanks to you.'

'What do you mean?'

'I mean he'd have quit by now if you hadn't persuaded him to fight on. And you're right, because he can't lose and things can only get better.'

'Well, he just had to believe in himself again, and he does now.'

I decided to be mischievous and feed her a trap.

'Not good news for Gordon, then.'

'No, it's not, is it?' she laughed.

'Well, take care Cherie – I'm so glad we're best friends now.'

'Oh, so am I, Piers, so am I!'

END

CAST OF CHARACTERS

There are hundreds of people mentioned in these diaries, often only by their first name. To help you keep track of who I am talking about, you may find it useful to refer to the following Cast of Characters.

Some are now dead, and others have lost or changed their jobs. But I decided to keep things simple and give them their most recognisable descriptions.

3AM GIRLS – *Daily Mirror* gossip columnists
A. A. (ADRIAN) GILL – TV critic
ADAM BOULTON – Sky News political editor
ADAM FAITH – actor and singer
ADAM INGRAM –Armed Forces Minister
ADDISON CRESWELL – agent to stars including Jonathan Ross
ADOLF HITLER – former Nazi leader
ALAN BROOKE (LORD ALANBROOKE) – British Field Marshal in the Second World War
ALAN CLARK – former Tory minister and best-selling diarist
ALAN FARTHING – gynaecologist; was fiancé of Jill Dando
ALAN MILBURN – Labour Cabinet minister
ALAN MOGG – my *News of the World* driver
ALAN PARTRIDGE – spoof TV broadcaster character
ALAN RUSBRIDGER – editor of the *Guardian*
ALAN SUGAR (SIR) – Amstrad business tycoon, Spurs chairman and *Daily Mirror* columnist
ALASTAIR CAMPBELL – director of communications at No. 10 Downing Street
ALASTAIR MORTON (SIR) – chairman of Eurotunnel PLC
ALEC STEWART – England cricket captain
ALEX FERGUSON (SIR) – Manchester United manager
ALEX MARUNCHAK – *News of the World* executive
ALI COCKAYNE – rugby star Will Carling's former lover
ALI ISMAEEL ABBAS – young Iraqi boy who lost his arms in the Iraq war and came to Britain to get new ones
ALICIA KEYS – American singer
ALISON HARKESS – judge's daughter who had affair with Alan Clark
ALLY MCCOIST – Scottish soccer star and TV pundit
ALUN MICHAEL – Labour Cabinet minister
ALVIN KALLICHARRAN – former West Indies cricket star
AMANDA DE CADENET – TV presenter
AMANDA HOLDEN – TV actress, formerly married to Les Dennis
ANDREW (PRINCE) – The Queen's second son
ANDREW BONAR-LAW – former British Prime Minister
ANDREW CALDECOTT – top QC
ANDREW GILLIGAN – BBC reporter famous for his report on the 'sexed-up' Iraq dossier
ANDREW GOWERS – editor of the *Financial Times*
ANDREW MARR – BBC political editor and ex-editor of the *Independent*
ANDREW NEIL – ex-*Sunday Times* editor, now a broadcaster and newspaper adviser to *Telegraph* owners, the Barclay brothers
ANDY COULSON – editor of the *News of the World*

ANDY HARRIES – TV producer
ANDY LINES – *Daily Mirror* executive
ANDY MCNAB – former SAS soldier, now best-selling author
ANGUS DEAYTON – TV presenter
ANIL BHOYRUL – former *Daily Mirror* City Slicker columnist
ANITA DEBNEY – former nanny to Paula Yates
ANITA RODDICK – founder of the Body Shop
ANJI HUNTER – former aide to Tony Blair, now works for BP
ANN LESLIE – *Daily Mail* foreign correspondent
ANN WIDDECOMBE – former Tory minister
ANNA FERRETTI – fiancée of James Hewitt
ANNA PASTERNAK – journalist who wrote book with James Hewitt
ANNABEL ELLIOTT – sister of Camilla Parker-Bowles
ANNE BULLEN – former PA to Robin Cook
ANNE ROBINSON – TV presenter and former *Daily Mirror* journalist
ANNE SHEVAS – No. 10 press officer
ANTHEA TURNER – TV presenter
ANTHONY LAIKER – my stockbroker
ANTON ANTONOWICZ – *Daily Mirror* foreign writer
ANTONIA DE SANCHA – former lover of Tory MP David Mellor
ARCHER – man who organised the beach facilities at the Sandy Lane Hotel, Barbados
ARNIE SLATER – *Daily Mirror* photographer
ARSENE WENGER – Arsenal manager
ARTHUR BALFOUR – former British Prime Minister
BAHA MOUSA – Iraqi hotel receptionist allegedly killed by British soldiers in Basra
BARBARA WINDSOR – TV star
BARRY DILLER – American media tycoon
BARRY GEORGE – Jill Dando's murderer
BEN MERCHANT – American email correspondent
BEN VERWAAYEN – chief executive of British Telecom
BENJAMIN PELL – man who collects celebrity rubbish
BENJAMIN WEGG-PROSSER – former aide to Peter Mandelson
BERNARD DOHERTY – PR to rock stars like Mick Jagger
BERNARD INGHAM (SIR) – former spindoctor to Margaret Thatcher
BERNARD MANNING – comedian
BERNICE RUBENS – former Booker Prize winning author
BERTIE PUGHE-MORGAN – my youngest son
BIENVENIDA BUCK (LADY) – lover of former Chief of Defence Staff, Sir Peter Harding
BILL ANSLOW – *News of the World* production executive
BILL BATESON – former *News of the World* sports editor
BILL CLINTON – former US President

BILL DEEDES (LORD) – *Daily Telegraph* columnist
BILL SHANKLY – former Liverpool manager
BILLIE PIPER – pop star married to Chris Evans
BOB BLAIR – *Daily Mirror* sports executive
BOB GELDOF – rock singer and Live Aid creator
BOB HOPE – American comedian
BOB PAISLEY – former Liverpool manager
BOB STEWART – former British commander in Bosnia
BOB WARREN – *News of the World* executive
BOB WILLIS – cricketing legend
BOBBY CHARLTON (SIR) – former Manchester United and England football legend
BORIS YELTSIN – former President of Russia
BOY GEORGE – transvestite pop star in the 1980s
BRENDON PARSONS – *Daily Mirror* deputy editor 1995–98
BRIAN BOSTOCK – *Daily Mirror* reader
BRIAN EPSTEIN – former manager of the Beatles
BRIAN HARVEY – pop star
BRIAN HITCHEN – former editor of the *Daily Star* and *Sunday Express*
BRIAN READE – *Daily Mirror* columnist
BRIDGET ROWE – former editor of the *Sunday Mirror* and *Sunday People*
BRITNEY SPEARS – American pop star
BROOKLYN BECKHAM – son of Victoria and David Beckham
BRUCE GROBBELAAR – former Liverpool goalkeeper accused of match-fixing
BRUCE WILLIS – American movie star
BRUNO LANGLEY – *Coronation Street* star
BUDDY HOLLY – singer
CAMILLA PARKER-BOWLES – Prince Charles's lover
CARINE REID – wife of Labour Cabinet minister John Reid
CARLOS THE JACKAL – notorious international assassin
CAROL VORDERMAN – TV presenter
CAROLE CAPLIN – former lifestyle adviser to Cherie Blair
CAROLE HEWITT – official at the All-England Club
CAROLE MALONE – *Sunday Mirror* columnist
CAROLINE MCATEER – PR aide to Victoria Beckham
CARRIE FISHER – American movie star
CATHERINE ZETA-JONES – British movie star, married to Michael Douglas
CECIL PARKINSON – former Tory minister
CHARLES – Prince of Wales
CHARLES COLLIER-WRIGHT – Mirror Group lawyer
CHARLES DUNSTONE – founder of Carphone Warehouse
CHARLES GRAY – a leading judge
CHARLES KENNEDY – leader of the Liberal Democrats
CHARLES MOORE – former editor of the *Daily Telegraph*
CHARLES SAATCHI – advertising guru and art dealer
CHARLES SPENCER (EARL) – Princess Diana's brother
CHARLIE DRAKE – comedy star
CHARLIE FALCONER (LORD) – Labour Cabinet minister and former flatmate of Tony Blair
CHARLIE GEORGE – former Arsenal soccer legend
CHARLIE KRAY – East End gangster, brother of twins Ronnie and Reggie
CHARLIE RICHARDSON – former South London gangster
CHARLIE WHELAN – former spindoctor to Gordon Brown, now a broadcaster
CHARLIE WILSON – former editor of *The Times* and managing director of Mirror Group Newspapers
CHARLOTTE TOMLINSON – my sister
CHERIE BLAIR – wife of Prime Minister Tony Blair
CHRIS BLYTHE – former *News of the World* reporter
CHRIS EUBANK – former boxer
CHRIS EVANS – TV and radio star
CHRIS GENT – former boss of Vodafone
CHRIS MAYBURY – former News International executive
CHRIS MULLIN – Labour MP
CHRIS ROYCROFT-DAVIS – leader writer for the *Sun*
CHRIS SEARLE – Olympic gold medal-winning oarsman
CHRIS TARRANT – TV presenter
CHRIS VERNON – British army spokesman during Iraq War
CHRIS WADE – *Mirror* PR executive
CHRISTINE HAMILTON – wife of former Tory minister Neil Hamilton
CHRISTOPHER HITCHENS – columnist
CHRISTOPHER MEYER (SIR) – former spokesman for John Major, now head of the Press Complaints Commission
CILLA BLACK – TV star

CINDY CRAWFORD – American supermodel
CITIZEN KANE – fictitious megalomaniac media tycoon
CLAIRE HALL – transsexual who had affair with *Emmerdale* star Stan Richards
CLARE SHORT – former Labour Cabinet minister
CLEMENT FREUD – writer and broadcaster, father of PR guru Matthew
CLEO ROCOS – TV star
CLIFF RICHARD – singer
CLIVE ANDERSON – TV comedian
CLIVE GOODMAN – royal editor of the *News of the World*
CLIVE LLOYD – former West Indies cricket star
COLIN MYLER – former editor of the *Daily Mirror* and *Sunday Mirror*
COLIN STAGG – man wrongly accused of killing Rachel Nickell on Wimbledon Common
COLIN WALSH – *Have I Got News For You* producer
COMBAT 18 – extreme right-wing English organisation
CONOR HANNA – *Daily Mirror* executive
CONRAD BLACK (LORD) – former owner of the *Telegraph*
CRAIG MACKENZIE – former *Daily Mirror* executive, brother of Kelvin
DAD – my father, Glynne Pughe-Morgan
DALE WINTON – TV presenter
DANIEL TAYLOR – News International lawyer
DANNII MINOGUE – singer, sister of Kylie Minogue
DAVE BALMFORTH – former *Daily Mirror* sports editor
DAVE BANKS – former *Daily Mirror* editor, now broadcaster
DAVE HILL – chairman of Fox Sports in America, former head of Sky Sports
DAVE WARWICK – Paul Burrell's agent
DAVID BECKHAM – footballer
DAVID BLACK – former commander of the Queen's Lancashire Regiment
DAVID BLAINE – magician and illusionist
DAVID BLUNKETT – former Labour Home Secretary under Tony Blair
DAVID BOWIE – rock star
DAVID BRENT – fictitious boss from hit comedy show *The Office*
DAVID DEIN – vice-chairman of Arsenal Football Club
DAVID DIMBLEBY – TV broadcaster
DAVID ENGLISH – former editor of the *Daily Mail*
DAVID FROST (SIR) – TV star
DAVID GINOLA – French football star
DAVID HILL – No. 10 spokesman
DAVID ICKE – former football star turned turquoise-clad conspiracy theorist
DAVID KELLY – government scientist whose death led to the Hutton report
DAVID LEIGH – former news editor of the *Daily Mirror*
DAVID LLOYD GEORGE – former Prime Minister
DAVID MELLOR – former Tory Cabinet minister
DAVID MONTGOMERY – former chief executive of Mirror Group Newspapers
DAVID PUTTNAM (LORD) – Labour peer and Oscar-winning movie producer
DAVID SCHUMAKER – *News of the World* investigative reporter in America
DAVID SEAMAN – former Arsenal and England goalkeeper
DAVID SEYMOUR – *Daily Mirror* leader writer
DAVID STEVENS (LORD) – former owner of Express Newspapers
DAVID YELLAND – former editor of the *Sun*
DAVINA MCCALL – TV presenter
DAVINIA MURPHY – TV actress
DAWN ALFORD – former *Daily Mirror* investigative journalist
DEIRDRE BARLOW – fictitious *Coronation Street* character
DELLA BOVEY – ex-wife of Grant Bovey, who left her for Anthea Turner
DENNIS SKINNER – Labour MP
DENZEL WASHINGTON – American movie star
DEREK JAMESON – former newspaper editor and broadcaster
DEREK LEWIS – former boss of the prison service
DERRY IRVINE (LORD) – former Lord Chancellor
DES KELLY – *Daily Mirror* executive
DES LYNAM – TV presenter
DESMOND BROWNE – top QC
DEVON MALCOLM – former England cricket star

DI BUTLER – Welsh *Daily Mirror* reader
DIANA – the Princess of Wales
DIANA ROSS – American singer
DIANE ABBOTT – Labour MP
DICK EMERY – TV comic
DIVINE BROWN – American prostitute caught with Hugh Grant
DODI FAYED – Mohammed Al Fayed's oldest son, who died in car crash with Princess Diana
DOMINIC LAWSON – editor of the *Sunday Telegraph*, and old boy of my prep school
DON BRADMAN (SIR) – Australian cricket legend
DON CORLEONE – Mafia family boss in *The Godfather* movie
DON MACKAY – *Daily Mirror* news reporter
DON REVIE – former England football manager
DONALD TRUMP – American business tycoon
DONATELLA VERSACE – sister of murdered fashion guru Gianni
DORIS DAY – Hollywood legend
DORIS STOKES – famous dead medium
DOUGLAS HURD – former Tory minister
DOUGLAS JARDINE – captain of England's 1932/33 bodyline tour to Australia
DUNCAN LOVETT – *Daily Mirror* picture desk executive
DUSTIN HOFFMAN – American movie star
DYLAN JONES – editor of *GQ* magazine
EAMONN HOLMES – GMTV presenter
ED HENTY – *News of the World* photographer killed by IRA bomb
EDDIE IZZARD – TV comic
EDWARD (PRINCE) – youngest son of The Queen
EDWARD PICKERING (SIR) – former newspaper editor and consultant to Rupert Murdoch
EDWINA CURRIE – former Tory minister
ELAINE BEDEL – 'friend' of TV star Jeremy Clarkson
ELISABETH MURDOCH – Rupert Murdoch's daughter, married to Matthew Freud
ELIZABETH BUTLER-SLOSS (DAME) – head of the Court of Appeal's Family Division
ELIZABETH HURLEY – British model
ELIZABETH TAYLOR – Hollywood legend
ELLIS WATSON – managing director of Trinity Mirror
ELTON JOHN – singer
ELVIS PRESLEY – American singer
EMILY BARR – journalist and former parliamentary researcher
EMMA NOBLE – TV star, and former wife of John Major's son James
EMMANUEL PETIT – former Arsenal football star
ERIC CLAPTON – rock star guitarist
EUAN BLAIR – son of Tony and Cherie Blair
EUGENE DUFFY – *Daily Mirror* executive
EVA SIMPSON – *Mirror* 3am Girl
F. S. MAUDE (GENERAL) – commander of the British forces in Iraq, 1917
FERGIE – Sarah, Duchess of York
FINLAY TOMLINSON – my sister's son
FIONA BRUCE – BBC newsreader
FIONA MCTAGGART – Labour MP
FIONA MILLAR – former aide to Cherie Blair and partner of Alastair Campbell
FIONA PARKER – *Daily Mirror* letters editor
FIONA PHILLIPS – TV presenter
FRANCES CLARKSON – wife of Jeremy Clarkson
FRANCES SHAND-KYDD – Princess Diana's mother
FRANCIS WHEEN – newspaper and magazine columnist who works for *Private Eye*
FRANK BRUNO – former world heavyweight boxing champion
FRANK DOBSON – former Labour Cabinet minister
FRANK FIELD – former Labour Cabinet minister
FRANK LONGFORD (LORD) – former Labour peer
FRANK SINATRA – singer
FRANK SKINNER – TV comedian
FRANK WARREN – boxing promoter
FRANKIE FRASER ('MAD') – former London gangster
FREDDIE MERCURY – rock star with Queen
GABRIEL BATISTUTA – Argentinian footballer
GAIL PORTER – TV presenter
GARETH GATES – pop star
GARRY BUSHELL – TV critic
GARRY SOBERS – former West Indies cricket legend
GARY FARROW – executive at Sony Music

GARY HERBERT – former Olympic rowing champion, now a lawyer
GARY JONES – former *News of the World* reporter, now *Daily Mirror* chief reporter
GARY LINEKER – former England soccer hero, now TV presenter
GARY NEVILLE – Manchester United star
GAVYN DAVIES – business tycoon and former BBC chairman
GAZZA – Paul Gascoigne, former England footballer
GEOFF BAKER – former PR aide to Paul McCartney
GEOFF HOON – Labour Cabinet minister
GEOFF LAKEMAN – former *Daily Mirror* reporter
GEOFFREY ROBINSON – business tycoon and former Government minister who lent Peter Mandelson money to buy a house
GEORGE – owner of the Dover Street Wine Bar, who sits next to me at Arsenal
GEORGE BEST – football legend
GEORGE BUSH – American President
GEORGE CARMAN – libel QC
GEORGE CUSTER (GENERAL) – famous for his last stand
GEORGE FOREMAN – former boxing champion
GEORGE GALLOWAY – Labour MP
GEORGE GRAHAM – former manager of Arsenal
GEORGE MICHAEL – singer
GERALD CORBETT – former boss of Railtrack
GERALD KAUFMAN – Labour MP
GERALD MCCLELLAN – former American boxing star
GERI HALLIWELL – pop star
GERRARD TYRRELL – celebrity lawyer
GERRY ADAMS – Sinn Fein party leader
GERRY AGAR – former assistant to Paula Yates
GIANNI VERSACE – Italian head of fashion empire, murdered in 1997
GILL HORNBY – wife of writer Robert Harris, and sister of writer Nick Hornby
GLENN GOODEY – *Sun* newspaper executive
GLENN HODDLE – former England football manager
GORDON BROWN – Chancellor of the Exchequer
GORDON WHITE (LORD) – business tycoon
GRACE KELLY – movie star who married Monaco's Prince Rainier
GRAHAM BURRELL – brother of Paul Burrell, Diana's former butler
GRAHAM TAYLOR – former England football manager
GRAND-MERE OR GRANDE FOR SHORT– my grandmother, Margot Barber
GRANDPA – my grandfather, Major Matthew Oliver
GRANT BOVEY – husband of Anthea Turner
GRANT MITCHELL – fictitious hardman character in *EastEnders*
GREG BENNETT – *Daily Mirror* picture executive
GREG DYKE – former BBC Director-General
GRIFF RHYS-JONES – TV comedian
GUY BLACK – former director of the PCC, now Michael Howard's spindoctor
GUY RITCHIE – film director and husband of Madonna
HALLE BERRY – Hollywood actress
HANNIBAL LECTER – fictitious cannibal killer
HANS BLIX – United Nations chief weapons inspector
HAROLD SHIPMAN – serial killer GP
HAROLD WILSON (LORD) – former Labour Prime Minister
HARRIET HARMAN – Labour MP and former Cabinet minister
HARRY (PRINCE) – youngest son of Prince Charles and Princess Diana
HARRY CARPENTER – former boxing commentator
HARRY ENFIELD – TV comedian
HARRY HARRIS – football reporter for *Daily Express*, formerly for the *Daily Mirror*
HARRY SCOTT – *News of the World* executive
HARTLEY BOOTH – former Tory MP
HEATHER MILLS-MCCARTNEY (LADY)– Sir Paul McCartney's wife
HELEN ADAMS – *Big Brother* TV star
HELEN ROLLASON – TV sports presenter
HENRI PAUL – French driver of the car that crashed and killed Princess Diana
HENRY CAMPBELL-BANNERMAN (SIR) – former British Prime Minister

HENRY CARLING – son of rugby star Will Carling
HENRY KISSINGER – American presidential adviser
HERMANN GOERING – Nazi chief
HILARY RYAN – former PA to Will Carling
HILLARY CLINTON – wife of former President Bill Clinton
HOLLY WELLS – murdered Soham schoolgirl
HOWARD DAVIES – former boss of the Financial Services Authority
HUGH CUDLIPP – legendary former editor of the *Daily Mirror*
HUGH GAITSKELL – former leader of the Labour Party
HUGH GRANT – British movie star, former lover of Liz Hurley
HUGHIE GREEN – former presenter of TV talent show *Opportunity Knocks*
HUTTON (LORD) – judge who oversaw report into No. 10's 'sexed-up' Iraq dossier
HUW EDWARDS – BBC newsreader
IAIN DUNCAN SMITH – former leader of the Tory Party
IAN BEALE – character in *EastEnders*
IAN BOTHAM – cricket legend
IAN BRADY – infamous Moors murderer
IAN HISLOP – editor of *Private Eye* and presenter of *Have I Got News For You*
IAN HUNTLEY – killer of schoolgirls Holly Wells and Jessica Chapman
IAN LUCAS – lawyer for Princess Diana car crash bodyguard Trevor Rees-Jones
IAN WALKER – Premiership goalkeeper
IAN WOOLDRIDGE – *Daily Mail* sports columnist
IAN WRIGHT – Arsenal and England football star
IMRAN KHAN – former Pakistan cricket legend, and ex-husband of Jemima Khan
IRENE CLARK – TV star Michael Aspel's lover
JAAP STAM – former Manchester United soccer star
JACK DANIEL'S – my favourite drink, with coke and ice
JACK KENNEDY – former American President, assassinated in 1963
JACK NICHOLSON – Hollywood legend
JACK PROFUMO – former Tory Cabinet minister who resigned over callgirl scandal in the 1960s
JACK STRAW – Foreign Secretary
JACQUES CHIRAC – President of France
JAMES BOND – fictitious spy hero
JAMES HARKESS – former judge whose wife and two daughters all had affairs with Alan Clark
JAMES HEWITT – former lover of Princess Diana's
JAMES HIPWELL – former *Daily Mirror* City Slicker columnist
JAMES MAJOR – son of former Tory Prime Minister John Major
JAMES MURDOCH – younger son of Rupert Murdoch, now running BskyB
JAMES PRICE – top QC
JAMES SCOTT – *Sunday Mirror* executive, former *Daily Mirror* showbiz reporter
JAMES WHITAKER – royal correspondent of the *Daily Mirror*
JAMIE DALTREY – son of Who rock star Roger Daltrey
JAMIE PYATT – *Sun* reporter
JANE ATKINSON – former PR assistant to Princess Diana
JANE GOLDMAN – TV presenter and wife of Jonathan Ross
JANE KERR – *Daily Mirror* royal reporter
JANE MOORE – *Sun* columnist and broadcaster
JANET DESMOND – wife of *Express* owner Richard Desmond
JANET STREET-PORTER – TV presenter
JASON DONOVAN – Australian TV star and singer
JASON FRASER – paparazzi photographer
JEFF BEZOS – founder of internet business Amazon
JEFF RANDALL – former editor of *Sunday Business*, now BBC business editor
JEFFREY ARCHER – author and former Tory politician jailed for perjury
JENNIE BOND – former BBC royal correspondent
JENNIFER BROWN – daughter of Gordon and Sarah Brown who tragically died just a few days after birth
JENNY JOHNSTON – *Daily Mirror* feature writer
JEREMY BOWEN – BBC presenter and war reporter
JEREMY CLARKSON – TV presenter
JEREMY PAXMAN – TV presenter
JEREMY PUGHE-MORGAN – my brother, a major in the Royal Regiment of Wales
JEREMY SANDELSON – my lawyer at Clifford Chance

JERRY HAYES – former Tory MP
JESSICA CHAPMAN – murdered Soham schoolgirl
JESSICA LYNCH – American soldier captured and later rescued in Iraq
JILL COLLINS – former wife of pop star Phil Collins
JILL DANDO – TV presenter shot dead outside her home
JO BRAND – TV comic and former *Daily Mirror* columnist
JO MOORE – former adviser for Stephen Byers
JOAN COLLINS – British actress
JOAN MULCASTER – journalist on the *Sutton Herald*
JODIE KIDD – supermodel
JOE JOSEPH – TV critic for *The Times*
JOHN ALLWOOD – former chief executive of Mirror Group Newspapers
JOHN BROWN – baby son of Gordon and Sarah Brown
JOHN CANTOPHER – my great-uncle
JOHN CLEESE – TV and movie star
JOHN DENHAM – Labour MP
JOHN DUX – former managing director of News International
JOHN FRASER – assistant to film mogul Michael Winner
JOHN HOLMES – sporting agent to stars like Will Carling and David Gower
JOHN HOWARD – *Daily Mirror* circulation executive
JOHN HUMPHRIES – BBC broadcaster
JOHN JUNOR – former editor of the *Sunday Express*, and *Mail on Sunday* columnist
JOHN KAY – chief reporter of the *Sun*
JOHN LENNON – former member of the Beatles, murdered in 1980
JOHN LEWIS – former headmaster of Eton College
JOHN MAJOR – former Tory Prime Minister
JOHN MCNAMARA – security chief for Mohammed Al Fayed
JOHN MONKS – former leader of the TUC
JOHN MORTIMER – lawyer famous for *Rumpole of the Bailey* books
JOHN PILGER – foreign correspondent
JOHN PRESCOTT – Deputy Prime Minister
JOHN REDWOOD –Tory MP and former Cabinet minister
JOHN REID – Elton John's former manager
JOHN REID – Labour Cabinet minister
JOHN SAVIDENT – *Coronation Street* star
JOHN SIMPSON – BBC foreign correspondent
JOHN SMITH – former Labour leader
JOHN STEVENS (SIR) – boss of the Metropolitan Police
JOHN WAYNE – Hollywood cowboy legend
JOHN WITHEROW – editor of the *Sunday Times*
JOHNNY HUNTER – brother of Blair aide Anji
JOHNNY SPENCER (EARL) – father of Princess Diana
JON MOORHEAD – *Daily Mirror* production executive
JONATHAN AITKEN – former Tory minister, jailed for perjury
JONATHAN CAINER – astrologer
JONATHAN DIMBLEBY – TV political journalist
JONATHAN MEADES – food critic
JONATHAN POWELL – No. 10 chief of staff
JONATHAN ROSS – TV presenter and former *Daily Mirror* film critic
JONATHAN ROTHERMERE (LORD) – owner of the *Daily Mail* newspaper group
JONATHAN WOODGATE – England football star
JORDAN – model with very large breasts
JORDAN RIOS – American man
JOSE LUIS RODRIGUEZ ZAPATERO – Prime Minister of Spain
JOSE MARIA AZNAR – former Prime Minister of Spain
JOSEPH MENGELE – Nazi torture expert
JOSEPHINE HARKESS – judge's daughter who had affair with Alan Clark
JUDAS – man who betrayed Jesus Christ
JUDITH KEPPEL –first £1 million winner of *Who Wants To Be a Millionaire?*
JUDITH MELLOR – former wife of David Mellor
JUDY MCGUIRE – *News of the World* executive
JULIA CARLING – former wife of rugby star Will Carling
JULIET GELLATLEY – founder of the anti-vivisection group VIVA
JULIUS FRANCIS – British boxer
JUNE WHITFIELD – British comedy actress
JURGEN KLINSMANN – former Spurs and Germany soccer star
JUSTICE MORLAND (LORD) – High Court judge

JUSTIN DUNN – former *Daily Mirror* reporter
KARREN BRADY – chief executive of Birmingham City FC and Sport Newspapers
KATE HOEY – former Labour Cabinet minister
KATE WINSLET – British actress
KATHRYN BLAIR – daughter of Tony and Cherie Blair
KATHY BOTHAM – wife of cricket legend Ian Botham
KATHY LLOYD – former Page Three model
KAY BURLEY – Sky TV presenter
KAY KENDALL – British movie actress
KAZUYA ENDO – Japanese spokesman for culture in UK
KEITH WILLIAMS – Harley Street eye surgeon
KELVIN MACKENZIE – former editor of the *Sun*, now owns Talksport
KEN BATES – former chairman of Chelsea Football Club
KEN CLARKE – former Tory Chancellor
KEN LIVINGSTONE – London Mayor and former Labour MP
KENNETH STARR – American lawyer and independent prosecutor
KENNY GOSS – boyfriend of pop star George Michael
KENT GAVIN – *Daily Mirror* photographer
KERRIE BUCKLEY – my PA at the *Mirror*
KEVIN COSTNER – American movie star
KEVIN MAGUIRE – former political editor of the *Mirror*
KEVIN O'SULLIVAN – *Mirror* features executive
KIM PHILBY – British spy who double-crossed us with the KGB
KIRSTY GALLACHER – TV presenter
KOFI ANNAN – Secretary-General of the United Nations
KRIS THYKIER – PR executive for Freud Communications
KRISHNAN GURU-MURTHY – Channel 4 News presenter
KYLIE MINOGUE – pocket-sized pop phenomenon
LACHLAN MURDOCH – older son of Rupert Murdoch
LANCE PRICE – former No. 10 spindoctor
LARRY GRAYSON – camp TV comic
LAURA BRUNO – Frank Bruno's ex-wife/partner
LEDLEY KING – Spurs soccer star
LEE BOWYER – Newcastle soccer star
LEE CHAPMAN – former soccer star, married to Leslie Ash
LENNOX LEWIS – boxing legend
LENNY HENRY – TV comic
LEO BLAIR – youngest son of Tony and Cherie Blair
LEONARDO DA VINCI – Italian painter
LES DENNIS – TV comedian
LES HINTON – chairman of News International
LESLIE ASH – TV actress, married to former soccer star Lee Chapman
LESLIE PHILLIPS – British movie star
LESTER PIGGOTT – legendary jockey
LIAM FOX – Tory MP and health spokesman
LIAM GALLAGHER – star with rock group Oasis
LINDA MCCARTNEY – wife of Beatles star Paul McCartney who died of cancer
LINFORD CHRISTIE – former British sprinting champion
LIZ BREWER – society party fixer
LIZ ROSENBERG – spokeswoman for Madonna
LLOYD EMBLEY – *Daily Mirror* production executive
LOIS BLASENHEIM – partner of Labour MP Dennis Skinner
LORRAINE HEGGESSEY – controller of BBC1 Television
LOU YAFFA – *News of the World* production executive
LOUIS XIV – longest-reigning French king
LUALUA – Newcastle striker
LUKE ALLSOPP – British soldier killed in Iraq
MADAME RIDAUDO – fantasy star of Alastair Campbell's erotic journalism
MADAME VASSO – psychic used by Fergie, Duchess of York
MADONNA – American singer
MAGDI YACOUB (PROFESSOR) – heart surgeon and friend of Princess Diana
MALCOLM RIFKIND – former Tory Cabinet minister
MANDY ALLWOOD – mum who conceived and then lost eight babies
MARCEL DESAILLY – former French football captain
MARCO PIERRE WHITE – master chef and restaurateur
MARCUS PARTINGTON – Mirror Group legal manager
MARGARET (PRINCESS) – The Queen's sister
MARGARET MCDONAGH – former aide to Tony Blair
MARGARET THATCHER (LADY) – former Tory Prime Minister

MARGOT BARBER – my grandmother
MARILYN MONROE – Hollywood superstar
MARION PUGHE-MORGAN – my wife
MARJE PROOPS – legendary *Daily Mirror* agony aunt
MARK BOLLAND – former aide to Prince Charles
MARK BOOTH – former chief executive of BskyB
MARK HAYSOM – former managing director of Mirror Group Newspapers
MARLON BRANDO – movie superstar
MARTIN CRUDDACE – former legal manager of Mirror Group Newspapers
MARTIN DUNN – former *Sun* executive and editor of *Today* newspaper
MARTIN EDWARDS – former chairman of Manchester United
MARTIN KEOWN – Arsenal football star
MARTIN LUTHER KING – American civil rights icon
MARTIN MCGUINNESS – leading Sinn Fein official
MARTIN PARKINSON – my *Daily Mirror* driver
MARTY SINGER – Hollywood lawyer
MARY NIGHTINGALE – ITV newsreader
MATI WHITE – wife of Marco Pierre White
MATT KELLY – *Daily Mirror* executive
MATT PRITCHETT – *Daily Telegraph* cartoonist
MATTHEW FREUD – PR mogul, married to Liz Murdoch
MATTHEW HARDING – former insurance tycoon and Chelsea Football Club boss
MATTHEW KELLY – TV star
MATTHEW NORMAN – newspaper columnist
MATTHEW PARRIS – former MP, now newspaper columnist
MATTHEW WRIGHT – TV presenter and former *Daily Mirror* columnist
MAURICE SAATCHI – advertising guru
MAX CLIFFORD – PR guru
MAXIMUS – fictitious character in the movie *Gladiator*
MAXINE CARR – girlfriend of childkiller Ian Huntley
MEKON (THE) – See DAVID YELLAND
MEL B – pop star
MEL SMITH – TV comedian
MELANIE CANTOR – agent to stars like Ulrika Jonsson
MICHAEL ASPEL – TV presenter
MICHAEL BARRYMORE – TV presenter
MICHAEL BROWN – former Tory MP, now columnist for the *Independent*
MICHAEL CAINE (SIR) – British movie star
MICHAEL COLE – former BBC royal reporter and spokesman for Mohammed Al Fayed
MICHAEL CORLEONE – fictitious character in the *Godfather* gangster movies
MICHAEL DOUGLAS – Hollywood star, married to Catherine Zeta-Jones
MICHAEL FLAHETY – *Daily Mirror* reader
MICHAEL FOOT – former leader of the Labour Party
MICHAEL GIBBINS – former adviser to Princess Diana
MICHAEL GREEN – TV mogul
MICHAEL HESELTINE – former Tory minister
MICHAEL HOLDING – former West Indies cricket star
MICHAEL HOWARD – leader of the Conservative Party
MICHAEL HUTCHENCE – rock star with Australian band, INXS
MICHAEL JACKSON – American singer
MICHAEL LEVY (LORD) – Labour peer
MICHAEL OWEN – England football star
MICHAEL PARKINSON – TV chat show host
MICHAEL PAYNE – father of murdered schoolgirl Sarah Payne
MICHAEL PEAT (SIR) – aide to Prince Charles
MICHAEL PORTILLO – former Tory Cabinet minister, now TV presenter
MICHAEL WATSON – former British boxing star
MICHAEL WINNER – film mogul and columnist
MICK JAGGER – rock star singer with the Rolling Stones
MIKE BANNISTER – Concorde pilot
MIKE JACKSON (GENERAL) – Chief of the General Staff
MIKE KEHOE – New York fireman on day of 9/11
MIKE MCCARTNEY – Paul McCartney's brother
MIKE MCCURRY – White House spokesman under Clinton
MIKE MOLLOY – former *Daily Mirror* editor
MIKE MOORE – war photographer
MIKE MOORE – American anti-war author and filmmaker
MIKE O'BRIEN – Home Office minister
MIKE TYSON – American heavyweight boxing champion

MIKHAIL GORBACHEV – former President of Russia

MILES CALDWELL – friend from my Sussex village

MILLS AND BOON – romantic novel firm

MIRIAM STOPPARD (DR) – *Daily Mirror* agony aunt, author and TV broadcaster

MO MOWLAM – former Labour Cabinet minister

MOHAMMED – Prophet of Islam

MOHAMMED AL FAYED – owner of Harrods

MOHAMMED SAEED AL-SAHAF – Iraq spokesman during the war

MONA LISA – painting by Leonardo da Vinci

MONICA LEWINSKY – White House intern who had an affair with President Clinton

MORAY MACLELLAN – M&C Saatchi chief executive

MUHAMMAD ALI – boxing legend

MUM – my mother, Gabrielle Pughe-Morgan

MYRA HINDLEY – Moors murderer

NANCY DELL'OLIO – lover of England football manager Sven-Goran Eriksson

NAOMI CAMPBELL – Streatham-born supermodel

NAYIM – footballer

NAYNESH DESAI – Ian Botham's lawyer

NEIL HAMILTON – former Tory minister

NEIL KINNOCK – former Labour leader

NEIL READING – top showbiz agent

NEIL WALLIS – deputy editor of the *News of the World*, former editor of the *People*

NELL MCANDREW – model

NELSON MANDELA – South African leader

NEVILLE CHAMBERLAIN – former British Prime Minister

NICHOLAS LYELL (SIR) – former Attorney General

NICK CLARKE – Radio 4 presenter

NICK FALDO – British golfer

NICK HORNBY – author and Arsenal fan

NICK LEESON – former City trader jailed for massive bank fraud

NICK LLOYD (SIR) – former newspaper editor, now top PR man

NICK MILNER-GULLAND – former headmaster of my prep school

NICKY BLAIR – son of Tony and Cherie Blair

NICOLA FORMBY – lover of TV critic A. A. Gill

NICOLA METHVEN – *Daily Mirror* TV editor

NIGEL BENN – former boxing champion

NIGEL DEMPSTER – *Daily Mail* gossip columnist

NIGEL TAIT – top QC

NIGELLA LAWSON – TV chef

NOEL EDMONDS – former TV presenter

NOEL GALLAGHER – star with rock group Oasis

NOOR (QUEEN) – Queen of Jordan

NORMA MAJOR – wife of former Tory Prime Minister John Major

NORMAN LAMONT – former Tory minister, now Lord Lamont

NORRIS MCWHIRTER – co-creator of *Guinness Book of Records*

ODYSSEUS – hero of Greek mythology

O. J. SIMPSON – American sporting icon cleared of killing his wife

OLIVER HOARE – art dealer, former close male friend of Princess Diana

OLLIE PICTON-JONES – fashion director of *Daily Mirror*

OLLIE REED – British hellraising actor

OONAGH BLACKMAN – *Daily Mirror* political journalist

ORIANNE CEVEY – third wife of pop star Phil Collins

OSAMA BIN LADEN – terrorist

PADDY ASHDOWN – former leader of the Liberal Democrats

PADDY POWER – bookmakers

PAMELA ANDERSON – American TV star

PATRICK DEMARCHELIER – French photographer, a favourite of Princess Diana's

PATRICK TOMLINSON – my sister Charlotte's husband, an army colonel

PATRICK VIEIRA – Arsenal football captain

PATSY CHAPMAN – former editor of the *News of the World*

PATSY KENSIT – British actress

PAUL BURRELL – former butler of Princess Diana's

PAUL DACRE – editor of the *Daily Mail*

PAUL FOOT – columnist

PAUL GILFEATHER – *Daily Mirror* political journalist

PAUL HANDLEY-GREAVES – security man for Mohammed Al Fayed

PAUL INCE – footballer

PAUL MCCARTNEY – singer

PAUL MERSON – footballer, formerly with Arsenal

PAUL MERTON – presenter of *Have I Got News For You*

PAUL RIDLEY – former sports editor of the *Sun*

PAUL ROUTLEDGE – *Daily Mirror* political commentator

PAUL SCHOLES – Manchester United star

PAUL VICKERS – company secretary of Trinity Mirror

PAULA HAMILTON – former model

PAULA YATES – former TV star and ex-wife of Bob Geldof

PENELOPE COBHAM (LADY) – David Mellor's lover

PENNY RUSSELL-SMITH – press secretary to The Queen

PETE WATERMAN – record company mogul

PETER BOTTOMLEY – Tory MP

PETER CARTER-RUCK – famous libel lawyer

PETER COX – former *Sun* and *Mirror* executive

PETER DONALD – young male model who died in tragic circumstances

PETER ESTCOURT – my GP in Sussex

PETER FOSTER – notorious conman who helped Cherie Blair buy some flats

PETER HAIN – Labour MP and leader of the House of Commons

PETER HARDING (SIR) – former Chief of Defence Staff

PETER HILL – editor of the *Daily Express*

PETER HOUNAM – former *Daily Mirror* journalist

PETER MANDELSON – former Labour spindoctor and Cabinet minister, now Trade Commissioner for the European Union

PETER POWELL – top showbiz agent and former husband of Anthea Turner

PETER PRESTON – former editor of the *Guardian*, now a media commentator for the *Observer*

PETER WILLIS – *Daily Mirror* executive

PETRONELLA WYATT – magazine columnist

PHIL COLLINS – pop superstar

PHIL HALL – my former deputy editor on the *News of the World*, replaced me as editor

PHIL NEVILLE – Manchester United star

PHIL TAYLOR – *News of the World* reporter

PHIL TUFNELL – former England cricket star

PHILIP (PRINCE) – The Queen's husband

PHILIP GRAF – former chief executive of Mirror Group Newspapers

PIERCE BROSNAN – movie star

PIERS MERCHANT – Tory MP

POPE (HIS HOLINESS THE) – John Paul II, leader of the Catholic Church

PUFF DADDY – rap star

QUEEN (THE) – our monarch

QUEEN MOTHER – The Queen's mother

QUENTIN WILLSON – TV and newspaper car expert

RACHEL HUNTER – Australian model, and former wife of rock star Rod Stewart

RACHEL STEVENS – pop star

RAGEH OMAAR – BBC reporter, became famous during Iraq War

RAINE SPENCER – Princess Diana's stepmother, and executive at Harrods

REBECCA LOOS – alleged girlfriend of David Beckham and my second cousin

REBEKAH WADE – editor of the *Sun* and former *News of the World* executive

REGGIE KRAY – East London gangster, twin of Ronnie

REINALDO DE SILVA – Peter Mandelson's boyfriend

REX HARRISON – British actor

RHODRI MORGAN – First Minister of Wales

RICHARD AND JUDY (MADELEY AND FINNEGAN) – husband and wife TV presenters

RICHARD BRANSON – Virgin tycoon

RICHARD CURTIS – British movie script writer

RICHARD DESMOND – owner of Express Newspapers

RICHARD E GRANT – British actor

RICHARD INGRAMS – former editor of *Private Eye*

RICHARD JOHNSON – jockey and former lover of royal Zara Phillips

RICHARD KAY – *Daily Mail* gossip columnist, former *Mail* royal reporter

RICHARD SPRING – Tory MP

RICHARD WALLACE – replaced me as editor of the *Daily*

Mirror

RICHARD WHITELEY – TV presenter
RICHARD YOUNG – top showbiz photographer
RICHIE BENAUD – cricket commentator
RICHIE RICHARDSON – former West Indies cricket star
ROBBIE WILLIAMS – pop superstar
ROBERT CLARK (SIR) – former chairman of Mirror Group Newspapers
ROBERT HARRIS – war historian and columnist
ROBERT MAXWELL – former owner of the *Daily Mirror* until he fell off his yacht
ROBIN COOK – former Foreign Secretary
ROD EDDINGTON – chief executive of British Airways
ROD HULL – TV ventriloquist, famous for his puppet Emu
ROD RICHARDS – Tory MP
ROD STEWART – rock star
ROGER ALTON – editor of the *Observer*
ROGER DALTREY – rock star with the Who
ROGER EASTOE – former managing director of Mirror Group newspapers
RON DAVIES – former Labour minister forced to resign over sex scandal
RON MORGANS – former *Mirror* picture editor
RONALDO – Brazil and Real Madrid football superstar
RONNIE FLANAGAN – former RUC chief
RONNIE KRAY – East End gangster, twin of Reggie
RORY BREMNER – TV impressionist
RORY CAMPBELL – son of spindoctor Alastair Campbell
ROSE – grandmother used as political football in 2001 election
ROSE WEST – wife of mass killer Fred West
ROSIE BOYCOTT – former editor of the *Daily Express*
ROSS KEMP – TV star, married to *Sun* editor Rebekah Wade
ROY GREENSLADE – former editor of the *Daily Mirror*, now media commentator for the *Guardian*
ROY KEANE – Manchester United soccer star
RUDY GIULIANI – former mayor of New York
RUPERT ALLASON – former Tory MP and spy-writer
RUPERT MURDOCH – chairman of News Corporation
RUPERT PUGHE-MORGAN – my little brother
RYAN GIGGS – Manchester United soccer star
RYAN PARRY – *Daily Mirror* undercover reporter who worked as a footman at Buckingham Palace
SADDAM HUSSEIN – deposed ruler of Iraq
SALLY MORGAN – aide to Tony Blair
SAM CARTER – friend from Sussex
SAM CHISOLM – former head of BskyB
SANDRA HOWARD – wife of Tory leader Michael Howard
SANDY HENNEY – former aide to Prince Charles
SARA KEAYS – former lover of ex-Tory minister Cecil Parkinson
SARA PAYNE – mother of murdered schoolgirl Sarah Payne
SARA WOODHATCH – assistant to Liz Hurley
SARAH BOTHAM – daughter of cricket legend Ian Botham
SARAH BROWN – wife of Gordon Brown
SARAH CHATTO (LADY) – the late Princess Margaret's daughter
SARAH MCCORQUODALE – Princess Diana's sister
SARAH SANDS – deputy editor of the *Daily Telegraph*
SARAH VAUGHAN-BROWN – *Daily Mirror* PR executive
SCARLETT JOHANSSON – American film actress
SCOTT MITCHELL – boyfriend of TV star Barbara Windsor
SEAN MACAULAY – writer, and brother of Sarah Brown
SEARLE BROTHERS – Olympic rowing champions
SHANE RICHIE – TV star
SHANE WARNE – Australian cricket superstar
SHERWIN CAMPBELL – West Indies cricket star
SHERYL KYLE (GASCOIGNE) – Paul Gascoigne's former wife
SID JAMES – Carry On movie star
SIDNEY POITIER – American movie star
SIEGFRIED SASSOON – First World War poet
SIMON COSYNS – former *Daily Mirror* executive, now works for the *Sun*
SIMON HOGGART – *Guardian* columnist
SIMON JONES – England cricket star
SIMON KELNER – editor of the *Independent*
SIMON OLIVER – my uncle and godfather
SIMON WESTON – Falklands veteran
SIMON WIESENTHAL – Nazi-hunter who survived the Holocaust

SINEAD BURKE – PA in the *Daily Mirror* deputy editor's office
SINEAD O'CONNOR – Irish singer
SITA WHITE – former lover of cricket legend Imran Khan
SLOBODAN MILOSEVIC – deposed leader of the Serbs
SLY BAILEY – chief executive of Trinity Mirror
SLY STALLONE – Hollywood superstar famous for *Rocky* and *Rambo* movies
SOL CAMPBELL – Arsenal and England soccer star
SOPHIE MONTGOMERY – wife of David Montgomery
SOPHIE RAWORTH – BBC newsreader
SOPHIE RHYS-JONES (COUNTESS) – wife of Prince Edward
SPENCER PUGHE-MORGAN – my oldest son
SPIKE MILLIGAN – comedian
SPOCK – fictitious character in *Star Trek* famed for his lack of humour and emotion
SRICHAND HINDUJA – Indian business tycoon
STAN COLLYMORE – soccer star
STAN RICHARDS – *Emmerdale* TV star
STAN THOMAS – Welsh tycoon
STANLEY PUGHE-MORGAN – my middle son
STELIOS HAJI-IOANNOU – Easyjet tycoon
STELLA BLYTHE – widow of *News of the World* reporter Chris Blythe
STEPHEN BYERS – former Labour Cabinet minister
STEPHEN DORRELL – former Tory Cabinet minister
STEPHEN FRY – comedian
STEPHEN GLOVER – former editor of the *Independent on Sunday*, now media commentator for the *Spectator*
STEPHEN LANDER – former boss of MI5
STEPHEN LAWRENCE – young black boy killed by racists in south London
STEPHEN MILLIGAN – former Tory MP
STEPHEN NORRIS – Tory MP
STEPHEN SPIELBERG – movie mogul
STEVE BELL – *Guardian* cartoonist
STEVE BING – former lover of actress Liz Hurley
STEVE COOGAN – comic famous for creating Alan Partridge
STEVE DENNIS – *Daily Mirror* reporter and co-writer of Paul Burrell's book on Diana
STEVE PURCELL – *Daily Mirror* features executive
STEVE PURDEW – business tycoon
STEVE SAMPSON – former *Sun* executive
STEVE WHITE – Northern news editor of the *Daily Mirror*
STEVEN GERRARD – British soldier
STING – rock star
STUART HIGGINS – former editor of the *Sun*, now a PR man
STUART KUTTNER – managing editor of the *News of the World*
STUART PEARCE – former England soccer star
STUART WHITE – *News of the World* executive
STUART WILLIAMS – West Indies cricket star
SUE BREALEY – showbiz PR woman
SUE CARROLL – *Daily Mirror* columnist
SUE DOUGLAS – former editor of the *Daily Express*
SUE NYE – aide to Gordon Brown and wife of former BBC chief Gavyn Davies
SUE THOMPSON – former news editor of the *Sun*
SUGGS – star of pop band Madness
SUSANNAH YORK – British movie star
SUSIE ORBACH – one of Diana's therapists
SUZY JAGGER – City reporter who first revealed my share-dealing activities
SVEN-GORAN ERIKSSON – England football manager
SYD YOUNG – former *Daily Mirror* news reporter
SYDNEY POITIER – American movie legend
SYLVESTER BOLAM – former editor of the *Daily Mirror*
TANITH CAREY – *Daily Mirror* executive
TARA FITZGERALD – actress
TARA PALMER-TOMPKINSON – TV presenter and former 'It' girl
TED OLIVER – former *Daily Mirror* reporter
TERRY LLOYD – former ITN news reporter who was killed in Iraq
TERRY VENABLES – former England football manager
TERRY WOGAN – radio star
THIERRY HENRY – Arsenal star
TIGER WOODS – American golf star
TIGER-LILY HUTCHENCE – daughter of Paula Yates and Michael Hutchence
TIGGY LEGGE-BOURKE – former assistant to Prince Charles

TIM GILL – friend from Sussex

TIM YEO – Tory shadow cabinet minister

TINA BROWN – former New York magazine publisher

TINA O'BRIEN – *Coronation Street* star

TINA WEAVER – my deputy editor on the *Daily Mirror*, now the *Sunday Mirror* editor

TOM CRONE – News International legal director

TOM HANKS – American movie star

TOM KING – former Tory Defence Minister

TOM NEWTON-DUNN – former *Daily Mirror* reporter, now on the *Sun*

TOM PETRIE – former *Sun* news editor

TOM SHRAGER – American investor in Trinity Mirror

TONY BANKS – former Labour sports minister

TONY BENN – Labour MP

TONY BLACKBURN – legendary DJ

TONY BLAIR – Prime Minister

TONY PARSONS – top-selling author and *Daily Mirror* columnist

TONY SNOWDON (LORD) – former husband of Princess Margaret

TREVOR KAVANAGH – political editor of the *Sun*

TREVOR MCDONALD – TV newsreader

TREVOR REES-JONES – bodyguard who survived crash that killed Princess Diana

ULRIKA JONSSON – TV presenter

VALERIE FALDO – third wife of golf legend Nick Faldo

VALERIE GROVE – *Times* journalist

VALERIE HARKESS – woman who cheated on her judge husband with Alan Clark

VALERIO VICCEI – notorious Knightsbridge bank robber

VANESSA FELTZ – former TV presenter

VERE ROTHERMERE (LORD) – press baron who owned the *Daily Mail*

VIC WAKELING – sports chief of BskyB

VICKY JARAMILLO – lover of Chelsea tycoon Matthew Harding

VICTOR BLANK – chairman of Trinity Mirror

VICTOR CHANDLER – bookmaking legend

VICTOR LEWIS-SMITH – TV critic and broadcaster

VICTORIA (QUEEN) – one of Britain's longest-reigning monarchs

VICTORIA BECKHAM – pop star and wife of David Beckham

VICTORIA HERVEY (LADY) – 'It' girl

VICTORIA SPENCER (COUNTESS) – ex-wife of Earl Spencer

VINNIE JONES – footballer and movie star

VIRGIN MARY – mother of Jesus Christ

VIRGINIA BOTTOMLEY – former Tory Cabinet minister

WAHEED ALI – Labour peer and TV mogul

WASIM AKRAM – former Pakistani cricket star

WAYNE – the worst builder in London

WAYNE FRANCIS – former *Daily Mirror* news reporter

WAYNE ROONEY – England soccer star

WENDY DENG – third wife of Rupert Murdoch

WENDY SPENCE – best personal trainer in London

WILL CARLING – former England rugby captain and 'friend' of Princess Diana

WILL WHITEHORN – Richard Branson's right-hand man

WILLIAM (PRINCE) – heir to the throne

WILLIAM CASH – journalist

WILLIAM HAGUE – former Tory leader

WILLIAM HISLOP – son of *Private Eye* editor Ian Hislop

WILLIAM SHAWCROSS – author

WILLIAM STRAW – son of Foreign Secretary Jack Straw

WINSTON CHURCHILL – former British Prime Minister

WOODROW WYATT – columnist for *News of the World*, and former MP

YASMIN LE BON – supermodel and wife of pop star Simon Le Bon

YORKSHIRE RIPPER – mass murderer Peter Sutcliffe

ZARA PHILLIPS – daughter of Princess Anne

ZOE LUCKER – star of TV show *Footballers' Wives*

ZSA ZSA GABOR – Hollywood legend

INDEX